D1591129

STUDIES IN THE ENGLISH RENAISSANCE

John T. Shawcross, General Editor

DARKE HIEROGLIPHICKS

Alchemy in English Literature from Chaucer to the Restoration

STANTON J. LINDEN

THE UNIVERSITY PRESS OF KENTUCKY

Copyright © 1996 by The University Press of Kentucky

Scholarly publisher for the Commonwealth,
serving Bellarmine College, Berea College, Centre
College of Kentucky, Eastern Kentucky University,
The Filson Club, Georgetown College, Kentucky
Historical Society, Kentucky State University,
Morehead State University, Murray State University,
Northern Kentucky University, Transylvania University,
University of Kentucky, University of Louisville,
and Western Kentucky University.

Editorial and Sales Offices: 663 South Limestone Street
Lexington, Kentucky 40508-4008

96 97 98 99 00   5 4 3 2 1

Library of Congress Cataloging-in-Publication Data

Linden, Stanton J., 1935-
    Darke hierogliphicks : alchemy in English literature from Chaucer
to the Restoration / Stanton J. Linden.
        p.   cm. — (Studies in the English Renaissance)
    Includes bibliographical references and index.
    ISBN 0-8131-1968-5 (alk. paper)
    1. English literature—Early modern, 1500-1700—History and
Criticism. 2. Alchemy in literature. 3. English literature—Middle
English, 1100-1500—History and criticism. 4. Chaucer, Geoffrey, d.
1400—Knowledge—Occultism. 5. Renaissance—England. I. Title.
II. Series.
PR428.A44L56   1996
820.9'37—dc20   96-14574

Contents

Illustrations

Acknowledgments

During the long labor of writing this book, I have received help from many individuals, libraries, and institutions whose assistance I wish to acknowledge. To the staffs of the Huntington Library, the Folger Shakespeare Library, the Wellcome Institute for the History of Medicine, the Bodleian Library, and, especially, the North Room of the British Library, I am grateful for supplying the many books and manuscripts that I have requested. Travel for research has been supported in part by the National Endowment for the Humanities, the American Council of Learned Societies, and Arts and Humanities Travel Awards from Washington State University. Washington State granted me a sabbatical leave for the 1992-93 academic year, during which writing and much of the revision was completed; the Dean of the College of Liberal Arts has also provided funds for the illustrations.

Parts of chapters 4, 5, 7, and 8 have appeared in different versions in *Ambix* and the *Journal of the History of Ideas,* whose editors I wish to thank for permission to reprint these materials. Chapter 9—indeed, much of my thinking about relationships between the hermetic and scientific worldviews—was clarified through invited participation in an interdisciplinary symposium at the Herzog August Bibliothek at Wolfenbüttel, Germany, in October 1992.

The late Gordon W. O'Brien of the University of Minnesota first kindled my interest in Renaissance hermeticism, and Allen G. Debus, Michael J.B. Allen, Thomas S. Willard, and many others, have helped sustain it. Thanks are due and gratefully given to John Shawcross for his extremely thorough and incisive readings of early and late drafts of the manuscript. For help in obtaining illustrations, I would like to thank Laila and Miro Vejzovic of Washington State University, Timothy D. Murray of the Special Collections Department of the University of Delaware Library, and the staffs of the Huntington Library and Wellcome Institute. Thanks are also due to the editorial and production staffs of the University Press of Kentucky for the care and efficiency they have shown in producing this book.

My debt to the following Washington State colleagues and friends who have contributed to this book is large, of long standing, and too complex to order and particularize: Rhonda Blair, Thomas Faulkner, Diane Gillespie, Virginia Hyde, Nicolas Kiessling, Louise Schleiner; and Winfried Schleiner of the University of California at Davis. Finally, for continuing encouragement and support, I owe very special thanks to my wife Lucy and son Steve.

Introduction

In broadest terms, this book investigates the influence of alchemy in English literature of the late Middle Ages and the sixteenth and seventeenth centuries through detailed study of references and allusions that occur in the literary works produced during this three-hundred-year period. That this historical era, which marked the height of interest in alchemy and related forms of occult and hermetic thought, should also be the one in which English literature emerged from the confines of insularity and foreign domination to attain, in the reigns of Elizabeth, James I, and their successors a period of its greatest genius and brilliance, provides opportunity to examine the impact of a familiar and controversial subject on a new and flourishing tradition of popular, vernacular literature. It is an opportunity to study ways in which the artistic imagination seizes upon a body of knowledge that is rich and varied in literary potential and shapes it for its own special purposes; it offers occasion for studying these purposes as well.

But in addition to providing means for studying poetic processes and the operation of the literary imagination upon a subject matter that is today obscure and inaccessible, an examination of alchemy's influence on medieval and Renaissance literature rewards us in other ways. To a considerable extent, for the modern, post-Enlightenment reader, alchemy represents the medieval "science" par excellence. Along with astrology, natural magic, and witchcraft, it stands as a prime example of the superstitiousness, credulity, and irrationality of the medieval mind, a mirror of the state of intellectual confusion from which the progressive, rational, and scientific mind of the present has evolved. In this respect, the "science" of chemistry represents all that the "art" of alchemy does not. Besides witnessing the flowering of English literature, the historical period that is the focus of this study is notable for greater revolutions, of which this transition from alchemy to chemistry, from "pseudo-science" to "science," is but a minor symptom. These greater changes touched every aspect of life directly or indirectly and involved a complex of rejections, revisions, and compromises in cosmology and astronomy, philosophy and metaphysics, religion and theology, and views of self and society. Such revolutionary shifts, their causes and implications, have been described by numerous students of intellectual history, from A.O. Lovejoy, E.A. Burtt, and Basil Willey to Thomas Kuhn, Keith Thomas, and Charles Webster; it is not my intention to explore the factors that led to the decline of medieval outlooks and habits of mind and the eventual rise of modernity. Rather, I wish to

1

place literary reflections of alchemy—that typically "medieval" pursuit—into the larger context of intellectual revolution and foment in order to see how they evolve with the passing of time. Such references and allusions can serve as valuable guides and indices to changing outlooks and patterns of ideas that were an important part of the intellectual milieu of the late Middle Ages and the early modern period.

My primary concerns are thus with alchemy as a subject of literary treatment and with literary references to alchemy—the results of this treatment—as objects of study that yield insights into aspects of English medieval and Renaissance thought. The specific period of investigation extends from roughly 1385 to the time of the Restoration, the three-hundred-year period in which literary references to alchemy are most abundant. I have chosen 1385 as my starting point because the earliest, and possibly finest, example of alchemically inspired literature is included in *The Canterbury Tales,* and 1385 is usually regarded as the approximate year Chaucer began writing his major work. As I will argue in chapter 2, the importance of *The Canon's Yeoman's Tale* results not only from Chaucer's genius in adapting the subject of alchemy to the demands of literature but also from the fact that this tale stands at the beginning of a long tradition of alchemical satire that continues throughout much of the entire period. To a considerable extent, the history of alchemy's literary presence is the history of a satirical tradition. As I will show in chapter 3, which is devoted to the fifteenth and sixteenth centuries, many of the subjects and themes, images, attitudes, and representational modes that later writers incorporate in their works occur for the first time in Chaucer. For this reason he holds a special position as founder of a satirical tradition kept alive in the works of Lydgate, Barclay, Erasmus, and many of the Elizabethan poets, playwrights, and writers of prose fiction. But among the latter writers—e.g., Sidney, Lyly, Shakespeare, Greene, and Nashe—alchemical allusions are rarely derived simply and directly from earlier ones; in the final decades of the sixteenth century the interaction of alchemy and literary genius produces a great variety of original and highly effective themes, motifs, images, and ideas to accompany the emergence of new literary forms.

Occupying the largest place in the book is the literature of the seventeenth century and the changing course of alchemy therein reflected. I have included chapters on Bacon, Jonson, Donne and Herbert, Henry Vaughan and Milton, and, in the ninth chapter, given special attention to works by Samuel Butler. The reasons for this seventeenth-century emphasis are complexly interesting and sometimes yield surprises. For example, Bacon's central position in this portion of the study is obviously justified because of his reputation as a founder of the new, inductive, experimentally based science, one antithetical to our preconceptions of alchemical theory and practice. Yet, expectations of his hostility to alchemy are only partially realized: not only does Bacon share with his age many of its magical and occultist aspects but he also takes a somewhat positive view of the possibility of transmutation *if* reforms are brought about in alchemical method and procedure. Such toleration of occultist thought did not characterize Bacon's devoted followers at the time of the Restoration because, as I will show in chapter 9, most writers associated with the Royal Society and university reform indiscriminately condemned all manifestations of occultism.

The poems of Donne and Herbert represent a marked shift away from the satirical use of alchemy that had so dominated its literary expression for more than two centuries. Although both poets occasionally invoke alchemy for purposes of satire, Donne's poems and those of *The Temple,* especially, are much more interesting for new, highly original applications of alchemical subjects and ideas wholly unrelated to this tradition. Their employment of alchemy to suggest spiritual growth, purification, regeneration, and millenarian ideas reflects several important new emphases in late sixteenth- and seventeenth-century alchemical, medical, and occultist writing, what Allen Debus has called the "chemical philosophy." Thus, their alchemical verse is much more a foreshadowing of the hermetic poetry of Henry Vaughan and the powerfully complex expressions of Milton than a continuation of the tradition that was begun by Chaucer and persisted almost without interruption through Jonson. Donne and Herbert represent an important turning point in the course of alchemy's literary influence. This new tradition of spiritual alchemy is not sustained throughout the century, however, and in the penultimate chapter I argue that the return to satire in the works of Samuel Butler reflects the antagonism of scientific and religious rationalists and the Royal Society to philosophical enthusiasm and the entire occultist milieu. It is important to note, however, that Butler's satirical victims are nearly as often experimental scientists as occult charlatans. For this reason, his treatment of the practitioners of alchemy and experimental science in *Hudibras* and "An Hermetic Philosopher" anticipates Swift's satire in Lemuel Gulliver's third voyage.

This is an inductive study and, insofar as possible, one guided by the principle of allowing the many examples of literary alchemy to speak for themselves: to reveal what they might about their creators' knowledge of alchemy, what was thought about it, and how this knowledge and these attitudes could be given artistic form and meaning. For this reason, I quote generously from primary sources, both alchemical and literary. In the case of the former, full quotation often followed by explanation is essential in making difficult material comprehensible; for the same reason, literary passages—especially those likely to be unfamiliar to readers—are presented with some degree of fullness and concern for context. Although I focus quite narrowly on alchemical influences, it has often been necessary and desirable to refer to related bodies of knowledge, such as astrology, natural magic, Neoplatonism, and Rosicrucianism. Sharp distinctions among aspects of these fields were much less apparent in the Renaissance than they are today, and as Elias Ashmole, the seventeenth-century antiquarian, collector of alchemical poetry, and student of the occult noted, "*Iudiciall Astrologie* is the *Key* of *Naturall Magick,* and *Naturall Magick* the *Doore* that leads to this Blessed Stone.*" [1]

Because one of my objectives is to demonstrate the sheer weight of alchemy's influence on the literature in question, it has been necessary to examine as many instances of its appearance as possible. I have sought a wide range of examples rather than being narrowly selective. At the same time, I have chosen not to discuss a few works, such as *The Faerie Queene, King Lear,* and *The Tempest,* the overall alchemical interpretation of which seems to me to rest on slender textual evidence. For reasons nearly opposite I have excluded commentary on alchemical implications in the poetry of Andrew Marvell; with the recent publication of Lyndy Abraham's *Marvell and Alchemy,* this topic has received thorough and incisive criticism. I have no pretensions that my search for alchemical allusions is exhaustive or complete; nonetheless, I believe I have located and examined enough examples to draw conclusions or point directions that have been unexplored in the few extended studies of alchemy and English literature previously published.[2]

While copiousness and inclusiveness have been crucial to illustrating the pervasiveness of alchemy's literary presence, I have also organized this study chronologically to suggest possible influences of earlier writers on those who followed and thereby the development of literary patterns and traditions. This book is not primarily a study of direct alchemical borrowings and questions of indebtedness, yet such concerns arise when, as in the case of Reginald Scot and Chaucer, we find later writers drawing on earlier works to reinforce their own attitudes toward alchemy. Generally, I have not been greatly concerned with making distinctions between writers who are regarded as "major" and "minor" today; Lyly and Breton appear alongside Chaucer, Jonson, and Donne. All confirm alchemy's popularity as a subject for literary treatment. I have also included alchemical references found in a wide range of genres and modes: epic and mock epic, comedy and tragedy, pastoral and masque, sacred and secular poetry, didactic and moralistic prose as well as satire and the literature of roguery. Alchemy was not confined within the boundaries of a few genres.

Another purpose of this study concerns the "uses" to which alchemical materials are put once they have entered a literary context. One is immediately impressed by the great diversity in the literary applications of this subject, and I have sought to develop at least tentative answers to questions like the following: What artistic potential does alchemy possess? What kinds of literary situations cause an author to have recourse to alchemy? And having done so, which of its associated ideas, themes, and images does he most often borrow? What are some of the things that alchemy "does" in a literary context? How does alchemy, a highly visual art, impart this quality to a literary medium? Do the distinctive visual forms and motifs associated with alchemy have counterparts in literary contexts? In an effort to answer these and other questions I have relied primarily on close textual analysis of the literary works, analysis undertaken following much reading in the alchemical and hermetic traditions, in the broader occult, magical milieu of the Renaissance and seventeenth century, and the general history of this period.

Combining many of these topics, my final concern is with patterns or tendencies that emerge when one examines alchemical references and resonances scattered throughout literature written over three centuries. My aim here is to investigate such topics as the beginning, flourishing, and decline in the literary use of alchemy; changes in its emphasis and treatment and possible links between these shifts and those occurring within the occult fields themselves; and the influence that certain writers and dominant intellectual currents may have had on alchemy's literary reflections.

To conclude, my purpose is not to study alchemy as such or to provide a history of its theory and practice during the period of focus. (In the first chapter, I supply only enough history and background to make the following discussions of literary alchemy and its context easier to follow.) Nor, except in my discussion of Jonson's *Mercury Vindicated from the Alchemists at Court* in chapter 5, am I especially concerned with identification of analogues and possible sources of alchemical references in literature. Rather, my intentions are to examine literary reflections of alchemy in an attempt to discover their meanings, explore their contributions to literary art, and investigate the insights they provide into important but obscure habits of thought present in English culture from the late Middle Ages to the Restoration.

I

"A *CLEW* AND A *LABYRINTH*"

Backgrounds, Definitions, and Preliminaries

In many ancient Bookes there are found many definitions of this Art, the intentions wherof we must consider in this Chapter. For *Hermes* saith of this Science:
Alchimy is a Corporal Science simply composed of one and by one, naturally
conjoyning things more precious, by knowledge and effect, and converting them
by a naturall commixtion into a better kind. A certain other saith: *Alchimy* is a
Science, teaching how to transforme any kind of mettall into another: and that
by a proper medicine, as it appeareth by many Philosophers Bookes. *Alchimy*
therfore is a science teaching how to make and compound a certaine medicine,
which is called *Elixir*, the which when it is cast upon mettals or imperfect bodies, doth fully perfect them in the verie projection.
— *The Mirror of Alchimy* [trans. 1597][1]

For *Halchymie* tradeth not alone with transmutation of metals (as ignorant
vulgars thinke: which error hath made them distaste that noble Science) but
shee hath also a chyrurgical hand in the anatomizing of every mesenteriall veine
of whole nature: Gods created handmaid, to conceive and bring forth his Creatures.
—Thomas Tymme, Dedication to Joseph Quercetanus's
The Practise of Chymicall, and Hermetical Physicke [1605][2]

The task of defining alchemy, of indicating its major types and varied interests is
formidable, sufficient, certainly, to challenge not only modern scholars of the
subject but the early alchemists themselves. Fortunately, my concern in this book
does not require undue attention to questions of historical definition or to those
of type and classification; nonetheless, some consideration of these problems is
appropriate at the outset if only to prepare the reader for the diverse conceptions
of alchemy and the variety of alchemical ideas and images that the literature of
the late Middle Ages, the Renaissance, and seventeenth century presents. This
introduction, accordingly, seeks to provide a *brief* background to a range of subjects that bear most directly on later discussion and analysis: definitions, varieties, and traditional goals of alchemy; its origin and development; some of its
leading personalities; and selected aspects and motifs that made alchemy particu-

larly attractive (or vulnerable) and adaptable to literary treatment. Overall, then, my purpose is not to provide a thorough and systematic treatment of this complex subject, which others have done with varying success,[3] but to plot a more selective and pragmatic guide to alchemy's presence in a broad range of literary contexts. In the case of many of these specific appearances, however, additional background will be provided at the point where it is needed.

As the first of the epigraphs to this chapter indicates, authors of alchemical treatises have long puzzled over alchemy's essential nature and definition. In this quotation from the popular *Mirror of Alchimy,* long misattributed to the thirteenth-century Oxford polymath and Franciscan monk Roger Bacon,[4] the unknown author—drawing upon two different authorities—speaks of alchemy as both an "Art" and a "Corporal Science" concerned with changing inferior or "imperfect" bodies, especially metals, into superior ones by means of a "proper medicine" or "*Elixir.*" Although the *Mirror's* definition was not formulated until several hundred years after alchemy was first practiced, it contains the key concepts associated with *exoteric* alchemy, which is concerned with the physical transmutation of "inferior" metals into ones more precious and, therefore, more "perfect." For centuries before and after composition of this treatise, metallic transformation supposedly achieved through use of a powerful transmuting agent, the philosopher's stone, was alchemy's primary signification, although not its only one, and aspects of this type most often inform literary references, especially those that are satirical in intention. The distinction between this practical type and *esoteric* alchemy, to be discussed shortly, receives further clarification in Roger Bacon's authentic work, the *Opus Tertium,* where it is placed within the context of the claims of "nature" versus those of "art" and, secondly, with searches for a miraculous *elixir vitae,* which was thought to cure all diseases and prolong human life indefinitely. Thus, utility and the betterment of the human condition enter the discussion. Exoteric alchemy, Bacon states, "teaches how to make the noble metals, and colours, and many other things better or more abundantly by art than they are made in nature. . . . For not only can it yield wealth and very many other things for the public good, but it also teaches how to discover such things as are capable of prolonging human life for much longer periods than can be accomplished by nature."[5]

In the art-nature debate, Bacon affirms the superiority of art, as do all believers in alchemy, and in emphasizing its common material and medical benefits, he is voicing arguments that remained current well into the seventeenth century. However, until the time of Paracelsus (1493-1541) and the beginning of the era of iatrochemistry, with its concentration on medicines chemically prepared and derived from minerals (as distinguished from herbal medicines), alchemy's primary concern was with attempts to transmute base metals into gold.[6]

Nevertheless, other kinds of alchemy existed. Following Thomas Tymme's statement that comprises my second epigraph, to the effect that alchemy is not solely concerned with metallic transmutation, historians often distinguish between practical or exoteric alchemy and a second type of esoteric, spiritual, or philosophical alchemy. Although these two traditions are often intermingled in the writings of the alchemists themselves, the distinction between them is important when examining the portrayals of alchemy and alchemists in medieval and Renaissance literature. Central to this second type is *knowledge* of the secrets of nature, not for the purpose of achieving dominion over nature, as with the philosopher's stone or a magical elixir, but rather a disinterested, unpragmatic knowledge of the origin, composition, and secret operations of all aspects of creation. Tymme's emphasis on knowledge to enable informed analysis of nature ("the anatomizing of every mesenteriall veine") is anticipated in Roger Bacon's discussion, again in the *Opus Tertium,* of speculative alchemy, which "treats of the generation of things from the elements and of all inanimate things and of simple and composite humours, of common stones, gems, marbles, of gold and other metals, of sulphurs and salts and pigments, . . . and other things without limit, concerning which we have nothing in the books of Aristotle."[7]

More important than knowledge of the natural world is esoteric alchemy's concentration on spiritual and philosophical values and ideals, especially as they impinge on the inner life of the individual adept. For E.J. Holmyard, this type with its strong religious and mystical overtones has its origins in the exoteric alchemist's recognition that divine grace is requisite to obtaining the philosopher's stone; this in turn, "gradually developed into a devotional system where the mundane transmutation of metals became merely symbolic of the transformation of sinful man into a perfect being through prayer and submission to the will of God. The two kinds of alchemy were often inextricably mixed; however, in some of the mystical treatises it is clear that the authors are not concerned with material substances but are employing the language of exoteric alchemy for the sole purpose of expressing theological, philosophical, or mystical beliefs and aspirations."[8] The close proximity of the two types of alchemy is evidenced in pictorial art as well. The circular engraving from Heinrich Khunrath's *Amphitheatrum sapientiæ* (1609) shows the sacred side in the figure of the adept praying in the oratorium, to the left of the central axis; the laboratorium with its clutter of apparatus is to the right (fig. 1). A similar format reinforces the relation between library and laboratory—esoteric and exoteric—in figure 2 from Michael Maier's *Tripus aureus* (1618).

Reflecting the diverse strands of magic, Gnosticism, Neoplatonism, and Christianity that had entered Greek alchemy between the time of Bolus and Zosimos (ca. 200 B.C.-300 A.D.), esoteric alchemy became a way of life for its most devout disciples: a vast religious and philosophical system aimed at the purification and regeneration of their lives. But in addition to being an internal, salvationist process, esoteric alchemy also set forth a worldview, which, as summarized later in this introduction, placed special emphasis on the unity of all things as created by God and the harmonious relationship between the greater world and the lesser world of man.

Figure 1. Laboratory and Oratory. Heinrich Khunrath, *Amphitheatrum sapientiæ* (1609). By permission of the University of Delaware Library, Newark, Delaware.

For mystically minded adepts, the purely chemical operations and reactions occurring within their vessels symbolized deeper spiritual meanings. Imperfect substances used as the proximate ingredients of the stone were thought, for example, to undergo death and corruption in the initial stage of the alchemical process. But following the blackness and death of this *putrefactio* (and continuing the analogy with Christ's death, resurrection, and man's salvation), these base materials later appeared to be "reborn" in the form of perfect, pure, and incorruptible gold. The progress from decay to growth, from death to resurrection, might be seen, furthermore, as a confirmation of the biblical commonplace: "Verily, verily, I say unto you, except a corn of wheat fall into the ground and die, it abideth alone: but if it die, it bringeth forth much fruit" (John 12:24).

This vein of religious allegorizing occurs frequently in alchemy's written tradition. It is present in the *Dialogue of Cleopatra and the Philosophers,* one of the

Figure 2. Library and Laboratory. Michael Maier, *Tripus aureus* (1618). By permission of the University of Delaware Library, Newark, Delaware.

earliest alchemical fragments dating from perhaps the second century A.D.,[9] and also in the "Visions" of Zosimos included in his treatise *Of Virtue*.[10] The characteristically pious tone of the majority of medieval alchemical treatises results largely from the art's religious associations, and the mystical language and allegorical mode of such Renaissance hermeticists as Jakob Boehme, Michael Maier, Robert Fludd, and others to be considered in chapter 7 is an expression of esoteric alchemy. It is this tradition that informs the selection from Martin Luther's *Table-Talk* quoted at the beginning of that chapter, and in the seventeenth century it is manifest in the hermetic writings of Thomas Vaughan and in the hermetically inspired poetry of his brother, Henry.

While it is convenient and historically justifiable to divide alchemy according to these two basic orientations, exoteric and esoteric, it is also essential to recognize that these types are often combined in the writings of the same author. As the secrets of transmuting base metal are cryptically unfolded, the discourse's allegorical and moral level imparts directions for the practitioner's spiritual purification and salvation; or, more commonly, the evolving "stone" becomes the symbol for, or direct reflection of, stages in the subject's inner purification. Useful examples of this duality of expression are contained in Patrick Scot's *Tillage of Light* (1623), one of the most interesting treatises belonging to the tradition of spiritual and philosophical alchemy in the seventeenth century, and a work to which I will return in chapter 7. Although Scot categorically denies the possibility of physical transmutation of metals, he nonetheless adapts the principles of exoteric alchemy to a moral, salvationist context. His moral and philosophical analysis is unusual in its detail, but his method is entirely representative of a large number of alchemical treatises of this period.

Given the problematics of definition, it is useful to think of alchemy as pluralistic rather than singular, as "alchemies" rather than "alchemy." If the latter, it must be recognized that along the continuum bounded by the poles "exoteric" and "esoteric" there are many intermediate points and permutations. For example, as Robert Schuler has shown, a large number of distinguishable "spiritual alchemies" coexisted in the seventeenth century alone, each having its foundation in various theological doctrines or political ideologies rather than in alchemical theories as such.[11]

Complicating problems of definition is the fact that alchemical processes and techniques were often put to service in diverse ways by members of other occupational groups, such as physicians and apothecaries. These groups might be further subdivided according to their allegiance to either Galen or Paracelsus with their corresponding prescriptions of either herbal or chemical medications. The literary consequences of such divisions are seen in works like John Lacy's play *The Dumb Lady* and in the many poetic references to "potable gold" or *aurum potabile*.[12] In a more generalized sense, alchemists often referred to themselves as physicians, restoring health to diseased, "leprous" base metals. Thus, the link between alchemy and medicine was close in the writings of alchemists, surgeons, apothecaries, and poet-physicians like Henry Vaughan.

If, in the final analysis, a comprehensive definition of alchemy is deemed necessary, it is useful to bear in mind one recently proposed by H.J. Sheppard and grounded in the notion that alchemists thought of themselves as making conscious "alterations of duration in some linear time scale," either shortening it (in the case of the artificial production of metals), lengthening it (in the case of life-prolonging elixirs), or, in the case of redemption, removing the subject from time's sway entirely. He states "Alchemy is the art of liberating parts of the Cosmos from temporal existence and achieving perfection which, for metals is gold, and for man, longevity, then immortality and, finally, redemption. Material perfection was sought through the action of a preparation (Philosopher's Stone for metals; Elixir of Life for humans), while spiritual ennoblement resulted from some form of inner revelation or other enlightenment (Gnosis, for example, in Hellenistic and western practices)."[13]

Although alchemy may have been called the "medieval" science by its detractors, the adjective is inaccurate if applied to the art's historical origins. While it flourished throughout the Middle Ages, Renaissance, and seventeenth century, it was during much of that time enjoying its final phase of popularity and credibility. The theory and practice of alchemy go back thousands of years, and its place of origin, its initial nature and aims, and the early phases of its development—shrouded in the uncertainties of pre-history—are still matters largely for scholarly speculation rather than solid fact.

Briefly, one widely held view places the birth of alchemy somewhere in the Middle East, perhaps in Mesopotamia, after which it spread to Egypt, Greece, and the Orient.[14] According to this theory it was initially an outgrowth of experimentation in metalworking, which is known to have been practiced as early as 3500 B.C.[15] The name "alchemy" itself suggests that the art may have had Egyptian origins: according to John Read, "*Khem* was the ancient name of Egypt and *al* is the Arabic definite article. For this reason, Egypt, or *Khem,* the country of dark soil, the Biblical Land of Ham, has often been held to have given birth to alchemy, the 'art of the dark country.'"[16] In opposition to this etymology, Holmyard argues that the Arabic *kmt* and *chem* were not alchemical at all and that the word *kimia* has Greek origins, deriving from *chyma*, "meaning to fuse or cast a metal."[17] Whether or not either of these views is correct, alchemy is known to have been practiced in Egypt at an early date by artisans whose trades, such as metallurgy, dyeing, and glass-making, required some knowledge of the principles of chemistry. Also pointing toward alchemy's Egyptian origin is the centrality of Hermes Trismegistus in its written tradition; the Greek counterpart of the Egyptian god Thoth (also identified with Athothis or Imhotep), Hermes, the Roman Mercury, has an extremely rich and diverse role in alchemical theory and practice. His mythological, iconographic, and chemical associations will be examined in detail in the discussion of Ben Jonson's alchemical drama in chapter 5.

Recent publication of early Chinese alchemical treatises suggests that the origin of alchemy might be traceable to China. That it was practiced there at an early date—perhaps the fourth century B.C.—is evidenced by the fact that an injunction prohibiting counterfeiting gold and threatening offenders with dire punishment was issued in 144 B.C.[18] But Chinese alchemy, in contrast to that practiced in the West, was chiefly concerned with discovering the elixir vitae, a miraculous "medicine" that could confer immortality or prolong life indefinitely. Subordinate to this aim was the search for the key to metallic transmutation, although Taylor notes that even though gold was not used for monetary exchange in China, its imperishability was associated with the possibility of human longevity and immortality.[19] A second major difference in ancient Chinese alchemy was its essentially mystical character, a result of its links with Taoism, which dates from about 300 B.C. Holmyard states that "the Taoists wished for long life, the better to prepare themselves for Paradise, and to this end practised meditation, control of breathing, and various physical exercises, as well as frugality of diet. By a natural evolution, the desire for longevity grew into the hope of immortality, and the disciples of the cult were thus led to the study and practice of alchemy."[20]

A final important feature of Chinese alchemical theory was its doctrine of the two opposing principles, the *Yin* and the *Yang,* which have their origins about the sixth century B.C. According to this dichotomy, the "*Yin* is feminine, watery, heavy, passive, and earthy, while *Yang* is masculine, fiery, light, and active"; the former was associated with the moon, the latter with the sun, and the interaction of the two resulted in the five elements of which all creation was composed.[21] In their sexual and planetary differentiations as well as qualitative meanings, these principles have close counterparts in the sulphur-mercury theory of Western alchemy; at the same time, the mystical emphasis of Chinese alchemy has parallels in the esoteric traditions of the West.

Greatly simplified, these are three of the leading theories concerning the origin of alchemy, but it should not be assumed that its rise in the West and the East occurred in a state of total independence and isolation from the other. It is possible that knowledge of alchemy passed between East and West, by way of Egypt, Mesopotamia, or India, but if it did we can only speculate as to the nature of that knowledge or when transmission first occurred.[22]

Much more significant for the rise of Western alchemy were various Greek philosophical traditions beginning in about the fourth century B.C. and continuing until several centuries after the time of Christ. Theory, rather than practice, constituted the ancient Greeks' chief contribution to alchemy's development. In addition to the theory of the four elements and their interchangeability, A.J. Hopkins has outlined several additional "psychic influences" that mark alchemy's Greek inheritance. From them, alchemy derived its *hylozistic* conception of the universe, the idea that external nature is alive and sentient. Alchemy also posited a harmonious relationship between *macrocosm* and *microcosm,* the cosmos and the little world of man being guided by the same power and principles. The alchemists also derived from the Greeks their beliefs in the efficacy of *astrology* and in an *animistic* world, the view that "any event apparently spontaneous is really due to some personality—fairy, wood spirit, hobgoblin, etc."[23] Not only are these principles basic to alchemical theory, they are also the ones upon which the worldview of the Middle Ages and Renaissance is predicated.

As will be shown in more detail at the beginning of chapter 2, copies of many early Greek alchemical writings survived in medieval and Renaissance England, lending the weight of their authority to the art and its practitioners. In addition to the genuine works of Plato and Aristotle, the two most eminent Greek authorities, dozens—perhaps hundreds—of spurious works were attributed to them by later writers seeking prestige and notoriety resulting from association with the venerable ancients. There were other important early treatises as well, such as the *Physika* of Bolos Democritos (Pseudo-Democritos, or Bolos of Mendes), a Greek living in Egypt around 200 B.C. when Alexandria was enjoying its height as a center of learning.[24] Widely read in antiquity—rivalling Aristotle as an authority on natural history—Bolus's works combine fact and fancy and appear to be unsystematic collections, but in the practical tradition of the earlier artisans of Mesopotamia and Egypt, they contain recipes for making gems and purple dyes, as well as silver and gold.[25] Bolus is set apart from these early craftsmen, however, through his interest in transmutation, his belief that the very nature of metals could be altered, and that these fundamental alterations were indicated by changes in the colors of metals during the process.[26] This belief that substances could be changed in essence is the single most important principle of alchemy and figures prominently in a wide range of literary treatments. The idea that stages in the alchemical process were signaled by color changes constitutes a second important motif.

The continuity of alchemical interest among later Greeks is evidenced by the writings of Zosimos of Panoplis (d. ca. 300 A.D.) and, later, Stephanos of Alexandria, who lived during the seventh century. Chief among Zosimos's works is a twenty-eight book encyclopedia addressed to his "spiritual sister," Theosebeia, which contains material that is both original and drawn from earlier sources. Some of Zosimos's works take the form of highly cryptic symbolic and allegorical visions that appear to set forth instructions for the alchemical work.[27] His interest in arcane symbolism is also revealed in the famous Formula of the Crab, which "was reported to embody the secret of transmutation, [but] was probably a cipher used by Egyptian craftsmen engaged in making imitative gold."[28]

Thus, during the five hundred years separating Bolus and Zosimos, several important changes occurred in the way alchemy was conceived, practiced, and written about. During this time it seems to have been transformed from what was essentially a metallurgical craft to a secret and mysterious hermetic art. According to Holmyard,

> We now find [in the writings of Zosimos] a bewildering confusion of Egyptian magic, Greek philosophy, Gnosticism, Neo-platonism, Babylonian astrology, Christian theology, and pagan mythology, together with the enigmatical and allusive language that makes the interpretation of alchemical literature so difficult and so uncertain. . . . In order to give some show of authority to their nebulous doctrines, alchemists busied themselves in composing treatises that they then attributed to any philosopher or celebrity of earlier times whom their whim led them to select. Thus works on alchemy were ascribed to Hermes, Plato, Moses, Miriam his sister, Theophrastus, Ostanes, Cleopatra, and Isis. . . . Legends and myths were given alchemical interpretations: the golden fleece, which Jason and the Argonauts carried over the Pontic Sea to Colchis, was claimed to have been a manuscript on parchment, teaching the manner of making gold by alchemical art, and even the 'Song of Solomon' was supposed to be an alchemical treatise couched in veiled language.[29]

Eclecticism in content and style typifies Western alchemical treatises written during the following centuries.

This outline of the early development of alchemy must include some mention of the contributions of Arabian scholars. For the most part, these occurred from the seventh to the tenth centuries when the political and military power of Islam was at its height. As a result of the conquest of Alexandria (642) and other centers of Greek learning, the Moslems came into possession of the corpus of Greek philosophical and scientific knowledge. In the case of alchemy, Greek writings were to provide the basis for all subsequent advances of their own, and Arabian scholars enhanced the knowledge of alchemy in the West through preserving, translating, and transmitting the Greek heritage.

Important among them was one Khalid (d. 704), under whose direction Arabian translations of alchemical treatises originally written in Greek and Coptic were completed. He is also said to have personally studied alchemy under the tutelage of the Christian scholar Morienus and to have composed alchemical poems.[30] But the most significant advances that grew out of Arabian interest in alchemy were made by Jabir ibn Hayyan in the eighth or ninth century A.D. Like Khalid, Jabir was inspired by the wealth of Greek learning that came to Islam with the conquest of Alexandria, and he, in turn, produced many treatises on astronomy, philosophy, logic, medicine, and mathematics.[31] Jabir is now rejected as the true author of all of the works that bear his name. Indeed, it is likely that many of these were writings, not of an individual author, but of an entire school, such as the Brethren of Purity or the Faithful Friends, that flourished in the tenth century.[32] Nonetheless, they were attributed to the legendary Jabir. It is now the practice among experts such as M. Plessner to distinguish between this earlier, Greek-inspired Arabic body of writings, the *Corpus Jabirianum,* and the highly influential body of Latin writings that appeared under the name of "Geber" in the thirteenth and fourteenth centuries. It is the latter group that includes such well-known works as the *Summa perfectionis magisterii, Liber de investigatione perfectionis, Liber de inventione veritatis, Liber fornacum,* and the *Testamentum Geberi.*[33]

To pass over these problems of authorial identity and attribution, Jabir's view of the origins of metals, which was grounded in the paired opposition of qualities implicit in the Aristotelian theory of the four elements, led to formulation of the sulphur-mercury theory, the most widely accepted account of the generation of metals until the rise of the phlogiston theory late in the seventeenth century.[34] According to this view, metals were produced beneath the earth's surface through the union of the two great "parent" principles, sulphur and mercury. Of these, the former represents the qualities of hotness, dryness, and masculinity, and the latter, coldness, moistness, and femininity.[35] This theory provided alchemy with its theoretical basis until the sixteenth century, when it came to be modified by the addition of Paracelsus's third principle, salt. For Jabir and subsequent alchemists, however, sulphur and mercury were not the common substances that bear these names; rather they were abstract and hypothetical principles—represented in alchemy by a host of fanciful names—which, when joined under the favorable influence of the planets, gave rise to the known metals. Sophic (i.e., "philosophical") sulphur was generally associated with the property of "combustibility or the spirit of fire, and sophic mercury [with] that of fusibility or the mineral spirit of metals."[36] The production of specific metals depended on the purity of these two interacting and sexually differentiated principles. Impure sulphur and mercury could produce only the baser metals, such as iron and tin; parent principles of higher purity would give rise to silver and gold. But, as Read notes, "when each of the two principles was of superfine purity they yielded the Philosopher's Stone. Thus the Stone was so much purer than ordinary 'gold from the mines' that a small quantity of it could, by virtue of a species of leavening, transmute or 'tinge' an indefinite quantity of a base metal into ordinary gold."[37]

In the century following Jabir, further contributions were made by the celebrated physician, teacher of medicine, and authority on all of the arts and sciences, Rhazes (ca. 864-925). These were of the nature of improvements in laboratory equipment and practice, accuracy of experiment, and classification of the substances used in alchemy.[38] The Persian-born Avicenna (ca. 980-1036), called the "Aristotle of the Arabians," is also known for his studies of alchemy as well as his achievements in philosophy, medicine, and other scientific fields. Like Jabir, Avicenna appears to have accepted the sulphur-mercury theory, but surprisingly he expressed total disbelief in the possibility that the essences of metals could be changed through alchemical transmutation. The "gold" that alchemists produced, he stated, merely has the appearance of the genuine metal; in his estimation alchemy is an art of clever imitation and forgery.[39] Thus, as early as the eleventh century we have a precedent for the charge against alchemy and alchemists that was most common in the works of English medieval and Renaissance satirists.

It was chiefly through the efforts of such Arabian scholars as Khalid, Jabir, Rhazes, and Avicenna that knowledge of alchemy entered Western Europe during the Middle Ages, and to these must be added, above all, the name of Geber. The texts that appeared in the latter part of the thirteenth century under the name of this "most famous Arabian Prince and Philosopher," while not identical with the earlier *Corpus Jabirianum,* are of Arabian provenance, and the *Summa perfectionis* has been called "the most important source for medieval alchemy and chemistry."[40] As I will show at the beginning of chapter 2, many of the original treatises of these Arab authors and the bulk of Greek alchemical texts that they helped preserve and transmit were widely known and studied in England during the period that is the focus of this study. The names of "Geber's cooks" appear even in English alchemical satire, as testimony to the fact that if the satirists were wholly skeptical and unsympathetic in their attitudes toward the art, they at least recognized the inestimable role Islam had played in bringing it to their attention.

In the Middle Ages and Renaissance, alchemy in England, though controversial, was popular and thriving. It was borne on a tide of Continental writings, both ancient and contemporary, which lent their respectability, and was also enhanced by a relatively small but important group of native authorities, which included Roger Bacon, Thomas Norton, and George Ripley. But more critical to alchemy's continuing vitality was the fact that the "old" philosophy still held sway and had not yet been "called in doubt" by the new, for it was the traditional medieval and Renaissance worldview that the theory and practice of alchemy depended upon for plausibility and perpetuation. This dependency was grounded in such widely held doctrines as the four elements theory, the sulphur-mercury theory, correspondences between macrocosm and microcosm, and the unity of matter, to each of which I will give brief attention.[41] With the weakening and eventual disappearance of these beliefs in the seventeenth century, alchemy necessarily lost its basis for survival.

Generally associated with Aristotle, although clearly traceable in earlier writers such as Empedocles and Plato, the theory of the four elements (earth, air, water, and fire), the opposing qualities that comprise them, and their relative positions in the universe, constitute the foundation of medieval and Renaissance physics, metaphysics, medicine, and psychology. These principles play an equally vital role in alchemy and the "hermetic" worldview. In contrast to Robert Boyle's modern conception of the elements as primary and discrete nonreducible substances, the four elements theory regarded them as different "appearances" or forms of the underlying matter or *prima materia* from which all visible, material objects are derived, each composed of a different combination of hotness, dryness, coldness, and moistness. Boyle's notion of chemical elements precluded the possibility of transmutation by definition: they are "certain Primitive and simple, or perfectly unmingled bodies; which not being made of any other bodies, or of one another, are the Ingredients of which all those call'd perfectly mixt Bodies are immediately compounded, and into which they are ultimately resolved."[42]

In contrast, the idea of alchemical transmutation is implicit in the four elements theory because of the "convertibility" of the elements that comprise all substances: earth could be changed to water if its characteristic "dryness" were replaced by "wetness" and "coldness" remained a constant; similarly air would become fire if "dryness" came to replace "wetness." The ease of this conversion is suggested by the diagram of the four elements from Petrus Bonus's *Pretiosa margarita novella* (Venice, 1546), which includes, along the bottom edge, primitive representations of alchemical vessels and, above, uses symbol to enhance visualization of the four elements, the qualities of which they are composed, and their relationship (fig. 3). In figure 3, as in the following quotation from Plato's *Timaeus*, 49, c, each of the elements is conceived as merely a form or changing manifestation of an underlying prima materia: "In the first place, we see that what we just now called water, by condensation, . . . becomes stone and earth; and this same element, when melted and dispersed, passes into vapour and air. Air, again, when inflamed, becomes fire; and again fire, when condensed and extinguished, passes once more into the form of air; and once more, air, when collected and condensed, produces cloud and mist; and from these, when still more compressed, comes flowing water, and from water comes earth and stones once more; and thus generation appears to be transmitted from one to the other

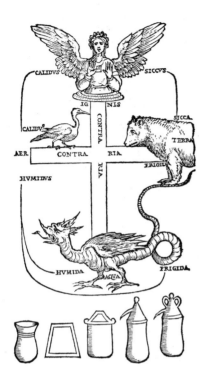

Figure 3. The Four Elements Symbolized. Petrus Bonus, *Pretiosa margarita novella* (1546). By permission of the University of Delaware Library, Newark, Delaware.

in a circle."[43] Alchemists patterned their cyclical transmutation process upon this platonic model, referring to it as the philosophical circle or wheel. Thus the view of unceasing terrestrial transformation provided, by analogy, sanction for the possibility of transmutation of one metal into another.

Boyle's publication of the *Sceptical Chymist,* which contains the critical re-definition of an element, has been called "the death-warrant of alchemy."[44] In view of its devastating effect on alchemical theory it is curious (yet altogether characteristic of the most eminent seventeenth-century scientists) that Boyle, like Newton, should have taken keen interest in alchemy. Unwilling to make dogmatic pronouncements on the nature of truth, he is said to have believed in the possibility of transmutation and to have helped repeal a medieval ordinance that outlawed multiplication of precious metals.[45] His attack on the foundations of alchemy had been foreshadowed, as I will show in chapter 4, by Francis Ba-con, who appears to have believed in transmutation but who attempted to dis-sociate it from the superstition-ridden ways of the alchemists. In addition to Bacon, Boyle, and Newton, a long procession of sixteenth- and seventeenth-century writers, works, and intellectual currents contributed to the demise of alchemy. Most of these are a part of the "new" philosophy with its increasingly empirical investigation of nature, and among them are Copernicus, Kepler, Galileo, Mersenne, Harvey, Hobbesian materialism, Cartesian rationalism, the experimentalism of the Royal Society, and the correct dating of writings long attributed to Hermes Trismegistus. The collective effect of these influences was actually and symbolically the death of alchemy, the "medieval" science.

The sulphur-mercury theory also derives from aspects of the old worldview and is the basis for Renaissance notions of the natural formation of metals and minerals in the earth and their artificial production through alchemy. If all sublunary substances are in a state of flux as the result of the imposition of different forms upon prime matter, it follows that metals, too, could be changed through recombining or altering the proportion of the elements that comprise them. The sulphur-mercury theory also draws on the idea of primary opposition inherent in the Aristotelian view: "sulphur" is identified with fire and possesses the qualities of hotness and dryness; "mercury," identified with water, possesses coldness and moistness. These two principles interact in the form of subterranean vapors or exhalations (the former "male," the latter "female"), and if the conjunction occurs under proper conditions—the degree of heat is especially crucial—new metals are produced within the womb of the earth.[46] The analogy between the natural and alchemical processes and related doctrines is visually represented in the engraving entitled, in translation, "Just as nature, art makes metals out of sulphur and mercury" (fig. 4), from Michael Maier's *Symbola aurea Mensæ* (1617).

For the alchemists, two extremely important corollaries developed from the four elements theory. Because in alchemy manipulation of the elements is conducted by human agents rather than nature, they came to consider their art as an imitation of nature, an artificial duplication of the subterranean processes that cause the conception and growth of metals. Second, because these artificial efforts were thought to produce gold more rapidly than the natural processes, alchemists continually described themselves as improvers or perfecters of nature, able to accomplish in a few weeks or months what nature had taken centuries to produce. Elias Ashmole, for example, states that "As *Nature* in her work below used two hot *Workmen* so will I; and because we cannot tarry her leisure, and long time she taketh to that purpose, we will match and countervail her little *Heats* with proportions answerable and meet for our time, that we may do that in fourty dayes which she doth in as many years."[47] For this reason, as noted earlier, H.J. Sheppard sees alchemy as effecting "alterations of duration in some linear time scale." Thus, alchemy was an important manifestation of the Renaissance debate on the relative powers of "art" versus "nature" although it has not generally been considered in this context.

Another alchemical doctrine that was wholly compatible, in fact synonymous, with the medieval-Renaissance worldview was that of the macrocosm and microcosm and the complex system of correspondences and "sympathies" that link them. The primacy of this relationship in alchemy, however, is much less familiar than its presence in Renaissance and seventeenth-century literature. As previously mentioned, the possibility of transmutation was predicated on the idea that underlying all "forms" in which substances appear there is only one

Figure 4. Nature and Art. Michael Maier, *Symbola aureæ Mensæ*
(1617). By permission of The Huntington Library, San Marino,
California.

prima materia. The macrocosm-microcosm idea is an extension of this theory
and of equally ancient origin. "The One is All"—and its visual counterpart, the
ouroboros—is one of the oldest motifs in alchemy, pervading the *Tabula
Smaragdina* or *Emerald Table of Hermes,* which according to two different versions was either found in the tomb of Hermes Trismegistus by Alexander the
Great or else "taken from the hands of the dead Hermes in a cave near Hebron,
some ages after the Flood, by Sarah the wife of Abraham."[48] Its supposed antiquity and semidivine authorship caused it to be regarded as the most sacred book
of alchemy, revealing cryptically the means of producing the philosopher's stone.
Its opening precepts emphasize the correspondences between the greater world
and the lesser: "That which is beneath is like that which is above: & that which
is above, is like that which is beneath, to worke the miracles of one thing. And
as all things have proceeded from one, by the meditation of one, so all things
have sprung from this one thing by adaptation."[49] Explicit in this passage is the
idea of resemblance and analogy between the celestial and sublunary spheres
and their creation by a single divine being or principle acting upon a common
underlying substance and for a single purpose.

      Because of their reliance on these common assumptions, natural magic and
alchemy were often linked together. Like the *magus,* the alchemist saw himself
as one who, although operating within the traditional worldview, was able to
alter and manipulate the normal course of nature through highly specialized

knowledge and experience. Thus the alchemist believed he could shorten the
natural process of goldmaking within the bowels of the earth by bringing base
metals to perfection through secret formulas and recipes, just as the magus believed it possible to accomplish unusual feats through the help of familiar spirits
invoked by occult powers. In each case "art" was decidedly an "improver" of nature.

Resting on a common foundation, it was inevitable that the two bodies of
knowledge should have many points of contact and that, as a result, attitudes
toward them tended to be similar. This kinship is evidenced by the fact that
from the time of Hermes Trismegistus—as it was traditionally conceived—on,
both magical and alchemical powers were thought often to reside in the same
individual. Frances Yates's remarks on the interplay of macrocosm and microcosm in Ficino's astral magic apply equally well to the relationship between the
alchemist (or the practitioner of Renaissance medicine) and the universe:

> For the All was One, united by an infinitely complex system of relationships.
> The magician was one who knew how to enter into this system, and use it, by
> knowing the links of the chains of influences descending vertically from above
> and establishing for himself a chain of ascending links by correct use of the
> occult sympathies in terrestrial things, of celestial images, of invocations and
> names, and the like. The methods and the cosmological background presup-
> posed are the same whether the magician is using these forces to try to obtain
> concrete material benefits for himself, or whether he is using them religiously, . . .
> for insight into the divine forces in nature and to assist his worship of them.[50]

This network of correspondences is illustrated with brilliant concision in
figure 5, a well-known diagram from Robert Fludd's *Utriusque cosmi maioris*
(Oppenheim, 1617, 19), in which the link between God, the goddess Nature,
and Art or Man, the "ape" of Nature, is established by means of a Christianized
version of Homer's golden chain. These figures are superimposed upon a symbolic representation of the macrocosm and microcosm, e.g., three angelic orders, the fixed stars, the planetary spheres arranged according to the Ptolemaic
ordering; and, in the microcosm, the four elements in descending order, the
three kingdoms with representative members, and the liberal arts, arranged so as
to illustrate ways in which they supplement, assist, or correct Nature's operations within the three kingdoms.[51] Upon this comprehensive and divinely created network the magus (or the alchemist) projects his will and specialized knowledge in order to bring about supernatural effects.

Besides providing man with a link to the divine, the macrocosm-microcosm correspondence was commonly employed by the alchemists in describing
their own position in the universe and even the composition of the philosopher's
stone. For example, in the *New Light of Alchymie* by Michael Sendivogius, a
popular seventeenth-century alchemist to be discussed in chapter 5, we have, on
the one hand, what appears to be a commonplace representation of man as microcosm. Sendivogius states that men are "created after the likeness of the great

Integræ Naturæ ʃpeculum,Artisque imago.

Figure 5. Fludd's Universal Correspondence Theory. *Utriusque cosmi . . . historia* (1617, 1619). Courtesy of the National Library of Medicine, Bethesda, Maryland.

World, yea after the Image of God. Thou hast in thy Body the Anatomy of the whole World, thou hast instead of the Firmament the Quintessence of the four Elements, extracted out of the Chaos of Sperms into a Matrix, and into a Skin, which doth compass it round, . . . thou hast a Heart in stead of the Earth; where the Central Fire continually works; and preserves the Fabrick of this Microcosm in its Being; . . . and all thy Members answer to some Celestials."[52] What gives the description uniqueness, however, is its effective use of concepts and terminology drawn from alchemy (as in "quintessence," "extracted," "Chaos of Sperms") to render the traditional picture of man's relation to the larger world. Or, in the following passage from *The Ordinall of Alchimy,* Thomas Norton of Bristol, one of England's most highly regarded late medieval alchemists, applies the same concept to the "*Stone Microcosmos*" itself. His lines contain an unusually clear statement of the macrocosm-microcosm and four elements theories, their relationship to alchemical theory, and final accommodation to Christian doctrine:

> Noble Auctors men of glorious fame,
> Called our *Stone Microcosmus* by name:
> For his composition is withouten doubt,
> Like to this World in which we walke about:
> Of Heate, of Cold, of Moyst and of Drye,
> Of Hard, of Soft, of Light and of Heavy,
> Of Rough, of Smooth, and of things Stable,
> Medled with things fleetinge and moveable;
> Of all kinds Contrary broght to one accord,
> Knit by the doctrine of *God* our blessed *Lord*:[53]

In Norton's representative view, the most striking feature of this remarkable stone's composition is the very commonness of its components. It is a synthesis of all sublunary opposites, which have been brought together by God into a unified whole. Here truly is unity within multiplicity.

Another link between alchemy and the medieval-Renaissance worldview is a shared animistic perspective, which posited a universe filled with life and sentiency. The Florentine Neoplatonists traced this notion back to Hermes Trismegistus and made it an integral part of their thought. For Tommaso Campanella, animism also descended from Hermes, who first taught "that the world is a living animal,"[54] and it served as the foundation for Campanella's natural magic. Michael Sendivogius accommodates this idea with Christianity, asserting that the spirit of God fills nature: "Therefore I say Nature is but one, true, plain, perfect, and entire in its own being, which God made from the beginning, placing his spirit in it."[55] A hylozoistic conception of matter is present even in Francis Bacon's work, although much more obvious in the hermetic poetry of Henry Vaughan and works of the "chemical philosophers," which I will treat in later chapters. Nonetheless this ancient doctrine rapidly declined in the face of assaults by increasingly rationalistic and mechanistic forces, as seen in Marin Mersenne's attacks on the hermeticism of Robert Fludd.[56]

Alchemy also relied on animistic ideas, often combined with anthropomorphism, in a variety of ways. They are basic to the notion that both natural and artificially produced metals possess sex, soul, and feeling. Sulphur and mercury are the sexually differentiated "parents" whose union produces offspring, which are other metals. Their birth from the womb of Mother Earth (or analogically from the "womb" of the alchemists' alembics) results after "gestation," which follows the impregnation or *conjunction,* has run its course. In Maier's *Emblema* II, "His nurse is the earth" (fig. 6), this doctrine is curiously depicted through combining this precept from the *Emerald Table* with the myths of Mother Earth and Romulus and Remus, and the notion of the philosopher's stone as microcosm. Lead and iron are base metals because their "maturation" is incomplete; gold and silver are purer because they have "grown ripe" over a prolonged period. An important axiom of alchemy and pre–seventeenth century natural history is that nature always "strives" to make gold, and the "souls" of base metals continually aspire to this state of perfection. Further, the volatility of substances within the alchemists' vessels is seen as evidence of the "spirits'" desire to escape the torture of the furnace. Such terms and concepts, often reminiscent of primitive myth and folklore, are commonplaces of alchemical animism and anthropomorphism and appear frequently in literary and visual representations of the art. In short, animism and hylozoism, together with the theories of the four elements, universal correspondences, and the unity of matter, were the links that securely bound alchemical theory to the common worldview of the Middle Ages and Renaissance.

Literary authors of the late Middle Ages and early modern period were usually more interested in the distinctly human aspects of alchemy than in its theory and history. While isolated theoretical and historical details appear frequently enough in literary treatments—as a basis for imagery, simile, or metaphor; to lend an element of concreteness and realism; to create an aura of "learnedness" or its opposite—such details are most often subordinated to the overall demands of portrayal of character and distinctly human situations. At its most successful, literary alchemy has the human condition as its prime concern, but it is the human condition as touched, or "worked upon," by recognizable aspects of the theory and practice of the art. Chaucer, Erasmus, Jonson, and Samuel Butler, to name only four, used alchemy to represent the flawed nature of mankind, creating characters corrupted less because of their involvement in alchemical matters than by the presence of deeper evils that have led them to this involvement. For example, in Chaucer's Canon's Yeoman, in Jonson's Face and Subtle and their victims, or in Butler's Hudibras and Ralph, alchemy may be both a cause and an effect of human corruption, but it is more frequently a means of objectifying the *consequences* of original sin than of representing the evil itself. Alchemy is splendidly equipped to represent moral transformation and transmutation, sometimes from evil to good, but also, in works belonging to the satirical tradition, from good or potential good to evil.

Just as there are varieties of alchemy corresponding to differing definitions and objectives, so there exists a wide range of types of alchemists, distinguished from each other according to their practices and intentions. These types are present in the works of both alchemical writers and in the creations of the literary authors whom I will be considering. Because the portrayal of alchemical

EMBLEMA II. *De secretis Naturæ.*
Nutrix ejus terra eſt.

EPIGRAMMA II.

Romulus hirta lupæ preſſiſſe ſed ubera capræ
Jupiter, & factis, fertur, adeſſe fides:
Quid mirum, teneræ SAPIENTUM viſcera PROLIS
Si ferimus TERRAM lacte nutriſſe ſuo?
Parvula ſi tantas Heroas beſtia pavit,
QUANTUS, cui NUTRIX TERREUS ORBIS, *erit?*

Figure 6. The Earth as Nurse. Michael Maier, *Atalanta fugiens* (1617).
By permission of the University of Delaware Library, Newark, Delaware.

characters is grounded in several of these types, each with its own distinctive context and associations, it will be useful to sketch some of them briefly, drawing primarily upon the writings of alchemical authors.

The earlier distinction between esoteric and exoteric alchemy provides a useful point of departure because the alchemists seemed never to tire of classifying and categorizing themselves while stating (and defending) their own positions. For example, as already noted, Patrick Scot, in asserting the primacy of spiritual alchemy and philosophical stoicism in *The Tillage of Light,* concludes with a warning to practitioners of physical alchemy to abandon their quests for artificial gold and turn to the perfection of their own souls: "If truth may have trust, all their *Ignitions, Calcinations, Dissolutions, Amalgations, Circulations, Sublimations, Fixations, and Multiplications,* otherwise then in a *spirituall* sense, are but borrowed words of *Art,* to make *unguent* for *Jadish itching diseases, smoake* to ruine craz'd estates, or trumpery to uphold *Mountebanckes* upon the charges of the more curious then wise."[57] The alchemists who are singled out for treatment by medieval and Renaissance satirists are generally adherents of the practical or exoteric type. More accurately, they are *pretenders* to alchemical wisdom who, like Scot's "*Mountebanckes,*" drew upon the art's mysterious processes and substances, its associations with magic, who utilized its revered authorities and exotic jargon, and, most of all, its promise of limitless wealth, in order to cheat the credulous and greedy. From the time of *The Canon's Yeoman's Tale* to the alchemical drama of Ben Jonson, it is the pseudo-alchemists who dominate English literature, and the absurd pretentiousness of their claims and the deceptiveness of their methods are repeatedly castigated by literary and alchemical authors alike. In the dedication to his *Fasciculus Chemicus* (1650), Arthur Dee observes that "The Art of Chymistry . . . is so much defamed, disparaged, and brought into disgrace, by the fraudulent dealings of Imposters, as that whosoever professes it, shall still be stigmatized with Publike Reproach."[58] And in his Prolegomena to the same work, Elias Ashmole notes that "the dignity of this infallible *Mystery* [i.e., alchemical secrets] lies open to many hard *Censures,* and profane *Scandals,*" but, adding the alchemists' conventional claim to legitimacy, he states that he will "endeavor to remove, and purge this pure and heroick *Science* (almost generally contemptible) from the dross, and corruption of an *Imposture.*"[59] These prefatory materials to the *Fasciculus Chemicus* are valuable for their information on the contemporary state of alchemy and clearly suggest that Dee, Ashmole, as well as other hermetic disciples, saw themselves as under a cloud of suspicion and mistrust. But at the same time, Dee's observation about charlatanism must be recognized as part of a very long tradition of such warnings reaching back to Avicenna and the beginning of alchemical writing in the West. Indeed, these admissions of alchemy's present debasement are so common as to constitute an important motif within the tradition of alchemical writing and give rise, in turn, to a more familiar topos: alchemical adepts boast that through requisite knowledge, hard work, and the grace of God, they will reveal the secret of transmutation to the worthy and endeavor to restore the debased art to its former state of glory. Thus we find a persistent tension within alchemy's written tradition between truth and falsity, honesty and chicanery, and ethical idealism and depravity. To cite only one example, these moral implications are present in Ashmole's summary of the true meaning of an alchemical master's passing on the secrets of his art to an initiate "son": "Furthermore, this *Learning* is not *revealed* by any *Master,* but under the most weighty *Ties* and *Obligations* of an *Oath;* and that by long *tryal* and *experience* of a mans *fidelity, vertue, judgment, discretion, faithfulness, secresie, desires, inclinations,* and *conversations;* to sift and try whether he be *capable* and *deserving.*"[60]

Although Ashmole's statements are conventional, his views are repeated with such urgency by his contemporaries that we sense that alchemy was undergoing a special crisis brought on as much by corruption within its practice as by the emerging New Philosophy. Examples of outcries against charlatanism in the mid- and late seventeenth century abound, and the following are only a few representative ones. In the Preface to his *Art of Distillation* (1651), the prolific medical writer and Paracelsian, John French, speaks of the "multitude of Artists [i.e., alchemists] there are in this Nation," of a "glut of Chymicall books, but a scarcity of chymicall truthes." His ire is directed especially at the quacks and imposters who have invaded the medical profession (fig. 7): a "sort of men by whom this Art hath been much scandalized, and they indeed have brought a great Odium upon it by carrying about, and vending their whites, and reds, their sophisticated oils, & salts, their dangerous and ill prepared *Turbithes,* and *Aurum vitae's.*" He further announces his dedication to the restoration of alchemy's reputation and its service to the art of healing.[61]

Also concerned about the consequences of medical quackery, Theodore Kirkringius, the annotator of the *Triumphant Chariot of Antimony* by the mysterious and pseudonymous authority on preparations of antimony, Basil Valentine, speaks out against the "*Clamours* [that] *arise against* Chymists, *as if the impious rashness of some false* Chymists *were to be imputed to the Art, which* Pseudochymists *care not how many Houses they fill with Funerals, provided one or two that are healed will blaze their Fame, and they can hear themselves called* Doctors, *and rob the simple of their money.*"[62] William Cooper, author, editor, printer, and seller of occult books, expresses the wish in his *Philosophical Epitaph of W.C. Esquire* (1673), that "the laws were not so strict, nor the snares so many, against the honest Practisers of this Art, but to punish the others more severely that abuse the same."[63] Similarly, John Frederick Houpreght's *Aurifontina Chymica* (1680) contains the exhortation to "shun such Sophisters, Cheats and Impostors, as much as the grand Impostor the Devil, and avoid them as carefully as a terrible burning Fire, and Poyson. . . . For though a man should spend a whole Province or Kingdom upon such deceitful processes, yet all would be consumed in vain, and no firm truth thereby be obtained."[64]

Finally, to trace this line of attack up to the beginning of the eighteenth

Figure 7. Itinerant Seller of Medicines. Engraving by T. Kitchin (fl. 1750), after David Teniers. By permission of the Wellcome Institute Library, London.

century, the pseudonymous Cleidophorus Mystagogus, author of *Mercury's Caducean Rod,* uses a treatise by Sendivogius, to be discussed in chapter 5, to attack charlatans and false commentators on alchemical authorities: "O vain wretches, may not I properly apply to you the words of *Sandivogius,* where Nature speaks to the Alchymist in his Treatise of Mercury, *for your falseness you deserve the Halter,* equally as well as those who rob on the high-way, for of the two, you are the greatest Thieves."[65]

It would be inaccurate to conclude from the above that all alchemists were either charlatans, incompetent iatrochemists, or men devoted to various forms of spiritual and moral improvement that they identified with the pursuit of the philosopher's stone or elixir vitae. During the seventeenth-century Paracelsian vogue in England, which saw heated controversy in the medical community as well as publication of many new editions and translations of Paracelsus's works, we find numerous vitriolic attacks on the Swiss reformer and his followers as well as occasional tributes to them. The latter, usually written by those who were of the Paracelsian persuasion, take pains to represent iatrochemists as ones who emphasize painstaking experimentation in the search for effective medications, conscientious care of patients, and a sober lifestyle. Such portraits are vastly different from those of doctors who were officially licensed by the College of Physicians. The translation of Paracelsus's *Nine Books of the Nature of Things,* published with a Sendivogian treatise in 1674, presents a highly sympathetic portrait of these medical practitioners:

> For they are not given to idleness and sloth, nor go in a proud habit, or Plush & Velvet Garments, often shewing their Rings upon their fingers, or wearing Swords

with silver hilts by their sides, or fine and gay Gloves upon their hands, but
diligently follow their labours, sweating whole nights and days by their Furnaces.

. . . They are not talkative when they come to the Sick, neither do they extol
their Medicines: seeing they well know that the Artificer must not commend
his Work, but the Work the Artificer, and that the Sick cannot be cured with
fine words.[66]

As we have observed, several of the images and stereotypes of chemists and
alchemists recently cited situate these types within a medical context. In this
respect, the examples drawn from John French, Basil Valentine, and Paracelsus
reflect a reorientation of alchemy and alchemical writing that was occurring in
the seventeenth century: medical and pharmacological concerns were coming to
supplant pursuit of the philosopher's stone and magical elixirs as primary interests. In addition, the terms "chemist" and "chemistry," although by no means
completely replacing the earlier forms, were becoming common and brought
with them associations of modernity, progress, and scientific respectability. The
literary implications of this evolution from the "art" of alchemy to the "science"
of chemistry will be discussed in chapter 9; at present I will anticipate only parts
of that discussion by giving brief attention to a final pair of portraits that relate
to the medical and scientific topics recently mentioned.

Considerable uncertainty has always surrounded the career of George Starkey
(1628-65?). Born in Bermuda and recipient of a B.A. and M.A. from Harvard,
Starkey (or Stirk) practiced medicine for a time in America and emigrated to
England about 1650, where he became active in the scientific circle of Samuel
Hartlib and an associate of Robert Boyle. At some point, probably before his
arrival in England, he began to promote the work of a mysterious adept who
wrote under the pseudonym "Eirenaeus Philalethes," with whom Starkey is usually, but not universally, identified. The Starkey controversy is centered in the
identity of "Philalethes," his relationship to Starkey, and authorship of the many
works that appear under each of their names.[67] One of these is the lengthy alchemical poem, *The Marrow of Alchemy,* which appeared in two parts in 1654-
55 under the name of Eirenaeus Philoponos Philalethes, generally regarded as
Starkey's pseudonym. A champion of chemical medicine at a time when its efficacy was being hotly debated, Starkey's prolific writings also include *Pyrotechny
Asserted and Illustrated, to be the surest and safest means for Arts Triumph over
Natures Infirmities* (1658). Of special interest for this study are the two prose
characters that Starkey included in *Pyrotechny,* for while my major concern is
alchemical influences in literature, it is also important to note those few instances in which distinctly "literary" influences are present in alchemical writing. Obviously aware of the vogue of the Theophrastan character in seventeenth-
century England and the works by Sir Thomas Overbury, John Earle, and their
successors, Starkey's carefully drawn contributions to this genre are entitled, first,
"The Character of a Praeposterous searcher after Natures secrets," followed im-

mediately by "The Character of him, who so searcheth Natures Secrets, as to reap profit thereby, and so attends Pyrotechny, *as to be made,* Per Ignem Philosophus."[68] (Not above self-congratulation, Starkey refers to himself on the book's title page as one *"who is a Philosopher by Fire."*)

The portrait of the "praeposterous" alchemist or iatrochemist analyzes its subject-type from the standpoint of psychology and character as much as by professional practice; Starkey's bases for evaluation appear to reflect something of the New Science as well as views and standards that were emerging in contemporary medical controversy. This "Searcher" lacks "due discretion, . . . and manageth his undertaking without prudence, or Reason" (57). Being "generally credulous, and confident" (i.e., rash) he is prone to be deceived by authors and works that promise greater and more spectacular cures and secrets. In marked contrast to the Paracelsian practitioner described earlier, Starkey's subject is "for the most part garrulous, and vainly glorious, . . . oft declaiming of his *Art,* . . . of which he is before hand as sure, as he who sold a Bearskin before he had killed the Bear" (58). His pride inspires him only to the highest ends, but incapable of attaining them for reasons of impatience and contempt for requisite training and preparation, he "verifies the Proverb of him, who *reaching at a star stumbles at a straw,* resolving to appear nothing, unless he may equal the highest, he lives all his life in obscuritie, care, and anxiety" (60). In the end, he becomes the *type* of the deluded adept of the tradition of alchemical satire, "daily impoverished, by expence of Coals, and Instruments of Glass, Earth, Iron, &c. And the Charge of the Materials he useth, besides Labourers Wages, and various Furnaces daily made and altered, which will soon sink a fair estate" (60).

The subject of the second of Starkey's characters (and both are true representatives of the genre) is also an iatrochemist. Predictably, however, and owing to the pairing of these sketches, "The Character of him, who . . . attends Pyrotechny," embodies all that the "Praeposterous" searcher lacks. Unlike his predecessor, he is not obsessed with the *"grand Arcana's"* but patiently studies in "Natures Book," secure in the belief that he who has "Gods blessing, will have his searches crownd with success" (63). Throughout, the details of this portrait are highly moralistic and pietistic: for example, "Such a one is from his childhood given to studiousness, & from the first of his yeers of *maturity,* his *mind* is busie, and his *thoughts* pensive, how he may live serviceable to *God* and *mankind,* according to the *Talents*" (63). He avoids *"temporal preferments"* (63), and next to the glorification of God, "accounts Medicine to be the most desirable, and highest attainment" (64). Finally, his piety and conscientious medical practice meet in his recognition of Christ as the type of the "good physician," the only pattern worthy of man's imitation (64).[69]

While this second character is informed primarily by traditions of protestant piety, the two together derive a moral meaning that owes something to the surrounding context of medical controversy and Baconian science's insistence on observation and experimentation rather than reliance on authority. In contrast to the first character's rash "praeposterousness," the second confronts differences in medical opinion with patience and a determination to test the worth of the contending theories for himself. Unlike his foil, his instinctive reaction is not simply to deprecate the traditional Galenic view that had long held sway: "He doth not (as many do) for company sake, rail at, & crie down the old way, received in the *Schools;* but makes trial of it according to the Scholastick promises, to bring about (with sincere intentions) his patients expectations" (65). His concern for his patients' recovery takes precedence over the politics of medicine—or so it would seem. Only after he has conducted a thorough examination into the grounds of controversy does it become clear that the careful searcher is Paracelsian in orientation, and this enables Starkey to end the sketch on a note of satiric humor at the expense of his academic opponents: "But alas! upon proof, he finds the whole *Art,* as it is *Academically* taught, to be but an Embleme of that *Stable* which was cleansed by *Hercules, a miscellaneous Hotchpotch,* partly false, partly ridiculous, generally desperate and dangerous" (65). Surely, given his own medical orientation, Starkey must have regarded his second character as a virtual self-portrait, as is suggested by the fact that this man who "so searcheth Natures Secrets, as to reap profit thereby, . . . [also] attends Pyrotechny."

Just as there are several definitions and types of alchemy and a variety of alchemists who practice (or malpractice) them, so there is a multiplicity of alchemical writing styles that evolve from the individual author's personality and orientation toward his subject, his purpose in writing, and view of his audience. While recognizing the existence of these styles, it is impossible here to analyze many of them, and I will conclude this chapter with brief discussion of a few distinguishing features of alchemical writing, particularly those that receive literary treatment. It is alchemical style that, perhaps more than anything else, is the measure of this art, the means by which it is known.

The title of this book is derived from a passage in Patrick Scot's *Tillage of Light,* where, in discussing the manner in which writers have attempted to communicate and accommodate the idea of Divine Wisdom to the human understanding, Scot notes that "least [sic] *Wisdome* might Prophesie to the *winde;* or that shee will not be apprehended but of sound mindes; that a glorious spirit will not appear but in her owne kinde, and that a precious seed requires pure earth, these Philosophers did sometimes pourtrey *Wisdome* in darke *hierogliphicks,* sometimes in fabulous attire, they have deified her, entituling her to the names of *Mercury, Pallas, Minerva,* begotten by *Jupiter;* all which doe mystically imply that true *Wisdome* commeth, and by us received from *heaven.*"[70] As noted earlier, Scot's concern throughout the *Tillage* is esoteric alchemy: he categorically rejects physical transmutation in favor of spiritual and philosophical realities to which, in his view, alchemy has primary reference. Nonetheless, the problems that Scot notes in communicating moral and ethical wisdom, as portrayed in the figure of Minerva, are similar to those faced by alchemical writers of all types:

the concerns with revelation and concealment. For writers who believed they possessed secrets of the art and, for whatever reason, wished to communicate them, there was great anxiety about the moral, spiritual, and intellectual "worthiness" of the recipient. Wisdom must not be allowed to prophecy in vain, after all it is sent from heaven, nor must her truths be apprehended by those who are not of "sound mindes." The secrets of the art must be passed on, therefore, by adept fathers to initiate sons who resemble them as closely as possible in—to cite Ashmole again—"*fidelity, vertue, judgment, discretion, faithfulness, secresie, desires, inclinations,* and *conversations.*" Only in this way can the adept be assured that wisdom's integrity will not be traduced, that this "precious seed" will be planted in "pure earth."

The seriousness with which this transmission of arcane wisdom was regarded is reflected in Robert Vaughan's engraving of an alchemical initiation that Ashmole included in his *Theatrum Chemicum Britannicum* (fig. 8), in which, beneath the Holy Spirit and two angels, the adept places the book of secrets into the hands of the initiate with the words: "Take God's gift under the holy seal." The initiate responds: "I will preserve the alchemical secrets in secrecy." Above, the scroll surrounding the angel on the left states: "Thou hast loved justice and hatest wickedness, therefore the Lord thy God hath anointed thee with oil"; that on the right states, "Await the Lord, play the man, and He will strengthen thy heart."[71] Alchemical authors are, then, centrally concerned with problems of selected revelation and concealment: with ensuring that their wisdom is passed only to those who are pure and pious and not to the ignorant, vulgar, and degenerate. To prevent the latter, alchemical works employ devices of concealment and disguise: cryptic imagery and symbol, fanciful simile and metaphor, pervasive allegory, arcane renderings of classical myth, biblical stories and fable and, as Brian Vickers has recently argued, a persistently analogical habit of mind.[72] The emblems and diagrams that comprise alchemy's rich pictorial tradition feature many of these same qualities, as often demonstrated in the illustrations included in this volume.

In his Prolegomena to Arthur Dee's *Fasciculus Chemicus,* Ashmole lists four types of alchemical authors, and it is significant that the distinctions among them have to do entirely with questions of revelation and concealment. First, there are those writers who "lay down the whole Mystery *faithfully* and *plainly;* giving you a *Clew,* as well as shewing you a *Labyrinth.*" Second are those who deal clearly only with a part of the whole, who write mainly to reveal their mastery and not to teach others. Third are those "who out of *Ignorance* or *Mistake,* have delivered blinde and unbottomed *Fictions,* which have too much deluded and abused the credulous *World.*" And, finally, "the last and worst of all, . . . who through *Envy* have scattered abroad their unfaithful *recipies* and false *glosses;* (taking for president [sic] the *Devil* that can sow *tares,* and transform himself into an *Angel of Light*) with intent to *choak* and *obfuscate* the more evident *light* of the plain dealing *Philosophers.*"[73] Ashmole's third and fourth types of alchemi-

Figure 8. Alchemical Master and Disciple. Elias Ashmole, *Theatrum Chemicum Britannicum* (1652). By permission of The Huntington Library, San Marino, California.

cal writers have, throughout English literary history, attracted the greatest amount of scornful criticism; from Chaucer to Erasmus, Jonson, and Butler, ignorance and deliberate misrepresentation are the qualities for which alchemical language is best known.

The following chapters will provide ample opportunity to observe these stylistic categories, because commentaries and attacks upon the alchemists frequently focus on the obscurity of their writing. Thus the tradition of *ignotum per ignocius,* explaining the unknown by the more unknown, is a vital part of the satirical tradition that goes back at least as far as Chaucer. Indeed, the bizarre catalogues of terms, processes, materials, and pieces of laboratory equipment that are the satirist's stock in trade through the time of Jonson have their basis in this aspect of alchemical lore. Attacks on the alchemists' obfuscation were not limited to literary authors, however, and, particularly with the New Science's insistence on clarity and plainness of style in the later seventeenth century, we find that the exotic idiom of the alchemists played an important role in its demise. As I will show in chapter 9, this idiom was associated with irrationality and philosophical enthusiasm and was frequently attacked in the treatises of Joseph Glanvill, John Wilkins, Seth Ward, Thomas Hall, Samuel Parker, and other Restoration intellectuals and scientists, many of whom were fellows of the newly founded Royal Society.

But even as the New Science and other forces demanding prose reform were hastening the demise of alchemy through insisting on perspicuity, other influences were working at least to perpetuate temporarily the exotic excesses of alchemical rhetoric. These influences were not, however, associated with the willful deceptions of practicing charlatans or medical quacks but with the various strains of religious and mystical alchemy that flourished throughout the seventeenth century. Especially important, as Christopher Hill and others have noted, were alchemy's links with biblical allegory and doctrines of millenarianism, which were associated primarily, although not exclusively, with the religious sectarians.[74] But even outside the radical sects and before their proliferation, we find a tradition of alchemical allegorization of biblical topoi extending throughout the seventeenth century from early to late. Thomas Tymme, who, as previously noted, emphasized the art's spiritual and philosophical dimensions, frequently employs alchemical glosses in his readings from the Old and New Testaments. The following quotation views the Mosaical account of the Creation in Genesis, chapter 1, from the perspective of Paracelsus's *tria prima,* or salt-sulphur-mercury theory: "For God in the beginning, as *Moses* testifieth, . . . devided waters from waters; that is to say, the more subtill, airie, and Mercurial liquor, from the more thicke, clammy, oyle-like, or Sulfurous liquor. After that, *Moses* telleth us that God separated from the more grosse waters, the *Earth,* which standeth apart by it selfe, like *Salt.* And thus in the bosome of the worlde, God included these three simple bodies, *Salt, Sulphur,* and *Mercurie,* as the first formes of things."[75] Here, Tymme uses Paracelsus's "three principles," which he ultimately attributes to Hermes Trismegistus, to subvert Aristotle's four elements theory and to lend support to his own belief that "all things exist in the number of three," a "most holy and potent number, and the number of perfection."[76] Writers also brought alchemical perspectives to bear on Christ's nativity, crucifixion, and, especially, the Last Judgment.

Closely related to scripturally based alchemical allegory is the parallel phenomenon of millenarian and eschatological doctrine conceived alchemically, which appears frequently in English and Continental treatises of the sixteenth and seventeenth centuries and finds occasional resonance in the poetry of Henry

Vaughan and Milton.[77] Vital to this concept is the perceived analogy between Christ and the philosopher's stone, both notable for their regenerative potency and ability to "cleanse" and "heal" imperfect matter, whether human or metallic. Around this center are clustered several related ideas, which will be examined in detail in chapter 7, but which can now be briefly introduced, again through a passage from Thomas Tymme. After citing several eschatological verses, such as Romans 8:19 and 2 Peter 3:7, 10, and 13, Tymme provides an unusually thorough alchemical gloss on the theme of the day of judgment,

> when Christ our Lord shall come to judgment, in the last period of time, the foure Elements (whereof all creatures consist) having in them matter both combustible, and incombustible, as the Heaven, shall by the wonderfull power of God, be changed. For the combustible having in it a corrupt and drossie matter, which maketh them subject to corruption, shall in that great and refining day be purged through fire, and then God will make new Heavens and a new Earth, . . . that all things may be brought to a Quintessence of eternitie: So that the world, as touching the Nature thereof, and substance, shall not perish, but be made new, to a greater perfection then now it hath.[78]

The figure of Christ as the "almighty chymist," descending to purge the world of its "corrupt and drossie matter" and make it new is frequently employed in seventeenth-century alchemical literature. Besides Tymme, we find versions of it in Nicolas Flamel, Cooper, Houpreght, Sendivogius, John French, Boehme, Starkey, Eirenaeus Philaletha, and Cleidophorous Mystagogus, and this list is not exhaustive. While these alchemical eschatologists present nothing like a uniform description of the impending day of wrath, collectively they reveal many of the themes and motifs traditionally associated with this event: the period of persecution and wickedness that will precede the Second Coming; the successive rises and falls of the three monarchies (eastern, southern, western) preceding the present emergence of the northern; the revelation of long-hidden secrets that will come to pass during the northern monarchy, making it a time of great hope and moral, material, and scientific progress; and the ushering in of this era by the figure of Elias or Elias Artista.[79]

What was the response of the alchemical millenarians to what was widely seen as the imminent destruction and reordering of the existing world? Tymme's notion of a world not "perishing" but wrought "to a greater perfection then now it hath" reflects the joyful hope that is commonly expressed at this prospect. Other writers explain in greater detail their reasons for optimism, statements usually based on expectations of improved conditions for human beings while on earth, not an escape from a temporal "vale of tears" into a conventional Christian afterlife. Drawing heavily on a millenarian passage included in the Preface to Sendivogius's *Treatise of Sulphur,* John French states that the "fourth Monarchy which is Northerne, is dawning, in which (as the ancient Philosophers did divine) all Arts and sciences shal flourish, and greater and more things shal be discovered then in the three former. . . . the Northerne is the last, and indeed is

no other then the golden age, in which all tyranny, oppression, envie, and covetousness shall cease, when there shal be one prince and one people abounding
with love and mercy, & flourishing in peace: which day I earnestly expect."[80]
For William Cooper, "the time is come, or not far off, when the true *Elias* is or
will be revealing this and all other Arts and Mysteries more plainly and publickly
then before,"[81] and his following dialogue between "Elias the Artist, and the
Physitian" suggests that Elias can reveal even the secret of the philosopher's stone
to select persons.[82] This idea is popular in treatises written during the remaining
years of the seventeenth century; and, at the beginning of the eighteenth, in his
great vision of millenarian peace, prosperity, and justice in human society, the
pseudonymous Cleidophorus Mystagogus affirms that "the Gold-making Art,
so call'd, will become common to the men of the new World, when Wisdom
shall be esteemed for Wisdom's sake."[83] Thus the prevailing optimism among
alchemical millenarians was rooted in confidence of learning the art's greatest
secret. As Christopher Hill states, "the cosmic hopes which the Hermetic philosophy seemed to open up were not wholly unreasonable in the mid-seventeenth century when magic and science were still advancing side by side."[84] The
philosopher's stone would become the vehicle for the return of the Golden Age.

In the final analysis, alchemy presents us with a series of irreconcilable para-
doxes, many of which have persisted to complicate, enrich, and enliven its literary reflections. It is both an art and a science, ancient and modern, God-sent
and satanic, esoteric and exoteric, remote and accessible: a subject—to draw
once more upon the words of Michael Scot—that is sometimes portrayed "in
darke *hierogliphicks,* and sometimes in fabulous attire." For these reasons, it is
difficult, perhaps impossible, to pursue a *single* line of development or argument in the following chapters. At one time or another, alchemy and alchemists
reflect all of these aspects and many more, depending on the particular mirror
that the author is using, on what he is concerned with revealing or concealing.
Yet in spite of such variations in authorial vision, a rough pattern emerges when
we trace alchemy's literary portrayal from the late Middle Ages to the end of the
seventeenth century. From the time of Chaucer to Jonson, alchemy is quite consistently the object of, or the vehicle for, satire. However, beginning with Bacon's
scientific prose and the poems of Donne and Herbert, this singleness of vision is
scattered and replaced by what are usually more serious religious, philosophical,
and medical adaptations. At a time when alchemical, iatrochemical, and hermetic writing was much concerned with these new directions, it is natural to
find Vaughan and Milton following them as well. This line of development does
not continue to the end of the century, however, and owing to the New Science,
Rationalism, and the general attacks on philosophical enthusiasm in the Restoration period and beyond, we find a return to satire in the works of Samuel
Butler, Shadwell, and Swift. This time the objects of satire are not only alchemy
and alchemists but also the New Science and its projectors with whom they
have been merged.

II

"CONCLUDEN EVEREMOORE AMYS"

Chaucer and the Medieval Heritage of Alchemical Satire

Withouten doute,
Though that the feend noght in our sighte hym shewe,
I trowe he with us be, that ilke shrewe!

The philosophres sworn were everychoon
That they sholden discovere it unto noon,
Ne in no book it write in no manere.
For unto Crist it is so lief and deere
That he wol nat that it discovered bee,
But where it liketh to his deitee
   —*The Canon's Yeoman's Tale*[1]

As has been shown, the commonly accepted medieval and Renaissance worldview, those ideas and assumptions that were held concerning the universe, God, and man, also constituted the supportive framework upon which alchemical theory and practice depended. Commanding the authoritative weight ascribed to "traditional" thought ascending from antiquity, the theory of the four elements and the *prima materia,* the macrocosm-microcosm idea with its intricate system of correspondences and the *anima mundi,* and the sulphur-mercury explanation of the generation of metals, was, as much medieval and sixteenth-century literature shows, a matter of comfortable belief although not impervious to doubt. This sense of security was to fade with the coming of the seventeenth century, but until that time the general attitude toward these principles was much closer to the line of thought represented by Ficino, Bruno, Paracelsus and, later, Robert Fludd, than to that of the English and Continental innovators who soon followed.[2]

Although references to alchemy are found in several medieval English writers, notably Chaucer, Langland, and Gower, this body of knowledge came to be widely used in literary prose, poetry, and drama only late in the sixteenth century. However, when one examines the references throughout the works of Greene, Nashe, Lyly, Dekker, and Lodge, it becomes apparent that their treatment of

alchemy is often similar to that of their medieval predecessors. Parallels in subject, attitude, method, and often specific detail reveal that Renaissance writers
frequently drew on a tradition of alchemical satire that originated in the fourteenth century. The cultivation of this vein of satire during the fifteenth century
and its emergence in the sixteenth will be the subject of chapter 3. My purpose
here is, first, to investigate the bibliographical basis for the frequent occurrence
of alchemy in medieval and Renaissance literature and, second, to examine several of the early literary works that are the foundation of this satirical tradition.

Although a high degree of compatibility existed between alchemical theory
and its cosmological, philosophical, and scientific context, this compatibility does
not alone account for the keen interest in alchemy during the period of this study.
A summary review of alchemical bibliography may, at least, begin to explain why
literary references to alchemy and alchemists began appearing with increasing
frequency toward the end of the sixteenth century and continued at an accelerat-
ing pace in the seventeenth. In comparison to countries on the Continent, England produced relatively few important alchemists and alchemical writings before and during the Renaissance. Yet, despite this scant native tradition, an abundance of alchemical manuscripts and printed treatises existed in England throughout this period. Dorothea W. Singer's *Catalogue of Latin and Vernacular Alchemical Manuscripts,*[3] a massive three-volume work of nearly 1,200 pages, contains
entries for over 1,100 manuscripts of original treatises, copies, translations, and
commentaries at present in England and Ireland and dating from the twelfth
through the fifteenth centuries. In addition, there are short references to over
200 "Alchemical and Technical Recipes and Notes" dating from the same period.

Singer's *Catalogue* demonstrates that while the number of English alchemical authors is small (the chief representatives being Roger Bacon, John Dastin,
Gower, Chaucer, George Ripley, and Thomas Norton), the range of materials
dating from this time, in terms of both number and authorship, is immense. If
we are to judge by the extant manuscripts cited by Singer, few treatises considered significant today were not then available in manuscript either as originals or
copies or had not been subject to commentary and translation. Among copies of
works dating from the ancient Egyptian, classical, and Hellenistic periods are
those ascribed to Plato, Aristotle, and Hermes Trismegistus (including the *Tabula
Smaragdina*).[4] Similarly, the English Middle Ages were in possession of numerous treatises written by the Arabian scholars of the eighth, ninth, and tenth centuries, mentioned in chapter 1: Jabir, Rhazes, Avicenna, and Artephius.[5] Through
translation into medieval Latin beginning in the mid-twelfth century, these works
were preserved, studied, and incorporated into the alchemical corpus of the West,
just as assimilation of the more legitimately scientific Arabian contributions to
medicine, mathematics, and astronomy helped lay the foundations for Western
interest in natural and experimental science. Finally, there were the Latin works
of the Western alchemists themselves: Hortulanus, Albertus Magnus, Aquinas,
Roger Bacon, Arnald of Villanova, Raymond Lull, and John of Rupescissa.[6]

Problems involving attribution and pseudepigrapha are outside the scope of this study, and I have mentioned only a few of the most famous writers whose work comprises a small fraction of the total amount of alchemical literature. Yet this brief review indicates that long before the invention of printing, a vast amount of writing on alchemy existed in England, and if medieval English authors added comparatively little to the volume it was not because the subject was unknown to them.

As expected, the sixteenth century saw the printing of many alchemical writings that had previously existed only in manuscript, but again production of these works in England did not keep pace with their appearance on the Continent. Early in this century, John Ferguson observed that "In fact, in the sixteenth century, Alchemy was either not cultivated and pursued energetically in England or its literature was rigidly preserved and concealed in manuscript."[7] In view of the large number of manuscripts known to have existed in England at this time, the royal statutes that were issued to curb or outlaw the practice of alchemy, and the special licenses that occasionally permitted practice in spite of the general ban, Ferguson's second reason accounts for the scarcity of sixteenth-century English printed alchemical books more plausibly than his first. Even so, the two works printed during this century that he does cite, George Ripley's *Compound of Alchymy* (1591) and the *Mirror of Alchimy* collection (1597), are an unrealistically small number, overlooking translations of, or works written in English by, Hieronymous Braunschweig, Joseph Duchesne (Quercetanus), Paracelsus, Conrad Gesner, John Hester, Sir Hugh Platt, and others.[8]

On the Continent, alchemical books began to appear only slowly in the early years of the sixteenth century, the rate of publication perhaps resulting, according to Thorndike, from "the prejudice against Arabic and medieval Latin authors which prevailed in the fields of medicine and astrology and the lack of any authentic texts of ancient Greek writers in the field of alchemy comparable to Galen, Hippocrates and Ptolemy." In contrast, "the dubious name of Hermes was all that alchemy had to offer by way of a focus for a classical revival."[9] This line of reasoning is, I think, again open to question. In addition to works ascribed to Hermes, the Middle Ages were in possession of manuscript copies of alchemical works *thought* to have been written by Plato and Aristotle as well as other eminent Greeks. The fact that such attributions were false and the works spurious, even had this been known, would have been of little concern to devotees of alchemy in the Middle Ages and early Renaissance. Unlike modern chemistry, alchemy never depended on the systematic study and development of a body of knowledge from century to century; interest in it could be stimulated merely by reports of spectacular successes, by the fanciful stories and legends that evolved from the careers of famous adepts, and the regard for it that was expressed in the writings of traditionally revered *auctors*. To those ignorant of Greek and untrained in the techniques of textual attribution, it was sufficient to know only that the greatest of classical philosophers had had their names attached—however erroneously—to alchemical treatises. The sanction of such authorities counted far more than the specialized knowledge that their writings added to the tradition. Returning to Thorndike's remarks on the stature of Hermes Trismegistus in the fifteenth and sixteenth centuries, it seems likely that his name and reputation were "dubious" in a way that increased rather than diminished his influence on alchemy, magic, and related fields. As Frances Yates has shown, the reason for the extreme veneration of Hermes up to, and after, the time his writings were correctly dated in 1614 was that he was believed to have been of great antiquity, an omniscient Egyptian priest who antedated Plato and Aristotle and possibly even Moses, and who prophesied the coming of Christianity.

Whatever the reasons, the number of alchemical books published on the Continent steadily grew as the sixteenth century progressed. In 1500 Hieronymus Braunschweig's *Buch zu Distillieren* was first printed. One of the earliest printed works to appear on the subject, this popular book is notable for having been written in the vernacular as well as for the numerous woodcuts that illustrate its many editions (fig. 9).[10] Such illustrations become increasingly prominent in early printed texts. Three years later the *Margarita philosophica,* an "influential general textbook," was printed; and in 1504 four alchemical treatises ascribed to Arnald of Villanova were included in the first edition of his work.[11] The writings of this Catalonian court physician, traveler, student of the occult, and theological controversialist, who died in 1311, are expectedly diverse in subject matter, and Arnald's reputation is attested to by the fact that at least seven complete editions of his works were printed in the sixteenth century.[12] Arnald is one of the authorities most frequently mentioned by later commentators on the art, and a work by him figures prominently in the concluding lines of *The Canon's Yeoman's Tale.* Interest in alchemical writings falsely ascribed to Raymond Lull,[13] Arnald's contemporary and compatriot, also began early in the century; a work on the fifth essence, *De secretis naturae,* was first printed in a collection of medical treatises in Venice in 1514 and six more times during the next thirty years.[14]

Increasing interest in alchemy is also evidenced by the number and types of texts that poured from Continental printing presses in the first half of the sixteenth century. Appearing frequently are complete editions of writers who had come to be accepted as authorities and also single- and multi-volume collections of alchemical treatises by different authors. In 1518 in Oppenheim, Albertus Magnus's *De mineralibus* appeared, following several printings during the previous century.[15] Geber's influential works, which account for a large portion of alchemical incunabula, were printed in Rome (1525), Strasburg (1529, 1531), Venice (1542) and Berne (1545).[16] These two writers, along with Roger Bacon, Arnald of Villanova, and Lull, constitute the most important group of authorities up until 1550, when the writings of Paracelsus and his followers began to draw alchemy into close alliance with medicine.[17]

Important among the sixteenth-century alchemical anthologies was Philip Ulstad's *Coelum philosophorum,* which appeared in Fribourg between 1525 and

Figure 9. Outdoor Scene. Hieronymus Braunschweig, *Liber de arte Distillandi de Compositis* (1512). By permission of the Wellcome Institute Library, London.

1528. It includes writings of Lull, Arnald, and Albertus Magnus, was often re-printed in the original Latin, and soon translated into French and German.[18] *De Alchemia Volumen,* published at Nuremberg by Petreium in 1541, provides additional evidence that medieval English alchemical authors were respected on the Continent in the early Renaissance, for it contains selections by Bacon and Richard of England along with those of Geber, Hermes, and Hortulanus.[19] The two-volume *Alchimia Opuscula,* printed at Frankfurt in 1550, contains selections attributed to Avicenna, Lull, and Aristotle as well as Arnald of Villanova's popular *Rosarium Philosophorum,* which is cited by Chaucer's Canon's Yeoman.[20] Fifty-three treatises, many by the aforementioned writers, were printed in Guglielmo Gratarolo's *Veræ Alchemiæ Artisque Metallicæ* (Basel, 1561).[21] The *Artis Auriferae* (Basel, 1572) included the increasingly standardized canon of authorities as well as works attributed to Mary the Prophet and the *Turba Philosophorum,* a medieval Latin translation of Arabian versions of Greek alchemical treatises.[22] It is convenient to end this enumeration with 1602, when the *Theatrum Chemicum* first appeared in Ursel. The most comprehensive anthology that had yet been printed, it included four volumes in the first edition, added a fifth in 1622, and a sixth in the edition of 1659-61. This brought the total number of printed items to nearly two hundred and ensured preservation, in a single set of volumes, of nearly every noteworthy alchemical treatise that was known to have been written.[23]

The preservation of these works demonstrates an abiding interest in alchemy throughout the centuries and guaranteed a wealth of detailed knowledge from which both alchemical writers and literary authors who used alchemy could draw. But for purposes of this study, the abundance of alchemical texts is also important as the means to achieving a serious, respectable reputation for the art and its followers. The weighty discussion of alchemical theories with their cosmological and metaphysical implications, the bewildering (but tantalizing) practical directions and recipes, the promise of riches and longevity, the injunctions to lead a pious life, the appeal to revered authorities—all of these are characteristic of alchemical writing and helped to establish its reputation as a worthy subject for study and pursuit. Yet, ironically, when alchemy passed into the tradition of popular literature in the fourteenth century, these are precisely the attributes that made it a common subject of satire. In Chaucer's *Canon's Yeoman's Tale* and in the writings of his contemporaries, satire becomes the dominant mode in which alchemy is given literary expression; this, in turn, marks the beginning of a clearly defined satirical tradition that extends through the later Middle Ages and Renaissance and to the time of Jonson and beyond to Samuel Butler. For these reasons a study of the literary use of alchemy in the sixteenth and seventeenth centuries must begin with its fourteenth-century antecedents.

While never among the most critically popular of Chaucer's works, the *Canon's Yeoman's Tale* has over the last thirty years or so been the subject of an increasing amount of shrewd and interesting criticism. During this time, enough has been written to redirect attention, once and for all, from conjecture about Chaucer's possible victimization at the hands of a real alchemist to explain the sudden appearance of the Yeoman and his Canon in the company of those with whom they alone did not set out from Southwark.[24] Among other biographical topics that have received intensive and fruitful investigation by the earlier of the "modern" critics are Chaucer's knowledge of alchemy, the sources of this knowledge, the accuracy of his statements, and his attitude toward alchemy.[25]

Recent critical emphases have been more varied and include such textual problems as the authenticity of the *Canon's Yeoman's Prologue* and *Tale* within the Chaucerian canon and the possibility that Chaucer first composed them for purposes independent of the *Canterbury Tales*. Necessarily, these investigations have explored the circumstances of composition and relations between its three parts (*Prologue, pars prima, pars secunda*), as well as to other *Tales,* such as that of the Second Nun.[26] The unusual qualities of the language of this tale have long been recognized and analyzed not only from the viewpoint of Chaucer's use of alchemical terminology, but from that of the irony, puns, and musical effects present in Chaucer's verse.[27] However, recent criticism has shown the greatest interest in Chaucer's extensive use of allegory and metaphor in the *Canon's Yeoman's Tale* and his subtle and elusive portrayal of character. Several critics have noted that Chaucer presents the pursuit of alchemy and, especially, the false "chanoun of religioun" of the pars secunda as diabolical and fiendish, thus deepening the satire and making more difficult the reconciliation between the problematical final section of this part (ll. 1428ff.) and everything that has preceded it. Perhaps the first to note this pattern of demonic imagery was Charles Muscatine. He states: "That the victim is a priest and the alchemists also canons may be owing to current events. . . . But the poetic effect is to suggest that their activity is a deep apostasy, a treason, a going over to the devil himself. They are Judases. The falseness of mere deceit is not enough to account for the Yeoman's passionate insistence on 'this chanons cursednesse,' and the ubiquity of 'the foule feend' in the Yeoman's discourse."[28] Much attention has also been given to the complexity of Chaucer's characters and the Yeoman in particular. He has been variously seen: as the simple, "lewed" man that he says he is, without "the faintest glimmer of spirituality or mysticism about him"; as a clever man who has come to renounce alchemy; as a morally developing character who is "trying to give up a bad habit" and is attempting to warn others; as an unstable character who, still addicted to alchemy, fluctuates between hope and despair; or as a blind and troubled sufferer of *acedia,* the sin of sloth that leads to despair.[29] Most recently, the Yeoman and alchemy itself have been approached as cultural phenomena, representing in various ways the spirit of approaching modernity, an ideological and social "site where modernizing values could take root."[30]

While critics generally agree that Chaucer's knowledge of alchemy was extensive, sufficient to cause some Renaissance commentators to regard him as an adept, and that he was familiar with a few of its leading authorities, there is little critical consensus on larger matters such as the Yeoman's character, his reasons for telling his tale, and its overall unity. In the following pages I wish to isolate and discuss aspects of the tale that became persistent motifs in the works of subsequent literary authors who used alchemical subject matter. Further, I will offer a reading of the entire Canon's Yeoman's section, the *Prologue* and the two parts of the *Tale* proper, that emphasizes its artistic unity and consistency of attitude toward alchemy throughout, including the final portion of the pars secunda.

In the *Canon's Yeoman's Prologue* and *Tale* we have the earliest significant artistic use of alchemy and the beginning of a long tradition—extending from the fourteenth century through the sixteenth and well into the seventeenth—in which a negative attitude toward the art and its practitioners is assumed and the reasons for this attitude exploited. Alchemists, their mystifying processes and jargon, as well as their unwitting victims, are treated in a pejorative manner that ranges from gently ironic humor to outrage and bitter contempt. The art itself becomes synonymous with poverty, treacherousness, avariciousness, self-deception, fiendishness, and moral depravity. In short, from the fourteenth century until the early seventeenth, when exoteric alchemy was enjoying its greatest vogue and its authorities received great respect and veneration, in the hands of literary authors it was transformed into an absurdly comic pseudoscience, rich primarily in its potential for humor and satire. When the *Tale* is viewed as the beginning of a long and influential comic and satiric tradition, we can reach a clearer understanding of its place in literary history.

Despite our prevailing distrust of issues concerning authorial intention in literature, such questions almost inevitably arise when considering the problem of unity in the *Canon's Yeoman's Tale*. On the one hand, it has most often been interpreted as Chaucer's wholesale condemnation of the art; however, some scholars, drawing attention to the seemingly incongruous fifty-six lines that conclude the *Tale,* argue that here the author is endorsing "true" alchemy as opposed to the "false" alchemy that he had castigated throughout the earlier part of the poem.[31] Except for this apparent inconsistency in its conclusion, the overall structure of the *Prologue* and *Tale* is carefully designed to promote and reinforce the satirical attack. In the *Prologue* Chaucer's use of the complementary points of view of the pilgrim-narrator and the Host immediately begin to draw out the comic and satiric possibilities present in the hurried arrival of the Yeoman and his master. The Canon's "clothes blake" and his abundant perspiration ("His forheed dropped as a stillatorie," l. 580) suggest the appearance of one who might as easily have stepped from the doorway of an alchemist's laboratory as from a horse that he has "priked miles three." They may also indicate that this pair of tricksters is in urgent pursuit of new victims, a conjecture strengthened by the Canon's first speech: "Faste have I priked, . . . for youre sake, / By cause that I wolde yow atake, / To riden in this myrie compaignye" (ll. 584-86). It is curious that this eager Canon who so loves "desport" and "daliaunce" should remain silent for the next hundred lines, while his supposedly "lewed" Yeoman takes the spotlight. Although the Canon's true profession is not immediately revealed, the Yeoman's opening lines intimate that his master's specialized knowledge and skill make it possible for him to accomplish great and unusual enterprises:

> also, sire, trusteth me,
> And ye hym knewe as wel as do I,
> Ye wolde wondre how wel and craftily

> He koude werke, and that in sondry wise.
> He hath take on hym many a greet emprise,
> Which were ful hard for any that is heere
> To brynge aboute, but they of hym it leere. [ll. 601-7]

Continuing in the vein of a perhaps too confident confidence man, the Yeoman also intimates that it would be to the Host's advantage to get to know his master, for through the "subtilitee" of the Canon's wit the roadway to Canterbury could be transformed to silver and gold. Having heard the Yeoman boast of his master's rare knowledge and capacity to perform miracles, the Host can restrain himself no longer. Through the deliciously naive questioning of the Host, Chaucer makes his first assaults on the discrepancies that appear to exist beween the penurious Canon's attire and the financially rewarding talents that he is said to possess:

> His overslope nys nat worth a myte,
> . . . .
> It is al baudy and totore also.
> Why is thy lord so sluttissh, I the preye,
> And is of power bettre clooth to beye,
> If that his dede accorde with thy speche? [ll. 633, 635-38]

The illuminator of the Ellesmere manuscript of the *Canterbury Tales* (fig. 10) also makes the Yeoman "baudy and totore," providing him with a knee patch as well as a darkened complexion resulting from his incessant minding of his master's alchemical furnace. The master's and servant's hasty ride to catch up with the pilgrims is also suggested by the Yeoman's large spur in this miniature.[32]

Under further questioning of the Host, the Yeoman's revelation that the Canon is forced to dwell on the outskirts of town ("Lurkynge in hernes and in lanes blynde, / Whereas thise robbours and thise theves by kynde / Holden hir pryvee fereful residence," ll. 658-60) ironically underscores the incongruity between his alleged talents and what they have brought him. But Chaucer's satire, even at this early stage, is not limited to the Canon's appearance and place of residence. Before the Canon makes his abrupt departure and the *Prologue* ends, the Yeoman reveals that his master is a victim of intellectual and moral perversion. Like Dr. Faustus, his intelligence has been corrupted through misapplication; to the extent that his learning has overstepped the boundaries proper to man, Chaucer's Canon is guilty of one of the most common charges leveled against the alchemists:

> He is to wys, in feith, as I bileeve.
> That that is overdoon, it wol nat preeve
> Aright, as clerkes seyn; it is a vice.
> Wherfore in that I holde hym lewed and nyce.
> For whan a man hath over-greet a wit,
> Ful oft hym happeth to mysusen it. [ll. 644-49]

Figure 10. Ellesmere MS Canon's Yeoman. By permission of The Huntington Library, San Marino, California.

The passage thus foreshadows the theme of forbidden knowledge and the parallel between the practice of alchemy and the demonic that are developed in the *Tale* proper.

Equally important in deepening the satire is Chaucer's introduction of two additional themes: that of the deception of self and others and that of the addictiveness of the whole alchemical enterprise. He has the Yeoman report, through his own voice and based on seven years' experience with the Canon, his final assessment of alchemy. In the end, both the alchemists and their victims are duped by the false prospect of alchemical success, the *ignis fatuus* that motivates their dreams and desires. More insidiously, this illusion of "good hope" persists despite the repeated failure of experiments and mounting poverty. Each experiment brings them no closer to the desired "conclusioun"—a key word in the *Tale*—because the "science" of alchemy remains unintelligible to them. It is "so fer us biforn" that there is no realistic prospect that their understanding will overtake it and achieve mastery; as a result they are doomed always to "lakken oure conclusioun" (l. 672).

Comic masterpieces though the *Canon's Yeoman's Prologue* and *Tale* are, they also contain serious overtones because of the repeated emphasis on alchemy's futilely addictive quality and the self-deception of charlatan and victim. Both are prototypes of those who, six centuries later, would be suitable candidates for Gamblers Anonymous, for as the Yeoman confesses at the end of the *Prologue:* "And yet, for al my smert and al my grief, / For al my sorwe, labour, and meschief, / I koude nevere leve it in no wise" (ll. 712-14). Chaucer's emphasis on alchemy's refusal to allow its victims to "leve it" dominates the two parts of the *Tale* proper. In his account of his apprenticeship to the Canon, the Yeoman reiterates that despite repeated attempts to gain the secret of transmutation, the philosopher's stone refuses to yield itself up to them, and their life has become a cycle of failures to achieve "conclusion." He states that "For al oure craft, when we han al ydo, / And al oure sleighte, he [the Stone's secret] wol nat come us to" (ll. 866-67). These failures notwithstanding, they have been drawn on to new efforts by the dream of success: "But that good hope crepeth in oure herte, / Supposynge evere, though we sore smerte, / To be releeved by hym afterward. / Swich supposyng and hope is sharp and hard" (ll. 870-73).

The poignancy of their inability to escape psychological addiction is seen nowhere more clearly than in the aftermath of the vessel's explosion near the end of the pars prima. Here, following sharp recriminations concerning who and what is to blame (it is not the first time that the "pot" has shattered and all been lost), the group literally "picks up the pieces" of the failed experiment and, under the direction of the Yeoman's Canon, prepares for a new beginning:

> "Be as be may, be ye no thyng amased;
> As usage is, lat swepe the floor as swithe,
> Plukke up youre hertes and beeth glad and blithe."
> The mullok on an heep ysweped was,
> And on the floor ycast a canevas,
> And al this mullok in a syve ythrowe,
> And sifted, and ypiked many a throwe.
> "Pardee," quod oon, "somwhat of oure metal
> Yet is ther heere, though that we han nat al.
> And though this thyng myshapped have as now,
> Another tyme it may be well ynow.
> Us moste putte oure good in aventure." [ll. 935-46]

Thus, although the Yeoman and his group "concluden everemoore amys," they nevertheless return to the laboratory for another attempt—and another failure.

In the *Prologue* then, Chaucer not only introduces the Yeoman but ridicules alchemy as it was practiced by the corrupt adepts of his day, poor men, meanly dressed and living on the fringes of society, who, in spite of repeated failure, cultivated grandiose illusions of wealth in their own minds and those of their victims. In contrast to this generalized commentary, the satire in both parts of the *Tale* proper is much more incisive and particularized. Once the Canon has ridden off, his Yeoman no longer has reason to keep his comments guarded. Besides, he states that he has abjured his master's company forever. While the prima pars of the *Tale* that follows is an autobiographical account of the Yeoman's experiences in the employment of the Canon, the pars secunda should, I think, be regarded as a kind of exemplum, a short narrative tale serving to underscore the folly of pursuing alchemy.

The opening lines of the prima pars reveal that the Yeoman's seven years of apprenticeship have been an exercise in futility. He has lost all the money he ever possessed and is now deeply in debt for money borrowed; he reiterates the transformation that his appearance has undergone, a kind of reverse alchemy from "fressh and reed" to leaden:[33] "And wher my colour was bothe fressh and reed, /

Now is it wan and of a leden hewe— / Whoso it useth, soore shal he rewe!— / And of my swynk yet blered is myn ye" (ll. 727-30). (Donne's speaker in "A nocturnall upon S. Lucies day" has undergone the psychological equivalent of this reverse alchemy.) Yet the Yeoman's "swynk" and suffering have brought knowledge, and even though he may be incapable of renouncing alchemy forever because of its addictive power, he is fully aware of its evil and willing to set himself as an example to warn others.[34] In this respect, the epithets that the Yeoman uses to designate the art provide a telling commentary on it: "slidynge science" (l. 732), "elvysshe craft" (l. 751), "cursed craft" (l. 830) and "elvysshe nyce loore" (l. 842). Considered together they suggest a pursuit that is "slippery" and deceptive, mysterious, unnatural, foolish, perhaps leading even to damnation. These descriptive phrases unquestionably contain diabolical and satanic overtones, as several critics have noted;[35] in fact, this association comes to be the central technique in Chaucer's attack upon alchemical charlatanism.

That the Yeoman deliberately identifies fraudulent alchemy and alchemists with the demonic is further evidenced by numerous references to "feend," "feendly" and the "devel." As the Canon rides off, he takes with him the curse of the Yeoman: "the foule feend hym quelle!" (l. 705). Later, the Yeoman concludes one of his lengthy catalogs of alchemical substances with the following lines: "Of alle thise names now wol I me reste, / For, as I trowe, I have yow toold ynowe / To reyse a feend, al looke he never so rowe" (ll. 859-61). The passage describing the laboratory explosion near the end of the prima pars suggests that the volatility of metals may be the work of the devil, who is ever present in the laboratory: "Withouten doute, / Though that the feend noght in oure sighte hym shewe, / I trowe he with us be, that ilke shrewe! / In helle, where that he is lord and sire" (ll. 915-18). This emphasis on the ubiquity of the demonic in matters alchemical is linked to similar image patterns that are applied to the false Canon of the pars secunda, and I will pursue this connection before turning to a few remaining alchemical topics in the pars prima.

As mentioned earlier, the pars secunda constitutes the tale proper and takes the form of an exemplum that vividly illustrates the lesson the Yeoman has learned (and which he relates) in part one. (The structure of the *Canon's Yeoman's Prologue* and *Tale* is in some ways comparable to those of the Wife of Bath and the Pardoner.)[36] The two most controversial problems in the pars secunda are the identity of the "chanoun of religioun / Amonges us" and the seeming inconsistency of the final fifty-six lines of the tale with what has preceded them.[37] The Yeoman introduces the mysterious Canon in the following way:

> There is a chanoun of religioun
> Amonges us, wolde infecte al a toun,
> Thogh it as greet were as was Nynyvee,
> Rome, Alisaundre, Troye, and othere three.
> His sleightes and his infinite falsnesse
> Ther koude no man writen, as I gesse,

Though that he myghte lyve a thousand yeer.
In al this world of falshede nis his peer;
For in his termes he wol hym so wynde,
And speke his wordes in so sly a knynde,
Whanne he commune shal with any wight,
That he wol make hym doten anonright,
But it a feend be, as hymselven is.
Ful many a man hath he bigiled er this,
And wole, if that he lyve may a while;
And yet men ride and goon ful many a mile
Hym for to seke and have his aqueyntaunce,
Noght knowynge of his false governaunce. [ll. 972-89]

Critics have puzzled over the identity of the Canon, who is presumably one of the party at the time of the telling of the *Tale*. But the original group of twenty-nine people who comprised the pilgrimage included no Canon, and the Yeoman's Canon has left before the tale begins. Furthermore, at line 1090 the Yeoman makes it clear that the Canon in doubt is not his master. Who, then, is he? Keeping in mind the Yeoman's propensity to link alchemy with the demonic, it seems likely, as Gardner and others have suggested, that this alchemist-canon is the devil himself or at least a satanic agent.[38] This identification is made explicit at line 984 ("But it a feend be, as hymselven is"), although it can be argued that given the Yeoman's experience, he would naturally liken any supremely treacherous alchemist to a devil. But evidence within the passage itself strongly suggests that the use of "feend" is not metaphoric. In the first place, we note that the Yeoman presents this alchemist as appearing in the guise of a "chanoun of religioun." As is usually true in Chaucer (we have only to recall the Pardoner's preaching and selling of false relics) the greatest sinners practice their wiles while disguised in the pious robes of ecclesiastical positions. Furthermore, this Canon is said to possess a superhuman capacity to "infecte," for the greatest cities of the ancient world and, ironically, some of the most corrupt, are vulnerable to him. His "sleightes" and "infinite falsnesse," which defy human accounting, clearly point to the archetypal Tempter. Yet Chaucer is able to prevent the Canon from becoming merely an allegorical devil-figure; while his confusing "termes" and "wordes in so sly a kynde" (ll. 980-81) recall the Edenic Satan, they apply equally well to the exotic jargon of alchemy. In fact, the lengthy descriptions of alchemical processes and materials in the pars prima were sufficient, by the Yeoman's own admission, "To reyse a feend, al looke he never so rowe" (l. 861). The alchemists' talk of winged dragons, black crows, and the tail of the peacock, like the words of Satan to Eve, proved to be destructively tantalizing.[39]

This introductory description, reinforced by several additional descriptive phrases and curses—the Canon as "roote of al trecherie" (l. 1069); "Swiche feendly thoghtes in his herte impresse—" (l. 1071); "this chanons cursednesse!" (l. 1101); "this feendly wrecche," (l. 1158); "This false chanoun—the foule feend hym fecche!" (l. 1159); "devel of helle" (l. 1238); and "the devel out of his skyn / Hym terve" (ll. 1273-74)—all serve to make the association clear. The Yeoman's experience results in knowledge that the fraudulent practice of alchemy is the work of the devil, whose presence is universal: "he is heere and there; / He is so variaunt, he abit nowhere" (ll. 1174-75). And even though his own addiction is so great that he is unable decisively to break off from further practice, he nonetheless ends the tale of the Canon and the duped priest with a powerful warning to his audience: "Medleth namoore with that art, I mene, / For if ye doon, youre thrift is goon ful clene " (ll. 1424-25). As later chapters will show, Chaucer is not alone in linking alchemy and the demonic; literary satirists and alchemical authors alike make the connection, and it appears occasionally in pictorial tradition as well. Figure 11, a woodcut from a block-book in the British Library (1480[?]), shows the Antichrist and a beckoning Satan near the furnace, along with two workers in an alchemist's laboratory.[40] Figure 12, an engraving by Adriaen Matham (1590-1660), serves as a vivid corrective to conventional professions of piety and depicts a nodding alchemist and a female temptress, between whom lurks the devil.

I turn now to the seemingly contradictory conclusion. The final fifty-six lines of the tale are made up largely of two quotations from alchemical authorities that *appear* to corroborate the Yeoman's own conclusion. The first is taken from Arnald of Villanova's (i.e., "Arnold of the Newe Toun's") *De lapide philosophorum* or *De secretis nature*, although the source cited by the Yeoman is Arnald's *Rosarie*, i.e., the *Rosarium Philosophorum*.[41] The quotation is complete with a reference to the "philosophres fader," Hermes, and a cryptic instruction for the "mortification" (fixation) of mercury with the help of "brymstoon" (sulphur), these being the "dragon" and "his brother." From these two philosophical principles—which, for Chaucer, are derived from gold and silver, Sol and Luna (l. 1440)—the philosopher's stone may be formulated *if* the adept possesses requisite knowledge. Lacking this, man must avoid the lure of alchemy. Of very great importance is the qualification that Chaucer next adds concerning the existence of a form of the art higher than physical transmutation:

> 'Lat no man bisye hym this art for to seche,
> But if that he th'entencioun and speche
> Of philosophres understonde kan;
> And if he do, he is a lewed man.
> For this science and this konnyng,' quod he,
> 'Is of the secree of the secretes, pardee.' [ll. 1442-47]

These lines are not a contradiction of the denunciation of alchemy that has preceded them; nor is the entire tale an exemplification of the thesis that the "pursuit of alchemy is the pursuit of a false religion," as has sometimes been argued.[42] The Canon of the pars secunda *is* the devil because of his wily and treacherous nature and because he infects his prey with insatiable greed and moral corruption. He is the universally and eternally "false" alchemist, the prototype of the many mortal ones who lived in Chaucer's time, and the public should be warned

Der anthycrist lernet hye em meister gold machen vnnd andere owentpre do mpt er dye menschen betrugt/Das geschpht in der stat Corrosapm Das stet in dem compedio theologpe/dpe stat verfflüchet got do er spralye in dem ewangelp/wee dpr corosaim

Figure 11. Satan, Alchemist, and Antichrist. *Antichristus* (IB.15343, 1480?). By permission of the British Library.

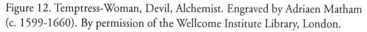

Figure 12. Temptress-Woman, Devil, Alchemist. Engraved by Adriaen Matham (c. 1599-1660). By permission of the Wellcome Institute Library, London.

against them. The warning is extended especially to those who fancy themselves
knowledgeable in the idiom used by the "philosophres" or alchemists: for the
man who pursues alchemy without understanding "th'entencioun and speche /
Of philosophres" is an ignorant fool, i.e., a "lewed" man.

This "secree of the secretes," which is the mysterious essence of true alchemy,
is also the subject of the Yeoman's second quotation, one drawn from a Latin
translation of an Arabic treatise entitled *Senioris Zadith Tabula Chimica*.[43] The
short section of dialogue in which Plato "answers" questions put to him by one
of his disciples imitates the *ignotum per ignocius* technique that characterizes discussions of the philosopher's stone in alchemical treatises. Plato's final statement
"quoted" by the Yeoman, in keeping with the alchemists' traditional insistence
on secrecy, refuses to elucidate the mystery but instead places it within the safe
confines of Christ's omniscience:

> 'The philosophres sworn were everychoon
> That they sholden discovere it unto noon,
> Ne in no book it write in no manere.
> For unto Crist it is so lief and deere
> That he wol nat that it discovered bee,
> But where it liketh to his deitee
> Men for t'enspire, and eek for to deffende
> Whom that hym liketh; lo, this is the ende.' [ll. 1464-71]

This quotation from a revered authority serves to draw the *Tale* to a piously enigmatic close: because the secret of the philosopher's stone rests in Christ and is
dear to him, it is his to dispose. Will it ever be revealed to man and, if so, under
what circumstances? Only, Plato responds, where it pleases his godhead ("deitee")
to "reveal it to one man by inspiration and withhold it from another."[44] Despite
this crucial qualification, the Yeoman's final position is, for all practical purposes,
clear: because God has ordained that philosophers not reveal the secret of the
stone, man should desist from the search or be subject to God's wrath for prying
into areas of forbidden knowledge. Thus the ultimate meaning of the pars secunda
is a warning against dabbling in the two opposing types of alchemy: one the gift
of God, the other the product of the devil's treachery. There is no inconsistency
in the tone of this section, in the character of the Yeoman-narrator, or in the
views of alchemy that have been presented. Experience has taught the Yeoman
that futility, poverty, and self-deception result from addiction to the demonic
sort, so he renounces it with harsh satire, even though he is still unable to extri-
cate himself entirely from its grip. But authority has also taught him that a true
form may exist, one that is shrouded in the mystery of God's will and wisdom;
his response to this is that of the humble, God-fearing Christian: "For whoso
maketh God his adversarie, / As for to werken any thyng in contrarie / Of his
wil, certes, never shal he thryve" (ll. 1476-78).

While it is the satirical attacks on "false" alchemy and fraudulent alchemists that appear most often in later literature, the *Canon's Yeoman's Tale* includes a number of other motifs that are commonly found in writers who followed Chaucer. For example, as a result of the alchemists' poverty and toil in the laboratories, their threadbare appearance and fulsome odor are frequently emphasized. The hellish associations of brimstone and the demonic associations of the goat serve to reinforce the link with the devil:[45]

> Men may hem knowe by smel of brymstoon.
> For al the world they stynken as a goot;
> Hir savour is so rammyssh and so hoot
> That though a man from hem a mile be,
> The savour wole infecte hym, trusteth me. [ll. 885-89]

At times, as earlier noted in the Ellesmere miniature, their ragged clothes even serve the alchemists as protective coloration, for if they wore the finery that was purchased from the boasted proceeds of their art they would be slain (ll. 892-96). Another serious hazard of the profession is madness, which commonly afflicts the alchemists of literature. The Yeoman speaks of the art that makes one's purse empty and "his wittes thynne" (l. 741) and of the dashed hopes that "For sorwe . . . almoost we wexen wood" (l. 869). In fact, throughout the *Tale* a devastating sense of doom and futility is attached to alchemical labors because of the inability to reach a successful "conclusioun": "But, be it hoot or coold, I dar seye this, / That we concluden everemoore amys. / We faille of that which that we wolden have, / And in oure madnesse everemoore we rave" (ll. 956-59).

As has been shown in several articles, Chaucer possessed a remarkably wide acquaintance with the technical aspects of alchemy.[46] This is revealed in the lengthy lists of substances, equipment, and processes that the Yeoman recites at lines 755-818 and 852-56. His knowledge includes alchemy's theoretical basis in the discussion of the "foure spirites and the bodies sevene" (l. 820). The former, quicksilver, "orpyment" (arsenic trisulphide), "Sal armonyak" (sal ammoniac), and "brymstoon" (sulphur), are substances that volatize completely when heated; the "bodyes" are the seven metals. There is also the short but graphic description of a laboratory explosion, similar to the one Jonson uses as the climactic incident in *The Alchemist*, and the "bechen cole" trick that the Canon employs to cheat the priest in the pars secunda appears in exactly the same form in one of Erasmus' *Colloquies*. Finally, the bizarre jargon of the secret fraternity—the "termes . . . so clergial and so queynte"—continued to be in frequent use by later writers of alchemical satire, as additional evidence of the varied richness of the Chaucerian legacy.

Of the several literary treatments of alchemy that date from the medieval period, Chaucer's is unquestionably the most interesting and original. The *Canon's Yeoman's Tale* combines familiarity with alchemical terminology, theory, and authorities and a detailed understanding of how a corrupted form of the art was often prac-

ticed in his time. These elements are in turn presented with a very certain literary
sense of plot, character, tone, and situation. The result is a work in which humor,
satire, theme, and moral message grow unobtrusively and naturally out of "story."
For these reasons the *Canon's Yeoman's Tale* occupies a primary place at the beginning of the tradition of literary alchemy.

To the extent that it possesses all of these virtues the *Canon's Yeoman's Tale*
must be regarded as an anomaly when placed beside other literary depictions of
alchemy dating from the fourteenth and fifteenth centuries. In turning to three
such works—a short selection from *Piers Plowman,* a passage from Gower's
Confessio Amantis, and a translation by John Lydgate—we find that many of the
topics and ideas first presented by Chaucer are also discussed, and often the underlying attitudes toward alchemy are similar. The chief difference is that in these
writers emphasis is on the mere reporting of what was commonly known and
thought about alchemy; treatment is "encyclopedic" rather than artistic, explicitly expository and didactic rather than balanced. Yet, despite the absence of distinctive literary qualities, these works also served to place the subject of alchemy
within the tradition of popular literature, and for this reason they warrant consideration in this study.

Alchemy plays only a slight role in *Piers Plowman.*[47] At the beginning of
passus 11 of the A-text, Wit's wife, Dame Study, decries the state of corruption
and spiritual decay that exists in the world. She deprecates her husband's attempts
to teach wisdom to fools and mourns the fact that preachers of Christian truths
are "Luytel . . . loved." According to her, men's hearts are set wholly on materialism and pleasure: "Bote Munstralsye and Murþe . A-Mong Men is nouþe; /
Lecherie and losengrie . and loseles tales, / And geten gold with grete oþes . beoþ
gamus nou A dayes" (11:35-37). After giving Piers directions to the house of
Clergy, who will teach him the meaning of "Dowel" (Do Well), Dame Study
enumerates the many gifts that she has given to man. To Clergy's wife, Scripture,
she has given the Psalter, logic, law, music, and "sapience" itself. She has been the
teacher of Plato and Aristotle and has taught masons and carpenters their trades
(11:103-35). After extolling Theology, which teaches humility, Christian brotherhood, and the bounties of God's love, Dame Study lists several kinds of knowledge, which, for various reasons, must be avoided:

> Bote Astronomye is hard þing . *and* vuel to knowe,
> Gemetrie and Gemensye . is gynful of speche,
> þat worcheþ with þeose þreo . þriueþ he late,
> For sorcerye Is þe souereyn [bok . þat to þat science longiþ,
> Yet arn þere febicchis of Forellis] . of mony mennes wittes.
> Experimentis of Alconomye . Of Alberdes makynge,
> Nigromancye and perimancie . þe pouke to Rise makeþ;
> Yif þou þenche Dowel . dele with hem nevere.
> Alle þeose sciences . siker, I my-seluen
> Haue I-founded hem furst . folk to deceyue. [11:152-61]

This quotation presents several interpretive problems. Astronomy and astrology were more or less synonymous during the Middle Ages, and in this context we can be quite certain that Dame Study has the latter in mind primarily. But Langland's linking of geometry and geomancy, implying that they are equally "gynful," i.e., guileful or deceitful, presents a difficulty for the modern reader. No doubt geometry's reliance on figures that were thought to possess magical properties, such as circles and pentangles, explains its association here with the magic and divination implicit in geomancy. (In Lydgate's translation of *Secrees of Old Philisoffres,* to be considered shortly, fortune-telling, geomancy, physiognomy, pyromancy, and *geometry* are all classified as secret crafts associated with Circe and Medea.[48])

The phrase "febicchis of Forellis" in line 156 is more difficult. The *Middle English Dictionary* cites this line as the only example of the use of "febicchis" and defines it tentatively as "some kind of alchemical manipulations or tricks."[49] The origin of the word is conjecturally traced to "Pebichios," the name of an early alchemist whom I have been unable to locate. According to the same dictionary, "Forellis" is the plural form of "forel," i.e., "1) a sheath or case for a weapon, or 2) a covering or box for books or documents; a bound volume." Thus in lines 154-55 Langland appears to be saying that the "souereyn bok" of sorcery, which is the guiding spirit of these three sciences, is nothing more than a volume of deceptive tricks.[50]

The connection between "Experimentis of Alconomye," associated here with Albertus Magnus, and necromancy and pyromancy is easier to explain because in the popular mind the three were thought to rely on black magic. All "the pouke to Rise maketh." "[P]ouke," in this line, may be a variant spelling of "pouce," flax dust or fine dirt that blinds the eyes; or it may be a variant of "pouche" or purse, which vanishes through the trickery of false practitioners. It is also possible that here "pouke" is intended as a variant of "puck," the devil of English folklore. It appears in this sense in line 341 of Spenser's "Epithalamion": "Ne let the Pouke, nor other evill sprights, / Ne let mischivous witches with theyr charmes / . . . / Fray us with things that be not." This meaning, more than any of the others, suggests the demonic associations of these pursuits through the image of magical conjuration.

A close reading of the passage shows consistency of meaning. Considered together, these forbidden arts are supremely and deliberately deceptive: they cause men to fail to prosper and are the ruin of their minds. They are associated with the devil and, as Dame Study's revelation about the result of pursuing them suggests (l. 159), may cause man's damnation, for to "Do Well" is the key to salvation. Thus, Dame Study's denunciation of alchemy and her reasons for doing so have much in common with the attack by Chaucer's Yeoman.

In 1652 Elias Ashmole published his *Theatrum Chemicum Britannicum,* the largest, richest, and most important collection of English alchemical poetry that has ever been printed. Although the poems included are predominantly the works of alchemical rather than "literary" authors, Ashmole did see fit to include *The Canon's Yeoman's Prologue* and *Tale* ("Written by our Ancient famous English poet, *Geoffry Chaucer*") and selections from Gower and Lydgate. The "Annotations and Discourses, Upon Some part of the preceding Worke," which appears at the end of the volume, explains Ashmole's reasons for including the selection from Chaucer: "One Reason why I selected out of *Chaucer's Canterbury Tales,* that of the *Chanon's Yeoman* was, to let the *World* see what notorious *Cheating* there has beene ever used, under pretence of this true (though Injur'd) *Science;* Another is, to shew that *Chaucer* himself was a *Master* therein. For, in this *Tale Chaucer* sets forth the deceipts in *Alchimy* to the life, and notably declaimes against all such villanous *Pretenders,* who being wholly ignorant of *Art,* have notwithstanding learnt the *Cunning,* to abuse the World."[51] It is expected that Ashmole should have included this work because of its attack on the "Quacking Mountebanks," for he was a believer in and a defender of alchemy as a *"Divine Science."* It is also clear from his notes that Ashmole viewed the objectives of alchemy as being remote from the practical attempts to turn base metals into gold. Referring to the disillusionment of those "that have been Decoy'd into the *snare*" of false alchemists, Ashmole states: "Let me tell them they may become *happier* and expect a *Blessing* in what they seeke; . . . if they can study this *Science* and not pursue it for Transmutation of Metals sake only, . . . [for] certainly the lucre of that will fix a *Curse* upon their *Endeavours,* and plunge them headlong into an unfathom'd depth of *Misfortune.*"[52]

Although the *Theatrum Chemicum Britannicum* appeared almost three hundred years after the *Canterbury Tales* had been written, these quotations reveal important similarities between their authors in regard to alchemy. Chaucer (or, at least, his point-of-view character, the Yeoman) and Ashmole agree that there are two kinds of alchemy: "false" alchemy as practiced by quack imposters and "true" alchemy, which is associated with the Sacred. Both agree that the reputation of the latter has been injured by the former, and both write for the explicit purpose of denouncing the former. The chief difference between them is that Chaucer's Yeoman hints vaguely at the nature of true alchemy through references to Arnald of Villanova and the "booke *Senior*"; but reflecting the piety of his age and his awareness of alchemy's dangers, he states that its divine nature makes it unsuitable as an object of human study. On the other hand, Ashmole, the sympathetic experimenter of the late Renaissance, asserts the worthiness of the *"Divine Science"* as a subject of study.

More important than these general resemblances in attitude, however, is the fact that Ashmole regarded Chaucer as a *"Master"* of the science, a *"Judicious Philosopher,"* and one who fully knew the *Mistery."* A final quotation from his notes to *The Canon's Yeoman's Tale* serves to emphasize this fact and also to relate Chaucer's reputed alchemical expertise to his friend, John Gower: "Now as Concerning *Chaucer* (the *Author* of this *Tale*) he is ranked amongst the *Hermetick Philosophers,* and his *Master* in this *Science* was Sir *John Gower,* whose familiar and neere acquaintance began at the *Inner Temple* upon *Chaucer's* returne into England."[53] It is essential to explore this relationship.

The chief source for study of Gower's knowledge of alchemy is book 4 of the *Confessio Amantis,* where the subject is included under the heading "Discoverers and Inventors." This passage (which Ashmole also included in the *Theatrum Chemicum Britannicum*) is 175 lines in length and immediately follows a brief section on mining and metallurgy.[54] Although their conclusions about corruption in the contemporary practice of alchemy are similar, Gower's discussion, unlike Chaucer's and like Langland's, is matter-of-fact, nonhumorous, and nonsatirical. In Chaucer, alchemy is "transmuted" into a glorious fiction; that the narrative is also didactic is almost incidental. In contrast, the "moral Gower" is interested in relating what is *generally* known about the subject: its history, theoretical bases, processes, authorities, and ultimate validity. He is informative but scarcely entertaining. Yet despite these differences in intention, the two works have many points of contact.

In speaking of the introduction of metals into human society, Gower states that "Philosophres wise" were responsible first for mining and later for the production of metal by artificial means:

> Ferst forto gete it out of Myne,
> And after forto trie and fyne.
>   And also with gret diligence
> Thei founden thilke experience,
> Which cleped is Alconomie,
> Wherof the Selver multeplie
> Thei made and ek the gold also. [4:455-61]

Gower is plainly more interested in "Alconomie" than in the processes of mining, testing, and refining. Using the terminology of Chaucer, he proceeds at once to discuss the "bodies sevene" and "foure spiritz," which are the subject matter of the alchemist. As in Chaucer, the seven primary metals are linked with the planets from which they "ben begonne" (4:2466-75): gold—Sun, silver—Moon, iron—Mars, lead—Saturn, brass—Jupiter, copper—Venus, and quicksilver—Mercury. Gower's linking of brass with Jupiter, rather than tin, is his only departure from the traditional planetary correspondences, and the list of "spiritz" included by each author is identical: quicksilver, orpiment, sal ammoniac, and brimstone. Each author also counts mercury (quicksilver) as both "body" and "spirit."

While there is little approaching orthodoxy in alchemical theory, until the time of Paracelsus it was commonly accepted that sulphur and mercury alone were the "spirits" or active "principles" that accounted for the presence of metals. Traditionally, the primary qualities of hotness and dryness, which are the essence of Fire, become "philosophical" or "sophic" sulphur; coldness and moistness, the essence of water, become "philosophical" or "sophic" mercury. These are the "spirits" or active principles that, when conjoined beneath the earth's surface, result in the natural production of metals or, within the alchemist's alembic, in the philosopher's stone.[55] In increasing the number of spirits to four, then, Chaucer and Gower are not following the most widely accepted theory. Nonetheless, they are in accordance with such authorities as Vincent of Beauvais, who placed their number at four: mercury, sulphur, arsenic, and sal ammoniac.[56]

Gower is, however, entirely conventional in stating that gold and silver are the "extremites" toward which all impure metals naturally incline and that the secret of transmutation is removal of these imperfections (ll. 2487-97). This, he states, is accomplished through a seven-stage process: distillation, congelation, solution, descension, sublimation, calcination, and fixation (ll. 2513-20). The alchemist continues the process "With tempred hetes of the fyr, / Til he the parfit Elixir / Of thilke philosophres Ston / Mai gete" (ll. 2521-24).

Gower's encyclopedic discussion of the philosopher's stone extends to material that is not included in *The Canon's Yeoman's Tale*. In accordance with many authorities, he states that there are three distinct types of stones.[57] The first is the *lapis vegetabilis*, which has the power to preserve man's health and prolong his life; it is commonly called the Elixir of Life. The second or *lapis animalis* is responsible for the well-being of the five senses. Gower's third or "Minerall" stone has the capacity to cleanse imperfect metals "of rust, of stink and of hardnesse" (l. 2557) and, following this, to bring about the multiplication of gold.

In theory, at least, Gower seems to have no doubts that successful transmutation is possible. In former times, he states, when men were wise it was accomplished, but this is no longer true. Like Chaucer, he concludes that, practically speaking, the pursuit of alchemy is destined to failure and should be avoided:

> To get a pound thei spenden fyve;
> I not hou such a craft schal thryve
> In the manere as it is used:
> It were betre be refused
> Than forto worchen upon weene
> In thing which stant nought as thei weene. [4:2591-96]

The final lines of the alchemical section of the *Confessio Amantis* are similar in two ways to the last lines spoken by the Yeoman: in each there is an affirmation of the truth of the science and an appeal to authority. Gower's statement that "The science of himself is trewe / Upon the forme as it was founded" (ll. 2598-99) precedes a list of the most highly venerated authorities. As in Chaucer, Hermes is regarded as the father of the science, and is followed by Geber, Hortulanus, Morienus, and Avicenna. These authorities, Gower concludes, have supplied him with all that he has related:

> Bot thei that writen the scripture
> Of Grek, Arabe and of Caldee,
> Thei were of such Auctorite
> That thei ferst founden out the weie

> Of al that thou hast herd me seie;
> Wherof the Cronique of her lore
> Schal stonde in pris for everemore. [4:2626-32]

For Elias Ashmole, this section from book 4 of the *Confessio Amantis* provided sufficient evidence to place Gower "in the *Register* of our *Hermetique Philosophers:* and one that adopted into the Inheritance of this *Mistery,* our famous *English Poet, Geoffry Chaucer.*" "In this litle *Fragment,*" Ashmole continues, "it appeares he fully understood the Secret, for he gives you a faithfull account of the *Properties* of the *Minerall, Vegitable,* and *Animall Stones,* and affirmes the *Art* to be true.[58] While it is true that Gower shows familiarity with many of the terms, processes, objectives, and authorities of alchemy, for him they seem nothing more than lists of abstractions culled from traditional sources. In some areas, Gower's alchemical knowledge appears to be more extensive than Chaucer's, but one would hesitate to designate him, as Ashmole does, Chaucer's "*Master* in this *Science.*"

John Lydgate and Benedict Burgh's translation of the *Secrees of Old Philisoffres* is not a work that commands great interest today. During the Middle Ages, however, it was considered to be an extremely important book because it is a version of the *Secreta Secretorum,* which purported to be a treatise written by Aristotle to his pupil, Alexander the Great. As is the case with many such works, the attribution is spurious, and Robert Steele has noted of the text's true history that it was originally compiled from Syriac sources in the eighth century, then translated into Arabic by the author. Philip of Paris translated the work into Latin in the thirteenth century, after which it was turned into French. Lydgate's English verse translation was perhaps prompted by Henry VI.[59]

The contents of the work make it difficult to classify, but the central focus is on the advice and practical and theoretical knowledge, given by "Aristotle," which would enable Alexander to become a great and successful ruler. Topics of discussion include the importance of religion and chastity, the proper appearance of a king, the principles of wise governing, the means to good health, physiognomy, astronomy, and alchemy. Like many other works of the Middle Ages it combines the functions of an encyclopedia with those of a "how-to-do-it" book. Its popularity is attested by the fact that it appeared in many manuscripts and printed editions and was often imitated, expanded, and translated.[60] In England alone Gower drew upon it in book 7 of the *Confessio Amantis,* and Thomas Hoccleve included portions in his translation of Egidio Colonna's *De Regimine Principum* in 1412. The first separate English translation was done by James Young about 1420; it was followed by several others in the fifteenth and sixteenth centuries.[61] Of these, the most important is the version known as the *Secrees of Old Philisoffres,* begun by Lydgate shortly before his death and completed afterwards by Benedict Burgh.

As in the *Confessio Amantis,* the alchemical passages in the *Secrees* are important for this study because they illustrate the removal of the subject from a highly specialized branch of occult writing and its placement in a popular literary tradi-

tion. Although the alchemical sections are admittedly only a small part of the
entire work (and the work itself perhaps continued to exist only because Aristotle's
name was falsely attached to it), the importance of these sections is demonstrated
by the fact that they were reprinted in Ashmole's *Theatrum Chemicum
Britannicum,* two hundred years after Lydgate's translation.

The work takes the form of an exchange of letters in which Alexander re-
quests information and Aristotle dispenses his wisdom. In the second of his epistles,
Alexander asks his master for knowledge of the workings of nature as well as of
the occult:

> Poweer of planetys / And mevying of al sterrys,
>   And of every / hevenly intelligence,
> Disposicioun / of pees and ek of werrys,
>   And of ech othir / straunge hyd science
>   As the sevene goddys / by ther Inffluence,
>   Dispoose the Ordre / of Incantaciouns,
>   Or of Sevene metallys / the transmutaciouns [ll. 491-97]

This quotation—with its tendency to link astronomy and astrology, magical in-
cantation and alchemy, macrocosm and microcosm—leads to a discussion of the
three stones, mineral, vegetable, and animal, the last of which is wrought out of
the four elements aided by fire. It is unlike any other stone "ffound in the
lapydarye" (l. 539), and is unsurpassed in its powers to cure man of diseases, a
view that is affirmed in many later alchemical treatises.[62]

The section on the virtues of the animal stone is followed by one in which
Aristotle hints at how it is produced (ll. 561-67), but more specific instructions
are given in a later passage entitled "How Aristotil declarith to king Alisaundre of
the Stoony." The first stage of the process involves manipulation of what was
earlier described as the philosopher's circle, e.g., separation of water from air, air
from fire, and fire from earth; once separated, the elements are purified and "preserved / ffrom Corrupcioun" (l. 992). If the work is done carefully the resulting
stone will be either white or citron in color: "The Citren Colour / for the sonne
bryght, / Whyte for the moone / that shyneth al the nyght" (ll. 1007-8). In accordance with traditional alchemical theory, the yellow stone, gold, and the sun
are associated, as are the white stone, silver, and the moon. But the narrator emphasizes that the secret of making the stone is known only to a select few, such as
Aristotle and Hermogenes, the tutor of Philip. He, himself, disavows any intention of aspiring to forbidden knowledge; in fact, he asserts that ignorance makes
him incapable of doing so:

> And for I have / but litel Rad or seyn,
>   To wryte or medle / of so hih materys,
> ffor presumpcyoun / somme wold have disdeyn
>   To be so boold / or Clymbe in my disirys,
>   To scale the laddere / above the nyne sperys,

> Or medle of Rubyes / that yeve so cleer a lyght
> On hooly shrynes / in the dirk nyght. [ll. 547-53]

As with the conclusion of Chaucer's Yeoman, alchemy is associated with the Sacred or, at least, with supernal mystery; it is not a proper subject for human investigation because it is categorized as forbidden knowledge.

Alexander's "secund pistil" concludes with the conventional warning to the ignorant of the dangers inherent in the pursuit of alchemy. For the uninitiated, "fals Erryng" is unavoidable and results in great expense, poverty, and madness: "ffor lak of brayn / they wern maad so wood / Thyng to be-gynne / which they nat undirstood" (ll. 573-74). The words that Lydgate uses to end this section are, in fact, remarkably similar to the Yeoman's indictment of false alchemy:

> It is no Crafft / poore men tassaye,
>   It Causith Coffres / and Chestys to be bare,
> Marryth wyttes / and braynes doth Affraye;
>   Yit be wryting / this book doth declare,
>   And be Resouns / lyst nat for to spare,
>   With goldeyn Resouns / in taast moost lykerous,
>   Thyng per ignotum / prevyd per ignocius. [ll. 582-88]

The selections that I have dealt with in this chapter are drawn from a number of the most popular literary works of the English Middle Ages. Although only one, *The Canon's Yeoman's Tale,* is explicitly comic and satiric, considered collectively these passages illustrate the characteristic treatment that alchemy receives when it passes into the tradition of popular literature. In contrast to the serious and worshipful mood and the optimistic attitude concerning success that prevails in the writings of the alchemists themselves, Chaucer and his contemporaries invariably concentrate on negative and deceptive aspects of the art. While conceding that a higher form of alchemy may exist or that transmutation is possible in theory, for them the pursuit of "practical" alchemy can result only in poverty, disillusionment, even madness. Ultimately, because it is based in forbidden knowledge, it may lead to the damnation of the overreaching adept. At the very least the alchemist of literature becomes an object of ironic derision because his immense learning results in so little material gain, the very discrepancy that Chaucer alludes to in the portrait of the Clerk of Oxenford in the *General Prologue:* "But al be that he was a philosophre, / Yet hadde he but litel gold in cofre" (ll. 297-98).

III

POSERS AND IMPOSTORS

=========

Sixteenth-Century Alchemical Satire

"[John Dee] being setled againe at *Mortelack,* the *Queene* used to call at his *House* to visit him, and shewed her self very Curteous to him, upon all Occasions. Against *Christmas* 1590, she sent him *Two hundred Angels* wherewith to keep his *Christmas,* and a hundred Markes against *Christmas* 1592, she likewise sent him word by Mr. *Thomas Candish,* to doe what he would in *Alchymie* and *Philosophy,* and none should controule or molest him: and not unlike by the *Queenes example,* diverse *Personages* of *Honour* at *Court,* frequented his *Company,* and sent him many *Guifts,* from time to time.
                    —Elias Ashmole, *Theatrum chemicum Britannicum*[1]

From Chaucer, the Renaissance inherited two very different traditions of alchemical thought and expression that approximate the two types developed within the *Canon's Yeoman's Prologue* and *Tale:* the sacred and the profane. The latter, which is the subject of this chapter, is the satirical tradition that is expressed in popular literature written throughout the sixteenth century and beyond. The former, derived from the final lines of the *pars secunda,* is the esoteric, holy type of alchemy that is "so lief and deere" to Christ and is his to reveal or conceal. Of this type, Elias Ashmole stated that "he that Reads the latter part of the *Chanon's Yeoman's Tale,* wil easily perceive him [Chaucer] to be a *Iudicious Philosopher,* and one that fully knew the *Mistery.*"[2] Recent scholarship has confirmed that this view was widely held by alchemical writers in the Renaissance. Thus the notion that the learned Chaucer possessed the secret of the philosopher's stone, that he had authored alchemical treatises, and that he should be regarded as an authority, originated and was cultivated within the relatively "closed" circles of alchemical authors, not disseminated in popular literary tradition.

Gareth Dunleavy and Robert M. Schuler have demonstrated a number of ways in which Chaucer's Renaissance reputation as an alchemical master developed. Dunleavy's discovery of Trinity College Dublin MS. D.2.8, bearing the title "Galfridus Chauser his worke" and dating from the sixteenth century, while making no real claim to legitimacy as a Chaucerian attribution, adds significantly to the store of evidence that links Chaucer with alchemy. The fact that the manuscript includes two recipes for making the purported "Yeoman's Elixir" helped strengthen belief that Chaucer was a successful adept and "complements the sixteenth- and seventeenth-century printings of the *Canon's Yeoman's Tale* on which the tradition of Chaucer the alchemist has rested."[3] Chaucer's Renaissance reputation as an alchemical authority has been delineated more sharply and completely by Robert M. Schuler, who has shown that long before Ashmole, in fact as far back as Thomas Norton's *Ordinall of Alchimy* (1477), Chaucer's reputation as a "magus and master alchemist" was carefully asserted by occultist writers.[4]

But the tradition of alchemical satire, begun by Chaucer and continued by Langland, Gower, and Lydgate, flourished much more vigorously in the sixteenth century. In this chapter, I will show that writers throughout the period continue to cultivate, adapt, and enlarge upon many of the alchemical themes, subjects, and associations that were first given popular expression by their fourteenth- and fifteenth-century forebears. Occasionally, as in the case of Reginald Scot, the debts of later writers to earlier ones are obvious and even acknowledged; thus, at times, we have a clear sense of the perpetuation of an attitude toward alchemy and alchemists through means that are primarily literary. But the satirical tradition is not entirely a product of conscious literary borrowing. Far more often, Renaissance authors simply *assume* an unfavorable attitude toward alchemy and its devotees. Their satirical treatment takes the form of a conditioned reflex, prompted through no critical examination of the subject and offered without reasons and explanations. As a result, in the sixteenth century an alchemical stereotype emerges, according to which the complexities of the art are reduced and simplified to the point where it is viewed as little more than a crude form of deception; its practitioners come to be universally known as cheats and imposters. This uncritical attitude contrasts sharply with that of Francis Bacon in the next century.

In all probability the reasons for the nearly formulaic portrayal of alchemists in literature had much to do with the state of the art itself. There is reason to believe that Chaucer's narrative of the false canon in the pars secunda presents an accurate picture of the abuses that alchemy sustained at the hands of corrupt and dishonest charlatans. This is evidenced by the numerous prohibitions against the practice of alchemy that were enacted during the Middle Ages and Renaissance. Furthermore, authors of alchemical treatises often take pains within their works to dissociate themselves from the deceits practiced by pseudo-alchemists. In *The Ordinall of Alchimy*, for example, Thomas Norton carefully draws the distinction between the true "philosophical" alchemist or the honest seeker of the key to transmutation and the confidence man whose greed and cunning were boundless. Of the former Norton says, according to the text of his work reprinted in Ashmole's *Theatrum Chemicum Britannicum:*

> All trew searchers of this *Science* of *Alkimy,*
> Mustbe full learned in their first Philosophie:

. . . .
And for that thei would that no Man shulde have losse,
They prove and seeke all at their owne Coste;
. . . .
With greate Patience thei doe proceede,
Trusting only in *God* to be their speede. [pp. 16-17]

On the contrary,

The fals man walketh from Towne to Towne,
For the most parte in a threed-bare-Gowne;
. . . .
And ever they rayle with perjury;
Saying how they can Multiplie
Gold and Silver, and in such wise
With promise thei please the Covetise. [p. 17]

Of these two species of alchemists, the latter rather than the former is the object of satirical attack. Nevertheless, the philosophical alchemist was often included as an unwitting victim because, unlike Chaucer and Norton, few men of letters took the trouble to make (or were even aware of) the distinction between them.

Although the first significant use of alchemy in sixteenth-century literature is to be found in Erasmus, it is also present in works of the English and Scottish poets who were born in the latter 1400s and lived on into the next century. In the poetry of Dunbar, Skelton, Douglas, Barclay, and Lindsay, references to alchemy and alchemists appear for purposes of satire and humor, and many of the alchemical topics included in medieval literature continue to be used.

William Dunbar's "As yung Awrora with cristall haile" (the "Ballat of the Fenyeit [False] Freir of Tungland") is a satire on John Damien, a real alchemical charlatan in the court of James IV of Scotland, and it is an unusually interesting example of the post-Chaucerian literary use of alchemy.[5] Cast in the form of a dream vision, no sooner has the speaker been lulled to sleep by "yung Awrora" than he is assailed by a vision of a "sonis of Sathanis seid"—in reality a Turk—leaving Barbary and taking up a fugitive's existence in Lombardy. Displaying at once all of the stereotyped barbarism of his nationality, he proceeds to murder a religious ("Fra baptasing for to eschew") and dons his victim's habit. When his dissembling nature is discovered he flees to France with a small quantity of "Lombard leid" (lead) and here practices treachery in a variety of ways. At first he appears in the guise of a leech, leaving "mony a man [to] rew evirmair; / For he left nowthir seik nor sair / Unslane" (ll. 18-20). Departing France, he next travels to Scotland:

He come his cunnyng till assay;
To sum man thair it was no play,
    The preving of his sciens.
In pottingry he wrocht grit pyne,

> He murdreist mony in medecyne;
> The jow was of a grit engyne,
>   And generit was of gyans. [ll. 26-32]

Like Dunbar's younger contemporary Paracelsus (1493-1541), the false friar is an iatrochemist, one who applies chemical principles to the practice of medicine. The important difference is that the friar's "pottingry," i.e., his work as an apothecary or alchemist, is not performed in the service of mankind: "His practikis nevir war put to preif, / But suddane deid, or grit mischeif" (ll. 45-46). Like Chaucer in the *Canon's Yeoman's Tale*, Dunbar associates the treacherous ingenuity of this "jow," i.e., juggler or trickster, with the supernatural: he has sprung from a race of giants and is referred to as a son of Satan's seed. Similarly, his great cunning and deceptiveness ("grit engyne") result from his posing as a religious man, but one who, in reality, avoids the celebration of the mass in order to pursue his craft in a smoky smithy. The fourth stanza reveals the futility of the friar's experimentation in alchemy but at the same time attributes to him other magical traits:

> And quhen he saw that nocht availyeit,
>   A fedrum on he tuke,
> And shupe in Turky for to fle;
> And quhen that he did mont on he,
> All fowill ferleit quhat he sowld be
>   That evir did on him luke. [ll. 59-64]

The concluding stanzas describe the fate of the friar after he has donned the "fedrum" or feathered wings in order to make his escape. While flying Icarus-like through the skies he is attacked by birds, who are astonished at his appearance. Some think him to be Daedalus, some the Minotaur, some Vulcan, and others, Saturn's cuckoo. Unable to withstand the attacks of the clamorous birds, the friar at last slips off his wings and plummets ingloriously to the earth: "And in a myre, up to the ene / Amang the glar did glyd" (ll. 107-8). At this point the dreamer awakens. Early emblem writers like Alciati commonly used the Icarus myth to represent the foolish pride of astrologers in pursuing forbidden knowledge (fig. 13), and Dunbar is only slightly modifying this tradition to accommodate the related charlatanism of his alchemist-friar.

Alchemy is also alluded to in a second short poem entitled, "Schir, ye have mony servitouris" (or "Dunbar's Remonstrance to the King"), the first part of which lists retainers who serve the King well, bringing honor and riches to his court. Included are doctors of law and medicine, philosophers, artists, knights, carpenters, masons, astrologers, and "potingaris." In contrast to these richly deserving members of the trades and professions are men of a different sort who also attach themselves to the court: feigners, flatterers, idle talkers, scoffers, gentlemen of France, beggars, robbers, and coaxers. These people, who have no claim to knowledge and bring confusion to the court, are the ones against whom Dunbar

116 AND. ALC. EMBLEM. L 1 P.

In Aſtrologos.

Iǽre per ſuperos qui raptus & aera,donec
In mare præàpitem cæra liquata daret.
Nunc te cæra eadem feruensẜ refuſàtat ignis,
Exemplo ut doceas dogmata ærta tuo.
Aſtrologus aueat quicquam prædiciare,præceps
Nam adet impoſtor dum ſuper aſtra uehit.

Liuret des Emblemes de   117
Andre Alciat.

Contre Aſtrologues.

Icarus cheut dedans la mer
Par trop grande exaltation:
Cil qui veult le ciel entamer,
Eſt trop plain de preſumption:
Doncques ſur ceſte fiction,
Doibuent garder les aſtrologues,
Que leur haulte diſcuſſion,
Les mette ou dieu reduit tous rogues:
H iij

Figure 13. The Fall of Icarus (Against Astrologers). Alciati, *Les Emblemes de Maistre Andre Alciat* (1540). By permission of The Huntington Library, San Marino, California.

remonstrates. Although alchemists are not included in this group, Dunbar chooses an alchemical metaphor to describe their effects upon the court; they exist only

> Bot to mak thrang, schir, in your duris,
>
> . . . .
>
> In quintiscence eik ingynouris joly
> That far can multiplie in folie,
> Fantastik fulis bayth fals and gredy,
> Of toung untrew and hand evill diedie. [ll. 52, 55-58]

Thus, while acknowledging the rightful place of apothecaries and alchemists in the court and praising the services they perform, Dunbar resorts paradoxically to the peculiar terminology of alchemy ("quintiscence," "multiplie") to express his indignation against corrupt courtly attendants. This method was to be used again in Jonson's *Mercury Vindicated from the Alchemists at Court.*

A similar but more universalized context informs Gavin Douglas's use of alchemy in the *Prologue* to the eighth book of his translation of the *Aeneid* (1512-

13, printed 1533).[6] Each of the books of Douglas's *Aeneid* is preceded by a "pro-logue," which amounts to an original, independent poem on any one of a variety of topics. The *Prologue* to book 8 takes the form of a dream vision in which the speaker decries the falseness of the world and how all things have turned from virtue to vice. The introductory lines convey a feeling of conventional melan-choly and despair: reason, right, friendship, and peace have fled from the earth and are replaced by lies, stupidity, and lust (ll. 8-13). Disquieting studies have taken away the joy of life, and man spends his time expressing discontent and practicing villainies. The dreamer remonstrates that "This cuntre is full of Caynis kyne, / And sic schyr schrewis. / Quhat wickitnes, quhat wanthrift now in warld walkis!" (p. 144, ll. 25-26; p. 145, l. 1). When enumerating the consequences of the untuning of the string of order, Douglas gives special attention to alchemists, placing them in a category with "tinters" of metal and counterfeiters: "Sum latit lattoun, but lay, lepis in laud lyte, / Sum penis furth a pan boddum to prent fals plakkis; / Sum goukis quhill the glas pyg grow ful of gold yit, / Throw cury of the quentassens, thocht clay mugis crakis" (p. 145, ll. 14-17). Although the allusion is brief, the treatment of alchemy is familiar: the alchemist is victimized as much by his delusions as his avarice; he peers expectantly into the "glass pitcher" watching for gold or searches after the quintessence even as the clay mugs crack.

The *Eclogues* of Alexander Barclay were written about 1515 and served to introduce the pastoral convention into English literature.[7] For this study, the *Fifth Eclogue*, entitled *Amintas and Faustus, of the disputation of Citizens and men of the Countrey*, is most important. A lengthened imitation of one by Mantuan, this eclogue takes the form of a midwinter debate between two impoverished young shepherds: Amintas, who is familiar with the ways of the city, and Faustus, long a dweller in the fields and villages. The central question concerns the original "diversitie" that led humans to take up each kind of existence, rural or urban, and the relative superiority and blessedness of life in each place. Faustus, the pastoralist, eventually gains the upper hand by attacking the "Envy, fraude, mal-ice and suche iniquitie / Which reigne in cities" (ll. 42-43) and citing the promi-nence of rural environments in the lives of many biblical and mythological char-acters. Additionally, he argues, God chose shepherds to be the first witnesses of the Nativity.

At this point Faustus discourses on the follies of city dwellers, particularly the "cloked foolishness" that causes them to dress elegantly in public while living beggarly lives at home. When Amintas objects that men driven by poverty are compelled to resort to wickedness to live, Faustus replies that not even extreme necessity justifies law-breaking. Furthermore, the lengths to which men will go to satisfy their greed are exemplified by the alchemists,

> wening by pollicy
> Nature to alter, and coyne to multiply.
> Some wash rude metall with licours manifolde
> Of herbes, wening to turne it into golde.

> All pale and smoky be such continuall,
> And after labour they lose their life and all: [ll. 601-6]

To these traditional charges against alchemy, Faustus adds another common allegation. The alchemists are like the practitioners of the "wretched art magike," who through their art attempt to find treasure

> Which many yeres is hid within the grounde.
> What is more foolish, more full of vanitie,
> Or more repugning to fayth and probitie,
> Because they would flye good busynes and payne,
> They use such trifles and wretched thinges vayne. [ll. 610-14]

Considering its nature, the translation of *The Ship of Fools,* for which Barclay is most famous, has surprisingly little to say about alchemy. Such commentary as is included is found in a chapter entitled "Of falshode, gyle, and disceyte, and suche as folowe them,"[8] which has to do with the general state of corruption that exists in all trades and crafts. The chapter heading contains a woodcut (retained from Brant's original) showing two alchemists in fool's caps at work at their furnace, while a third rogue is busily adulterating a cask of wine; the caption beneath emphasizes the prevalence of corruption (fig. 14). Barclay's theme of the universality of dishonesty is also emphasized through an alchemical invocation wherein the muses are asked to multiply the narrator's wit and tongue a hundred-fold so that he is better able to record "The fraude, and disceyt, whiche is by gylefull wayes / Among all chraftis used nowe adayes" (p. 220, ll. 6-7). Against this background of corruption brought about by greed, Barclay, like Douglas, places alchemists with makers of false coins or those who debase the value of currency by "clipping" and "washing":

> in many a regyon
> Suche folys stody to mengle and multyply
> Eche sort of metall men to disceyve therby
>
> And in theyr wretchyd ryches to abounde
> The clyp, they coyne, and that: counterfayt metall
> And the right kynde of golde they oft confounde
> . . . .
> Thus over the worlde is nought but gyle and sleyght [p. 222, ll. 5-10, 14]

Among these transitional writers alchemical subject matter is not limited to nondramatic verse but is also present in drama written long before such material was given popular expression in the comedies of Lyly and Jonson. An allusion to it occurs in David Lindsay's long and popular morality play, *Ane Satyre of the thrie Estaits,* acted before James V, on January 6, 1540.[9] As is often the case in works surveyed in this chapter, Lindsay's play focuses on the exposure of all manner of vice and corruption, particularly as it exists among representatives of the

Of falshode, gyle, and disceyte, and suche as folowe them.

The vayne and disceytfull craft of alkemy
The corruptynge of wyne and other merchandyse
Techyth and shewyth vnto vs openly
What gyle and falshode men nowe do exercyse
All occupyers almost, suche gyle dyuyse
In euery chaffar, for no fydelyte
Is in this londe, but gyle and subtylte

Figure 14. Alchemists. Alexander Barclay, translation of Sebastian Brant, *Ship of Fools* (1509).

three estates: Lords Spiritual, Lords Temporal, and Burgesses. Its 5,630 lines provide amply for an enormous cast of allegorical characters who variously tempt Rex Humanitas to do evil (e.g., Wantonness, Placebo, Solace) or exhort him to reform (e.g., Chastity, Divine Correction, Verity). Early in the play Rex Humanitas is tempted by the guile of three evil counselors: Flattrie, who specializes in philosophy, astronomy, and palmistry; Dissait, whose talents are in physiognomy and prophecy; and Falset, who states:

> And I have greit intelligence
> In quelling of the quintessence.
> Bot, to preif my experience,
>   Sir, len me fourtie crownes,
> To mak multiplicatioun. [ll. 886-90]

The satirical tone of the passage and the name of the speaker assure that granting Falset's request for forty crowns will result only in the multiplication of deception. Later in the play, when the overthrow of Vice necessitates the hanging of Falset, he laments that his passing will cause the craftsmen to starve, so dependent have they become on his guile. He enumerates the lessons in deceit taught to tradesmen, suggesting, as does Barclay in *The Ship of Fools,* that no craft has been left untainted. Finally, he exhorts all surviving goldsmiths to continue to mix less precious metal with their gold:

> Gold Smythis, fair-weill! above them all.
> Remember my memoriall,
> With mony ane sittill cast.
> To mix, set ye nocht by twa preinis,
> Fyne Ducat gold with hard Gudlingis,
> Lyke as I lernit yow last. [ll. 4166-71]

John Skelton's *Garlande or Chapelet of Laurell*[10] (written and printed in 1523) will serve as a final example of the literary use of alchemy among the transitional poets. Adopting the form of the dream vision, like Dunbar, Skelton's narrator describes falling asleep in the forest of Galtres and overhearing the debate between Pallas Athene and the Queen of Fame concerning his right to wear the laurel. Later, Fame's servant, the "gentilwoman" Occupacyoun, welcomes Skelton and conducts him on a tour of a walled field through whose gates people of all nations can enter (ll. 533-81). Looking over the wall to the world outside the field, Skelton sees masses of people pressing against the gates awaiting admission. To his inquiries as to their identity, Occupacyoun replies that they are base and ribald fellows ("haskardis and rebawdis") who are guilty of all manner of deceits and follies: "Dysers, carders, tumblars with gambawdis, / Furdrers of love, with baudry aqueinted, / Brainles blenkardis that blow at the cole, / Fals forgers of mony, for kownnage atteintid" (ll. 608-11). In classifying alchemists, these

"brainles blenkardis [men with blinking eyes] that blow at the cole," with counterfeiters and cheaters of all sorts, Skelton reveals an attitude that is entirely compatible with those of his late-medieval, early-Renaissance contemporaries. In the
works here considered, one theme—the decay of honesty and morality in all aspects of human existence—is prominent. Whether the context is Dunbar's narrative of the false friar, the disaffected *weltschmerz* of his "Remonstrance" and
Douglas's *Prologue*, the pastoral lament of Barclay's shepherds, or the bitter sar-
casm of his *Ship of Fools*, the practice of alchemy is regarded as convincing evidence that evil has triumphed over honesty and virtue.

Clearly, these references suggest that the connotative meaning of alchemy
and alchemists has shifted slightly from what it had earlier been. In comparison
to Chaucer, Gower, and Langland, the transitional poets appear to have known
relatively little about the art. Detailed references to arcane processes of transmutation, the complex materials and laboratory apparatus, and even the exotic jargon are missing. There are few mentions of theoretical bases and principles and
no allusions to traditional authorities. Above all, there is no hint of recognition
that a "truer" kind of alchemy exists. Although the obvious affinities between
alchemists and apothecaries, goldsmiths, and dealers in natural magic are briefly
explored in some of these later writings, generally the meaning of alchemy is
reduced to a few catchwords such as "quintessence" and "multiply." It is through
this process of semantic simplification that its rich and varied literary potential is
drastically reduced. In striking contrast to the *Canon's Yeoman's Tale*, in works of
the transitional poets alchemy becomes merely an objective correlative for evoking a vision of poverty, folly, and deception. Thus, at the same time that its frequency in popular literature was "multiplying," its rich suggestiveness fell into a
state of "mortification."

While the transitional poets accomplished little in the way of transmuting the
subject matter of alchemy into new and highly original kinds of literary experience, they did assure its survival as a literary motif through frequent references in
a variety of poetic forms. But at the same time that many of these works were
being written and printed, a greater writer was utilizing the subject of alchemy in
ways that are far more interesting. Although Desiderius Erasmus was not an En-
glishman, his works warrant consideration here because of his impact on sixteenth-century intellectual life in England, an impact that resulted from the popularity of his writings as well as his association with leading Renaissance human-
ists. Moreover, the discussions of alchemy included in his works constitute the
most important literary adaptations of the subject between Chaucer and Jonson
and Donne.

The *Moriae Encomium*, written in 1509 while Erasmus was on his third visit
to England, was composed in seven days while the author was recuperating from
illness in the home of Sir Thomas More. He was, as he tells us, "too sick to do
any serious work."[11] That was also the year in which Pynson printed Barclay's

Ship of Fools, and together these works constitute two of the most extensive and popular depictions of fools and folly in literary history. The success of the *Encomium* is demonstrated by the fact that seven editions followed shortly the printing of the Latin original in Paris in 1511, and there were also numerous translations, including the first one into English by Sir Thomas Chaloner in 1549.

Although the aims and methods of the *Encomium* and *The Ship of Fools* differ,[12] the satire in both is directed against many of the same targets, and in each work the targets are many. In the Preface to his translation Chaloner remarks that his purpose in Englishing the work was "not so muche to please all men, as rather to shew how evin this Foly toucheth all men."[13] Referring to Erasmus's satiric method, Chaloner states "he maketh Folie to speake at randon, without sparying of any estate of men: but yet indifferent eares will heare their faultes paciently, aslong as they maie chose, whether they will take the faulte uppon theim or not: or be aknowne to be those, whom Folie noteth" (5). As is not the case in *The Ship of Fools,* Folly's auditors are not forced "to wear the shoe" but may if they choose to do so. Chaloner's statement thus reveals the key to the work's devastating charm: in presenting Folly as a goddess, in having her address the "notable assembly" and list the "benefits" she has conferred upon mankind as well as her principal followers, Erasmus sharpens the satire through the irony of self-revelation. Both the goddess and her followers are condemned simultaneously. This method is similar to the one that Lindsay was later to use in his character "Falset" in *Ane Satyre of the thrie Estaits.*

Folly places alchemists in a category with men who are truly mad: those who are deceived not only in their senses but also habitually in the "judgement of the mynde." Such is the man who believes he hears the chiming of chapel bells whenever an ass brays or the beggar who thinks he possesses the wealth of Cresus (53). Yet, ironically, hope can be derived from even the profoundest state of self-delusion and in this Swiftian sense is especially applicable to the "Alcumistes, or multipliers," who

> by theyr newfound secrete science, go about to chaunge metall into metall, serchyng bothe by sea and by lande, a certaine Quintessence. These men are so enticed by an hope they have to bringe theyr feate to passe, as neither labour, nor cost maie withdraw theim from the same, but wittily ever they dooe devise some new thyng, wherwith to begyle theim selves again, till at last, havyng spent all they coulde make, there remaineth not to theim so muche silver, as wherwith to bie bechen coles for their fornace. Natheles they leave not to dreame still of wonderous pleasant invencions, encourageyng others, as muche as in theim lieth, to the same trade of felicitee. (55)

Aside from the mention of "bechen coles," recalling the trick played by Chaucer's Canon, the passage might be seen as a previously unnoticed extended analogue for the alchemical simile in Donne's "Loves Alchymie." In emphasizing the pathos of the alchemists' futile quest, Folly strikes a note that is missing in the writings of the transitional poets. For her, they are not merely evidence of the ways men abuse their fellows or symptoms of the corruptness of the times, but rather an affirmation of the universal infirmity of the human mind. In them, we see the persistence of hope notwithstanding repeated failure to reach a "conclusioun," the waste of labor and money, the empty dreams, and self-protective rationalizations. In presenting alchemy as this *ignis fatuus* of the human mind, Folly reveals a complex attitude that combines comedy and satire, but also Swiftian pessimism and the existentialists' tragic view of life.

Compared to the *Moriae Encomium,* Erasmus's treatment of alchemy in the *Colloquies* is more extensive and more squarely in the satirical tradition. Employing the techniques of dramatic realism, these short dialogues are pedagogically useful, morally instructive and entertaining, and were to be enduringly popular. Along with his *Copia* and *De Conscribendis Epistolis,* the *Colloquies* formed an important part of the curriculum of the Elizabethan grammar school[14] and exerted what T.W. Baldwin has called "a powerful influence on English literature."[15] Their popularity is demonstrated by the early history of their publication. The *Familiarium colloquiorum formulae* first appeared in an unauthorized edition of 1518. Although annoyed that his friend Johannes Froben of Basel should have printed it without permission, Erasmus appears to have at first taken little serious interest in the work. After all, it consisted largely of "formulae" or exercises of use in teaching colloquial Latin to young pupils. But the work was immediately successful. Reprints of the unauthorized edition appeared shortly in Paris and Antwerp, and Erasmus himself wrote a preface for a new edition that was published in Louvain in March 1519; at least sixteen editions were printed by 1533 and eighty-seven by 1536, the year of Erasmus's death (xxiv-xxv). Throughout these years the nature of the collection changed drastically, and after March 1522, new editions were augmented with dialogues "that might serve boys as models of speech and writing both, and would appeal to men as much as to boys; it became a book of colloquies instead of exercises. For the next two centuries or longer it had a double career, as a schoolbook and as adult literary entertainment" (xxv-xxvi). A more strategic medium for the discussion of alchemy could hardly be imagined.

Incidental references to alchemy and alchemists are present in several of the *Colloquies,* and in two, "Beggar Talk" and "Alchemy," this subject comprises the heart of the work. In "A Marriage in Name Only, or the Unequal Match," first printed in March 1529, mention is made of a masklike protective device, worn by alchemists, that "admits light through glass windows and allows you to breathe through mouth and nose by means of a tube extending from the mask over your shoulders and down your back" (411). This brief allusion is humorous because the device is prescribed, not to protect artisans from the perils of the furnace, but to guard citizens against the deadly vapors of syphilis. A second dialogue, "The Art of Learning" (459-61), concerns the attempts of a lazy student, Erasmius, to find an easy shortcut to mastering his studies. He tells his learned tutor, Desiderius, of an intricate mnemonic system (of the type popular during the Renaissance) that will enable him to learn the entire liberal arts curriculum in fourteen days. Desiderius replies that reliance on artificial means to wisdom is as futile as expecting riches through alchemy and counsels Erasmius to adopt hard work and perseverance instead (460).

It is not surprising that Desiderius should invoke alchemy in condemning both Erasmius's memory system and the book that sets it forth: one filled with "various figures of animals—dragons, lions, leopards—and various circles with words written in them, partly Greek, partly Latin, partly Hebrew, and others in barbarous tongues" (460). From this generalized description it appears that the illustrations Erasmius has seen are typical of the intricate diagrams common in Renaissance memory books.[16] The animals, circles, and inscriptions in foreign languages also recall numerous alchemical illustrations. In fact, as Yates has shown, during the Renaissance the mnemonic art was frequently associated with the hermetic arts: all rested on common philosophical assumptions that were platonic and Neoplatonic in origin, and these, in turn, were connected with a far more ancient and inspired source, Hermes Trismegistus. That Erasmus had more than a passing acquaintance with the art of memory we know from correspondence with his friend Viglius Zuichemus, who described the "Memory Theater" of Giulio Camillo in enthusiastic detail.[17] And Camillo's Theater provides an excellent example of how solidly the art of memory was built upon the foundations of Renaissance platonic and hermetic philosophy. Yates notes that "Camillo brings the art of memory into line with the new currents now running through the Renaissance. His Memory Theatre houses Ficino and Pico, Magia and Cabala, the Hermetism and Cabalism implicit in Renaissance so-called Neoplatonism. He turns the classical art of memory into an occult art."[18]

Given this close association, it follows that skepticism about the mnemonic art as an easy way to wisdom should be accompanied (and reinforced) by an allusion to an allied art, alchemy. For Erasmus, this juxtaposition was probably a well-conditioned reflex. In other *Colloquies* Erasmus also expands the associations of alchemy to include more of the occult arts. For example, in "Exorcism, or The Specter" the "occult arts, alchemy, and magic" are grouped comically together (236). This traditional connection is repeated in "The Usefulness of the Colloquies" (first printed in June 1526), where, in justifying their composition, he states: "By no means the slightest of human afflictions is alchemy, a disorder so intoxicating, once it strikes a man, that it beguiles even the learned and prudent. Related to it is magic, which goes by the same name but entices us by the additional title of 'natural.' I denounce similar impostures in *The Cheating Horse-Dealer* and in *Beggar Talk;* again in *The Fabulous Feast*" (631).

"Beggar Talk," first printed by Froben in the August-September 1524 edition of the *Colloquies,* is essentially satirical social criticism that attacks the problem of poverty and the prevalence of begging in particular. Yet it is alchemy, or rather the humorous exposé of the tricks used by alchemists, that provides the foundation for both dialogue and action. Although there appears to be only one specific borrowing, Erasmus's use of wit, irony, and comic characterization strongly recall Chaucer's treatment of the subject, and like the *Canon's Yeoman's Tale,* "Beggar Talk" touches upon several themes that were traditionally linked with alchemy. The dialogue occurs as a result of a chance meeting between Irides ("son of Irus," named after the beggar Irus in the *Odyssey*) and Misoponus ("hater of work"), who, unlike his friend, has recently graduated from the order of "down-and-out" (248). In response to Irides' question as to where his new clothes, handsomeness, and "strange sleekness" came from, Misoponus reveals that he has taken up the profession of alchemy, which is infinitely more lucrative than picking pockets. From a drinking crony he has learned to become an adept in two weeks' time, and the remainder of the dialogue relates how his knowledge is utilized (251).

Misoponus's boasts about his talents always assure him a plentiful number of victims for his confidence game. After carefully selecting them, he allays suspicion by warning them "not to trust practitioners of this art too readily, since many of them are cheats who play tricks to empty fools' purses" (252). He also urges them to believe only what they see with their own eyes; to this end, like Chaucer's "Chanoun of religioun," he lets his victims do most of the work of the experiment while he acts as overseer. He supplies only the technical know-how and the "fine powder" that acts as the transmuting agent. The trick that Misoponus uses to bring about the miraculous result is also that of Chaucer's Canon:

> The whole trick turns on one coal prepared for this purpose. I hollow it out and insert molten silver, the amount I predict must be yielded. After the powder is spread over this, I make ready the pot so that it's surrounded by live coals not only below and on the sides but also above. I convince them this is part of the art. Among the coals placed on top I lay the one containing silver or gold. Melted by the heat, this flows down on the other stuff, say tin or bronze, which liquefies. When refining takes place, what was mixed with it is discovered. (252)

Should the experiment fail, Misoponus says that he can fall back on the alchemists' traditional rationalizations: the utensils were dirty, the coals were imperfect, or the fire did not attain the proper temperature. Finally, he admits that "part of [his] professional acumen is not to stay too long in the same place!" (253). These hazards notwithstanding, Misoponus's "practice" of alchemy is sufficiently rewarding to discourage him from returning to the order of beggars.

Although Erasmus reveals an acquaintance with some of the most obvious alchemical terms and processes (e.g., "refining," "trying," "liquefaction," and "tinting"), it is obvious that in "Beggar Talk" he regards the art as nothing more than a crude form of charlatanism. Any serious interest or specialized knowledge that he may have had is subordinated to alchemy's rich comic and satiric potential. For this reason, Erasmus's references to alchemy illustrate an important tendency in its literary use that was to be adopted by writers throughout the sixteenth century. Although his references are numerous and their sources were frequently reprinted and therefore well known, the reputation of alchemy could only suffer immeasurably from this treatment. Cut off from those philosophical bases that lent it at least the appearance of validity, divested of its traditional authorities, alchemy becomes synonymous with deceit, poverty, and degradation. The process of simplification evident in the writings of the transitional poets is therefore continued and intensified in the prose of their more celebrated contemporary.

Erasmus's dialogue "Alchemy," which also first appeared in the August-September 1524 edition of the *Colloquies,* is his most extensive treatment of this subject and also his best example of the reductive process I have been describing (239-45). To a much greater extent than in "Beggar Talk," narration and characterization are skillfully developed and grow organically from the alchemical context. (The chief flaw in "Beggar Talk" is the way in which Misoponus's "profession of alchemy" is somewhat arbitrarily imposed upon him.) Because of its harmonious blending of story and character with alchemical background, "Alchemy" represents the finest achievement of this kind between Chaucer and Jonson and, for this reason, I am summarizing the dialogue in some detail. Like "Beggar Talk," it enjoyed the popularity resulting from inclusion in later editions of the *Colloquies,* and it also appeared in Reginald Scot's *Discoverie of Witchcraft* of 1584.

"Alchemy" opens with Lalus ("talkative") eager to share with Philecous ("fond of hearing") a story about Balbinus, who is described as "the gentleman [who] has this slight blemish: that for a long while he's been mad about the art called alchemy." To this Philecous replies that such a weakness cannot be considered a mere blemish, but "a notorious disease" (239). In the past Balbinus has often fallen victim to the wiles of alchemists but has not learned discretion. Recently, Lalus continues, Balbinus was approached by a priest who tells him that he has studied alchemy—"that core of all philosophy"—from his boyhood on, but now he is sorrowful because he has chosen the wrong path to success: "longation" rather than "curtation." The priest falsely flatters Balbinus for his profound knowledge of both ways and begs to be shown the secret of the shorter method: "And so I've hurried here to you in hopes that you might take pity on me and deign to share with me that most blessed way of curtation. . . . Do not conceal so great a gift of God from a brother about to die of grief. So may Jesus Christ ever enrich you with great gifts!" (240).

When Balbinus confesses that he doesn't know either method, the priest tells him that one is "shorter but a little more risky; the other takes longer but is safer." This information whets Balbinus's desire, causing him to lose his fear of fraud: "Finally, unable to restrain himself, he says, 'Away with that curtation! I've never even heard of it, let alone mastered it. Tell me straight: do you understand longation well?'" (240). The priest confides that he does, but warns Balbinus that this process takes at least a year. With that, "like persons initiated into secret rites," they agree to begin the experiment in Balbinus's house, Balbinus providing the money and the priest the work: "Money is counted out then and there for the operator to buy pots, glasses, charcoal, and other equipment needed for the laboratory. This money our alchemist squanders enjoyably on whores, dice, and drink" (241).

When all is spent, more gold is needed to construct the laboratory, and Balbinus, still seized with greed, willingly gives it. He has decided to invest 2,000 ounces of gold in hopes that it will yield fifteen to one. This, too, is wasted, the priest confessing that he has erred in the purchase of charcoal. Months later, when the experiment should have been completed and much gold has been spent, the priest suggests that an offering be made to the Virgin Mother: "For the art is a sacred one and cannot prosper without the blessing of heaven" (241).

With Balbinus's money in hand, the priest sets out on his "pious journey"— to a neighboring village—and "there spent the votive money in riotous living. Home again, he announces he has the highest hopes that their enterprise will prosper, . . . so pleased did the Holy Virgin seem with his offering" (242). Predictably, the venture fails, and the priest finally confesses that failure may result from negligence in fulfilling his religious duties. As penance "the expert undertook to hear twelve Masses for the two he had missed, and in place of a single salutation to make ten" (242).

The cycle of duplicity is repeated many times, and after all possible excuses for requesting more money have been exhausted, the priest hits upon a final plan. He tells Balbinus that court officials have discovered their scheme and that he will be hanged, for "to practice alchemy without royal permission is a capital crime in these parts" (242). In the face of this threat, the priest suggests that the officials might be bribed, and Balbinus gladly counts out "thirty gold crowns to stop their tongues." This done, the experiment is supposedly resumed, and again, time and money are wasted. Meanwhile the alchemist is having an affair with the wife of a courtier, who eventually becomes suspicious and arrives at his bedroom door at an inappropriate moment. The priest escapes through a window, but word of the escapade reaches Balbinus. Being a straight-laced person, Balbinus rebukes him severely: "'There's no mystery about what the trouble is,' he says[,] 'Your sins block the success of what should be handled by pure men in a pure way'" (244). The priest at once confesses his wickedness but is as quick to supply excuses:

> At this word the alchemist dropped to his knees, beating his breast repeatedly, and with tearful looks and tone said, "Balbinus, you've spoken the absolute truth. My sins, I admit, are the hindrance. But they're my sins, not yours, for I shan't be ashamed to confess my disgrace before you, as before the holiest priest. Weakness of the flesh overcame me; Satan drew me into his snares, and—O wretched me!—from priest I am become an adulterer. Yet the offering we made to the Virgin Mother was not altogether wasted. I would certainly have been killed if she had not come to my rescue. The husband was breaking down the door; the window was too narrow for me to slip through. In so imminent a danger I thought

of the Most Holy Virgin. I fell on my knees and implored her, if the gift had been acceptable, to help me. Without further delay I tried the window again— my plight forced me to do so—and it was wide enough for my escape." [244]

Not prepared to disbelieve so powerful a demonstration of divine providence, Balbinus forgives him, and thinking that the priest is now truly repentant, he supplies him with more money so that the cycle of deception can begin anew. After much time has passed Balbinus is warned by a friend who knows of the priest's reputation, upon which he urges the priest to leave the country, offers him "travel money," and implores him "by everything sacred not to blab about what has happened" (244).

The success of this dialogue results as much from a certain knowledge of human nature as from familiarity with alchemical lore. Details of the latter are fused with the former in such a way that the entire work has enough unity, coherence, and realism of sorts to make a valid statement about human nature. The four characters—the teller of the tale, the listener, the trickster, and the greedy and credulous victim—are all "types." Yet, although their actions, speeches, and psychology are totally uncomplicated by the vagaries of real existence, they retain enough vestiges of humanity to be immediately recognizable and satisfying. But the uncommon merit of the dialogue is brought about through the grafting of numerous alchemical details onto these simplified specimens of humanity. For example, the priest's plea that Balbinus grant him this "gift of God" (the key to transmutation) is not merely an extravagant metaphor that is incidentally congruent with his "profession." Alchemical treatises habitually refer to the secret of the philosopher's stone in this manner, as seen in the following passage from Thomas Norton's *Ordinall of Alchimy* (1477):

> For *Gods* Conjunctions Man maie not undoe,
> But if his Grace fully consent thereto,
> By helpe of this *Science,* which our *Lord* above
> Hath given to such Men as he doth love;
> Wherefore old *Fathers* conveniently
> Called this *Science Holy Alkimy.*
>   Therefore noe man shulde be too swifte,
> To cast away our *Lords* blessed guift:[19]

Similarly, a translated passage from Hermes' *Tractatus Aureus* included in William Salmon's *Medicina Practica* (London, 1692) states: "*Even Hermes himself saith, . . . I obtained the knowledge of this Art, by the Inspiration of the Living God only, who esteeming me his Servant worthy, did reveal and open the Secret to me.*"[20] Or again, the fact that Balbinus and the priest enter into an agreement resembling those used for initiations into secret societies and complete with an oath of secrecy is based on the alchemical tradition of deliberate obscurity. Seen in connection with passages like the following from Artephius's *Liber Secretus,* this agreement takes on new and delicious ironies: "However, that he might not profligate his Art, nor prostitute it to the Abuses of Impious, Ignorant, and Evil Men, he has drawn, as it were, a thin Veile before the Illustrious and Dazling Face of Truth; in nothing more pregnant than in the Principles of this Science."[21]

A reason for secrecy more compelling than the *ignotum per ignocius* commonplace are the royal and ecclesiastical prohibitions of the practice of alchemy frequently enacted during the Middle Ages and Renaissance. While the setting of "Alchemy" is uncertain, the priest's fear of imprisonment or hanging would be understandable were he subject to the statute enacted by Henry IV in 1403-1404 and not formally repealed until 1689: "Item, It is ordained and stablished, That none from henceforth shall use to multiply Gold or Silver, nor use the Craft of Multiplication: And if any the same do, and be thereof attaint, that he incur the Pain of Felony in this Case."[22] Thorndike records the enactment of a similar statute in Venice in 1468 or 1488, which sought to prevent activities of the type Balbinus and the priest are guilty of.[23] But if he is apprehended by the authorities, the priest can envision a fate even worse than death: being forced to pursue his experiments in prison for the benefit of his captors. "Is there any death," he says, "not preferable to such a life?" (242). Although the priest's effusive rhetoric is wholly an attempt to gain Balbinus's sympathy, the fate he alludes to is known to have befallen numerous alchemists. Robert Steele records a writ of Edward III that commands two alchemists to perform their services in his behalf, for "they by this art can be of great benefit to us and to our kingdom by the making of this metal, if it can be truly done." Should they refuse to come, the writ continues, Thomas Cary, the King's sheriff, "shall take them and bring them to us, wherever we may be, in aforesaid form."[24] Although it is difficult to distinguish fact from legend, historians of alchemy record numerous severe punishments that adepts received at the hands of cruel magistrates and kings. An alchemist named Gustenhover spent the last years of his life in the White Tower of Emperor Rudolph II, and before his death in 1603 or 1604 the Scottish alchemist Alexander Seton was subjected to torture by Christian II, Elector of Saxony.[25] In chapter 5 I will discuss the adventures of Seton and his links with Michael Sendivogius, whose *Dialogus Mercurii, Alchymistae et Naturae* is the likely source of Ben Jonson's masque, *Mercury Vindicated from the Alchemists at Court.*

A final detail that confirms Erasmus's familiarity with alchemical lore occurs near the end of the dialogue where Balbinus, after learning of the priest's affair with a married woman, castigates him for moral impurity. Moreover, he attributes the experiment's failure to these sinful acts: alchemical experiments, Balbinus says, "should be handled by pure men in a pure way" (244). This idea is repeated often enough in alchemical treatises to become a commonplace, and, as will be shown, it contributes to the successful duping of Sir Epicure Mammon by Face and Subtle in Jonson's *The Alchemist.* Because the secret of the philosopher's stone was regarded as a gift of God, it followed that only those who led exemplary lives would be able to achieve it. These two assumptions account for the pietistic tone

usually present in alchemical treatises as well as for the rigid insistence on pure
and moral lives and the severe condemnation of charlatans who, like Erasmus's
priest, attempt to satisfy their greed through any means possible. All of these
points are illustrated in the following passage from the anonymous *Glory of the
World, or Table of Paradise:*

> If then you would obtain this knowledge at the hand of God, you must
> confess yourself a miserable sinner, and implore His blessing, which alone can
> enable you to receive His Gift worthily, and to bear in mind that He has be-
> stowed it upon you out of pure mercy, and that any pride or presumptuous
> insolence on your part will most certainly entail its loss, in addition to His wrath,
> and eternal condemnation. . . . For this treasure, which is above all other earthly
> treasures, is granted to him alone who approves himself humble, honest, gentle,
> and faithful, as far as the weakness of human nature allows, and keeps the laws
> of God through God's bounty and blessing, and who is not likely to mistake the
> true nature of the gift, or to abuse it against his own eternal welfare.[26]

This insistence on righteous living is stated more succinctly in *The Great
Stone of the Ancient Sages,* one of many popular works attributed to the mysterious Basil Valentine. Here the author states that God reserves the gift of the Stone
"for those favoured few, who love the truth, and hate falsehood, who study our
Art earnestly by day and by night, and whose hearts are set upon God with an
unfeigned affection."[27] Finally, *The Twelve Keys . . . With Which We May Open
The Doors of the Knowledge of the Most Ancient Stone,* the most famous of all the
works ascribed to Valentine, suggests another reason for the importance of purity
in the life of the adept, and, in doing so, presents an aspect of the correspondence theory that is wholly compatible with the aims of "philosophical" (as opposed to "exoteric") alchemy. Because alchemy is an "art of purification," it follows that the presence of things of "leprous nature" will retard the process, whether
they exist in base metals or in the adept himself. Using a simile derived from the
practice of medicine, Valentine argues that successful transmutation depends on
the wholesomeness of both art and artist: "As the physician purges and cleanses
the inward parts of the body, and removes all unhealthy matter by means of his
medicines, so our metallic substances must be purified and refined of all foreign
matter, in order to ensure the success of our task. Therefore, our Masters require
a pure immaculate body, that is untainted with any foreign admixture, which
admixture is the leprosy of our metals."[28]

In one sense Erasmus's "Alchemy" is merely another literary work that nar-
rows and depreciates its subject. Its conclusion leaves one no alternative but to
equate the art with folly and deception. There is no recognition that it may be
practiced by types who differ from the priest and no suggestion that a higher
form may exist. In this sense Erasmus's treatment is thoroughly conventional.
But the key to the work's success and its high place in the tradition of alchemically
inspired literature is the way in which this diminution is brought about. Erasmus

borrows accurately (but unobtrusively) numerous ideas common in alchemical writing and experience; these he blends carefully with character and clever plot, thereby creating opportunities for comic and ironic interplay. The overall effect is akin to burlesque or to that achieved in Samuel Butler's mock-heroic *Hudibras,* as will be shown in chapter 9. Considered apart from the context of the dialogue, the borrowed material is serious and elevated, but when it is juxtaposed with "low" characters and broad comic situations one recognizes the incongruity that has been created. Although alchemy is deflated in the process, the result is a small masterpiece of comedy and satire, one of the finest examples of the thorough and intelligent integration of alchemical subject matter with literary technique.

About Reginald Scot, whose *Discoverie of Witchcraft* (1584) will be considered next, C.S. Lewis made the following statement:

> Genuine humanity was clearly his motive when he began [to write the *Discoverie*]. He is the champion of 'manie poor old women' against those 'unnatural people' who delight 'to pursue the poore, to accuse the simple, and to kill the innocent.' But I think he was also actuated, intermittently, by a quality of mind which, if it had come to dominate him completely, would have lifted him right out of his own century and made him more at home in the period of Sprat and Locke. At times he seems on the verge of rejecting the whole outlook which made witch-craft credible.[29]

Although cautiously phrased, Lewis's supposition about Scot's intellectual kin-ship with some of the leaders of the New Science is open to question on two counts. First, his characterization of the "period of Sprat and Locke" is greatly oversimplified, for implicit is the idea that England of the later seventeenth cen-tury was so dominated by rationalistic philosophy that belief in witchcraft and other occult arts was no longer possible. He also implies that the outlook of the sixteenth century was exactly opposite. Although there is surely a degree of truth here, Lewis overlooks the fact that the period of the Royal Society and Locke was very near that of the *Theatrum Chemicum Britannicum* and the hermetic (and hermetically inspired) writings of Henry and Thomas Vaughan. Moreover, as will be shown in chapter 9, the period was exactly contemporaneous with the time when John Webster, author of the *Academiarum Examen* (1654), was calling for educational reform that included a significant role for the occult arts. Nor does Lewis's picture of seventeenth-century intellectual history take into account the fact that both Boyle and Newton possessed very serious interests in alchemy or that Francis Bacon, the self-proclaimed "*buccinator novi temporis,*" had at times resorted to an animistic interpretation of nature and also harbored positive thoughts concerning the ultimate objectives of alchemy. Second, Lewis's view of Scot's skepticism, his assertion that the author of the *Discoverie* seems "at times. . . on the verge of rejecting" the outlook that made belief in witchcraft possible, is contradicted by some of Scot's own statements. For example, in discussing the central concern of his book Scot remarks, "My question is not (as many fondly suppose) whether there be witches or nay: but whether they can do miraculous works as are imputed to them." Or again, "Because I mislike the extreme cruelty used against some of these silly souls [those accused of witchcraft], it will be said that I deny punishment at all to be due to any witch whatever. Truly I deny not that there are witches . . . but I detest the idolatrous opinions conceived of them."[30] Yet, despite affirmations of the existence of witches, Scot's reputation among his contemporaries was that of a skeptic. The *Discoverie* prompted King James I to write his *Demonology*, the famous argument for the existence of witches and demons, and one of James's first orders upon ascending the throne in 1603 was for the burning of all copies of the *Discoverie* (Introduction, 23).

Scot's discussion of alchemy is contained in book 14, entitled "Of the art of Alcumystrie, of their woords of art and devises to bleare mens eies, and to procure credit to their profession." The title effectively signals the nature of Scot's treatment of the "craft," which is satirical and utterly skeptical. But Scot's skepticism is not reached by following the methods of empirical investigation soon to be set forth by Bacon; instead, his view of alchemy is derived entirely from received opinion and authority. It is the use of authority that is of special interest in the *Discoverie*, for his attack is based almost entirely on purely literary sources. For Scot, Erasmus, Chaucer, and other poets become serious and persuasive authorities whose works count as convincing evidence in the "discovery" or exposure of alchemy.

Scot's utilization of Chaucer is acknowledged at the outset of the *Discoverie* and is the strongest evidence for the continuing influence of the *Canon's Yeoman's Tale* in shaping the tradition of alchemical satire in the sixteenth century. He states, "Chaucer, of all other men, most lively deciphereth the craft of Alcumistrie, otherwise called Multiplication" and proceeds to draw the connection between alchemy, witchcraft, and conjuration, "whereby some cousen others, and some are cousened themselves." This statement, in turn, is supported by a nine-line "quotation" from Chaucer, which in actuality is a composite of four different passages—often slightly altered—from the *Prologue* and *Canon's Yeoman's Tale*.[31] This method of selecting material for quotations is typical of Scot's use of his sources; by removing individual lines or small groups of lines from their proper contexts, he is able to piece together a statement that is more forceful than the original and one that will better serve his purposes.

One of Scot's favorite targets is the *ignotum per ignocius* tradition, wherein alchemists who "would be thought wise, learned, cunning, and their crafts maisters, . . . have devised words of art, sentences and epithets obscure, and confections so innumerable (which are also compounded of strange and rare simples) as confound the capacities of them that are either set on worke heerein, or be brought to behold or expect their conclusions" (297). Of the hundred or so names of substances, processes, preparations, "bodies," "spirits," and pieces of equipment that Scot cites as examples, only two, "termination" and "yest," are not either directly drawn or adapted from the Yeoman's lists in the *pars prima.*[32]

The beginning of chapter 2 of book 14 provides an even more revealing example of Scot's use of Chaucer as an alchemical authority. Although he does not mention "Arnold of the Newe Toun," Plato, or the "book Senior" as ultimate sources, the following passage on the aims of alchemy is obviously reformulated from lines 1428-71 of the *Canon's Yeoman's Tale,* lines which, as previously argued, suggest the existence of a higher form of alchemy identified with the sacred:

> Now you must understand that the end and drift of all their worke, is, to atteine unto the composition of the philosophers stone, called Alixer, and to the stone called Titanus; and to Magnatia, which is a water made of the foure elements, which (they saie) the philosophers are sworne neither to discover, nor to write of. And by these they mortifie quicke silver, and make it malleable, and to hold touch: heereby also they convert any other mettall (but speciallie copper) into gold. This science (forsooth) is the secret of secrets; even as *Salomons* conjuration is said among the conjurors to be so likewise. And thus, when they chance to meete with yong men, or simple people, they boast and brag, and saie with *Simon Magus,* that they can worke miracles, and bring mightie things to passe. (298)

But unlike the original, Scot's version is harshly condemnatory and skeptical. His scoffing attitude is given some emphasis through the ironic effect of the parenthetical asides. Furthermore, Scot makes no mention of the authorities that Chaucer had included. The "despiritualization" (and corresponding vulgarization) of the art is also achieved by omission of such lines from Chaucer as "For unto Crist it is so lief and deere" (l. 1467), as well as by associating the art with the diabolical powers manifested in Solomon's conjuration and in the account of Simon the sorcerer in Acts 8. Scot concludes this chapter with a summary of the *Canon's Yeoman's Tale,* which he calls "a perfect demonstration of the art of Alcumystrie or multiplication."

Scot then notes that he could cite many additional examples of imposture wrought by a Dr. Burcot and one Feates, whom I have not been able to identify. But instead, he resorts to fiction once again and tells three entertaining stories to corroborate his skepticism. The first concerns a naive yeoman who is cheated "by a notable cousening varlot, who professed Alcumystrie, juggling, witchcraft, and conjuration." In this instance, the deceit is accomplished through use of specially designed balls of wax that hide the "multiplied" gold. I can find no other source for this story or for the second, in which a king is made the object of an alchemist's treachery. Scot's third example, however, is a lengthy and detailed retelling of Erasmus's "Alchemy." Here, as throughout the *Discoverie,* his skeptical viewpoint is underscored through the inclusion of numerous notes placed strategically in the margins of the text: "The Alcumyster bringeth Balbin into a fooles paradise" or "Marke how this Alcumyster goeth from one degree of cousenage to another" (306-7).

In the final chapters of book 14 Scot cites several additional authorities—both literary and otherwise—to prove his contention. He first reports the views of Avicenna, as recorded in Albertus Magnus's *Book of Minerals,* to the effect that alchemy cannot change the fundamental substance of metals, only their external appearances. Thus in practice alchemy is nothing more than the tinting of metals, an attempt to give less valuable metals the appearance of those that are more precious.[33] He also quotes from a dialogue of Petrarch ("a man of great learning and no less experience; who . . . in his time . . . saw the fraudulent fetches of this compassing craft" [309]), identified marginally as *lib. de remed. utr. fort.I. cap.10.,* which asserts that expecting wealth from alchemy is a painful delusion. Finally, Scot refers to "an ancient writer of a religious order, who lived above a thousand yeares since,"[34] who calls alchemists *Falsificantes metallorum & mineralium,* witches and counterfetters of metals and minerals." Further, he attacks the art not only because its grounds are uncertain, but because it leads to covetousness, the devaluation of legal currency, and the cheating of the innocent.

Thus, Scot's work is of special importance because it was the means by which two of the finest examples of the literary use of alchemy from the past were brought to the attention of Elizabethan writers and readers. That the *Discoverie* was popular among many types of writers is demonstrated by the fact that sections were used in the plays of Shakespeare and Middleton, references to it are found in prose pamphlets, and at least one book was dedicated to "Mr. Reginald Scot that wrote *The Discovery of Witchcraft.*"[35] Its serious reputation is attested by the fact that it was both the inspiration of James I's *Demonology* and the object of his suppression; yet it endured to be republished in 1665 with additions "by a believing magician."[36] But its chief importance for this study lies in the support it added to the already well-established tradition of the satirical and skeptical treatment of alchemy, a strength that resulted mainly from its use of literary evidence.

The literature of the last two decades of the sixteenth century contains many allusions to alchemy and a variety of images that have alchemy as their basis. These we find occasionally in the sonnets and plays but most frequently in prose fiction and pamphlet literature. With the notable exception of John Lyly's *Gallathea,* the majority of these allusions are brief, revealing little knowledge of the theoretical and technical aspects of the art. Nonetheless they show that the satiric possibilities inherent in the subject were ever-present in the minds of many of the period's principal writers.

Alchemy was particularly well-suited to the needs of late Elizabethan prose writers, especially those whose personal invective, prose fiction, and realistic accounts of London lowlife demanded material that was colorful, racy, malleable to different contexts, and familiar to all classes of readers. In these respects as well as in its rich comic potential, alchemy perfectly suited the interests and styles of Robert Greene and Thomas Nashe. Two of the works that Greene wrote while he was still under the spell of Lyly's euphuism use alchemy in a way that is atypically restrained and unsatirical. In *The Carde of Fancie* (1587), the extraordinary prodigality of the hero, Gwyndonius, causes the natives of his adopted country to suspect that he is a successful alchemist.[37] In *Perimedes the Blacke-Smith* the poor but virtuous sage of Memphis alludes to the medicinal capabilities of alchemy in prescriptions for a useful and worry-free life. He states that "the auncient Alcumists reposed great trust in their Philosophers stone, as the most necessarie iewell to drawe out quintesses for restoratives," making this one of the earliest literary references to iatrochemistry (7:20).

But as Greene's interest turned from the romance in the late 1580s, his references to alchemy become less neutral and objective, more in keeping with the lively spirit of his rogue literature and autobiography in the next decade. Nashe's preface to *Menaphon* contains a passage that, in a sense, is indicative of his master's changing treatment of alchemy. In castigating the decay in the writing of his contemporaries—the abhorrence of native English, the use of "solemne periphrasis" and inkhornisms—Nashe uses an original and effective alchemical simile. The "vainglorious tragoedians" who supply the models so slavishly imitated by lesser playwrights are termed "alcumists of eloquence": "But herein I cannot so fully bequeath them [the imitators] to follie, as their idiote art-masters, that intrude themselves to our eares as the alcumists of eloquence; who (mounted on the stage of arrogance) think to outbrave better pens with the swelling bumbast of a bragging blank verse" (6:10). Nashe's thrust at Marlowe is successful only because the art itself (and by implication the idiom of the alchemists) is disparagingly equated with falseness. This familiar motif is present in a number of Greene's later writings. In the transparently autobiographical *Greenes Groatsworth of Wit*, the dying usurer Gorinius, after disinheriting Roberto, bestows his fortune on Luciano with the following advice: "Multiply in wealth my sonne by anie meanes thou maist, onely flie Alchymie, for therein are more deceites then her beggerly Artistes have wordes; and yet are the wretches more talkative then women" (12:107-8). In *A Quippe for an Upstart Courtier* (1592) Greene's social satire encompasses both goldsmiths and alchemists. The former, he says, are for the most part "skilde in alcumy, & can temper mettales shrewdly, with no little profite to themselves & disadvantage to the buier" (11:277). *The Blacke Booke's Messenger* humorously alludes to the alchemists' vaunted scrupulosity about laboratory procedures, which is like the care Ned Browne exercises in planning his crimes: "The most expert and skilful Alcumist, never tooke more pains in experience of his mettalls, the Phisition in his simples, the Mecanicall man in the mysterie of his occupation, than I have done in plotting precepts, rules, axiomes, and principles, how smoothly and neately to foist a pocket, or nyppe a bung" (11:20). And in a later passage from the same work Browne reveals the deceit his companions use to cheat covetous men and the result that invariably follows: "If they see you covetously bent, they wil tel you wonders of the Philosophers stone, and make you beleeve they can make golde of Goose-greace: onely you must bee at some two or three hundred pounds cost, or such a trifling matter, to helpe to set up their Stylles, and then you need not care where you begge your bread, for they will make you doo little better if you followe their prescriptions" (11:25).

Thomas Nashe's references to alchemy are more numerous and interesting than Greene's, generally revealing a sophisticated knowledge of the art and a capacity to treat materials more imaginatively. Thus alchemy's comic and satiric potential is greatly expanded, as evidenced by the number of pamphlets that Nashe wrote during the controversy with Gabriel Harvey. Nashe's employment of alchemy to attack Harvey was, in all probability, not an arbitrary choice. From the time of his years at Cambridge under the tutorship of Sir Thomas Smith, Harvey had shown keen interest in mathematics and the occult arts, as has been brought to light in recent investigations of Harvey's notes and marginalia in books and manuscripts that passed through his hands.[38]

As a preface to *Strange Newes* (1593), Nashe wrote a satirical epistle dedicatory to a Maister *Apis lapis,* whose generosity as a patron of old poets is as well known as his expenditures on "the durt of wisedome, called Alcumie."[39] Here Nashe seeks *Apis lapis*'s aid in bearing the pamphlet to the author of a "*certaine foure penniworth of Letters and three farthing-worth of Sonnets*" (1:257). In a second preface to *Strange Newes,* Nashe makes his attack on Harvey more specific, at the same time enlarging it to include all who have wilfully distorted the meaning of his works: "What ever they [his detractors] be that thus persecute Art (as the Alcumists are said to persecute Nature) I would wish them to rebate the edge of their wit, and not grinde their colours so harde: having founde that which is blacke, let them not, with our forenamed Gold-falsifiers, seeke for a substance that is blacker than black, or angle for frogs in a cleare fountaine" (1:261).

In attacking those who criticized his writings, Nashe echoes an accusation that was traditionally levied against alchemists: those who, through their use of artificial processes that simulated the natural production of gold, regarded themselves as imitators of nature, were, in fact, her persecutors. They are, therefore, *unnatural,* a charge that Mercury, in Jonson's *Mercury Vindicated,* frequently uses in attacking the ignorant alchemist. Furthermore, Nashe's reference to "blackness" in the latter part of the quotation hints at the importance alchemists assigned to maintaining a strict sequence of changing colors that marked stages in the stone's preparation. According to the most common theory, black was associated with the initial stage, known variously as the "putrefaction," "mortification," or *nigredo.* This stage involved the "death" of the metal—the decomposition of its recognizable physical characteristics—that occurred when heat was applied to the alembic. Following this, a succession of variously colored steps saw the "resurrection" or "revivification" of the soul of the metal, which endured after the destruction of the body in the putrefaction. The anonymous *Stone of the Philosophers* states that

[w]hen the putrefaction of our seed has been thus completed, the fire may be increased till glorious colours appear, which the Sons of Art have called *Cauda Pavonis,* or the *Peacock's Tail.* These colours come and go, as heat is administered approaching to the third degree, till all is of a beautiful green, and as it ripens assumes a perfect whiteness, which is the White Tincture, transmuting the inferior metals into silver, and very powerful as a medicine. . . . [The alchemist] goes on increasing his fire till it assumes a yellow, then an orange or citron colour; and then boldly gives a heat of the fourth degree, till it acquires a redness like blood taken from a sound person, which is a manifest sign of its thorough concoction and fitness for the uses intended.[40]

Because black symbolizes the first stage, Nashe's mention of the "Gold-falsifiers [search] for a substance that is blacker than black" is a remonstrance against those critics who would obfuscate his works, supplying interpretations that the originals do not warrant. Later in *Strange Newes,* in the *Foure Letters Confuted* section, Nashe alludes to the story of King Midas's golden touch, as recorded in Ovid's *Metamorphoses,* which serves to mock the futile attempts of the alchemists to achieve success (1:286).

References to alchemy also appear in Harvey's rejoinders. For example, in *Pierces Supererogation,* his reply to *Strange Newes,* alchemy serves to sharpen and coarsen the invective. In a long scatological passage that attempts the "assification" of his opponents, Harvey speaks of the medicinal and restorative properties of various parts of the anatomies of asses as if they were the universal medicine of the alchemists. This "Secret in Philosophie" he gleefully bestows on the "sonnes of the Art," and in a following section he associates alchemists with empirics, spagirics, cabalists, magicians, and occult philosophers, all of whom "wrap up their profoundest, and Unrevealable mysteries in the thickest skinne, or rather in the closest intrals of an Asse."[41]

In *Have with You to Saffron-Waldon* Nashe again uses alchemy to ridicule Harvey, whose quotations are printed and followed by satirical glosses. Thus when awakening from a sleep Harvey is made to say, "*O Humanitie, my* Lullius, *and Divinitie, my* Paracelsus," the exclamation is followed by the comic asides of the three interlocutors, Consiliadore, Carneades, and Importuno:

> *Consil:* As much to say as all the humanitie he hath is gathered out of *Lullius,* and all his divinitie or religion out of *Paracelsus.*
>
> *Carnead:* Let him call uppon *Kelly,* who is better than them both; and for the spirites and soules of the ancient Alchumists, he hath them . . . emprisoned in the firie purgatorie of his fornace, . . .
>
> *Import:* Whether you call his fire Purgatorie or no, the fire of Alchumie hath wrought such a purgation or purgatory in a great number of mens purses in *England* that it hath clean fir'd them out of al they have. [3:51-52]

It is mildy amusing that Consiliadore should attribute Harvey's humanity and divinity to Lull and Paracelsus, for the reputation of the latter in particular was

dubious in late sixteenth- and seventeenth-century England. But Carneades' statement that "Kelly . . . is better than them both" provides the ultimate in the dis
paragement of both alchemy and Harvey. Edward Kelley or Kelly (1555-c.1595),
who is mentioned in a number of literary works,[42] was widely known as a charlatan throughout Elizabeth's reign. His career included apprenticeship to an apothecary, the fraudulent practice of law, necromancy, counterfeiting (for which his
ears were cropped on the pillory), and alchemical experimentation with his repu-
table companion, Dr. John Dee.[43] In any event, Carneades' reference to Kelley
provides a fitting transition to Importuno's final assessment of the effects of alchemy in England.

Although the majority of Nashe's allusions to alchemy are negative and skep-
tical, there are important exceptions. In *The Terrors of the Night,* for example,
Nashe speaks of the benign spirits of fire that help man to ward off gloom and
melancholy, as resulting from "the excellent restorative distillations of wit and of
Alcumie" (1:351). But in a later passage in the same work, he recognizes that the
"unskilfuller cousning kind of Alchumists, with their artificiall and ceremoniall
Magicke" thrive by picking men's purses (1:367). In *Christs Teares over Jerusalem,*
Nashe alludes to the "musicall gold" of the alchemists;[44] but in his exhortation
against the sin of delicacy—the inordinate fondness for luxury and ostentation
common among London women—he states that such indulgences are a "kind of
Alchymical quintessensing a heaven out of earth. It is the exchaunging of an
eternall heaven for a short, momentary, imperfect heaven" (2:145).

Nashe's imaginative use of alchemical ideas and their increasing adaptability
to a variety of literary contexts is also present in his prose fiction, where conventionally satiric examples appear with those that are fresh and innovative. In *The
Unfortunate Traveller,* alchemy helps to emphasize the extraordinary miserliness
of Dr. Zachary and the shabbiness of his practice. Jack Wilton's visit to the doctor is the occasion for the following description: "Miserable is that Mouse that
lives in a Phisitions house; *Tantalus* lives not so hunger-starved in hell, as she
doth there. Not the verie crums that fall from his table, but *Zacharie* sweepes
together, and of them moulds up a Manna. Of the ashie parings of his bread, he
would make conserve of chippings. Out of bones, after the meate was eaten off,
hee would alchumize an oyle, that hee sold for a shilling a dram" (2:306).

In another passage, Geraldine, the mistress of Jack Wilton's master, is the
force that inspires the impassioned "alcumy of his [the master's] eloquence." This
phrase had been used earlier in the preface to *Menaphon,* but here Nashe expands
it into a short conceit that is elegant and humorously ironic in its exaggeration,
similar to several in Shakespeare's sonnets and plays. The master's visit to
Geraldine's birthplace has this effect on him: "O, but when hee came to the cham-
ber where his *Geraldines* cleere Sunbeames first thrust themselves into this cloud
of flesh, and acquainted mortalitie with the puritie of Angels, then did his mouth
overflow with magnificats . . . . The alcumie of his eloquence, out of the incom-

prehensible drossie matter of cloudes and aire, distilled no more quintescence than woulde make his *Geraldine* compleat faire" (2:270). Jack Wilton's own encounter with a mistress who proves false provides occasion for an alchemical metaphor that has decidedly bawdy overtones and humorous plays on "trying" and "testing" as used in goldsmithery: "There was a delicate wench named *Flavia Aemilia* lodging in saint Markes street at a goldsmiths, which I would faine have had to the grand test, to trie whether she were cunning in Alcumie or no. . . . To her I sent my golde to beg an houre of grace: ah, graceles fornicatres, my hostesse and shee were confederate, who having gotten but one peece of my ill golde in their handes, devised the meanes to make me immortal" (2:258).

The nature and diversity of Nashe's writings make it difficult to determine exactly what his attitude toward alchemy is. Approximately fifteen references to the subject are scattered throughout his work, but most are brief and the contexts in which they appear fail to provide opportunities for serious discussion. In fact, Nashe's allusions to alchemy nearly always take the form of short humorous anecdotes, satirical thrusts, bases for metaphor and imagery, or other forms of decoration and embellishment. It appears that he gave little, if any, serious thought to the subject, as such. Yet, at the same time, these references demonstrate that Nashe possessed an unusual familiarity with at least the surface details of the art, details that must have been acquired from reading alchemical works or from more immediate experience.

We are certain from internal and external evidence that Nashe had read both Erasmus's *Colloquies* and Scot's *Discoverie of Witchcraft*;[45] however, there is no evidence in his writings that he borrowed from the alchemical sections of these works. In all probability his major source of knowledge was Cornelius Agrippa's *De Incertitudine et Vanitate Scientiarum*, which had been translated into English by James Sandford in 1569 and enjoyed great popularity in Elizabethan and Jacobean England. Agrippa is said to be the modern author from whom Nashe borrowed most,[46] and, in the case of alchemy, we find a number of ideas, topics, and phrases in chapter 90 ("Of Alcumie") of the Sandford translation that he either borrowed directly or that undoubtedly served as strong hints in the framing of his discussion. Such passages from Agrippa account for many of the most obscure allusions to alchemy that we find in Nashe, among them the references to Midas, the "substance that is blacker than black," "the durt of wisedom," "musical gold," and the "quintessensing [of] a heaven out of earth."

Although the majority of Nashe's remarks on alchemy are negative and satirical, we never find in him the sustained hostility and bitter rejection that pervades Agrippa's treatise as is illustrated in his conclusion: "Alcumie then whether it ought to be termed an Arte, or a counterfaite colouringe, or a pursuite of nature, is doubtlesse a notable and a suffered deceipt."[47] In fact, a passage from Nashe's last work, *Nashe's Lenten Stuffe*, despite its mocking humor and irony, may suggest that he believed transmutation possible:

Howe many bee there in the worlde that childishly deprave Alchumy, and cannot spell the first letter of it; in the black booke of which ignorant band of
scorners, it may be I am scorde up with the highest: . . . the *probatum est* of
whose transfiguration *ex Luna in Solem,* from his duskie tinne hew into a perfit
golden blandishment, onely by the foggy smoake of the grossest kind of fire
that is, illumines my speculative soule, what muche more, not sophisticate or
superficiall effects, but absolute essentiall alterations of mettalles there may bee
made by an artificiall repurified flame and diverse other helpes of nature added
besides. (3:220-21)

Although none of the remaining Elizabethan writers of literary prose treats
alchemy with the imagination, wit, and sophisticated insight of Nashe, we do
continue to find many conventionally satiric references in the prose of his contemporaries. In *Pappe With An Hatchet,* John Lyly tells an amusing anecdote about
an alchemist who approached an Italian duke with the boast that he could produce gold faster than the duke could spend it. (Conventionally, his own shabby
appearance is rationalized by his alleged inability to find a laboratory hidden
from the eyes of authorities.) The duke supplies him with both a place in which
to experiment and money, which predictably is soon wasted. However, Lyly gives
a clever turn to the story's conclusion: "This Alcumist, in short time consumed
two thousande pound of the Dukes gold, and brought him halfe a Ducket: whie
(quoth the Duke) is this all? All quoth he my Lord, that I could make by Art.
Wel said the Duke, then shalt thou see my cunning: for I will boyle thee, straine
thee, and then drie thee, so that of a lubber, that weighed three hundred weight,
I will at last make a dram of knaves powder. The Duke did it."[48]

Thomas Dekker's *Lanthorne and Candle-light* contains an account of a cheating rogue named "*Jack in a boxe,* or this Devill in mans shape" whose sleight-of-
hand methods of fleecing London citizens recall the practices of the alchemists of
Chaucer and Erasmus.[49] Dekker decries the growing numbers of these charlatans
who "carrie the Philosophers stone about them, and are able of fortie shillings to
make fortie pound" (3:289). Similar to these works in its satirical treatment,
Dekker's "old Enterlude of Iniquitie," *The Seven deadly Sinnes of London,* likens
the cheating of the Politick Bankrupt to that of the alchemist, who "having taken
a hundred pound to multiply it, he keepes a puffing and a blowing, as if he
would fetch the Philosophers stone out of it, yet melts your hundred pound so
long in his *Crusibles,* till at length he either melt it cleane away, or (at the least)
makes him that lends it thinke good, if every hundred bring him home five, with
Principall and Interest" (2:28-29).

Dekker's most interesting and extended allusion to alchemy occurs in *A Strange
Horse-Race,* which will conclude discussion of alchemy in late sixteenth- and early
seventeenth-century literary prose. Dekker's purpose in writing this work, he tells
us in the dedicatory epistle, is to "*beget mirth*" (3:312). And before the masques
that end the piece are presented, he invites the reader to witness a variety of races.
These include races on foot and chariot competitions in the Roman manner;

Apollo's daily ride through the heavens is included, as is that of the Queen of Night. Next Dekker presents the sublime race of the four elements, "proportioned to more diverse waies, and with strange turnings, yet all to meete in one delicate tune within *Mans body*" (3:326). Finally, in a passage that beautifully reveals Renaissance thought concerning the formation of minerals, he likens to a race the "aspirations" of the various metals to become purer and more valuable. The passage shows not only the common view of the workings of nature but also the processes that the alchemists believed they could duplicate artificially: "Againe, if I should rifle this Treasure-house of living Creatures, and looke into the depth of it, I could bring you to those hidden *Races of Minerals,* and *Mettals,* which the *Sunne* never sees, yet can they not live without him: there should you behold a *Mine of Lead,* labouring to turne it selfe into *Tynne,* and so to rise to preferment; but like a poore Man, that workes day and night to grow rich, hee strives with impossibilities, and is at the yeares end no better then at the biginning" (3:326-27). Likewise, tin labors to enhance its position in the great chain of being and become more like her sister, silver; and silver herself "ambitiously aspir[es] to bee as glorious *Gold:* but she workes like an Alchimist, watches long, and looses her labour; yea, though shee were able to passe through those twelve gates" (3:327). Dekker's mention of the "twelve gates" reveals at least his passing familiarity with *The Compound of Alchymy* written by Sir George Ripley, a canon of Bridlington and one of the most famous alchemists of late medieval England. According to Ashmole, who reprinted it in the *Theatrum Chemicum Britannicum,* Ripley wrote the *Compound* in 1471.[50] Each of its twelve main chapters is termed a "gate" and describes the mastery of a stage in the process leading to transmutation. Dekker recounts these steps exactly as they appear in Ripley: Calcination, Dissolution, Separation, Conjunction, Putrifaction, Congelation, Cibation, Sublimation, Firmentation, Exaltation, Multiplication, and Projection (3:327-28). But even if silver were to pass through all of these gates, Dekker concludes, it would still be silver; only gold, "(the eldest child of the *Sunne*) . . . who being King of *Mettals,* never aspires to bee higher, because it knowes, there is none above him" (3:328). Thus by rejecting the view that metals can change their essence through the operations of nature, Dekker indirectly denies that similar changes can be brought about through alchemy.

This survey of the use of alchemy in Elizabethan literary prose reveals that the continuity of the satirical tradition, begun late in the fourteenth century, remains unbroken to the end of the sixteenth. Throughout this two-hundred-year period it is strengthened and solidified in several ways, such as by the borrowing of fragments or the retelling of larger portions of key works by older poets such as Chaucer, whose *Canon's Yeoman's Tale* figured prominently in Scot's skeptical attack in *The Discoverie of Witchcraft.* The satirical impulse is also fostered by the popularity of works like Erasmus's "alchemical" dialogues, which were widely read by the Elizabethans. Furthermore, treatises by later writers in the occult tradition, such as George Ripley and Cornelius Agrippa, served as sources of knowledge for authors whose allusions to alchemy tended to be "learned." Finally, current interest in alchemy (and suspicion of it) could not fail to have been stimulated by the notoriety of those like Edward Kelley, whose exploits were widely known and held up to scorn. These factors were most important in shaping and sustaining this rich and influential satirical tradition into the dawn of the seventeenth century.

The literary use of alchemy among later Elizabethan writers was not, however, restricted to prose and prose fiction, and I now turn to examples of its appearance in poetry. With the notable exceptions of Jonson and Donne, whose alchemical interests will be dealt with in following chapters, references to the art occur infrequently in the poetry of this period. A major reason for this is that the conventionally satiric use of alchemy was almost totally alien to the nature and intent of love sonnets and lyric verse, dominated as they were by themes and conventions derived ultimately from Petrarch and other Renaissance Italians, the courtly love tradition, and classical literature. It would seem that English authors were only now beginning to realize alchemy's potential for enriching kinds of poetry other than satire. As a result, poetic references to alchemy are much more common in satiric verse than in lyrics and sonnets, although the latter genres contain a few interesting applications that foreshadow the highly original achievements of Donne that were shortly to follow.

  "Sonnet 28" in Sidney's *Astrophil and Stella*[51] subtly and unobtrusively incorporates diction from alchemy and magic for the purpose of affirming the speaker's devotion to Stella and the sincerity of his love. The "Stella" of his sonnet is not to be interpreted allegorically, he states at the outset; rather she is the "Princesse of Beautie, for whose only sake / The raines of *Love* I love." Through contrast, the allusions to alchemy in the sestet ("hid wayes to guide Philosophie," l. 10; "quintessence," l. 11; and "art," l. 14) serve to reinforce the speaker's complete and genuine absorption in Stella. They suggest a background of false and shallow artifice against which the "pure simplicitie" of his love is projected:

> I beg no subject to use eloquence,
> Nor in hid wayes to guide Philosophie:
> Looke at my hands for no such quintessence;
> But know that I in pure simplicitie,
>   Breathe out the flames which burne within my heart,
>   *Love* onely reading unto me this art. [ll. 9-14]

In "Sonnet 77" alchemy is used to heighten the speaker's compliments to Stella, and in this instance it has no unfavorable connotations: her words "do sublime the quintessence of blisse," enhancing the purity and perfection of that beauty and goodness that is already perfect.

  More interesting is Shakespeare's "Sonnet 33," in which the description of the dawning of a new day is embellished by the common sun—king—gold correspondence and the alchemical metaphor: "Full many a glorious morning have I seen / Flatter the mountain tops with sovereign eye, / Kissing with golden face the meadows green, / Gilding pale streams with heavenly alcumy" (ll. 1-4).[52] Yet, just as this vision of natural beauty is soon to be obscured by the appearance of the "*basest* clouds" (italics mine), the speaker's moment of bliss is lost through the cruelty of his friend. The transiency of moments of beauty (suggested by "Gilding" in l. 4) is paralleled by the transiency of moments of joy (suggested by the emphatic use of "stain" and "staineth" in l. 14). Both terms are applicable to alchemy and therefore serve to reinforce the specific reference in line 4.

Again in "Sonnet 114" alchemy is used as a metaphor for change, though here Shakespeare exploits the traditional prejudices against the art, particularly the illusory nature of apparent transmutations, which, in this poem, figure forth the eclipsing of reason by the passions:

> Or whether doth my mind being crown'd with you
> Drink up the monarch's plague, this flattery?
> Or whether shall I say mine eye saith true,
> And that your love taught it this alcumy,
> To make of monsters and things indigest
> Such cherubins as your sweet self resemble,
> Creating every bad a perfect best
> As fast as objects to his beams assemble? [ll. 1-8]

Similarly, in "Sonnet 119" the supremacy of destructive passion in the speaker results from "potions . . . drunk of Siren tears / Distill'd from limbecks foul as hell within," causing him to "[apply] fears to hopes, and hopes to fears, / Still losing when I saw myself to win!" The technical basis for this image, which involves the emission of distilled fluids from an alchemist's vessel, is also present in Spenser's humorously allegorical portrayal of Winter in *Faerie Queene*, 7, 7, 31:

> Lastly, came *Winter* cloathed all in frize,
> Chattering his teeth for cold that did him chill,
> Wil'st on his hoary beard his breath did freese;
> And the dull drops that from his purpled bill
> As from a limbeck did adown distill.[53]

By including the description of the old man's dripping nose Spenser seems to be indulging in a rather common joke about the appearance of alchemists, for we find similar versions in Agrippa and Lodge.

The alchemical imagery in Sir John Davies' *Nosce Teipsum*, like that of Shakespeare's sonnets, represents a marked departure from the satiric norm.[54] In this long philosophical poem, Davies often resorts to alchemy to describe the particularly rarefied nature of the human soul and to distinguish its composition from both sense and the bodily humors. In the section entitled "*That the soule is more then the temperature of the humours of the bodie*" the poet asks: "Who can in

Memorie, or *wit,* or *will,* / Or *aire,* or *fire,* or *earth,* or *water* find? / What *Alchimist* can draw with all his skill, / The *Quintessence* of these out of the mind?" (ll. 465-68). And in the following section he asserts that the soul is a spirit far more excellent and rare than those the alchemists attempt to draw from the substances they work upon: "She is a spirit, yet not like *aire,* or *wind,* / Nor like the *spirits* about the *heart* or *braine,* / Nor like those spirits which *Alchimists* do find, / When they in every thing seeke gold, in *vaine*" (ll. 497-500). A later passage made famous through inclusion in Coleridge's *Biographia Literaria* utilizes the process of sublimation to enrich description of the mind's expansiveness and its capacity to "transmute" concrete experience into intellectual abstraction. This process, through which substances underwent radical conversion from solid to vapor through the application of heat, is an extremely effective metaphor within this context and again anticipates several of the highly original, nonsatirical alchemical figures in the poetry of Donne and Herbert: the mind's power of transformation, Davies states,

> could not be, but that she turnes
> Bodies to spirits, by *sublimation* strange;
> As fire converts to fire, the thinge it burnes,
> As we our meates into our nature change.
>
> From their grosse *matter* she abstracts the *formes,*
> And drawes a kind of *Quintessence* from things;
> Which to her proper nature she transformes,
> To bear them light on her celestiall wings.
>
> This doth she when from things *particular,*
> She doth abstract the *universall kinds;* [ll. 537-46]

Finally, in the first of his *Hymnes of Astræa,* entitled "Of Astræa," Davies again uses alchemy metaphorically in the manner of Shakespeare. The image of transmutation concludes his tribute to Queen Elizabeth, combining the idea of her capacity to refine the crudity of her age with the myth of the return of the Golden Age:

> R udenesse it selfe she doth refine,
> E ven like an Alchymist divine,
> G rosse times of Iron turning
> I nto the purest forme of gold:
> N ot to corrupt, till heaven waxe old,
> A nd be refin'd with burning. [ll. 11-16]

The most remarkable aspect of this figure, within the tradition I have been tracing, is not the ingeniously successful Elizabeth—Astraea—"Alchymist divine" analogy but that Davies should have seen fit to use this much disparaged art at all in the praise of his queen.

Examples of the more conventionally satirical use of alchemy are found in the works of Joseph Hall and Thomas Lodge. "Satire 4" in book 2 of Hall's *Virgidemiarum,*[55] a poem included in the earlier collection of "toothless" satires first printed in 1597, alludes to the use of alchemical preparations in the art of healing. In so doing, it may well reflect the controversy that resulted when iatrochemistry and Paracelsian medical and pharmaceutical practices were introduced into England in the latter years of the sixteenth century.[56] Essentially Hall's poem takes the form of a complaint in which the speaker, a physician or would-be physician, laments the unpleasantness of the services he performs and the scant financial rewards it brings him. He asks himself:

> Should I on each sicke pillow leane my brest,
> And grope the pulse of everie mangie wrest:
> And spie out marvels in each Urinall:
> And tumble up the filths that from them fall,
> And give a *Dose* for every disease,
> In prescripts long, and tedious *Recipes:*
> All for so leane reward of Art and mee? [ll. 9-15]

While one cannot prove with certainty that Hall's physician is a follower of Paracelsus, a number of details point to this conclusion. For example, it is known that Paracelsian physicians attached great importance to careful examination of a patient's urine and used their findings in diagnosing illnesses.[57] If this is the principle that is humorously reflected in line 11 of the satire, it is quite probable that lines 13-14 allude to the Paracelsians' meticulous care in formulating and prescribing their medicines. Debus again remarks that "if the remedies of Paracelsus himself were not always original, his use of them was laudable, for Paracelsus and his followers called attention to the fact that they went to great pains to determine the correct dosage with their medicines."[58]

As if these grievances were not enough, Hall's speaker complains that when a patient dies, even after conscientious treatment, murmurs arise that "Th'unskilfull leech murdred his patient, / By poyson of some foule *Ingredient*" (ll. 23-24). While this may be another instance of a common charge against physicians that goes back at least as far as Chaucer, in this poetic context it has special applicability to Paracelsian methods of treatment. According to their underlying theory, poisons could be remarkably successful cures, a view that prompted cries of outrage from followers of Galen, who believed that illness resulting from humoral imbalance could be cured by the application of contraries, and many others who were suspicious of Paracelsus. Debus summarizes Paracelsus's theory as follows: "Germanic folk tradition suggested an opposed theory, that like cures like. Here it was assumed that the poison that caused the complaint would—in proper dosage—also cure it. With his distrust of the ancients, and his sympathy for folk medicine, Paracelsus accepted this principle as valid, and it became one of the most distinctive hallmarks of his followers."[59] In the face of these unpleasant experiences, Hall's speaker is forced to conclude that his services should be available only to those who are able and willing to pay handsomely for them. Provided that this were the case, the "sickly *ladie,* and the gouty *Peere*" would receive his closest attention, even to the extent that he would

> conjure the *Chymick Mercurie,* [to]
> Rise from his hors-dung bed, and upwards flie:
> And with glas-stils, and sticks of *Juniper,*
> Raise the *Black-spright* that burns not with the fire:
> And bring *Quintessence* of *Elixir* pale,
> Out of sublimed spirits minerall.
> Each poudred graine ransometh captive Kings,
> Purchaseth Realmes, and life prolonged brings. [ll. 39-46]

The details of these lines—even down to the rising of the mercurial spirit from the horse dung fire—make it clear that this magical medicine is the philosopher's stone of traditional alchemical theory. But certain of these same details suggest affinities with Paracelsian medicine. As will be shown in chapter 9, in the minds of many in the late sixteenth and seventeenth century, Paracelsus and his followers were closely linked with witchcraft and black magic,[60] recalling the earlier illustration featuring the devil, alchemist, and wanton woman (fig. 12). Although Paracelsus himself is said to have rejected conjuring, some of his adherents apparently used it or were thought to have done so.[61] The representation of the "*Chymick Mercurie,*" similar to the more highly developed character in Jonson's *Mercury Vindicated,* is also in accordance with the role of mercury in alchemical theory and in Paracelsus. In Paracelsus's doctrine of the three primary principles, or *tria prima,* it stands for the active, vaporous, spiritual quality, in contrast to "sulphur," which gives a body structure and substance, and "salt," which imparts color and solidity.[62] Furthermore, Paracelsus is known to have prescribed medicines of specially prepared mercury for the cure of diseases like syphilis,[63] and at the heart of his theory of pharmacology was his insistence that cures can best be effected through administering carefully prepared compounds of metals and other minerals,[64] a view that Hall seems to be alluding to in lines 43-44 of the quotation.

For these reasons I would conclude that Hall is attacking Paracelsian medicine and alchemically derived cures and that his poem, like the curing scene in *All's Well that Ends Well* (1602-3), is a literary reflection of an important and highly controversial topic of late Renaissance debate in England.[65] While in this satire Hall is exploiting an aspect of alchemy that appears infrequently in literature, his "Satire 3" in book 4 of the *Virgidemiarum* contains an allusion that is thoroughly traditional. Here he attacks those who display inordinate pride in the nobility of their ancestry and those who hastily squander their inheritances through foolish ventures. Some men, the speaker relates, stake all they have in foreign trading expectations, while others like

> Wiser *Raymundus* in his closet pent,
> Laughs at such danger and adventurement;
> When halfe his lands are spent in golden smoke,
> And now his second hopefull glasse is broke.
> But yet if haply his third fornace hold,
> Devoteth all his pots and pans to gold;
> So spend thou *Pontice,* if thou canst not spare,
> Like some stout sea-man or *Philosopher:* [ll. 34-41]

The probable allusion to Raymond Lull and the tone of the poem make it unmistakably clear that the pursuit of practical alchemy is tantamount to financial ruin.

Both of the alchemists' preoccupations that Hall includes in these satires—concern with chemical medicines and transmutation—are also present in Nicholas Breton's long poem "I would and would Not."[66] In stanza 49, he warns of the dangers that can result from taking chemically prepared medicines and speaks in favor of the more orthodox herbal cures:

> No, I had rather bee an Herbalist,
>   To know the Vertue both of Hearbs and Rootes.
> Then be the bold and desperate Alchymist;
>   That ofte his weight and measure over-shootes,
> And so, by either want of Care or skill,
>   In steede of *Curing,* give a killing-Pill.

In stanza 127 alchemy is equated with delusion and quakery:

> Nor would I be a golden *Alchymist,*
>   To studie the *Phylosophers* faire stone:
> And feede a sight of Fooles, with *Had-I-wist,*
>   To weepe for Silver, when theyr Golde is gone,
> Poope noddy, never was there such an other,
>   To make a Couzen of a simple Brother.

The most complete poetic assessment of alchemy dating from the 1590s is "Epistle 7" of Thomas Lodge's *A Fig for Momus;*[67] it is entitled "The Anatomie of Alchymie" and stands as a comprehensive summary of reasons for the disparagement of the art and its satirical treatment in literature. For purposes of this study it can be regarded as a catalog of most of the important themes and motifs that have already been discussed in connection with other works; for this reason my treatment will be brief.

Because "Anatomie" owes many of its ideas to Sandford's translation of Agrippa's *De Incertitudine et Vanitate Scientiarum,* it provides further evidence of the influence of this important book on writers of the English Renaissance.[68] The speaker's announced intention is to reveal his "opinion" about alchemy, and

this is followed, after the manner of Agrippa, by an exposé of its fraudulent claims
to being a science grounded in nature:

> This fruite of foolish innovation
> Is first condemn'd by deepest-red divines,
> Not as an art, but as the seale of shift,
> The persecution of natures power,
> Divine in show, in proofe, a subtill drift,
> To cousen slight-beleevers everie hower:
> For if with jealous eies we justly prie
> Into the scope, and issue of the same
> Nature, (the mistres of Philosophie)
> Is lost therein, and wanteth power, and name. [3:66-67]

According to the poem, the aims of the alchemists are to produce gold artificially, to restore youthfulness to aged men, and to give fruitfulness to barren plants;
but "al these promis'd mountaines prove a mouse," and in the end the "silly idi-
ots" who work these deceptions lose wealth and wits and often kill themselves in
laboratory explosions. Yet, like the majority of alchemists represented in literature, they do not suffer for lack of victims: "They by their words enritch beleeving
sots, / Whereas in deede they emptie all their chists, / . . . They beg for groats,
and part with empty fists." The effects of the art on its practitioners are described
by Lodge in words very similar to those of the Sandford translation:

> At last through losse of substance, and of time,
> Robb'd, and bereft of rent, and olde receite,
> Are like a crased clocke, that cannot chime:
> Olde, clothles, meatles, smelling brimstone still,
> Besmeer'd with cole-dust, from their furnace brought,
> Plagu'd with the palsie, (letchers common ill)
> By tempring of quick-silver quickly cought:
> Their riches are the droppings of their nose,
> Where els beside, the slaves are brought so low. [3:68]

In the remainder of the poem, Lodge, following Agrippa, attacks alchemy in many
of the places where it had traditionally been most vulnerable: he castigates its
"authorities," men such as Geber and Roger Bacon as well as Hermes, the "father
of this Fraud." He scourges the *ignotum per ignocius* tradition and shows the criminality into which its adepts fall. Finally, he warns readers of the corruption resulting from the misapplication of the human mind to things that are beyond its
proper sphere: "Alas, alas, how vanitie hath power / To draw mens minds from
vertue, under hope / Of fading treasures? *Danaas* golden shower / Doth ravish
wits, and leades them from their scope" (3:69-70).

The following discussion of alchemy in late Elizabethan drama draws on a small
sampling of plays. I have selected works by its most popular playwrights—

Marlowe, Greene, Lyly, and Shakespeare—that illustrate uses of alchemy in a variety of dramatic contexts and genres. Generally speaking, alchemy does not play a prominent role in any of these works; we find nothing approaching the centrality it assumes in *The Alchemist* or in *Mercury Vindicated.* It appears most conspicuously in the hermetic subplot of Lyly's *Gallathea.* In other works it is used to motivate serious if minor action, provide earthy humor and satire, or serve as a basis for metaphor and embellishment.

Perhaps the most serious context in which it appears is the minor incident that occurs at the end of act 4, scene 2, of Marlowe's *Tamburlaine, Part II.*[69] Here Olympia, grief-stricken over the death of her husband and son, is faced with escaping Theridamas's assault upon her honor. As a last resort she cleverly promises him "a present of such price, / As all the world cannot affoord the like" (4.2.3937-38). It is a magical-chemical potion that will supposedly make the user invulnerable to violent death, something perhaps distantly related to the "weapon salve" popularized by Paracelsus, Robert Fludd, and Sir Kenelm Digby:

> An ointment which a cunning Alcumist
> Distilled from the purest Balsamum,
> And simplest extracts of all Minerals,
> In which the essentiall fourme of Marble stone,
> Tempered by science metaphisicall,
> And Spels of magicke from the mouthes of spirits,
> With which if you but noint your tender Skin,
> Nor Pistol, Sword, nor Lance can pierce your flesh. [4.2.3940-47]

Olympia persuades the gullible Theridamas to let her put the ointment to a test: she spreads it on her throat, he stabs her fatally, and she thereby escapes her fate through death.

For all of his devotion to "magic and concealed arts" and lust for power and wealth, it may seem surprising that Marlowe's Faustus fails to pursue alchemy. His mastery of medicine, law, and divinity—to say nothing of magic—would seem to have promised extraordinary success; yet alchemy is scarcely mentioned in the play.[70] The question of why this is the case is moot, but speculations upon it reveal something important about the relationship between literature and alchemy at this point in the English Renaissance. In using black magic and necromancy as the means to bring about Faustus's fall, Marlowe is choosing depravities of such magnitude that they had to be taken seriously. (That the "black arts" were so regarded is demonstrated by the innumerable treatises, witch trials, and persecutions that appeared in Europe, England, and Scotland following the first printing of the *Malleus Maleficarum* in 1486.) On the other hand, alchemy's ruinous effects could be lamented and at times its practitioners and victims could be regarded with pity, but among Renaissance authors who stood outside the occult tradition the art could never be taken seriously enough to serve as the principal motivating force behind a central character in a serious literary work.

This lack of "high seriousness" is why, I think, alchemy's literary potential was, at this time, almost invariably channeled into satire and comedy rather than tragedy and epic.

A typically brief and unserious example of the way alchemy is used in serious drama occurs in *The Jew of Malta,* when Barabas, visiting the slave market, quibbles about the price of a Turkish slave. He asks the slave if he possesses the philosopher's stone—as if only this could account for the price that is being asked. This resort to alchemy in attempting humor is far exceeded in Greene's *Friar Bacon and Friar Bungay* where, as in Nashe's *The Unfortunate Traveller,* the vocabulary of alchemy (i.e., "multiply") is manipulated to produce delightfully humorous sexual innuendoes and double entendres. Friar Bacon facetiously explains Dr. Burden's frequent trips to Henley in this way:

> Masters, for that learned Burden's skill is deep,
> And sore he doubts of Bacon's cabalism,
> I'll show you why he haunts to Henley oft:
> Not, doctors, for to taste the fragant air,
> But there to spend the night in alchemy,
> To multiply with secret spells of art.
> Thus private steals he learning from us all.
> To prove my sayings true, I'll show you straight
> The book he keeps at Henley for himself.[71]

The mysterious "book" to which Burden is attracted is immediately revealed when Bacon conjures up the Hostess of Henley, who arrives carrying a shoulder of mutton.

In Shakespearean drama, alchemical bawdry is also present in the Fool's reply to Varro's servant's question "What is a whoremaster?" in *Timon of Athens,* 2.2.108-14: "A fool in good clothes, and something like thee. 'Tis a spirit; sometime't appears like a lord, sometime like a lawyer, sometime like a philosopher, with two stones moe than's artificial one. He is very often like a knight; and, generally, in all shapes that man goes up and down in from fourscore to thirteen, this spirit walks in." Later in 5.1.114-15, Timon chases the Poet away from his cave with the words: "You are an alcumist, make gold of that. Out, rascal dogs!" In *Henry IV, Part II,* Falstaff's threats to Justice Shallow in 3.2.328-32 incorporate an ambigous reference to the art: "Well, I'll be acquainted with him if I return, and't shall go hard but I'll make him a philosopher's two stones to me. If the young dace be a bait for the old pike, I see no reason in the law of nature but I may snap at him: let time shape, and there an end."

But in Shakespearean drama, alchemy is most effective when, as in the sonnets, it is used to suggest beauty, richness, and change. In the following passages from *King John* and *Julius Caesar* the magnificent imagery of the opening quatrain of "Sonnet 33" is clearly visible. In the first of these plays, King Philip speaks in 3.1.75-82:

> 'Tis true, fair daughter, and this blessed day
> Ever in France shall be kept festival.
> To solemnize this day the glorious sun
> Stays in his course and plays the alchymist,
> Turning with splendor of his precious eye
> The meagre cloddy earth to glittering gold.
> The yearly course that brings this day about
> Shall never see it but a holy day.

In *Julius Caesar,* Casca, speaking to Cassius in 1.3.157-60, says this of Brutus:

> O, he sits high in all the people's hearts;
> And that which would appear offense in us,
> His countenance, like richest alchymy,
> Will change to virtue and to worthiness.

And a related image in *Antony and Cleopatra* (1.5.36-37) suggests to Cleopatra that Alexas, coming to her from Antony in Rome, has derived a certain lustre from being in her lover's presence: "that great med'cine hath / With his tinct gilded thee."[72]

In each of these examples from the drama, alchemical allusions are short and easily separated from the larger work; with the exception of Olympia's trick in *Tamburlaine,* they perform no vital role in motivating the action of a play, in promoting characterization, or in establishing a significant pattern of imagery. In contrast, their part in John Lyly's *Gallathea*[73] is much more ambitious and interesting. Although the main action involving the virgin sacrifice and Cupid's mischief among Diana's nymphs is played out against a background of the most rarefied blend of classical myth and pastoral romance, the comic subplot is grounded in the homely and concrete realism of occult chicanery. As in the *Canon's Yeoman's Tale* and many of its descendants, the theme of Lyly's subplot might be termed the education of a would-be adept.

The subplot is limited to brief scenes in four of the five acts. In 1.4 the clownish characters, Rafe, Robin, and Dick, are introduced as having just been cast up on the shores of Lincolnshire following a shipwreck. They agree to go their separate ways and reunite after a year has passed. In 2.3 Rafe, now separated from the other survivors, meets Peter, a boy unhappily in service to an alchemist. He complains of his lot in life: "Nothing but blowing of bellows, beating of spirits, and scraping of crosslets!" (2.3.8-9). In order to entice Rafe into taking his place in his master's service, Peter regales him with the mystifying terms of this "very secret science." The items in Peter's lengthy lists of processes, instruments, metals, and spirits are very obviously drawn from Chaucer, although in places their spelling appears to have been consciously distorted for the sake of humor.[74]

For Peter, alchemy has proved to be "a beggarly science . . . so strong on multiplication, that the end is to have neither gold, wit, nor honesty" (2.3.27-9). Nonetheless for Rafe's benefit, he describes his master as being "a little more than a man and a hair's breadth less than a god" (2.3.37-8). Like the Yeoman's Canon, this alchemist has the power to pave large tracts of land with gold, if initially he has gold and beechen coals with which to work (2.3.43-5).

The appearance of the master himself provokes comments that recall many works in the tradition of alchemical satire: his beggarly appearance is merely a disguise, for without it alchemists would "be compelled to work for princes and so be constrained to bewray their secrets" (2.3.71-73). Certain of this alchemist's powers appear to be original, yet they fall quite within the conventional limits of alchemical hoax: of a pottle-pot, he can make "a whole cupboard of plate"; from a "leaden plummet he hath framed twenty dozen of silver spoons." He can make golden bracelets from his breath and silver drops from smoke; even the shower of gold in which Jupiter appeared to Danaë was the work of this master (2.3.81-95). With blandishments such as these Rafe is easily persuaded to begin his apprenticeship in the "mystery," unaware of the raggedness and hunger that await him. Meanwhile Peter rejoices in his escape: "I am glad of this, for now I shall have leisure to run away. Such a bald art as never was! Let him keep his new man, for he shall never see his old again. God shield me from blowing gold to nothing, with a strong imagination to make nothing anything!" (2.3.130-34).

During the passing of time between 2.3 and 3.3, Rafe's education in the ways of alchemists is completed. Like Chaucer's Yeoman and Peter of this play, Rafe has become thoroughly disillusioned. The promised "cupboard of plate" and "silver steeple" wrought from a Spanish needle have not materialized. Even the master's excuses—the faulty "degree" of the fire and, more imaginatively, the disharmony existing between experiment and experimenter ("they that blow must beat time with their breaths, as musicians do with their breasts, so as there must be of the metals, the fire, and workers a very harmony" [3.3.16-18])—cannot persuade him to remain. He too runs off, only to fall at once into another circle of deception through the wiles of an astrologer.

In 5.1, we see the fruits of this second segment of Rafe's education. Even alchemy, he states, is to be preferred to astrology: "well fare the alchemist, for he keeps good fires though he gets no gold. The other [i.e., the astrologer] stands warming himself by staring on the stars" (5.1.3-5). Throughout this scene Rafe is reunited with the other clowns, and a humorous bit of dialogue that ends this section combines several strands of alchemical bawdry similar to those already noted in plays by Greene and Shakespeare:

Rafe.   I have had two masters, not by art but by nature.
            One said that by multiplying he would make of a penny ten
            pound.
Robin.   Ay, but could he do it?
Rafe.   Could he do it, quoth you! Why, man, I saw a pretty wench come

	to his shop, where with puffing, blowing, and sweating he so plied her that he multiplied her.
Robin.	How?
Rafe.	Why, he made her of one, two.
Robin.	What, by fire?
Rafe.	No, by the philosopher's stone.
Robin.	Why, have philosophers such stones?
Rafe.	Ay, but they lie in a privy cupboard. [5.1.15-26]

With this the subplot concludes; its characters touch the main action only at the very end of the play when they appear in time to sing at the wedding of Gallathea and Phyllida.

This chapter has revealed the pervasiveness of alchemical interest shown by authors of the sixteenth century. As we have seen, it frequently appears in the works of major and minor writers who span the entire century, from the early transitional poets and imitators of Chaucer down through the late Elizabethans. Furthermore, its popularity is evidenced by the fact that alchemical references are present in nearly every genre that gained prominence at this time: satire written in prose and verse, allegory and pastoral, comedy and tragedy, didactic prose, rogue literature, and prose fiction—even in selections from the sonnet sequences. It is hardly an overstatement to say that virtually every author of the period found occasion at one time or another to draw upon this body of knowledge.

Given the extreme diversity in the authors who employ alchemy and the types of literature in which it appears, it is even more remarkable that such uniformity and consistency exists in the uses to which alchemy is put. Although the specific treatment varies considerably from author to author, the underlying purpose is, with few exceptions, satirical. In the sixteenth century, the tradition of alchemical satire begun by Chaucer is strengthened and solidified to the extent that the alchemist becomes a stock literary figure who is synonymous with trickery, deception, futility, and poverty. His art is also assumed to reflect these qualities and is therefore held up as an object of ridicule and amusement.

These are the qualities most basic to the meaning of alchemy as it is reflected in English literature of the sixteenth century, and it is these meanings and assumptions that inform the alchemically inspired writings of Ben Jonson in the century that followed. But before discussing the works of Jonson, which, historically, point toward the closing of the tradition of alchemical satire, it is necessary to examine Francis Bacon's views on alchemy. Bacon's thought and the directions in seventeenth-century intellectual life that it helped establish are crucial in determining the future of the art.

IV

THE REFORMATION OF VULCAN

=================

Francis Bacon and Alchemy

Francis Bacon thought in this manner. The knowledge whereof the world is now possessed, especially that of nature, extendeth not to magnitude and certainty of works. The Physician pronounceth many diseases incurable, and faileth oft in the rest. The Alchemists wax old and die in hopes. The Magicians perform nothing that is permanent and profitable. The Mechanics take small light from natural philosophy, and do but spin on their own little threads. Chance sometimes discovereth inventions; but that worketh not in years, but ages. So he saw well, that the inventions known are very unperfect; and that new are not like to be brought to light but in great length of time; and that those which are, came not to light by philosophy.

—Francis Bacon, *Filum Labyrinthi, Sive Formula Inquisitionis*[1]

Evidence presented thus far has shown that English writers of the Middle Ages and Renaissance were familiar with alchemy, were aware of its literary potential, and came to use it extensively, the frequency of its appearance increasing with the passing of time and the proliferation of printed books. Thus, for the author of the late sixteenth and early seventeenth century, alchemy was a "current" topic: knowledge about its theoretical and practical aspects could be gained from a variety of manuscript and printed sources, both ancient and modern, Continental and English. Along with astrology and natural magic, it was also the subject of considerable interest, albeit on an unofficial level, within the two universities, where tutors and pupils, such as Gabriel Harvey, could study these subjects in a relatively hospitable environment.[2] Furthermore, romanticized accounts of the lives and reported successes of practicing adepts provided an abundance of vivid and concrete detail, which added color and contemporaneity to a given work. But most important, the author of this period was the recipient of a long and highly developed heritage of alchemically inspired literature, whose authors included Chaucer and Erasmus. Thus it is no accident that allusions to alchemy appear so frequently and in such a great variety of genres and literary contexts.

While in a few instances, as in Shakespeare's sonnets and Sir John Davies's *Nosce Teipsum,* alchemy was used neutrally as a basis for metaphor or embellishment, this was uncommon; generally, the attitude of Elizabethan writers toward the art ranged from bitter hostility to mirthful skepticism. Crucial to an understanding of the reasons for this negative treatment is the fact that authors typically took an interest only in the *exoteric* aspects of alchemy: the making of the philopher's stone, the possibility of transmuting base metals, and the efficacy of universal medicines and elixirs. Because the possibility of success in these areas seemed unlikely and reported successes were difficult to verify, and because serious adepts were nearly indistinguishable from the stereotypical charlatans, "multipliers," and "bellows-blowers," it is easy to see why the entire art was subject to sweeping condemnation. Little, if any, concern was shown for the philosophical bases upon which practical alchemy rested; indeed, it would seem that until Francis Bacon this side of the art was virtually unknown to men of letters.

Because of Bacon's crucial position at the beginning of the seventeenth-century scientific movement and his impact on subsequent English thought, it is now necessary to step outside the purely literary tradition to analyze his views on alchemy.[3] Bacon is, I believe, the first English writer to give alchemy an impartial hearing through careful consideration of its physical and metaphysical foundations; yet at the same time he was keenly interested in its practical aspects and potential benefits to mankind. Not content to rely on the conventional portrayals of alchemy and alchemists in literature, although undoubtedly aware of them, Bacon is notable for his cautiousness and objectivity in treating the subject. From a study of the many references to alchemy scattered thoughout his works there emerges a new complexity and ambiguity of attitude: in regard to alchemy he is scarcely the *buccinator novi temporis* as we might expect him to be, any more than he is a sympathizer with what had passed for science during the Middle Ages. In fact, in him we see some of the intellectual "amphibiousness" of Sir Thomas Browne.

Basil Willey has written the following about the nature of Bacon's intellectual mission: "It was not the living core of mediaeval thought—its witness to other than empirical realities—that Bacon wished to kill. There was so much else to criticise in the mediaeval tradition—so much pseudo-science, magic, alchemy, astrology, and the like—that Bacon and his age generally cannot be blamed for feeling that their task was simply the separation of truth from error, fact from fable, reality from fiction."[4] It is inaccurate to imply, as this statement seems to, that Bacon's attitude toward magic, alchemy, and astrology was wholly condemnatory. Rather, by means of cautious and unprejudiced examination, he wished to separate what was genuinely useful and scientifically valid in these traditions from what was worthless and deceptive. His final attitude toward alchemy is by no means simple and unequivocal, and it can be arrived at only by placing his references to the art in the context of his views on the relationship between the divisions of the human mind and their corresponding disciplines, on experimentation, reliance on authority, the composition of all bodies, and the operations of nature.

Like several other writers whom we have investigated, Bacon frequently treats alchemy, astrology, and natural magic collectively, categorizing them, as in the third book of the *De Augmentis* (1623), as "sciences which hold too much of imagination and belief" (4:367). Although at present they exist in a debased condition, Bacon readily acknowledges that their ancient pasts have been respectable, and he argues, furthermore, that they should be restored to their former eminence. This interest in the restoration of alchemy and the other occult sciences is grounded, significantly, in a willingness to consider alchemy's theoretical and practical aspects, distinctions that satirical writers had generally failed to observe. Bacon states, however, that their "means and theory are ever more monstrous than the end and action at which they aim" (4:367). An example of how such a reconstruction can be brought about also occurs in the discussion of natural magic in book 3 of the *De Augmentis;* here, by showing the causes of its present low esteem, Bacon points toward a method through which "its ancient and honorable meaning" can be returned to the eminence it enjoyed among the ancient Persians, who associated it with "sublime wisdom, and the knowledge of the universal consents of things" (4:366). That Bacon's lament over the decline in the reputation of natural magic was not unique is apparent when comparing this statement to Cornelius Agrippa's *Dedicatory letter to Johannes Trithemius:* "The outstanding question was this: why is it that although magic originally occupied the pinnacle of excellence in the judgement of all the ancient philosophers and was always held in the highest veneration by those great sages and priests of antiquity, subsequently (from the beginning of the rise of the Catholic Church) it became an object of hatred and suspicion to the holy Fathers, and was at last hissed off the stage by the theologians, condemned by the sacred canons and, in fine, outlawed by the judgement of all laws?"[5] Bacon begins this discussion with a definition that sees magic as "the science which applies the knowledge of hidden forms to the production of wonderful operations; and by uniting . . . actives with passives, displays the wonderful works of nature" (4:366-67). The "hidden forms," knowledge of which is the key to this restorative undertaking, appear to be certain underlying principles or "fixed laws" that explain and provide the basis for the operations of the natural world, and, Bacon asserts, they are knowable.[6]

But this very positive conception of magic has become debased through the infiltration of what he terms "credulous and superstitious traditions and observations concerning sympathies and antipathies" that abound in books as well as through "frivolous" experiments (4:367). Of its practitioners, Bacon says

> So they who are carried away by insane and uncontrollable passion after things which they only fancy they see through the clouds and vapours of imagination, shall in place of works beget nothing else but empty hopes and hideous and monstrous spectres. But this popular and degenerate natural magic . . . . lays the understanding asleep by singing of specific properties and hidden virtues, sent

as from heaven and only to be learned from the whispers of tradition; which makes men no longer alive and awake for the pursuit and inquiry of real causes, but to rest content with these slothful and credulous opinions; and then it insinuates innumerable fictions, pleasant to the mind, and such as one would most desire,—like so many dreams. [4:367]

(The plight of these deluded men closely parallels that of the lover in Donne's "Loves Alchymie," dreaming "a rich and long delight," but getting "a winter-seeming summers night.") In this passage on natural magic—and its implications hold true for alchemy and astrology as well[7]—Bacon attributes the cause of debasement to undue reliance on imagination and belief. The perpetrators of this corruption have chosen to follow "high and vaporous imaginations" rather than "a laborious and sober inquiry of truth" (3:362) and following in the train of this first calamitous decision are manifold errors and defects—susceptibility to illusion, false hope, intellectual sloth, adherence to traditional "authority"— that assure further failures in experiment. Quite simply, in their present state the pseudosciences and occult arts are doomed because they rest on improper foundations. Bacon's objection to magic is not, as has been recently stated, primarily "ethical," in that supernatural appeals would "enable man to achieve his material ends without labour."[8] His condemnation is much more pragmatic: experimentation in the occult arts will not bear fruit because it is grounded in "imagination and belief."

Bacon's diagnosis of these reasons for past failure and his prescriptions for recovery reverberate throughout the century. For example, as will be shown in chapter 9, the majority of Restoration writers and intellectuals who are associated with the Royal Society repeat essentially the same criticisms of alchemy and hermetic ideas that Bacon here articulates. For them, alchemy and alchemists are also identified with philosophical enthusiasm, a defect so fatal to the cause of experimental science that it must be banished entirely. There is, however, one important difference between Bacon's views on alchemical experimentalism and those commonly held in the Restoration period: Bacon believes that methodological reform can bring about recovery and productive results. On the other hand, Restoration thinkers, with few exceptions, see scientific progress as necessarily requiring eradication of *all* traces of magical, alchemical, and astrological thought. For them, occult ideas have become synonymous with all that is contrary to scientific advancement.

Standing behind Bacon's censure of natural magic is his theory concerning the division of all learning as it accords with the three principal parts of the human understanding. As expounded in book 2 of the *Advancement*, History has its seat in the Memory, Poesy in the Imagination, and Philosophy in the Reason (3:329). Governed by this "judicial place or palace of the mind," Philosophy may be further divided into Divine, Human, and Natural; and Natural Philosophy itself is subdivided into two parts, theoretical and applied (3:351).

It is significant that Bacon should draw on alchemy to clarify the two parts resulting from this final subdivision of Natural Philosophy, i.e., the speculative as opposed to the operative, or the "Inquisition of Causes" as opposed to "the Production of Effects." He states: " . . . if it be true likewise that [which] the Alchemists do so much inculcate, that Vulcan is a second nature, and imitateth that dexterously and compendiously which nature worketh by ambages and length of time; it were good to divide natural philosophy into the mine and the furnace, and to make two professions or occupations of natural philosophers, some to be pioners and some smiths; some to dig, and some to refine and hammer" (3:351). Bacon's allusion to Vulcan, his metaphor for art or "second nature," is symptomatic of his views on both alchemy and the practical side of Natural Philosophy. He regards "art" as a perfecter of "nature" just as he sees the efforts of the alchemists as parallel to nature's slower and more dependable subterranean production of gold. But on a deeper level, the Vulcan metaphor has an appropriateness that Bacon failed to see, at least he doesn't mention it: for just as Vulcan, the Roman counterpart of the Greek craftsman-god Hephaestus, fell (or was thrown) from the top of Mt. Olympus, so the crafts, mechanical trades, and occult arts have fallen from a once-eminent position. They, too, have been "lamed" and are subject to the laughter and ridicule of the enlightened. However, unlike the Olympian father of the gods, Bacon intends to aid in the restoration and reformation of the lost and fallen, a mission to be accomplished mainly through the use of Reason.

That the Reason is the only appropriate faculty for governing scientific inquiry can be demonstrated by examining the areas of faith and religion wherein the Imagination is exalted over the Reason. Here the supremacy of imagination results in "parables, visions, and dreams" (3:382). The quotation continues, "I find not any science that doth properly or fitly pertain to the Imagination." Similarly, in poetry and "in all persuasions that are wrought by eloquence and other impression of like nature, which do paint and disguise the true appearance of things, the chief recommendation unto Reason is from the Imagination" (3:382). The deceptiveness of the Imagination and its unfitness for guiding scientific inquiry receive even stronger emphasis in a corresponding passage from book 5 of the later *De Augmentis Scientiarum*: "And again it is no small dominion which imagination holds in persuasions that are wrought by eloquence; for when by arts of speech men's minds are soothed, inflamed, and carried hither and thither, it is all done by stimulating the imagination till it becomes ungovernable, and not only sets reason at nought, but offers violence to it, partly by blinding, partly by incensing it" (4:406).

Bacon's general distrust of belief and imagination as bases for Natural Philosophy is closely related to two major reasons for his suspicion of alchemy: its reliance on authority and the chanciness of its experimental methods. His desire to liberate present inquiry from the errors of the past and the "customs and institutions of schools" is well known[9] and is exemplified especially well by the alchemist in the *Filum Labyrinthi,* who "dischargeth his art upon his own errors, either supposing a misunderstanding of the words of his authors, which maketh him listen after auricular traditions; or else a failing in the true proportions and scruples of practice, which maketh him renew infinitely his trials; and finding also that he lighteth upon some mean experiments and conclusions by the way, feedeth upon them, and magnifieth them to the most, and supplieth the rest in hopes" (3:497).

While it is true that "[c]hance sometimes discovereth inventions" (3:496), serendipity obviously cannot be considered a certain guide to progress in natural science. Chance discoveries are too infrequent and uncertain; moreover they breed false hope and ultimately despair. Nonetheless, Bacon applauds those alchemists who have chosen to rely on experiment rather than the authority of books. In book 2 of the *De Augmentis,* he states: "I will now notice another defect, wherein I should call in some alchemist to help me; one of those who advise the studious to sell their books and build furnaces, and forsaking Minerva and the Muses as barren virgins, to rely upon Vulcan. But certain it is that for depth of speculation no less than for fruit of operation in some sciences (specially natural philosophy and physic) other helps are required besides books" (4:287). Bacon's injunction to rely upon experimentation (Vulcan) rather than traditional teachings (Minerva) reveals the proximity of his own thinking to that of many alchemical authorities who extol the virtues of the laboratory over those of the library. Again in book 1 of the *Advancement,* Bacon credits the alchemists for inadvertently bringing valuable new discoveries to light:

> And yet surely to alchemy this right is due, that it may be compared to the husbandman whereof Æsop makes the fable, that when he died told his sons that he had left unto them gold buried under ground in his vineyard; and they digged over all the ground, and gold they found none, but by reason of their stirring and digging the mould about the roots of their vines, they had a great vintage the year following: so assuredly the search and stir to make gold hath brought to light a great number of good and fruitful inventions and experiments, as well for the disclosing of nature as for the use of man's life. [3:289]

For Bacon, the aims of science and the means to achieve them do not differ greatly from those that he proposes for a reformed alchemy.

Bacon's reference to reliance on "auricular traditions" suggests indirectly another traditional charge against alchemy that made it subject to his criticism as well. The jargon of the alchemists and particularly the *ignotum per ignocius* tradition might be classified as one of the "Idols of the Market-place," a defect that has crept into the human understanding "through the alliances of words and names" (4:61). In book 1 of the *Advancement,* he attacks those who have "sought to veil over and conceal [their errors] by enigmatical writings" and thus prevent exposure (3:289), and his discussion of the "first distemper of learning" in the same book would necessarily include the emphasis on words over matter present in alchemical discourse. These criticisms of the alchemists' deliberate use of obscurity directly anticipate similar charges that were made with increasing frequency during the course of the seventeenth century. To cite only two examples, part 4 of Robert Boyle's *Sceptical Chymist* (1661) repeatedly attacks the obscurity of Paracelsus and the "chemists":

> For I find that even eminent writers (such as Raymund Lully, Paracelsus, and
> others) do so abuse the termes they employ, that as they will now and then give
> divers things, one name; so they will oftentimes give one thing, many names. . . .
> chymists write thus darkly, not because they think their notions too precious to
> be explained, but because they fear that if they were explained, men would discern, that they are farr from being precious. And indeed, I fear that the chief
> reason why chymists have written so obscurely of their three principles, may be,
> that not having clear and distinct notions of them themselves, they cannot write
> otherwise than confusedly of what they but confusedly apprehend:[10]

Furthermore, every feature of alchemical discourse would be subject to censure by the Royal Society, whose members, in the familiar words of Thomas Sprat, have resolved to "reject all amplifications, digressions, and swellings of style; to return back to the primitive purity and shortness, when men deliver'd so many *things* almost in an equal number of *words*. They have exacted from all their members a close, naked, natural way of speaking; positive expressions, clear senses, a native easiness, bringing all things as near the Mathematical plainness as they can, and preferring the language of Artizans, Countrymen, and Merchants, before that of Wits, or Scholars."[11] Thus Bacon's censures of the style of alchemical discourse were historically important in making distinctions between the "closed," secretive mode of transmitting knowledge in the occult arts and the "open" mode of the exact sciences in which progress depended on the collection, analysis, and revision of knowledge passing easily among people.[12]

As a spokesman for the unbiased investigation of the nature of *things* and the necessity of practicality in the mechanical arts, Bacon believed that improvements in experimental techniques would produce greater and more consistent results than haphazard efforts. In the *Aphorisms* that introduce the *Novum Organum* he acknowledges that "operative" studies presently conducted by mechanics, mathematicians, physicists, alchemists, and magicians alike have met with "scanty success" as a result of poor experimental methods, such as the tendency to ground generalizations in too few experiments, or "premature hurry" in leaping from raw datum to "universals and principles of things" (4:48, 65, 70-71). Yet, in book 3 of the *De Augmentis,* he maintains that if the professed aims of alchemy can ever be realized, it will be done by men whose knowledge of the art is gained through careful investigation: "The conversion of silver, quicksilver, or any other metal into gold, is a thing difficult to believe; yet it is far more probable that a man who . . . has also made diligent search into the first seeds and menstruums of minerals, may at last by much and sagacious endeavour produce gold; than that a few grains of an elixir should in a few moments of time be able to turn other metals into gold by the agency of that elixir" (4:367-68). This passage clearly shows Bacon's emphasis on the application of unimpassioned knowledge, sustained effort, and careful methodology if alchemical success is to be attained;[13] and while transmutation "is a thing difficult to believe" in, there is the admission that under the right conditions it may occur. This passage, then, summarizes nicely the paradoxical nature of Bacon's discussions of alchemy: as it is currently practiced success is extremely unlikely; however, if reformed experimental methods are combined with more certain knowledge, the possibility of success exists.

It is now necessary to examine Bacon's views on those principles and assumptions that constituted the foundations upon which the theory and practice of alchemy traditionally depended. As has been shown in chapter 1, these are also the ones most vital to the perpetuation of the general medieval-Renaissance worldview and the continuation of serious belief in all forms of occult and hermetic doctrine. If, as Bacon asserts in book 2 of the *De Augmentis*, "Gold is sometimes refined in the fire and sometimes found pure in the sands" (4:295), it must follow that he either shared with his age those assumptions that made transmutation credible or else substituted new axioms that could produce a similar effect. Thus it is necessary to turn from Bacon as the proponent of new experimental methods to some aspects of his thought that were age-old.

Like the traditional alchemists, Bacon accepted the view that art could be an improver of nature. In book 2 of the *De Augmentis* he asserts that a "subtle error" has entered the human mind through its acceptance of the belief that art is merely nature's "assistant," a "finisher" or "corrector" of nature's processes. In opposition, Bacon says that art, which he defines as "nature with man to help" (4:295), has the capacity to "change, transmute, or fundamentally alter nature." The former view has brought about "a premature despair in human enterprises" (4:294), and as a countermeasure to prevailing pessimism, Bacon argues that man should regard art and nature as being parallel in their essential features and recognize his own power as an efficient cause: "the artificial does not differ from the natural in form or essence, but only in the efficient; in that man has no power over nature except that of motion; he can put natural bodies together, and he can separate them; . . . Nor matters it, provided things are put in the way to produce an effect, whether it be done by human means or otherwise" (4:294-95). Here Bacon's description of the role that humans may play in helping nature "artificially" produce new creations through joining or dividing natural bodies not normally together or separated is virtually identical to his description of the magician's *modus operandi* cited earlier, suggesting perhaps that he sees little difference in the powers of the knowledgeable natural philosopher and those of the magician. The latter may produce "wonderful operations," the former may "do everything." For both (and the situation holds for the alchemist as well), knowledge is the key.

Besides regarding art as an "improver" of nature, Bacon—again in accordance with traditional alchemical doctrine—also relied heavily on "spirits" to account for natural phenomena whose appearance could apparently be explained in no other way. Thus his view of the operations of nature is by no means solely mechanical; to a significant degree Bacon's world is the animate and hylozoistic world of magic and the occult and is complete with a "pneumatic" theory of matter. In the *Experiment solitary touching the secret processes of nature* included in the *Sylva Sylvarum,* he states that these invisible "spirits or pneumaticals" are present in *all* "tangible bodies" and are the forces that "govern nature principally" (2:380).[14] The spirits associated with tangible matter are actually imprisoned within it and are "struggling to break free, promote many of the changes that take place in the terrestrial world"; on the other hand, "pure spirits," those unconfined to tangible matter, "completely fill the rest of the universe from the surface of the Earth to the furthest reaches of the cosmos."[15] On the exact nature of these spirits Bacon is less clear, a fact that undoubtedly betrays his reluctance to attribute significant powers to anything that is immaterial in nature or cannot be validated by the methods of scientific empiricism. He remarks that different authors construe the nature of spirits variously, as vacuum, air, heat, fire, soul, or "the virtues and qualities of the tangible parts [of the substances] which they see" (2:381). Bacon's own view is that they are greatly rarefied natural bodies that permeate the tangible body and are almost always in motion. From these spirits and their motions "principally proceed arefaction, colliquation, concoction, maturation, putrefaction, vivification, and most of the effects of nature" (2:381). The connection between spirits and most of these vital processes is discussed in detail in the *Historia Vitæ et Mortis* (5:321-22), but it is certain from the following passage in the *Sylva Sylvarum* that the existence of all substances is dependent upon them: "tangible parts in bodies are stupid things," he states emphatically, "and the spirits do (in effect) all" (2:381).

Closely related to Bacon's animism is another doctrine that he appears to have shared with disciples of the occult: the doctrine concerning sympathies, antipathies, and their correspondences. On these matters we must be careful not to generalize too quickly about his final view (if indeed there was one) and also to be watchful for inconsistencies. While there is ample evidence of Bacon's keen interest in, and occasional adoption of, a doctrine of sympathies, it is also true, as Graham Rees has noted, that "the theory of 'consent' is a version of a doctrine which Bacon criticized severely—the magical doctrine of sympathies and antipathies."[16] Of primary importance here, as in his thoughts on alchemy and the occult arts generally, is Bacon's willingness to call forth, carefully evaluate, utilize wholly or in part, adapt, or dismiss a large body of disparate material that has potential significance for his topic. In the *Experiments in consort touch-*

ing the secret virtue of sympathy and antipathy, included in century 10 of *Sylva Sylvarum,* he states that "there be many things that work upon the spirits of man by secret sympathy and antipathy" (2:660). Many examples of the efficacy of sympathetic virtues of various articles are given: precious gems, chiefly diamonds, emeralds, the jacinth oriental, and the gold stone, may serve to "comfort and exhilarate" their wearers, working "by consent" upon their spirits (2:661). Bracelets and beads may affect the spirits in a variety of different ways owing to their particular virtues (2:661); because the wolf is "a beast of great edacity and digestion," applying his guts or skin to one's belly may cure the colic (2:664); the wound caused by a weapon may be healed by the weapon itself, though Bacon adds that he "as yet, [is] not fully inclined to believe it" (2:670). These are only a few examples of the cures and restoratives that Bacon either accepts or recommends as subjects for further investigation. They are by no means the most fantastic, and I do not list them primarily as examples of Bacon's credulity. Rather, they are a testimony to the strength of his interest in the power of occult sympathies and correspondences. Lynn Thorndike has stated that in Bacon "the supposed action of the spirits borders on the occult, on fascination and the evil eye, on natural magic. As an attempt to explain nature they may represent something of an improvement on the occult virtues and specific forms of the scholastic period, but it is a slight one. They are still semi-occult themselves."[17] Having seen that Bacon embraced a concept of nature that included a place for the operation of invisible spirits and, at least to some degree, occult sympathies, we must now examine his views on the correspondence theory and especially those principles related to the production of metals.

In the *Sylva Sylvarum* he refers to sulphur and mercury as the "two great families of things" that Paracelsian chemists use to designate a variety of opposing qualities: inflammability and uninflammability, refined as opposed to crude, and oily as opposed to watery. (According to Bacon, Paracelsus's third principle, salt, is unnecessary because "it is a compound of the other two" [2:459].) For Bacon, sulphur and mercury are the primordial principles that give rise to all matter and in different forms, or "consents," "occupy or penetrate" the entire universe. Underground they are known as brimstone and mercury; in the plant and vegetable kingdoms they are oil and water; in the sublunary regions of the atmosphere they are flame and air, and in the celestial regions they are the starry bodies and pure ether (2:459). Because of the diametrically opposite qualities of sulphur and mercury, Bacon asserts that the transformation of water or watery substances into oil or oily substances is one of the greatest "*magnalia naturæ,*" far greater than the transformation of "silver or quicksilver into gold" (2:459). Yet, he acknowledges that such changes commonly occur in nature, examples being the fruition resulting when a mixture of earth and water is acted upon by the sun or the production of nutriment in the digestive systems of plants and animals (2:460).

Although there are enough rudiments of a correspondence theory in Bacon to make transformations in natural bodies—and therefore alchemical transmutation—possible, he firmly rejects the exhaustive sytem of macrocosmic-microcosmic analogies proposed by Paracelsus and hermetic writers, such as Robert Fludd (see fig. 5). Speaking of the uncertainty of medical cures in book 4 of the *De Augmentis,* Bacon states: "Not that I share the idle notion of Paracelsus and the alchemists, that there are to be found in man's body certain correspondences and parallels which have respect to all the several species (as stars, planets, minerals) which are extant in the universe; foolishly and stupidly misapplying the ancient emblem (that man was a *microcosm* or epitome of the world) to the support of this fancy of theirs. But yet this much is true, that . . . of all substances which nature has produced man's body is the most multifariously compounded" (4:379-80).[18] Again in book 5 of the *De Augmentis* Bacon ridicules belief in a thoroughgoing correspondence theory, stating that "the chemists have marshalled the universe in phalanx; conceiving, upon a most groundless fancy, that in those four elements of theirs (heaven, air, water, and earth,) each species in one has parallel and corresponding species in the others" (4:432). And in century 10 of the *Sylva Sylvarum* he condemns this theory in that it is the basis for the occult practices of Paracelsus and other "darksome authors of magic" (2:641). Curiously, however, even as Bacon was roundly rejecting these aspects of Paracelsian thought, he was drawing significantly upon other aspects of the Swiss alchemist's theories in formulating his own eclectic views on cosmology. As Rees has demonstrated, Bacon's "Bi-Quaternion" theory, according to which cosmological correspondents of sulphur and mercury extend throughout the universe, thus giving it a "chemico-physical" structure, are rooted in Paracelsus's thought. Yet this "Semi-Paracelsian Cosmology" also differs in important ways, rejecting salt as a third principle and, more generally, "the quasi-religious strain in Paracelsian philosophy [and] all its esoteric, mystical and visionary manifestations."[19]

Thus Bacon accepts to a significant degree a view of nature that upheld the theoretical principles of alchemy. He embraced a correspondence theory of sorts, but one divested of the fantastically complicated system of analogies adopted by Paracelsus and the magicians. Similarly, his worldview included invisible spirits, sympathies, and antipathies, and these play a vital part in the operations of nature. Finally, Bacon's conception of the relationship between art and nature, as expounded in book 2 of the *De Augmentis,* allows for the possibility of alchemical transmutation, and the possibility of achieving this "through much and sagacious endeavor" is made explicit in book 3 of the same treatise. But while transmutation would seem to be theoretically possible, in practice it is rare because of the alchemists' faulty experimental methods and their excessive reliance on authority, belief, and imagination.

It is within the context of these qualifications and variables that one must approach the question of whether Bacon truly believed it possible to produce gold artificially. I have already noted several passages in which he explicitly or implicitly expresses his belief in the possibility of transmutation *if* attempted under the proper conditions. In the *De Augmentis* he professes that "gold is sometimes refined in the fire," and in the same work and parallel passages from *The Advancement of Learning* he admits that industrious and knowledgeable men are far more likely to learn the secret than those who rely on chance and hope. (In only two places, the allegorical interpretation of the Proserpina myth in *De Sapientia Veterum* and a brief passage in the *Historia Densi et Rari,* does he appear to deny the possibility altogether.)[20]

The most reliable sources of knowledge concerning Bacon's thoughts on gold-making are two passages from century 4 of the *Sylva Sylvarum.* Their importance is increased by the fact that in both Bacon is concerned exclusively with this subject, whereas in most other references alchemy is ancillary to other topics and concerns. In the *Experiment solitary touching the nature of gold* he notes that the chief characteristics of this metal are heaviness, denseness, "fixation," malleability, "immunity from rust," and yellowness and concludes the description by reaffirming the necessity of possessing clear and certain knowledge of the experiment's objective: "Therefore the sure way (though most about) to make gold, is to know the causes of the several natures before rehearsed, and the axioms concerning the same. For if a man can make a metal that hath all these properties, let men dispute whether it be gold or no" (2:450).

In an adjoining section of the same work, entitled *Experiment solitary touching the making of gold,* Bacon gives his fullest account of the subject. He begins by stating that gold can be produced artificially, but the remarks that follow again indicate why experimenters in the past have fallen into error:

> The world hath been much abused by the opinion of making of gold: the work itself I judge to be possible; but the means (hitherto propounded) to effect it are, in the practice, full of error and imposture; and in the theory, full of unsound imaginations. For to say that nature hath an intention to make all metals gold; and that if she were delivered from impediments, she would perform her own work; and that if the crudities, impurities, and leprosies of metals were cured, they would become gold; and that a little quantity of the medicine, in the work of projection, will turn a sea of baser metal into gold by multiplying: all these are but dreams; and so are many other grounds of alchemy. [2:448]

The most remarkable advance reflected in this passage is the idea that gold can be made, but *without* the aid of the philosopher's stone. This "medicine" is but one of the many "dreams" with which alchemists delude themselves, and in a continuation of the same passage he states that such delusions are fostered by the alchemists' adoption of "many vanities out of astrology, natural magic, superstitious interpretations of Scriptures, auricular traditions, feigned testimonies of ancient authors, and the like" (2:448).[21]

Having dispelled the errors of the past—having, in fact, rejected much of the very concept of alchemy as it was traditionally conceived—Bacon confidently announces his intention to "lay open the true ways and passages of nature, which may lead to this great effect" (2:448). (It is ironic that he phrases this claim in a way so similar to the conventional boasts of the alchemists.) He acknowledges that gold is exceedingly difficult to make because of its "most ponderous and materiate" nature, stating that in performing the experiment, knowledge of the principles of maturation is highly important as is the selection of the baser metals to be worked upon (2:449). Like the alchemists, Bacon emphasizes the importance of using fires of an exacting degree of heat. He recalls an unnamed "Dutchman," whom he has known, who claimed that alchemists commonly overfired their works and who recommends instead that the heat be gentle and even. Bacon accepts this commonplace of exoteric alchemy, adding that in using temperate heats he is also following nature: natural gold is formed underground "where little heat cometh" and where the work can progress over a long period of time (2:449).

The *Experiment solitary* concludes with a series of six "axioms of maturation" that serve as practical and theoretical guides to the making of gold (2:449-50). These are not to be confused with the progressive stages leading up to transmutation as set forth in most alchemical treatises. Rather, they are Bacon's "reformed" principles and techniques growing out of his reasoned and careful investigation of the attributes of gold and the operations of nature. They may be briefly summarized as follows:

1. "Temperate" heats are to be used because these are most effective in digesting and maturing metals.

2. Base metals are changed to more precious ones through "quickening" the spirit and opening the "tangible" parts of the former. Without this, "the spirit of the metal wrought upon will not be able to digest the parts."

3. An even heat is required to "open" the tangible parts so that the spirits can be ingested and evenly spread. Unless this is done the spirits will be distributed irregularly and the metal will not remain pliant.

4. Loss of pliancy will also result if the spirits escape; a temperate fire and a closed vessel will prevent this.

5. "The likeliest and best prepared" metals must be selected as the basic materials. Silver, rather than quicksilver, is preferred.

6. Ample time must be allowed for the experiment to work, "not to prolong hopes (as the alchemists do), but indeed to give nature a convenient space to work in."

These "most certain and true" axioms are followed by a short description of an experiment for making gold. Here Bacon recommends that silver be used as the basic material because in nature it approximates gold more closely than any other metal. To silver should be added a tenth part quicksilver, the metal richest in spirit, and a twelfth part of nitre for the purpose of quickening and opening the body. A temperate heat must also be used to keep the metals "perpetually molten," and the experiment should be continued for at least six months. Finally, Bacon adds that periodically "an injection of some oiled substance" is needed to open the tangible parts so that the spirit can be absorbed evenly and smoothly (2:450).

Bacon's attitude toward gold-making is then a complicated mixture of doubt and confidence, traditional belief and innovation, credulity and skepticism. Moreover, in his thinking on this subject there appears to be no progressive development toward a "final" position. The cautious ambiguity that characterizes references in the *Advancement of Learning* persists in the later *De Augmentis* as well as in the *Novum Organum*. The confidence in the possibility of transmutation clearly present in the descriptions of experiments in the late *Sylva Sylvarum* (published posthumously in 1627) is countered by brief negative statements in both the early *De Sapientia Veterum* and the late *Historia Densi et Rari*,[22] unpublished until 1658. Skeptical remarks about the powers of an alchemically prepared elixir of life appearing in the *De Augmentis*[23] seem completely incompatible with a potable gold recipe in the *Medical Remains*, which contains three ounces of "perfectly refined" gold, some nitre, and "good claret wine" (3:827). Muriel West has accurately stated that "Bacon's remarks on alchemy show considerable confusion of mind. . . . He contradicts himself at every turn."[24]

It is true that Bacon's mind, like Salomon's House in the *New Atlantis*, is furnished not only with places for alchemists' furnaces and fountains dispensing the miraculous Water of Paradise (3:158) but also with the apparatus for producing "new profitable inventions" (3:166). In this respect he is very much a part of an age that could easily reconcile the findings of belief, imagination, and reason. But my concern has been not only with what Bacon thought about alchemy but also with the nature of the thought processes themselves. In the latter we see major advances over the treatment of alchemy accorded by both earlier and contemporary literary authors. Unlike them, Bacon seriously believed that gold could be produced artificially. More importantly, however, he arrives at this position through a process of reasoned investigation that, although error-ridden and scientifically invalid by modern standards, anticipates both the spirit and practice of modern science. His conclusions may be fraught with "medieval" superstitiousness but the means to them point surely in the direction of Robert Boyle, the Royal Society, and, ultimately, the twentieth century. In the broadest sense, for Bacon the restoration of Vulcan necessitated the "de-alchemization" of alchemy.

"ABSTRACT RIDDLES OF OUR *STONE*"

═══════════════════════════

Ben Jonson and the Drama of Alchemy

If all you boast of your great art be true,
Sure, willing poverty lives most in you.
—Ben Jonson, "To Alchemists"[1]

To make things, that are not perceived, but lie hid in the shadow, to appear, and to take from them their vail, is granted to an intelligent Philosopher by God through Nature. . . . All these are done, and the eyes of the vulgar do not see them; but the eyes of the understanding and imagination perceive them, and that with a true sight.

—Michael Sendivogius, *A New Light of Alchymy*[2]

If, after examining the thoughts of Francis Bacon on alchemy's need for rehabilitation, English readers of the early seventeenth century still possessed doubts about the art's debased condition, these could immediately have been dispelled through attendance at performances of Ben Jonson's *The Alchemist* and *Mercury Vindicated from the Alchemists at Court*. First presented in 1610 and early 1616 respectively, these two works, city comedy and courtly masque, public theater and private entertainment, constitute the most brilliant, incisive, and perpetually engaging adaptations of alchemical materials that had yet been written. They are direct descendants of the *Canon's Yeoman's Tale*, Erasmus's alchemical dialogues, the fourteenth book of the *Discoverie of Witchcraft*, and the great variety of other literary treatments that have been previously considered. They also reflect a view of alchemy wholly compatible with the one that prompted Bacon's program of reform. Together, *The Alchemist* and *Mercury Vindicated* are the greatest—and among the last—works contained in the tradition of alchemical satire. As I will show in chapter 6, the attacks on charlatanism they included might be regarded as having been seriously injurious to alchemy as a practical pursuit, for the literary interest in alchemy that was beginning to flourish in the poetry of Donne and Herbert was strikingly different from that which had dominated the preceding centuries.

Yet, despite their common subject and shared satirical purpose, *The Alchemist* and *Mercury Vindicated* differ markedly in the precise objects of their attacks, just as in their dramatic forms and techniques. The masque, to be discussed in the last half of this chapter, is an adaptation of a popular seventeenth-century alchemical dialogue by Michael Sendivogius and represents Jonson's principal contribution to the Renaissance controversy concerning the claims of Art and Nature. It is his splendidly theatrical, complimentary, humorous, satirical, seemingly unserious treatment of a serious, much-debated issue, one that Jonson had also addressed expositorily in the *Discoveries,* under the title *Natura non effæta:* "I cannot thinke *Nature* is so spent, and decay'd, that she can bring forth nothing worth her former yeares. She is alwayes the same, like her selfe: And when she collects her strength, is abler still. Men are decay'd, and *studies:* Shee is not."[3] Given its subject and Jonson's strong support of the "Nature" side of the dichotomy (his opposition, that is, to the position of Bacon and the emerging New Science), *Mercury Vindicated* is deserving of a small place in the philosophical and scientific controversial writing of this period. The success of *The Alchemist,* on the other hand, is owing to Jonson's genius in transforming a wide range of rather conventional alchemical materials into an enduring statement on the effects of human greed and hypocrisy.

For all of its brilliance and originality, *The Alchemist,* more than any other work considered in this study, is a compendium of commonplace ideas, motifs, situations, and images derived from the traditions of alchemical writing and alchemical satire.[4] The play is, of course, infinitely more than this, and the fact that it is so thoroughly grounded in traditional materials in no way compromises its artistic originality or diminishes Jonson's creative genius. That much of the specifically alchemical subject matter he incorporates had appeared previously either in alchemical treatises or satire does not lessen the freshness of his treatment but rather provides a background against which the originality of his achievement contrasts the more vividly: quite simply, among literary authors Jonson is unsurpassed in the range, depth, and accuracy of his knowledge as well as in his ability to transmute this knowledge into an incisive commentary on human nature.[5]

No doubt for Jonson, as for the skeptical Surly, alchemy was "a pretty kind of game, / Somewhat like tricks o'the cards, to cheat a man, / With charming" (2.3.180-82). There is every reason to believe that his view of the art coincided with that of the satirical writers and that in his mind it was equivalent to the confidence games practiced by Face, Subtle, and Dol.[6] It is a form of deception practiced by cheating rogues whose victims are gullible fools. However, it is important to note that in this play Jonson is concerned with exposing the "victims" of this deceit, whose greed draws them to the alchemists' lair, quite as much as he is with attacking the art and its practitioners.[7] In this way the play provides a universal comment on the frailty of human nature: the art is represented as being supremely and transparently ridiculous, and its adepts are relentlessly but obviously wily; yet for all of this obviousness man is drawn to them through his lust for riches, power, and "success," the entire range of aspirations that motivates all of the gulls, from Dapper and Drugger to Sir Epicure Mammon and the Puritan brethren. That Jonson is even less sympathetic with the deceived than the deceivers is demonstrated at the end of the play when Face is forgiven by the recently returned Lovewit, Subtle and Dol are allowed to escape (albeit without their loot), but the victims must undergo large material and psychic losses. They have had ample exposure to the truth that Tribulation intimates to Ananias at the beginning of act 3: "And for his [Subtle's] *Stone*, it is a worke of darknesse, / And, with *Philosophie*, blinds the eyes of man" (3.1.9-10).

Yet despite this recognition of the truth about alchemy, the victims have not been enabled by their experience to reach greater self-understanding as they emerge from the "seat of false-hood, and this cave of cos'nage" (5.5.115), which is Lovewit's house. They have not been morally or psychologically refined and regenerated through their experience of the "transmutational" process conducted by the three conspirators, a process that produces gold only for the conspirators and ultimately Lovewit. Their eyes may have been opened to the deceits of the alchemical confidence game but they remain blind to their own internal flaws and vices. Although Face, in his role as Subtle's "puffer," Lungs, eventually receives "manumission" from the furnace promised early in the play (2.2.18) and forgiveness by his master, the numerous other conversions and transformations promised throughout the first four acts do not occur—base metals remain base. Even the neighbors who appear in the final act to report the activities that have been taking place in Lovewit's absence are a thoroughly leaden lot; and the audience, whom Face invites to frequent feastings and enlargement with his newly gotten "pelfe," gives little promise of potential transformation or of becoming agents of change. According to Face's final speech (5.5.162-65), as jurors having the power to sentence or "[ac]quit" him and the play, audience members are residents of his own "countrey" and are here enjoined, I think, to enter a compact with a trickster whose rehabilitation is unproven and unlikely. One may be unable to accept, with clear conscience, a dinner to be paid for with tainted money, even when the invitation is extended by a countryman. As Anne Barton has written, "*The Alchemist* is a play about transformation, as it affects not metals, but human beings." "Yet," she continues, "at the end of the day, no Shakespearean miracle has occurred."[8]

While *The Alchemist*, like the experiments of Chaucer's Yeoman, appears to lack a satisfactory "conclusion"[9] or a convincing transformation scene such as we find in *Mercury Vindicated*, its alchemy serves nonetheless as a *potential* source of illumination as well as a vehicle for satiric attack and high comedy. In designing this elaborate construct to achieve these ends, Jonson draws heavily on materials derived from both alchemical writings and the literature of satire. The sophistication of his knowledge of alchemy as well as the play's brilliantly "recapitulative" quality may be seen, first of all, by investigating several examples of this creative adaptation of materials relating to alchemical theory and background; the art's practical aspects; and adepts and their clients. These references will not necessarily be considered in the order in which they appear in the play, but I will briefly indicate the contexts in which they are found so as to suggest the care the playwright has taken in constructing his alchemical microcosm.

Though Jonson is much more interested in presenting alchemy as it was actually practiced, the play also incorporates a substantial body of theoretical material that we have encountered in other forms and writers. For example, he is careful to explain the popular theoretical basis for the growth of metals and transmutation, and this is done according to the conventional ideas about the relationship between Art and Nature and the sulphur-mercury theory. As Mammon approaches Lovewit's house early on the day of the *magisterium's* supposed completion, Subtle informs Dol of the great—and not entirely ignoble—deeds that Mammon has promised to perform:

> He will make
> Nature asham'd, of her long sleepe: when art,
> Who's but a step-dame, shall doe more, then shee,
> In her best love to man-kind, ever could.
> If his dreame last, hee'll turne the age, to gold. [1.4.25-29]

As is appropriate to an alchemist, Subtle asserts the superiority of Art to Nature, just as his counterpart does in *Mercury Vindicated.* And in both comedy and masque, the philosophically conservative Jonson will take pains to refute this notion. As a corollary, at least twice in the play—more often in the masque—the alchemist's experimental efforts are seen as a persecution of the operations of Nature: at 1.3.100, Face refers to Subtle as a "smoky persecuter of nature!" and in Subtle's remarkable alchemical catechism of Face before the astonished Ananias in act 2, scene 5, the details of this persecution are vividly rendered through the torturing of language:

> SUB. Sirah, my varlet, stand you forth, and speake to him,
> Like a *Philosopher:* Answere, i'the language.
> Name the vexations, and the martyrizations
> Of mettals, in the worke. FAC. Sir, *Putrefaction,*
> *Solution, Ablution, Sublimation,*
> *Cohobation, Calcination, Ceration,* and
> *Fixation.* [2.5.18-24]

Like Chaucer in similar passages in the *Canon's Yeoman's Tale,* Jonson creates an alchemical idiom that is simultaneously expository (accurately naming these "martyrization" processes according to alchemical terminology) and comically satirical (employing tortuous, polysyllabic words expressive of the idea of persecution).[10] Moreover, this passage and the lines that precede and follow are evocative of the motif of explaining the obscure by the more obscure, which is vital both to establishing Ananias's state of confusion and in keeping with alchemical lore. For him, words such as *cucurbite, sapor pontick, pamphysick, panarchick,* and *oleositie* can only be "*heathen Greeke*" ("All's *heathen,* but the *Hebrew,*" 2.5.17).

Closely related to the theme of Art versus Nature is Jonson's attention to the topic of the origin of metals. He has Subtle tell the impressionable Mammon and Surly about the nature of the "remote matter" from which metals evolve:

> It is, of the one part,
> A humide exhalation, which we call
> *Materia liquida,* or the *unctuous water;*
> On th'other part, a certaine crasse, and viscous
> Portion of earth; both which, concorporate,
> Doe make the elementarie matter of gold:
> Which is not, yet, *propria materia,*
> But commune to all mettalls, and all stones.
> For, where it is forsaken of that moysture,
> And hath more drynesse, it becomes a stone;
> Where it retaines more of the humid fatnesse,
> It turnes to *sulphur,* or to *quick-silver:*
> Who are the parents of all other mettalls. [2.3.142-54]

The passage continues in this vein for an additional fifty lines, becoming increasingly detailed in its account of the origin of metals from the sexually differentiated "parents," sulphur and mercury; of nature's desire to produce gold, the perfect metal, through a gradual evolution from "imperfect" ones (ll. 155-59); and of the slowness of this process. In the rather complicated context of the dramatic moment—the drawing of Mammon ever deeper into the alchemists' confidence game; the introduction of the "piety" ploy to explain, later, why the experiment has failed; and the establishment of Surly as a resistance figure—Subtle's speech serves as a marvelous instance of alchemical foolishness, one of the myriad examples of the hocus-pocus characteristic of the *ignotum per ignocius* tradition. Its inherent humor is underscored by the contrasting responses of Surly and Mammon, Subtle's "son" in the hermetic sense (2.3.1-5, 19, 55). But the passage is also a very accurate reflection of alchemical theory: sulphur and mercury account for the "ductile, malleable, [and] extensive" properties of gold (l. 166), and at times their masculinity and femininity are replaced by "*hermaphrodeitie*" (l. 164).

Lines 167-70 of the same scene recapitulate two additional beliefs that are correlatives of the doctrine of the generation of metals: that alchemists attempt to duplicate artificially the processes of nature and that their results are superior. Referring to "sophic" sulphur and mercury, Subtle states,

> for we doe find
> Seedes of them, by our fire, and gold in them:

> And can produce the *species* of each mettall
> More perfect thence, then nature doth in earth.

The assumption that Art is superior to Nature is central to the conflict of *Mercury Vindicated* and often asserted in *The Alchemist* by the three predators and the infected Sir Epicure Mammon. In 1.4.25-29, Subtle states that Art, Nature's "step-dame," will put Nature to shame; and, according to Mammon, Face's job as Subtle's "fire-drake, / His lungs, his *Zephyrus*" is to puff "his coales, / Till he firke nature up, in her owne center" (2.1.26-28). Art's superiority to "dull" Nature is also evident through the production of an elixir, by means of which man will be able to prolong his life unnaturally, a dream that obsesses Mammon nearly as much as infinite riches and sex. Drinking this elixir, he tells Dol, will "renew / Our youth, and strength" and so allow them to "enjoy a perpetuitie / Of life, and lust" (4.1.163-66). Jonson did not feel the need to rebut this position verbally—the play, in fact, includes no character sufficiently uncompromised to be entrusted to this task—preferring to let its truth be demonstrated through the action.

Again, Subtle's alchemical catechizing of Face for the benefit of Ananias in act 2, scene 5, also reveals the breadth of Jonson's knowledge not only of the surface terminology but also the underlying concepts of the art. Here, as in other scenes, his tendency to overwhelm the audience with details of alchemical theory and practice is apparent, much in the manner of Chaucer's Yeoman. For the audience, as well as for Ananias, this rhetorical display may sound like "*heathen Greeke,*" but it is used not only in brilliant imitation of the tradition of deliberate obscurity, but with accuracy as well. Subtle's reply that the *magisterium* involves the "shifting" of the elements, "Drie into cold, cold into moist, moist in- / to hot, hot into drie" (2.5.38-39), is based on the possibility of transmutation provided in the four elements theory.[11] The philosopher's stone is explained in the form of a riddle, as is often the case in alchemical tracts (ll. 40-44), and the stages in its making are recounted in the order in which they traditionally occur (ll. 20-25). Even the volatile spirit of Mercury causes him to be described as "fugitive" (l. 32), a role that Jonson develops at great length in *Mercury Vindicated,* and it is this characteristic of mercury that is responsible for the "*great crack and noise within*" that marks the climactic explosion at 4.5.55:

> FAC. O sir, we are defeated! all the *workes*
> Are flowne *in fumo:* every glasse is burst.
> Fornace, and all rent downe! as if a bolt
> Of thunder had beene driven through the house. [57-60]

Evidence of Jonson's detailed knowledge of alchemy's theoretical background could easily be multiplied, the only useful purpose being, perhaps, to demonstrate in new ways his extraordinary cleverness in transmuting leaden principles and methodology to golden comedy and satire while still retaining the recogniz-

able attributes of their *prima materia.* The case is similar with his utilization of
the techniques and materials of alchemical practice; again, the evidence of Jonson's
familiarity is too abundant to require specific documentation beyond that which
would suggest his transmutative genius. At the time of Drugger's first appearance in Lovewit's house-turned-alchemist's-lair, Subtle speculates that his tobacco
shop is equipped with "*arsnike, / Vitriol, sal-tartre, argaile, alkaly, / Cinoper*" and
other substances that could lead to his becoming a "great distiller" and even
attempting the philosopher's stone (1.3.75-80), the suggestion serving to awaken
the dull druggist's latent greed. Boasts about the efficacy of the philosopher's
stone and the elixir, such as those of Mammon in 2.1.37-41, 45-61, are legion
in alchemical writing; the extent of Jonson's knowledge is perhaps better revealed
in Face's description of the colors that mark the stages in the alchemical processes. Speaking to Mammon, he says:

> FAC. I have blowne, sir,
> Hard, for your worship; throwne by many a coale,
> When 'twas not beech; weigh'd those I put in, just,
> To keepe your heat, still even; These bleard-eyes
> Have wak'd, to reade your severall colours, sir,
> Of the *pale citron,* the *greene lyon,* the *crow,*
> The *peacocks taile,* the *plumed swan.* [2.2.21-27]

But the fullest demonstration of the range of Jonson's knowledge of practical alchemy occurs in act 2, scene 3, where, in the manner of Chaucer's Yeoman
and his descendants, we find a tremendous outpouring of technical names for
laboratory equipment, substances, and processes. Recited by Subtle and Face,
these terms threaten to engulf the deluded Mammon and, at the same time,
they call forth cynical retorts from Surly: "What a brave language here is? next
to canting?" (2.3.42). Jonson's catalog of pieces of laboratory apparatus includes
registers, aludels, bolt's heads, athanors, pelicans, and gripe's eggs. Among the
chemical substances are *lac Virginis,* oil of Luna, calxes, and philosopher's vin-
egar. There are references to a variety of baths and allusions to such processes as
calcination, digestion, and inceration. The comic and satiric effect is enhanced
by Surly's mocking recitation of his own long list (ll. 182-98) "of other strange
ingredients, / Would burst a man to name." Indeed, the "vexed" and "martyred"
language of the alchemical laboratory—so similar, according to Surly's intuition,
to the cant of thieves—is one of the major thematic and satiric components in
the play. For Jonson plainness and clarity of expression are the most essential
marks of style, and his many critical pronouncements against obscurity could
only fall heavily on the varieties of deliberate obfuscation that appear in *The
Alchemist.* For example, though focused specifically on the fashion for the metaphysical style in his time, Jonson's statement, "now nothing is good that is naturall:
Right and naturall language seemes to have least of the wit in it; that which is

writh'd and tortur'd, is counted the more exquisite," is equally reflective of his contempt for the "vexed" and "martyred" language of alchemy.[12] And the moral foundation beneath this linguistic aversion is Jonson's Baconian contempt for "deceit, or the likenesse of truth; Imposture held up by credulity."[13] Thus, Subtle's later insistence that Face's responses in his alchemical catechism be spoken "Like a *Philosopher:* Answere[d], i'the language" (2.5.18-19) is Jonson's means of exposing the fraudulence and emptiness that is lightly veiled by the beguiling surface.

In addition to being familiar with alchemical theory and practice, Jonson, like Chaucer and Erasmus, was keenly aware of the nature of those who, according to the stereotype, practiced the art and those who sought them out. Thus, the success of *The Alchemist* depends largely on a multiplicity of subtle details that serve to represent the art in terms that are very human and concrete: never is alchemy evoked simply through lists of colorful and fanciful abstractions and generalizations. Examples such as the following are highly effective in giving the play a strong sense of the reality of the art and its human dimension. In act 1, Dapper's request that he be given a "familiar" and his ensuing relationship with the "queene of *Faerie*" are plausible within the play's context because, as has often been shown, alchemy was commonly linked with magic and even witchcraft. Even more than Face with his many faces, Subtle, with his "dosen of trades," is responsible for the phantasmagoria of deceit and the *comprehensive* charlatanism present in Lovewit's house. Face draws our attention to Subtle's occupational versatility early in the play:

> FAC. When all your *alchemy,* and your *algebra,*
> Your *mineralls, vegetalls,* and *animalls,*
> Your conjuring, cosning, and your dosen of trades,
> Could not relieve your corps,
>
> . . . .
> [I] Built you a fornace, drew you customers,
> Advanc'd all your black arts; lent you, beside,
> A house to practise in —— [1.1.38-41, 45-47]

Subtle's "dosen of trades" are, of course, only narrowly diverse: for Surly, he is the operator of a bawdy house (2.3.226) and "Captaine *Pandar*" (5.5.19); for Mammon, "a rare physitian" and an "excellent *Paracelsian*" (2.3.229-30) but at play's end, "the *Chymicall* cousoner"(5.5.19); for Kastril, a marriage broker and fortune-teller (3.4.101-4); for others, a pickpocket (4.5.108-10), astrologer (5.4.128), and one versed in dicing and the legality of coining and casting money. His supposed efforts in behalf of Dapper involve a witch's familiar and those in behalf of Drugger require some knowledge of necromancy, astrology, and physiognomy; more negligible talents appear in his own self-description at 1.1.74-76. Most tellingly, he is for Surly,

the FAUSTUS,
That casteth figures, and can conjure, cures
Plague, piles, and poxe, by the *Ephemerides,*
And holds intelligence with all the bawdes,
And midwives of three shires. [4.6.46-50]

All of these diverse roles evolve naturally enough from Subtle's primary identity
as alchemist. His portrayal is a comic adaptation of many of the assocations
(Faustian magic, satanism, bawdry, astrology) previously noted in A. Matham's
engraving, "The Alchemist" (fig. 12).

Jonson's familiarity with the distinctly human aspects of alchemy extends to
other areas as well. In a quite different vein, Subtle's pretensions to piety and his
attendance at prayers are frequently iterated and extremely effective in capturing his boundless hypocrisy,[14] but at the same time the success of the alchemical
opus demanded that the adept be a "*homo frugi,* / A pious, holy, and religious
man, / One free from mortall sinne, a very virgin" (2.2.97-99). The same alchemical doctrine lies behind Face's admonition to Mammon that the house be
used for no sinful purposes: "The very house, sir, would runne mad. You know
it / How scrupulous he is, and violent, / 'Gainst the least act of sinne" (4.1.13-
15). And it is again present when Mammon assumes the responsibility for the
destruction of the experiment following the explosion and also in Subtle's remonstrance against "the curst fruits of vice, and lust" (4.5.77).

We have already noticed Jonson's frequent and effective imitation of alchemical jargon, the "brave language . . . next to canting." His knowledge of several of
the art's real or legendary authorities is also skillfully incorporated at 2.1.80-104
where Mammon reherses, for the benefit of Surly, the names of Moses, Miriam,
Salomon, and Adam, to whom treatises were actually ascribed: "Will you beleeve
antiquitie? recordes? / I'll show you a booke, where MOSES, and his sister
[Miriam the Jewess], / And SALOMON have written, of the art; / I, and a treatise penn'd by ADAM." The play also contains brief references to a number of
recent or contemporary practitioners. "The spirits of dead HOLLAND, living
ISAAC," to whom Subtle alludes in 1.2.109, is a glance at two fifteenth-century
Dutch alchemists, Isaac and John Isaac Hollandus, whose works were printed in
the early seventeenth century.[15] At the opening of act 2, scene 5, the names of
Raymond Lull, the thirteenth-century Spanish missionary to whom many alchemical treatises were erroneously ascribed, and George Ripley, the fifteenth-
century author of *The Compound of Alchemy,* are invoked. The name of Dr. John
Dee, the most famous student of hermetic philosophy in Elizabethan England,
is important in devising the "thriving signe" for Drugger's shop (2.6.19-23),
and Dee's disreputable companion Edward Kelley is mentioned at 4.1.90.[16] (In
chapter 3 it was noted that word of Kelley's notoriety had many years earlier
reached Gabriel Harvey, who refers to him in *Pierces Supererogation* of 1593.)
However, in creating Drugger's sign, Subtle rejects the use of popular astrologi-

cal sigils as "stale, and common," preferring instead to incorporate Drugger's name in a magical configuration that will attract customers through occult influences: "Form'd in some mystick character; whose *radii,* / Striking the senses of the passers by, / Shall, by a vertuall influence, breed affections, / That may result upon the partie ownes it" (2.6.15-18). Not the least of the delights in this little episode is Jonson's exquisite use of inflated language for comic purposes; the abysmally crude design for Drugger's sign is accompanied by Subtle's remark: "That's his signe. / And here's now *mysterie,* and *hieroglyphick!*" (2.6.23-24).

Jonson's inclusion of several references to alchemical interpretations of myth effectively recapitulates this familiar feature of Renaissance alchemical writing. For example, Mammon's detailed allegorical interpretation of Jason's quest for the golden fleece would arouse neither humor nor special interest if it remained in its original context within the alchemical tradition.[17] Such, however, is not the case when it is transformed into blank verse and spoken by Mammon to the skeptical Surly:

> I have a peece of IASONS fleece, too,
> Which was no other, then a booke of *alchemie,*
> Writ in large sheepe-skin, a good fat ram-vellam.
> Such was PYTHAGORA'S thigh, PANDORA'S tub;
> And, all that fable of MEDEAS charmes,
> The manner of our worke: The Bulls, our fornace,
> Still breathing fire; our *argente-vive,* the Dragon:
> The Dragons teeth, *mercury* sublimate,
> That keepes the whitenesse, hardnesse, and the biting;
> And they are gather'd, into IASON's helme,
> (Th'*alembeke*) and then sow'd in MARS his field,
> And, thence, sublim'd so often, till they are fix'd.
> Both this, th'*Hesperian* garden, CADMUS storie,
> JOVE's shower, the boone of MIDAS, ARGUS eyes,
> BOCCACE his *Demogorgon,* thousands more,
> All abstract riddles of our *stone.* [2.1.89-104]

Equally comic, if less detailed in analysis, is Jonson's incorporation of the myth of Jove, Danaë, and the golden shower in the seduction speeches Mammon delivers to his "great lady," Dol, in 4.1.25-31, 125-28. An alchemical interpretation of this myth is included in Michael Maier's emblem, *Aurum pluit, dum nascitur Pallas Rhodi, & Sol concumbit Veneri* from *Atalanta Fugiens* (fig. 15).[18] Thus to the alchemical tradition of *ignotum per ignocius,* Jonson joins other modes of "dark" discourse: mythological allegory, the hieroglyphics of Drugger's sign, the Puritan idiolect of the Anabaptist brethren, the impenetrable babble of the inspired Dol once the fit of Hugh Broughton's rabbinical knowledge has descended on her, Surly's Spanish, and Kastril's language of the quarrel.[19] Jonson, in fact, draws our attention to this aspect of the play by having Subtle explain to Mammon the various means that alchemical authors have used deliberately to conceal and reveal their secrets:

> Was not all the knowledge
> Of the *Egyptians* writ in mystick *symboles?*
> Speake not the *Scriptures,* oft, in *parables?*
> Are not the choisest *fables* of the *Poets,*
> That were the fountaines, and first springs of wisedome,
> Wrapt in perplexed *allegories?* [2.3.202-7]

This linguistic Tower of Babel, which, for Jonson, stands as a monument to the dangers of personal eccentricity and moral and religious deviation from the norm of his conservative ethics and religion, is finally cast down by the explosion of the furnace, the return of Lovewit, and the unmasking of the charlatans.[20]

Another important evidence of Jonson's keen awareness of the political and religious associations of contemporary hermetic thought is his linking of occult interests with radical protestantism. The research of such scholars as Christopher Hill, Keith Thomas, Charles Webster, and P.M. Rattansi has clearly established this connection though analysis of largely nonliterary sources, and I will have more to say on literary reflections in chapters 8 and 9.[21] It is therefore historically plausible that in Jonson's play the Anabaptists, Ananais and Tribulation, should be drawn to the occult charlatans residing in Lovewit's house, and it is natural to find the many scathing references to radical protestantism and the Dutch revolutionaries, John of Leyden and Bernt Knipperdollinck (e.g., 2.5.13 and throughout 3.1 and 3.2). Given the association of occult ideas and nonconformist religion it is also not surprising that Mammon's inadvertent reference to the philosopher's stone should trigger Dol's millenarian tirade: "Alas I talk'd / Of a fift *Monarchy* I would erect, / With the *Philosophers stone* (by chance) and shee [Dol] / Fals on the other foure [monarchies], straight" (4.5.25-28). And at the end of the play, Mammon announces that he "will goe mount a turnep-cart, and preach / The end o'the world, within these two months" (5.5.81-82).[22] References to the various "monarchies" and other millenarian and utopian themes abound in the writings of sixteenth- and seventeenth-century alchemical authors, just as they do in works of the radical sectarians. John S. Mebane has recently written that *The Alchemist* "sets out to ridicule the claim of occult philosophers that human beings are demigods who can literally perfect their own personalities, control time and change, or perfect the fallen world through magical arts. The center of the play is the deflation—or perhaps explosion—of the illusion that the individual can realize a godlike potential through a series of self-transformations and that this perfection of the soul can lead directly to the radical reformation of nature and society."[23] Thus, while keeping within the satirical tradition, Jonson's linking of the themes of alchemical transformation and millenarian expectations, most notably in the episodes involving

EMBLEMA XXIII. *De secretis Naturæ.*

Aurum pluit, dum naſcitur Pallas Rhodi, & Sol concumbit Veneri.

EPIGRAMMA XXIII.

RES eſt mira, fidem fecit ſed Græcia nobis
    Ejus, apud Rhodios quæ celebrata fuit.
Nubibus Aureolus, referunt, quòd decidit imber,
    Sol ubi erat Cypriæ junctus amore Deæ:
Tum quoque, cùm Pallas cerebro Jovis excidit, aurum
    Vaſe ſuo pluviæ ſic cadat inſtar aquæ.

Figure 15. Athena's Birth, Jove and Danaë. Michael Maier, *Atalanta fugiens* (1617). By permission of the University of Delaware Library, Newark, Delaware.

Ananias and Tribulation, also significantly extends the usual boundaries of this mode in the direction of contemporary religion and politics. In this sense as well, *The Alchemist* anticipates the attacks on alchemy as manifestations of philosophical enthusiasm that were to become common during the Restoration.

A variety of other allusions common in literary treatments of alchemy from Chaucer onward also serve to invest the play with a sense of the art's reality. The quarreling at the beginning of the play provides Jonson with opportunity to associate Subtle with desperate poverty, from which he has been lifted through Face's beneficence:

> But I shall put you in mind, sir, at *pie-corner,*
> Taking your meale of steeme in, from cookes stalls,
> Where, like the father of hunger, you did walke
> Piteously costive,
>
> . . . .
> When you went pinn'd up, in the severall rags,
> Yo'had rak'd, and pick'd from dung-hills, before day,
> Your feet in mouldie slippers, for your kibes,
> A felt of rugg, and a thin thredden cloake,
> That scarce would cover your no-buttocks. [1.1.25-28, 33-37]

That Face, like Chaucer's Yeoman, has also suffered from his work as Subtle's "lungs" is made plain by Mammon's promise that he will "manumit thee [Face], from the fornace; / I will restore thee thy complexion, *Puffe,* / Lost in the embers; and repaire this braine, / Hurt wi'the fume o'the mettalls" (2.2.18-21). Following the explosion later in the play Face confesses that his brain is "quite un-done with the fume" (4.5.69).[24] Another type of alchemy-induced madness afflicts Mammon, who has "talk'd, as he were possess'd" for a month about the riches to be gained through the philosopher's stone; and, as previously noted, Dol's feigned rabbinical madness also results from hearing Mammon speak of the stone.

Along with madness, Face's attacks on Subtle in the play's first scene serve unequivocally to link alchemists with cheating and deception, the primary association developed throughout. Before setting up practice in Lovewit's house, Subtle has plied "conjuring, cosning, and [a] dosen of trades" (1.1.40); and for his ungratefulness, Face says that he will cause all of Subtle's past villainies to be written up in red letters for public view:

>   all thy tricks
>   Of cosning with a hollow cole, dust, scrapings,
>   Searching for things lost, with a sive, and sheeres,
>   Erecting *figures,* in your rowes of *houses,*
>   And taking in of shaddowes, with a glasse, (1.1.93-97)

For his violation of a statute forbidding sorcery enacted by Henry VIII, Subtle could receive severe punishment, perhaps even hanging, for defacing legal coins ("laundring gold, and barbing it," 1.1.114). In fact, all of the crimes that Subtle is charged with (including the Chaucerian hollow coal trick) are those that alchemists were guilty of according to writers of satire. And another glance at Chaucer is present in the aftermath of the laboratory explosion in act 4, scene 5. Just as Chaucer emphasized alchemy's powerfully addictive quality through the Yeoman's description of sweeping up the remains of the failed experiment for use in another attempt ("And though this thyng myshapped have as now, / Another tyme it may be well ynow," [ll. 944-45]), so Mammon's hopeless obsession is figured forth in identical terms in the dialogue with Face:

> MAM.   Will nought be sav'd, that's good for med'cine, thinkst thou?
> FAC.   I cannot tell, sir. There will be, perhaps,
>   Something, about the scraping of the shardes,
>   Will cure the itch: though not your itch of mind, sir. [4.5.90-93]

Finally, in all of the victims of Subtle, Face, and Dol—in Dapper, Drugger, Kastril, Ananias and Tribulation, but most strikingly in the voluptuous exoticism of Sir Epicure Mammon—are revealed the weaknesses of human nature that guaranteed alchemists a perpetual source of materials with which to experiment.[25] Each of these characters is drawn into the alchemist's lair by a hope or dream, craftily expanded by Subtle and Face to the proportion of an obsession,[26] that his thirst for wealth and power will be satisfied. Unlike Surly, who early in the play exclaims that "Your *stone* / Cannot transmute me" (2.1.78-79), each of the gulls is transmuted by his obsessions into a blind, dehumanized creature whose loss of reason makes his victimization inevitable.[27] Jonson is therefore suggesting that the world of alchemy, of which Lovewit's house is the microcosm, is a world of illusion, madness, and self-deception. All who enter must be resigned to the cheating, rascality, disappointment, and poverty that await them. Thus the matter and expectations of Jonson's alchemical world are very close to those of earlier satirical writers, only his world is richer, more varied, and infinitely more comic than any created before him.

Quite apart from its intrinsic merits, Jonson's *Mercury Vindicated from the Alchemists at Court,* the masque performed before King James at Whitehall early in January 1616 and first printed in the folio edition of that year,[28] is an unusually interesting and profitable work through which to investigate the artistic potential inherent in alchemy. Like *The Alchemist,* it serves as an example of the operation of Jonson's imagination upon alchemical subject matter; furthermore, it shows how, in the hands of the alchemical "poet par excellence,"[29] this body of knowledge could be adapted brilliantly to the requirements of this genre. *Mercury Vindicated* possesses all of the elements necessary to the masque form: liveliness, courtly compliment, humor, song, and colorful spectacle, staging, and costume. But in addition to these attributes that evolve so harmoniously from alchemical materials, this masque contains a seriousness resulting from its examination of a much-debated question: the claims of Art to superiority over Nature. Jonson treats an idea that had been one of the underlying beliefs of the alchemists—that Art was a perfecter of Nature and was therefore superior to it—and one that Francis Bacon and other proponents of the New Philosophy were currently affirming in their prose works. In *Mercury Vindictated,* however, this assumption is categorically denied and, accordingly, alchemy and Vulcan (the symbol of both alchemy and "the second nature," art) are denounced.

That this question concerning Art's superiority to Nature is central to the masque has been noted by editors of Jonson's works and more fully studied in an essay by Edgar H. Duncan, where it is linked to the controversy over the Decay of Nature common in Jacobean England.[30] In addition, Herford and Simpson as well as Duncan have suggested a few analogues and possible sources for portions of the masque. Nonetheless it is true that *Mercury Vindicated* has received little attention from scholars, and the state of its neglect is indicated by the fact that it is given only brief mention in several modern studies of Jonson's masques.[31] My concern is twofold: first, I will demonstrate that in both the design and execution of *Mercury Vindicated* Jonson relied heavily on a treatise written by the celebrated Polish or Moravian alchemist Michael Sendivogius (Sędzimir or Sedziẃoj) (1566-1636). The degree of his indebtedness is sufficient, in fact, to warrant claiming Sendivogius's work as the direct source of the masque. Secondly, by means of close comparison of treatise and masque, I will try to illustrate the proximity of the "alchemical imagination" to the literary imagination, thereby enabling us to see how two authors—one an alchemist, the other an outspoken foe of the art—create a fiction to achieve their respective purposes and how, in the case of *Mercury Vindicated,* alchemy's rich suggestiveness could contribute to achieving objectives that are ultimately political in nature. For Jonson, in accordance with the tradition that he and Inigo Jones established, masques were not merely vehicles for royal flattery; they were "festal embodiments of [the] concept of monarchy."[32] The realization of this conception in *Mercury Vindicated* involved examination and rejection of Art's claims to superiority over Nature.

In the quotation that serves as the second epigraph to this chapter, Sendivogius himself describes the reliance of the alchemist on a kind of mystical insight, one combining intellect and imagination, to apprehend and explain the reality of things unseen; but the terms he uses might apply equally well to the literary artist's attempts to represent concretely the products of his mind and imagination. For Sendivogius and other members of the brotherhood of alchemists, the reality of the art depended on the possession of this imaginative vision; Jonson, though totally skeptical, could imaginatively participate in the mythology of alchemy to the extent that his satire is invested with a sense of its reality.

In its general design, *Mercury Vindicated* progresses from conflict to resolution: from the attempts of a tyrannical Vulcan to enslave Mercury to the liberation of Mercury from the false claims of his would-be master. This progression, like the conflict itself, is achieved largely through the dialogue of a few highly symbolic and allegorical characters. Action, while adding immeasurably to the spectacle and entertaining qualities of the masque, serves also to clarify and intensify the dispute concerning Art and Nature. In respect to theme, characterization, primacy of dialogue, and many specific details as well, *Mercury Vindicated* is strikingly similar to Sendivogius's satirical *Dialogus Mercurii, Alchymistae et Naturae*. There is no direct evidence in Jonson's writings or in the records of books known to have been included in his "well-furnisht" library that he knew Sendivogius's works.[33] Yet it is likely that the legend and notoriety surrounding Sendivogius during his lifetime and the popularity of his writings, as indicated by numerous seventeenth-century editions, translations, and references, could not have failed to reach Jonson's attention.

Accounts of Sendivogius's life published prior to the important corrective studies of Włodzimierz Hubicki, to which I will turn shortly, rest on the doubtful assumption that it was closely linked to the career of the mysterious Scottish alchemist Alexander Seton. According to the romanticized version set forth by A.E. Waite and essentially repeated by John Read, E.J. Holmyard, and others,[34] the flamboyant and much-traveled Seton allegedly produced gold alchemically in Enkhuizen, Holland, in 1602, and during the next two years his reputation grew as a result of transmutations performed in other Continental cities. Gaining the epithet "Cosmopolite" as a result of his extensive travels and having recently married, Seton, late in 1603, arrived in Krossen, Germany, and the court of Christian II, Elector of Saxony. Here he suffered the fate common to adepts who fell into the hands of avaricious monarchs; Seton was imprisoned and tortured for his denial of Christian's request for the secret of the transmuting powder that Seton had used so successfully. While in prison, Seton was frequently visited by Michael Sendivogius, a Moravian-born student of chemistry who usually resided in Cracow, Poland. Together they plotted Seton's escape and eventually accomplished it through generous bribes of money and wine to the guards; Sendivogius is said to have carried the enfeebled Seton out of the prison himself. After reaching safety in Cracow, Seton reportedly turned over the remaining supply of transmuting powder to his rescuer and died shortly thereafter.

At the time of Seton's death in late 1603 or early 1604, Sendivogius was about thirty-seven years old. Born in 1566 and trained in mining and pigment manufacturing, his interest in alchemy may have begun only after meeting Seton in Christian's prison. In fact, there is reason to believe that his personal interest in Seton was inspired more by a desire to gain the secret of gold-making than concern for the welfare of the captive. This supposition is strengthened by the allegation that shortly after Seton's death Sendivogius married his widow, hoping, perhaps, to learn from her the secret of the philosopher's stone. (At the time of his death, Seton had given his rescuer only his supply of the transmuting powder and not the formula for its preparation.)

As a result of transmutations performed in public and at court, an ostentatious manner of travel and dress, and the companionship of a beautiful young wife, Sendivogius's life—at this point in his career—resembled that of a hero of romantic melodrama. It is therefore not surprising that he soon attracted the attention of Emperor Rudolf II at Prague, whose interest in the occult caused him to be known as "the German Hermes." In 1604 Sendivogius is reported to have produced gold before Rudolf and his court and to have been rewarded with the title of counsellor to the Emperor. This event was "celebrated in verse" by Rudolf's court poet, Mardochie de Delle, and commemorated through the installation of a marble tablet inscribed with the words: *Faciat hoc quispiam alius, / Quod fecit Sendivogius Polonus!* ("Let another do that which Sendivogius of Poland has done!").[35] Figure 16, a nineteenth-century painting by W. Brozik, shows Rudolf II in the laboratory of his alchemist.

According to the Waite version, Sendivogius's life then came to be an alternating cycle of courtly triumph and squalid imprisonment. Honors and rewards were lavished upon him; his reputation rapidly increased, and, like Seton before him, he became known as the "Cosmopolite." However, between 1605 and 1607, eight to ten years before Jonson wrote *Mercury Vindicated,* a series of events occurred that marked a turning point in Sendivogius's career. While visiting the court of Duke Frederick of Württemberg at Stuttgart, he fell victim to a plot carried out by a rival alchemist named Müllenfels (but possibly instigated by Frederick himself), which resulted in the theft of Sendivogius's valuables, including a diamond necklace and much of the remaining transmuting powder. Although he was eventually restored to honor through appeal to Rudolf and Müllenfels was hanged, Sendivogius's career as an eminent alchemist seems to have been near its end. His supply of transmuting powder was exhausted and, not possessing the secret of its preparation, he appears to have degenerated into the living embodiment of the alchemist of literary satire. He disappears from view until 1625; then, in Warsaw, we find him employing "the tricks of the vulgar charlatan, selling marvellous nostrums, conterfeiting silver, and borrowing money from the credulous on the strength of false promises to make the philosophers' stone."[36] Sendivogius, who had been "counsellor of state to four emperors successively," died in 1646 (or 1636) when he was eighty years old.[37]

If Jonson's attention was not drawn to the *Dialogus* through the fanciful episodes that comprise the Sendivogian legend, it is very probable that his interest would have been aroused by the plainer, though scarcely unromantic, facts surrounding the adept's life. Biographical accounts of both Sendivogius and Seton based on archival research have recently been published by Włodzimierz Hubicki and contain findings suggesting that Jonson could scarcely have been unaware of Sendivogius. Most important, Professor Hubicki identifies Seton as the Italian imposter-charlatan-illusionist Girolamo vel Hieronymus Scotto of Parma (b. ca. 1540), whose appearances in numerous Continental cities and courts created sensations prior to his death after 1606.[38] While not absolutely denying

Figure 16. Rudolph II in the Laboratory of His Alchemist. Painting by W. Brozik (1881). By permission of the Wellcome Institute Library, London.

that "Seton"/Scotto and Sendivogius were acquainted, Hubicki minimizes the importance of this relationship to Sendivogius's career: he rejects totally the story of Seton's imprisonment by Christian II and consequently that of Sendivogius's assistance in his escape;[39] moreover, he states that Sendivogius's interest in alchemy began long before he had any contact with Seton.[40] In opposition to the version recorded by Waite and his successors, Hubicki denies the rumor that Sendivogius married Seton's widow and asserts that he was solely responsible for the *Novum Lumen Chymicum,*[41] to be discussed in the following section. In summary, Hubicki's investigation has reoriented our understanding of Sendivogius on at least two major points. His name is vindicated from charges of involvement in the seamier aspects of alchemical charlatanism. Second, much attention is given to the honor and notoriety he acquired as a result of extensive travels and personal contacts growing out of his employment as a courier—diplomat in the courts of Rudolf II, Sigismond III, and Ferdinand II.

If Hubicki's identification of Alexander Seton with Girolamo vel Hieronymus Scotto is correct, it would indirectly suggest the likelihood of Jonson's awareness of Sendivogius's *Dialogus*—at times attributed to Seton—because, quite apart from the bibliographical evidence cited below, Jonson was keenly aware of Scotto and capitalized on his notoriety in *Volpone* (performed 1605). In act 2, scene 2, the disguised Volpone "mounts the bank" beneath the window of Corvino's house to woo Celia and identifies himself as "Scoto *Mantuano*" (l. 34). Here the "quack-salver, [that lives] by venting oyles, and drugs" (ll. 5-6) performs his medicine show before Sir Politic Would-Be, Peregrine, and the gullible citizens: "Pol: Is not his language rare? Per: But *Alchimy*, / I never heard the like: or Broughton's bookes" (2.2.118-19). (See fig. 17, "Le Marchand d'orviétan de Campagne," for a French version of a comparable mountebank.) Volpone's sales pitch is replete with the obfuscating jargon of both medicine and alchemy, clearly indicating that Scotto/Seton was linked in Jonson's mind with alchemy. And because the common view, whether accurate or not, closely associated Seton and Sendivogius, it makes all the more likely Jonson's awareness of Sendivogius's *Dialogus.*

While we lack conclusive evidence that Sendivogius traveled to England,[42] it is difficult to believe that a career so marked by adventure, intrigue, and courtly recognition would have gone unnoticed there. It is especially likely that it would have been known to those who, like Jonson, were interested in alchemy and keenly aware of contemporary events.[43] But Sendivogius's reputation was unquestionably established through works written by him or attributed to him. Problems of attribution result again from his supposedly close association with Seton. The manuscript of the *Novum Lumen Chymicum,* for example, is often considered to have been written by Seton and to have been passed on to Sendivogius by Seton's widow at the time of their rumored marriage. Sendivogius is then alleged to have published the treatise as his own under the anagram, *Divi Leschi genus amo,* which contains all of the letters in his full name.[44] Nonetheless, seventeenth-century authorities frequently assign the *Novum Lumen* to Sendivogius, and under his authorship it proved to be extremely popular in Europe and England.

According to Thorndike, the *Novum Lumen Chymicum* first appeared in Prague in 1604 and other editions in the original Latin followed: in Paris (1608), Frankfurt (1611), Cologne (1614), Geneva (1628), and Venice (1644). A French translation appeared in 1609, 1618, 1639, 1669, 1691, and 1723.[45] A German commentary on the work was issued in 1624, translated into Latin, and later printed in the 1661 edition of Zetzner's voluminous collection of alchemical treatises, the *Theatrum Chemicum.*[46] Another alchemical anthology, the *Biblioteca Chemica Contracta,* printed in Geneva in 1653, contained several of Sendivogius's works, including the *Novum Lumen.*[47] The latter was also translated into English in 1650 and reprinted in 1674 and again in 1722.

But my primary concern is with the *Dialogus Mercurii, Alchymistae et Naturae,* about which there is also reasonably ample bibliographical information. Read states that "this dialogue was published as a separate tract [i.e., independent of the *Novum Lumen*] at Cologne, so early as 1607, under the anagrammatised name of Michael Sendivogius as it appears on the title-page of the *New Light.*"[48] John Ferguson supports this claim by citing the complete bibliographical entry for the 1607 edition;[49] furthermore, Thorndike reports that the *Dialogus* "ran through several Latin editions and was translated into French and English," the Latin appearing in Paris (1608), Cologne (1612, 1614), Wittenberg (1614, 1623),

Figure 17. "Le Marchand d'orviétan de Campagne." By Bonnet (19th century) after P. Careme (1734-96). By permission of the Wellcome Institute Library, London.

and Venice (1644).[50] The congruence between these dates and places of publication and several of those for the *Novum Lumen* would indicate that the two works were often published together, an inference that is supported by Ferguson.[51] The first of these was translated by John French and printed in London in 1650; a second edition was issued in 1674. Information on the title page pertaining to selections by Sendivogius included in the latter volume is as follows: "A NEW LIGHT OF ALCHYMY: Taken out of the Fountain of NATURE and MANUAL EXPERIENCE. To which is added A TREATISE of SULPHUR Written by Micheel [sic] Sandivogius [sic]: i.e. Anagrammatically, DIVI LESCHI GENUS AMO. . . . All which are faithfully translated out of the *Latin* into the *English* Tongue, By *J.F.* M.D. London, Printed by *A. Clark,* for *Tho. Williams* at the Golden Ball in Hosier-Lane, 1674." As can be seen, the title page makes no mention of the inclusion of the *Dialogue;* however, it is placed between the *New Light* and the *Treatise of Sulphur,* occupying pages 60-75 of this edition. A similar practice is followed in the printing of the English version of the *Dialogue* included in A.E. Waite's edition of *The Hermetic Museum, Restored and Enlarged,* which is itself a translation of the Latin *Musaeum Hermeticum* published at Frankfurt in 1678. Additional evidence of the early popularity of this dialogue as well as of the fact that it was, at times, printed apart from the *Novum Lumen* is its inclusion in the fourth volume of Zetzner's *Theatrum Chemicum*, published in Strasburg in 1613.[52]

The date of the earliest English translation obviously precludes its use by Jonson. Nonetheless, excluding translations and the "unacknowledged" inclusion of the *Dialogue* in several early editions of the *Novum Lumen*, we find no fewer than five separately published Latin editions originating from various cities on the Continent before 1615, to which should be added its appearance in at least one popular collection of alchemical treatises. In short, we can confidently state that by the time Jonson wrote *Mercury Vindicated* there were a significant number of copies of the *Dialogue* in existence and available to him. That Sendivogius's works were available and that their author enjoyed high regard throughout the seventeenth century is evidenced by both library records and an abundance of contemporary references. The existence of the *Novum Lumen* in England at about the time of the composition of *Mercury Vindicated* is proven, for example, by the presence of a copy of the 1614 Cologne edition, which did include the *Dialogue,* in the library of Henry Percy, ninth Earl of Northumberland (d. 1632).[53] It may well have been part of the extensive collection of alchemical books that the Wizard Earl provided for his lengthy confinement in the Tower of London.

In 1624, Sendivogius was enshrined among "The Champions of Alchemy and the Principal Alchemists of Twelve Nations" in Daniel Stolcius's alchemical emblem book, the *Viridarium Chymicum.* The verse accompanying an engraving representing him states in part: "Though this name in the past / Has been kept in oblivion, / Its praise now penetrates the darkness, / As it ought to be, indeed."[54] Sir Thomas Browne discusses the *Treatise of Sulphur* knowledgeably in the *Pseudodoxia Epidemica* (1646),[55] and beginning in the mid-seventeenth century, Sendivogius is one of the contemporary authorities most often cited by English alchemical writers. Invariably his works are referred to with awe and respect: for example, he is "that most Excellent Author of Twelve Tractates upon the Stone";[56] "*Cosmopolite Sendivogius* . . . in whose obscure words the Truth lyes hidd";[57] the "great Philosopher Michael Sendivogius";[58] or "Michael Sandivogius [sic], that noble Polander, . . . in whose hands [are shown] . . . the wonderful Virtues and Operation of the Philosopher's Tincture."[59] Finally, the availability of the 1650 translation of the *Novum Lumen* is indicated by its inclusion in the *Catalogue of Chymicall Books,* which that curious alchemical bibliophile, William Cooper, published to advertise the wares of his bookshop at the sign of the Pelican in Little-Britain.[60]

The most striking parallels between the *Dialogue* and Jonson's masque are, as noted earlier, those of theme, character, and the dialogue form itself. If Jonson drew on Sendivogius in the writing of *Mercury Vindicated,* he would have found a model that was not only filled with dramatic potential but also in its existing form amounted to a compact and witty little drama. It is, in fact, quite accurate to refer to it as a *ludibrium,* the term that Frances Yates applies to the genre exemplified by Johann Valentin Andreae's *Chymische Hochzeit Christiani Rosencreutz* (Strasburg, 1616) and that designates a play, comic fiction, or jest "of little worth."[61] Both works are short: the masque runs to 268 lines and the *Dialogue* occupies sixteen pages in the 1650 English edition.[62] In each, the main characters are the same in number, role, and delineation. Mercury, the protagonist, is a small masterpiece of alchemical and mythological complexity; Vulcan, the antagonist (known only as the "Alchymist" in Sendivogius), epitomizes the foolish alchemist of satirical literature. In addition, both works include a third identical character, Nature, who serves as the agent of Mercury's vindication. Except for the vision of an old man who appears briefly, this constitutes the entire cast of the *Dialogue;* Jonson's work adds several minor characters—a cyclops, Prometheus, and the members of the two antimasque groups—largely for the purpose of satisfying the genre's demand for color and spectacle.

In addition to providing a ready-made basis for the theme and characterization that Jonson wished to develop, the *Dialogue* also has an unusual style that would no doubt have attracted Jonson's attention. In giving dialogue the most prominent place in his work, Sendivogius was departing abruptly from the conventional form used in alchemical literature. Typically, such treatises are written in a weighty and solemn expository style, frequently in the first person, and are heavily laden with admonitions to piety and quotations from authorities. While the presence of dialogue is by no means unique to Sendivogius,[63] in no other alchemical author I have read are form and style suited so admirably to the requirements of drama. In both the *Dialogue* and the *Treatise of Sulphur,*[64] where the amount of dialogue is far less, we find speeches emanating from characters who are actually speaking to each other, and their lines often have the qualities of dramatic repartee: brevity, liveliness, irony, and humor. When these formal and stylistic properties, which make the *Dialogue* unusual among alchemical treatises, are combined with further parallels to Jonson in setting, action, and theme, we have convincing evidence that Jonson drew on it in writing his masque.

Sendivogius's work begins with a brief description of a group of alchemists meeting "in the open aire, in a certaine meadow, on a faire cleer day" (*Dialogue,* 59). The narrator tells us that they are disputing about which is the prime ingredient in the making of the philosopher's stone. Following tradition, some claim that it is sulphur, and others mercury. But before the debate can be settled a "very great tempest, with stormes, showers of rain, and an unheard of wind" (*Dialogue,* 60) disperses the assembly, and the scene quickly changes to a place where one alchemist, with glasses and fire, "began to work." Similarly, after "lowd musique" (perhaps in imitation of the *Dialogue*'s tempest) has subsided, the setting of *Mercury Vindicated* is revealed as "*a laboratory, or Alchymists workehouse*" (l. 2), and as the masque opens we find Vulcan, the alchemist, overseeing the labours of a fire-tending cyclops. While Sendivogius's alchemist is unnamed it is not surprising that Jonson should have used "Vulcan," "old *Smug* here of *Lemnos,*" to designate his archetypal alchemist. The identification of the Roman god of fire and metalwork with the alchemist and his art is, as Duncan has noted, common in alchemical writing.[65] As seen in the preceding chapter, this association is also made by Francis Bacon, for whom Vulcan is the "second nature," Art, whose intention is to improve and perfect the original, a claim that the conservative Jonson chose to reject.

This claim, so important in setting forth the Art-Nature conflict, is first asserted in *Mercury Vindicated* in the cyclops' opening song in praise of fire, the dying rhythms of which reinforce the decay-of-Nature idea:

> Soft, subtile fire, thou soule of art,
>   Now doe thy part
> On weaker Nature, that through age is lamed.
>   Take but thy time, now she is old,
>   And the Sunne her friend growne cold,
> She will no more, in strife with thee be named. [ll. 6-11]

At the close of the second verse Mercury appears, *"thrusting out his head, and afterward his body, at the Tunnell of the middle furnace"*; thereupon Vulcan cries out for assistance in an attempt to "fix" him, i.e., to reduce this volatile metal to a permanent state that will resist further change. His fears that Mercury "will bee gon, he will evaporate" and his pleas, "be fixt; be not so volatile" (ll. 24-26), are well founded because Mercury does escape, dramatizing his freedom by running furtively around the room. In Sendivogius's tract, shortly after the alchemist has begun to work we find that "Mercury as it is wont to do, vapoured away." This the foolish alchemist takes as a hopeful sign because he has read that "the first matter of the Philosophers Stone must be volatile" (*Dialogue*, 60-61).

But these resemblances in the use of dialogue, in setting, and even in diction (e.g., "volatile," "evaporate," "vapoured away") give rise in later parts of both works to parallels that demonstrate more conclusively Jonson's debt to Sendivogius. Chief among these is the portrayal of Mercury himself: in both works, but especially in Jonson's, he is an extremely subtle and complex blend of the varied representations found in alchemical and mythological tradition. Pictorially, several of these iconographic components are combined in figure 18, from Basil Valentine's *Duodecim Claves*, where Mercury's wings and caducei, his uniting of opposing principles, and also the suggestion of his ascendency over the two threatening (or astonished) "mortal" alchemists are portrayed in ways similar to both Jonson and Sendivogius.

On the most obvious level, in both Jonson and Sendivogius, Mercury's presence is essential to the conflict because he, as Nature's son, is her representative and stands in opposition to Vulcan; and it is from this opposition that the theme evolves: (1) Mercury and Vulcan are at war with each other; (2) Vulcan's attempts to capture Mercury reveal his cruel, tyrannical character; (3) Mercury, in

Figure 18. Mercurius. Basil Valentine, *Duodecim Claves,* in *Musæum Hermeticum* (1678). Courtesy of the National Library of Medicine, Bethesda, Maryland.

the end, triumphs over his oppressor. This three-part development yields the conclusion that Nature is superior to Art. But it is equally apparent that this conflict is played out within the specific context of alchemy, and in both works the satirical intent is predicated on the reader's or viewer's recognition of the alchemical meaning of each of the characters. In accordance with the most fundamental doctrine of alchemy, Mercury is synonymous or closely associated with quicksilver; it, along with sulphur, is the "parent" of all other metals or it is one of the two philosophical "principles" that, when conjoined with its opposite, results in the production of the philosopher's stone. True to alchemical theory, both Jonson and Sendivogius give Mercury the attributes of spiritedness, volatility, and fusibility, properties that must be removed or transformed if Mercury is to be efficacious in preparing the stone. Given this natural state, efforts to enslave Mercury must necessarily be harsh and unnatural. For this reason, in many examples of alchemical satire, alchemists are depicted as persecutors of Nature.

In his first long speech in *Mercury Vindicated* (ll. 30-109), Mercury presents himself as the object of Vulcan's persecution. As the section opens we find him looking for a place of asylum: "I will stand, close, up, any where, to escape this polt-footed *Philosopher,* old *Smug* here of *Lemnos,* and his smoaky familie.

. . . O the variety of torment, that I have endur'd in the reigne of the *Cyclops,* beyond the most exquisite wit of *Tyrannes*" (ll. 36-40). He further relates that "[t]he whole household of 'hem are become *Alchymists* (since their trade of armour-making fail'd them) onely to keepe themselves in fire, for this winter" (ll. 41-43)—lines that glance humorously at James's pacifistic policies and also remind us that the masque was performed at court during the winter season. The "punishments" Mercury has been subjected to are those that result from a variety of alchemical processes: "I am their Crude, and their Sublimate; their Præcipitate, and their unctuous; their male and their female; sometimes their *Hermaphrodite;* what they list to stile me. It is I, that am corroded, and exalted, and sublim'd and reduc'd and fetch'd over, and filtred, and wash'd, and wip'd . . . never Herring, Oyster, or Coucumer past so many vexations: my whole life with 'hem hath bene an exercise of torture" (ll. 51-62).[66] Physically, Mercury is experiencing the variety of "vexations" and "martyrizations" that were the subject of Subtle's interrogation of Face in *The Alchemist* (2.5.18-24), and Jonson's humorously vivid portrayal of these tortures effectively captures the cycle of solutions and coagulations that the volatile principle was thought to experience while in the alembic. The description, with its allusions to mercury's "crude" and "philosophical" states, mercury's exposure to different chemicals and degrees of heat, and even its sex changes, again recapitulates an important alchemical *topos.* But Jonson's success in this passage depends less on his talent for merely dramatizing details culled from alchemical treatises than on his adoption of an animistic perspective that enables him to render concretely and interestingly the feelings and experiences of an abstract principle. As a kind of literary alchemist, he realizes that his hero is not an inanimate metal but one that possesses a distinctly human nature, spirit, and personality. Nor does Jonson allow his description to dissipate into a cloud of meaningless alchemical jargon, for the "vexed" terminology with which it begins quickly gives way to homely and concrete salts, vinegars, oysters, and cucumbers. As this long speech continues, we also come to see that Mercury's punishments are spiritual and psychological as well as physical.

Sendivogius's *Dialogue* contains several descriptions of Mercury's persecution that might easily have provided sources for corresponding passages in the masque. Although generally they tend to be less colorful and flamboyant than Jonson's, many of the same terms for materials and processes are used. The first example occurs just after the Alchymist, recognizing the volatility of his victim, begins to work upon him with renewed effort: "Hee began now to work upon Mercury boldly, he learned afterwards to sublime it, and to calcine it divers ways, as with Salt, Sulphur, and Metalls, Mineralls, Bloud, Haire, Corrosive waters, Herbs, Urine, Vineger, but could find nothing for his purpose" (*Dialogue,* 61). The number of duplicated, specialized terms that appear in this passage and in the passage from Jonson is sufficient to suggest the possibility of direct borrowing. "Salt," "Sulphur," and "Vineger" appear in both, and "sublime it" and "Corrosive waters" in Sendivogius are paired off with "sublimed" and "corroded" in Jonson.

Two passages occurring slightly later in the *Dialogue* contain parallels that are both general and quite specific. In the first, Mercury recalls the confusion and torment that he has suffered under the Alchymist: "O my Master, hee hath done many evill things to mee, for hee hath mixed mee, poor wretch as I am, with things contrary to mee: from whence I shall never bee able to recover my strength, and I am almost dead, for I am tormented almost unto death" (*Dialogue,* 64). A few lines later, Sendivogius's narrator relates that now the Alchymist "began to sublime Mercury, distil, calcine, make Turbith of him, precipitate, and dissolve him divers wayes, and with divers waters" (*Dialogue,* 65). Further on we find Mercury posing two short rhetorical questions, "Am I not sublimed? Am I not precipitated?" (*Dialogue,* 68), which are echoed at the beginning of the last-quoted passage from Jonson ("I am their Crude, and their Sublimate; their Præcipitate, and their unctuous").

There are further parallels in the hero's portrayal that reveal each author's awareness of the complex of alchemical and mythological interpretations that stands behind his own creation. Jung's remarks on the historical changes in the conception of Mercury and the diversification of his roles illuminate Mercury's characterization in these works:

> Something . . . happened to the classical *paut* of the Greco-Roman or Babylonian gods in the post-classical age, when the gods were degraded to demons and retired partly to the distant stars and partly to the metals inside the earth. It then transpired that Hermes or Mercurius possessed a double nature, being a chthonic god of revelation and also the spirit of quicksilver, for which reason he was represented as a hermaphrodite. As the planet Mercury, he is nearest to the sun, hence he is pre-eminently related to gold. But, as quicksilver, he dissolves the gold and extinguishes its sunlike brilliance. All through the Middle Ages he was the object of much puzzled speculation on the part of the natural philosophers: sometimes he was a ministering and helpful spirit, a πάρεδρος (literally "assistant, comrade") or *familiaris;* and sometimes the *servus* or *cervus fugitivus* (the fugitive slave or stag), an elusive, deceptive, teasing goblin who drove the alchemists to despair and had many of his attributes in common with the devil.[67]

Both the *Dialogue* and *Mercury Vindicated* present Mercury as the *servus* or *cervus fugitivus* and also the *familiaris.* Although the threats and punishments of the foolish alchemist of the *Dialogue* might seem to mark him as the superior force, he is utterly helpless without the cooperation of Mercury. Ironically, he is unable to realize that Mercury cannot help him because his pride and arrogance (as seen in his constant boast that he is a "philosopher") have blinded him to his own ignorance. As a result, the alchemist wastes vast amounts of time and money; furthermore, he falls victim to "false visions" that declare to him that Mercury can be fixed through conjuration. The alchemist rationalizes his acceptance of this advice by saying that he has often seen Mercury "painted with Serpents . . . so it must bee conjured as the Serpents" (*Dialogue*, 62), an association based on the serpent-entwined staff or caduceus vital to his iconography in both mythology and alchemy. Mercury's laughter and ironic responses in a number of subsequent scenes illustrate well his role as the *servus fugitivus*. The following passage, for example, shows Sendivogius's skillful use of the dialogue technique to emphasize the "teasing" nature of Mercury and the credulity of the alchemist:

> [*Alch.*] . . . thou wicked beast Mercury, &c. At which words Mercury began to laugh, and to speak unto him saying, What wilt thou have, that thou thus troublest mee my Master Alchymist? *Alch.* O ho, now thou callest me Master, when I touch thee to the quick, now I have found where thy bridle is, wait a little, and by and by thou shalt sing my song, and he began to speak to him, as it were angerly, Art thou that Mercury of Philosophers? *Merc.* (as if he were afraid answered) I am Mercury, my Master. *Alch.* Why therefore wilt not thou obey mee? and why could not I fix thee? *Merc.* O my noble Master, I beseech thee pardon mee, wretch that I am, I did not know that thou wast so great a Philosopher. *Alch.* Didst not thou perceive this by my operations, seeing I proceeded so Philosophically with thee? *Merc.* So it is, my noble Master, although I would hide my selfe, yet I see I cannot from so honourable a Master as thou art. [*Dialogue*, 63]

Mercury's mockery of the alchemist runs consistently through the *Dialogue* and additional examples could be cited, but brief attention must also be given to other qualities that characterize Mercury in his role as *servus fugitivus*. Keeping in mind Jung's description, we see that Sendivogius's Mercury is associated with the devil and has the ability to vanish and change his shape. We have already noted that he "vapoured away" shortly after the alchemist begins his work; slightly later we are told that Mercury "vanished away" as a result of being combined with unclean "mixtures," i.e., dung; and in a related passage Mercury states: "Thou sowest mee in dung, and in time of harvest I do vanish away, and thou art wont to reap dung" (*Dialogue*, 67). His protean talent for shape-shifting is also a cause of vexation to the alchemist: "O ho, it [the torture] doth not hurt thee, . . . although thou turnest thy self inside out, yet thou dost not change thy selfe, thou dost but frame to thy selfe a new shape" (*Dialogue*, 68). Finally, the diabolical aspects of Mercury—closely related to these other powers—are manifest in the following bit of dialogue: "*Alch.* O thou art but a devill, and wilt seduce mee. *Merc.* Truly my Philosopher thou art a devill to mee, not I to thee: for thou dost deale most sordidly with mee, after a devillish manner. *Alch.* O what doe I hear? this certainly is a devill indeed" (*Dialogue*, 66). Here the wordplay on "devil" aptly summarizes the qualities that both Jonson's Mercury and his alchemist find in their opponent, providing another link with the demonic conception of alchemy present in literature from the time of Chaucer on. In *The Alchemist* the connection between alchemy and the demonic is indirect but no less clear: for Ananias, Subtle "beares / The visible marke of the *Beast*" and the philosopher's stone is a "worke of darknesse" (3.1.7-9); for Tribulation, the Devil's very devilishness results from the alchemical environment in which he lives: "What makes the Devill so devillish, I would aske you, / *Sathan*, our common enemie, but his being / Perpetually about the fire, and boyling / *Brimstone*, and *arsnike?*" (3.1.24-27).

Mercury's primary role in both the dialogue and the masque is that of the *servus fugitivus;* he is derived from the "cunning trickster" archetype of classical mythology: the sly baby of the *Homeric Hymn to Hermes* who steals Apollo's cattle on the day of his birth, or the crafty slayer of Argus in book 1 of the *Metamorphoses.* But Sendivogius also places him in the subordinate role of the *familiaris,* the "ministering and helpful spirit." If we were to trace this role back to classical myth, we would find there Hermes as the swift and dependable messenger of Zeus or as the faithful conductor of the souls of the dead to their abode in the underworld. Sendivogius acknowledges this side of Mercury in the latter's reply to the alchemist's charges that he has been inconstant: "Dost thou say, that I am inconstant, I resolve thee thus, I am constant unto a constant Artificer; fixed to him, that is of a fixed mind, but thou, and such as thou art, are inconstant, running from one thing unto another, from one matter unto another" (*Dialogue,* 67). His steadfastness is also shown in his statement that "Whatsoever is with mee I love as a friend; and whatsoever is brought forth with mee, to that I give nourishment, and whatsoever is naked, I cover with my wings" (*Dialogue,* 69). There is even the suggestion that through Mercury's assistance the alchemist has received specific material benefits: "By vertue of me thou hast milk, flesh, bloud, butter, oyl, water, and which of all the metalls, or mineral can do that which I do alone?" (*Dialogue,* 68). In *Mercury Vindicated,* the hero's first long speech (ll. 30-109) reveals that much of his psychic suffering results from the fact that his many gifts to the alchemist and his "smoaky familie" have been received with ingratitude, to say nothing of cruel torture.

Jonson's Mercury is also both the *servus fugitivus* and the *familiaris,* but owing to the difference in genre these roles are at times presented otherwise than in Sendivogius. How better could one demonstrate his teasing elusiveness and volatility than to have him *"run once or twice about the roome"* as Jonson does in the stage directions at lines 27-28, just prior to his first speech? At its conclusion, Jonson again relies on dramatic action to reveal these qualities as well as Mercury's warfare with alchemy. Here, in the performance of the first antimasque, he arranges to have *"a troupe of threedbare* Alchymists" dance *"about* Mercury *with varietie of changes, whilst he defends himselfe with his* Caducæus" (ll. 110-11, 115-16). But Mercury's role as *servus fugitivus* is also conveyed through speech. Seeing the troupe arriving just before the antimasque begins, he cries out for the protection of King James: "See, they begin to muster againe, and draw their forces out against me! The *Genius* of the place defend me! You that are both the *Sol* and the *Iupiter* of this sphære, *Mercury* invokes your maiesty against the sooty Tribe here; for in your favour onely, I growe recover'd and warme" (ll. 104-9). The "*troupe of threedbare* Alchymists" that comprises this first group of antimasquers furthers the masque's thematic design by representing, through contrast, the tawdriness of Art's claims in the face of Nature's bounty and royal munificence. In contrast to the universal, life-giving "warmth" and light of Sol and the power and protection of Jupiter—the cosmic attributes of King James, the "*Genius* of the place"—the "sooty Tribe" represents an art whose powers are trivial, dark, and mean, capable of producing only the abortive "*imperfect creatures*" who perform the second antimasque. Thus the masque's complimentary function depends on the identification, by means of planetary imagery, of King James with Nature and Mercury (Nature's son) and the subsequent triumph of Nature over Art, as embodied in Vulcan and alchemy.

Mercury's role as the *familiaris* is most prominent in the two long speeches that constitute the central portion of the masque. In this section Jonson's castigation of alchemy and alchemists is extremely severe, and for the first time we see its corruption spreading into society. This attack is pointed enough to lead one to suspect that in 1615-16 court and palace were suffering from an infestation of alchemy or a similarly noxious form of corruption, which the masque was attempting to purge; Vulcan's laboratory is, after all, located in the lower regions of Whitehall, the scene of the masque's performance. However, in the absence of specific evidence that this was the case, the sharpness of satire might well be an appeal to James's known contempt for, and fear of, witches and the occult arts.[68] On the other hand, Jonson, especially with Sendivogius's *Dialogue* in mind and the writing of *The Alchemist* behind him, was well equipped to write an alchemical masque with ease and on short notice.

What is clear is that in this portion of the masque, the attack on alchemy is inseparable from a withering critique of the effects of materialism and commercialization on the manners of court and society. Because of his importance in the alchemical process and hence in the production of gold, Mercury must assume some of the responsibility for the ruin that results from materialistic preoccupations. In a passage that is remarkably similar to ones from Sendivogius last quoted (*Dialogue*, 68, 69), Jonson's Mercury recounts the "benefits" he has brought to the alchemists: "I am their turne-spit indeed: They eate or smell no rost-meate but in my name. I am their bill of credit still, that passes for their victuals and house-roome. It is through mee, they ha' got this corner o' the Court to coozen in, where they sharke for a hungry diet below staires, and cheat upon your under-Officers, promising mountaines for their meat, and all upon *Mercuries* security" (ll. 65-72). Jonson's mention of the "corner o' the Court" and the "hungry diet below staires" serves to remind us of the full title of the masque: *Mercury Vindicated from the Alchemists at Court*. The corrupting power of alchemy is such that even Whitehall, the scene of the masque's first performance, has become infected. The lowliest employees are victimized by false dreams of wealth and power. In this world of deception, "a poore *Page* o'the Larder" is made to believe that he will possess an alchemical medicine that will cure all ills. A "child o' the Scullery" who steals coals for the alchemists' furnaces is promised a bit of the philosopher's stone in return. Even members of the court guard have illusions of prolonging their lives indefinitely through a magical elixir. And all of this, Mercury takes pains to tell us, is only what is taking place "below the staires" (ll. 91-92).

In much of the balance of this speech Jonson turns his attention to the scene that exists "above the stairs," having Mercury address directly the courtly audience in attendance. For this group, the alchemists' promises of a plenitude of "beauty . . . health, Riches, Honours," are nothing. Rather, their promises are aimed (as is Jonson's humorous satire) at the corruption of the manners of this society:

> They [the alchemists] will calcine you a grave matron (as it might bee a mother o' the maides) and spring up a yong virgin, out of her ashes, as fresh as a *Phoenix:* Lay you an old Courtier o' the coales like a sausedge, or a bloat-herring, and after they ha' broil'd him enough, blow a soule into him with a paire of bellowes, till hee start up into his galliard, that was made when *Mounsieur* was here. They professe familiarly to melt down all the old sinners o' the suburbes once in halfe a yeere, into fresh gamesters againe. Get all the crack'd maiden-heads, and cast 'hem into new Ingots, halfe the wenches o' the towne are *Alchymie.* [ll. 94-104]

While the poor servants who lived downstairs are attacked for their corrupt and unrealistic mercenary aspirations, the aristocrats residing "upstairs" are chided for their pretensions and hypocrisy: aging and decrepit courtiers of both sexes become, by means of this perverse art of societal transformation, younger but idle and licentious versions of themselves. Their confidence in the restorative and life-extending powers of an alchemical elixir are as unrealistic as Sir Epicure Mammon's dream that the possessor of this "perfect *ruby*" can "confer honour, love, respect, long life, / . . . safety, valure: yea, and victorie, To whom he will" (2.1.48-52). The representation of the masque's courtly audience is not a flattering one. Jonson's manner of conceiving this scene demonstrates his brilliant talent for combining the subject of alchemy with satire. In constructing a microcosm that is being devastated by the charlatanism and deception of Art—the falseness and artificiality induced by all forms of materialism and pretension, and epitomized by alchemy—Jonson is, of course, echoing Chaucer, Barclay, Erasmus, and many other alchemical satirists who dealt with its social implications. I do not discount the influence of this tradition on Jonson's general design. However, I would point again to passages from Sendivogius that might very easily have provided Jonson with the inspiration for placing *Mercury Vindicated* in a courtly setting.

As we have seen, Sendivogius's foolish alchemist suffers most from pride that blinds him to his own ignorance; in his mind, he is not an alchemist but a "philosopher." Sendivogius plays at length on the irony stemming from this confusion, as does Jonson.[69] But to a great extent the pride of Sendivogius's alchemist also results from having practiced his art at court, a small but crucial detail that argues strongly that Jonson drew on the earlier *Dialogue*. In replying to one of Mercury's wry comments, the Alchemist states: "Thou speakest to mee as to some simple man, perhaps thou dost not know that I have worked with Princes, and was accounted a Philosopher with them" (*Dialogue,* 64). And the connection between alchemy and the court (and between the *Dialogue* and *Mercury Vindicated*) is made even more apparent in the following exchange: "*Merc.* Thou art very blind, for thou canst not see thy selfe, how then canst thou see mee? *Alch.* O now thou art proud, I speak civilly to thee, and thou contemnest mee: thou dost not know perhaps that I have worked with many Princes, and was esteemed as a Philosopher amongst them. *Merc.* Fools flock to Princes Courts, for there they are honoured, and fare better then others. Wast thou also at the Court?" (*Dialogue,* 66)

Jonson's social and political satire necessarily had to be less direct, but the ideas conveyed in Mercury's second long speech (especially ll. 139-72) are strikingly similar to this section of the *Dialogue*. It is as if Jonson were here making a list (and later illustrating it through performance of the second antimasque) of Sendivogius's "Fools [that] flock to Princes Courts." Returning to the Art-Nature controversy, Jonson, through Mercury, attacks the arrogance of those who believe they can produce creations that rival those of the sun and Nature in excellence and perfection. Near at hand are men of the court, "not common or ordinary creatures, but of rarity and excellence, such as the times wanted, and the *Age* had a speciall deale of neede of" (ll. 140-42). Among these proud and hypocritical fools is the Kastril-like "master of the *Duel,* a carrier of the differencies," whose ingredients are presented, as Duncan has noted,[70] in the form of an alchemical recipe. Also present are the "fencer i' the *Mathematiques*"; "the townes-cunning-man" who is also a "creature of arte"; and a "supposed secretary to the starres" given to dabbling in astrology, whose components include "iuyce of almanacks, extraction of *Ephemerides* . . . a graine of skill, and a drop of trueth" (ll. 157-59, 161-64). Generalizing the satire at the end of his speech, Mercury also finds in this alembic of society a collection of contemptible "vegetals" and minerals, such as "adders tongue, title-bane, nitre of clyents, tartar of false conveyance, *Aurum palpabile* . . . to which they added tincture of conscience, with the fæces of honesty" (ll. 166-69).

Following his denunciation, Mercury is set upon by a second antimasque group: these are Art's "*imperfect creatures*" who, wearing "*helmes of lymbecks on their heads,*" visually represent the defective society that has just been described. Consciously recalling the artificial, laboratory-produced *homunculi* of Paracelsus, they are thus the perfect embodiment of the imperfections of Art, as Jonson wishes to represent it. In addition, as the creations of the "*threedbare* Alchymists" who danced the first antimasque, they provide an element of continuity in the central portion of the masque and also dramatize the increasing degree of fire that is to serve as the instrument of the "slanderer's" torture (ll. 176-79). At a comparable point in the *Dialogue,* the alchemist also calls for a more severe degree of thermal punishment: "Wife, bring hither the hogs dung, I will handle that Mercury some new wayes, untill hee tell mee how the Philosophers Stone is to bee made of him" (*Dialogue,* 71).

The transformation scenes of both works contain further parallels in action, characterization, and dialogue that are remarkably close. In the *Dialogue,* Mercury's mother, Nature, enters to castigate the alchemist for the cruel treatment of her son and for his ignorance of her ways: "What dost thou with my son, thou fool thou? Why dost thou thus injure him? Why dost thou torment him? who is willing to doe thee any good, if thou couldst understand so much" (*Dialogue,* 71). In the masque, the scene is "*changed to a glorious bowre,*" in which Nature, Prometheus, and the twelve masquers are placed. As a means of emphasizing the theme, Prometheus, the traditional personification of Art, is positioned at the feet of Nature (l. 197), whose lovely song, "How yong and fresh am I to night," includes her plea to "wise *Prometheus*" to help her assert her superiority, to prove that Nature is "no stepdame, but a mother." Numbered among her children will be Mercury, whose final speech, delivered just before the transformation, continues to integrate attack on alchemy with courtly compliment: Vulcan's shameful "creatures more imperfect, then the very flies and insects" are commanded to disappear in anticipation of the coming "Sunne" and Nature: "Vanish with thy insolence, thou and thy Imposters, and all mention of you melt, before the Maiesty of this light, whose *Mercury* henceforth I professe to be, and never againe the *Philosophers.* Vanish, I say, that all who have but their senses, may see and judge the difference betweene thy ridiculous monsters, and his absolute features" (ll. 189-95).

Comparable to this speech is one Sendivogius's Nature addresses to the Alchymist, in which she carefully draws the (for him) difficult distinction between an "alchemist" and a true "philosopher": "O fool ful of pride, the dung of Philosophers, I know all Philosophers, and wise men, and I love them, for they love me, and doe all things for me at my pleasure, and whither I cannot goe they help me. But you Alchymists, of whose order thou also art one, without my knowledg, and consent, doe all things contrary unto me; wherefore it falls out contrary to your expectation. You think that you deal with my sons rationally, but you perfect nothing" (*Dialogue,* 71). Sendivogius's distinction between the ignorant "Alchymist" and the knowledgeable "Philosopher" is, we see, his chief means of clarifying the relationship that should obtain between Art and Nature. The task of Art is to *assist* Nature, helping her in places "whither [she] cannot goe." For Jonson, Nature is inherently superior to Art, as is evident from Prometheus's reclining position at the beginning of the transformation scene; nonetheless, Art's assistance is important if rendered rationally and in accordance with Nature's principles. Without these qualities, the Alchymist can "perfect" nothing; like Chaucer's Yeoman, his experimentation is destined to lack a conclusion.

In *Mercury Vindicated,* Nature's song "How yong and fresh" appears to go some distance in recognizing Art's role in the "perfection" of Nature, yet this acknowledgement stops well short of the relationship delineated by Sendivogius. Jonson's Nature refers to the "Art" figure, Prometheus, as "wise" (l. 205), capable of helping reveal that her twelve "sonnes" are "creatures of the Sunne" (l. 206), and that she, herself, is "no stepdame, but a mother" (l. 209).[71] Beyond this, however, Jonson's employment of the Art-Nature motif in this song is channeled into powerful, yet graceful and witty, compliment, a purpose more important than, but related to, the conflict between Nature and Art. King James is the source of illumination that makes night seem day and the "Maker" in whose presence the twelve masquers stand; deriving their courtly existence—even their brotherly relationship—from him, they are truly "creatures of the Sunne." The number of these "sonnes," their kinship to the "Sun"/"Maker" James, and their movement around him, all serve to represent the masquers as the months of the year or signs of the zodiac. In this way, their presence serves to heighten and universalize the courtly compliment. But it is probable that Jonson also intended the scene to attain a higher level of representation and flattery. The number of "sonnes" recalls that of Christ's disciples, thus deepening our response to Mercury's portrayal throughout the masque as the suffering martyr undergoing a "variety of torment," even to death. Moreover, we have noted that in addition to physical torture, Mercury's psychic suffering stems in large part from the ingratitude of those whom he has helped, the alchemist himself and his "smoaky familie." In the end, however, Jonson's Mercury/Christ has escaped the permanent "fixation" of crucifixion and death and is now vindicated—in a sense, resurrected to triumph over his persecutors. The masque is an enactment of the Passion of both Mercury and Christ, with both of whom James is identified, and we can be quite certain that the dates of its first two performances, January 1 and 6, 1616—the Feasts of the Circumcision and the Epiphany—were chosen to strengthen this identification. Thus, the strategy of praise that Jonson adopts in *Mercury Vindicated* is far more serious than might be thought if the masque is read in the same comic context as *The Alchemist.*

Nature's appeal to Prometheus to show his "winding wayes and artes" is for amatory and complimentary purposes, dissolving into a witty conceit on his stealing of fire "from Ladies eyes and hearts" (l. 215). In this way, Jonson preserves Prometheus's reputation and respectability without suggesting that he is Nature's competitor; in fact, their sharing, with the Chorus, in the final songs that accompany the dances (ll. 225ff.) implies a harmonious resolution resulting from the acknowledgement of Nature's superiority: "PRO. *Nature* is motions mother, as she is your's. / CHO. The spring, whence order flowes, that all directs, / And knits the causes with th'effects" (ll. 242-44).

For all practical purposes, the serious discussion and interplay among Mercury, the alchemist, and Nature end, in both works, with the last pair of passages quoted. These may also be used to point out their one important thematic difference. In *Mercury Vindicated,* the alchemists are banished forever; Mercury announces his future allegiance to King James and Nature only, and alchemy is flatly equated with imposture. Jonson refuses to consider the art and its practitioners in any other way. However, as an alchemist himself, Sendivogius is naturally unwilling to go to this extreme. For this reason he has his Nature draw the distinction between the foolish and ignorant "alchemist," who is rightfully banished, and the true alchemical "philosophers" and "wise men," who are placed under her benevolent patronage. By her own admission they have the knowledge to help her "whither [she] cannot goe." Sendivogius is thus in full agreement with Michael Maier's familiar *Emblema 42* on the necessity of the alchemist's following of Nature: *In Chymicis versanti Natura, Ratio, Experientia & lectio, sint Dux, scipio, perspicilia & lampas* (fig. 19).[72]

On the basis of these many similarities in form, theme, character and action, language, and descriptive detail, I would argue that it is extremely likely that Jonson knew Sendivogius's *Dialogue* and used it as his direct source. In this work, Jonson found a fully drawn model that was to serve him extremely well in realizing the primary objectives and overall design of his masque. It provided, first of all, a pattern for a fanciful and humorous fictive treatment of the themes of Nature versus Art and the Decay of Nature that had recently been explored in such works as *The Winter's Tale* and Donne's *First Anniversary. An Anatomy of the World.* Inherent in Sendivogius's treatment of these themes was, of course, a heavy admixture of satire at the expense of alchemical charlatanism, a subject for which Jonson needed no model. Finally, the *Dialogue* suggested, but did not develop, the idea of a courtly setting for the practice of alchemy, and from this, in combination with the earlier themes, there followed the masque's encompassing design of courtly compliment. Given this inheritance from a likely source, Jonson's greatest challenge was undoubtedly the problem of how to evoke courtly compliment from materials that were traditionally allied more to satire than the idealizing mode of the masque.[73] His solution involved, first of all, recognition and utilization of many of the important oppositions that were implicit in the philosophical and alchemical materials at hand: e.g., Art/Nature, Vulcan/Mercury, alchemist/philosopher, ignorance/knowledge, fools/princes, torture/liberation, deformity/perfection, *Alchymists workehouse/glorious bowre,* Prometheus/charlatan, and the devil/Christ. After establishing these antitheses, Jonson needed only to relate King James to the "honorific" side of the dichotomy as it was crystallized in the transformation scene with its triumph of Nature and Mercury over Art and Vulcan. Having thus positioned James, having represented him as the "Maiesty of this light" who transforms the sooty laboratory into the "*glorious bowre,*" royal compliment and flattery could only result in denigration of Art, alchemy, and all of the objects of Jonson's satire.

Whether Jonson actually drew upon Sendivogius's *Dialogue* and, if he did,

EMBLEMA **XLII.** *De secretis Naturæ.*

In Chymicis verſanti Natura, Ratio, Experientia & lectio,
  ſint Dux, ſcipio, perſpicilia & lampas.

EPIGRAMMA XLII.

DUx Natura tibi, túque arte pediſſequus illi
    Eſto lubens, errás, ni comes ipſa viæ eſt.
Det ratio ſcipionis opem, Experientia firmet
    Lumina, quò poſſit cernere poſta procul.
Lectio ſit lampas tenebris dilucida, rerum
    Verborúmque ſtrues providus ut caveas.

Figure 19. Alchemist following Nature. Michael Maier, *Atalanta fugiens* (1617).
By permission of the University of Delaware Library, Newark, Delaware.

whether it was in the manner I have suggested, will perhaps never be positively determined. Nonetheless, *Mercury Vindicated,* like the "recapitulative" *Alchemist,* reveals an intimate knowledge of the theoretical and practical aspects of alchemy and of its disciples and their victims that was assuredly derived from sources within its written tradition. But Jonson's use of alchemy amounts to much more than the accurate recording of arcane terms drawn from obscure treatises. The key to the success of his alchemical drama lies in his possession of the vision of the adepts. Through his informed imagination he could see, concretely and vividly, the operations within the glass, and through his literary genius he could impart what he saw to his audience.

VI

"A TRUE RELIGIOUS ALCHIMY"

The Poetry of Donne and Herbert

And wee in us finde the'Eagle and the dove.
The Phoenix ridle hath more wit
By us, we two being one, are it.
So, to one neutrall thing both sexes fit.
Wee dye and rise the same, and prove
Mysterious by this love.
—John Donne, "The Canonization"[1]

And (like a good Husband-man with Corn) Sow the pure grain of Gold (not common Gold) in its pure Mercurial virgin Mother *Earth* (not common Earth) but a white Crude, Golden Water or Essence, brought to them by the help of Eagles, or else by the mediation of the Doves; . . . And so the Masculine and Feminine, or ☉. ☽. & ☿ being in perfect health, and in their prime and Sperme, as one thing, willingly embrace, and joyn to spiritualize themselves into a Sprout, or living Seed, to grow up to the highest degree of the power, energy, and virtue of ☽. and Gold, and of the spiritual Stone of Philosophers, and to do whatsoever else the Philosophers have need of.
—William Cooper, *The Philosophical Epitaph*[2]

The year 1633, which saw publication of the collected *Poems* of John Donne and George Herbert's *The Temple,* marks a turning point in this study of alchemy in literature of the Middle Ages and early modern period. As heirs to a tradition of popular literature that had, during the course of more than two of its most brilliant and formative centuries, drawn often on alchemical subject matter and ideas, it is only natural to expect Donne and Herbert to be aware of its literary potential. And owing to the fact that these borrowings—from the time of Chaucer on—had been primarily for the purpose of humor and satire, we would likewise expect such conventional uses to be evident in their works. While the poetry of Donne and Herbert fulfills both of these expectations, it is most important in this study for pointing new directions in alchemy's literary use, providing further evidence of its richness and versatility as a source of poetic subject matter and modes of expression.

154

In the poetry of Donne and Herbert, the once nearly monolithic tradition of alchemically inspired satire is broken and replaced by the appearance of alchemy in a multitude of new forms, images, and uses. Although, as I will show in chapter 9, later instances of alchemical satire do appear in the works of Samuel Butler and other writers, it is not with the concentrated force or frequency that we find in Jonson and his predecessors. Donne, in particular, marks this point of transition; although alchemical references are common in his poetry, many of the most interesting are not satirical in function. While nonsatirical uses of alchemy have been noted in writers discussed earlier, as in the imagery of Davies' *Nosce Teipsum* and certain of Shakespeare's sonnets and plays, these uses are exceptional. In both Donne and Herbert nonsatirical uses outweigh those that are satirical in nature, pointing the direction to be followed in the alchemical imagery of Milton and Vaughan, to be discussed in chapter 8.

Although Donne and Herbert are aware of the rich legacy of alchemical satire and often draw upon it, for them alchemy rarely becomes merely a formula for producing an automatic, predetermined response of mirth, scorn, or amusement. Rather, both poets tend to use alchemy with an understanding of its full range of denotations, connotations, and associational nuances as well as its potential in meeting the intellectual, spiritual, and imagistic demands of the new metaphysical poetry that they were creating.

Generally in metaphysical poetry the alchemical image operates in a way something like the following. It is placed in a poem in such a way that only its root meaning of *change and transformation* and its *energizing potential* are initially present and visible; that is, rid of its narrowly satiric conventional associations, it is at first emotionally and intellectually "neutral"—rarely imparting to its context a "meaning" or emotional coloration of its own. Although seemingly dormant, its potential vitality and energy can be channeled in a number of different directions, wherever the poetic situation calls for the idea of change and transformation: e.g., the dawning of the emotion of powerful love, the transforming power of God's grace, or the devastating effects of human loss. Within the same poem this core of meaning may, in fact, be released in several directions, sometimes simultaneously, more often in a close chronological progression. Typically, then, as it functions within a given poem, the alchemical image moves from a state of potentiality to one of actuality, the state of being or actuality that it finally achieves being dependent upon the poem's total emotional and intellectual content as well as its structure. The principal difference between this type of alchemical image and the conventional satirical one is that the former subordinates and defers its implicit transformative meaning and its energy to the larger demands of the work in which it appears, whereas the latter tends to color its immediate context or the entire work with the satiric associations of charlatanism, folly, self-deception, and penuriousness, as we have amply seen in previous chapters.

The metaphysical image's subordination to the whole and its constant malleability and adaptability serve to determine the form it finally achieves. But as the image develops, it imparts its own richness, complexity, and diversity of meaning to the whole in such a way that the direction of the poem itself is shaped by the image's growth and "extension." Thus, the relationship between the two—vehicle and tenor—is organic and symbiotic. The fusion or contiguity of the two produce, as is the case with other varieties of "metaphysical" imagery, the tension and energy for which this poetry is notable. In this way, alchemical imagery is particularly well suited to the complex wit of metaphysical poetry. At times, as in "The Sunne Rising" and "Loves Alchymie," its function is conventionally satirical; more often, however, it is a metaphor for change, growth, transformation, and spiritual regeneration.

Before examining many of the works in which Donne uses alchemy, with some attention to the genres in which they are found, I should note that I am little concerned with possible sources of Donne's alchemical ideas or with analogues to his work contained in alchemical authors. Among these the influence of Paracelsus is especially important, as has been shown in a number of earlier studies.[3] Similarly, I am not interested in assessing the extent to which Donne actually believed in alchemy and other aspects of the "old" and "new" philosophies;[4] rather, I am concerned with the multiplicity of alchemical ideas that appear in his poetry and the ways in which he uses them. The diversity of Donne's uses of alchemy and the adaptability of this body of knowledge to the demands of a variety of poetic contexts and genres can be demonstrated by examining a number of poems that fall into each of the following categories: (1) poems treating alchemy satirically; (2) poems that reveal alchemical ideas about the nature, attributes, and production of gold; (3) poems that make reference to the types of equipment, materials, and procedures that alchemists used in their experiments; and (4) poems especially concerned with transmutation and the making of elixirs and philosophers' stones.[5] These categories should not be regarded as mutually exclusive.

Poems in which Donne uses alchemy in the manner of the traditional literary satirists are scattered within the *The Songs and Sonets,* the *Elegies,* and the *Divine Poems.* In the first group, the familiar reference at the beginning of the third stanza of "The Sunne Rising" is especially interesting and effectively placed: "She is all States, and all Princes, I, / Nothing else is. / Princes doe but play us; compar'd to this, / All honor's mimique; All wealth alchimie" (ll. 21-24). As in several of Donne's major love poems, "The Sunne Rising" depends heavily on the developing contrast between the "we-ness" of the speaker and his beloved (probably Ann More) and the "otherness" of all else: on the discrepancy between the genuinely noble and the tawdrily artificial and mundane, e.g., the temporally bound activities of tardy schoolboys, shopkeepers' apprentices, and royal huntsmen. The speaker argues—although with some bitterness and a lack of conviction perhaps borne of Donne's own insecurities about his future—that through the intensity of their love, he and his lover have been able to establish their own superior, private world, isolated from such trivial ambitions and intrusions.[6] Indeed, the transforming power of their love is so great that, hyperbolically, they become the real world, in contrast to which the honor and wealth of the shadowy, impermanent one is "mimique" and "alchimie." "Alchimie" in this case, then, obviously functions as a restrictive and exclusionary term of disparagement, delimiting *all* that is false, deceptive, and of little value from the one true reality, the couple loving "all alike" (l. 9) within their bedchamber.

Although "Loves Alchymie," a palinode that reflects, perhaps, a male, coterie audience,[7] assumes an attitude toward romantic experience that is precisely opposite that of "The Sunne Rising," the effect and meaning of their alchemical images are nearly identical. Here the speaker's cynicism concerning women's intellectual faculties and the coarseness of his treatment of sexual experience are conveyed, initially, through his combining of alchemy and the historically related art of mining. In lines 1-6 the speaker's bitterly reductive view of love is introduced through the association of lovers with miners: his own "deep digging" in "loves Myne" (the female genitals, as Shawcross suggests[8]), however, has produced only the painful realization that to expect to find a "centrique happinesse" in love is an illusion. The search for it is futile, an "imposture." In the next six lines, his disillusionment is further intensified by means of alchemical simile:

> And as no chymique yet th'Elixar got,
>   But glorifies his pregnant pot,
>   If by the way to him befall
> Some odoriferous thing, or medicinall,
>   So, lovers dreame a rich and long delight,
>   But get a winter-seeming summers night. [ll. 7-12]

Into the first four lines of this quotation Donne compresses several familiar ideas from the satirical tradition: the flat denial that any alchemist has ever obtained the "Elixar," i.e., the *elixir vitae*, which could miraculously cure all ills, prolong life indefinitely, and transmute base metals; the womb-like vessel, which in the eyes of the ever-hopeful operator is worthy of praise when it accidentally produces anything, no matter how trivial;[9] even the noxious odors of the happily accepted substitute product and its medicinal associations are included. And it is this impression of manifest squalor and delusion that is directly applied to the case of the lovers' "winter-seeming summers night," an image that recalls descriptions of false alchemical hopes arising from diseased imaginations previously noted in the *Praise of Folly* and Bacon's *De Augmentis*. Thus the meaning of "Alchymie" in the poem's title is precisely the same as in "The Sunne Rising."

These two examples reveal Donne's skillful, although entirely conventional, use of alchemy for satirical purposes. This is not to say that his aim is to satirize alchemy itself, but rather to employ the art's traditional associations of deception and falseness in attacking a romantic view of love and sexual experience in

"Loves Alchymy" and, on the other hand, to defy the claims of politics and materialism and assert the transcendence of love and romantic experience in "The Sunne Rising." Thus in Donne, the nearly formulaic use of alchemy of earlier periods is already beginning to break down.

Three additional poems that combine satiric references with those intended for newer, more original purposes are "The Bracelet," "The Comparison," and "The Crosse." In the first of these, Donne's wit plays with dazzling ingenuity on the subject of the lost bracelet and the "twelve righteous Angels" ("good" coins) that must be surrendered by the speaker so they can be melted down and recast to fashion a new ornament. Adopting an even harsher anti-romantic attitude than "Loves Alchymie"—the monetary value of the bracelet is the *only* reason for mourning its loss—the speaker states that he would mourn less if the gold coins he is to give up were of the debased currencies of France or Spain, or were constituted of

> such gold as that wherewithall
> Almighty *Chimiques* from each minerall,
> Having by subtle fire a soule out-pull'd;
> Are dirtely and desperately gull'd:
> I would not spit to quench the fire they'are in,
> For, they are guilty of much hainous Sin. [ll. 43-48]

Yet even as he speaks contemptuously of "alchemists' gold," of the squalor and self-deception that mark attempts to produce it, and of alchemists' deserved damnation, the elegy incorporates other more positive—or at least neutral—references to alchemy and allied topics. For example, this quotation also mentions one of the underlying theories of alchemy that has been noted in Chaucer and his contemporaries: each mineral or metal contains a "soul" that can be extracted by fire, and this soul, e.g., "sophic" mercury or "sophic" sulphur, can, in the projection stage, be combined with the philosopher's stone to effect metallic transmutation. A related image appears in a salacious context in another early elegy, "The Comparison," although there the attitude toward alchemy is less skeptical than in "The Bracelet." The inviting sexuality of the speaker's mistress is vivified (and contrasted, in lines 39-42, with the scalding, disease-ridden genitalia of his rival's mistress) by means of a simile based on the idea of *conjunctio*. The action of the chemist's "masculine" fire upon the *prima materia* ("earths worthlesse durt") within the feminine "Lymbecks warme wombe" inspires production of something precious: "Then like the Chymicks masculine equall fire, / Which in the Lymbecks warme wombe doth inspire / Into th'earths worthlesse durt a soule of gold, / Such cherishing heat her best lov'd part doth hold" (ll. 35-38).

Returning to "The Bracelet," we find in later lines several images that have their basis in such "neutral" topics as the physical properties of gold or the powers it was thought to possess, but which Donne effectively adapts to the satiric and comic requirements of the poem. Lines 69-70, "Thou say'st (alas) the gold doth still remaine, / Though it be chang'd, and put into a chaine," allude to the incorruptibility of gold and the impossibility of changing its essence even though its outward form is altered. In lines 93-94 Donne bases an image on the heaviness of gold, punning on it effectively to intensify his bitterness against the finder of the lost bracelet: "Gold being the heaviest metal amongst all, / May my most heavy curse upon thee fall." Finally, in addressing the finder of the bracelet in the last four lines of the poem, he puns wittily on two medicinal properties of gold: "But, I forgive; repent thee honest man: / Gold is Restorative, restore it then: / Or if with it thou beest loath to'depart, / Because 'tis cordiall, would twere at thy heart" (ll. 111-14). The "restorative" properties of gold, he argues, require that the finder return the bracelet to him. However, the introduction of "cordiall" and the idea of "cordiality" in the final line are more problematical: gold is a cordial because of its capacity to affect the heart positively in several ways, as a medicinal preparation, through its monetary value, beauty, etc.—all reasons for the finder's reluctance to part with the jewelry. While gold is "cordial" or "of the heart" in this sense, Donne's concluding phrase, "would twere *at* thy heart" (emphasis mine), has sinister overtones, suggesting, perhaps, the desired death of the finder through the well-known toxicity of gold.[10]

A similar combination of images that both incorporates alchemy as a means of satire and refers to the curative powers of some of its by-products occurs in "The Crosse," a poem that criticizes, according to Grierson, "the aversion of the Puritan to the sign of the cross used in baptism."[11] This poem is a witty attack on religious dogmatism, particularly on those who attempt to obliterate all manifestations of the symbol in religious art and ritual. The futility of such action results from the ubiquitousness of the cross in nature and the life of man: "Who can deny mee power, and liberty / To stretch mine armes, and mine owne Crosse to be? / Swimme, and at every stroake, thou art thy Crosse, / The Mast and yard make one, where seas do tosse" (ll. 17-20). Donne's wit then leaps from these concrete symbols of the cross, which are "good physicke" in that they call to mind Christ's sacrifice, to "crosses" that are spiritually efficacious; the rest of the poem treats the role of affliction in the life of the Christian:

> Materiall Crosses then, good physicke bee,
> And yet spirituall have chiefe dignity.
> These for extracted chimique medicine serve,
> And cure much better, and as well preserve;
> Then are you your own physicke, or need none,
> When Still'd, or purg'd by tribulation. [ll. 25-30]

Like Paracelsian medicines that have superior potency because they are derived from preservative substances by chemical extraction, Donne's spiritual crosses have great salutary effect: these adversities of the spirit, internal to the sinner and "[di]Still'd, . . . by tribulation," enable the sinner to provide his own source of healing, his own "physicke" or "Crucifixe." In a final image derived from alchemy, Donne employs the common charge that alchemists were involved in counterfeiting ("as oft Alchimists doe coyners prove," l. 37) to illustrate the idea that spiritual pride may spring from self-abnegation. Thus, the poem punningly continues, "Crosse / Your joy in crosses, else, 'tis double losse" (ll. 41-42).

The alchemical images contained in these six poems are largely satirical in intent although, as we have seen, in several Donne widens considerably the associations of the art to include its processes, the attributes of gold, and connections with medicine. Furthermore, in none of the poems is the main theme or subject even remotely related to alchemy, but in each the images drawn from some aspect of the art have been used to enhance, intensify, and clarify the meaning and total experience of the poem.

A more original contribution to poetic alchemy is Donne's cultivation of a non-satirical mode in which alchemy, purged of its negative associations, becomes a basis for metaphor in representing a great variety of generally positive qualities and characteristics. This diversification increasingly characterizes literary alchemy in the seventeenth century, and its early stages can be traced through examination of a number of brief references present in the *Verse Letters* written to several of his friends and patrons.

"To Sr. *Henry Wotton*" ("Sir, more then kisses, letters mingle Soules;") is addressed to Donne's courtier-friend on the subject of impediments to one's moral independence and development, in particular the ways in which "Countries, Courts, [and] Towns are Rockes, or Remoraes" (l. 8) threatening personal integrity on the voyage of life.[12] Following vivid analysis of the types of corruption posed by each environment, Donne admonishes his friend to cling to his independence: "Be thou thine owne home, and in thy selfe dwell; / . . . . / Bee thine owne Palace, or the world's thy gaile" (ll. 47, 52). He then invokes contemporary medical controversy to point the way in which one's honesty and integrity can be retained: "Onely'in this one thing, be no Galenist. To make / Courts hot ambitions wholesome, do not take / A dramme of Countries dulnesse; do not adde / Correctives, but as chymiques, purge the bad" (ll. 59-62). Following the teachings of the Paracelsian "chymiques" in line 62, Donne encourages his friend to purge the corrupting influences of all three environments. He is not to imitate the method of the Galenists who attempt to reclaim health by administering a dose of the medicine that stands contrarious to the condition causing the "illness," i.e., he should not counteract the "hot ambitions" of courtly life with an antidote of "country dulness." Although this poem may not be the earliest poetic evidence of the Paracelsian-Galenist controversy in Elizabethan England, its date, c. 1597-98, marks it as one of the earliest and shows Donne as sympathetic toward the Swiss alchemist's position.

In "*H.W. in Hiber. belligeranti,*" another poem addressed to Sir Henry Wotton, then fighting with Essex in the Irish campaign of 1599,[13] Donne draws a concise, but vivid, picture of a confusing array of laboratory vessels and tubing to evoke the devious and potentially corrupting influences of "schools and courts" on his friend's life (see fig. 20, with its great range of alembics, "pelicans," and other equipment for distillation): "Lett not your soule (at first with graces filld / And since and thorough crooked lymbecks, stild / In many schooles and courts, which quicken it,) / It self unto the Irish negligence submit" (ll. 13-16). At the same time, "stild" and "quicken" indicate the transformation that is taking place within this alembic and thus the refining and invigorating effect of these institutions on the natural graces of the recipient's soul. But as seen in the final four lines, the letter is less a bit of moral instruction to Wotton than a remonstrance for his failure to maintain correspondence with Donne.

Donne obviously saw alchemy as a usefully varied source of imagery in the *Verse Letters,* one responsive to their diverse situations, contents, and moods. In a third poem addressed to Wotton, "To Sir *H.W.* at his going Ambassador to *Venice,*" dating from July 1604 when Wotton was knighted by King James and he set sail for his diplomatic post, Donne draws upon the related art of the goldsmith to mark Wotton's emergence into the active life: "'Tis therefore well

Figure 20. Alchemical Laboratory (16th century?). By permission of the Wellcome Institute Library, London.

your spirits now are plac'd / In their last Furnace, in activity; / Which fits them (Schooles and Courts and warres o'rpast) / To touch and test in any best degree" (ll. 29-32). The imagery of this stanza is the final stage in a progression of alchemical images that we have traced in the three verse letters to Wotton. Throughout, Donne has used alchemy to analyze and chart the growth and development of his courtier friend: through the morally dubious environments of country, city and court; to the enlivening effects of court and school; and, finally, to his emergence into the active life as a diplomat in the service of James I. In alchemical terms, this development has been presented as a process of progressive refining: through purging and distilling (resulting in "quickening"), which are now to be followed by his final testing in the "Furnace" of "activity." As the goldsmith assays gold, Wotton's "metal" will be subjected "To touch and test" though experience. Whether consciously or unconsciously employed on Donne's part, alchemical imagery thus provides a powerful link among three letters to the same courtier-friend, written over a period of six or seven years.

Alchemical imagery or that derived from closely related fields also plays an important role in the series of poems that Donne addressed to his famous patroness, Lucy Russell, the Countess of Bedford.[14] Arthur Marotti has described the first of these, "*To the Countesse of* Bedford" ("Reason is our Soules left hand, Faith her right"), as a "witty complimentary act of a man aware of Lady Bedford's power to assist him socially, politically, and economically."[15] But it is also an occasion for an excess of flattery of the most high-flown sort: the Countess is expressly deified (l. 2) and approachable only through the dual means to theological knowledge, reason and faith. Her courtiers are "Saints," "whom your election glorifies" (ll. 9-10); she is "The first good Angell, since the worlds frame stood, / That ever did in womans shape appeare" (ll. 31-32) and "Gods masterpeece" (l. 33). In contrast to this vein, Donne's incorporation of Paracelsian ideas in explaining the role of her heredity and beauty appears modestly restrained: "In every thing there naturally growes / A *Balsamum* to keepe it fresh, and new, / If 'twere not injur'd by extrinsique blowes; / Your birth and beauty are this Balme in you" (ll. 21-24). While Paracelsus's notion of an inherent life-preserving force or *"Balsamum"* is effective in presenting her external features, making her courtly appearance "fresh, and new," it is the deeper stamp of her character—her learning, religion, and virtue—that constitutes an antidote against evil, a "methridate" that "Keepes off, or cures what can be done or said" (ll. 27-28).[16] Donne's accurate use of terms derived from contemporary medical practice, especially that of the Paracelsian camp, provides at once a much-needed tonal corrective to a surfeit of tasteless hyperbole and a means of distinguishing between the superficial and more enduring features of the frivolous and manipulative countess.[17]

A second *Verse Letter* to the countess ("Honour is so sublime perfection") is more successful as a poem and interesting in its use of alchemy. In the first nine lines, alchemical imagery is brought to bear on the question of the nature of courtly praise and the relationship between the giver of praise and its recipient. Donne's theme, that honor exists only in an environment in which there are those to bestow and receive it and that praise has its origin in the lower social classes and ascends to the superior, is, in fact, vividly expressed through the vehicle of alchemical purification:

> Honour is so sublime perfection,
> And so refinde; that when God was alone
> And creaturelesse at first, himselfe had none;
>
> But as of the'elements, these which wee tread,
> Produce all things with which wee'are joy'd or fed,
> And, those are barren both above our head:
>
> So from low persons doth all honour flow;
> Kings, whom they would have honour'd, to us show,
> And but *direct* our honour, not *bestow*. [ll. 1-9]

That honor is the most rarefied of courtly sentiments is announced at the outset: this "perfection" is produced by the processes of sublimation and refining, from which it derives its purity. Further, honor's human contingency is shown in that before the sixth day of creation, God was without honor since there were as yet no creatures to bestow it. With the nature of honor established, Donne proceeds, in the next three stanzas, to shift the setting from heaven to earth and the actors from God and the "creatures" to patroness and suitor. The shift itself is accomplished largely through the clear, almost Herbertian simile in the second stanza, with its distinction between the "barren" elements, fire and air, and the (to man) more "serviceable" water and earth. Having set forth his argument and structure so carefully, Donne needs only to state explicitly the particular, courtly application of his theme in the third stanza ("So from low persons doth all honour flow"), and, in the fourth, summarize the content thus far by means of a return to imagery derived from alchemical distillation: "For when from herbs the pure part must be wonne / From grosse, by Stilling, this is better done / By despis'd dung, then by the fire of Sunne" (ll. 10-12). With the suitor's subservient utility ("despis'd dung") established through reference to alchemy's reliance on "lowly dung" as an agent of gentle warmth—as opposed to the extreme "fire of [the] Sunne"—Donne may then proceed to praise the countess in a manner that is more typically learned, hyperbolic, and complex. It is a style highly appropriate, as Mauer has argued, "to prescribe as well as praise this delicate balance between '*Beeing* and *seeming*' (l. 32) in the Countess."[18]

Donne's employment of alchemical images as instruments for defining and analyzing honor, praise, self, and the courtier's relationship to the court and his patroness continues in brief but critical references in three additional verse letters to Lucy, Countess of Bedford. In "Madame, / You have refin'd mee, and to worthyest things," the speaker acknowledges that he has undergone "refinement" through his suits to the countess; she has assumed the role of alchemist, he the base metal, and one consequence of her practice is a change in his perception and valuation of "worthyest things," such as "Vertue, Art, Beauty, [and] Fortune" (ll. 1-2). Formerly, the speaker had judged their worth according to an absolute scale determined by their intrinsic "nature" (l. 3). Now, as a result of his experience with the court and countess, he sees that "Rareness, or use, not nature value brings; / And such, as they are circumstanc'd, they bee" (ll. 3-4). Absolutes have given way to relativism and, as David Aers and Gunther Kress have stated, "*Now* he sees that value is the product of contingent social relationships. Already there may be hints, clarified later in the poem, that value, being generated by rareness or use, is an aspect of market transactions. Even seemingly transcendent, platonic forms, Vertue, Art, Beauty, 'worthyest things' indeed, get their worth in this way. . . . But before his 'refinement' he had assumed, in good idealist (platonic or stoic) fashion that value transcended the contingent placings of social practice; he had assumed that value was a reflection of the object or person's intrinsic nature, that, in his own words, 'nature value brings.'"[19] The fact that in this "two world" model the court decidedly belongs to the "real" one and not the ideal allows for several possible interpretations. On the one hand, the existence of a court "which is not vertues clime" (l. 7) enables Donne easily to heighten the countess's brilliance and worthiness against this darker background (stanzas 3 and 4); his own role as the countess's courtier-poet, the singer of her praises to a "fallen" court, is simultaneously elevated: "For, as darke texts need notes: there some must bee / To usher vertue, and say, *This is shee*" (ll. 11-12). On the other hand, the poem's opening stanzas are rich in possibilities for irony and subtle criticism: if Lucy is included among the "worthyest things," then she too must be valued on a relative scale and not an absolute one, as things are "circumstanc'd," not as "nature value brings." Her worth is all the more ambiguous because of her importance in the circle of the court, which, as we have seen, "is not vertues clime." Within this world of contingency, Donne's actual (or desired) service as the means for praising a suspect subject before a suspect audience places his own role in an ambiguous light. He is, after all, the "creation" of her transmutative power: "Since a new world doth rise here from your light, / We your new creatures, by new recknings goe" (ll. 21-22). At the very least, the speaker recognizes that without "use" as Lucy's praiser—in a sense then as her "creator"—he will not have value. Thus employment by a patron is key to Donne's very concept of being, a concern made more urgent by his desperate financial situation in 1608/9, when the poem was probably written.[20]

The very slight alchemical allusion in "*To the Countesse of* Bedford. *On New-yeares day*" is related in both form and function to that of the preceding poem. Conjecturally dating from January 1610,[21] the poem opens with the speaker contemplating the emblematic relevance of the temporal setting to his confused state of being—the waning of the old year and the birth of the new: "Some embleme is of mee, or I of this, / Who Meteor-like, of stuffe and forme perplext,

/ Whose *what,* and *where,* in disputation is" (ll. 2-4). Donne then states, in the third stanza, that he *would* herald the virtues of the Countess to future ages, showing "What you were, and teach[ing] them to'urge towards such. / Verse embalmes vertue;'and Tombs, or Thrones of rimes, / Preserve fraile transitory fame, as much / As spice doth bodies from corrupt aires touch" (ll. 12-15). "Verse embalmes vertue" is a somewhat unusual instance of Donne's asserting the great Renaissance theme of poetry's power to perpetuate the memory of the worthy;[22] here it does not, unfortunately, apply to his own lines, for he admits that "Mine are short-liv'd" (l. 16). His explanation depends on a difficult alchemical figure:

> the tincture of your name
> Creates in them, but dissipates as fast,
> New spirits: for, strong agents with the same
> Force that doth warme and cherish, us doe wast;
> Kept hot with strong extracts, no bodies last: [ll. 16-20]

The presence of Lucy's name in Donne's poetry is regarded as a preservative, but only up to a point; like the alchemical tincture or elixir, it is a spiritual principle "whose character or quality may be infused into material things" *(OED,* 6a); or, as Milgate suggests, "The Countess's name is like the tincture made by refining gold to the highest degree, so that it has power to transform other substances to itself. It does this by changing the 'spirits' of those substances into 'new spirits.'"[23] Interpretive difficulties begin, however, with the idea that the very potency of Lucy's name in Donne's verses may eventually cause the "dissipation" of these preserving "New spirits," just as it was responsible for creating them in the first place. When such "dissipation" has reached a certain stage the death of the body, or the loss of the immortalizing capacity of the verses, will result. How may the same "tincture" act as both preserver and destroyer? Donne's answer has to do with the strength and temperature of these "agents" (l. 18). The success of alchemical experiments, it was thought, depended largely on moderate, carefully controlled fires that would provide gentle warmth for the contents of the alembics. Success was threatened by fires that were too hot as well as by materials that were too "strong" and powerful.[24] For example, George Ripley's famous and influential *Compound of Alchymy* (first published 1591) cautions the practitioner never to allow the vessel containing the experimental liquids to become too hot to touch:

> Then must thou know the measure of firing [the furnace],
> The which unknowne thy worke is lost each deele:
> Let never thy glasse be hotter than thou maist feele
> And suffer still in thy bare hand to hold.
> For feare of losing, as Philosophers have told.[25]

In "Honor is so Sublime perfection" we have noted that distillation can best be carried out with heats created "By despis'd dung, then by the fire of Sunne"; it seems probable that a similar idea stands behind his statement in the "New-yeares day" poem that bodies "Kept hot with strong extracts" do not "last." While the alchemical metaphor is, itself, reasonably clear, its precise application to the tenor of the passage remains somewhat uncertain: Donne appears to be flatter-ing the countess by saying that the disparity between his verse and the subject they enshrine (her name and person) is too great to assure their permanence. In general, the difficulties that Donne appears to have had in writing this poem may be reflected in its concluding section, where, in Marotti's words, "having reached an impasse, he switches from compliment to advice-giving, a function he does not openly undertake (since that would have been presumptuous): he pretends to 'turne to God' (33) as the source of instruction for his noble patron-ess and, through this fiction, he authoritatively instructs Lady Bedford in the last six stanzas of the poem."[26]

A final poem to the Countess of Bedford ("You that are she and you, that's double shee") from the *Epicedes and Obsequies* is at once a consolation addressed to Lady Bedford upon the death of a friend[27] and an extravagant compliment to the patroness herself. Following an image that is grounded on the fabled rich-ness of the Indies (one similar to that found in stanza 2 of "The Sunne Rising"), Donne praises his grieving patroness by comparing her character to the perfec-tion, incorruptibility, and irreducibility of gold:

> And as no fire, nor rust can spend or waste
>   One dramme of gold, but what was first shall last,
> Though it bee forc'd in water, earth, salt, aire,
>   Expans'd in infinite, none will impaire;
> So, to your selfe you may additions take,
>   But nothing can you lesse, or changed make. [ll. 35-40]

The equation of gold with perfection is based on its permanence, beauty, rarity, and economic value, as well as its traditional position in the great chain of be-ing. Occupying the highest position in the segment of the chain encompassing inanimate matter, the "King of Metals" is the most appropriate (and the only conceivable) metallic correspondent to Lady Bedford.

Donne's use of alchemical ideas and imagery as means of praising the Count-ess of Bedford extends to other noble women as well, as is seen in many ex-amples from the *Verse Letters, Epicedes and Obsequies,* and, most spectacularly, in the two *Anniversaries.* From the first of these collections, "*To the Countesse of Huntingdon*" ("Man to Gods image") effectively conflates the Astraea myth, the idea of the death of the world, and alchemical transmutation in order to cel-ebrate its subject's virtue and goodness. Building on conventional antifeminist notions of the rarity of "milde innocence" (a "seldome comet") and "active good" (a "miracle") in women (ll. 9-11), Donne moves rapidly to the myth of virtue's (Astraea's) removal to the heavens, noting, in keeping with the poem's compli-mentary purpose, that her scattered remnants are now concentrated in the "heavenly" Countess of Huntingdon: "But she's [virtue's] not stoop'd, but rais'd; exil'd by men / She fled to heaven, that's heavenly things, that's you; / She was in all men, thinly scatter'd then, / But now amass'd, contracted in a few" (ll. 21-24). The following stanza carries us into the realm of transformation and transmutation that is glimpsed in the preceding lines, making this one of the finest examples of the new uses of alchemical ideas that emerge in Donne's poetry: "She [virtue] guilded us: But you are gold, and Shee; / Us she inform'd, but transubstantiates you; / Soft dispositions which ductile bee, / Elixarlike, she makes not cleane, but new" (ll. 25-28). Virtue's powers of moral transformation, like the stone's capacity to transmute base metals, do not operate everywhere alike, the degree of renewal being dependent on the purity of the substance acted upon. Thus Donne posits that some—the implied "we" of line 25—are superficially gilded by the tincture of virtue, receiving only its surface coloration; "informed" by virtue, we take on only its appearance (*OED*, I.2). The countess, by contrast, being of the nature of "gold" to begin with, and possessing the "soft," "ductile" disposition most suited to alchemical change, has been completely "transubstantiated" into a new substance, becoming virtue itself.[28] The use of "transubstantiate" in a specifically alchemical context is rare; the *OED* lists only one such entry (dating from 1670), but there are others in *The First Anniversary. An Anatomy of the World* and "Twicknam garden." However, in the presentation of the Countess of Huntingdon, its primary theological sense reinforces its alchemical meaning perfectly. She is therefore suited to take on the role of moral guide for "baser" humanity: "By vertues beames by fame deriv'd from you, / May apt soules, and the worst may, vertue know" (ll. 15-16).

Among the *Epicedes and Obsequies,* the "*Elegie on the Lady* Marckham," while not one of Donne's most successful tributes to the dead by reason of the intricacy of its overfreighted conceits and servile flattery, contains nonetheless a striking image that combines alchemy and eschatology.[29] It thus exemplifies another distinctly innovative use of alchemical ideas that emerges early in the seventeenth century with the dissipation of the satiric tradition. Lines 21-28 read:

> As men of China,' after an ages stay,
>   Do take up Porcelane, where they buried Clay;
> So at this grave, her limbecke, which refines
>   The Diamonds, Rubies, Saphires, Pearles, and Mines,
> Of which this flesh was, her soule shall inspire
>   Flesh of such stuffe, as God, when his last fire
> Annuls this world, to recompence it, shall,
>   Make and name then, th'Elixar of this All.

As in "Resurrection, imperfect," to be considered later, the death-resurrection motif inherent in alchemical theory is central to the conceit. Here, however, Donne's daring metaphor is introduced by means of a more decorous simile based on the natural, subterranean transformation of clay into fine porcelain through the agency of time and heat. In order to demonstrate that Lady Marckham's "flesh [has been] refin'd by deaths cold hand" (l. 20), her grave is represented as an alembic, a vessel of rebirth and regeneration. And notwithstanding the preciousness of her physical remains, the process of putrefaction will ultimately yield a far more perfect substance through the operation of her exquisite soul upon the entombed flesh. It is this "Elixar" that God on Judgment Day will use to transmute all mortal bodies into heavenly ones. Lady Marckham died on May 4, 1609, and in another poem of about this period, Donne uses a related conceit.

In the "Epitaph on Himselfe. To the Countesse of Bedford," perhaps written during the serious illness of 1608 (Shawcross) or on a less serious occasion,[30] Donne once again presents the grave as a vessel of both putrefaction and generation in which we lie to "ripe[n] and mellow" (l. 12): "Parents make us earth, and soules dignifie / Us to be glasse; here to grow gold we lie" (ll. 13-14). The word "gold," like "Elixar" in the previous poem, signals the beginning of a shift from death to hope and regeneration, a movement implicit not only in the prospect of alchemical transmutation but of the natural striving of base metals to become gold in the bowels of the earth. On the moral and religious level, the putrefaction of the bodies in their graves will condition and glorify them for resurrection "when the Trumpets ayre shall them exhale" (l. 20).[31] This poem fits closely into the pattern of poems addressed to the Countess of Bedford in that, once more, Donne engages in advice-giving couched in alchemical imagery. He says, in conclusion, "Heare this, and mend thy selfe, and thou mendst me, / By making me being dead, doe good to thee, / And thinke me well compos'd, that I could now / A last-sicke houre to syllables allow" (ll. 21-24).

Although "*To* E. of D. *with six holy Sonnets*" is classified among the *Divine Poems,* it may be considered here because it takes the form of a poetic address, and its brief alchemical reference is the vehicle for a highly original and specialized form of flattery. "E. of D.," the recipient of the poem and the accompanying sonnets, is lavishly praised for his literary judgment and invention.[32] In fact, the following lines are one of few instances in which alchemical terms are applied in a purely literary context and to the creative faculties:

> I choose your judgement, which the same degree
>   Doth with her sister, your invention, hold,
> As fire these drossie Rymes to purifie,
>   Or as Elixar, to change them to gold;
> You are that Alchimist which alwaies had
>   Wit, whose one spark could make good things of bad. [ll. 9-14]

In submitting his "drossie" verses to E. of D.'s judgment for critical "purification," Donne expects that they will be transformed into gold by this poetic "Alchimist" and potential patron.[33] The transmuting agent will be the philosopher's stone ("Elixar") of the addressee's judgment and invention. Would E. of D. have been dismayed at Donne's having assigned him to the same "profession" that had long been mercilessly satirized? Would drawing this connection have placed potential patronage in jeopardy, or would it have been laughed off as a coterie joke? While these questions can never be answered with certainty, the important point, I think, is that Donne and a few of his contemporaries, like Shakespeare and Davies, were initiating a new and very different species of literary alchemy: rid of its satirical associations, their "purified" alchemy was seen as a fit vehicle for praising the likes of E. of D., the Countess of Bedford and other noble women and patronesses, and the soon-to-be dead daughter of Sir Robert Drury. Not too many years later, the youthful Abraham Cowley was to praise Charles I in similar terms:

> Where dreaming *Chimicks* is your paine and cost?
> How is your oyle, how is your labour lost?
> 　　Our *Charles*, blest *Alchymist* (though strange,
> 　　Beleeve it future times) did change
> 　　The *Iron* age of old,
> 　　Into an age of *Gold*.[34]

Scholars and critics who have dealt with alchemical and hermetic ideas in the *Anniversaries* have usually treated this topic as an aspect of the poems' varied and complex intellectual background. Because of their resemblances to, and close assimilation of, this broader background, the specialized ideas and images associated with alchemy and hermeticism are difficult, if not impossible, to separate out. For this reason, critics like Joseph Mazzeo and Eluned Crawshaw treat such representative topics as the macrocosm and microcosm and their correspondences as part and parcel of the "Elizabethan world picture"; the "hermetic" doctrines of universal magnetism and sympathies are seen as aspects of the hylozoistic view of the universe; or the preserving balm that connects all matter is identified with Paracelsian philosophy and medicine. At the same time, the work of E.H. Duncan and a number of Donne's editors has been invaluable in clarifying the meanings of specific passages and in providing sources and analogues for Donne's references.[35] Thus, between the more general and the more specific types of scholarly treatment, this important source of imagery and ideas has been covered with reasonable thoroughness.

As in the preceding discussion of alchemy in the *Epicedes and Obsequies,* my concern in the *Anniversaries* is with Donne's innovative use of this body of knowledge and its place in the tradition of literary alchemy. In neither *An Anatomy of the World* nor *Of the Progres of the Soule* does the amount of specifically alchemical content weigh heavily, although both poems are suffused with the kinds of background ideas that provide the foundation for alchemy. However, despite the relative dearth of specific references, alchemy plays a vital part in the praise of Elizabeth Drury. Thus, there are close similarities in the ways in which it is used in the *Anniversaries* and the *Verse Letters* and shorter poems of patronage recently discussed.

In *An Anatomy of the World* alchemy serves in the praise of Elizabeth Drury in two closely related ways: by contributing to the "disestimation" of the world as it is pictured following Elizabeth's death and as a vehicle of direct praise. (Because the two intentions are antithetically structured in the totality of the poem, the "dispraise" of the former will necessarily result in the praise of the latter.) This structural principle can be demonstrated, first of all, in the Paracelsian reference to Elizabeth as the preserving balm, similar to that responsible for keeping the Countess of Bedford's image "fresh, and new" in the *Verse Letter,* "Reason is our Soules left hand." Donne notes "But though it be too late to succour thee, / Sicke world, yea dead, yea putrified, since shee / Thy'intrinsique Balme, and thy preservative, / Can never be renew'd, thou never live" (ll. 55-58). Thus, the loss of the world's "intrinsique Balme" through Elizabeth's death is the cause of the world's death as well, an extension of the "languishing" effect of its earlier loss of "vitall spirits" (ll. 11-13). In this way throughout the poem, the linking of Elizabeth's death with the world's demise obviously serves to elevate her position and meaning considerably beyond that of the girl, unknown to Donne, who died in December 1610, shortly before her fifteenth birthday.

Alchemy is again employed to vivify the idea of the world's degeneration in the passage describing the decline in the physical height of its inhabitants, man's having "Contracted to an inch, who was a span" (l. 136). But, Donne adds, the fact that "We're scarse our Fathers shadowes cast at noone" could be overlooked had we retained the amount of virtue and godliness possessed by our ancestors. Such, however, is not the case:

> But this were light, did our lesse volume hold
> All the old Text; or had we chang'd to gold
> Their silver; or dispos'd into lesse glas,
> Spirits of vertue, which then scattred was.
> But 'tis not so: [ll. 147-51]

Here the doubling of alchemical images, our failure to transmute silver to gold, and our unwillingness to concentrate into the smaller vessell ("lesse glas") of our reduced height the elixir-like "Spirits of vertue"[36] reinforces man's physical and moral degeneration. Paracelsian medicine also informs a subsequent line in which recently introduced "new diseases," e.g., syphilis, have prompted "new phisicke, a worse Engin farre" (ll. 159-60): either the often lethal, chemically prepared medicines associated with Paracelsus, his "ignorant, and torturing Physitians" that Donne speaks of in *Biathanatos,* or both.[37]

Donne's loftiest praise of Elizabeth is conveyed through two striking extended conceits that draw upon nearly all of the important associations of the "purified" alchemy that was emerging early in the seventeenth century:

> She, of whom th'Auncients seem'd to prophesie,
> When they call'd vertues by the name of shee;
> She in whom vertue was so much refin'd,
> That for Allay unto so pure a minde
> Shee tooke the weaker Sex, she that could drive
> The poysonous tincture, and the stayne of *Eve,*
> Out of her thoughts, and deeds; and purifie
> All, by a true religious Alchimy;
> Shee, shee is dead; [ll. 175-83]

The starting point of this conceit's development is, of course, the identification of Elizabeth with virtue: not, however, virtue as it is conceived in the degenerate present but as it was prophesied by the "Auncients," virtuous men living in virtuous times, to be embodied at some future date. Thus, in the representation of Elizabeth as the fulfillment of this prophecy there already inheres a very high degree of virtuousness.

Alchemy is now invoked to elevate Elizabeth's purity even higher, albeit in the direction—and with the assistance—of traditional antifeminism. As the result of alchemical refinement, the purity of her virtue is such that she willed herself to take "the weaker Sex." The "economy" of her constitution (or of the universe) demanded that virtue be kept in balance or proportion, as if an excess of it would threaten or destroy decorum. In order to satisfy this requirement for proportion even in virtue *and* to redeem the female sex, she assumed womanhood. Donne adopts the metallurgical term "Allay" (l. 178) to contrast Elizabeth's purity of mind and the defects of the sex she consciously chose: according to the *OED,* it designates a mixture of base and precious metals, more specifically the intrusion of an alien substance that debases the worth of the original, purer metal. Nonetheless the purity and potency of Elizabeth, now figured forth as an elixir or philosopher's stone, is such that it can eradicate the taint of Eve's fall from her mind and action, countering Eve's "poysonous tincture" with her own salutary one. But Donne's extravagant wit carries the hyperbole one step further: the potency of Elizabeth as elixir is so great that "All [is transformed] by a true religious Alchimy" (l. 182). Thus she has become the agent for universal transformation and redemption. Not since Chaucer's description of esoteric alchemy as the art so dear to Christ (*Canon's Yeoman's Tale,* l. 1467) have we seen alchemy treated with such reverence and respect.

Elizabeth's potency as a transmuting agent is again manifest in a second image occurring near the end of the poem:

> She from whose influence all Impressions came,
> But, by Receivers impotencies, lame,
> Who, though she could not transubstantiate
> All states to gold, yet guilded every state,
> So that some Princes have some temperance; [ll. 415-19]

This point is part of Donne's larger argument that the heaven "forbeares" its influence in the microcosm (l. 378), signaling barrenness in the lower world as evidenced by the fact that the common hermetic image of the creation of the world as a dove-like hatching or infusion of a "balmy showre" now engenders only infertility (ll. 381-84). Among the many evidences of this loss of contact is the fact that natural magic, which depends on the existence of sympathies and correspondences between the macrocosm and microcosm, is now abandoned by the "Artist" (ll. 391-92). This severing of lines of communication now prevents the influence of Elizabeth, even in her death, from being felt in the lower world. In the preceding extract and following the principle of structural opposition that undergirds the poem, Donne's celebration of Elizabeth as the source of all "Impressions"—by which he means not "sensations" but positive moral impulses—is contrasted with the impotency of mankind to receive these guides and utilize them effectively. Given such severe impairment, it is little wonder that Elizabeth's restorative influence cannot "transubstantiate / All states to gold"; nonetheless it is a testimony to her transmuting power that she can at least "guild" or bring some appearance of morality to "every state." Here the word "transubstantiate" draws together the same theological, alchemical, and moral meanings that are present in the verse letter "*To the Countesse of Huntingdon*" (ll. 25-26). Later in the poem, Elizabeth's purifying effect is extended even to poetry in that her "name refines course lines, and makes prose song" (l. 446), somewhat in the manner of the refining wit of "*To E. of D. with six holy Sonnets.*"

In *Of the Progres of the Soule: The Second Anniversary* Donne again uses both alchemical and nonalchemical allusions to gold to draw the connection between Elizabeth Drury and the idea of perfection.[38] Early in the poem he employs a very conventional image based on the golden age of classical literature, of which Elizabeth becomes the emblem: "Shee, to whom all this world was but a stage, / Where all sat harkning how her youthfull age / Should be emploid, because in all, shee did, / Some Figure of the Golden times, was hid" (ll. 67-70). Since *The Second Anniversary* is concerned with extolling the spiritual nature of the dead girl as well as her physical beauty and virtuous character, Donne is faced with a problem of achieving the proper balance in his praise of these dual aspects. If "in all, shee did," she recalled "Some Figure of the Golden times," then how does one proceed in expressing the perfection of her soul? That Donne was not wholly successful in solving this problem of decorum was first observed in the celebrated remark by Ben Jonson, who told William Drummond: "that Dones Anniversarie was profane and full of Blasphemies[;] that he told Mr Donne, if it had been written of ye Virgin Marie it had been something to which he answered that he described the Idea of a Woman and not as she was."[39] One of Donne's solutions involves the use of an alchemical image, the only true example of this type in the entire poem. In lines 241-43 he writes: "Shee, of whose soule, if we may say, t'was Gold, / Her body was th'Electrum, and did hold / Many degrees of that." In likening Elizabeth's soul to gold and her body to an

"Electrum," Donne again demonstrates his familiarity with alchemical terminology. According to Paracelsus, "electrum" is, for some, a synonym for gold or an alloy of silver and gold. In Paracelsus's own writings it is often a compound of the seven metals "mixed together, and united in the fire." In this sense it "conjoin[s] and link[s] together all the virtues of the seven metals. . . . Its efficacy, power, and operations, moreover, shew themselves to be much greater, even supernaturally so, than exist in a latent form grafted by Nature on metals in their rude condition."[40] Donne's use of the word "electrum" to describe Elizabeth Drury's body follows Paracelsus closely. It is an alloy that falls between crude ore and refined metal, "neither wholly perfect nor altogether imperfect."[41] It does not possess the perfection and nobility of gold, just as Elizabeth's body does not possess the perfection and nobility of her soul. Yet for Donne the proportion of "gold" contained in the girl's body was assuredly higher than in those of ordinary mortals.

It has been the purpose of this section of the chapter to discuss the new and diverse nonsatirical uses to which alchemy is put in poems drawn primarily from the *Verse Letters* and the *Epicedes and Obsequies.* Before turning to several additional poems from the *Songs and Sonnets* and *Divine Poems,* I wish to consider one additional conceit that links Donne's alchemy with one of the few nonsatirical images present in earlier authors and in at least two of his successors. The idea that nature strives to produce gold in the bowels of the earth but succeeds in doing so only occasionally and with the sun's help is given literary expression in Donne's epithalamium "*Ecclogue. 1613. December* 26," where it suggests the animating and transforming power of royal favor when it is focused upon common man: "The earth doth in her inward bowels hold / Stuffe well dispos'd, and which would faine be gold, / But never shall, except it chance to lye, / So upward, that heaven gild it with his eye;" (ll. 61-64). As noted earlier, the familiar alchemical doctrine that informs this image is given extensive and original treatment in Dekker's *A Strange Horse-Race,* leading to the corollary that art is an improver of nature. Donne's image also recalls the "golden face" and gilding powers of the sun in Shakespeare's "Sonnet 33" and *King John,* 3.1.77-80, and points as well to related images in poems by Marvell and Milton. In "Eyes and Tears," for example, Marvell's argument that all states of mind and varieties of experience—joy, beauty, laughter—are reducible to weeping is buttressed by the idea that the sun's powers of "chemical" distillation yield a uniform "Essence," and the circularity implicit in the process of distillation is effectively developed in the idea of the "extracted" vapor being returned to earth in the form of showers: "So the all-seeing Sun each day / Distills the World with Chymick Ray; / But finds the Essence only Showers, / Which straight in pity back he powers"[42] (ll. 21-24). Similarly, for Milton in *Paradise Lost,* 3:606-12, a portion of a complex alchemical passage that will be discussed further in chapter 8, the brilliance of the sun's surface is intensified through the narrator's reflection upon the sun's extraordinarily powerful effects upon the distant earth:

> What wonder then if fields and regions here
> Breathe forth *Elixir* pure, and Rivers run
> Potable Gold, when with one virtuous touch
> Th' Arch-chemic Sun so far from us remote
> Produces with Terrestrial Humor mixt
> Here in the dark so many precious things
> Of color glorious and effect so rare?[43]

In each of these passages the sun plays the alchemist, and the effects of its macrocosmic transmutation are manifest in different ways: in Donne, through the baser metals' subterranean progress toward gold; in Marvell, through the continuous circulation of water on and above the earth; and in Milton, through the beauty and goodness of the earth and the production of precious gems and metals beneath its surface. Clearly, the new metaphoric uses for alchemy that were being discovered in the seventeenth century extended to poetic description of natural phenomena, even as the New Science was rejecting the foundations upon which this vocabulary was based.

Among the poems of the *Songs and Sonnets,* two of Donne's most complex and original uses of alchemical themes and symbols occur in "The Canonization" and "A nocturnall upon S. Lucies day, Being the shortest day." Both poems treat strikingly different aspects and manifestations of love and, in each, alchemical terms and ideas are used to sharpen and intensify the moods of the speakers and to clarify their contrasting romantic experiences and attitudes toward love. The use of alchemy in the third stanza of "The Canonization" is particularly subtle and elusive:

> Call us what you will, wee'are made such by love;
>   Call her one, mee another flye,
> We'are Tapers too, and at our owne cost die,
>   And wee in us finde the'Eagle and the dove.
>   The Phoenix ridle hath more wit
>   By us, we two being one, are it.
> So, to one neutrall thing both sexes fit.
>   Wee dye and rise the same, and prove
>   Mysterious by this love. [ll. 19-27]

Very likely Donne is here drawing on alchemical materials, quite possibly on illustrations from its rich visual tradition. As several critics and editors have observed,[44] in contrast to all other stanzas in the poem, the third has a strong emblematic quality that sets it apart in tone and content from both the exasperated speaker's defense of his love affair in stanzas 1 and 2 and the quiet, conciliatory tone of the last two. It marks a transition between the speaker's shrill protest against the encroachment of the affairs of the world on his love and the peace with the world that follows canonization. Thus, it occupies a pivotal position; in it the speaker must demonstrate to the auditor and the reader why he should be left alone with his love, and looking toward the final stanzas, he must also show why he and his mistress are worthy of canonization.

Citing numerous imagistic parallels from Petrarchan and Neoplatonic tradition, Donald Guss has shown convincingly that the general progression of meaning in the third stanza is from death to life, moving "to a glorious statement of love's mysteries, establishing the ground for the final conceit of the poem, the lovers' canonization."[45] My reading of stanza 3 and the entire poem is similar to Guss's; however, it is derived primarily through an alchemical interpretation of several of the symbols and images that are most crucial to Guss's "Petrarchan" analysis. This death-resurrection pattern is reinforced by the structural division of the stanza into three parts of four, three, and two lines each, my division differing slightly from Guss's as a result of his following the 1633 text, which places a comma after "dove" in line 22 rather than a period. (This period marks the end of the first part.) As if conceding the charge of his interlocutor concerning the ruinous effects of this love affair, the speaker's imagery in the first four lines is strongly suggestive of lechery and self-consumption ("flye," "Tapers"), death and sexual intercourse ("die" in both senses of the word).[46] Following in line 22, the summarizing "Eagle *and* the dove" (emphasis mine) reinforces these images of destruction by emphasizing the (albeit complementary) *separateness* of the lovers.

In contrast, the second part (ll. 23-25) suggests harmony, reconciliation, and regeneration, the key words being "Phoenix," "we two being one," and "neutrall thing." Lines 26-27, which conclude the stanza, serve again to summarize and emphasize both the contrast and the relationship between the two groups of images: "Wee dye and rise the same, and prove / Mysterious by this love." If an alchemical metaphor were applied to the stanza's structure it might be said to move from the death or *putrefactio* stage to the *exaltatio* stage in which the elixir or philosopher's stone is actually produced. But the one most crucial to the meaning is the intermediate *conjunctio*.

The alchemical interpretation of the stanza rests entirely on the symbolic meanings of the three birds—eagle, dove, and phoenix—and their interaction. Edgar Duncan's reluctance to pinpoint the body of knowledge that serves as background to this passage stems from his inability to find any sources—either in the bestiary or alchemical traditions—that link all three symbolic birds. He does, however, cite a passage from Paracelsus that combines eagle and phoenix and suggests the death-regeneration theme in a manner quite parallel to Donne.[47]

Considered separately, the three birds are among the most common symbols in alchemical literature and pictorial art and are often, as here, used to represent substances and stages in the alchemical process. The dove has an unusually large number of meanings: it is sometimes referred to as the "'salt [i.e., body] of the metals;'"[48] it is often associated with whiteness and is said to be female in sex, as in Grasseus's *Arca arcani* where it is personified as "'the chaste, wise, and rich Queen of Sheba, veiled in white, who was willing to give herself to none but King Solomon.'"[49] In a number of alchemical illustrations it represents the spirit escaping from the heating metals,[50] and it is also one of the most common symbols for mercury.[51]

The iconography of the eagle is equally diverse, and at times we find that its meanings overlap those of the dove. It, too, can stand for the mercurial spirit;[52] but more often than the dove, it is masculine in sex or even hermaphroditic.[53] However, it is unnecessary to try to establish which of these specifically alchemical meanings, if any, Donne had in mind when he made reference to the "Eagle and the dove." From the variety of alchemical significations presented and from the context of the poem itself, it seems certain that he intended them as two independent, sexually differentiated bodies that are joined, as in the alchemical conjunction of opposites. This merging, which entails the loss of the lovers' individual identities, thus embodies a new unified perfection, analagous to what Donne in "The Extasie" sees as the evolution of a single "abler soule" through love's "interinanimat[ion]" of the two separate souls of the lovers (ll. 41-44). As Stella Revard has stated, "The point is that union annihilates the differences between war and peace, male and female, for love makes the two, now become one, indistinguishable in feeling and being."[54]

We have seen that alchemists commonly depicted the interaction of the opposing principles involved in making the philosopher's stone as a form of coition that brought death to the individual partners but birth to the product of their union. In figure 21, for example, an illustration of the *conjunctio* from the *Rosarium Philosophorum* (1550), the crowned subterranean lovers are accompanied by symbolic representations of sulphur and quicksilver. Or again, alchemical "death" is vividly represented by the entombed king and queen in an engraving from Mylius's *Philosophia Reformata,* published in Frankfurt in 1622 (fig. 22).[55] Often, too, the product of this conjunction is represented as a phoenix, symbolizing the final stage of the process in which the stone either appears or is projected upon baser metals in order to "multiply" them. In this respect figure 23, from Libavius's *Alchymia* (1606) is instructive: it shows the phoenix at the very top of the design (indicating its ultimacy in the process), "cremating itself" and from it, "many gold and silver birds fly out of the ashes," indicating multiplication.[56] This illustration might also provide indirect evidence of the alchemical provenance of Donne's third stanza in that it is a relatively rare instance of the presence of all three symbolic birds in a single design: the phoenix sits on its burning nest at the top of the design and from it doves or, at least, dove-like birds are released into the clouds, and "G," near the middle of the large globe and to the right, identifies a triple-headed eagle. Although not in so clear a sense as in the "Canonization," the Libavius illustration suggests a progression from the "separateness" of the eagle—here paired with the red lion at "K"—to the

CONIVNCTIO SIVE
Coitus.

① Luna durch meyn vmbgeben/vnd ſuſſe mynne/
Wirſtu ſchön/ſtarck/vnd gewaltig als ich byn.
① Sol/ du biſt vber alle liecht zu erkennen/
So bedarffſtu doch mein als der han der hennen.

Figure 21. Conjunctio. *Rosarium
Philosophorum* (1550).

Figure 22. Entombed King and Queen. Johann Mylius, *Philosophia Reformata* (1622).
By permission of the University of Delaware Library, Newark, Delaware.

Figure 23. Stages in the Alchemical
Process. Andreas Libavius, *Alchymia*
(1606). Courtesy of the National Library
of Medicine, Bethesda, Maryland.

unity and ultimacy of the phoenix. Anthropomorphically, this movement is presented through the robed and crowned alchemical king and queen who are inscribed on the globe that supports the phoenix.

When the alchemical signification of the birds is kept in mind, the following meaning emerges: if a love relationship is to be worthy of "canonization," all
inherently opposing qualities in the partners—even those that confer their individual identities—are destructive and must be removed because they prevent
the unified transcendence that is the heart of canonized love. The eagle and the
dove must give way to the phoenix.

The sense of destructive separateness to be banished if the the lovers are to
achieve this state of transcendence is reflected at line 20, which associates each
of them with a fly: "Call her one, mee another flye." In spite of the range of
meanings and connotations uncovered by A.B. Chambers, "flye" has here the
primary signification of lust, as in Lear's "the small gilded fly / Does lecher in
my sight" (4.6.112-13), and lust's destructiveness is implicit in the notion of the
fly's transiency as well as its prolific breeding. While Chambers's discovery of the
fly's hermaphroditic and resurrectable qualities may point in a cleverly Donne-

ish way to the phoenix, the phoenix's primary meanings relate to the death and destructiveness of lust and separateness, specifically emphasized in the reference to the wasting of the tapers in line 22. On the physical level, the removal of these individualizing qualities is accomplished through the "death" of sexual intercourse, the "neutrall thing both sexes fit." But implicit in this stanza and those that follow is the idea that other individualizing attributes must also disappear. In the broadest sense, everything that accounted for their separate identities—the eagle *and* the dove—must be eradicated: "two-ness" must be replaced by "one-ness." From this death of the isolated selves a new mysterious creation arises, just as the phoenix is born out of the alchemical conjunction of opposites. This offspring is the perfectly unified love that is worthy of canonization.

The alchemical parallels to this "avian" death of self and the resulting generation of an ennobled love in stanza 3 is further clarified through the following verses from the emblematic *Book of Lambspringk*. They accompany an illustration in which two birds, representing body and spirit (fig. 24),[57] are in a state of violently amorous war with each other:

> In India there is a most pleasant wood,
> In which two birds are bound together.
> One is of a snowy white; the other is red.
> They bite each other, and one is slain
> And devoured by the other.
> Then both are changed into white doves,
> And of the Dove is born a Phoenix,
> Which has left behind blackness and foul death,
> And has regained a more glorious life.
> This power was given it by God Himself,
> That it might live eternally, and never die.
> It gives us wealth, it preserves our life,
> And with it we may work great miracles,
> As also the true Philosophers do plainly inform us.[58]

The mysterious transformation of Donne's lovers from destructive doubleness to unified transcendence has interesting parallels in this alchemical narrative of the rapturous raptors—*nobiles and magni pretii*. The two birds, symbolizing body and spirit, are initially set apart by the colors white and red, exist in a state of conflict leading to the death and ingestion of one of them, and are resurrected as a pair of doves and eventually the phoenix. In this final state, all marks of individuality and conflict have been effaced. Furthermore, the philosopher's stone, for which the phoenix stands as symbol, possesses the additional attributes of having been resurrected into glorious immortality and has the god-given powers of performing miracles and conferring wealth and immortality upon men. Thus, in likening canonized love to the alchemical phoenix, Donne is asserting that it transcends time and exists outside of history; for this reason, if the lovers' "leg-

OCTAVA FIGURA.

Figure 24. Symbolic Birds. *Book of Lambspringk,* in *Musæum Hermeticum* (1678). By permission of the University of Delaware Library, Newark, Delaware.

end" proves to be "no peece of Chronicle" (l. 31), it will be "fit for verse" and qualify them for canonization. It is this selfless, transcendent, and immortal love for which earthly lovers from "Countries, Townes, [and] Courts" will beg as a pattern for themselves.

"A nocturnall upon S. Lucies day, Being the shortest day" contains Donne's wittiest and most original adaptation of alchemical subject matter. The poem is an extravagant expression of sorrow caused by the death of a loved one (perhaps Anne More), and it is totally dominated by the voice of the grief-ridden speaker. In the "Nocturnall" Donne combines the subject of grief with the vehicle of alchemy to produce an elaborate and hyperbolic conceit that is expanded throughout most of the three central stanzas. Alchemical metaphor becomes the chief means of intensifying the grief, of showing the destructive effects of a boundless love that is fixed in mortality, and of illustrating the impact that the loss of the loved one has on the speaker.[59] For these reasons, Donne's employment of alchemical concepts is contrary to their function in "The Canonization" and the majority of poems recently considered. Rather, alchemy in "Nocturnall" most resembles its use in "Twicknam garden," in which love has produced a curious "reverse alchemy" in the speaker's life. Entering the garden in search of a Paracelsian panacea for his disappointment—"such balmes, as else cure every thing"—the speaker notes bitterly: "But O, selfe traytor, I do bring / The spider love, which transubstantiates all, / And can convert Manna to gall" (ll. 5-7). Here the alchemical "transubstantiat[ion]" wrought by the "spider love" in converting life-sustaining "Manna" to bitter "gall" is exactly opposite the positive morally and theologically charged process found in "*To the Countesse of Huntingdon*" and *The First Anniversary*. Donne's highly original use of a kind of reverse alchemy as metaphor for the debilitating effects of love in "Twicknam garden" and the "Nocturnall" is, however, not without precedent in the writings of alchemical and chemical authors.

In 1678, a brief tract entitled *[An Historical Account] of a Degradation of Gold Made by an Anti-Elixir: A Strange Chymical Narrative* (Wing 3984) was published in London. Not a serious experimental treatise by Robert Boyle, to whom it has been attributed, this rare pamphlet might more accurately be classified as a *ludibrium* (derision, mockery, or sport), a joke or "comic fiction," as exemplified by Sendivogius's *Dialogue* or as Frances Yates has described Michael Maier's *Lusus serius* and *Jocus severus*.[60] Set at a conference of virtuosi undoubtedly modeled on the Royal Society, the tract consists of a report by Pyrophilus of an experiment in which a piece of gold is debased or transmuted into a cruder metal, a bizarre instance of reverse alchemy produced by an "anti-elixir." In Pyrophilus's narrative, the experiment proceeds with all of the accuracy and objectivity associated with the Royal Society and Robert Boyle, the founder of modern chemistry, but at a crucial moment a tiny portion of reddish powder (given to Pyrophilus by a mysterious stranger) is added to the two drams of gold originally placed in the crucible. When the substance cooled, Pyrophilus reports, "I was somewhat surpriz'd to find . . . that we had not lost any thing of the weight we put in, yet in stead of *fine Gold*, we had a lump of Metal of a dirty colour, and as it were overcast with a thin coat, almost like *half vitrified Litharge*."[61] This "odd" metal is taken to a goldsmith for testing and found to be far less precious than the original gold; its specific gravity has been reduced and it resembles bell-metal or brass. There seems little doubt that a "reverse" transmutation has been effected through the use of an anti-elixir. However, no less than in a conventional projection, where base metals are transmuted into gold, Pyrophilus's experiment must be interpreted as a victory of art over nature.[62] Curiously, Boyle's alchemical jest was anticipated many years earlier in Donne's love poetry,[63] but in contrast to the long tradition of alchemical satire, both Donne and Boyle argue the negative consequences of alchemical practice by affirming the essential truth and validity of the art itself.

The temporal setting of the "Nocturnall" described in stanza 1 provides a perfect mirror of the psychological state of the speaker. It is the eve of St. Lucy's Day, December 13, commonly regarded as the shortest day of the year and, accordingly, the sun's rays are visible for only seven hours. But in addition to its being "the yeares midnight," the poem's melancholy is intensified through imagery that evokes the death of creation as well as time: "The worlds whole sap is sunke: / The generall balme th'hydroptique earth hath drunk" (ll. 5-6). And with the absorption of the "generall balme" into the earth's surface the vital force that sustains all life is fled: "shrunke, / Dead and enterr'd." Yet paradoxically this universalized picture of death and decay can only be seen by the speaker as a mockery of himself, for he is "their Epitaph" (l. 9).

Donne's indebtedness to alchemical ideas extends throughout much of the second, third, and fourth stanzas and first appears just after line 12. Addressing those whose love will bloom with the awakening of the spring to follow, the speaker implores them to study him because he can serve as a valuable object lesson in the effects of love:

> For I am every dead thing,
> In whom love wrought new Alchimie.
>   For his art did expresse
> A quintessence even from nothingnesse,
> From dull privations, and leane emptinesse:
> He ruin'd mee, and I am re-begot
> Of absence, darknesse, death; things which are not. [ll. 12- 18]

As Duncan has observed, the poem "deals altogether with the process of [the] alchemical preparation of Quintessence," that most concentrated essence of all substances in nature.[64] The potency of this process, which becomes the metaphor for conveying the effects of love upon the speaker, is seen as infinitely great. Love's new alchemical art has been able to "expresse" (i.e., extract or draw out) a "quintessence" even from something that was nothing to begin with.[65] Unlike the impure metals alchemists used as proximate materials, which possess form and substance, the speaker entered the alembic already as the personification of "nothingnesse"—mere "dull privations, and leane emptinesse" (l. 16). But from this initial, seemingly complete state of negation the "new Alchimie" of love has produced a quintessence. Like the corrupted materials of the early stages of the alchemical process, the speaker has been putrefied (i.e., "ruin'd") into a state of even greater nothingness and then resurrected ("re-begot"), but owing to the material from which he has been prepared, he emerges as the "elixir" of all nothings. For Duncan, in contrast to what was traditionally expected of an elixir, "Donne applies the terms of the figure to a situation which is the complete reverse of the alchemist's dream. Instead of the 'Elixir of All' we have here the quintessence of nothingness."[66]

This state of incredibly rarefied annihilation provides the basis for extensions of the conceit that occur at the beginning of stanzas 3 and 4:

> All others, from all things, draw all that's good,
> Life, soule, forme, spirit, whence they beeing have;
>   I, by loves limbecke, am the grave
>   Of all, that's nothing. [ll. 19-22]

and

> But I am by her death, (which word wrongs her)
> Of the first nothing, the Elixer grown; [ll. 28-29]

Existing in defiance of logic as a state of absolute negation, the speaker's only positive attribute is, perhaps, his capacity to produce an infinite regression of ever more absolute vacuity. This is the implication of "grave" in lines 21-22, in which, as in the illustrations from Mylius's *Philosophia Reformata* and the *Rosarium Philosophorum,* the place of putrefaction and death is also the place of resurrection and rebirth. However, instead of anticipations of the birth of something good from the grave/alembic, Donne's lines resonate much more with the awfulness of Lear's "Nothing will come of nothing" (1.i.90).

In the remaining lines of these stanzas the speaker reveals the means by which love has transformed him. The love that he and the woman shared so intensely resulted, at times, in weeping, in distractions by other things, and in absences from each other. As a consequence, their state occasionally *approximated* nothingness: their tears "Drownd the whole world" and presumably they, too, were victims of this flood; and at times they became "Chaosses" and even "carcasses." But as related at the beginning of stanza 4, these were only approximations of that quintessential nothingness to which he has fallen through the death of the beloved. From this event—the anachronism nothwithstanding—he has become the elixir from which was produced the "first nothing," the void that preceded the creation of the world.

In the concluding lines the speaker continues to elaborate, using nonalchemical terms, on the state of nothingness that he has become. Donne's wit plays ingeniously on the concept of an "ordinary nothing," which in the speaker's mind would be a more desirable state. But practically speaking, the reduction of self can be carried no further than it has been in the quintessence conceit. It is this that gives the poem its meaning and depth of feeling.

Among other poems in the *Songs and Sonets,*[67] the "Valediction of the booke" contains two brief allusions to alchemy. In line 13 an injunction is given to "all whom loves subliming fire invades" to study the lovers' celebrated book of "Annals" derived from their love letters, because in it will be found the "Rule and example" of love. The line in question is nonsatirical, alluding to the stage of sublimation in which matter is purified through conversion, by means of heat, from a solid to a vaporous state. In alchemy, as in Donne's line, the term suggests elevation, refinement, and rarefaction: a state, according to Ruland's *Lexicon,* of "improvement of quality and virtue, as when Sol is made out of Luna, and is called that which is elevated, that which is above on the heights."[68] In this instance the alchemical allusion has a function obviously opposite that in "Nocturnall"; love is here seen as possessing the capacity to cleanse and elevate those it works upon, not reduce them to a state of nothingness.

However, Donne is sometimes inconsistent in his attitude toward alchemy, even within a single poem. Later in the "Valediction of the booke," he satirizes the extremes to which alchemists (and, by extension, statesmen and lovers) will go to find a basis for the practice of their "arts," a foundation that is wholly chimerical: "In this thy booke, such will their nothing see, / As in the Bible some can finde out Alchimy" (ll. 53-54). Statesmen (or at least "they which can reade"), Donne is saying, will attempt to find in the lovers' "Annals" the basis of their political practice, just as alchemists at times search the Bible for the grounds of their art. Typically employing a heavy overlay of religious metaphor, symbolism, and allegory, alchemical treatises also occasionally make use of the Bible as an authority, as the following excerpt from one of Donne's sermons makes clear: "And as our Alchymists can finde their whole art and worke of Alchymy, not only in Virgil and Ovid, but in Moses and Solomon; so these men can find such a transmutation into golde, such a foundation of profit, in extorting a sense for Purgatory, or other profitable Doctrines, out of any Scripture."[69]

Ranging outside the *Songs and Sonets,* another small group of images have generally to do with the nature and properties of gold, both natural and artificial, and ways to produce it. We have already seen that in "The Bracelet," gold's heaviness and incorruptibility are alluded to. In the indecently misogynistic "Loves Progress" this list of attributes is greatly expanded. The speaker argues that love's progress will be easier and more rapid if, rather than "beginning at the face," one instead "set[s] out below" (ll. 72-73). For the speaker, women are, at best, mere sex objects, and his single-mindedness about them (we may admire their virtue, speech, and beauty, "but we love the Centrique part," l. 36) is wittily clarified and intensified by the expression of his attitude toward gold:

> preferr
> One woman first, and then one thing in her.
> I, when I value gold, may think upon
> The ductilness, the application,
> The wholsomness, the ingenuitie,
> From rust, from soil, from fire ever free:
> But if I love it, 'tis because 'tis made
> By our new nature (Use) the soul of trade. [ll. 9-16]

Donne's virtuosity is demonstrated in his introducing several positive properties of gold (malleability, versatility, salubriousness, nobility, incorruptibility, etc.)

that might, however remotely, apply to the nature of women and then undercutting the developing analogy by dismissing these similarities and substituting an entirely physical and mercenary middle term: "(Use) the soul of trade." In applying this pejorative new term to the equation, Donne succeeds in denying any possibility that romantic and idealistic qualities might be present in the speaker's attitude toward women. "Search every sphear / And firmament," Donne asserts, "our *Cupid* is not there: / He's an infernal god and under ground, / With *Pluto* dwells, where gold and fire abound" (ll. 27-30).

A number of the images in the poems examined thus far reveal Donne's familiarity with materials and equipment found in alchemists' laboratories and with the processes involved in the *opus magisterium*. At times such references are very general, and at times a note of disparagement is conveyed simply through the term selected, as in the "pregnant pot" of "Loves Alchymie." But more often Donne's references to alchemical processes and equipment are specific, accurate, and extremely vivid, as in "sublimed" and "still'd" (i.e., distilled) already quoted in passages from "Valediction of the booke" and "The Crosse." Yet the range of Donne's knowledge of practical alchemy is narrower than Chaucer's and Jonson's. In Donne, the reader is never overwhelmed with lengthy catalogues of metals, minerals, planets, spirits, and processes or with the mystifying idiom of the *ignotum per ignocius* tradition. Rather, his use of the technical vocabulary of alchemy is notable for its clarity, precision, economy, and ingenuity, which, along with his extraordinary imaginative powers, enable his rather limited stock of allusions and images to contribute disproportionately to his poetry.

Donne's most frequently used images derived from alchemical apparatus involve the physical appearance of the alembic (originally the still-head, but in later times usually referring to the still as a whole)[70] or the creative processes that take place therein.[71] As an example of the latter, the "Lymbeck's warme wombe" of the previously cited quotation from "The Comparison" powerfully and humorously suggests the fecundity of the speaker's mistress's "best lov'd part" and in so doing comments on her sexual attractiveness. But the image is also accurate in the alchemical sense: alembics, by virtue of their placement on the furnaces, constantly received varying degrees of heat and were often described anthropomorphically or in organic terms as a womb (or egg or living microcosm) in which the gestation of the philosopher's stone took place. Jung, for example, states that

> Although an instrument, [the *vas Hermetis*] nevertheless has peculiar connections with the *prima materia* as well as with the *lapis,* so it is no mere piece of apparatus. For the alchemists the vessel is something truly marvellous: a *vas mirabile.* Maria Prophetissa says that the whole secret lies in knowing about the Hermetic vessel. "*Unum est vas*" (the vessel is one) is emphasized again and again. It must be completely round, in imitation of the spherical cosmos, so that the influence of the stars may contribute to the success of the operation. It is a kind

of matrix or uterus from which the *filius philosophorum,* the miraculous stone, is to be born. Hence it is required that the vessel be not only round but egg-shaped.[72]

Donne again makes brief poetic use of the interior operations of the alembic in the twenty-seventh stanza of the "Infinitati Sacrum, 16. *Augusti* 1601." At this stage in the metempsychosis, the soul's receptacle is a dolphin-like fish whose respiratory system is cause for speculation. Donne suggests that its alembic-like lung or gill system has the capacity to "refine" water to an air-like state so that it can be inhaled (ll. 263-68). And near the end of the poem, Donne resorts— with an equally humorous effect—to the ingenious simile that he had used in "The Comparison" (ll. 35-36) to describe Eve's pregnancy that was to produce Themech, the wife of Cain: "*Adam* and *Eve* had mingled bloods, and now / Like Chimiques equall fires, her temperate wombe / Had stew'd and form'd it" (ll. 493-95).

Lines 21-26 of "Satyre III" (Religion) provide further evidence of Donne's attraction to alchemists' laboratory equipment and alembics as imagistic sources, and they are richly allusive. The speaker asks—

> Hast thou couragious fire to thaw the ice
> Of frozen North discoveries? and thrise
> Colder then Salamanders, like divine
> Children in th'oven, fires of Spaine, and the'line,
> Whose countries limbecks to our bodies bee,
> Canst thou for gaine beare?

Here Donne employs a pair of contrasts to demonstrate and satirize the extremes to which man will go to exercise his courage and assert his will in pursuit of material gain. These include contrasts in geographical location or direction ("North," "Spaine," and "the'line" [i.e., the equator]) with their related extremes in temperature or climate ("frozen," "thaw," "oven," "fires"), all of which serve to emphasize the discomfort, danger, and death that man will voluntarily face to achieve his goals. This is especially true in Spain and the equatorial countries where, as the passage is usually interpreted, the adventurer is threatened with being "roasted alive" in the alembic-like fires of the autos-da-fé of the Inquisition or succumbing to the extremely high temperatures of the tropical climate. Donne thus attacks self-motivated pursuits of the ignoble or, more in keeping with the poem's overall theme, externally imposed methods of coersion that threaten the autonomy of the religious conscience. In any case, the alembic image functions effectively to convey this sense of intense heat, destruction, and confinement.

Although the "countries limbicks" metaphor is the only positively identifiable alchemical figure, the passage likely contains a small cluster of allusions to the art, which serves to sharpen and vivify the central image of man's penchant for self-destruction in pursuit of ignoble ends. The most important of these are "Salamanders" and "divine / Children in th'oven." In alchemical symbolism, sala-

manders are closely related variants of dragons, serpents, and the *ouroboros*, the
tail-eating serpent of ancient Egyptian iconography. Within this class of creatures, the dragon is notable for its extreme antiquity and multiplicity of meaning. According to Jung, its documented past dates back to the *Codex Marcianus*
of the tenth or eleventh centuries, where it is accompanied by the caption ἕν τὸ
πᾶν (the One, the All),[73] and its tail-biting pattern traditionally symbolizes the
circularity of the alchemical process: "Time and again the alchemists reiterate
that the *opus* proceeds from the one and leads back to the one, that it is a sort of
circle like a dragon biting its own tail. For this reason the *opus* was often called
circulare (circular) or else *rota* (the wheel). Mercurius stands at the beginning
and end of the work: he is the *prima materia*, the *caput corvi*, the *nigredo;* as
dragon he devours himself and as dragon he dies, to rise again as the *lapis.*"[74]

The association of the salamander with this alchemical meaning is present
in emblem 29 of Michael Maier's *Atalanta Fugiens* (fig. 25), which bears the
motto: "Just as the Salamander, the stone lives in the fire."[75] For Meier, as for
Patrick Scot in the passage quoted in chapter 1, the salamander thus symbolizes
the philosopher's stone in that it is made by fire and is also indestructible. There
are further visual and verbal parallels in the symbolism of the salamander as set
forth in Lambsprinck's *De Lapide Philosophico Libellus* (Frankfurt, 1625).[76] In
David Person's *Varieties, or, a Surveigh of rare and excellent matters* (London, 1635),
the fifth book is entitled *Salamandra, or a short Treatise of the Philosophers Stone,*
and, finally, the link between salamanders, alembics, and their contents is confirmed in the following passage from an anonymous eighteenth-century French
manuscript: "How often did their pleasure in the wonderful discoveries I made
concerning the abstruse doctrines of the ancients move them to reveal unto my
eyes and fingers the Hermetic vessel, the salamander, the full moon and the
rising sun."[77] As the mercurial spirit, the salamander represents imperishability
and ultimately regeneration because, although like the *ouroboros* it can suffer
death through self-consumption, it is reborn in the form of the philosopher's
stone. In the context of Donne's satire, man and his desperate courage are mock-
ingly compared to this miraculous creature.

Closely related to the salamander is Donne's allusion to the "Divine / Children in th'oven." In this regard, the link established in Ruland's *Lexicon* should
be noted; the entry for "Salamandri or Saldini" begins: "Fiery Men or Spirits,
Beings sustained by the influence and nourished by the element of fire."[78] While
obviously primary reference is to the presence of Shadrach, Meshach, and
Abednego in the fiery furnace as told in the third chapter of the book of Daniel,
this story was at times given an allegorical interpretation by writers on alchemy.[79]

The relation of this story of the three Jewish youths to Donne's third satire
is unquestionably on the moral and narrative, rather than the alchemical, level.
He is not using the narrative for any symbolic or allegorical signification that
has to do with alchemy per se, but he is mocking the arrogance that causes man
to assume that he possesses the same protection from death and disaster that

EMBLEMA **XXIX.**   *De secretis Naturæ.*
Ut Salamandra vivit igne sic lapis:

EPIGRAMMA XXIX.

D *Egit in ardenti Salamandra potentior igne,*
    Nec Vulcane tuas æstimat illa minas:
Sic quoque non flammarum incendia sæva recusat,
    Qui fuit assiduo natus in igne Lapis.
Illa rigens æstus extinguit, liberáque exit,
At calet hic, similis quem calor inde juvat.

Figure 25. Salamander. Michael Maier, *Atalanta fugiens* (1617). By permission of the
University of Delaware Library, Newark, Delaware.

had preserved the Old Testament youth. Nonetheless I would point out that within three lines (23-25) Donne makes four references to alchemical tools or symbols: one ("limbecks") is unequivocal; the second ("fires") is the most necessary of aids to alchemists; the remaining two ("Salamanders" and "Children in th'oven") occur commonly enough in alchemical treatises. It is altogether possible that these lines are the product of the fusion of a number of diverse alchemical ideas in the mind of the poet, each of which conveys forcefully the impression of heat and destruction.

The death and regeneration motif that is hinted at in "Satyre III" makes it possible to regard this as a transitional poem, pointing the way to two *Divine Poems* in which images concerned with the process of transmutation, the making of elixirs, and philosopher's stones are used metaphorically to suggest regeneration, purification, or at least a crucial change in essence. In the first section of "A Litanie," entitled "The Father," the speaker implores God to "purge away / All vicious tinctures, that new fashioned / I may rise up from death, before I'am dead" (ll. 7-9). Donne contrasts this view of "tincture," as death-dealing sin that can only be assuaged through the grace of God, with an opposing view in "Resurrection, imperfect." In this poem, indebtedness to esoteric alchemy is more pronounced in that the themes of death, resurrection, and purification are conveyed through alchemical images akin to those in *The First Anniversary* and the "*Elegie on the Lady* Marckham." Furthermore, as a recent critic has noted, these images are of central importance in contrasting the order of nature with the order of grace.[80] Just as the planetary sun's role is subordinate to that of the "better" Son in "enlightening" the world, so is Christ's entombed, "minerall" state of less efficacy than his resurrected state as the "elixir":

> Whose body having walk'd on earth, and now
> Hasting to Heaven, would, that he might allow
> Himselfe unto all stations, and fill all,
> For these three daies become a minerall;
> Hee was all gold when he lay downe, but rose
> All tincture, and doth not alone dispose
> Leaden and iron wills to good, but is
> Of power to make even sinfull flesh like his. [ll. 9-16]

As "perfect man," Christ is appropriately represented as "minerall" gold during the three days' entombment. However, this mineralogical figure has unobtrusively "absorbed" into itself the earlier sun/Son conceit (ll. 1-8), to be presented at this time. For as base metals are transformed to gold through the sun's action in the subterranean region, so the power of the Son is such that even his own body is transformed from a state of gold to a more perfect and powerful "tincture" upon rising from the tomb. In these lines, "tincture" is equivalent in meaning to the elixir or philosopher's stone, a fitting metaphor to suggest the operation of the grace of the resurrected Christ upon the "Leaden and iron wills" of sinful mankind.

In contrast to the poems of Donne, those of George Herbert contain few al-chemical references and allusions, and those that are present are typically used in an uncomplex manner and with a limited number of associational meanings. As is not the case in "Canonization" and "Nocturnall," Herbert seldom invokes alchemy to bear a substantial part of the intellectual and emotional weight of his verse; unlike Donne, he shows little interest in alchemy's richness as a source of symbol and figurative language. Generally, his use of alchemy is simple and not showy, always subordinate to the larger requirements of plainness and clar-ity. Nonetheless, the poems of *The Temple*[81] require consideration in this study because they indicate an important tendency in the poetic use of alchemy in the seventeenth century. As in Donne, we find that Herbert's alchemical allusions represent a sharp break from the satiric tradition; in fact, only in "Vanitie" (I), is the reference colored by such overtones. Rather, we find that alchemical ideas and concepts are applied in ways that had rarely been attempted by writers out-side of the metaphysical tradition. Thus Herbert's alchemical poems support my argument as to the waning of the satirical vogue that occurs with the metaphysi-cal poets' rise to prominence; at the same time they demonstrate the adaptabil-ity of alchemy to diverse types of poetic subjects, themes, and genres.

"The Sinner" is an example of what is for Herbert a common poetic theme: the relative proportions of good and evil in the human heart. The speaker in this case finds that within his own there are whole "quarries of pil'd vanities, / But shreds of holinesse" (ll. 5-6). Alluding slightly to the terminology of al-chemy, he states that "In so much dregs the quintessence is small: / The spirit and good extract of my heart / Comes to about the many hundred part" (ll. 9-11). The signification of "quintessence" is defined in the context, and its mean-ing need not be restricted to alchemy. It is the disproportionately small quantity of good in his own heart, which may nonetheless—with God's help—transmute the "dregs" to a state of Christian purity.

"Easter," like Donne's "Resurrection, imperfect," relies on alchemy to con-vey Christian views of death, resurrection, and salvation. In both poems Christ is represented as the transmuting agent who, through his death, acquired the potency to purify the baser bodies that he chooses to touch:

> Rise heart; thy Lord is risen. Sing his praise
> >Without delayes,
> Who takes thee by the hand, that thou likewise
> >With him mayst rise:
> That, as his death calcined thee to dust,
> His life may make thee gold, and much more, just. [ll. 1-6]

In lines 1-5, "calcined" is effective in accounting for the "dust" or abject and hopeless state that sinful man was reduced to at the time of the crucifixion be-cause, in alchemy, calcination brings about reduction of something solid to a fine powdery state. Yet this image is somewhat flawed in that it fails to suggest a source of intense heat, on which the alchemical process necessarily depended.

The emblematic quality of the first stanza of "Whitsunday" and its mention of the dove faintly recall the third stanza of "The Canonization." Although the primary reference in Herbert's poem is to the Holy Spirit, the image of hatching, birth, and flight may owe something to the dove of alchemical iconography or emblem literature. Alchemical illustrations quite commonly depict rebirth as the hatching of an egg;[82] and at times the divine guidance that alchemists considered necessary to the success of their work appears in the form of a dove, as in the previously discussed figure 8, Robert Vaughan's engraving for Ashmole's *Theatrum Chemicum Britannicum.*[83] Such concepts may be the inspiration for the Christianized version that we find in the imagery of the following passage: "Listen sweet Dove unto my song, / And spread thy golden wings in me; / Hatching my tender heart so long, / Till it get wing, and flie away with thee" (ll. 1-4). A brief metaphor in "To all Angels and Saints" draws effectively on the familiar belief in gold as the universal medicine and applies it to Christian doctrine. Addressing the Virgin Mary, the speaker states: "Thou art the holy mine, whence came the gold, / The great restorative for all decay / In young and old;" (ll. 11-13).

An interest in herbal cures is present in "Man," which is a powerful assertion of the complexity of macrocosmic-microcosmic correspondences and belief in universal sympathies:

> Man is all symmetrie,
> Full of proportions, one limbe to another,
> And all to all the world besides:
> Each part may call the furthest, brother:
> For head with foot hath private amitie,
> And both with moons and tides.
>
> . . . .
>
> He is in little all the sphere.
> Herbs gladly cure our flesh; because that they
> Finde their acquaintance there. [ll. 13-18, 22-24]

Herbert's most specifically alchemical poem is "The Elixir," in which several of the art's central concepts are applied to spiritual regeneration: God is seen as the "famous stone," his will is the "tincture," and man is the "mean" substance upon which the tincture is projected:

> All may of thee partake:
> Nothing can be so mean,
> Which with his tincture (for thy sake)
> Will not grow bright and clean.
>
> . . . .
>
> This is the famous stone
> That turneth all to gold:

> For that which God doth touch and own
> Cannot for lesse be told. [ll. 13-16, 21-24]

The great majority of Herbert's alchemical references apply aspects of the art to Christian doctrine, particularly that of regeneration. In only one poem, "Vanitie" (I), is the treatment satiric, and here Herbert's satire is indirect because the poem's main purpose is not to attack alchemy but to expose human pride and arrogance and especially man's misapplication of his intellectual faculties. Following two stanzas that describe the acquisition of planetary knowledge by the "fleet Astronomer" and the foolhardy "nimble Diver" who risks his life to find a pearl, Herbert turns his attention to

> The subtil Chymick [who] can devest
> And strip the creature naked, till he finde
> The callow principles within their nest:
> There he imparts to them his minde,
> Admitted to their bed-chamber, before
> They appear trim and drest
> To ordinarie suitours at the doore. [ll. 15-21]

Herbert's image is based on the commonly used figure of the alchemist who, eager in his search for the principle inherent in a metal or elixir, analytically "undresses" the object of his investigation to discover its secret.[84] At the same time, however, Herbert is mocking the natural philosopher who, following the injunctions of Francis Bacon and the New Science, was increasingly concerned with the "rational" and empirical investigation of the world. No longer is it possible to accept nature at face value, or as she had appeared to the "ordinarie suitours" who once investigated her. Her secrets must now be examined and quantified in an attempt to understand her inner workings.

The ambiguity concerning the exact profession of Herbert's experimenter is interesting in other ways. Quite possibly we have here an early literary reflection of the historical passage of alchemy into chemistry; if this is the case, the distinction between the practitioners of the art and the science is nearly imperceptible. The meaning of the passage applies equally well to either. Herbert's "subtil Chymick" may belong with either the old or the new. Looking backward he belongs with a great number of "durtily and desperately gull'd" alchemists and their victims who populate English literature from the time of the Canon's Yeoman on. Looking forward, he finds his place among the "projectors" of Samuel Butler's "Satyr upon the Royal Society" and those of Lemuel Gulliver's third voyage. It would seem most likely that Herbert's alchemist-chemist is a combination of both ancient and modern.

VII

"THAT GREAT & GENERALL REFINING DAY"

Alchemy, Allegory, and Eschatology
in the Seventeenth Century

The science of alchymy I like very well, and, indeed, 'tis the philosophy of the ancients. I like it not only for the profits it brings in melting metals, in decocting, preparing, extracting, and distilling herbs, roots; I like it also for the sake of the allegory and secret signification, which is exceedingly fine, touching the resurrection of the dead at the last day. For, as in a furnace the fire extracts and separates from a substance the other portions, and carries upward the spirit, the life, the sap, the strength, while the unclean matter, the dregs, remain at the bottom, like a dead and worthless carcass; even so God, at the day of judgment, will separate all things through fire, the righteous from the ungodly. The Christians and righteous shall ascend upwards into heaven, and there live everlastingly, but the wicked and the ungodly, as the dross and filth, shall remain in hell, and there be damned.

—Martin Luther, *Table Talk*, DCCCV[1]

For the Grace of God is a blessed Alcumist, where it toucheth it makes good, and religious.

—Richard Sibbes, *A Learned Commentary* (1656)[2]

Neither the weight of a two-hundred year tradition of alchemical satire, nor Bacon's attempts to reform alchemy's experimental methods, nor the dramatic triumphs of Ben Jonson were sufficient to cause seventeenth-century writers to abandon the use of alchemical ideas and images. Similarly, the complex of scientific, religious, and social forces that gives this century its revolutionary, antiauthoritarian, "modern" character—although ostensibly antagonistic to the art's theory and practice—was unable to dispel the fond hope of alchemical success or dissipate the exotic jargon, arcane symbolism, and recondite allegory in which such aspirations were usually expressed. On the contrary, with the emergence of many new writers pursuing both new and traditional subjects and themes and engaging in new controversies, the production of alchemical treatises flourished

in the middle decades of the seventeenth century. As in the past, literary allusions continue to reflect current topics and tendencies in alchemical thought
and writing; for this reason, the context for reading many such references must
be enlarged to include the continuing hostility between Galenists and Paracelsians,
the efforts to reform university curricula to enhance the position of scientific
and, especially, chemical studies, and the profound influence of the writings of
the spiritual and philosophical alchemists with their inclinations to link alchemy
with millenarianism and religious allegory and mysticism. These are some of the
new directions that will be examined in the works of Henry Vaughan, Milton,
and Samuel Butler in chapters 8 and 9.

    Yet in spite of the fact that the most novel and interesting literary allusions
reflect such tendencies, alchemical satire of the traditional sort is occasionally
written by those who followed Donne and Jonson. It appears, for example, in
the concluding lines of Cowley's "Hope"[3] to dramatize the illusory nature of this
quality in human experience, as exemplified by the futile quests of alchemist
and lover. Hope is the

> child of fond desire
> That blow'st the chymick & the lover's fire.
> Still leading them insensibly'on
> With the strong witchcraft of Anon.
> By thee the one does changing nature through
> Her endlesse labyrinth's pursue,
> And th'other chases woman; while she goes
> More wayes & turnes then hunted nature knowes. [ll. 33-40]

Crashaw's companion poem, "Mr. Crashaws Answer for Hope," also represents
alchemy's futility but for the purpose of emphasizing the existence of true hope
in the world. In phrasing that closely parallels Cowley's, Crashaw asserts true
hope's presence even "Though the vext chymick vainly chases / His fugitive gold
through all her faces" (ll. 44-45). Brief as these references are, it is obvious that
both poets draw heavily upon traditional satirical motifs and attitudes. Similarly, Dryden concludes Aureng-Zebe's famous expression of hopelessness ("When
I consider Life, 'tis all a cheat," IV, 33-44) with a metaphor that identifies
humanity's illusory happiness with alchemical cozenage: "I'm tir'd with waiting
for this Chymic Gold, / Which fools us young, and beggars us when old."[4] Also
within this conventionally satiric mode is Marvell's early poem "Upon the Death
of Lord Hastings" (published 1649), where alchemy is again employed to intensify a feeling of hopelessness and futility: Aesculapius, the god of healing, is
brought to a state of shame and self-condemnation by Hastings's untimely death
(ll. 47-48), and the disconsolate "Mayern" (i.e., the physician Theodore de
Mayerne, whose daughter was to have married Hastings the next day), "Like
some sad chemist, . . . prepared to reap / The golden harvest, sees his glasses
leap" (ll. 49-50).[5] Marvell's choice of the word "leap" to mean burst or crack

recalls laboratory explosions that appear in satirical works from Chaucer to Jonson, and it occurs in a similar alchemical context in chapter 6 of Ashmole's edition of Norton's *Ordinall of Alchimy,* included in the *Theatrum Chemicum Britannicum.* Norton cautions that certain laboratory vessels made of clay "woll leape in Fier, / Such for Vessells doe not desire."[6]

In addition to equating the pursuit of alchemy with folly and futility, mid–seventeenth-century subscribers to satiric convention, at times, and with varying degrees of seriousness, use alchemical allusions in commenting upon varieties of sexual experience. In a didactic vein, for example, Henry King, in "Paradox. That Fruition destroys Love," argues that illicit sex ("fruition") is antithetical to long and lasting love and inimical to desire itself: "After Fruition once, what is Desire / But ashes kept warm by a dying fire?" (ll. 73-74).[7] The iatrochemical metaphor that follows likens coition to the philosopher's stone, which, if it exists at all, "still [i.e., always] miscarries at Projection" (l. 76); it continually fails to transmute into a more exalted form the baser matter upon which it is projected. Thus, ironically, the lover robs himself of the fuel "and corrupts the Spice / Which sweetens and inflames Love's sacrifice." In developing the image throughout the next four lines (77-80), King associates the burning of lust with the intensely hot eighth degree ("Heat ad Octo") of alchemists' fires; the result is that the desire to sustain love is attacked with the same force that is visited upon the body by violent fevers of a "Third [i.e., tertian] Ague."

In a very different vein, the lover in Carew's "A Rapture"—transformed temporarily into a bee—ranges over the garden-like body of his mistress in search of sweets from which to produce an erotic elixir. The description of this "panacea" unquestionably derives from the Paracelsian preoccupation with universal medicines prepared from chemicals by means of distillation: "I will all those ravisht sweets distill / Through Loves Alimbique, and with Chimmique skill / From the mixt masse, one soveraigne Balme derive, / Then bring that great *Elixir* to thy hive" (ll. 75-78).[8]

Some of the century's most successful examples of alchemically derived satire appear in writings by Samuel Butler and will be reserved for discussion in chapter 9 with other works that attack religious and philosophical enthusiasm; however, John Lacy's satirical comedy *The Dumb Lady*[9] (written 1669, acted 1672) requires brief consideration here because of its use of Paracelsian themes and ideas that were being generated in current medical controversies. This aspect of Lacy's play had been slightly anticipated much earlier in Robert Burton's Latin play, *Philosophaster* (written 1606; performed February 16, 1617, at Christ Church, Oxford), which includes brief references to Paracelsus, iatrochemistry, and urinalysis, as well as other motifs from the tradition of alchemical chicanery. Moreover, there are direct borrowings from Erasmus's dialogue, *Alchemy.*[10]

The plot of Lacy's admittedly obscure play involves attempts to "cure" the heroine, Olinda, first of her inability to speak and later her madness, both of which are feigned to prevent marriage to the inane Squire Softhead. Since her

condition has been pronounced incurable by the "professed" (i.e., officially licensed) members of the College of Physicians, other types of medical assistance
must be sought. Much of the play's humor and satire against contemporary medical practice result from the fact that Olinda's cure is finally effected by one Doctor Drench, a farrier in disguise, and Leander, a disguised apothecary who will
eventually marry the heroine. The assumption of these positions by rude mechanics provides opportunities for many thrusts at current "official" medicine.
For example, at the outset, Drench is confident of his ability to impersonate a
doctor since he once served a mountebank who taught him some "canting terms"
that should prove him "as good a physician as if I'd served an apprenticeship at
Padua" (29). (We recall that in the sixteenth and seventeenth centuries—at least
until 1640—the training of English physicians occurred much more frequently
on the Continent, especially at Padua, Bologna, Leyden, Montpellier, and Paris,
than at Oxford and Cambridge.)[11]

Lacy's play also reveals an awareness of controversies in medical theory that
had raged since the introduction of Paracelsian ideas early in the century. Like
Galenical physicians, for example, Drench at first considers prescribing herbal
medicine for Olinda: the "powder of a dried dockleaf with apothecaries' hard
name to it" (30), and his later reference to traditional "humoral" medicine suggests a similarly anti-Paracelsian position: "Then, I say, 'tis generally held at Padua,
that women, when they take physic, ought to have their potions much more
stronger than men, because physic cannot work so well upon cold and phleg-
matic bodies as upon hot and dry" (63). Sympathetic medicine, a third approach
to curing the sick, is mentioned briefly: "when any man or woman is sick in
Greenland, they always send the next of kin to the doctor; and by that pulse the
disease is known and the patient cured" (37), causing one to recall Bacon's remarks on medical theories involving sympathies and antipathies and also those
of Robert Fludd and Sir Kenelm Digby.

Aware of the leading medical and pharmacological theories that flourished
in seventeenth-century England, Lacy, above all, uses the controversy between
Galenists and Paracelsians as a source of dramatic conflict and satire. Leander,
Doctor Drench's accomplice, adopts the disguise of an "apothecary's apprentice,
or a disciple of Paracelsus" (92), who stands in opposition to the several learned
"professed" doctors who are brought in to attempt Olinda's cure. At this point,
Leander's brother, Parson Othentick,[12] identifies these properly licensed members of the profession with "strict Galen[ism]" and with a Paduan medical education (95). In contrast, he, his brother, and Doctor Drench will assume the
roles of Paracelsian "chemists."

As the research of Rattansi and Charles Webster has shown, however, the
rivalry between Galenical physicians and Paracelsian apothecaries did not stem
alone from their preferences for either herbal or chemical cures or the site of
their professional training. Social factors were also important. The increasing
population of London during the seventeenth century created a need for doc-

tors that could not be met given the stringent licensing regulations of the College of Physicians, which limited the number of its Fellows by statute.[13] The result was rising demand for the services of apothecaries, who formed their own company, the Society of Apothecaries, in 1617[14] and who illegally prescribed medical treatment in defiance of the College of Physicians. Webster notes that the incorporated apothecaries "tended to trespass into medical practice quite as much as their brother surgeons. Their effective exploitation of the newly imported drugs and plants from the New World gave them a proprietary interest in an important branch of knowledge which was at that time inadequately appreciated by the physicians."[15] In Lacy's play, this intense professional rivalry between physicians and apothecaries in the middle decades of the century is reflected in the slighting references, including the academic Latinism, to Doctor Drench made by the three learned Galenists:

> *1 Doct.* Why, ay, for if he [Dr. Drench] be a chemist, his opinion and ours must needs differ, and consequently not agree in consultation. . . .
> *1 Doct.* If he be a chemist, sir, he is, *eo nomine,* a declared enemy to the Galenical way, to all truth and learning, and a denyer of principles, and therefore not to be consulted with.
> *2 Doct.* Right, sir; *contra principia negantem non est disputandum.* He that replies but with submission to *sic dixit Galenus* is not to be looked on as a physician.
> *3 Doct.* Pardon me, gentlemen, I have known some chemical physicians learned and rational men; and, although not strict adherers to the Galenical method, proceed with great reason and good success, which, I take it, answers all we can say or do.
> *2 Doct.* I profess I think it as bad as murder to cure out of the methodical way. Oh, what satisfaction 'tis to have a patient die according to all the rules of art! [98-99]

Earlier discussion of verse satires by Joseph Hall and Burton's *Philosophaster* has revealed that English authors were aware that Paracelsus and his followers attached great importance to the use of urinalysis in diagnosing disease. But whereas Hall's persona in Satire 4, book 2, of the *Virgidemiarium* had spoken only of "spie[ing] out marvels in each Urinall," Lacy uses this Paracelsian principle to bring about the denouement of his comedy. In act 5, the search for the cause of Olinda's madness results in dispute as to whether examination of the pulse or the urine can best serve diagnostic purposes. Opinion is divided, with the physicians favoring the pulse and Doctor Drench and his assistants championing urinalysis. Adopting the Paracelsian view, Stirquilutio (really Parson Othentick, but in the guise of an apothecary's assistant) states that "the urine above the pulse gives the most manifest, certain, and general signification of all diseases, because with the blood it is conveyed into all parts of the body, and from thence returns back again in the veins to the liver and vessels of urine, and so brings some note of the state and disposition of all those parts from whence it comes" (102-3). The play concludes with the Paracelsian apothecaries duping the physicians by means of a "rigged" test of urine, in which a specimen supposedly belonging to Olinda is really that of her mother, the Nurse. According to the Nurse, the purpose of the scheme was to determine who, Drench or the physicians, was the ablest doctor, and Drench is pronounced winner (105). The romantic plot concludes with the tricking of Squire Softhead and the promised marriage of Olinda and Leander.

While Lacy's play is obviously deficient in literary and purely dramatic qualities, it marks new directions in the tradition of alchemical satire. Although it is concerned with the traditional themes of charlatanism and chicanery, these occur in a context of iatrochemistry rather than gold-making. It could not have been written or successfully staged without the public's awareness of both Paracelsian ideas and controversial issues in the contemporary practice of medicine. Thus the play serves as evidence for the view that medical applications come to supplant gold-making and magical elixirs in the endeavors of mid–seventeenth-century experimenters. Paracelsian controversy was one—but only one—of the many strains of medical, alchemical, and hermetic writing that provide a richly diverse background for the literary allusions of the period. The purpose of the remainder of this chapter is to discuss some of these background topics and to attempt to give a sense of the diversity of alchemical thought and writing during, roughly, the period between Francis Bacon and the Restoration.

Serious mid-century students of alchemy as well as the public at large were no doubt as aware of the art's dubious reputation as their counterparts in previous centuries. Writing in the *Fasciculus Chemicus* of 1650, Arthur Dee, as previously noted, laments that chemistry is "much defamed, disparaged, and brought into disgrace, by the fraudulent dealings of Imposters."[16] While freely admitting that this "infallible *Mystery*" is "open to many hard *Censures,* and profane Scandals," Elias Ashmole, translating the *Fasciculus* under the pseudonym James Hasolle, declares that the volume's purpose is "to remove, and purge this pure and heroick *Science* (almost generally contemptible) from the dross, and corruption of an *Imposture.*"[17] But while successful alchemical satire of the mid-century often derives from such conventional charges, or, as in *The Dumb Lady,* has its basis in Paracelsian ideas and contemporary medical controversy, the latter sources are also employed to produce strikingly different literary effects. In the poetry of Vaughan and Milton, for example, iatrochemical ideas as well as those originating in the multifarious forms of mystical and spiritualized alchemy are frequently invoked to serve religious ends. It is these sources that account for the most original and interesting allusions to alchemy in literature of this period.

In the *Preface* to his *Art of Distillation,* published in 1651, John French comments that "there is a glut of Chymicall books, but a scarcity of chymicall truthes."[18] Like Arthur Dee and Elias Ashmole, French views the current state of alchemy with both despair and guarded optimism. *The Art of Distillation,* like most of French's other works, has a practical emphasis; it is subtitled *A Treatise of the choicest Spagyricall Preparations performed by way of Distillation . . . Together with the Description of the chiefest Furnaces and Vessels used by Ancient, and Moderne Chymists.* French (1616?-57), the self-styled "Dr. of Physick" who practiced his profession in the Parliamentary army, accepts the traditional claims of the alchemists as to the possibility of metallic transmutation, the curing of disease in both plants and animals, and restoration of youth to the aged.[19] He speaks of his "long, and manuall experience" in chemical experiment; and, in the Baconian tradition, he decries the vain and trivial nature of the sciences as they are taught in the universities:

> This [alchemy] is that true naturall philosophy which most accurately anatomizeth nature and natural things, and ocularly demonstrates the principles and operations of them. That empty naturall philosophy which is read in the Universities, is scarce the meanest handmaid to this Queene of arts. It is pity there is such great encouragement for many empty, and unprofitable arts, and none for this, & such like ingenuities, which if promoted would render a University farre more flourishing, then the former. I once read or heard of a famous University beyond sea, that was faln into decay, through what cause I know not: but there was a generall counsell held by the learned, how to restore it to its primitive glory. The *Medium* at last agreed upon, was the promoting of Alchymie, & encouraging the arts themselves. But I never expect to see such rationall actings in this nation.[20]

Like Francis Bacon, French vigorously attacks the tyranny of Galen, Hippocrates, and Aristotle over the study of nature; and in matters of medical theory and practice, he enthusiastically aligns himself with Hermes and Paracelsus: "That which I cannot allow of in them [the followers of classical authority] is their strict observation of the quudraplicity [sic] of humours (which in the schoole of *Paracelsus,* and writings of *Helmont,* where the anatomy of humours hath been most rationally and fully discussed, hath been sufficiently confuted) and their confining themselves to such crude medicines, which are more fit to be put into Spagyricall vessels for a further digestion, then into mens bodies to be fermented therein."[21] While French sees many reasons for despair, he is encouraged by the revival of interest in alchemical studies, the "multitude of Artists there are in this Nation." Adopting the rhetoric of alchemical millenarianism, to be discussed shortly, French "rejoyce[s] as at the break of the day after a long tedious night, to see how this solary art of Alchymie begins for to shine forth out of the clouds of reproach, which it hath a long time undeservedly layen under."

Further confirmation of French's belief in the truth of alchemy is contained in his address to the reader, prefixed to the first edition of the English translation of *The Divine Pymander of Hermes Mercurius Trismegistus,* that of John

Everard, and published in 1650. French begins his address by affirming categorically the authenticity of the translation's original, which can "justly challenge the first place for antiquity, from all the Books in the World, being written
some hundreds of yeers before *Moses* his time."[22] He reviews Hermes' claim to
have been the inventor of writing and master of all learning and philosophy and
follows with a passing reference to the discovery of the *Emerald Table*.[23] In short,
French—nearly forty years after the correct dating of the Hermetic writings by
Isaac Casaubon—was disposed to argue forcefully for the authenticity of alchemy's
most revered text, and he could proudly claim that some Englishmen, e.g., Ripley,
Roger Bacon, and Norton, had actually discovered the secret of the stone's preparation.[24]

   Reasons for French's optimism about the growing interest in alchemy at
mid-century and his concern about the "glut of Chymicall books" are to be found
in the works of both seventeenth- and twentieth-century bibliographers. John
Ferguson has noted that in contrast to the dearth of English alchemical books
printed prior to the middle of the seventeenth century, their number increased
dramatically about 1650 and was augmented by a wide variety of mystical and
occult books. He concludes that "between the years 1650 and 1675 or 1680
more alchemical books appeared in English than in all the time before or after
those dates."[25] Strong support for Ferguson's generalization is found in William
Cooper's *Catalogue of Chymicall Books,* appended to his *Philosophical Epitaph of
W.C. Esquire,* first published in London, 1673. Cooper's *Catalogue* is the first
bibliography of alchemical, chemical, and medical books in England. Revised
and expanded in 1675, and to three parts in 1688 (the first and second containing "such *Chymical Books* as have been written Originally, or Translated into
English," the third listing chemical and scientific studies appearing in the *Philosophical Transactions* of the *Royal Society*), Cooper's bibliography contains over
400 titles and represents not only the first but also the largest and most defini-
tive listing of works in English dating from this period when alchemical studies
were at their height. In addition to these works, many of which the enterprising
Cooper must have offered for sale in his bookshop at the sign of the Pelican in
Little Britain, London, several of the chemical and alchemical books that Cooper published include listings of titles that supplement the *Catalogue of Chymicall
Books.* Taken together, these lists and the numerous entries for chemical and
alchemical books that appear in the sale catalogs that Cooper printed to advertise his thriving auctioneering business provide ample evidence of the extremely
large number of alchemical works that were available in mid–seventeenth-century England.[26]

   Along with other concerns, alchemical authors of this period were especially interested in setting forth the sacred implications of the art by devising or
reaffirming intricate systems of correspondence that existed (or were thought to
exist) between chemical processes and interactions occurring within their alembics

and spiritual transformations taking place within their own hearts and souls. In each case the desired end was purification and perfection: the attainment of the philosopher's stone or the moral and spiritual regeneration of a believer whose soul, through God's grace, has been fitted for salvation. Central to this analogical system is the ancient idea of Christ as the philosopher's stone: the agent of healing, deliverer from sin and baseness, rewarder of merit, author of grace and salvation, and creator of new heavens and a new earth "in that great & generall refining day," to borrow a phrase from Thomas Tymme's description of the Second Coming.[27] The successive stages in the preparation of the philosopher's stone are likened to Christ's nativity, crucifixion, and resurrection, and, by a curious extension of the analogy, the two major events in the world's past and future, the Creation and the Last Judgment, are often described in terms of alchemical process. This imagistic pattern is present in the quotation from Luther's *Table Talk* that provides the first epigraph for this chapter. In its most extreme form, this analogical mode of thought leads to a direct identification of Christ, or his attributes, or God, with the master alchemist who creates, directs, and will someday end the world and the course of human history. Eschatological passages in the poetry of both Vaughan and Milton, among others, utilize this curious analogy.

Among the English editions of earlier alchemical treatises that one might expect to have been influential in increasing seventeenth-century awareness of the sacred implications of alchemy was Hortulanus's *A briefe Commentarie* on the *Smaragdine Table of Hermes Trismegistus,* printed in London in 1597. An English translation of a Latin text that first appeared in 1541, Hortulanus's *Commentarie* was one of "certaine other worthie Treatises" (including the *Smaragdine Table* itself) printed with the *Mirror of Alchimy,* traditionally, but falsely, attributed to Roger Bacon. But unlike the *Mirror,* which is concerned wholly with the transmutation of base metals, Hortulanus consistently uses divine analogy to explain the production of the philosopher's stone. In the following passage, for example, we find these processes likened to God's actions at the time of the Creation. Speaking of the author of the *Emerald Table,* Hortulanus states: "He giveth us also an example of the composition of his Stone, saying, *So was the World created.* That is, like as the world was created, so is our stone composed. For in the beginning, the whole world and all that is therein, was a confused Masse or Chaos . . . but afterward by the workemanship of the soveraigne Creator, this masse was divided into the foure elements, wonderfully separated and rectified, through which separation, divers things were created: so likewise may divers things bee made by ordering our worke, through the separation of the divers elements from divers bodies."[28] Hortulanus's version of the Creation—like Ovid's account in the *Metamorphoses,* book 1, with its emphasis on the Creator's role as a separator and organizer of the "confused" pre-existing elements in chaos—is one of two different types of alchemical creation accounts favored by seventeenth-century writers. The second "hermetic" type, derived from Genesis 1:2 and the *Corpus Hermeticum*, frequently appears in the works of Robert Fludd, Vaughan, and Milton.

Together with alchemical Last Judgments and the less frequent alchemical nativities, Creation tropes come to be extremely popular in treatises of the next century. An elaborated version appears in 1605 in Thomas Tymme's English translation of Joseph Quercetanus's *The Practise of Chymicall, and Hermetical Physicke,* a work of major importance in promoting Paracelsianism and spagyrical medicine in France and England. In a passage that John French is likely to have drawn upon when asserting, in *The Art of Distillation,* alchemy's efficacy as a means of investigating nature, Tymme states that alchemy "tradeth not alone with transmutation of metals (as ignorant vulgars thinke: which error hath made them distaste that noble Science) but shee hath also a chyrurgical hand in the anatomizing of every mesenteriall veine of whole nature: Gods created handmaid, to conceive and bring forth his Creatures" (sig. A₃). Indeed, for Tymme, "*Halchymie* should have concurrence and antiquitie with *Theologie,*" a premise that rests on his "Mosaical" description of the world's beginning. At the time "that the *Spirit of God moved upon the water* [that] which was an indigested Chaos or masse . . . with confused Earth in mixture, . . . [was by God's] Halchymicall Extraction, Seperation[sic], Sublimation, and Conjunction, so ordered and conjoyned againe, as they are manifestly seen" (sig. A₃). But if "this Divine *Halchymie,* through the operation of the spirit . . . was the beginning of *Time,* & of *Terrestrial existence,*" so will it be the operative force at the world's dissolution. Tymme's alchemical description of the Second Coming, quite possibly the earliest of many seventeenth-century versions, is unusually complete and requires quotation in full:

> Moreover, as the omnipotent God, hath in the beginning, by his divine wisedom, created the things of the hevens & earth, in weight, number, & measure, depending upon most wonderfull proportion & harmony, to serve the time which he hath appointed: so in the fulnesse & last period of time (which approacheth fast on) the 4. Elements (whereof al creatures consist) having in every of them 2. other Elements, the one putrifying and combustible, the other eternal & incombustible, as the heaven, shall by Gods *Halchymie* be metamorphosed and changed. For the combustible having in them a corrupt stinking feces, or drossie matter, which maketh them subject to corruption, shall in that great & generall refining day, be purged through fire: And then God wil make new Heavens and a new Earth, and bring all things to a christalline cleernes, & wil also make the 4. Elements perfect, simple, & fixed in themselves, that al things may be reduced to a *Quintessence of Eternitie* (A₃).

This alchemical description of the "great & generall refining day" is repeated nearly verbatim seven years later in Tymme's *A Dialogue Philosophicall* (1612). Unlike his translation of Quercetanus, however, the *Dialogue* is not primarily an alchemical work, but a philosophical treatise on the nature of and relationships between form and matter, soul and spirit. As the subtitle indicates, the work also demonstrates "how all things exist in the number of three." Underlying Tymme's view of these relationships is the doctrine of the three principles that, curiously enough, he traces not to its most immediate source, Paracelsus, but to Hermes Trismegistus. In the *Dialogue Philosophicall,* as in the following passage from his Dedication to the Quercetanus translation, Tymme states that these basic principles "were by Hermes the most ancient Philosopher, called Spirit, Soule, and Body, ... The body is joyned with the spirit, by the bond of Sulphur: the soule, for that it hath affinitie with both the extreames, as a meane coupling them together" (C3$_c$). Like earlier alchemical writers, Quercetanus denies that these underlying principles are to be equated with common salt, sulphur, and mercury. Rather, they are "some other thing of nature, more pure and nimble," which possesses nevertheless "some conscience and agreement" with the common substances. These principles are present everywhere—in the heavens, elements, minerals, vegetables—and, as in Paracelsus, they provide the basis for a thorough and complex correspondence theory.

Although the name of Paracelsus is rarely if ever mentioned in *A Dialogue Philosophicall,* the assimilation of his ideas is obvious on nearly every page; and the favorable commentary on Paracelsian thought is usually accompanied by disparagement of Aristotle. For example, when Philadelph, the question-raising voice of the treatise, seeks to know how the Aristotelian quaternity of elements can be reconciled with the *tria prima,* Theophrast, the respondent, answers that salt, sulphur, and mercury originated as "the first formes of things" when God divided waters from waters and waters from earth at the time of the creation. Applying an alchemical interpretation to the Mosaical account, Theophrast speaks of God's separation of "the more subtill, airie, and Mercurial liquor, from the more thicke, clammy, oyle-like, or Sulfurous liquor" (31). From the "more grosse" waters God then separates the Earth, which is likened to salt, and the trinity of principles is complete. Thus, Tymme utilizes an alchemical interpretation of Genesis to support the three principles theory and refute Aristotle's metaphysics.

In a similar manner, by combining the authority of Moses and Hermes Trismegistus, Tymme's spokesman is able to dispose of such vexatious questions as the existence of the element of fire, the nature of the three principles, the operation of signatures, correspondences, astral influences, and the ubiquity and significance of the number three. Overall, Tymme's *Dialogue* is distinctly Christian in flavor, as is demonstrated in Theophrast's reply to Philadelph's question concerning the nature of felicity. Citing such millenarian passages as 2 Peter 3, Theophrast states that the true felicity of the future life is the restoration of all things to a greater perfection than they now possess. At the Lord's coming, the four elements whereof all consists will "melt with heate" and will be replaced by new heavens and a new earth "wherein dwelleth righteousnesse" (68-69). Passages such as this come to be repeated with increasing frequency during the middle decades of the seventeenth century.

In its combining of Hermetic and Judeo-Christian teachings with much familiar detail from Renaissance cosmology and natural philosophy, Tymme's *Dialogue* is quite typically Elizabethan. Its most unusual feature is the heavy emphasis given to the three principles theory, which provides the basis for much of Tymme's speculation and analysis. The fact that this theory is traced to Hermes rather than Paracelsus suggests the veneration in which the ancient authority was held, even two years before the correct dating of his writings by Isaac Casaubon in 1614, and the eagerness of Renaissance authors to enlist his support rather than that of more recent authorities.[29] As Tymme was a minister, as well as the author and translator of numerous religious and philosophical treatises,[30] the *Dialogue Philosophicall* also serves as evidence of the degree to which Hermetic and Paracelsian ideas were assimilated by Renaissance writers who were not primarily in the occult tradition.

Although the 1620s saw no great outpouring of alchemical books, those that were published tended to emphasize the art's philosophical and spiritual aspects much more than its traditional concerns with transmutation and iatrochemistry. For this reason, publication of works by Giovanni Lambye, Patrick Scot, and the shadowy Nicholas Flamel helped to provide both pattern and context for literary allusions marked by boldness of metaphor, mystical overtones, allegorical style, and, above all, a combination of alchemical image and Christian subject, theme, and doctrine. The first and least important work in this group, *A Revelation of the Secret Spirit* by John Baptista Lambye (Giovanni Lambi, a Venetian), was translated from the Latin original and Italian commentary by one "R.N.E. Gentleman" and published in 1623.[31] In his Epistle Dedicatory, the translator refers to the treatise as a "Philosophicall Apocalypse" that can be explicated only by one of such singular learning as the dedicatee, John Thornburgh, Lord Bishop of Worcester. An alchemized mythography of Atalanta (alchemy) and Hippomenes (a would-be adept) is included at the beginning of the dedication to demonstrate that "the dangerous course of *Alchymie* in many is manifestly seene, that who doth not overcome it, perisheth; and whosoever is to overcome it, must first receive three golden apples from *Venus*."[32] Five years earlier, Michael Maier had utilized the same mythography in the title and engraved title page of his most famous work, the *Atalanta Fugiens* (1618). Within the treatise proper, Lambye quickly turns to description and explication of his main subject, the World Soul. This dominant force in both macrocosm and microcosm is "the Spirit of the Quintessence," which Lambye figures forth as the agent of all natural and salutary effects. It is, variously, the "upholder of Heaven," "retainer of Earth," "container of all things and vertues," the remover of all evil, and the curer of all diseases. Citing Avicenna, Lambye states that this spirit "is called the soule of the worlde, because as the soule moveth the members, so this Spirit moveth all bodies; and as the soule is in every part of the body, so in every elementary thing this Spirit is found." Through possessing it, Adam and the patriarchs enjoyed health and long life.[33]

This platonic *anima mundi,* which Lambye soon identifies with the universal medicine and the philosopher's stone, as well as with light,[34] enables its possessor to perform God-like miracles, restoring health and prolonging life in the plant and animal worlds and perfecting imperfect metals. Although Lambye's approach to his subject is more philosophical, and specifically platonic, than that of most alchemical authors, the *Revelation* also contains much that is commonplace: chapter 8 deals with the preparation of the elixir, and the final chapter contains a conventional diatribe against corrupt practitioners of the art. Finally, Lambye asserts the need to pursue his quest in solitude, which offers the best way to find both the stone and God.

While Lambye's concern with explaining the world soul in alchemical terms is indicative of the new metaphoric uses to which the vocabulary of alchemy was being put in the seventeenth century, the *Revelation* is not unique in this respect. To cite only one additional example, Agricola Carpenter's *Pseuchographia Anthropomagica: or, A Magicall Description of the Soul* consistently employs such terms in its religious and philosophical speculations. In Carpenter's work, the spirit, soul, and body of man are referred to as the *tria omnia;* and the rational soul, a corporal substance extracted from "grosser materials by the Chymistrie of Nature," is a "Mercurial moisture that marries the two extreams of Spirit and Body."[35]

It is not strictly accurate to describe Patrick Scot's *Tillage of Light* (1623) as an alchemical treatise. Although it is addressed to students of alchemy and uses alchemical allegory and allusion pervasively, it is primarily an ethical work that achieves its strong moral tone largely through denial of the possibility of physical transmutation. Like Lambye in his treatise of the same year, Scot adopts a Hermetic view of the nature and origin of the soul and its relationship to the body: the world soul is a "quallity of brightnesse," derived from the sun, and implanted in the individual body at the time of Creation.[36] It is also identified with the logos: "This *Al-Seeing* light hath established a *rule* and certaine *law,* whereby all things must bee produced, disposed, and maintained in their own kind" (6). But whereas Lambye associates his secret spirit with the philosopher's stone and the universal elixir, Scot's quest is for philosophical truth and moral perfection: the "tillage of light" has as its end the cultivation of wisdom until soul and character become resplendently illuminated: "the full knowledge of the *tillage* of *light,* ariseth from the true notice of the first and last end of things: as man was created of pure earth, coagulat by pure ayre: so his last end is to shine as the *sunne.* . . . the true ends of *divine light* and Philosophy . . . [are] to exalt the *excellency* of *wisdome*" (3, 4-5).

Scot's denial of the possibility of transmutation is based on a conventional, but carefully reasoned, explanation of the respective roles of art and nature and their interrelationship. For him, nature is limited to instilling in its creatures initial perfection only; it produces natural effects by means of natural causes. Art, on the other hand, can only "dignifie and pollish" the works of nature. Adopting imagery derived from alchemy, Scot defines both the virtues and limitations of art, which can "by a kinde of *sublimation* separate the *grosse* parts from the *pure,* rectifyie the substance of things, & draw from vile things *wholesome* and good *effects,* but never adde essence to the first substance other then it had before" (5). While Scot admits that nature and art in combination may produce things of "glorious perfection," he goes to great lengths to reject the idea of alchemical transmutation. The "miraculous multiplication of unrefined substances," he states, is beyond the bounds of either nature or art, and such attempts are intrusions into forbidden knowledge and the domain of God (5).

Scot's attack on physical transmutation takes many forms but is centered in conventional philosophical and Christian apologetics: for example, nature, which must always be subsumed under God, can multiply only within a species and by means of propagation and putrefaction (6); or, nature cannot be forced by the fire of art or by an artificial elixir to produce something deviant from her normal course. To believe that art can "*Metaphysically* transmute" nature's work is a "fond conception" (8), Scot states, and "drives all wit out of harmony" (10): "Wee may as probably suggest, that art may enable *fish* to live and multiply upon the land, *beasts* in the ayre, and *foules* without ayre; as that *Mineralls* remooved from their naturall places, may by art bee brought to multiply in a great perfection, then by *nature* in the wombe of the earth, where the sunne applieth his force, according to the quallity and disposition of the matter; for *Mineralls* can never be said properly to *multiply* or *propogate*"(8).

Finally, Scot finds transmutation ethically repugnant: because the infinite multiplication of gold would produce "harmefull consequences," it is inconsistent that "philosophers" should devote so much time and effort in pursuing the philosopher's stone ("untwining a *Spider Web*") rather than questing for a greater good. Even supposing transmutation to be possible, what could be gained by it but "corruption of manners," loss of professional reputation, and the decline of "all *politike* government, mutuall commerce, and industrious exchange" (11-12)? In a more positive vein, Scot shares with many of his age the stoical ideal that is the end of the "tillage of light." In contrast to the alchemists' lusts for power and wealth, true greatness consists in the "moderation of *high fortunes* setled in *generous minds* by a due examination and contempt of base slyding vanities, and by the praise worthy aspiring to the *glory* of frugall imployment of its short time in those *Honourable Actions,* which onely challenge the name of greatnesse" (17).

It is a curious fact, although representative of the time in which *The Tillage of Light* was written, that although Scot was contemptuous of alchemy's traditional boast of physical transmutation, he nevertheless uses alchemical imagery to express the high value he places on philosophy. He speaks of philosophy's capacity for "refyning" man in the ways of virtue, of the transformation of man into a substance purer than "thrice purified *gold,*" of "*extract*[ing]" virtue from vice and "true *reputation*" from "*poverty* and *contempt*," and of multiplying "some few short *earthly crosses* into *Caelestiall* permanent *joyes*." Such transformation and purification, Scot claims, can result from philosophy, "*the upright couragious government of our selves in all our actions by the rule of reason*" (33).

The use of alchemical imagery to describe moral and ethical conditions and the efficacy of philosophy in bringing about spiritual transformation is pervasive in Scot's writing. Indeed, in several instances it is expanded and woven into a reasonably complete allegorical web. For example, after citing a lengthy list of alchemical authorities ranging from Hermes to Morienus and Calid to St. Thomas, Scot summarizes their four common teachings concerning the making of the elixir: mercury is the prime matter to be used; the vigorous physical labors in preparing the matter (to quicken and refine the spirits) are to be accompanied by incantations; the chief task is to fix the volatile; and the work is completed when the colors of red and white are conjoined in alchemical matrimony. At this point, however, Scot denies that such preparations will result in the birth of the expected "Salamander"; "let us not," he says, "bee deceived with such excursory survey" (23).[37] Scot replies that according to other authorities—Aristotle, Avulfanes, Daniell, Euclides—the true interpretation of such passages is on the moral and ethical level rather than in the context of physical transmutation. Scot's allegorizing, based as it is upon the aforementioned teachings, provides a practical guide to the life of reason:

> What then is the *Philosophers Mercury,* but *Wisdome the childe of heaven, and the glory of the earth? the pounding and mixing of the matter, is the beating downe and qualifying of our affections in the morter* of a wise heart; the feeding of it with more or lesse fire is, *the timely pressing and relaxing of our corrupt will,* the fixation of *volatile,* is the *reduction of our inconstant running Wits, to the solidity of true Wisedome:* Lastly the *Redde colour* joyned to the *white,* which crownes the worke, gives us to understand, that *perseverance in vertue will gaine us the garland of victorie over all foraigne incumbrances;* and subdue our unruly *domesticke affections, which unlesse they be overcome, pounded, qualified sublimat & fixed to a pure Syndon-like white, are ever ready to debord from the precinct of reason, to a soule-killing liberty* (24).

While the major emphasis of Scot's treatise is on the moral life, he is not oblivious to the demands of the physical and would not exclude human labor as a requirement for attaining the good life. In addition to the agrarian imagery with which the *Tillage* begins and ends—the human heart is a field "rough to plow"; his essay is an "ill cultur'd Farme" brought to the reader's view (*Preface*)—traces of Baconian utilitarianism are present. In phrasing that stands apart from the norm of alchemical expression and also recalls Bacon's insistence on industriousness and practicality, Scot states that "Every man ought to have a *sweating Browe,* to beget the necessities of life, or a *working Braine,* to advance the publique good; the most Blessed alloweth of no *Cyphers* in his *Arithmatique:*

Paradise was as well a Shop to exercise *Adams* hands with labour, as it was a Garden to feede his Senses with delight" (21).

The third in this group of representative texts dating from the 1620s that give special emphasis to alchemy's moral and spiritual dimensions is known chiefly for its allegorical style and symbolic illustrations. Nicolas Flamel's *His Exposition of the Hieroglyphicall Figures* was published in English translation in 1624. Speculations concerning Flamel's identity, career, and literary productions are as varied as they are exotic. According to the autobiographical account included in the *Exposition,* which is itself of dubious authenticity,[38] Flamel was born in 1330, worked as a Parisian scrivener, acquired great wealth through alchemy that he learned in part from a large "gilded book" containing cryptic illustrations by Abraham the Jew, was rumored to have lived centuries beyond the time of his reported death in 1417, and has endured in memory chiefly because of his charitable works.[39] This philanthropy, he tells us, resulted in the founding and endowment of fourteen hospitals, the building of three chapels, the enrichment "with great gifts and good rents" of seven churches, and the restoration of many churchyards. He adds that his and his wife's charitable acts in Boulogne were "not much lesse than that which wee have done heere," i.e., in Paris (14).

The title of Flamel's work refers to the "Hieroglyphical Figures" that are included and explicated in the *Exposition.* These figures are derived from the symbolic illustrations that Flamel found in "a guilded Booke, very old and large" that had come into his possession in 1357 (7). This book is said to have been the *Asch Mezareph* of Rabbi Abraham, a work of considerable importance in Cabbalistic tradition.[40] Flamel's successful transmutation, vividly described in the *Exposition,* resulted from the correct interpretation of these diagrams. Furthermore, the perpetuation of Flamel's memory and the importance of these symbolic drawings are explained and demonstrated through his commissioning of a series of colored murals to be painted in the *"fourth Arch* of the Churchyard of the *Innocents,* as you enter in by the great gate in *St. Dennis street"* in Paris (14-15). These paintings are in imitation of those figures in the gilded book, to which have been added representations of the kneeling Flamel and his wife, Perrenelle, together with Christ and Saints James and John, as seen in the full illustration of the tympanum in the 1624 edition of the *Exposition* (fig. 26). Waite, on the authority of Langlet du Fresnoy, states that this arch remained intact until 1742 and came to be regarded as a shrine by generations of alchemists.[41]

In marked contrast to the denial of the possibility of transmutation that characterizes Scot's *Tillage of Light,* Flamel's work is specifically addressed to the making of gold. Alchemy is advocated even on moral grounds: "would to God," he states, "every man knew how to make *gold* to his owne will, that they might live, and leade forth to pasture their faire flocks, without Usury or going to Law, in imitation of the holy *Patriarkes"* (46). Thus, the *Exposition* is in the pietistic tradition, and Flamel's own piety, as illustrated in his representation

Figure 26. Tympanum. Nicolas Flamel, *Exposition of the Hieroglyphicall Figures* (1624).

with the saints in the churchyard arch and through his numerous charitable acts, is sufficient proof of the personal and public benefits that can result from the practice of alchemy.

The dominant features of the *Exposition* are the "hieroglyphical figures" themselves and the accompanying description and explanation. Flamel's illustrations are simultaneously personal (representing him and his wife) and alchemical and religious, representing the process of making the stone and analogous Christian doctrines. The figures included in the Holy Innocents' arch are, he tells us, capable of twofold interpretation and are likewise intended to promote Christian morality and salvation in two different ways. They contain

> the most true and essentiall markes of the *Arte,* yet under *vailes* and *Hieroglyphicall covertures,* in imitation of those which are in the gilded Booke of *Abraham* the *Jew,* which may represent *two things,* according to the capacity and understanding of them that behold them: First, the *mysteries* of our future and undoubted *Resurrection,* at the day of Judgement, and comming of good Jesus, . . . And secondly, they may signifie to them, which are skilled in Naturall *Philosophy,* all the principall and necessary operations of the *Maistery.* These *Hieroglyphicke figures* shall serve as two wayes to leade unto the heavenly life: the first and most open sence, teaching the sacred *Mysteries* of our salvation; . . . the

other teaching every man, that hath any small understanding in the *Stone,* the lineary way of the worke; which being perfected by any one, the change of evill into good, takes away from him the roote of all sinne (which is, *covetousness*) making him liberall, gentle, pious, religious, and fearing God, how evill soever hee was before (15).

The combining of religious and alchemical levels of meaning in Flamel's allegory is furthered by a variety of conventional devices. For example, the small illustration of two intertwined dragons mortally biting each other becomes an apt symbol for the product of an alchemical *conjunctio* as well as for Christian doctrine concerning death and resurrection (fig. 26, on left beneath arch). As the double ouroborous suffers death through cruel bites and the release of venom, so their physical death and corruption are followed by transformation into a "new, more noble, and better forme" (27). In addition to employing such conventional symbols as the ouroborous, Flamel draws heavily on traditional alchemical color symbolism: although blackness symbolizes death and corruption in both the natural and spiritual worlds, it is desirable because generation stems from putrefaction (29). In chapter 6, green is appropriate as a background color for a figure representing the vegetable stone, which corresponds to the soul.

In several instances, Flamel's theological and alchemical allegorizing contains glances at millenarian and eschatological doctrine in a way that is characteristic of a common pattern of imagery in seventeenth-century religious poetry. In chapter 4, "Of the man and the woman clothed in a gowne of Orange colour upon a field azure and blew, and of their rowles," the following gloss accompanies the words, *Homo veniet ad judicium Dei,* contained in the rowles (fig. 26, second from left beneath arch):

> that is, *Man shall come to the Judgement of God:* . . . *Truly that will be a terrible day.* These are not passages of holy *Scripture,* but onely sayings which speake according to the *Theologicall* sence, of the *Judgement* to come, . . . and also it may serve for them, that gathering together the *Parables* of the *Science,* take to them the eyes of *Lynceus,* to pierce deeper then the visible objects. There is then, *Man shall come to the judgement of God: Certainly that day shall be terrible.* That is as if I should have said; It behoves that this come to the colour of *perfection,* to bee judged & clensed from all his *blacknesse* and filth, and to be *spiritualized* and *whitened.* (34-35)

A later gloss from the *Exposition* draws even closer the analogy between mercury's irrepressible fusibility and Christ's Second Coming, thus providing an obvious parallel with the quotation from Luther that serves as an epigraph to this chapter and also with the pattern of poetic imagery with which I am concerned. Referring to the central illustration of the standing Christ and the small disinterment beneath (fig. 26), Flamel states:

The [metallic] *Spirit* which likewise cannot bee put in a grave, I have made to bee painted in fashion of a man comming out of the *earth,* not from a Tombe. They are all white; so the *blacknesse,* that is, *death,* is vanquished, and they being whitened, are from hence-forward incorruptible. Now lift up thine eyes on high, and see our *King* comming, crowned and raised again, which hath overcome Death, the darkenesses, and moistures; behold him in the forme wherein our *Saviour* shall come, who shall eternally unite unto him all pure and cleane soules, and will drive away all impurity and uncleannesse, as being unworthy to bee united to his *divine Body.* So by comparison . . . see heere our white *Elixir,* which from hence-forward will inseparably unite unto himselfe every pure *Metallicke* nature, changing it into his owne most fine *silvery* nature, rejecting all that is impure, strange, and *Heterogeneall,* or of another kind (43).

In this quotation, alchemical allegorizing, based on Christ's resurrection and millenarian doctrine and presented through an emblem-like combination of text, visual illustration, and color symbolism, is a dominant feature. And if metallic transmutation is not denied, as it is in Scot's *Tillage of Light,* it is drastically subordinated to religious and ethical concerns. In fact, in the *Exposition,* transmutation assumes importance only as the means of accomplishing the famous philanthropic activities in Paris and Boulogne. Overall then, the import of the publication of the legend of Nicholas Flamel is similar to that of the two other works from the 1620s that I have discussed: as in Lambye and Scot, alchemy's traditional emphasis on the transmutation of base metals is redirected toward moral, spiritual, and philosophical transformation. These tendencies were, in turn, fostered by the growing influence of Paracelsus in the next few decades of the century.

Earlier consideration of poems by Hall and Breton and of Lacy's *Dumb Lady* has shown that Paracelsian ideas were particularly adaptable to comic and satiric modes and contexts in seventeenth-century literature. Here, the theories, practices, and personal associations of the Swiss physician (e.g., the *tria prima* and homeopathy, urinalysis, and the allegations of witchcraft and black magic) provided a basis for fresh and varied humor and satire that often reflected contemporary medical controversy. In this way the introduction of Paracelsian iatrochemical ideas serves as a means of shifting literary interest away from the traditional topics of transmutation and alchemical chicanery. But the influence of Paracelsus on seventeenth-century literature is a complex matter and often assumes forms directly opposite those present in the works of Hall and Lacy. In the 1650s and 1660s the extraordinary interest in Paracelsus, as reflected in new editions and translations of his works into English, and the growing number of English medical adherents contributed much to the changing direction in alchemy that we have already noted in works of Lambye, Scot, and Flamel. As much as these writers, the works of Paracelsus gave new emphasis to the spiritual and philosophical aspects of alchemy and often combined Christian themes of moral regeneration, salvation, eschatology, and millenarianism with alchemical imagery and allegory. It is this background, along with hermetic tradition, that provides the most valuable approach to alchemical ideas and allusions in the works of Vaughan and Milton to be discussed in the following chapter.

Before turning to several Paracelsian works dating from the 1650s, it is useful, as a way of demonstrating the growing skepticism about alchemical transmutation, to give brief attention to the 1633 edition of *The Secrets of Physick and Philosophy,* which is essentially a collection of Paracelsian recipes and medications, both herbal and mineral, that had appeared earlier (and under different titles) in editions of 1575, 1580, and 1596. The translator of this work was John Hester (d. ca. 1593), a practical distiller, promoter of chemical medicines, prolific translator, and, at this early date, the chief individual through whom the English could learn of advances in chemical medicine taking place on the Continent.[42] Despite his death forty years earlier, Hester's preface "To the Reader" was still included in the 1633 edition of *Secrets* and yields valuable insights into the status of alchemy from the viewpoint of one whose iatrochemical interests depended on its processes and methods. For Hester, as for Francis Bacon, alchemy is a true and "worthy science" but one whose reputation has suffered "disdain through lewd persons," and while granting that benefits had resulted from alchemical experimentation, he says of the transmutation of metals: "yet will I not affirme that it is possible to be done, for it seemeth unreasonable, that a man in so short time should doe that thing the which nature doth in many yeares. And that men should presume to doe that which God doth only himself, and not any of his creatures. Wee therefore will not affirme it to bee true or possible, nor yet will wee deny it utterly or condemne it as untrueth."[43] Aware of the implausibility of transmutation on both religious and scientific grounds, Hester challenges the conventional view that would restrict alchemy's aim solely to this end. Rather, as a proponent of the new chemical medicines, he states that alchemy "serveth to helpe those diseased both inwardly and outwardly, who of the common sort of Chirurgions are counted uncurable, and also given over of the Physitians. Those patients shall be holpen through the hidden mysteries & heavenly secrets of this science" (109). Finally, and in a manner that anticipates Bacon's fable of the vineyard owner's sons who increase their harvest through the cultivation resulting from their search for buried treasure, Hester asserts alchemy's efficacy in opening the "secondary" secrets of medicine even though the key to transmutation remains hidden: "Therefore is the Arte of *Alchymie* worthy to be praised, and the *Alchymist* to bee praised also, although they attaine not to their first intention, yet they have opened the way through the which this excellent cunning of preparation was knowne and found, and through the which there are a number of wonderfull secrets opened, the which without this Arte were all unknowne, to the great hinderance of the sicke and diseased persons" (114).

If Hester's attitude toward the possibility of metallic tranformation is cautious and skeptical in the Preface to *Secrets of Physick and Philosophy,* the same ambivalence generally characterizes seventeenth-century responses to Paracelsus, even as English translations were gaining popularity in the years 1650-75. In the preface "To the Reader" of *Paracelsus his Dispensatory and Chirurgery* (1656), the unknown translator, "W. D.," praises Paracelsus's contributions to medicine but is careful to state that he does not embrace his "Philosophical Opinions," especially those concerning supernatural phenomena. Indeed, his skepticism about Paracelsus's methods of driving away ghosts and evil spirits reveals his desire not to be too closely identified with this aspect of the author's thought: "These things are in deed very strange, I cannot say much for the probability of them; neither can I say, that they are impossible: I am not of that minde, as many are, who conclude those things to be impossible, or that they must be done by the Divel, which are extraordinary, and are such things which they cannot understand, for I know, that God can do many things."[44]

That English publishers were acutely conscious of charges of black magic and witchcraft levied against Paracelsus is demonstrated in another work of the following year. *Philosophy Reformed & Improved in Four Profound Tractates* (1657) contains three treatises by Paracelsus and a fourth, entitled *Discovering the Great and Deep Mysteries of Nature,* by Oswald Croll (1580-1609), a German follower of Paracelsus's theories of chemical medicine. The latter essay, which appears first in this collection, is of interest because, first, it undertakes to defend beneficent magic on religious grounds (and in so doing defends the reputation of Paracelsus), and, second, it sets forth theoretical aspects of Paracelsian medicine that had been neglected in the earlier collections of recipes and cures translated by John Hester. Together, the effect of these two tendencies is to strengthen the medical, religious, and esoteric associations of alchemy and weaken its connections with physical transmutation. On the first issue, Croll asserts that "Great things have been effected by True *Magicians* (by whom I doe not mean Nicromancers or them of the Black Art)." While "True *Magicians*" are defined as "accurate searchers out of Nature," their practice of natural magic is based on recognition of certain astrologically propitious characters and signs that connect the greater world and the lesser. These divinely appointed links were, Croll continues, "framed at a certaine time according to the power of Heaven, far from all superstition, which ariseth onely from ignorance, without any prophanation or scandall of the Divine Majesty, or any wrong to Faith and Religion; . . . For Characters or constellated Names according to *Agrippa,* have no force from the Figureors Pronunciation, but by reason of the Vertue or Office which God or Nature hath ordained to such a Name or Character."[45] In this way, magic and its theoretical underpinnings are attributed to God. The particular foundation of Croll's medical theory is, predictably, the Paracelsian notion of a harmonious correspondence between the macrocosm and microcosm, and thus he calls upon the chemists of his age to "be well acquainted with the true Fundamentall of the occult Phylosophycal Physick, because of this Harmonicall concord and conspiration between the superiour and inferiour things of the greater and lesser world" (74).

Ideas such as these, combined with the restorative power of the alchemical elixir and its prototype, Christ, inform the commendatory poem entitled "CROLLIUS" that prefaces the volume. Its author is anonymous and the crude verses were added, we are told, "by a Friend of the Publisher." The poem as a whole is representative of the large, interesting, but artistically uneven body of Renaissance alchemical verse,[46] and the following lines are characteristic of the Christ-philosopher's stone parallels and the themes of spiritual purification and transformation present in much alchemical writing of this era. The imagery recalls that used by contemporary poets such as Vaughan. Speaking of the book as a divinely inspired repository of medical and moral wisdom ("The Author was divinely taught that writ, / so likewise was he that translated it"), the poet states:

> Here may be seen, what nature is and grace,
>   what God his back parts are, and what his face.
> Here is both heaven and earth in Harmony,
>   a cure to ease us of our vanity.
> The true Elixir's here, the stone that doth
>   transmute the outward and the inward both:
> And make all heavenly like to Chrystall fine,
>   yea like to Christ the prototype divine.
> What is above is likewise here below,
>   as this Anatomy of man doth show.
> The man in all the parts of him consists
>   of what the Macrocosm composed it.[47]

Like Scot's *Tillage of Light*, Croll's treatise stresses the attainment of wisdom, rather than riches, as the proper end of a "Phylosopher's" endeavors. While Croll's work is far more positive about the possibility of transmutation than Scot's and lacks the platonic resonances of the latter, Croll adopts the allegorical mode and steadfastly asserts the primacy of wisdom: "A Phylosopher must covet Nothing but Wisdome, which is conversant about Divine things; therefore a true Phylosopher never sought after nor desired riches, but is rather delighted with the Mysteries of Nature" (183).

That the works of Paracelsus and his followers were vital in reorienting alchemical interests toward iatrochemistry and religious and philosophical knowledge is intimated by the few examples already surveyed. Unfortunately, a scattering of titles provides little indication of the tremendous impact of Paracelsian thought following 1650. To get a clearer idea of the sheer quantity of Paracelsian works then available, it is useful to recall Ferguson's statistical summary of "English

Editions of Paracelsus' Works," listing titles as they appeared during various periods throughout the sixteenth and seventeenth centuries: 1525-99 (seven); 1600-1649 (two); 1650-74 (thirteen); 1675-1700 (two).[48] More specific evidence of the increasing interest in Paracelsus is contained, once again, in William Cooper's authoritative *Catalogue of Chymicall Books,* which lists the following mid-century English editions: *Archidoxes* (1660, 1661, 1663), *Paracelsus his Aurora, & Treasure of the Philosophers* (1659), *Of Chemical Transmutation* (1657), *Paracelsus his Dispensatory and Chirurgery* (1656), and *Of the Supreme Mysteries* (1656). In addition—and Cooper's *Catalogue* does not purport to be complete—Paracelsian treatises appeared in numerous collections that were published throughout the century.

Among these works, the *Aurora,* a supposititious work probably by Gerhard Dorn, will provide the one example from many possible of the allegorizing tendencies in seventeenth-century Paracelsian mystical and religious alchemy. I have noted this characteristic in works of Scot and Flamel, and the combining of alchemical and religious ideas in allegory is no less a feature in Paracelsian tracts than in alchemical allusions in mid-century poetry and literary prose. By far the most interesting treatise included in the *Aurora* volume is not the title piece now attributed to Dorn but the *Water-Stone of the Wise Men; Describing the matter of, and manner how to attain the universal Tincture,* usually attributed to the early seventeenth-century German, Johann Ambrosius Siebmacher.[49] *The Water-Stone* provides an excellent theoretical framework for understanding the analogical modes of thought that underlie alchemical allegory, and for this reason it merits detailed consideration.

Siebmacher, like Croll, begins with the familiar assumption that alchemy is a holy art, revealed only by God and only to those of exemplary character:

> [I]f therefore any one thinks to attain to that high and unspeakable mysterie, let him know, that such an Art is not in the power of man, but consists in the most gracious will [and pleasure] of God, and that it is not the Will or Desire, but the meer Mercy of the Almighty that helps [man] thereunto.

> If therefore, now, thou wouldst know her [nature], then its behovefull that thou beest even as Nature her self is, *viz.* true, simple, constant, patient, yea pious, and no waies hurtful unto thy neighbor; but briefly, such an one must be a new and regenerated man.[50]

From this moral and ethical emphasis, Siebmacher turns to the foundation of his allegory with its intricate and fantastic equation of Christ with the philosopher's stone; his exposition will attempt to demonstrate "how the terrestrial Philosophical stone may be accounted as a true type of the true, spiritual, and heavenly stone, Jesus Christ, [and how] he is herein set before us, and discovered (as 'twere) in a visible shape by God, even in a Corporeal manner" (147).

While God has historically revealed his wisdom and goodness to man through the Book of Nature and the secrets of creation through parables, Siebmacher also contends that through "another certain wonderful and secret thing," i.e., the philosopher's stone, he has allowed man a glimpse, a "certain corporeal, visible, and apprehensible *idea* of those Celestial goods and benefits" (143-44). That this wondrous stone can be regarded as a type of Christ rests, first of all, on biblical evidence, the notion of Christ as the cornerstone: "a tried stone, a precious corner *stone,* a sure foundation" (Isaiah 28:16); or the contemptible "stone *which* the builders refused [which] is become the head *stone* of the corner" (Psalms 118:22; cf. Matthew 21:42, Acts 4:11). Following this identification, Siebmacher announces that he will demonstrate how the "precious, blessed and heavenly stone [i.e., Christ], doth artificially or harmoniously agree with this so-oft-mentioned terrestrial, Corporeal, Philosophical stone" (146-47). Siebmacher's argument for this identification takes the form of a dozen or so propositions—ranging from the obvious and redundant to the ingeniously obscure—that assert the purported similarities; there is no need to review all of them in detail. He notes, for example, that the search for both Christ and the stone requires wisdom and serious preparation; the search for each is conducted in the Scriptures and nature (147-48). Knowledge of both is hidden from the majority of men, and in each case the object of the search is "disesteemed" by the world, like the "refused" cornerstone (157). More interesting, and following Paracelsian theory, Siebmacher observes that the tripartite composition of the stone (body = salt, soul = sulphur, spirit = mercury) is a reflection of the trinity.

In seventeenth-century alchemical writing and visual illustration as well as in the religious poems that reflect these influences, the most fertile source of imagery is a series of events from the life of Christ that are regarded as having alchemical parallels. The "forty days" interval, for example, applies to Christ's sojourn in the wilderness as well as to the duration (according to some theories) of the alchemical process. More bizarre, but not without parallels in literary contexts and in the visual arts, is the treatment of the crucifixion-resurrection theme, which Siebmacher describes as follows: "And moreover, even as (in the Philosophick work) that said composition, the two essences being conjoyned now together, must be placed over the fire, and be putrified, ground or broken, and be well boiled, . . . Even so, this God-man and man-God person Jesus Christ, so appointed by God, his heavenly Father, in this world, was cast into the firie furnace of tribulation, and was therein well boyled (as 'twere) that is, he was encompassed with various troubles, reproaches, the Cross and tribulation, and was changed and transmuted (as 'twere) into various shapes" (170-71). Finally (although we will eventually discover additional parallels in other works), Siebmacher draws upon the alchemical possibilities present in the redemptive act of Christ, "whose efficacy, power, and rosey-coloured tincture is able to transmute us imperfect men and sinners even now in body and soul, to tinge, and more then perfectly to cure and heal us" (175-76). As already noted in the poetry of Donne and Herbert, the salvation of man is often presented as alchemical allegory. Not only is Christ the Good Physician, he is the Good Alchemist as well. This is precisely the conception that informs Robert Herrick's little poem, "Sin," from the *Noble Numbers:*

> There is no evill that we do commit,
> But hath th'extraction of some good from it:
> As when we sin; God, the great *Chymist,* thence
> Drawes out th'*Elixar* of true penitence."[51]

While Siebmacher's alchemical allegory in this section is not entirely consistent and thoroughgoing, it does include representations of sin, death, and Satan. Sin, that "Spiritual Leprosy," is analogous to "imperfect mettals" that receive cleansing and healing through the "one only terrene Saviour and Chymical King," the alchemical counterpart of Christ, who is "the only and alone Saviour and Mediatour." False doctrine, such as that which "Heathens, and other hereticks have published," is "false and Sophisticate Alchimy . . . by which we men are not purifyed, . . . [but] wholy mortifyed." Such heresies are like the false alchemy "which hath found out many and diverse tinctures and colours, by which men are not only deceived, but . . . oftentimes cast into the peril and danger of their good and corporal life" (179-80). The root cause of man's spiritual misadventures is "that terrible and lying false Chymist Sathan [who] doth there shew himself, and doth daily lay snares and gins for the new and regenerated Men and Sons of God" (189). Finally, the steadfast, regenerate man who is suffering from affliction is likened to substances within the alembic: "he is placed by God in the fornace of tribulation, and is so long pressed with straights of all kinds, and with various calamities and troubles, until he becomes dead to the old *Adam* and flesh, *Eph.* 4. and be like a truly new man, . . . If this now be done, and that a man doth daily cease to sin, that so by this means sin may bear no more rule over him, then doth the solution of the adjoyned body of gold (as in the terrene work) take its original in him" (199-200). The passage succinctly summarizes Siebmacher's alchemical rendering of the redemptive scheme: God, the "good" alchemist, places man in the purgative furnace to cleanse him of the corruption of original sin; when the impurities of the "old *Adam*" are removed and sin ceases to dominate, the "truly new man" emerges as gold transmuted from base metals. Victory over the "false alchemist" Satan has been achieved.

Among the biblical themes most frequently treated as alchemical allegory are the creation, crucifixion, and Last Judgment, and these are the ones that appear most frequently in literary contexts. Before turning to some examples closely related to the themes of eschatology and millenarianism, however, it remains to give brief notice to a final, unusual variation of the Christ-philosopher's stone analogy. Similar to Siebmacher's regenerate man suffering adversities as the alchemical *prima materia* undergoing thermal punishment in the "fornace of tribulation," for Dorn in *Aurora, & Treasure of the Philosophers* (one of two tracts that precede the much longer *Water-Stone*), Christ is represented as the antitype foreshadowed by the stone, suffering as it evolves within the alchemist's glass. The author vividly states that in the final stages of preparing the "animal" stone (so-called because it was thought to cure physical disease), the operations within the alembic cause the substance to sweat blood-like drops:

> In its . . . last operations, the virtue of this most noble fiery mystery causeth an obscure liquor to sweat forth out of that matter in their Vessel, drop by drop: From thence they presaged and foretold, that in the last times there should come a most pure man upon the earth, by whom the redemption of the world should be accomplished; and that this same man should emit or send forth bloody drops of a Rosie or red colour, by which means he should redeem the world from sin: After the like manner, also the blood of their stone (yet, in its own kind) did free the Leprous mettalls from their infirmities and Contagion (21-22).

The ingenuity with which seventeenth-century alchemical allegorists fused Christian theology with details of their art is at times remarkably baroque.

In the works of Thomas Tymme and, especially, Nicholas Flamel we have already noted the complicating presence of eschatological and millenarian threads woven into a fabric of alchemical allegory. The vividness and wit of Tymme's notion of a "great & generall refining day" and Flamel's visionary exhortation to "lift up thine eyes on high, and see our *King* comming, crowned and raised again" impart a quality of drama and originality to works that might otherwise be indistinguishable in a sea of writing on the Last Things. Not limited to works of the earlier part of the century, however, alchemical millenarianism and eschatology are especially prominent in English editions and translations of works by Paracelsus and Jacob Boehme and in writers whom they influenced. Even one of so tough-minded a bent as John French, for example, in the epistle dedicatory to *The Art of Distillation* (1651), sees the revival of interest in alchemy as a harbinger of a new Golden Age of moral perfection. Alluding to Sendivogius,[52] he speaks of the presently dawning Fourth (or Northern) Monarchy as a time when all the arts and sciences will flourish and more useful inventions will be discovered than in the three previous epochs. Moreover, this will be an era of moral reform, "no other then the golden age, in which all tyranny, oppression, envie, and covetousness shall cease, when there shal be one prince and one people abounding with love and mercy, & flourishing in peace: which day I earnestly expect."[53] Comparison reveals that French's millenarianism is here heavily indebted to Sendivogius's Preface to *A Treatise of Sulphur* as it appears in French's English translation of *A New Light of Alchymy* of 1674.[54]

Although otherwise conventional, *Secrets Reveal'd: Or, An Open Entrance to the Shut Palace of the King* (1669) by Eyraeneus Philaletha, a pseudonymous author with whom George Starkey is often associated or identified, incorporates extensive biblical analogy in setting forth the process for making the philosopher's stone. In addition to an alchemical account of the Creation,[55] the tract contains a detailed paralleling of the early stages of the stone's preparation and Christ's nativity, a relatively unusual feature in alchemical treatises of the time.[56] Its most striking aspect, however, is its association of alchemy with millenarian thought and doctrine concerning the Antichrist. Philaletha zealously decries the primacy of money ("that prop of the *AntiChristian Beast*") in the world, the mad ravings of people and nations, and the ascendency of false gods. He does, however, regard these as signs of "our so long expected and so suddenly approaching Redemption," the coming of the New Jerusalem. As in French and Sendivogius, the Millenium is also linked with a return of alchemical "*Adeptists . . . from the four Corners of the Earth.*" Speaking in a prophetic frenzy, Philaletha urgently appeals to his readers: "Believe me ye Youngmen, believe me ye Fathers, because the time is at the dore; I do not write these things out of a vain conception, but I see them in the Spirit. . . . Let my Book therefore be the fore-runner of *Elias,* which may prepare the Kingly way of the Lord" (48-49).

For the late seventeenth-century author, editor, translator, and collector and seller of alchemical books, William Cooper, the religious colorings of the art are also pervasive, as revealed especially in *A Philosophicall Epitaph in Hierogliphicall Figures,* published in 1673 and dedicated to Robert Boyle. In this work, the philosopher's stone, "the Glorified King (*Triply crown'd*)," like Christ with his purifying tincture, "shall vanquish his Enemies, and redeem his Brethren and Kindred, in all or any Nations from their vile Corruptions."[57] Cooper's description, as well as those of other alchemical millenarians, recalls the image of the resurrected Christ emerging victoriously from the tomb in the *Rosarium Philosophorum* (fig. 27). And in a passage that illuminates precisely the previously discussed alchemical conceit in Donne's "*Resurrection, imperfect*" (ll. 9-16), Cooper states that in preparing the stone, its constituent parts must undergo both the Passion and Resurrection of Christ: "Sol (though pure, perfect, and full of virtue in its self bodily) must be Reincrudate, Crucified, and die to Nature, that its Virtue and Tincture lockt up . . . might become exalted with its body and . . . extend and communicate more largely its powerful Virtues, and Tincture to imperfect Bodies, and Spirits to redeem them" (14-15). In exactly this way, for Donne, Christ's crucifixion and entombment "exalted" his incarnate "gold" to redemptive "tincture," enabling the transformation of "Leaden and iron wills to good" and even "sinfull flesh" to a state of Christ-like perfection. Just as the death and resurrection of Christ provide a metaphor for the making and operation of the philosopher's stone, so the individual Christian's spiritual evolution is modeled on the alchemical pattern of corruption, purification, and transcendance, the latter conceived as a platonic ascent from the elemental world, to the celestial realm, to final union with the One. Cooper urges his reader to "pray affectionately, That God, in and through Christs spirit, may enliven thee from dead works, and seperate light from thy dark body and Chaos of sin, that . . . thou maiest improve thy Talent, and mount through and above the quaternary defiling world into the Triune power, and at last come to the quintessential, or Super celestial Central circle of Peace, and Heavenly Beatitude" (sig. C3).

Cooper's millenarianism, which has close affinities with Philaletha's in *Secrets Reveal'd,* is most apparent in the dedicatory remarks to his abbreviated translation of Helvetius's *The Golden Calf,* also included in the *Philosophicall Epitaph.* Here he sees the golden age of moral perfection as being ushered in by the alchemists' revelations of nature's secrets. As is common in writings of late seventeenth-century millenarians, the biblical figure of Elias (Elijah) is presented as a forerunner of the new age, one whose long-awaited arrival betokens the renovation in human knowledge and morality that will shortly precede the Second Coming. Cooper writes that "manifest Tokens would perswade us that the time is come, or not far off, when the true *Elias* is or will be revealing this and all other Arts and Mysteries more plainly and publickly then before, . . . to prepare the way for a higher design, by which men may forsake their vain lusts and pleasures, to follow this and other laudable Arts. And Exercise more Justice, Honesty, and Love to their Neighbors, (hitherto very cool and remiss) til they come to be transformed into the perfect Image of Christ, in, by, and with whom he will Reign spiritually."[58]

Appropriating Elias's biblical function as chosen forerunner of the Messiah (the prophet sent before "the great and dreadful day of the Lord," Malachi 4:5-6; the "restorer of all things," according to Matthew 17:11), alchemical millenarians saw Elias as a mysterious luminary who would reveal the secret of the stone's preparation, thereby dispelling greed, lust, and other evils. The concept of a specifically alchemical or scientific Elias (*Elias artista*) originates with Paracelsus and is popularized by Renaissance utopian writers whose notions of social progress were predicated on scientific advancement. In the second half of the seventeenth century, works by the following writers, among others, contain references to this shadowy figure: Jacob Boehme, William Cooper, Arthur Dee, John Rudolph Glauber, Mystagogus, Paracelsus, Eirenaeus Philalethes, George Thor, and Basil Valentine. The most interestingly ambiguous remarks on the nature and identity of "Elias" belong to John Rudolph Glauber, who, on the one hand, associates this figure with military displays and radical politics throughout Europe and, on the other, identifies Elias/*salia*/salt as one of the proximate ingredients of the stone: Elias's coming "is not to be understood according to the Letter, and to be meant of some great Man in the World, but Magically; for the word *Elias* by transposition of Letters, makes out *Salia.* . . . *Elias Artista* therefore according to the style of Philosophers, signifies extraordinary and unknown Salts, by which great and incredible things may be performed, and accordingly when manifested, will be the cause of great Changes in the World."[59]

Brief consideration of two additional volumes will demonstrate the persistence of alchemical millenarianism throughout the remainder of the seventeenth century and into the early eighteenth. The very rare *Aurifontina Chymica: or, A*

PHILOSOPHORVM·

Nach meinem viel vnnd manches leiden vnnd marter
(groß/
Bin ich erstanden/ clarificiert/ vnd aller mackel bloß·
& à læß፥

Figure 27. Resurrected Christ. *Rosarium Philosophorum* (1550).

Collection of Fourteen small Treatises concerning the First Matter of Philosophers was published for William Cooper in 1680. It contains primarily tracts of older alchemical authorities, both anonymous and known (e.g., Ripley, Bernard Trevisan, Lull, and Flamel), which, when considered together, suggest that belief in the possibility of making the philosopher's stone was still strong late in the century. In fact, in dedicating the volume to Charles II, John Frederick Houpreght (a "student of, and searcher into the wonderful Secrets of Hermes") boasts that the work "prompt[s] us with the very Key, which alone is able to unlock the Philosophers Inchanted Castle" and that "The Philosophers Stone, or Elixir, hath been always counted, and is the highest Secret in Nature."[60]

Yet, despite the volume's emphasis on physical transmutation, certain of its treatises continue the tradition of alchemical allegorizing and millenarianism that we have been tracing. In the *Hydropyrographum Hermeticum,* written originally in German but now translated by Houpreght, the interaction of sulphur and mercury by means of fire is figured forth religiously and eschatologically through reference to God's impending destruction of the old world and creation of a new: "The Body of *Sol* is dissolved and burnt up, and of this dissolved and destroyed Body, a new World likewise is created and born, and the Heavenly-*Jerusalem*, . . . out of the broken corruptible Work of the dissolved Elements, a new Work will be born, which will be an everlasting Work; even so the Holy Trinity hath shewed and signified unto us likewise, a supernatural Fire in the Heavenly Stone" (16). A later treatise in the *Aurifontina Chymica,* the anonymous *Tractatus de Lapide,* unusual in its presentation of alchemy as a mystical, visionary art and its practitioners as magus-like in powers and omniscience, draws interesting parallels between the production of the stone and the hexameral account of the creation (137-38).

A final example among many possible, *Mercury's Caducean Rod,* written by the pseudonymous Cleidophorus Mystagogus and published in a second edition in 1704, will serve to summarize the various seventeenth-century biblical-alchemical parallels I have been tracing. As the work's full subtitle indicates, Mystagogus assumes the closest possible link between Mercury and Christ; it reads: "*The great and wonderful Office of the Universal Mercury, or God's Vicegerent, Displayed. Wherein is Shewn His Nativity, Life, Death, Renovation and Exaltation to an Immutable State.*" Likening the requisite death and regeneration of Mercury to a seed and citing John 12:24, Mystagogus argues that "nothing can be Animated and born again, unless it first suffer Mortification, Putrifaction and Corruption, by which dissolution . . . a more secret and noble change is brought about."[61]

For Mystagogus, as for many earlier seventeenth-century writers and illustrators of alchemical treatises, Mercury is a type of Christ, "implanted by God in Nature, even a true Emblem of the *Heavenly Jerusalem*." As believers look forward to the Second Coming, so this author "invite[s] all such, as desire to be Possessors of this great Mystery, to prepare themselves against the day of Mercury, God's Vice-gerent's appearance, who hath in one hand his Snaky Rod, and in the other a Triune Key, which unlocks the Mysteries of *Acetum, Elixir* and *Azoth*" (38). According to the alchemical millenarianism here set forth, the general and public manifestation of the stone will result in restoration of the natural order and of man's moral nature, no less than Christ's return will effect his spiritual regeneration. Echoing such eschatological passages as Isaiah 65:17, Mystagogus anticipates the coming of a "Spiritual *Jerusalem,* which shall be adorned with all the Glories of God; for all visibles we now see must pass away, and then will be seen what now is invisible, which hath been hid from the generality of Mankind, ever since the foundation of the World, which is the converting of a Quadrant into a Circle; . . . For the true knowledge of *Mercury's Triune Power* will shew man the true Emblem of the Garden of *Eden,* the Paradise of God, about which there is to this day such a clashing among the seeming Learned" (44). At this "now approaching universal day of Redemption," which will be signaled by the squaring of the circle, alchemical gold-making will become common among all men: "money shall be esteemed like Dross, and the prop of Antichrist dash'd in pieces"; "the Adeptists [will] return from all the Corners of the Earth," and "this great glorious Monarchy of the North [will be] established." Mystagogus earnestly prays for assurance that "*Elias* the *Forerunner* of these mighty things [will] come . . . [to] beat his Alarum and [sound] the Trumpet for the Preparation of the Kingly way of the Lord." He asserts in conclusion that every true philosopher beholds a type of this apocalyptic vision: "How the Elements are unbanded, Principles produced, Bodies Calcined and Purified, in order [that] those rich and living Metals, even that Gold, which St. *John* in the *Revelations* says, *The streets of the new Jerusalem* shall be layed with, all which is brought about by the knowledge of *Mercury* and his Regenerating Nature; for 'tis he that must deliver into your hand that Triune Key, that unlocks all the Mysteries of Nature" (64-65).

In concluding this chapter, although I do not want to leave the impression that transmuting base metals into gold and formulating magical elixirs disappear as interests for alchemical authors, I wish to emphasize that these traditional goals are, in many writings of the middle and late seventeenth century, subordinated to religious, esoteric, moral, reformist, as well as iatrochemical concerns. These works are often tinged with millenarian and eschatological ideas and figured forth through ingenious metaphor and striking allegory. Thus, contemporary alchemical writing provides a valuable context for study of the hermetic ideas and references in the poetry of Henry Vaughan and John Milton.

"UNDER *VAILES*, AND *HIEROGLYPHICALL COVERTURES*"

Alchemy in the Poetry of Vaughan and Milton

The smattering I have of the Philosophers stone, (which is something more then the perfect exaltation of gold) hath taught me a great deale of Divinity, and instructed my beliefe, how that immortall spirit and incorruptible substance of my soule may lye obscure, and sleepe a while within this house of flesh.

—Sir Thomas Browne, Religio Medici[1]

Among poets of the mid-seventeenth century, the subjects and modes that we have noted in contemporary alchemical writing—religious allegory, mystical and millenarian tendencies, a lessening interest in transmutation of metals paralleled by increasing iatrochemical concerns—are best seen in the poetry of Henry Vaughan. More than any other poet of this period, Vaughan's work has been investigated from the perspective of the hermetic and alchemical influences it is thought to reflect. In fact, along with the question of Herbert's influence and the nature of Vaughan's mysticism, hermeticism has been among the most interesting and rewarding approaches to the poems of *Silex Scintillans,* in particular.

Detailed investigations adopting this critical approach began with Elizabeth Holmes's pioneering study, *Henry Vaughan and the Hermetic Philosophy,*[2] and extend to the present. Narrowly focused as its title indicates, Holmes's brief monograph traces the hermeticism of the poems of *Silex Scintillans* chiefly to the works of the poet's twin brother Thomas, as well as to several of the most popular authors in the contemporary hermetic and alchemical milieu, Boehme, Agrippa, and Paracelsus. Drawing extensively on the notes included in L.C. Martin's edition of the poems,[3] first published in 1914, Holmes cites many parallels and verbal echoes to these writers in Vaughan's poetry, but the chief value of her study is the attention given to many of the major hermetic themes and image patterns that have continued to be subjects of scholarly investigation and debate: reflections in the verse of a doctrine of an immanent God and an all-pervading *anima mundi,* the notion of sympathies and correspondences linking macrocosm and microcosm, the presence of universal "signatures" or stamps that betoken this linkage of terrestrial objects with their celestial correspondents, and a doctrine of childhood innocence and purity.

The work of several later critics has consisted mainly of extensions and refinements of Holmes's hermetic approach. Richard H. Walters,[4] for example, finds in *Silex Scintillans* many parallels to ideas and terminology present in treatises of the *Hermetic Musaeum*, first published in 1622; while he provides little detailed discussion of individual poems, his isolation of such topics as analogies between transmutation and regeneration, ideas of the *anima mundi* and an ever-changing cosmos, and parallels between alchemy and medicine are at least relevant to the study of many poems. As shown in the previous chapter, such topics are dominant in seventeenth-century alchemical writing. For Alan Rudrum,[5] less concerned than Holmes and Walters with tracing hermetic allusions to their specific sources, this influence imparts a sense of energy, motion, and flux in Vaughan's verse. Thus, preoccupation with *change* and *process,* while not the only evidence of the poet's alchemical and hermetic interests, reflects "the latent possibilities of matter [that] are realized in a process of transformation through the various grades of existence. In its more purely philosophical aspect, hermeticism accounts for the created world in the Plotinian terms of emanation and return to source, in terms, that is, of endless cyclic movement."[6]

In contrast to these critics, for Frank Kermode the influence of hermeticism in Vaughan's poetry is incidental rather than central: "The object of the poet is hardly ever to make the hermetic or Dionysian idea [Kermode continually conflates the two] the central one; it is always illustrative, lighting and enriching the tenuous, often Herbert-inspired, argument of the poem."[7] Just as he discounts the evidence for, and hence the influence of, Vaughan's supposed "conversion," so he elevates the purely literary influences reflected in his verse, and chiefly the poetry of Herbert. Thus, while acknowledging the extensive reference to hermetic themes and images in *Silex Scintillans* and other collections, for Kermode, Vaughan's roots are planted in poetry rather than religious mysticism and philosophical obscurities.

Most of the authors of more recent studies of Vaughan's poetry have adopted a position on his hermeticism that falls somewhere between Holmes's and Walters's assertion of its importance and Kermode's skepticism about its central role. In the latter camp, Ross Garner's *Henry Vaughan: Experience and the Tradition,* although it presents detailed analyses of "Regeneration" and "Resurrection and Immortality" only, argues that hermeticism plays no major part in Vaughan's work. In "Regeneration" (and here I agree), hermeticism "is not inherent in the plain language of the poem; the poem makes very good traditional sense without it."[8] Clearly, the poem can be satisfactorily interpreted in the light of Christian mysticism alone. However, Garner's reductive view of the influence of hermeticism in "Resurrection and Immortality," as I hope to show, does not take into account the sheer number and importance of ideas from the *Hermetica* that are interwoven in this poem.[9] His larger point, that in using hermetic images Vaughan was not asserting their truthfulness *per se* but their aptness and validity in figuring forth the truths and "realities of Christian experience,"[10] is less disputable only because it is difficult to prove. On the whole, Garner's understanding of hermeticism in Vaughan is flawed by his failure to recognize that in the seventeenth century such ideas tend to be closely fused with those of Christianity. As has been shown, hermetic writings typically rely heavily on biblical themes, imagery, allegory, and analogy in setting forth their ideas; furthermore, as R.A. Durr reminds us, "Vaughan was entirely capable of absorbing elements of the amorphous hermeticism of the time into his fundamentally Christian belief without feeling heretical . . . just as it is possible for a man today to incorporate aspects of Freudian or Jungian psychology or Existential philosophy into a fundamentally Christian view of life."[11]

In contrast, E.C. Pettet in *Of Paradise and Light,* while not treating Vaughan's hermeticism in as much detail as Garner, is willing to grant it a greater role in *Silex Scintillans.* Drawing upon Holmes's study and hence upon the treatises of Thomas Vaughan, Pettet sees the influence in terms of a technical vocabulary (e.g., *balsam, exhalation, glance, grain, ray, magnetism, seed, sympathy,* etc.)[12] and, more importantly, of a conception of nature marked by such hermetic *topoi* as God's immanence and continuing operation within the natural world, the *anima mundi,* and the "sympathies" and "magnetism" that bind together all parts of the cosmos. While concluding, like Kermode, that Vaughan "was never primarily inspired by hermetic beliefs and ideas" and depended on them less than on Herbert and the Bible (84), Pettet nonetheless emphasizes hermeticism's importance in creating "a singular and unmistakable atmosphere about his poetry, a sense of mysterious activities and influences continuously at work, of integration and harmony—in short, a peculiarly living quality" (82).

More than most critics, especially those like Walters and Rudrum, James D. Simmonds's *Masques of God* denies that hermeticism exerted a serious and explicit influence; rather, that influence is most manifest when hermeticism is closely assimilated with Christianity and Neoplatonism.[13] As a result, it is rarely used as an approach or tool of explication for either the sacred or secular poems. Among authors of recent critical studies, and in striking contrast to Simmonds, Thomas O. Calhoun's *Henry Vaughan: The Achievement of Silex Scintillans* attributes to hermeticism a much more pervasive, although vaguely defined, influence. Pursuing further Rudrum's interest in the sense of change, process, and flux exhibited in Vaughan's conception of nature, Calhoun's intent is to isolate and analyze the "interior progress" of the poems, a quality of metamorphosis and transmutation that is both figuratively and literally magical. Unlike his contemporary Baconians in their attempts at mechanizing and quantifying nature, "Vaughan does not see objects or creatures as fixed entities, but as active and interacting. Instead of quantified elements he sees vapors, dews, exhalations, sympathies, antipathies, distillations, combustions, corruptions, purifications, and subtly changing colors. He sees nature as a sequence of transformations. The form of his thought is determined by the way he perceives this natural movement."[14]

The source of this phantasmagoria of sensation (and hence of Vaughan's poetic expression) is hermeticism, specifically the tradition of "hermetical physick" of Paracelsus and his followers, one of whom, Henry Nollius, Vaughan translated and knew through his own medical practice. It is the linking of the peculiar nature of the poet's processes of "associative thought and the analogical structure of his poems"[15] to the ancient Egyptian, hermetic, Platonizing, Paracelsian variety of homeopathic medicine that accounts for much of the originality of Calhoun's study. And if this study is occasionally weakened by the sheer tenuousness of the qualities whose presence he sets out to prove, by insufficient sketching of the seventeenth-century context of "hermetical physick,"[16] and by too little analysis of individual poems, Calhoun's linking of major principles and processes in Vaughan's verse to contemporary medical theory is nonetheless a significant contribution.

While the extent to which Vaughan's poetry is indebted to hermetic philosophy is thus a matter of critical controversy, the proximity of Vaughan's hermetic borrowings to the dominant ideas and images that appear in the treatises of his time is indisputable. In both we find abundant evidence of doctrines of an immanent God, a pervasive world soul, sympathies and correspondences connecting the greater world and the lesser, and imprints or signatures of the macrocosm visible in the Creation and the creatures. The presence of these general hermetic themes, Vaughan's adoption of an allegoresis that fuses religion and alchemy, and his use of medicine or "hermetical physick" along with millenarian and eschatological ideas, give to his poetry a consistency and individuality of idea, mood, movement, and outlook that sets it apart from all other hermetic and alchemical poems previously considered. We shall investigate examples of each of these tendencies in poems drawn from *Silex Scintillans.*

Among the poems that incorporate a variety of hermetic doctrines, "Resurrection and Immortality" has received far less attention than others like "Cockcrowing" and "The Night," although L.C. Martin and more recent editors have detected extensive parallels to ideas from the *Corpus Hermeticum.* But it is the way hermetic ideas are assimilated with Christian doctrine, how they are used, in fact, not merely to provide analogies but to clarify and vivify the nature and meaning of resurrection and immortality that makes the poem unusually powerful and representative of Vaughan's hermeticism at its best. Whereas editors and critics most often point to the concentration of hermetic parallels in sections 2 and 3 (the Soul's responses to the Body), one of the poem's underlying themes— the idea of an immanent God and the ties between Creator and creatures and among the creatures themselves—is asserted by the Body in the opening lines:

Body.

I.

Oft have I seen, when that renewing breath
That binds, and loosens death
Inspir'd a quickning power through the dead
Creatures a bed,

> Some drowsie silk-worme creepe
>   From that long sleepe
> And in weake, infant hummings chime, and knell
>   About her silent Cell
> Untill at last full with the vitall Ray
>   She wing'd away,
>
> . . . .
> Shall I then thinke such providence will be
>   Lesse friend to me? [ll. 1-10, 15-16]

In these lines, Vaughan's characterization of an immanent God whose breath re-news and quickens, injecting a "vitall Ray" into the lowest of the creatures (the "drowsie silk-worme") as well as the highest, recalls not only the role of the pre-serving and transforming demiurge or sun in the *Corpus Hermeticum,* 16,[17] but more the God of the heavily Christianized hermeticism of Vaughan's contempo-rary, Robert Fludd: "God operateth all in all. He vivifieth all things. He filleth all things. His incorruptible Spirit is in all things. . . . He sent his Spirit and created all things. He giveth breath unto the people, and Spirit unto the creatures that tread on the earth. . . . If thou hidest thy face, the creatures are troubled, if thou takest away their breath they die, if thou sendest forth thy Spirit they are re-created or revived."[18]

Even though the Body has "oft" seen such examples of metamorphosis and renewal in the natural world, these observations have failed to provide it with complete assurance of a similar transformation for itself, and its resulting insecu-rity is reflected in the very tentativeness of the question it poses in lines 15-16. The Body's lack of confidence, then, results from its ignorance of the promise of change and rebirth implicit in the law of nature according to both Christian and hermetic doctrine: God's "incorruptible Spirit is in all things"; "the permanence of every kind of body is maintained by change." Lacking reason, the Body can-not, like a well-trained natural philosopher, make the inductive leap from ob-served instances to general laws. Although its speculation in the final lines of this section reveals that its instincts are correct, the Body remains trapped in the world of appearance and sensation.

In addition to much else, "Resurrection and Immortality" is exemplary of the rules of decorum that demand that lines spoken be appropriate to the speaker's nature and character. While the Body's perspective is typically earth-bound (re-stricted in its observations to the lower "two whole Elements," earth and water), the Soul's speech in the second section of the poem is compact of air and fire in its abstract philosophizing. It is appropriate that its intellectual superiority and more comprehensive understanding should reflect close familiarity with the doc-trines of permanence and change set forth in the *Hermetica.* The Soul's perspec-tive, which could scarcely be more opposite to that of the Body, is initially established by its mode of empirical investigation. Whereas the Body's observa-tions have been superficial (like Caliban, "nurture" does not "stick" to his nature), the Soul's examination of nature has been keenly analytical, piercing deeply beneath the surface:

> was't for this
> I taught thee all that is?
> Unbowel'd nature, shew'd thee her recruits,
> And Change of suits
> And how of death we make
> A meere mistake [ll. 19-24]

Vaughan points the contrast between the speakers by means of a variation on the "unveiling of nature" motif, used by Herbert, Milton, and a variety of Renaissance alchemical writers, according to which nature is stripped naked by the skillful scientist to reveal her secrets, whereas she remains fully clothed to the casual observer.[19]

What this unveiling reveals to the "Poore, querulous handfull," the Body, is the "truth" of a range of doctrines that, while not incompatible with Christianity, are more directly expressive of concepts from several of the Libelli of the *Hermetica*.[20] For example, the study of nature reveals that all forms of life are subject to an endless series of renewals and rebirths, a Neoplatonic sequence of emanations from a source followed by returns to that source. Thus, to speak of death is "A meere mistake":

> For no thing can to *Nothing* fall, but still
> Incorporates by skill,
> And then returns, and from the wombe of things
> Such treasure brings
> As *Phenix*-like renew'th
> Both life, and youth; [ll. 25-30]

For the Soul in this role of pedagogue, the agent of renewal is the *anima mundi*, "a preserving spirit [that] doth still passe / Untainted through this Masse" (ll. 31-32). Although this spirit recalls "the radical Balsame, the vital seed, and the very root or fundamentall of humane Nature" that Vaughan encountered while translating Nollius's *Hermetical Physick*,[21] the entire stanza is essentially a versification of Libellus 8, entitled, "That none of the things that are is destroyed, and they are mistaken who say that changes are deaths and destructions."[22] While parallels are numerous, the similarities of the preceding lines to the following passage from the beginning of Libellus 8 are especially striking: "Death has to do with destruction, yet none of the things in the cosmos is destroyed. If the cosmos is a second god and an immortal living thing, it is impossible for any part of this immortal living thing to die."[23] Thus for the Soul, which speaks at a level of abstraction considerably higher than does the Body in the opening section, nature's lessons are that death and extinction are illusory and that the principles of continuing "incorporation" (the taking of bodily form) and return operating in the creatures

are grounds for firm belief in immortality for *all* life. The presence of the phoenix image to symbolize renewal of life and youth (l. 29), practically inevitable in
this context, is justified for reasons of the argument and the touch of concreteness it provides.

As the argument for resurrection develops in section 2, the obvious facts of
aging and physical corruption are necessarily subordinated to the liberation of
the Soul ("the more noble *Essence*") and its return to the One, "that spring, / And
source of spirits." Vaughan's conception of the reunion of Soul with Body, which
"Shall one day rise, and cloath'd with shining light / All pure, and bright / Re-
marry to the soule," has certain parallels with a kind of hermetic renewal described in Libellus 8,[24] and the section concludes with one of his favorite alchemical
images, refining, used in combination with the idea of renewal: "for 'tis most
plaine / Thou only fal'st to be refin'd againe" (ll. 49-50).

Vaughan does not explicitly identify the speaker of the final section (ll. 51-
70); on the one hand, it may be the Body, now speaking with the advantage of its
recently acquired knowledge. More likely, however, it is the Soul speaking of the
far greater vision and understanding to be enjoyed in a future state of blessedness
when it will be united with the resurrected Body. In either case, this section describes the experience of immortality, which has only been foreshadowed thus
far, but it begins by contrasting future omniscience with the finitude of ordinary
human knowledge and wisdom:

> Then I that here saw darkly in a glasse
> > But mists, and shadows passe,
> And, by their owne weake *Shine,* did search the springs
> > And Course of things
> > Shall with Inlightned Rayes
> > Peirce all their wayes; [ll. 51-56]

The strongly Christian outlook of this section, more pronounced than in either
of the two preceding, is attributable in part to the conscious echoes of I Corinthians
13:12. Again, however, it is incautious to trace the "Through a glass darkly" idea
to one source alone. Given the hermetic provenance of the poem, Vaughan may
also have drawn upon a passage from the *Asclepius,* where the imperfection of
human knowledge is likened to seeing through a "mist" but which may dissipate
and evolve to a state in which glimpses of heaven and eternity are possible.[25] The
Soul's illumination in this future state also encompasses a kind of mental flight
that enables it to range freely throughout the universe, from the highest reaches
of the heavens to underground, to grasp the secrets of all things with angelic
intuition:

> I in a thought could goe
> To heav'n, or Earth below
> To reade some *Starre,* or *Min'rall,* and in State

> There often sate,
> So shalt thou then with me
> (Both wing'd, and free,)
> Rove in that mighty, and eternall light
> Where no rude shade, or night
> Shall dare approach us; [ll. 57-65]

The Soul's cosmic excursion, in which it is to be accompanied by the resurrected body, is not Vaughan's invention. As Martin has pointed out, the passage has parallels in the *Hermetica,* Libellus 11;[26] but Vaughan was also adopting a topos used by a host of classical and medieval authorities, including Plato, Xenophon, Posidonius, Horace, Ovid, Cicero, and Plutarch, who, in their encomia on the powers of mind, included descriptions of the soul's flights beyond time and space.[27] No less popular in the Renaissance, the best-known examples of this topos appear in Marlowe's *Tamburlaine, Part II,* act 5, 58-69 and *Dr. Faustus,* act 2, scene 3, 8-13 and in Milton's "At a Vacation Exercise," lines 33-52, and the celebrated passage from "Il Penseroso," lines 85-96, to be discussed later in this chapter, which may well have provided inspiration for Vaughan's imagery and cosmic itinerary.

However, the most immediate source, which is also the best gloss on the third section of Vaughan's poem, is his own translation of Archbishop Anselm's treatise, *Man in Glory: or, A Discourse of the blessed state of the Saints in the New Jerusalem,* which he had printed in 1652, two years following publication of part 1 of *Silex Scintillans* (in which this poem appeared), and three years before the collection was reissued with additions. In the following passages, Vaughan treats of the glories of the resurrected body in the life to come. After discussing its beauty, the type of which is the body of Christ, he speaks of its capacity for physical motion and activity and of the complete felicity that comes only at the "re-marrying" of the soul with the now-incorruptible body:

> As for *Activity,* which is every way as desirable as *Beauty,* we shall be indued with such a measure of it, as shall render us equall for swiftnesse to the very Angels of God, which in a moment passe from the highest heaven unto the earth, and from the earth again into heaven; . . . Again, it is a thing certainly known, that the souls of the Elect which are in the hand of the Lord, have not yet enjoyed the fulnesse of felicity, untill their bodies shall be restored unto them incorruptible; which when they shall enjoy, there will be nothing more left for them to wait for and desire.[28]

In the final analysis, "Resurrection and Immortality" is a "hermetic" poem. By that I do not mean that Vaughan necessarily subscribed to the ideas and doctrines from the *Corpus Hermeticum* that appear in it or that, as such, they were a dominant part of his private religious creed. Nonetheless, these hermetic borrowings are more than just a vehicle for Vaughan's expression of his religious vision, like the "drowsie silk-worme" of the opening lines. Vaughan, I think, saw no fundamental incompatibility or contradiction between his borrowings and the more traditional Christian ideas that he espouses in many of the poems of *Silex Scintillans.* For him, the description of immortality that concludes "Resurrection and Immortality," "One everlasting *Saboth* there shall runne / Without *Succession,* and without a *Sunne*" (ll. 69-70), reflects essentially the same state of being that Hermes describes in response to his son Tat's question concerning the nature of rebirth in Libellus 13:

> [Tat] "Tell me clearly the way to be born again." [Hermes] "What can I say, my child? I have nothing to tell except this: seeing {} within me an unfabricated vision that came from the mercy of god, I went out of myself into an immortal body, and now I am not what I was before. I have been born in mind. . . . Color, touch, or size I no longer have; I am a stranger to them. . . ." [Tat] "What is the true, then, Trismegistus?" [Hermes] "The unsullied, my child, the unlimited, the colorless, the figureless, the indifferent, the naked-seeming, the self-apprehended, the immutable good, the incorporeal."[29]

Both traditions are present and indissoluble in this poem.

At the conclusion of his chapter on "Hermetic Philosophy," E.C. Pettet observes that "Cock-crowing" and "The Starre" are the best examples of poems in which "hermetic conceptions have furnished an exceptionally powerful initial impulse that persists throughout the poem" (84). I argue for inclusion of "Resurrection and Immortality" in this small group, particularly because of its recollection of several key ideas and images from the *Corpus Hermeticum.* Although Pettet's commentary on "Cock-crowing" is very limited and indebted to Holmes's earlier study especially, he is correct in seeing the poem as exemplary of the "singular and unmistakable atmosphere . . . [and] sense of mysterious activities and influences continuously at work" that, for him, is hermeticism's principal effect in Vaughan's poetry (82).

The following discussion of "Cock-crowing," not intended as exhaustive, will concentrate on general hermetic topics that were of special interest to his age and which Vaughan became acquainted with through the writings of his brother Thomas and hermetic and alchemical books that were then proliferating in England. In terms of its hermetic interests, "Cock-crowing" is broadly comprehensive, nearly a catalog of ideas and images popular in his time. Chief among these are the closely related topics of the seed or tincture, sympathies and "magnetisme," correspondences between the macrocosm and microcosm, and the now-familiar flight of the disembodied soul. The poem's range of hermetic reference is thus greater than that of "Resurrection and Immortality," but like the latter it effects a fusion of occult and Christian ideas that resists attempts to make convincing distinctions between them. The result is a poem marked by the strangeness of atmosphere noted by Pettet and a powerful appeal for immediate union with God, a contact ironically allowed the lower creatures but denied to men imprisoned in the veil of flesh.

Vaughan's rooster with its matinal crowings could scarcely be a more effective vehicle to express the intimate bond that should exist between the Creator and his creatures. While Martin and others have noted close parallels of idea and phrasing between the poem's opening lines and a passage from Thomas Vaughan's *Anima Magica Abscondita,*[30] it remained to D.C. Allen to demonstrate the bird's many-layered richness of meaning in both Classical and Christian tradition.[31] It is not only a "solary" bird but also a holy and magical one, associated with the mysteries of the cosmos and guidance of the souls of the dead. Obviously linked with St. Peter's denial of Christ, it also "awakens men from spiritual slumber, warning them of the coming of light."[32] Through Plato, it is connected with the image of the soul as a "winged thing," and at times it may be a symbol for Christ. While all of these meanings inform the cock, its most important role in the poem, that of symbol for the "sympathy" or correspondence that obtains between the macrocosm or God and the creatures of the lower world, results from its possession of the "Sunnie seed," "glance of day," or "busie Ray":

> Father of lights! what Sunnie seed,
> What glance of day hast thou confin'd
> Into this bird? To all the breed
> This busie Ray thou hast assign'd;
>   Their magnetisme works all night,
>   And dreams of Paradise and light. [ll. 1-6]

Vaughan's vocabulary for expressing this natural, instinctive response of creature to its creator and source of light is varied throughout the first six stanzas of the poem: it is the "little grain expelling night" (l. 8), the "candle . . . / tinn'd and lighted at the sunne" (ll. 11-12), a "tincture" (l. 13), God's "seed" (l. 23), and a "Pulse [that] beats still for light" (l. 32). All these images are variations on divine sparks and seeds—manifestations of the divine implanted by God in his creatures—that should ensure fidelity and responsiveness to him. That part of the human soul or that imprint or "signature" within the lower creatures that is received from God, the theory goes, *is* God, and this share of divinity provides the means for conformity with God's will or the law of nature, at least in all creatures but man. Vaughan's use of the doctrine of *synteresis,* man's participation in the divine through the presence of the spark within his soul, is based not only on a long tradition of Christian theological commentary[33] but also on the Neoplatonic and hermetic commonplace that since all creation is the work of God, all creation is divine, and that "rays" and "seeds," emanating from the One, determine mortal thought and conduct.[34]

A final possible source for these images in Vaughan's poetry is the tradition of Greek and Roman Stoicism with its concept of God as the *spermatikos logos,* not only creating the material world but also disseminating the seeds of God-like qualities, identified with reason, throughout the cosmos. Or, in a related metaphor derived from Heraclitus, God is portrayed as a divine *pyr* or fire, which imparts to man sparks or small flashes (the Ciceronean *igniculus*) of divinity, serving as guides to rational thought and conduct. In either case, and the images of seeds and sparks are at times combined in Stoic thought, man carries within himself attributes of his creator, and the substance of his soul is divine.[35]

Whatever the immediate source for Vaughan's notion of the divine ray implanted within the creatures, its presence is the principle cause of tension and conflict within the poem as well as the chief means of communicating its theme. If the "Father of lights" has implanted his signature in the bird indelibly enough to ensure the bird's instinctive knowledge of and responsiveness to its creator ("Their little grain expelling night / So shines and sings, as if it knew / The path unto the house of light," [ll. 8-10]), why should man, God's "own image," lack steadfastness in watching for the Second Coming? Man, no less than the cock, contains within himself the divine imprint, albeit in the form of reason and thus subject to his own perfidious nature, rather than instinct. The tragedy of man's infidelity to God is intensified by his possession of the very reason that should ensure his obedience. In stanza 4, his reason leads him to awareness that the beauty of the world implies the goodness and wisdom of the creator, and in addition to the teleological argument, reason has also taught man of the damnation that certainly awaits those whose souls are beyond the state of grace: "In such a dark, Ægyptian border, / The shades of death dwell and disorder" (ll. 29-30). Yet, despite these potentially saving insights, man's stubborn blindness persists.

Man's tragedy, as delineated in "Cock-crowing," truly stems from his existence in a middle state, below that of the angels and above that of the humble creatures, for whom God has provided instinct.[36] Despite the fact that man's link with the divine has been weakened through the corruption of reason resulting from original sin, he retains a longing for God and yearns for the upward flight of his winged soul to God. The lines "who, but thee, knows / A love-sick souls exalted flight? / Can souls be track'd by any eye / But his, who gave them wings to flie?" (ll. 33-36) recall the similar image in section 3 of "Resurrection and Immortality," and, along with the rising rhythms of the two final stanzas, suggest the soul's urgent desire for unity with the One. However, except for partial glimpses ("onely gleams and fractions"), the soul is prevented from full vision and understanding by the veil of flesh that encompasses it:

> Onely this Veyle which thou hast broke,
> And must be broken yet in me,
> This veyle, I say, is all the cloke
> And cloud which shadows thee from me.
> > This veyle thy full-ey'd love denies,
> > And onely gleams and fractions spies. [ll. 37-42]

While the veil is obviously biblical in provenance and alludes to that which, in 2 Corinthians 3:14, darkens minds imprisoned in the law of the Old Testament, but which is dissipated by Christ; or, more directly, to the precedence that

Christ's fleshly sacrifice takes over the burnt offering of the law, as in Hebrews 10:19-20,[37] it is also hermetic. The eagerness of the speaker's appeal for the veil's removal in the final stanza ("O take it off! make no delay, / But brush me with thy light") anticipates a fullness of illumination to be experienced in the state of immortality, recalling the passage from *Asclepius* 3, in which mortal vision through a mist may yield to clearer sight of heavenly things.[38] Thus, while Vaughan's poetry generally reflects the extreme difficulty of attaining the highest state of mystical unity, the possibility of such vision is at least admitted in "Cock-crowing." Through cultivation of the seed containing God that dwells within the speaker, the fracture between the macrocosm and microcosm may be repaired, the sympathies (the "loose tye of influence" that prevails among creatures "that have no sence")[39] may again prevail, and man may once more know God as easily and instinctively as the crowing rooster.

Vaughan's essentially hermetic view of the cosmos—a world both created and permeated by the divine; that is alive and sentient; and that features a network of correspondences ("a tye of Bodyes")[40] linking the high and the low, the near and the remote—is present in many of his poems. For example, the bird in the poem of that name, after enduring the buffeting of a nocturnal storm, awakens, like the crowing cock, with instinctive praise for its creator, "whose unseen arm" protected it and kept it "well and warm" (ll. 9-10); later, in response to remote influences, all of nature including the dumb stones join together in a chorus of praise. Similarly in "The Starre," another work that begins in close observation of the natural world, this heavenly body is mysteriously attracted to some object in the microcosm, causing the star to twinkle and vary its course. The cause of this attraction (and here we see that the lines of force or magnetism extend upward as well as downward) is the occult resemblance between things of the great world and the lesser.[41] The propitious beams emanating from the star seek only objects that are receptive to them. Hence, to receive this astrological "commerce," the terrestrial object must be "well-disposed" and pure and active in its desire for the beams.[42] These qualities are the "Magnets which so strongly move / And work all night upon thy light and love" (ll. 21-22); they are the qualities in the human heart that God desires.

"Disorder *and* frailty," unlike the preceding poems, posits a relationship between God and man in which the chain of communication has been disrupted. The spiritual experience that the poem presents is consequently marked by shifts and vacillations in the speaker's mood as he is subject to the extremes of depression and joyous optimism in his attempt to heal the broken relationship with God. The "disorder and frailty" that thus marks his spiritual experience makes him acutely aware of his dependence on God for spiritual wholeness. However, this poem is akin to those preceding in that Vaughan again uses a variety of hermetic ideas and images to delineate these shifting states of mind. These references are skillfully incorporated into the larger image patterns of the journey and, more importantly, the growing plant.[43]

The metaphor of the journey provides a backdrop for the speaker's initial experiences, giving the poem superficial resemblances to "Regeneration." God is the soul's "guide, and Scout," who first conducted it on its journey from a brutish state of sin and animalistic passion. Early confidence, however, has declined in the face of spiritual hardship and loss of communication with God:

> And though here tost
> By winds, and bit with frost
> I pine, and shrink
> Breaking the link
> 'Twixt thee, and me; [ll. 6-10]

And in charting the speaker's spiritual vacillations in stanza 2, and in shifting the poem's major metaphor to a plant, Vaughan describes alternating states of optimism and aridity with images that, although predominantly botanical, contain potentialities for hermetic interpretation that will be fully realized only in stanzas 3 and 4. The persona's religious zeal, for example, is imaged as God's touching of a bud with his fire and breath (ll. 17-18); Christ's blood is both dew and "springing wel" (l. 19).

While the hermeticism of "Disorder *and* frailty" has received less attention than it warrants, Vaughan's editors have usually pointed out parallels between stanza 3 and an excerpt from the *Stobaei Hermetica* in which atmospheric vapors or "exhalations" are shown to be rising from the earth and returning to it, as the sun's heat is applied or withdrawn. The resulting fluctuations are analogous to the alterations in the speaker's spiritual state as his confident aspirations toward heaven, secure as he is in his knowledge of Christ's atonement, are blasted by spiritual disease:

> 3.
> Thus like some sleeping Exhalation
> (Which wak'd by heat, and beams, makes up
> Unto that Comforter, the Sun,
> And soars, and shines; But e'r we sup
>   And walk two steps
> Cool'd by the damps of night, descends,
>   And, whence it sprung, there ends,)
>   Doth my weak fire
>   Pine, and retire,
> And (after all my hight of flames,)
> In sickly Expirations tames
>   Leaving me dead
>   On my first bed
> Untill thy Sun again ascends.
>   *Poor, falling Star!* [ll. 31-45]

Whether Vaughan was consciously recalling the passage from the collection of hermetic fragments compiled by Joannes Stobaeus,[44] it might have served him well, for here the generation of "exhalations" (meteors or shooting stars) is explicitly associated, like the persona's changing moods, with frustration and futility:

> And below the moon are stars of another sort, perishable and inert, which are so composed as to last but for a little time, rising as exhalations from the earth itself into the air above the earth; and we can see their dissolution with our own eyes. . . . even so the stars which rise as exhalations from the earth do not attain to the region of heaven,—for they are not able to do that, because they rise from below,—and, as they have in them much heavy stuff, they are dragged down by their own matter, and are quickly dissipated, and being broken up, they fall down again to earth, having effected nothing except a troubling of the air above the earth.[45]

While I do not insist on Vaughan's familiarity with this particular excerpt, his use of the atmospheric image is at once so vivid and scientifically precise *and* psychologically valid in its suggestion of alternating spiritual states, that it is tempting at least to make note of this possible analogue. The imagery of stanza 3, then, richly contributes to what Pettet thinks of as the otherworldly atmosphere of Vaughan's poetry and to what Rudrum calls the emphasis on the soul's involvement in the cosmic process. In regard to the latter, Vaughan's imagery recalls parallels in at least two very well-known hermetic sources: Hermes' *Emerald Table* and Robert Fludd's *Mosaicall Philosophy*. The former, containing originals for many of the ideas and images we have been examining, includes this cryptic instruction for making the philosopher's stone: "The father of all the telesme of this world is here. His force and power is perfect, if it be turned into earth. Thou shalt seperate the earth from the fire, the thinne from the thicke, and that gently with great discretion. It ascendeth from Earth into Heaven: and againe it descendeth into the earth, and receiveth the power of the superiours and inferiours: so shalt thou have the glorie of the whole worlde."[46]

The vividness and precision of Vaughan's image may also owe something to the descriptions and illustrations of the weather-glass that his celebrated contemporary, Robert Fludd, included in the *Mosaicall Philosophy*. Fludd's "scientific" instrument, which combines the function of the barometer with the working principles of a thermometer, is exhalation-like in its linking of the rising and falling of its column of liquid to the presence or withdrawal of heat from the instrument. More than from its purely scientific description and illustration, however, the relevance of Fludd's account to Vaughan's hermetic context results from Fludd's view of his experimental apparatus as a replication of the laws of nature, an imitation of the way the forces of the macrocosm operate in the microcosm. This relationship is asserted in the descriptive title that Fludd gives to chapter 5 of the first book: "Here it is proved evidently, notwithstanding any objection

which may be made to the contrary, that not only this experimentall Organ hath
a relation unto the great world, but also the spirit included in this little modell
doth resemble and imitate the action of that which is included in the great or
macrocosmicall Machin."[47]

The final stanza of "Disorder *and* frailty" is no less daring in its attempt to
express the ineffable than the conclusions of "Resurrection and Immortality" and
"Cock-crowing," and, as in those poems, its effectiveness is largely dependent on
a highly skillful blending of hermetic idea and image with Christian teaching.
Whereas the two poems considered earlier conclude with the speakers' appeals to
be shown the state of immortality or to experience the presence of God that
exists beyond the veil of flesh, "Disorder *and* frailty" combines the "flight of the
soul" image with those of hermetic seeds and fires in order to express the soul's
desire to transcend the state of spiritual weakness earlier described. Lines 47-49
recall the cosmic excursion of "Resurrection and Immortality," the soul's roving
through heaven and earth "To reade some *Starre,* or *Min'rall,*" but are more
"mosaicall" in their notion of the soul's origin as an act of brooding or hatching
on the part of God's spirit. Furthermore, the flight of the fledged soul takes a
steadfastly upward direction, through the higher reaches of the celestial spheres
toward God: "O, is! but give wings to my fire, / And hatch my soul, untill it fly /
Up where thou art, amongst thy tire / Of Stars, above Infirmity" (ll. 46-49).
Vaughan's cosmic flight is not sustained, however, and "Disorder *and* frailty" ends
on a more humble strain. Having glimpsed the upward path to the Almighty, his
speaker is content to be taught the lesson of practical Herbertian piety. Appropriately, at this point in the poem where the verse is being "tuned" of its earlier
disorder, the central image shifts from the soul's flight to the humble plant:

> Let not perverse,
> And foolish thoughts adde to my Bil
> Of forward sins, and Kil
> That seed, which thou
> In me didst sow,
> But dresse, and water with thy grace
> Together with the seed, the place; [ll. 50-56]

Other poems in which hermetic themes and ideas appear must be glanced at
more briefly. As Pettet has noted, the seventh and eighth stanzas of "I walkt the
other day" are enriched by a variety of hermetic echoes, such as the notion of the
true reality, God, behind the multifarious "Masques and shadows" (l. 50) that
obstruct the way to him, or the concept of the world's creation as a result of
divine incubation and hatching. The latter idea, which is present in several of the
poems of *Silex Scintillans,* first appears in stanza 7 of "I walkt," when, having
earlier seen the "doctrine" of resurrection imaged in the "fresh and green" root
beneath the earth's surface, the speaker ponders the universal force that operates

in ways that are often hidden, employing creation as an hieroglyphical "second" book whereby man may recognize the true source of divine love and mercy. Here, Vaughan's God, "Who art in all things, though invisibly" (l. 54), is represented as the creating spirit of Genesis 1:2 that "move[s] upon the face of the waters," as well as in hermetic terms:

> O thou! whose spirit did at first inflame
> And warm the dead,
> And by a sacred Incubation fed
> With life this frame
> Which once had neither being, forme, nor name [ll. 43-47]

In Libellus 3, Hermes describes the Creation as the result of divine breath extending over chaos and the formless waters, accompanied by brilliant illumination. The elements then evolve through division and separation: "In the deep there was boundless darkness and water and fine intelligent spirit, all existing by divine power in chaos. Then a holy light was sent forth, and elements solidified [ ] out of liquid essence. . . . While all was unlimited and unformed, light elements were set apart to the heights and the heavy were grounded in the moist sand, the whole of them delimited by fire and raised aloft, to be carried by spirit."[48] And, similarly, for Robert Fludd, the "Mosaicall Principles" depict Creation as a type of "Spagiricall separation" effected in six days by God's Word or the "divine Spirit *Elohim*," spoken over the waters, "the common, or universall matter and subject of all things."[49] Creation proceeds according to the alchemical processes of condensation and rarefaction whereby "all things in this world are made to differ from one another, and are disposed and ordered by God, according to weight, number, and measure, in their proper rancks and places."[50] These two processes are, in turn, governed by the presence or absence of the sun, in a manner reminiscent of Fludd's "weather-glass," discussed earlier.

Containing many of these same echoes—from the *Corpus Hermeticum,* Robert Fludd, Thomas Vaughan's Creation description in *Magia Adamica,* and Genesis 1:2—"The Water-fall," like most of the nature poems here considered, is centrally concerned with the problem of human vision. How can man learn to read nature aright, as an hieroglyph of God, so as to be led upward to communion with the author of all creation? The answer Vaughan provides in "The Water-fall"—which, as nearly all critics have noted, is an emblem or hieroglyph by virtue of its visual shaping[51]—is that proper vision is itself a gift of God:

> What sublime truths, and wholesome themes,
> Lodge in thy mystical, deep streams!
> Such as dull man can never finde
> Unless that Spirit lead his minde,
> Which first upon thy face did move,
> And hatch'd all with his quickning love. [ll. 27-32]

Not only the explicit reference to the Creation as an act of brooding or hatching by the Holy Spirit upon the face of the waters,[52] but also the encompassing metaphor of the water's cyclical outflowing and return as analogue for the soul's imperishability mark "The Water-fall" as hermetic in inspiration. As a poem that begins in meditation on a natural object, "The Water-fall" has much in common with "Resurrection and Immortality" and its "drowsie silke-worme," with the crowing cock, and with "I walkt the other day" and its snugly growing root. As with these poems, the effectiveness of "The Water-fall" owes largely to Vaughan's consummate skill in fusing physical object, hermetic image and idea, and Christian theme. In lines 13-20, for example, the integration of all three elements is accomplished with a degree of effectiveness rarely exceeded or equalled by Vaughan or any poet of his age. The stream, often the object of the speaker's "pensive eye" and of his meditation, reveals to him the truth of the unending cycle of its liquid transport. From this initial recognition growing out of physical observation (recall the silk-worm's lesson to the Body), and facilitated by the connecting correspondences that link all creation, the stream may easily serve as an emblem for the immortality of the soul and the resurrection of the body. But assisting in this meditative progress from physical object to Christian truth and meaning, and as a kind of hermetic middle term, we are introduced to the essentially hermetic or Neoplatonic doctrine of permanence through change, of the soul's apparent pre-existence in a "sea of light," its emanation from that origin and eventual return:

> Why, since each drop of thy quick store
> Runs thither, whence it flow'd before,
> Should poor souls fear a shade or night,
> Who came (sure) from a sea of light?
> Or since those drops are all sent back
> So sure to thee, that none doth lack,
> Why should frail flesh doubt any more
> That what God takes, hee'l not restore? [ll. 15-22]

Thus far in discussing Vaughan's poetry, it has been the practice to speak of *hermetic* ideas and images and their *hermetic* sources. In contrast to nearly all the writers considered in earlier chapters, to whose works the terms alchemy and alchemical were freely applied, Vaughan's poetry with its philosophical and mystical emphasis can more properly be described by the term hermetic. However, if by alchemy we mean a practical application of some of the principles of hermetic philosophy that typically takes the form of the transmutation of base metals, the discovery of chemical cures, or the search for life-extending elixirs, it is clear that Vaughan's poetry reflects alchemical interests and knowledge as well. The relationships in meaning between hermetic and alchemical are vague at best, and distinctions become especially difficult when such classes of ideas present themselves in literary contexts. Even granted these semantic difficulties, however, the distinctions and the implications thereof set forth by M.M. Mahood in her chapter on Vaughan in *Poetry and Humanism* are greatly oversimplified and misleading. She observes that through the writings of Thomas Vaughan, "Henry Vaughan studied the Hermetic philosophy which, after sinking to the level of alchemy and magic during the Middle Ages, had been restored as a metaphysical system by Renaissance thinkers."[53]   I have no quarrel with Mahood's reference to Renaissance hermeticism as a "metaphysical system"; indeed, I hope my own discussion supports this designation. It is incorrect, however, to refer categorically to medieval hermetic thought as "*sinking* [emphasis mine] to the level of alchemy and magic," as if the art could be represented exclusively by the alchemical charlatans who actually practiced their deceptions in the Middle Ages or by the confidence men who appear so frequently in literary works from Chaucer through Ben Jonson and occasionally beyond. Mahood's statement overlooks the fact that alchemy was also considered to be a holy art and that there were doubtless honest seekers after the philosopher's stone.

The important distinction between hermeticism and alchemy is not between a crude form of charlatanism and a respectable metaphysical system, but between aspects of a large and complex body of thought that were now and again either more practical and utilitarian or more theoretical, religious, and philosophical in nature and purpose. Thus in Vaughan and in other Renaissance writers who were seriously interested in various forms of occultism, we find that beliefs in an immanent God whose divine presence penetrates the cosmos, in sympathies and correspondences that unite the macrocosm and microcosm, and in signatures and *synteresis* are important theoretical foundations upon which the practice of alchemy and magic depended. While among most recent critics it is more common to discuss Vaughan's hermeticism rather than his alchemy,[54] the latter, with its emphasis on transmutational processes and the philosopher's stone, on salutary cordials and elixirs, and on the allegorization of these subjects in light of Christian doctrine, must not be neglected. These conventional topics, while not often providing a basis for the larger philosophical and religious themes or the unusual atmosphere of Vaughan's poetry, serve well as sources for smaller details, such as specialized vocabulary and individual images.

The differences in the functions of hermeticism and alchemy can be clarified by a final glance at "Resurrection and Immortality," a poem that, as I have shown, is as deeply indebted to hermetic ideas and imagery as any that Vaughan wrote. In several places, however, Vaughan introduces the more technical and specialized vocabulary of alchemy, often drawing attention to these terms through the use of italics. As might be expected, most of these usages occur in the poem's second part, that spoken by the Soul. For example, the "*Nothing*" to which "no thing" can fall (l. 25), while undoubtedly appropriated from Donne's "The Broken Heart,"[55] also strongly suggests the alchemical "chaos" or "first nothing" to which Donne's persona in "A Nocturnall upon S. Lucies day" is reduced as a result of the woman's death. He is not an "ordinary nothing." Vaughan's use of the term, like Donne's, is freighted with overtones of absolute extinction and annihilation, and the allusion to the early stage in the alchemical process is highly effective. At line 29, the "*Phenix*-like" cycle of the rebirth and renewal of matter may share alchemical ancestry along with currency in mythographic and other traditions. Further, "*Essence*" (l. 39) (or *essentia* or quintessence) as a synonym for the soul is richly suggestive in alchemical tradition as, according to Ruland, it is "something higher than the elements, nor does it originate from these or from what is gross therein, but is divine in source and in effect."[56] In Vaughan's context, these connotations serve well in setting the nobler soul apart from the declining body. In the final and most unequivocally alchemical of all of these images, the process of refining is invoked to describe the condition of the resurrected body at the time of its remarriage to the Soul. The Body "Shall one day rise, and cloath'd with shining light / All pure, and bright / Re-marry to the soule, for 'tis most plaine / Thou only fal'st to be refin'd againe" (ll. 47-50).

Among the images derived from alchemical processes in other poems, those that refer to refining are most frequent. In "Dressing," the speaker pleads that God should "my gloomie Brest / With thy cleer fire refine" and follows directly with reference to the technical process of calcination ("burning to dust / These dark Confusions, that within me nest," ll. 5-7), the reduction of a substance to a powdery calx through the application of great heat, and very "serviceable to a speedy, marvellous healing."[57] In "To the Holy Bible," the book, which has been neglected during the speaker's spiritual rebellion, nonetheless exerts a force, conveying "A sudden and most searching ray / Into my soul, with whose quick touch / Refining still, I strugled much" (ll. 20-22). This poem also contains the image of the Holy Spirit as a brooding, fructifying dove (ll. 28-29) and is linked thematically and imagistically with "H. Scriptures." The latter poem in praise of the Bible, an English sonnet in form, contains a variety of hermetic and alchemical allusions. Following the feasting image that opens the first stanza, Vaughan adopts a term from alchemy to suggest that the Scriptures are an epitome of heaven: he states that "Heav'n extracted lyes in thee" (l. 2), Heaven's essence having been drawn forth and transfused into the book. A catalog of epithets in the manner of Herbert's "Prayer," the quatrain figures forth the concept of the Bible as a repository for the writings of those inspired by the Holy Spirit, which thus serves as the indispensable means for attaining salvation and eternal life. In Vaughan's curious, almost Crashavian, conceit, this aspect of the Bible is presented as "The Doves spotless neast / Where souls are hatch'd unto Eternitie."

The second quatrain contains alchemical allusions in even greater concentration: "In thee the hidden stone, the *Manna* lies, / Thou art the great *Elixir,* rare, and Choice; / The Key that opens to all Mysteries, / The *Word* in Characters, God in the *Voice*" (ll. 5-8). The first line of this quotation juxtaposes the imagery of the "hidden stone" and manna in a manner that recalls Revelations 2:17 ("To him that overcometh will I give to eat of the hidden manna, and will give him a white stone, and in the stone a new name written, which no man knoweth saving he that receiveth it"), which no doubt served as Vaughan's direct source. But the line also points to the allegorical motif of Christ as the philosopher's stone, previously discussed, which rests in part on the Scriptural metaphor of Christ as the cornerstone, the despised stone rejected by the builders. Vaughan's stone is quite properly "hidden" because of its disesteem in the biblical references to the cornerstone (e.g., Psalms 118:22, Isaiah 28:16, Matthew 21:42, and Acts 4:11) as well as its proximity to the "white stone" of Revelations that conceals the name written on it. But the fact that Vaughan's stone is hidden (in the verse from Revelations the manna is hidden) is more satisfactorily explained because preparation of the philosopher's stone is a secret known only to select initiates. The passage's alchemical background is confirmed by images that follow immediately. Like the alchemical allegorists, Vaughan conflates manna, the divinely sent food of the Israelites, with the spagyrical "manna," a balsam which, according to Ruland, "preserves bodies from putrefaction."[58] The Scriptures are also the "*Elixir,*" appropriately "rare, and Choice," and finally, echoing the titles of numerous alchemical treatises, they are "The Key that opens to all Mysteries."

Owing perhaps to Vaughan's career as a physician, to his work as a translator of Henry Nollius's *Hermetical Physick* and *The Chymists Key,* or to the fact that, increasingly, seventeenth-century alchemy came to be employed more in the formulation of chemical medicines than in the transmutation of metals, Vaughan's conception of the deity often has spagyric overtones. These are also the most probable reasons for the abundance of medical imagery in his poetry and for the frequent combining, in allegory, of medicine with Christian subjects and themes. Whatever the reasons for these characteristics, it is certain that Vaughan's familiarity with some of the leading medical theories of the day, as exemplified in his translations of Nollius, provided him with ideas to which he was poetically and medically receptive. To cite only a few examples, Nollius's *Hermetical Physick,* which the Westphalian pastor and professor of philosophy at Giessen first published in Latin in 1613,[59] was avowedly Paracelsian in orientation. However, as was the case with Tymme's *Dialogue Philosophicall* (1612), discussed in the previous chapter, Nollius traces his medical theory back to Hermes Trismegistus:

> It is termed *Hermetical Physicke,* because it is grounded upon *Principles* of true *Philosophy,* as the Physick of *Hermes* was. And for this very reason the true Philosophers applyed themselves wholly to the *Hermetic* science, that they might thereby lay a true foundation of Physick, for the *Hermetic* Phylosophy layes open the most private and abstruse closets of nature, it doth most exquisitely search and find out the natures of health and sickness, it provides most elaborate and effectuall Medicines, teacheth the just Dose of them, and surpasseth by many degrees the vulgar Philosophy, and that faculty which is grounded upon the principles of the common, supposititious knowledge, that is to say, it doth much exceed and outdo the *Galenical Physick.*[60]

For the hermetical physician, then, cures are discovered only by close observation of nature rather than received opinion. They take the form of universal medicines operating through correspondences upon the body's innate preservative or "radical balsam" and proceed according to homeopathic principles.[61]

The fullest investigation of Vaughan's poetry in the light of "hermetical physicke" appears in the work of Thomas Calhoun, who sees the hermetic (and Paracelsian) principle, "*Every like is cured by its like,*"[62] as the key to the patterns of thought and structure in many of the poems of *Silex Scintillans*. For Calhoun, "Individual lyrics seize upon immediate responses to events and, imitating nature's operation, move to transform transient sense into something durable and new. . . . The precepts and procedures of hermetical medicine affect the form of Vaughan's poems by shaping the way he understands natural metamorphoses."[63] I wish neither to accept nor challenge Calhoun's interesting thesis on the problematical issue of the origins of Vaughan's thought processes, vis-à-vis his poetry; rather, I will examine several of the poems from the point of view of their medical themes and images, since these constitute some of the most interesting aspects of his work and reveal the proximity of his thought to a number of the ideas that are central in the alchemical and medical literature of his time.

The final section of Vaughan's translation of Nollius's *Hermetical Physick* concludes with the words: "*When the Patient is delivered from his disease, and restored to his former health, let him heartily and solemnly give all the glory to the Supreme, All-mighty Physician: let him offer the sacrifice of Thankes-giving, and acknowledge the goodness and the tender mercies of the Lord.*"[64] The notion of Christ as the good physician serves either explicitly or implicitly as a dominant image in several of the poems of *Silex Scintillans*. For Vaughan, however, the familiar biblical metaphor, derived from such events as Christ's healing of the centurion's servant and Peter's wife's mother in Matthew 8, takes on overtones that are specifically hermetic and Paracelsian in nature. For example, in "The Sap," a poem that can be read as an extended spagyrical conceit, Christ is portrayed as a dispenser of the health-giving sap or cordial and is thus a type of the physician or apothecary:

> To shew what strange love he had to our good
> He gave his sacred bloud
> By wil our sap, and Cordial; now in this
> Lies such a heav'n of bliss,
> That, who but truly tasts it, no decay
> Can touch him any way,
> Such secret life, and vertue in it lies
> It wil exalt and rise
> And actuate such spirits as are shed
> Or ready to be dead,
> And bring new too. [ll. 25-35]

"The Sap" is Vaughan's brief version of man's fall from grace and his recovery through the agency of the restoring and preserving blood of the good physician. The effect of this "rare dew" (l. 40) or "balm for souls that ake" (l. 44) is exactly parallel to those of Nollius's universal medicine, which is an "infallible remedy against all infirmities, and the greatest and most proper restorative and comforter of the spirits in their functions."[65]

"The Agreement" contains a very similar image of God as a Paracelsian physician, curing likes with likes, opposing the speaker's "heynous sins and numberless" with medicines and methods that are suggestively harsh. Use of the specialized term *Cathartics* (l. 58) originated in the seventeenth century (see *OED*): "And this I hourly finde, for thou / Dost still renew, and purge and heal: / Thy care and love, which joyntly flow / New Cordials, new *Cathartics* deal" (ll. 55-58).

Other examples of imagery derived from medical theory and practice are common.[66] In his refining capacity, the Christ of "Love-sick" is implicitly likened to an alchemist's fire, purging the speaker's heart of its foulness (ll. 12-14). Much more explicit are the spagyric and Paracelsian overtones in "Affliction," where, ironically, God-given adversities are the "Pils that change / Thy sick Accessions into setled health, / This is the great *Elixir* that turns gall / To wine, and sweetness" (ll. 2-5). And in lines that are thematically and imagistically related, the speaker in the version of "Day of Judgement" appearing in the first edition of *Silex Scintillans* pleads to God for additional corrections before the fearful day is at hand: "Still more afflictions lend, / That pill, though bitter, is most deare / That brings health in the end" (ll. 34-36). Common among the charges levied against Paracelsian physicians was the bitterness of their metallic and mineral medicines, and central to Paracelsus's theory of healing was the view that cures resulted from administering potions of the same "poisons" that caused the illness in the first place. Thus, through additional adversities the speaker's sinful heart may be prepared for judgment before it is too late.

In the previous chapter, I discussed the common practice among alchemical writers of the early and middle seventeenth century to combine eschatological and millenarian ideas with alchemical allegory. Grounding their prophecies in the analogies between Christ and the philosopher's stone, Thomas Tymme, Nicholas Flamel, Philaletha, William Cooper, and others saw Christ's return as ushering in a period of unprecedented scientific and moral enlightenment, a golden age in which the secret of the stone's preparation would be publicly revealed after having been foreshadowed by the appearance of the mysterious *Elias artista*.[67] Vaughan's eschatological and millenarian interests are expressed in several poems, such as "Day of Judgement," with its recently noted Paracelsian overtones; in addition, "The Dawning" reflects concern about the exact time of the Second Coming, and in "The Jews," their conversion is seen as imminent. However, only in the Pentecostal poem "White Sunday" is Vaughan's millenarian interest firmly linked with alchemical tradition. In the first fifty-six lines, he describes his times as "this last and lewdest age" (l. 39), a period of sectarian conflict, false doctrine, greed, political disorder, and blindness to God's word. Against this background of evil, Vaughan sets his urgent appeal to God in the final stanzas:

> So let thy grace now make the way
> Even for thy love; for by that means
> We, who are nothing but foul clay,
> Shall be fine gold, which thou didst cleanse.
>
> O come! refine us with thy fire!
> Refine us! we are at a loss.
> Let not thy stars for *Balaams* hire
> Dissolve into the common dross! [ll. 57-64]

While the imagery of gold and refining in these two stanzas owes much to biblical prophecy (e.g., Malachi 3:1-3), the conception of God that informs this passage is also that of a master alchemist whose prevenient grace and ensuing love will effect moral transformation and salvation. As Pettet has noted, these lines reveal "the close correspondence, almost identity, between transmutation of the metals and regeneration, between the alchemic furnaces and the 'furnaces' of affliction."[68] Vaughan's plea is at once intensely personal and "publicly" millenarian in its overtones. Given the unmitigated evil of the times portrayed in the poem and Vaughan's detestation of the political and religious upheaval resulting from the Civil War, it is only natural that he should have drawn upon the techniques of contemporary alchemical millenarians to intensify the enormity of the existing evil and the urgency of its cessation. The combining of beliefs concerning Christ's return with alchemy was, as previously demonstrated, a popular topos in alchemical tracts written at the time of the poem's composition, and it was also used on occasion by Vaughan's contemporary, John Milton.

In contrast to Donne, Jonson, and particularly Vaughan, Milton's interest in alchemy and hermeticism appears slight, a surprising fact given the extraordinary breadth of his reading and the allusiveness of his literary style. Although learned and used with precision, these references are relatively few in number and may at first seem to support little of the substantive weight of the contexts in which they appear. As a result, there are relatively few modern scholarly investigations of Milton's alchemy, the topic having often been subsumed under the larger subjects of his science or philosophy.[69] A recent scholar, in fact, while discussing similarities in the ideas of Robert Fludd and Milton, states that "Milton was skeptical of occult phenomena and alchemical experiments (although he viewed digestion as a kind of natural alchemy),"[70] a judgment that, although true in part, fails to recognize the range and complexity of Milton's incorporations of alchemical ideas and images in his works. At the same time, it is perhaps excessively ingenious to see "L'Allegro" and "Il Penseroso" as fraught with "possible revolutionary Hermetic meanings," or *Comus* as being "in part about the achieving of the alchemical quest," as Douglas Brooks-Davies has argued.[71]

Milton was aware of and occasionally employed both the old, satirical uses of alchemy and the more recent metaphoric mode illustrated in the verse of Donne,

Herbert, and Vaughan. For example, that Milton, no less than Greene and Nashe, was capable of using alchemy as a weapon in savage attacks on others is shown in his reference to his adversary in the *Apology for Smectymnuus* as "an Alchymist of slander, [who] could not extract that, as well as the University vomit, and the Suburb sinke which his art could distill so cunningly, but because his Limbeck failes him, to give him and envie the more vexation, Ile tell him."[72] A few pages later his foe is represented as an "Empirick of false accusations [who would] try his poysons upon me whether they would work or no" (1:893). Milton's scathing attacks on prelatical corruption in *Of Reformation* incorporate the charge that "[t]heir trade [is], by the same Alchymy that the *Pope* uses, to extract heaps of *gold,* and *silver* out of the drossie *Bullion* of the Peoples sinnes" (1:592). Again, his attacks on book licensing in the *Areopagitica* are vivified through reference to Ramond Lull's reputation as an alchemist; he states, "I am of those who beleeve, it will be a harder alchymy then *Lullius* ever knew, to sublimat any good use out of such an invention [i.e., licensing]" (2:507). Or, finally, speaking of the folly of restricting even bad books, he states, "if it be true, that a wise man like a good refiner can gather gold out of the drossiest volume, . . . there is no reason that we should deprive a wise man of any advantage to his wisdom" (2:521). In each of these examples, Milton's employment of the terminology of the alchemical process, e.g., "extract," "distill," "sublimat," "refine," results in serious assaults on personal, religious, and political opponents, and the effect is the same whether alchemy is represented as being actually transmutative or not. (In the last quotation from the *Areopagitica,* as Kester Svendsen has noted, the ability to "gather gold out of the drossiest volume" is assigned to a "good refiner" and not an alchemist.)[73] If anything sets Milton's alchemical satire apart from tradition, it is the seriousness with which he wields it and the seriousness of the targets upon which it is directed. Unlike most of the authors who are a part of this tradition, Milton's alchemical satire is not composed primarily for the purpose of humor.

Milton's most interesting and original uses of alchemy are found in a half dozen or so passages in *Paradise Lost* that have been the subject of varying amounts of critical attention. I will pass over briefly the view of Michael Lieb concerning the dialectical role of alchemy in delineating the epic's contrasting types of creativity: the first, represented by the sun, is what Lieb terms "natural creativity"; the second, identified with Satan and false alchemists, is "unnatural."[74] To proceed with discussion of Miltonic alchemical allusions in the order in which they occur, the infernal setting of book 1 is made palpably uncomfortable, in part, by reference to sublimation at line 235. After Satan leaves the burning lake, Milton's description of the "dry Land / . . . that ever burn'd / With solid, as the Lake with liquid fire" (ll. 227-29) where he alights, is heightened by means of a volcanic simile; it appears

> as when the force
> Of subterranean wind transports a Hill

> Torn from *Pelorus,* or the shatter'd side
> Of thund'ring *Ætna,* whose combustible
> And fuell'd entrails thence conceiving Fire,
> Sublim'd with Mineral fury, aid the Winds,
> And leave a singed bottom all involv'd
> With stench and smoke: [1:230-37]

Milton's prototype of a nuclear firestorm, the result of violent winds and intense heat escaping from within the subterranean vault, is solidly grounded in Renaissance theories concerning these natural phenomena.[75] And while his "Sublim'd with Mineral fury" is extremely effective in rendering this holocaust of heat and wind, even suggesting hell's sulphurous stench, its sublimation offers no possibility of refining and purification. The traditional aims of this alchemical process have no place in the abode of one who is beyond hope and redemption. Also learnedly accurate, as Duncan has shown,[76] is the reference later in book 1 to the subterranean growth of metals. The fallen angels' search for materials with which to build Pandaemonium takes them to the hill where the "parent" principle of sulphur has been operative:

> There stood a Hill not far whose grisly top
> Belch'd fire and rolling smoke; the rest entire
> Shone with a glossy scurf, undoubted sign
> That in his womb was hid metallic Ore,
> The work of Sulphur. [1. 670-74]

The description recalls the illustration from Michael Maier's *Symbola aureæ Mensæ* of the mountain within which the vaporous exhalations of sulphur and mercury are producing ore, just as it is being produced alchemically on the mountaintop (fig. 4).

But much more original than this traditional view of metallic generation is Milton's reference to alchemy as a metal in 2:516-17, the first such use that I have found in a purely literary context. Here, following closure of the Stygian council, four cherubim-heralds blazon forth the results with infernal trumpets, "Put[ting] to thir mouths the sounding Alchymy." Duncan, citing earlier editors and the *OED,* has suggested two related lines of explanation. "Alchymy" appears at times in the Renaissance to designate an artifical, counterfeit or "mixed metal," an alloy of the sort used in the production of bells; hence it was referred to as "bell metal." Second, Milton's usage is metonymic; he is naming "the efficient for the effect."[77] Such explanations, however, fail to address the most important aspect of Milton's image: the *sound* of the "sounding Alchymy" and its effects. The linking of the sound of angelic trumpets with alchemy suggests the concept of "musical gold" and the role that music, based on Pythagorean concepts of harmony and proportion, played in alchemical ritual and process.[78] Henry Cornelius Agrippa, for example, notes the useful by-products that have resulted from alchemical experimentation: "I do not denie that of this Arte many most excellente workemanshippes had theire beginninge. From hence come the temperatures of Asure, of Cinnaber, of Sinople, of Purple, and of that which they call musicall golde, and of other Coloures."[79] Some alchemists were also composers of music that was intimately related to their art, such as the *Cantilena* of George Ripley, which have survived in many Latin and English versions,[80] and as Thomas Norton, the other famous late medieval alchemist, wrote in 1477: "Joyne them together also *Arithmetically,* By suttil Numbers proportionally . . . Joyne your Elements *Musically.*"[81] However, the best-known pairing of music and alchemy is Michael Maier's *Atalanta Fugiens* (Oppenheim, 1618), in which each of the fifty engraved illustrations is accompanied by an epigram and a fugue, complete with musical notation and words.

But beyond these matters of background, the appropriateness of this unusual use of "Alchymy" in its immediate context has not been discussed. The effects of the notes played by the angelic trumpeters are immediate and large in scope, producing a dramatically significant *change* in Satan's fallen legions:

> the hollow Abyss
> Heard far and wide, and all the host of Hell
> With deaf'ning shout, return'd them loud acclaim.
> Thence more at ease thir minds and somewhat rais'd
> By false presumptuous hope, the ranged powers
> Disband, and wand'ring, each his several way
> Pursues, as inclination or sad choice
> Leads him perplext [2:518-25]

While Milton intends the scene to be recognized as an infernal parody of the chorusing of heavenly angels, his masterstroke of irony is the momentary lifting of the demons' anxious minds by the "false presumptuous hope" inspired by the trumpets' "sounding Alchymy." Like the traditional victims of alchemical hoaxes they depart in sad confusion, a point that resonates in the twice-repeated "in vain" in the next alchemical image in 3:601-2.

For Milton, the primary association of alchemy is fundamental change, whether of the kind exhibited in the demeanor of the fallen angels upon hearing the heralds' "sounding Alchymy" or in the extended discussion of ontology and the operations of nature in book 5, to be discussed shortly. However, the passing of Satan through the shell of the universe in book 3, followed by his descent to the sun's surface, provides occasion for the epic's most spectacular alchemical allusion. In this universe, the sun is obviously the source and provider of the life force. In phrases that recall hermetic images of the dove brooding over the primordial waters at the time of the Creation, Milton also emphasizes the sun's impregnation of the universe with fructifying virtue; its "Magnetic beam" "gently warms / The Universe, and to each inward part / With gentle penetration, though unseen, / Shoots invisible virtue even to the deep:" (3:583-86). In accordance with traditional metallurgical theory, here and elsewhere in *Paradise Lost,* the sun's action extends to the production of metals and minerals in the "deep," far below the earth's surface.[82]

But Milton's sun—"great Luminary," "all cheering Lamp," "lucent orb"—is best known in the epic for its brilliant light "beyond expression bright," as Satan discovers when he walks upon its surface:

> Not all parts like, but all alike inform'd
> With radiant light, as glowing Iron with fire;
> If metal, part seem'd Gold, part Silver clear;
> If stone, Carbuncle most or Chrysolite,
> Ruby or Topaz, to the Twelve that shone
> In *Aaron's* Breastplate, and a stone besides
> Imagin'd rather oft than elsewhere seen,
> That stone, or like to that which here below
> Philosophers in vain so long have sought,
> In vain, though by thir powerful Art they bind
> Volatile *Hermes,* and call up unbound
> In various shapes old *Proteus* from the Sea,
> Drain'd through a Limbec to his Native form.
> What wonder then if fields and regions here
> Breathe forth *Elixir* pure, and Rivers run
> Potable Gold, when with one virtuous touch
> Th' Arch-chemic Sun so far from us remote
> Produces with Terrestrial Humor mixt
> Here in the dark so many precious things
> Of color glorious and effect so rare? [3:593-612]

Critics concerned with the sources of this brilliance have pointed to its possible indebtedness to Ovid's description of Hyperion's temple in the *Metamorphoses,* book 2, to the explicit allusion to Aaron's breastplate in Exodus 28:17-24, and to Milton's obvious invoking of several alchemical ideas and images.[83] Little has been said, however, on the links *between* the twelve stones placed on Aaron's breastplate and the philosopher's stone, "Imagin'd rather oft than elsewhere seen." Lieb is correct in noting that the philosopher's stone is here "associated with Urim and Thummim, the mysterious stones in '*Aarons* breastplate,'" but he does not explain the nature of the connection.[84] Exodus 28:30 is the earliest biblical reference to the Urim and Thummim and provides the basis for Milton's image, which he will use again in *Paradise Lost* 6:761 and *Paradise Regained* 3:14-16: "And thou shalt put in the breastplate of judgment the Urim and the Thummim; and they shall be upon Aaron's heart, when he goeth in before the Lord: and Aaron shall bear the judgment of the children of Israel upon his heart before the Lord continually." This biblical reference is followed by several others that link these mysterious objects to Aaron's breastplate or to the priesthood generally or associates them with the judgment of Israel or with a means of communication between the Lord and the human soul.[85] They have been called "oracular media by which the priest obtained God's decision for the people . . . and a symbol of the intercessory role of the priest."[86] Milton follows this description closely in the opening of book 3 of *Paradise Regained,* where Satan, speaking false words of flattery to Christ, states "Thy Counsel would be as the Oracle / *Urim* and *Thummim,* those oraculous gems / On *Aaron's* breast" (ll. 13-15).

However, in addition to their Old Testament meanings, the Urim and Thummim possessed alchemical associations, knowledge of which might have enabled Milton to make the transition easily from priestly stone to philosopher's stone at line 598 of the preceding quotation and thereby intensify the sun's brilliance. In 1655, an anonymous treatise entitled "Whether *The Urim & Thummim* were given in the Mount, or perfected by Art" appeared in a collection of alchemical treatises entitled *Chymical, Medicinal and Chyrurgical Addresses, made to Samuel Hartlib, Esquire,* printed by G. Dawson for Giles Calvert. The treatise offers no clue as to authorship or information as to the compiler of the collection, although this is generally assumed to have been Samuel Hartlib, the important educational reformer and dedicatee of Milton's *Of Education* in 1644.[87] Although the possibility of a Hartlib connection is intriguing, I am not contending that Milton's awareness of the alchemical interpretation of the Urim and Thummim must have been derived from this particular source, which is the only one that I have encountered that provides such an interpretation.[88] In any case, the listing of the treatise's title in the table of contents makes the alchemical association clearer than the interrogative form of the title previously cited, which was taken from the first page of the essay itself. The Contents title reads: "A Short Discourse, proving Urim & Thummim to be perfected by Art, and to be of like pure Snbstance [sic], with the White and Red Elixirs" (sig. A2).

This treatise belongs to the highly esoteric tradition of spiritual alchemy, extolling "the true Alchymist [who] excludes all vulgar operations to extract the internal beauty" (2). It has several points in common with the Miltonic context in which the Urim and Thummim appear, both originating in the same passages from the Old Testament. For example, like Milton at lines 594-98, the author of "Whether *The Urim & Thummim*" also discusses the twelve stones in Aaron's breastplate but elaborates on their cabalistic and numerological arrangement and meanings: "The four Elements . . . they [the Rabbis] express in Numbers and figures, for number is Unity folded up, and Unity is number unfolded . . . And number is said to be formed, and material signifying *Principia & Elementa,* because *vocabulum naturale est symbolum numeri,* which is expressed in the setting of the precious stones four rowes, three in a row, four to shew the natural perfection, and three the inward genreration [sic]; as three and four the artificial exaltation" (11-12). Both Milton and the author of this tract extensively employ images of the sun and brilliant light, the latter stating that the words Urim and Thummim themselves "signifie light and perfection," but they were also the "bright and perfect" substances that Moses put into the breastplate (5). "[P]ure sulphur," one of the proximate materials of the philosopher's stone, "should have regal power and rest, eternally visible, shining as the Sun in glory" (10). The *"occultum corporis, . . .* augmented and fixed, shines as the Sun in glory" (13). Or finally, "as the Sun is chiefest amongst celestial bodies, so his spirit doth raign over the fourfold nature, and being corporate is without shadow" (10). In short, "Whether *The Urim & Thummim"* provides an excellent example of the linking of these mysterious objects with alchemy and with the sun and light imagery, just as Milton does in *Paradise Lost* 3:593-612.[89] While other models for these associations may exist, this one has the advantage of proximity of date (1655) to the time of composition of *Paradise Lost* and the connection with Samuel Hartlib.

Milton's purpose in introducing alchemy and the philosopher's stone as similes in this description of the sun's surface is not merely to intensify the luminosity of the scene that Satan surveys, although it does contribute to this effect by means of implicit associations with the radiant and changing colors that mark crucial stages in the alchemical process: the tail of the peacock, the white stone, the red stone, and so on. The alchemical similes also help emphasize the solar setting's remoteness from human experience and, through Satan's contrasting darkness, his deceptiveness and alienation from humanity. At the beginning of the passage, the narrator takes pains to tell us that no astronomer peering through a telescope had ever seen a place such as that where Satan alights (3:589-90); similarly, the alchemists' "stone," closely juxtaposed with the mysterious Urim and the stones adorning Aaron's breastplate at line 598, is represented as existing only in the imaginations of its pursuers; it is an *ignis fatuus* rather than a reality, a point doubly emphasized through repetition of "in vain" at lines 601-2. The quest for the philosopher's stone, Milton concludes, must end in futility even though alchemists may succeed in "binding" (i.e., fixing) "Volatile *Hermes,"* the mercury that serves as one of the stone's components. Here Milton's ironic reference to the "powerful Art" used in this attempt recalls the alchemist's futile efforts to fix Mercury in Jonson's *Mercury Vindicated.* The adjoining reference to another classical deity, the invoking of "Proteus"—arguably the *prima materia* or another ingredient of the stone—again suggests the ultimate futility of adepts' attempts to purify or reduce their materials to their first essence through a process that resembles distillation.[90] Thus the alchemists' failures may be associated with the failures of Satan, whereas in contrast, the "Arch-chemic" sun, whose remote powers are manifest in the growth of gems and metals deep beneath the earth's surface, is capable of far more magnificent transmutations on its own surface: "fields and regions [that] / Breathe forth *Elixir* pure, and Rivers [that] run / Potable Gold" (ll. 606-8).

A suggestive interpretation of this entire passage appears in Svendsen's *Milton and Science,* which regards it as a locus of important, related images and symbols whose meanings extend throughout the poem. He sees the sun as a symbol of worldly perfection and an approximation (but only that) of heaven. In contrast to the sun's natural virtue is the deception and artificiality practiced by the alchemists, who fail to produce what the sun does naturally, and of these Satan is the type. Svendsen concludes: "A system of contrasts pervades the lines: reality against artificiality, physical brightness against spiritual darkness, Hebrew against pagan, the true dignity of the sun as lord of planets and natural creator against the false pride of the artful alchemists and Satan. All these implications come once we have perceived the metaphoric vocabulary imbedded in the curious and forgotten lore of the philosopher's stone, the fecundating sun, and alchemy."[91] Svendsen's view of these relationships is strengthened by the Satan-false alchemist correspondences noted in several of the literary works discussed earlier. On this level, the continuity extending from Chaucer to Milton appears unbroken.

In addition to falsity and artificiality, another primary association of alchemy for Milton is that of fundamental change and flux, whether of the kind exhibited in the demeanor of the fallen angels upon hearing the "sounding Alchymy" of the infernal trumpets or, as in book 5, that which is integral in the operations of the "universal Frame" and within man himself. Milton's optimistic and fluidic ontology is expressed most memorably in Raphael's familiar speech beginning "one Almighty is, from whom / All things proceed," (5:469ff.) with its famous image of the tree becoming increasingly "spiritous" and rarefied as it rises toward its divine source. This arboreal image—Milton's metaphor for the scale and operation of nature—along with other parallels, I have argued elsewhere, has a notable analogue, perhaps an immediate source, in the *Enchyridion Physicae Restitutae* by the French hermetic, scientific, and philosophical writer Jean d'Espagnet. The *Enchyridion* was first published in Latin in 1623, often reprinted in the first half of the seventeenth century, and translated into English in 1651.[92] But before considering Milton's use of alchemy in his metaphysical and ontological discussions, I will briefly reexamine the tree image's larger context, arguing that nearly all of the preceding part of book 5 is carefully designed to prepare Adam for the possibility of melioristic ascent from body to spirit that is figured forth so effectively in Milton's springing tree. This tree, then, serves not only as metaphor and model for the nature of Nature but also as a powerful and central moral symbol, the culmination of a consciously developed pattern, which introduces Adam to the possibility for human development and affirms its contingency on obedience to God.

As early as *The Reason of Church Government Urged Against Prelaty* (1642), Milton observes that God had carefully ranked and positioned the angels in the heavenly region from the time of their creation and that a similar, but less perfect, discipline and order extends to the "state also of the blessed in Paradise."[93] In *Paradise Lost,* this fixity of creation in the celestial spheres is forcefully asserted in the forms of address to angelic audiences used by three different speakers on three different occasions in book 5: "Thrones, Dominations, Princedoms, Virtues, Powers" is the salutation repeated by God (l. 601), Satan (l. 772), and finally Abdiel (l. 840) in his refutation of Satan's "argument blasphemous, false and proud!" And, as if to reify the idea of hierarchical rigidity in the celestial sphere, the epic narrator describes the angelic hosts bearing "Ten thousand thousand Ensigns high advanc'd, / Standards and Gonfalons, twixt Van and Rear / Stream in the Air, and for distinction serve / Of Hierarchies, of Orders, and Degrees;" (5:588-91). Over these legions, Christ is appointed "Head" (5:606). Later, Satan is described as "great indeed / [in] name, and high was his degree in Heav'n" (5:706-7); proud and jealous of his power, it is to his advantage that he should espouse a political doctrine in which hierarchical order is not incompatible with freedom. Included in the self-serving propaganda that Satan disseminates among his followers is the statement that "Orders and Degrees / Jar not with liberty, but well consist" (5:792-93); however, as Abdiel quickly notes, such a position is indeed ironic for one who places himself "so high above [his] Peers" (5:812). The faithful angel then continues to expose Satan's sophistry by reminding him of his position as a dependent being (5:822-25).

Thus from the moment of Christ's exaltation, Satan's growing pride and envy are stimulated by his acute awareness of heavenly hierarchy and degree and the threat of greater servitude. The Lord of the North scornfully envisions the progress of the "great *Messiah*, . . . / Who speedily through all the Hierarchies / Intends to pass triumphant, and give Laws" (5:691-93). He and his rebellious comrades fly among "the mighty Regencies / Of Seraphim and Potentates and Thrones / In thir triple Degrees" (5:748-50) en route to the lofty throne marked by the "great Hierarchal Standard" (5:701) from which Satan will address his legions. Finally, Abdiel again reminds Satan (and in terms that cannot fail to exacerbate Satan's sense of injured merit) of his ontological status:

> As by his Word the mighty Father made
> All things, ev'n thee, and all the Spirits of Heav'n
> By him created in thir bright degrees,
> Crown'd them with Glory, and to thir Glory nam'd
> Thrones, Dominations, Princedoms, Virtues, Powers. (5:836-40)

But for man the situation is very different. Throughout book 5, Milton outlines an ontology and cosmology in which, unlike the celestial scheme, the steps and gradations of creation—if they exist at all—are comforting and reassuring in their gradualness.[94] For example, one of the effects of Adam and Eve's morning hymn of praise is to blur sharp boundaries between the celestial and terrestrial spheres that might otherwise prove inhibiting to their upward aspirations. Here the entire scale of creation—angels, sun, moon, fixed stars and planets, the forces of nature, and the earthly creatures—joins them in a common act of praise for the Creator's "goodness beyond thought, and Power Divine" (5:159). Thus, through the intermingling of different categories of creation, we find, early in the book, a clear foreshadowing of Raphael's later, explicitly melioristic position. Further in the hymn, although no specifically alchemical terms are used, Milton's description of the four elements "that in quaternion run / Perpetual Circle" (5:181-

82), with its emphasis on their interconvertibility and "ceaseless change," figures forth precisely the alchemical concept of the "philosophical circle," the eternal interconvertibility of the elements, which is its theoretical foundation. In asserting the principle of permanence through continual change, recalling this topos in Vaughan's hermetic poetry, Milton's image provides the metaphysical basis for a dynamic universe of motion, fluidity, and continual flux, a setting in which human transformation and ascent are entirely possible. It is a metaphysics closely patterned on Plato's *Timaeus,* 49 c, cited in chapters 1 and 5.[95]

That the demarcations between the celestial and terrestrial spheres are greatly relaxed in contrast to distinctions between angelic orders is shown in Raphael's unimpeded descent to converse "as friend with friend" with Adam. However, cosmic and ontological fluidity is more subtly demonstrated in the account of the paradisiacal luncheon that follows. Adam's question concerning the suitability of human food for angelic constitutions leads to Raphael's exposition of their common spiritual essence and faculties of sense: "both [angels and humans] contain / Within them every lower faculty / Of sense, whereby they hear, see, smell, touch, taste, / Tasting concoct, digest, assimilate, / And corporeal to incorporeal turn" (5:409-13). Following these direct foreshadowings of the "nutritive" images in the ontological tree section (ll. 475-84), Raphael's further insistence on the commonality of sensory experience, the fact that *all* creation requires nutrition, is supported by the idea that in the elemental world "the grosser feeds the purer" (5:416), or through the example of "The Sun that light imparts to all, [which] receives / From all his alimental recompense / In humid exhalations, and at Even / Sups with the Ocean:" (5:423-26).

Moving easily from the great world to the lesser and from the realm of nature to the human sphere, but sharpening always his focus on matters of greatest spiritual import for Adam and Eve, Milton employs alchemical metaphor in describing the eating of the meal, which serves at once to erase barriers between seemingly opposing categories and to suggest the possibility of upward mobility. Raphael's consumption of human food, we are told, is not figurative but incontrovertibly real:

> So down they sat,
> And to thir viands fell, nor seemingly
> The Angel, nor in mist, the common gloss
> Of Theologians, but with keen dispatch
> Of real hunger, and concoctive heat
> To transubstantiate; what redounds, transpires
> Through Spirits with ease; nor wonder; if by fire
> Of sooty coal the Empiric Alchemist
> Can turn, or holds it possible to turn
> Metals of drossiest Ore to perfet Gold
> As from the Mine. [5:433-43]

Milton's conception of the digestive process—the "transubstantiation" of "baser" food to more precious "vital spirit" through the agency of "concoctive heat"— would be recognizably alchemical even without the derisive allusion to metallic transmutation near the end of the passage. (In the *Hermetical Physick*, incidentally, Nollius had referred to the stomach as "our internal natural Alchymist.")[96] Both vehicle and tenor establish, by means of a fluid and dynamic physiology, the possibility of evolutionary progress from corporal to spiritual in unfallen man.

Having set forth for Adam "the scale of Nature . . . / From centre to circumference," Raphael proceeds with his famous account of Creation and the first matter, an account aided by alchemical ideas and terminology:

> O *Adam,* one Almighty is, from whom
> All things proceed, and up to him return,
> If not deprav'd from good, created all
> Such to perfection, one first matter all,
> Indu'd with various forms, various degrees
> Of substance, and in things that live, of life;
> But more refin'd, more spiritous, and pure,
> As nearer to him plac't or nearer tending
> Each in thir several active Spheres assign'd,
> Till body up to spirit work, in bounds
> Proportion'd to each kind. So from the root
> Springs lighter the green stalk, from thence the leaves
> More aery, last the bright consummate flow'r
> Spirits odorous breathes: flow'rs and thir fruit
> Man's nourishment, by gradual scale sublim'd
> To vital spirits aspire, [5:469-84]

Milton, as reported here by Raphael, envisages a creative act that is Neoplatonic in its rhythm of emanation and return (ll. 469-70).[97] The result is a universe in which there is uniformity of matter ("one first matter all"); however, the *prima materia* is endowed with "various forms, various degrees / Of substance, and in things that live, of life;" (ll. 473-74). While Milton denies a difference in the *essence* of things spiritual and physical, he does assert that beings and objects in closer proximity to God are, by virtue of their placement, "more *refin'd* [emphasis mine], more spiritous, and pure / As nearer to him plac't or nearer tending" (ll. 475-76). The concrete embodiment of this chain of being, the gradual transformation from "body up to spirit," is the well-known tree simile of lines 479-85, where the evolutionary progress of degree (but not of kind) is again assisted by alchemical terminology.[98] Just as the earthiness and corporeality of the tree's root and trunk yield gradually to the increasing lightness and aeriness of its branches, leaves, and flowers, so "by gradual scale sublim'd" is mortal food converted to "vital spirits," the life-supporting principle in all of nature. Thus Milton's ontological discussion of mortal and angelic nutrition reaches the conclusion that "the grosser feeds the purer," a principle that applies to all creation. At the same time, the tree analogy has served to show that all things proceed from God and also return to him, "if not deprav'd from good" (5:471).

Although Raphael's exposition contains only two references that are unequivocally alchemical, "refin'd" and "sublim'd," this passage bears important general resemblances to certain alchemical and hermetic ideas that appear in Vaughan's poetry and in the works of contemporary occult writers discussed in the previous chapter. Among these, the concept of the *prima materia* and the convertibility of the four elements "that in quaternion run" is fundamental to alchemical theory and practice and also recalls the pattern of emanation and return that pervades the *Corpus Hermeticum* and the writings of the Neoplatonists.

Set in the context of universal history, Milton's great example of alchemical eschatology in *Paradise Lost* 12:545ff. has immediate reference to a moral climate that closely resembles that of Henry Vaughan's "White Sunday."[99] As described in the prophetic words of Michael, the last days are those when "Wolves shall succeed for teachers" (l. 508), when "lucre and ambition" gain ascendency over truth (l. 511), when conscience is forced (ll. 521-22), and liberty is bound (ll. 525-26). Only then will Christ appear—in the manner of the philosopher's stone—first to dissolve, and then to purge, refine, and (finally) recreate:[100]

> Last in the Clouds from Heav'n to be reveal'd
> In glory of the Father, to dissolve
> *Satan* with his perverted World, then raise
> From the conflagrant mass, purg'd and refin'd,
> New Heav'ns, new Earth, Ages of endless date
> Founded in righteousness and peace and love,
> To bring forth fruits Joy and eternal Bliss. [12:545-51]

Like Vaughan's, Milton's conception of Christ and the day of "respiration to the just, / And vengeance to the wicked" (12:540-41) was commonplace in alchemical books of the time. Moreover, in its representation of the Second Coming as a type of alchemical separation and purification (cf. "dissolve," "raise," "purg'd and refin'd"), Milton's image has a close visual counterpart in an intricate illustration that the contemporary engraver Robert Vaughan produced for inclusion in Ashmole's *Theatrum Chemicum Britannicum* (fig. 28). This engraving features a master alchemist, represented as God the Father, overseeing the operations within the glass; just beneath him, at the top of a crescent, is an enthroned judge figure—probably Hermes Trismegistus/Christ—on either side of whom winged, mitred, and cowled "blessed" angels and dignitaries behold the scene before them. In dramatic contrast, the central portion of the illustration features a tripartite orb design containing the elements of earth, air, and water, through which the damned plummet into the eternal fire beneath.[101] In this allegorical illustration, then, Robert Vaughan not only represents the alchemical process of separating the pure from the impure but also designates the art itself as sacred.

Figure 28. Last Judgment. Elias Ashmole, *Theatrum Chemicum Britannicum* (1652). By permission of The Huntington Library, San Marino, California.

Michael's prophetic words recall a passage from the much earlier "Il Penseroso" in which Milton also combines alchemical lore with knowledge and prophecy, thus suggesting a final category of alchemical meaning or association: that of arcane wisdom concerning man, the nature of the universe, and the future. "[O]utwatch[ing] the *Bear*" from his "high lonely Tow'r," Penseroso's nocturnal studies invoke the image and example of Hermes Trismegistus and platonic tradition as means to prophetic revelation:

> to unfold
> What Worlds, or what vast Regions hold
> The immortal mind that hath forsook
> Her mansion in this fleshly nook:

> And of those *Daemons* that are found
> In fire, air, flood, or underground,
> Whose power hath a true consent
> With Planet, or with Element. [ll. 89-96]

Penseroso's appeal to Hermes, although not connected with specifically alchemical detail, introduces several closely related platonic and "hermetic" topics that are linked in Milton's mind with the supposed author of the *Hermetica,* writings that had been correctly dated by Isaac Casaubon in 1614, less than twenty years before Milton's composition of "L'Allegro" and "Il Penseroso." To all appearances, Milton was unaffected by Casaubon's "bomb-shell" discovery, as Frances Yates has termed it,[102] as his hermetic allusions contain no hint of negativity or skepticism concerning the authenticity of the ancient authority and his works. On the contrary, Milton's references to the disembodied spirit's access to remote worlds, or to the "daemons," whose association with the four elements enables the magus to exercise control over the terrestrial world, or his suggestion at lines 85-92 that this hidden knowledge results from some type of mystical trance or conjuration are all presented without apology or embarrassment.[103]

Brooks-Davies has accurately stated that "Hermes Trismegistus is . . . the, literally, central character in *Il Penseroso,*"[104] as it is the contemplative ideal patterned on hermetic studies that shapes all aspects of the nature, interests, perceptions, and activities of the speaker. At the end of the poem, and under spell of the "studious Cloister" with its "pealing Organ" and "full voic'd Choir," these influences come to be identified with prophetic wisdom:

> And may at last my weary age
> Find out the peaceful hermitage,
> The Hairy Gown and Mossy Cell,
> Where I may sit and rightly spell
> Of every Star that Heav'n doth shew,
> And every Herb that sips the dew;
> Till old experience do attain
> To something like Prophetic strain. [ll. 167-74]

Thus, in the conclusion of "Il Penseroso," pagan philosophy and Christian asceticism, the contemplation of nature and mystical transport, hermetic magic and scriptural revelation, poetry and prophecy—all mingle and merge mysteriously into a new synthesis effected primarily through contemplative excursions guided by "thrice great *Hermes.*" Some thirty years after Penseroso's appeal to "Dissolve me into ecstasies, / And bring all Heav'n before mine eyes," Michael, as has been shown, would also resort to the language of alchemy to express his eschatological vision of Christ's return "in the Clouds from Heav'n to be reveal'd" and the ensuing "dissolv[ing of] / *Satan* with his perverted World." Although the visions differ in kind, the means of expressing them are very similar.

IX

"Teutonick Chimericall extravagancies"

==========================

Alchemy, Poetry, and the Restoration Revolt against Enthusiasm

The *Real Philosophy,* and *knowledge of Gods works,* serves *Religion* against *Enthusiasm,* another of its deadly enemies. Now *Enthusiasm* is a *false conceit of inspiration;* and all the bold and mistaken pretensions to the *Spirit* in our days, are of this sort. . . . It will be enough to say, in an Age that hath so much and such sad experience of it, that *Enthusiasm,* (I.) By crying up the *excesses,* and *diseases of Imagination* for the greatest height of *godliness.* And (II.) By the disparagement *of sober Reason,* as an enemy to the Principles of *Faith;* I say, by these two ways it hath introduc'd a *Religion* that is *Phantastical,* and made way for all imaginable follies, and even *Atheism* it self.

—Joseph Glanvill, *Philosophia Pia* (1671)[1]

This disease many of your *Chymists* and several *Theosophists,* in my judgement, seem very obnoxious to, who dictate their own Conceits and Fancies so magisterially and imperiously, as if they were indeed Authentick messengers from God Almighty. But that they are but Counterfeits, that is *Enthusiasts,* no infallible illuminated men, the gross fopperies they let drop in their writings will sufficiently demonstrate to all that are not smitten in some measure with the like Lunacy with themselves.

—Henry More, *Enthusiasmus Triumphatus* (1662)[2]

The spagyric, philosophical, and religious emphases that mark much alchemical and hermetic writing in the middle years of the seventeenth century and are also present in the poetic references of Vaughan and Milton were soon to be countered by powerful forces operating in the post-Restoration intellectual milieu. Thus the New Science and Rationalism were finally to accomplish what three centuries of alchemical satire were unable to perform. It is a curious fact that even as increasing numbers of occult books were published following 1660—evidence that a significant audience still existed—the general atmosphere for the reception of these works and ideas was becoming more hostile.[3] About this growing hostility there can be little doubt, despite the recent demonstration that, beginning with Charles II and his alchemical laboratory and extending through Royalist circles, alchemy found a number of important Royalist patrons and sympathizers. Alchemy and chemical medicine were not, in other words, automatically equated with radical theology and politics, and interest in alchemy did not cease with the Restoration.[4] While it is difficult to determine precisely what factors were responsible for this increasingly negative atmosphere, it is certain that some of the traditional reasons for distrust of alchemy continued to play a role after 1660: its lack of demonstrable successes, the faultiness of its experimental methods, the enigmatic quality of its prose style, and its association with magic and other occult arts. However, as my epigraph from Henry More suggests, an important related factor in the reaction against alchemy in this era of the New Science, the Royal Society, and an increasingly mechanistic worldview was its association with philosophical enthusiasm. It is the Restoration revolt against enthusiasm that will serve as a context for treating the occult themes in the works of Samuel Butler, the last major seventeenth-century writer to have dealt with these themes.

The notion of "enthusiasm" and the reaction against it are not, to be sure, peculiar to this time period. One need only look back to Robert Burton's attacks on the excessive devotion, superstition, blind zeal, and madness of "enthusiasticks, and desperate persons" in the discussion of religious melancholy in the Third Partition of *The Anatomy of Melancholy*[5] to be reminded that this deep distrust need not have resulted only from recent, direct experience with the dissenting sects and the Civil Wars. Burton's discussion of the effects of this manifestation of religious melancholy does not include specific contemporary examples; nonetheless, his concentration on the causes and symptoms of enthusiasm in "*Pythonissas, Sibyls, Enthusiasts, Pseudoprophets, Heretickes,* and *Schismaticks*"[6] is in agreement with Joseph Glanvill's identification of enthusiasm with atheism, as seen in the first epigraph to this chapter, and with Henry More's notion of enthusiasm as "a misconceit of being *inspired*." Similarly, for Meric Casaubon, who also associates it with melancholy, enthusiasm is "a participation of an extrinsecal and divine power, which is very light and superficial."[7]

For Glanvill, More, and their fellows, the experience of the Civil Wars and the emergence of the New Science, as well as their own Latitudinarian predispositions, figure strongly in their attacks on enthusiasm.[8] In the *Enthusiasmus Triumphatus,* for example, More recalls the example of the Fifth Monarchist "whose discourse was not onely rational, but pious, and he seemed to have his wits very well about him; nor could I discover the least intimation to the contrary, onely he had this flaw, that he conceited that he was by God appointed to be that fifth Monarch of which there is so much noise in this age; which imagination had so possessed him, that he would sometime have his servant to serve him all in plate and upon the knee, as a very learned and religious friend of mine told me afterward" (1:22). The unbridled imagination, here conceived as a dominant cause of enthusiasm, "is yet the Soul's weaknesse or unwieldinesse, whereby she so farre sinks into Phantasmes that she cannot recover her self into the use of her more free Faculties of *Reason* and *Understanding.*"[9] Although More's examples of religious melancholy are more contemporary and topical than Burton's, such as his inclusion of millenarians and the Quakers ("who undoubtedly are the most *Melancholy Sect* that ever was yet in the world" [1:19]), the characteristics of impetuousness, fervor, and zeal are common to all.

As seen in the second of the epigraphs that head this chapter, More reserves some of his sharpest attacks in the *Triumphatus* for Paracelsus, chemists, and theosophists, thus sounding a note frequently repeated by contemporary scientific and religious rationalists. His attack is thorough and severe, beginning with section 44 (in which he ironically lists "*A promiscuous Collection of divers odde conceits out of several* Theosophists *and* Chymists") and concluding with section 49. At the very time when English publishers were producing new editions and translations of Paracelsus in record numbers, the controversial Swiss doctor was at the center of More's target.[10] More opens his attack on Paracelsus by first presenting, immediately following the aforementioned "*promiscuous Collection,*" a list of additional "divers odde conceits" drawn exclusively from Paracelsus's writings. These "absurdities" cover a range of topics, including the stars, spirit world, the causes of thunder and lightning, and the making of the *homunculus* or artificial man. More's assessment of Paracelsus's influence is entirely consistent with those written at this time by traditional Galenists and members of the Royal Society: "These are the rampant and delirous Fancies of that great boaster of Europe *Paracelsus,* whose unbridled Imagination and bold and confident obtrusion of his uncouth and supine inventions upon the world has, . . . given occasion to the wildest *Philosophical Enthusiasms* that ever were broached by any either Christian or Heathen" (1:33). Further, discussion of Paracelsus's views on the supremacy of the stars and star worship leads directly to veiled allegations of atheism. More states: "I have observed generally of *Chymists* and *Theosophists,* as of several other men more palpably mad, that their thoughts are carryed much to *Astrology,* it being a fancifull study built upon very slight grounds, and indeed I do not question, but a relique of the ancient Superstition and Idolatry amongst the rude Heathens, which either their own *Melancholy,* or something worse, instructed them in" (1:30). Conceding that Paracelsus's writings have the appearance of religion, More is willing to grant them little more: whereas Paracelsus's followers "conceive themselves taught of God; . . . their brains are merely heated and infected by this strong spirit of *Phantastrie* that breaths in *Paracelsus* his Books" (1:33). Thus while refusing to call Paracelsus and his followers atheists, More, like Glanvill, unquestionably believes that enthusiasm can lead in that direction. The antidotes to this state of madness are three: Temperance, Humility, and Reason, the latter being "so settled and cautious a Composure of Mind as will suspect every high-flown & forward Fancy that endeavours to carry away the assent before deliberate examination" (1:38).

Although Paracelsus is the figure most frequently invoked in Restoration attacks on enthusiasm—attacks that typically focus less on his medical and pharmaceutical theories than on his religion and philosophy—the popular writings of Jacob Boehme are also singled out for censure.[11] For example, in Meric Casaubon's encyclopedic *Treatise concerning Enthusiasme,* the inadvertent encouragement of this theologian's "Teutonick Chimericall extravagancies" to disbelief among the ignorant is stressed: "I can easily believe that so holy a man, in his ordinary conversation, and so profound a Philosopher, as he shews himself by his writings, might make good use of such meditations, and elevations of thoughts; and yet keep himself within sobrietie, but . . . it is a dangerous book otherwise for ordinary capacities, apt to turn all Religion and all Scripture (in weaker brains) into mere phansie, and Teutonick Chimericall extravagancies" (126).

In the face of such insinuations, the responses of the defenders of Boehme were, at times, interestingly inconsistent. John Sparrow, one of the leading translators of Boehme, invokes the example of Francis Bacon in an attempt to make his author appear scientifically respectable in the dawning of the Royal Society. In the preface to his translation of *Forty Questions of the Soul* (1665) Sparrow argues that Bacon's exemplary scientific method might serve as a model for a history of divinity: "[Bacon] laid his foundation sure, and raised his building high; by his *Instauratio Magna,* he taught men, first to free themselves from the *Idola Mentis humanæ,* and then laid down the whole process of the Mind, from a Natural and Experimental History, to raise a Natural Philosophy: which doth shew the way to compose a Divine experimental History, to the building of a Divine Philosophy, or mystical Divinity."[12]

But while invoking the name of Bacon and the spirit of experimental science, Sparrow also places Boehme among the esoteric tradition's most revered authorities and seekers of the philosopher's stone. Ranking with the *prisci theologi,* Boehme has reached into the "Deepest Mysteries" of religious experience and nature, just as had "the Ancient Philosophers, *Hermes Trismegistus, Zoroaster, Pythagoras, Plato* and other deep Men, conversant in the Operative Mysteries of Nature, and the Modern, *Trevisanus, Raymundus Lullius, Paracelsus,* and others: by which men will be satisfied, that not only they have gotten, but that we also may get that *Lapis Philosophorum, the Philosophers Stone, indeed.*"[13] Sparrow believes, however, that a reconciliation between the experimentalists and the hermeticists can come about through study of Boehme's works. Just as it is possible to demonstrate that the "ancient theologians" are compatible with Christianity, so "all the real differences of Opinions, of all sorts, may be *reconciled;* even the nicest Differences of the most Learned Criticks of all Ages; that which seemeth different in the Writings of the Profound *Magical Mystical Chymick Philosophers,* from that which we find in the Experimental *Physicians, Philosophers, Astronomers,* may be reconciled by considering what this Author [Boehme] Teacheth."[14] From a very different perspective, Glanvill, too, had argued for the reconciliation of science and religion; but for him, reason was the true foundation of both and, in accordance with the teleological view, God is revealed through his creation.

However, serious belief, like Sparrow's, in the ultimate reconcilability of experimental science and the "Profound *Magical Mystical Chymick Philosophers*" was a rarity in the Restoration period, and for most commentators alchemy was linked with the irrational: enthusiasm, Platonism, and superstitiousness. Chemistry, on the other hand, was coming to be associated with reformed experimental methods, modernity, and the Royal Society. Symptomatic of these shifts in associations is Joseph Glanvill's *Plus Ultra: Or, The Progress and Advancement of Knowledge Since the Days of Aristotle* (1668), in which the Royal Society is given special credit for recent developments in chemistry, anatomy, mathematics, and scientific instrumentation. Glanvill's particular interest in chemistry ("by which *Nature* is *unwound*, and *resolv'd* into the *minute Rudiments* of its *Composition*")[15] is reflected in his brief account of its history and evolution. Tracing its supposed origins to Hermes Trismegistus and its later descent to the Egyptians and then the Arabians, where chemistry was "infinitely mingled with *vanity* and *superstitious devices*," Glanvill then observes that among "the *Paracelsians,* and some other *Moderns, Chymistry* was very *phantastick, unintelligible,* and *delusive;* and the *boasts, vanity,* and *canting* of those *Spagyrists,* brought a *scandal* upon the *Art,* and exposed it to *suspicion* and *contempt;* but its late *Cultivatours,* and particularly the *Royal Society,* have refin'd it from its *dross,* and made it *honest, sober,* and *intelligible,* an excellent *Interpreter* to *Philosophy,* and *help* to *common life.*"[16] For Glanvill the Royal Society has assumed the role of an alchemist, transmuting alchemy itself into the beneficial and scientifically respectable chemistry. Thus, the program for reform advocated by Bacon had attained at least partial fruition.

Keith Thomas has speculated that the great popularity of magical and other varieties of esoteric writing during the Interregnum may have hastened the rejection of these traditions following the Restoration, the enlightened investigators of the Royal Society being eager to put behind them all associations with sectarian enthusiasm.[17] Several aspects of this explanation require further study as the idea of "enthusiasm" is a complex one, and attacks upon it have revealing and far-reaching implications. It is necessary, therefore, to consider several additional authors and works that figured prominently in discussions of enthusiasm—Samuel Parker, George Castle, John Webster, Thomas Hall, Seth Ward, and John Wilkins, for example—and some of the issues that fueled the controversy. Among these issues are the perceived relationship between enthusiasm and hermeticism, Platonism, and alchemy; the question of authority; the ideal of stylistic clarity as opposed to obscurity and abstraction; the tradition of secrecy; and the persisting influence of Bacon as well as that of the Royal Society. Taken together, these issues constitute some of the most important ones discussed in works of Restoration-era intellectuals and thus provide a larger context for study of literary works that contain hermetic and alchemical references.

It is useful to begin with Samuel Parker's *Free and Impartial Censure of the Platonick Philosophie* (1666) as it provides a convenient and comprehensive summary of Restoration disparagement of Platonism and related forms of "occult-ist" thought as well as contrasting views of the Royal Society. In Parker, the lines of opposition are sharply drawn. Published in Oxford by its ambitious and con-troversial bishop, the *Free and Impartial Censure*'s stated intention is presenta-tion of "as satisfactory an account of the *Platonick Philosophie,* as I am able," and following a summary of the revival of this philosophy under Ficino, Parker ap-plauds certain aspects of its morality and ethics. However, the work quickly turns into a harsh attack on manifestations of Platonism, ranging from its "Second School" to contemporary Rosicrucianism. For Parker, the Neoplatonists deserve scorn because of their susceptibility to magical practices: "And yet the latter *Platonists,* or *second School of Plato,* degenerated into the basest and foulest Su-perstition, being the greatest Patrons of *Theurgical Rites* and *Magical Arts,* or rather *Jugling Tricks,* . . . especially those of them that did most *Pythagorise,* As *Apollonius Tyanaeus,* that grand stickler for *Ethnicisme; Jamblicus,* [and] . . . *Julianus* the *Syrian* . . . were great Zealots for the *Pythagorean Philosophie.*"[18] Here, the verb form "Pythagorise" carries the more negative connotations of magic, charlatanism, and paganism than that suggested by the entry in the *OED,* which is limited to the doctrine of transmigration of souls, after the manner of Pythagoras.

For Parker, a thoroughgoing empiricist and admirer of Francis Bacon and the Royal Society, the greatest weakness of platonic epistemology is its rejection of "the Testimony and Judgment of sense in matters of Philosophie" (53). As a result, condemnation of the platonic doctrine of universals, along with abstrac-tions of all sorts, is consistent throughout the work, as is his upholding of the empirical method followed by members of the Royal Society: "the truely wise and discerning Philosophers do not endeavour after the dry and sapless knowl-edge of abstracted Natures, but only search after the Properties, Qualities, Vertues and Operations of Natural Beings; the knowledge whereof may be acquired by Observations and Experiments; but there are no certain means or rational Meth-ods . . . to investigate the mysterious Ideas of bare and abstracted Essences" (64). These "wise and discerning" experimentalists, members of the Royal Soci-ety, have, Parker states, "discarded all particular *Hypotheses,* and wholly addicted themselves to exact Experiments and Observations" (45), thus laying the foun-dation for fruitful research according to the Baconian model. Methodologically, the Royal Society stands in diametric opposition to the unsystematic experi-mentation and *a priori* acceptance of authority that characterized the pursuit of alchemy.

Similarly Baconian is Parker's discussion of the connections between phi-losophy and linguistic style. The meaningless, abstruse abstractions of the Neoplatonists, he asserts, may be met with as well in the writings of Jacob Boehme and all writers who have, in imitation of Orpheus, Pythagoras, and Plato, "com-municated their Notions by Emblems, Fables, Symbols, Parables, heaps of Meta-phors, Allegories, and all sorts of Mystical Representations. . . . All which upon the account of their Obscurity and Ambiguity are apparently the unfittest signes in the world to express the Train of any mans thoughts to another" (68). Thus Parker's censure of what Hugh Ormsby-Lennon has termed "Rosicrucian linguistics" goes to the very heart of poetic language and representation.[19] Parker's position is close to that of Thomas Sprat, the historian of the Royal Society, for whom the ideal of language was to express "so many *things* almost in an equal number of *words*."[20] For Parker, the greatest defect in a style intended to communicate the truths of scientific discovery is "Allegorical and dark discourses," which predominate in the writings of the Rosicrucians and other contemporary occultists. His attack on groups and individuals who exhibit these weaknesses is carried on with great zeal and high spirits, as we see in the following quotation that targets the Rosicrucians, Eugenius Philalethes (i.e., Thomas Vaughan) and John Heydon, and alludes ironically to their current notoriety:

> methinks I may dare to add the same Censure of our late English *Rosie-Crusians*, but yet of all men I am most sorely afraid of angring these, because they seem to be of a very quarrelsome Humour, and to have a huge ambition to be esteemed the Polemical Scripturients of the Age; whereas I have been scared from Engaging with a *Rosie-Crucian*, ever since I first saw the Controversial Rencountres of *Eugenius Philalethes;* and besides, (to confess my fears to you) I know not but the Romantick Heroes of this Order may have retreiv'd the lost Invention of Enchanted Arms, especially that lovely Fairie Knight descended (as the Romance of his Life relates it, 'tis a prettier Tale then that of *Amadis de Gaul*) of the *Cesar Heydons of Rome*, and the venerable Author of the *Heydonian Philosophy*, as himself modestly stiles his own ignorant, uncouth, and ridiculous Scrible. [72]

Recalling Bacon's strictures against empty rhetoric, such as his remarks on "delicate learning" in the first book of the *Advancement of Learning*, Parker assails the Rosicrucians and their fellows not only for excessive figurative language and allegory but also for the arrogance that causes them to take seriously their pitiful investigations of nature: "when they pretend to be Natures Secretaries, & to understand all her Intrigues, or to be Heavens Privadoes, talking of the Transactions there, like men lately drop'd thence encircled with *Glories,* and cloathed with the Garments of *Moses* and *Elias,* and yet put us off with nothing but rampant Metaphors, and Pompous Allegories, and other splendid but empty Schemes of speech, I must crave leave to account them (to say no worse) Poets & Romancers" (73-74).[21] Thus the attacks on Platonism and enthusiasm come to include poetry itself, for that "*Platonisme* is almost nothing but an Allegorie, is too notorious to want a proof, [and] *Plato's* two famous Dialogues, *viz.* his *Symposium* and his *Phaedrus*, . . . treat of nothing but Love and Beauty, and of them too in Poetick Schemes and Fables" (74).[22]

A further censure of the poetic qualities of Neoplatonic language is semantic in nature and relates to the problem of analogy versus identity, which has recently been discussed by Brian Vickers as a means of distinguishing between scientific and occult discourse in the Renaissance.[23] Parker notes that "to Discourse of the Natures of Things in Metaphors and Allegories is nothing else but to sport and trifle with empty words" (75). Lacking concrete referents, such literary modes "do not express the Natures of Things, but only their Similitudes and Resemblances, for Metaphors are only words, which properly signifying one thing, are apply'd to signifie another by reason of some Resemblance between them. When therefore anything is express'd by a Metaphor or Allegory, the thing it self is not expressed, but only some similitude observ'd or made by Fancy" (75).[24]

Parker's wide-ranging attack on various manifestations of what he understood as Platonism includes three additional targets: Hermes Trismegistus, Egyptian hieroglyphics, and the cabala. The first he regards as a "supposititious" author, one who is proof of the "Vanity of all pretences to the more abstruse and mystical Learning of the Antients" (95-96). Along with the disparagement of Hermes, he debunks the entire notion of the wisdom of ancient Egypt and the *prisca theologia* (94-96, 108-9). Similarly, he mocks the Renaissance fascination with hieroglyphics, which had begun with the "discovery" of Horapollo's *Hieroglyphica* early in the fifteenth century: "What childish fooleries their [Egyptian] Hieroglyphicks were, Learned Men now prove from the lost labour and fruitless industry of *Kirchers Oedipus Ægyptiacus*. Certainly, if they had design'd to abuse and debauch this humour, they could scarce have contrived more fond and extravagant Emblems; and indeed their coarseness and unlikeness to the things they should resemble, sufficiently discover them to have been but the rude Essays of a barbarous and undisciplined Fancy" (97).[25] In the latter part of this passage, Parker's attack on the faulty representationalism of hieroglyphics reveals that he shares the Renaissance misconception that these visual designs were words representing the objects pictured and not representations of phonetic sounds. Further, we see his inability to conceive of language as a symbolic construct or of having any function other than the strictly utilitarian. Of students of the cabala, he states ironically that "he that could find all the Learning of the world in an *Egyptian Hieroglyphick* may find all the Articles of his Faith in a *Rabbinical Fable*" (105).

Finally, and most comprehensively, the Rosicrucians represent the excesses of enthusiasm and fanaticism at their worst, for "there is so much Affinity between *Rosi-Crucianisme* and *Enthusiasme*, that whoever entertains the one, he may upon the same Reason embrace the other; and what Pestilential Influences the Genius of *Enthusiasme* or opinionative Zeal has upon the Publick Peace, is so evident from Experience, that it needs not be prov'd from Reason. To conclude, I am confident, that from the beginning of time to this day, there has not been so great a Conjunction of Ignorance with Confidence, as in these Fellows, which certainly of all other Aspects is the most contrary and malignant to true knowledge" (72-73).

Thus, in summary, for Samuel Parker "Platonisme" has become an all-encompassing object of attack: it includes the writings of Plato and his forebears among the *prisci theologi,* as well as the Neoplatonists, writers of hieroglyphics, cabalists, and contemporary Rosicrucian writers like Thomas Vaughan and John Heydon. The attack is also carried out on several fronts: such writers are associated with magical practice, and, in their preoccupation with abstractions, they subvert the new scientists' proper application to particular, observable, quantifiable properties. Further, their style is wholly inappropriate for communicating exact scientific observation and experiment, being better suited to poetry and romance, where allegory and enigma are permitted. Finally, and most damningly, these writers are grounded in enthusiasm, unrestrained fancy, and fanaticism, from which all the foregoing defects proceed. In short, for Parker "Platonisme" is a code word for all that is unscientific and unprogressive. As the remainder of this chapter will show, he was not alone in holding these views.

In the year following Parker's treatise, George Castle published a work bearing a similarly compromising title, *The Chymical Galenist: A Treatise Wherein The Practise of the Ancients is reconcil'd to the new Discoveries in the Theory of Physick* (1667). True to his title, Castle does seek to accommodate the two warring medical theories; however, he displays no tolerance for the encroachment of enthusiastic tendencies into medical theory as they pose a threat greater than immoderate devotion to antiquity:

> We need not (I think) in our age, apprehend any danger to *Physick* from an over-fondness of Antiquity. The growing evil is the other Extream, a fancy of rejecting the wisdom of the Ancients, for the follies and whimsies of some phantastical *Pseudo-chymists,* which is, like the *Americans,* to barter Gold and Silver, for Beads and Glass.
>
> Sir, our Nation is of late grown as fond of Enthusiasts in *Physick,* as they were of those in *Divinity;* and Ignorance (amongst some men) is become as necessary a qualification for the practise of *Physick,* as it us'd to be for *Preaching.*[26]

Castle continues by narrowing this attack on enthusiasm in medical practice to *Mercurius Politicus,* i.e., Marchamont Nedham or Needham, author of the *Medela Medicina* (1665). Notorious for his own bold and scurrilous journalistic attacks on the Royalist cause and the College of Physicians, and for consorting with Fifth Monarchists, Nedham fits the profile of the enthusiast in both politics and medicine.[27]

Like Castle's work, the title of Walter Harris's *Pharmacologia Anti-Empirica: or a Rational Discourse of Remedies Both Chymical and Galenical. Wherein Chymistry is impartially represented* (1683) would also appear to offer reconciliation between opposing medical theories in late seventeenth-century England. Harris (1647-1732) was physician to both Charles II and William III, and attended Queen Mary during her final illness with smallpox. These facts, combined with the work's dedication to Prince Henry, Duke of Beaufort, mark Harris as a devoted Royalist and serve to explain why, despite the work's apparently conciliatory theoretical stance, it is, in fact, strongly anti-Paracelsian. Harris is conservative and traditionally Galenic in his prescribed cures, as is made clear in his early reference to the *"Ignorant Tribe of Impudent Empiricks."*[28] Despite this bias, Harris's account of the medical "wars" in his time is engaging and informative in its detail.[29]

With chapter 3, however, Harris begins a stinging attack on Paracelsus: he was a liar and given to great exaggerations, as well as to tremendous pride and egotism. He "chose to write like a *Heathen,* and in an *Ethnick Style.* . . . [calling] himself the (most absolute) *Monarch of Arcana's,* and commanded the World to follow him, as an unerring Leader" (16).[30] The vocabulary of his books includes "strained, affected, fantastical, unintelligible, and ill-coin'd Words" (17). His medical reforms were carried out "with all the Malice, and Ill-will, with all the hatred and Contempt, that a Beast and a Sot could possibly conceive against *Sober* men, whose *Seriousness* and *Sobriety* was the greatest *Reproach,* and declaration of Enmity to his dissolute and profligate Life" (18). Harris's attack on Paracelsus betrays his own traditional, Galenist bias:

> This *Cacophrastus,* or foul-mouth'd railer declares himself a Cursed Enemy to *Avicenna, Galen, Rhasis, Montagnana,* . . . to all that inhabit the *Rhine* and *Danube,* to *Italy, Dalmatia, Greece, Athens, Arabia,* and to all *Israel.* He Condemns *Galen* to the Pit of Hell, . . . Nay he threatned no less than to make the Dogs Piss upon them all. But know bold Wretch, their Names will be Consecrated to after-ages, and had in good Reputation by Wise, and Sober men, when thy *Bombastic* Names shall perish and be despised, when thy frantick folly, and miserable vanity, and ill-nature, shall with thy Dust be trampled upon by all men. [18-19]

Harris next turns to Paracelsus's disciple, Jean Baptiste van Helmont, "another Terror to all Antient Learning, and with as foul a mouth" (24). Even more than his master, van Helmont believed "that there was no Real Knowledge but by Inspiration, and *Enthusiasm,* and fancied he had no less than *Raphael* to Inspire him." Harris concludes that van Helmont "writ like a man of more than ordinary *Brains,* but his *Head* was Heated too much, with his *Over-Reading,* insomuch that he shewed himself a True Morose *Stoick,* and the worst sort too, the *Cynick,* all along his Works" (25). In contrast, he recommends chemical doctors of a more *"Dogmatical* or *Rational"* bent, Sir Theodore Mayern and Quercetanus (27). Thus, although more personally abusive, Harris continues the kind of attacks on Paracelsus and his enthusiastic followers that we first noted in the works of Henry More and Joseph Glanvill.

As I have already suggested, Harris's attack on chemical physic appears to be motivated primarily by his conservative position in the medical wars of his time, a position that necessarily required rejection of enthusiasm in favor of a rational approach to healing and formulation of medicines. From this it follows that he should regard alchemy and the possibility of transmuting metals with great skepticism, an attitude that is confirmed in his discussion of alchemy in chapter 6 of the *Pharmacologia*. Harris states that although the truth of transmutation is attested to by many authorities, he personally suspects that such accounts are the result of counterfeit and collusion. His evidence against the possibility of transmutation is conventional: few alchemists are enviably wealthy despite the fact that many were born into good estates, and "all after much *Bragging, Counterfeiting,* and *Lying,* have grown *Contemptibly Poor* and *Miserable.*" A case in point is that of Bernard Penotus who, having been a champion of alchemy throughout his life, died in poverty after confessing, "for the *Good* of the *Publick,*" that "if he had an *Enemy* he wish'd ill to, and did not dare to assail by force, he could wish him no greater a *Curse,* than that he would give himself up to the *Study* of *Alchymy*" (64). Harris, nonetheless, proposes one original argument against transmutation and the existence of the philosopher's stone; he wonders "whether it be consistent with the *Established* and *Unalterable Providence* of *God* over the World, that one man should have that advantage over his Fellow-creatures, as to multiply Riches without end, as it must be supposed that man may, who is Perfect Master of this *Secret. . . .* there are *Bounds* determined by *Providence,* beyond which the most *Ambitious Prince* can never pass. But granting the conceit of *All powerful Projection,* the *Laws* of *Nature* are subject to be *overwhelmed,* by the Inexhaustible *Purse* of a *Whimsical Philosopher Paramount*" (54-55). This argument places Harris in direct opposition to those alchemical millenarians, discussed in chapter 7, who joyously anticipated the return of Elias and common possession of the philosopher's stone as means of increasing public wealth, improving morality, and enhancing the general welfare of mankind. Nonetheless, it is interesting that while countering the notion of the millenarian dream and equitable distribution of wealth, Harris unexpectedly employs the language of populism in privileging the disadvantaged "Fellow-creatures" over the avariciousness of the "*Ambitious Prince*" "who is Perfect Master of this *Secret.*"

While arguments against alchemy, astrology, Rosicrucianism, Platonism, and other varieties of occult thought dominate the controversies of the Restoration era, these subjects were not without defenders. The most important of them was John Webster (1610-82), and it is to his works and the attacks they elicited—by Seth Ward and Thomas Hall—that I turn next. Webster, author of the well-known *Displaying of Supposed Witchcraft* and not the playwright, studied chemistry under John Huniades and was a lifelong reader in mystical philosophy. He was ordained in 1632, served as chaplain and surgeon for the Parliamentary army, and was known for his nonconformism and his interests in educational reform.[31] His place in the tradition I have been tracing is, like his background, curiously mixed: he is a defender of the occult arts and praiser of Paracelsus and Jacob Boehme and also one who, determined to purge the academies of their Aristotelian influence,[32] sees Francis Bacon as providing a model for reform. Most of these apparent contradictions are stubbornly asserted in his major work, *Academiarum Examen, or the Examination of Academies* (1654).

Webster opens with a highly rhetorical defense of astrology, which will recall the numerous strictures against stylistic enthusiasm that I have already discussed:

> 6. What shall I say of the Science, or art of *Astrology*, shall the blind fury of *Misotechnists*, and malicious spirits, deter me from giving it the commendations that it deserves? shall the *Academies* who have not only sleighted and neglected it, but also scoffed at it, terrifie me from expressing my thoughts of so noble and beneficial a Science? shall the arguments of *Picus Mirandula*, and others, who have bitterly inveighed against it, fright me from owning the truth? . . . No truly, I must needs defend that which my judgement evidences to me to be laudable, and profitable; not but that I utterly condemn the ignorance, knavery, and impostorage of many pretending *Sciolists*, that abuse the same. [51][33]

Such resounding defenses of the occult arts are unusual at this time, and Webster's embattled position forces him to exercise caution in framing his argument. Thus he is able to defend astronomy by attacking one of its attackers (Pico), and in the following passage he distinguishes between the praiseworthy art of chemistry and the imposters who have injured its reputation:

> but shall the art of medicine or *Chymistry* be condemned, and rejected, because many ignorant *Empericks* and false *Alcumists* do profess them? Surely no, let the blame be upon the professors, not upon the profession it self. For the art it self is high, noble, excellent, and useful to all mankind, and is a study not unbeseeming the best wits, and greatest Scholars, and no way offensive to God or true Religion. And therefore I cannot without detracting from worth and vertue, pass without a due *Elogy* in the commendation of my learned, and industrious Countrymen Mr. *Ashmole*, Mr. *William Lilly*, Mr. *Booker*, Mr. *Sanders*, Mr. *Culpepper*, and others, who have taken unwearied pains for the resuscitation, and promotion of this noble Science, and with much patience against many unworthy scandals have laboured to propagate it to posterity.[34]

Webster's reference to the "art of medicine or *Chymistry*" and the "false *Alcumists*" recalls a similar distinction in Glanvill's *Plus Ultra*, noted earlier; however, he is not prepared to sound alchemy's death knell. In both his defense of chemistry ("that sublime, and never sufficiently praised Science") and his program for educational reform, Webster's opponents are the Aristotelians as much as the greedy imposters. He recounts the authorities responsible for alchemy's honorable past— "*Trismegist, Geber, Raymund Lully, Arnoldus de villanova, Roger Bacon*"—whose passing was followed by a long period of decline. Webster then turns to alchemy's modern rebirth, proudly extolling the accomplishments of several figures most subject to attack by his contemporaries: "yet was it for many ages in a manner buried in oblivion, or banished to the Monastick cells, until, *Basilius Valentinus,* *Isaac Hollandus,* and *Paracelsus* that singular ornament of *Germany,* did revive and restore the same, and since more cleerly manifested by him, who is justly stiled *Philosophus per ignem* [i.e., George Starkey], and many other famous men" (70-71). To praise Paracelsus and this group of chemical philosophers so lavishly required great courage and conviction on Webster's part, especially given the near certainty of retaliation. He concludes this section with a plea for reform in the schools, which will include banishing all of the debilitating aspects of Aristotelianism: "I dare truly and boldly say, that one years exercise therein to ingenious spirits, under able Masters, will produce more real and true fruit, than the studying *Aristotelian Philosophy* hath brought forth in many centuries. O that the Schools therefore would leave their idle, and fruitless speculations, and not be too proud to put their hands to the coals and furnace, where they might find ocular experiments to confute their fopperies, and produce effects that would be beneficial to all posterities" (71).

Webster's insistence on direct experimentation and observation is one of the dominant themes of the *Academiarum Examen,* underlying his view of the weaknesses of the universities and informing his program for curricular reform and inclusion of chemical studies in particular. His Baconian insistence on the value of experiment is, in fact, at the center of his antagonism toward Aristotelianism: "This *School Philosophy* is altogether void of true and infallible demonstration, observation and experiment, the only certain means, and in-struments to discover, and anatomize natures occult and central operations; which are found out by laborious tryals, manual operations, assiduous observations, and the like, and not by poring continually upon a few paper Idols, and unexpe-rienced Authors: As though we could fathome the Universe by our shallow imagi-nations, or comprize the mysteries of mother nature in the narrow compass of our weak brains" (68).[35]

Webster's cultivation of chemical studies in the universities undoubtedly resulted from his own medical training, his inherently "enthusiastic" tendencies, and from the fact that chemistry was clearly an empiricist-reformer's subject *par* *excellence.* As in the following quotation, his imagination and rhetoric are kindled, no less than Bacon's and Milton's, at the prospect of youth being trained in the experimental methods that chemistry can provide: "That youth may not be idlely trained up in notions, speculations, and verbal disputes, but may learn to inure their hands to labour, and put their fingers to the furnaces, that the mysteries discovered by *Pyrotechny,* and the wonders brought to light by *Chymistry,* may be rendered familiar unto them: . . . that so they may not be *Sophisters,* and *Philosophers,* but *Sophists* indeed, true Natural *Magicians,* . . . which can never come to pass, unless they have Laboratories as well as Libraries, and work in the fire, better than build Castles in the air" (106).

Despite excoriating attacks by Thomas Hall and Seth Ward that followed immediately, and to which I will turn shortly, the strength of Webster's convictions was great, and his views remained consistent in his later works as did his ability to inhabit the worlds of both magic and science. The *Metallographia: or, An History of Metals* (1671), for example, is at once a practical treatise on mining and metallurgy and a discussion "of the most difficult Questions belonging to Mystical Chymistry." In its preface, Webster continues to champion anti-Aristotelianism and experimentalism, "that Mens judgments may no longer be fettered in Scholastick Chains, nor kept always in the Prisons of Academick Opinions."[36] In keeping with his first, practical aim, Webster notes that "the stile [of *Metallographia*] is low, and plain as the nature of such a subject would bear, whose harsh and unusual terms, suitable for the most part for the Miners themselves, could not well have admitted of Rhetorick, or more polite Language." Moreover, his insistence on the use of experiment and observation in the natural sciences is grounded in the Baconian assumption that "all the knowledge (doubtless) that is yet had, is but a small part of that which may be known, and lies yet undiscovered, or found out."

Such progressive assertions notwithstanding, Webster's treatment of his subject is often traditional: there is much quoting of sources, including a large debt to Paracelsus and frequent references to Boyle, Hooke, Harvey, Ashmole, and van Helmont, among contemporaries. He appears confident in his belief in the philosopher's stone, "to the search and enquiry of which, I humbly and heartily intreat all ingenious persons, and Sons of Art, to use their industry, and ultimate endeavour, and not to think it a *Chymical Chimaera*" (122). Chapters 12 and 29 contain his most extensive discussion of gold, its medicinal uses, and the possibility of transmutation. Here, however, his conclusions about the latter reveal a greater sense of caution and balance than his earlier "enthusiastic" pronouncements, although he still appears to accept the truth of transmutation on the authority of Paracelsus, van Helmont, and others.

In a final work, *The Displaying of Supposed Witchcraft* (1677), Webster reveals a broad understanding of chemical medicine as well as familiarity with the history of its reception in France and England. His sensitive account of the experiences of Josephus Quercetanus and Sir Theodore Mayern in introducing chemical medicine in Paris ("what cruel censures and scandals did they undergo by all the rest of the Physicians of the Colledge, so that they were accounted illiterate and ignorant Fellows and dangerous Empiricks")[37] may owe something to the ridicule that Webster had received earlier in his own career; and his treatment of the persecutions of Roger Bacon, Arnald of Villanova, Raymond Lull, John Dee, Robert Fludd, and other "divers persons that have written of abstruse and mysterious Subjects" rises to a conclusion that is unquestionably personal and deeply felt. This account of persecutions, Webster states, "I have produced to shew how inconsiderately and ignorantly the best learned of an Age may be, and often are wrongfully and falsely traduced and slandered, which may be a warning to all persons to take heed how they pass their censures, until they understand perfectly all that is necessary to be known about the Subject they are to give judgment of, before they utter or declare their sentence" (7).

Almost immediately upon publication of *Academiarum Examen* in 1654 John Webster learned that "dauntless Spirits that have adventured to cross the current of common opinion . . . have never wanted opposition and scandal" (8), as he was attacked swiftly and savagely by Thomas Hall and Seth Ward. For those highly sympathetic to the aims and ideals of the universities, the New Science, and the Royal Society, Webster's "true Natural *Magician*" was hardly an acceptable model for the natural philosopher.

Thomas Hall (1610-65) was educated at Oxford and a lifelong bibliophile and founder of libraries, as well as a Presbyterian preacher who was ejected from his position by the Act of Uniformity in 1662.[38] His *Histrio-Mastix. A Whip for Webster (as 'tis conceived) the Quondom Player: Or, An examination of one John Websters delusive Examen of Academies* (1654) was written shortly after completion of *Vindiciae Literarum*, his defense of the universities and humane learning. As the title indicates, *Histrio-Mastix* is primarily an *ad hominem* attack on Webster, who is ridiculed for his magical and chemical interests and his politics. He is "a great stickler for the fire and Furnace of Chymestry, for Magick and Physiognomy &c.,"[39] and one of the "Familisticall-Levelling-Magicall temper" (199). He is also condemned because of the disreputable company he keeps: "not only *Lilly* and *Booker,* but also *Fryor Bacon* . . . and *Paracelsus,* a Libertine, a Drunkard, a man of little learning, and lesse Latine; he was not only skilled in naturall Magick, (the utmost bounds whereof, border'd on the suburbs of Hell) but is charged to converse constantly with Familiars, and to have the Devill for his Purse-bearer; yet this is one of Mr. Websters society" (209).

Hall, who emerges as a strong supporter of Aristotle and Galen, has read Webster's critique of the universities and sarcastically cites several of its main points: "his extolling of Chymistry, and preferring it before *Aristotelian Philosophy,* and advising schollars to leave their Libraries, and fall to Laboratories, putting their hands to the coales and Furnace. [So they may quickly find *pro thesauro carbones,* beggary instead of Learning]" (209-10). In the most universal terms, "Mr. *Webster* is against learning, against *Aristotle,* against Magistracie, against Ministrie, against Physitians, and against all that is truly good" (214). Hall's ire even extends to Webster's publisher, Giles Calvert, for in the *Academiarum Examen,* "the world may here see, what stuffe still comes from Lame *Giles Calvers* [sic] shop, that forge of the Devil, from whence so many blasphemous, lying, scandalous Pamphlets, for many yeers past, have spread over the Land, to the great dishonour of the Nation" (215). Throughout the 1650s and 1660s, Calvert was a leading publisher of translations and editions of Boehme and Paracelsus.

For us, *Histrio-Mastix* has greater importance than simply being a cleverly malicious attack by one somewhat obscure seventeenth-century author against another. Significant, first of all, is the way in which Webster is made the focal point of such comprehensive condemnation: for his occult interests and kinship with Paracelsus and other "disreputable" authors, his politics and religion, his views on university curricula, and his elevation of experimental science over Aristotelian philosophy—even for his choice of book publisher. In Hall's mind, as he candidly states, Webster is "against all that is truly good." He and his *Academiarum Examen* represent interests and modes of thought that directly challenge the conservative science and humanistic academic traditions that Hall upholds, and these oppositions are deepened by their political and religious differences. The controversy between Webster and Hall is representative of many that were played out in often similar terms in the latter half of the seventeenth century. An important aspect of this particular debate for this study is that it is partially grounded in the transition from the pseudoscience alchemy to the science of chemistry.

By virtue of his education, politics, and personal associations, Seth Ward (1617-89) could only have occupied a position adversarial to that of John Webster. He had obtained two degrees from Sidney Sussex College at Cambridge, possessed outstanding mathematical skills and friendship with William Oughtred, one of England's leading mathematicians, received appointment as professor of astronomy at Oxford, and—in the company of Boyle, Thomas Willis, and Ralph Bathurst—held membership in the Philosophical Society of Oxford, which, with the Gresham College group in London, later evolved into the Royal Society, of which Ward was a charter member. Moreover, he had successive appointments as bishop of Exeter and Salisbury and had gained a reputation for acting harshly toward nonconformists. Ward was thus placed within the highest intellectual and scientific circles and occupied positions of power in both church and university.[40]

Ward's *Vindiciae Academiarum: Containing Some briefe Animadversions upon Mr Websters Book, Stiled, The Examination of Academies* was published at Oxford in 1654, the year of the *Academiarum Examen* and Hall's *Histrio-Mastix*. Like Hall's work, Ward's critique engages in *ad hominem* attacks but it is far more valuable because of its comprehensiveness and insights into how Webster's causes and interests were perceived by those who opposed him. For this reason, it merits detailed analysis. In a preface signed only "N. S.," Ward comments generally on both the content and style of the *Examen*, calling it little more than a "Torrent of affected insignificant tautologies with some peevish unworthy reflections, & the repetitions of some old & trite cavills, together with severall bundles of grosse mistaks."[41] The preface also charges Webster with ignorance of the true present state of the universities and, more important for our purposes, attacks him for having defended the occult: "But above all, the man doth give me the freest prospect of his depth and braine, in that canting Discourse about the language of nature, wherein he doth assent unto the highly illuminated fraternity of the *Rosycrucians*[,] [i]n his large encomiums upon *Jacob Behem,* in that reverence which he professes to judiciall Astrologie, which may sufficiently convince what a kind of credulous fanatick Reformer he is like to prove" (5). Webster's enthusiastic brand of reformation is, above all, reflected in his rhetoric, which Ward spoofs through allusion to Dapper and Dol Common in Jonson's *Alchemist* and other literary characters: "But making my approach to him, I find him at his distance, praying (like some moping Friar [to] the Lady of *Lauretto,* or like) the Nephew of the Queene of Faery, and uttering a speech to her, made by *John Dee* in his Preface, enough to satisfy mee, that she is yet pure and untouched by him, and hath not entertained him into any familiarity" (15).

Integral to Ward's attack on enthusiastic rhetoric is his ironic commentary on hieroglyphics and emblems; here, some twelve years before Samuel Parker's similar analysis of these "childish fooleries" in *Free and Impartial Censure,* Ward mocks the notion of a rhetoric of concealment:

> *Hierogliphicks* and *Cryptography,* were invented for *concealment* of things, and used either in mysteries of Religion . . . or in the exigences of Warre, or in occasions of the deepest secresy, . . . and Grammar is one of those Arts and Language one of those helps, which serve for *explication* of our minds and notions: How incongruous then is it, that the Art of *Concealment,* should not be made a part of the Art of *Illustration;* surely it would make much to the advancement of Children while they are learning the Elements of Grammar, to be put upon the speculation of the *Mensa Isiacae,* the *Canopi,* and *Obeliskes,* the *Thesaurus Hieroglyphicus,* or *Grosschedel's Magicall Calendar;* This would certainly effect, even in Children, what *Porta & Agrippa* have done to M. *Webster,* bring them to *Wonder* and *Amazement.* [18-19][42]

Speaking as one fully aware of the state of affairs within the universities, Ward then turns from rhetoric to Webster's championing of magic, chemistry, and the Rosicrucians. He asserts that chemistry is not neglected in the universities, that discoveries "of light and profit" are pursued that contribute to knowledge in both natural philosophy and medicine. But, he continues, "Mr. *Webster* expects we should tell him, that we have found the Elixar, (surely we are wiser then to say so) yet we can recommend him to one of his faith, who hath been threescore years in the pursuance of it, and two years since believed he was very neare it" (35).

Like Thomas Hall, Ward's close familiarity with Webster's book is reflected in the fact that his own essay often takes the form of a "chapter and verse" refutation of the original. For example, in chapter 10, *Of some helps in Naturall Phylosophy,* Webster's words are quoted and underscored, then followed by Ward's "refutation," in this case, of Webster's appropriation of Baconian inductive methods:

> 1. [Webster's] first [Remedy] is, *that my L. Bacons way may be embraced. That Axioms be evidently proved by observations, and no other be admitted &c.*
>
> I am wholly of his judgement, yet I have an itching desire to know what *Lilly,* and *Booker, Behmen,* and all the families of Magicians, Soothsayers, Can-

ters, and Rosycrucians, have done to vexe him, since he was writing of *Mathematicks,* and *Scholastick Philosophy,* that having cherished them then, and put them in hopes of his blessing, he should now of a sudden cast them off, betaking himselfe to their deadly enemy.

2. The Second Remedy is, *That some Physicall Learning may be brought into the Schooles, that is grounded upon sensible, Rationall, Experimentall, and Scripture Principles, and such an Author is Dr Fludd; then which for all the particulars, the World never had a more perfect piece.*

[Ward concludes] How little trust there is in villainous man! he that even now was for the way of strict and accurate induction, is fallen into the mysticall way of the *Cabala,* and numbers formall: there are not two waies in the whole World more opposite, then those of the L. *Verulam* and D. *Fludd,* the one founded upon experiment, the other upon mysticall Ideal reasons. [46]

Ward's final assessment of the antithetical methods of Bacon and Fludd— in fact, our view of the entire Webster, Hall, Ward controversy—serves to illuminate the uneasy relationship between the magical and scientific milieus in Restoration England. As has been shown, "enthusiasm" was an inflammatory term and, when employed by those in the scientific community, could easily suggest nearly universal contempt and disparagement. From this perspective, it encompasses a wide range of undesirable ideas, psychological conditions, movements, and individual authors; it suggests fanaticism and excesses of all sorts, irrationality, credulousness, faulty methodologies (or no methodologies at all), emptily rhetorical prose, Platonism, magic, Rosicrucianism, Paracelsianism and chemical medicine, nonconformism, even atheism. The question is not that Hall and Ward were being unfair to the substance of Webster's work or that they failed to recognize that he was, at least partially, operating in the tradition of Baconian reform, experiment, and cautious inquiry into the benefits to be derived from these methods; the mere levying of the term "enthusiasm" against Webster precluded objective evaluation. Ironically, in the works of the pre- and post-Restoration writers I have thus far discussed, scientific objectivity fell victim to its own concern with *a priori* standards.

The Webster controversy suggests another interesting aspect of the debate between partisans of the occult and the New Science in late seventeenth-century England. As charges of enthusiasm increased in intensity, it would seem that the targets (or potential targets) of these attacks at times went some length to distance themselves from "enthusiastic" associations. One of these strategies that we have seen in Webster is his determination to align himself with the aims and methods "so judiciously laid down by our learned Countreyman the Lord *Bacon,* . . . [which should be] set up for a rule and pattern."[43] John Sparrow, Boehme's translator, employed a similar means of diverting the opposition. More striking is the disclaimer issued by a prolific late seventeenth-century alchemical author, Eyraeneus Philaletha, who, in his pursuit of the elixir, would reject the methods of enthusiasts and traditional alchemical authorities and adopt those of the New

Science: "We have sequestred the Chymical Art from all the vulgar errours, and of the vanquished *Sophisms,* and the curious Dreams of the *Imaginarists;* . . . We have protested, and do again profess, That we do not declare these things from the faith we give to the Writings of other Men; the things we faithfully declare, are what we have both seen and known. We have made and do possess the *Stone,* the great *Elixir.*"[44]

On the other hand, those who were solidly positioned on the side of the New Science might refer to the effects of the emerging technology as if they were wrought by magic. This we note in John Wilkins's work entitled *Mathematicall Magick. Or, The wonders that may be performed by Mechanicall Geometry* (1648), in which the "miracles" performed by levers, wheels, pulleys, and screws are explained and illustrated. Wilkins states in his preface that "this whole Discourse I call Mathematicall Magick, because the art of such mechanicall inventions as are here chiefly insisted upon, hath been formerly so styled; and in allusion to vulgar opinion, which doth commonly attribute all such strange operations unto the power of magick."[45]

As is seen most notably in the attacks on John Webster by Hall and Ward and in Seth Parker's indictment of Platonism, critiques of the entire occult milieu that originated in scientific and university circles just before and following the Restoration were harsh, comprehensive, and little concerned with fairness and objectivity. The dominant tendency was to lump together the offending ideas, individuals, and movements and tar them over with a very wide brush. The remainder of this chapter will show that this method of castigation was not limited to leading scientists and intellectuals but had a counterpart in the works of one of the period's major satirists, Samuel Butler, the author of *Hudibras* and the last writer of the seventeenth century to utilize hermetic materials to a significant degree.

Butler's "An Hermetic Philosopher," with which I begin, is written in the popular genre of the prose character, which, by the time of Butler's contributions to the form, had already enjoyed considerable success. Through the pens of Sir Thomas Overbury, John Earle, and others, it was a genre associated primarily with wit and satire.[46] While "An Hermetic Philosopher" has most often been interpreted as an attack on Thomas Vaughan because of references to his works and concentrated ridicule of the Rosicrucians,[47] it also touches on many subjects and themes that had emerged in the Webster controversy and the work of Seth Parker. For this reason, Butler's prose character should be read in a wider context than as a narrowly focused personal attack; it is, after all, a representative of a literary form given to delineating generalized types rather than unique individuals.

Seth Parker's *Free and Impartial Censure* (1666), we recall, ironically complained of the "very quarrelsome Humour" of the English Rosicrucians, to the extent that Parker had been "scared from Engaging" with them; they had also exhibited a keen passion for writing and authorship: i.e., "a huge ambition to be esteemed the Polemical Scripturients of the Age."[48] Immediately thereafter, he alludes to the "Controversial Rencountres of *Eugenius Philalethes,*" clear reference to the dispute with Henry More.[49] Butler begins on a very similar note, leaving no doubt at the outset of his sketch that he has Vaughan specifically in mind: the Hermetic Philosopher "is a Kind of Hector in Learning, that thinks to maintain himself in Reputation by picking Quarrels with his gentle Readers"; he is also given to "baffl[ing] their Understandings," intimidating them with his great reputation and public declaration of *"concealed Truths"* (139-40). Although the Rosicrucian manifestos published in 1614-15 denied that alchemical transmutation was a goal of the fraternity,[50] some of Butler's richest humor is at the expense of the alchemists' insistence on linguistic obscurity, which has as its precedent *"Adam's* first green Britches; because Fig-leaves being the first Cloaths, that Mankind wore, were only used for Covering, and therefore are the most ancient Monuments of concealed Mysteries" (141). Also noted are the Hermetic Philosopher's attack on the Schoolmen and his devotion to Agrippa, Sendivogius, Lull, and Jean d'Espagnet, author of the *Enchyridion Physicae Restitutae,* to whom I referred in discussing *Paradise Lost,* book 5.

Butler turns next to his Philosopher's "adoration" of the *"Brethren of the Rosy-Cross,"* and from this point to the end the work shifts from being a character sketch to a humorous and satirical exposé of this magical order. This shift is logical since Vaughan (assuming that he is the satirical target at the beginning of the essay) was closely identified with the Rosicrucians through publication of *The Fame and Confession of the Fraternity of R: C:* in 1652, the first English translation of the manifestos to be printed. Butler's attack is many-sided, again recalling the range of charges against the Rosicrucians that appeared in the works of Parker and Ward. Like Parker, who had condemned the stylistic exuberances and elements of literary romance in Rosicrucian writing, Butler lashes out against the Brotherhood as "a Kind of *Philosophers Errant,* that wander up and down upon Adventures, and have an enchanted Castle, invisible to all but themselves, to which they are bound by their Order to repair at certain Seasons. In this Tabernacle rests the Body of their Prophet or Founder, who dying, as they affirm, hid himself in a Kind of invisible Oven, where after an hundred Years he was discovered . . . looking (like a Woodcock's Head stuck in the Lid of a Pye) as if he were alive. With him they found a World of most precious Secrets and Mysteries, with a deal of Treasure, and a Dictionary of all those Names, that *Adam* gave the Creatures" (145).

Employing broad humor, jarring associations of ideas, and absurdities of all sorts to render Rosicrucian beliefs nonsensical, Butler sees the order as little more than a catchall for ridiculous ideas and opinions, a view similar to the one Parker had of Platonism. For example, of the abstract, platonic cosmos of the Rosicrucians, Butler notes "they are better acquainted with the intelligible World, than they are with this [the terrestrial world]; and understand more of Ideas, than they do of Things" (146). This leads to his characterizing it as "a Kind of *Terra incognita,*" which, in turn, gives rise to discussion of correspondences between this intelligible world and the celestial and elemental ones. Cosmological absurdities are necessarily mirrored in the bizarrely futile terrestrial powers and practices of the members of this strange brotherhood: "They have fine Devices to make counterfeit Maggots of Lute-Strings, translate Agues into Dogs, or fright them away with Spiders; to cure the Tooth-ach or sore Eyes with Medicines laid to the Imagination; . . . blow the Philosophers Fire with Words of pure Wind, and draw the glorify'd Spirit of the Elixir not out of gross Matter, but the pure incorporeal Hope and Faith of the Credulous, which is the best and the most rational Way of Multiplication; for a small Dose so prepared and projected upon the dullest Metal, converts it presently into Gold ready coined" (147-48). Butler's satiric technique and prose style in this passage recall Jonson and Swift and, in its rushing torrent of language, Robert Burton. However, the ideas behind the satire are transformed commonplaces derived from alchemy, astrology, Neoplatonism, magic, and the cabala, and the stinging indictment of the human consequences of charlatanism (reflected in the final section of the quotation) recall many examples of earlier alchemical satire. For Butler, no less than for Chaucer, Erasmus, and Jonson, human misery and degradation are the final results of rapacious greed preying upon credulity. Thus Butler, the last seventeenth-century writer to treat alchemy and hermeticism at length and in detail, represents a return to the long tradition of alchemical satire.

Not sufficiently noticed, I think, is the manner in which Butler's imagination and satirical sense operate upon the material that he derived from occult tradition. Examples of this transforming power abound in "An Hermetic Philosopher," and I offer only a representative few. In the case of astronomy, satire of the numerous cosmological reconfigurations that were a major consequence of Renaissance scientific investigation takes the following form: "They [astronomers and/or Rosicrucian theorists] are now carrying on a *thorough Reformation* in the celestial World—They have repaired the old Spheres, that were worn as thin as a Cob-web, and fastened the Stars in them with a Screw, by which means they may be taken off, and put on again at Pleasure" (148). Charges of hermetic philosophy's demonic connections, such as were levied by Parker and Ward, as well as thrusts at the Jews and the cabala are present in Butler's statement that pious astronomers, having reassigned Christian, rather than pagan, names to the planets, may eventually "derive the Principles and Rudiments of their Science from divine Authority." In the course of time, this may "save the Charge of hiring old Mungrel Rabines, that are three Quarters *Jews,* to make their Art as lawful as they can, with mighty Arguments drawn from Etymologies and Anagrams. But their Intelligence in the upper World is nothing to what they have in the infernal; for they hold exact Correspondence with the Devils, and can give a perfect Account of their ecclesiastical, civil, and military Discipline" (149). Butler's attack on the Rosicrucian brotherhood includes many additional aspects: numerological methods are likened to having the assistance of "the better Sort of Spirits" who range throughout the Neoplatonic cosmos and "have a strange natural Allegiance to hard Words" and symbolic characters. The brotherhood's cabalistic interests also involve millenarian prophecy ("how long it is to the Day of Judgment, and, which is more wonderful, whether it shall be in Winter or Summer") and the casting of horoscopes (150-51).

Given these esoteric preoccupations, it is not surprising that members of the brotherhood should avoid empirical approaches to knowledge of the natural world. Butler, like Ward in his attack on "the mysticall way of the *Cabala,* and numbers formall," castigates the Rosicrucians for their condemnation of "any Knowledge, that is either derived from Sense or reducible to it," for regarding "Demonstration [as] too gross and low an Aim for the sublime Speculations of the Intellect" (153). Nonetheless, if deductive argument fails, the brotherhood has invented an optic that gives them strange powers. In a highly Swiftian passage, Butler speaks of "Spectacles to read *Jacob Boehmen* and *Ben-Israel* with, which, like those Glasses that revert the Object, will turn the wrong End of their Sentences upwards, and make them look like Sense" (154). He concludes his character not by summarizing the defining qualities of a typical hermetic philosopher but by listing many of the occult "bodies of knowledge" associated with the Rosicrucian order and by questioning the moral contradictions they present: "Philosophy, Magic, Divinity, Physics, Astrology, Alchimy, Bawdery, Witchcraft, &c. for, beside a rare Property they have to restore sinful old Age to Virtue, Youth, and Understanding, they are very sovereign to clear the Eyes of the Mind, and make a blear-ey'd Intellect see like a Cat in the Dark, though it be stark blind in the Light" (157). Adopting the role of the traditional satirist, Butler points out the discrepancies between what these secretive brotherhoods and individuals profess and their true motives. If, as members of the occult orders claim, they have taken a vow of secrecy not to reveal their God-given knowledge, why do they teach it to others? And, having taught it, why do they enjoin their pupils not to reveal it further? Finally, he notes that "after so many Precepts and Rules delivered with the greatest Confidence and Presumption of Certainty, they will tell you, that this Art is not to be attained but by divine Revelation, and only to be expected by holy and sanctified Persons, that have left behind them all the concernments of this World; whereby it seems, *this Shadow of Art follows those only that fly it, and flies from those that follow it*" (159). The statement aptly summarizes the relationship between the *ignis fatuus* alchemy and its victims throughout the duration of the satirical tradition from Chaucer to Butler, and beyond to Swift.

In *Hudibras,* Butler's major work, many of the objects of satirical commentary that are present in "An Hermetic Philosopher" appear once more, but the peculiarly "Hudibrastic" technique of this long poem results in a work of far greater humor, trenchancy, and originality. John Wilders has written that the poem's satirical mode is varied, combining such elements as invective, caricature, mock disputation, and farce within the encompassing vehicle of the mock heroic, which "depends for its effect on the violent contrast between subject and treatment."[51] As I hope to demonstrate, these qualities, as well as the attributes of the Hudibrastic style—gross distortions in meter and rhyme, colloquial language, and bizarre imagery—when applied to the materials of mid–seventeenth-century occultism, create a satirical method that is keen and incisive. They are well suited to the task of deflating and debasing those aspects of religious nonconformism that are the Royalist Butler's principal targets. In *Hudibras,* as in the finest examples of alchemical satire previously considered, the varied forms of occultism serve as an effective vehicle for commenting on a wide range of flaws in human character and behavior.

While alchemy, per se, plays virtually no part in Butler's mock-heroic, his main characters and several of their major adventures definitely exist within an occult milieu. For this reason, it is necessary to broaden my focus in order to encompass the diversity of satirical objects and methods, just as has been the case with his prose character. Thus in terms of his comprehensive treatment of many aspects of contemporary occultism—astrology, magic, Rosicrucianism, Platonism, the cabala, witchcraft—Butler is following the lead of several of the attackers of occultism whose works I have considered. There is, however, one important difference. Whereas Glanvill, Parker, Ward, and others championed the aims and achievements of the Royal Society, we see no such respect paid in *Hudibras.* Scientific experimentalism and the virtuosi are for Butler as worthy of condemnation as the perpetrators and victims of occult charlatanism. In fact, he draws no real distinction between them: both groups are victims of zeal and enthusiasm, whether imparted by the New Light or the New Science.

Like other Restoration (and Royalist) attackers of the occult arts, Butler establishes their connection with philosophical and religious enthusiasm at the outset. Not only is Sir Hudibras a "*Presbyterian* true blew," but in his absorption in arcane scientific knowledge and impractical schemes he is a close relative of his contemporary, Sir Nicholas Gimcrack, the protagonist of Thomas Shadwell's *Virtuoso.* No less than Gimcrack's designs for learning to swim on dry land and selling bottles of air, Hudibras's "learning" in the trivium and the quadrivium is palpably nonsensical, in the manner of the satire of the Rosicrucian brotherhood in Butler's prose character and Swift's scientific projectors in the third voyage of *Gulliver's Travels.* For Butler, Shadwell, and Swift, impractical and futile "scientific" ventures, even when (or especially when) associated with the Royal Society, come to replace the specific occult arts as objects of satire. Hudibras's intellectual bent amounts to an *idée fixe* that dooms him to impracticality:

> For he by *Geometrick* scale
> Could take the size of *Pots of Ale;*
> Resolve by Sines and Tangents straight,

> If *Bread* or *Butter* wanted weight;
> And wisely tell what hour o'th' day
> The Clock does strike, by *Algebra.* [part 1, canto 1, 121-26]

But if the Knight's absurdities take the form of comic self-deception, the flaws of his companion and squire, Ralph, strike much deeper, for in him we see eccentricities and deviations that are not only self-deceiving but also pose threats to social, religious, and political stability. Butler's principal means of demonstrating sectarian destructiveness is to present it as issuing forth in the form of dictates from the "New Light," which, in turn, is related to the absurdities seen in the contemporary occult milieu. Ralph is, therefore, a specific example of the character type represented in "An Hermetic Philosopher" and a concrete embodiment of the varied tendencies castigated in the treatises of Restoration opponents of occultism.[52] At the heart of both versions is the strong link between occult philosophy and enthusiasm; as Samuel Parker observed, "there is so much Affinity between *Rosi-Crucianisme* and *Enthusiasme,* that whoever entertains the one, he may upon the same Reason embrace the other:"[53]

> [Ralph's] *Knowledge* was not far behind
> The Knight's, but of another kind,
> And he another way came by't:
> Some call it *Gifts,* and some *New light;*
> A Liberal Art, that cost no pains
> Of Study, Industry, or Brains.
>
> . . . .
>
> A light that falls down from on high,
> For Spiritual Trades to cousen by: [1.1.473-78, 501-2]

As a result of Butler's insistence on the close links between religious nonconformity, occultism, and enthusiasm, the descriptions of Ralph's background, "learning," and interests become a comprehensive catalog of both current and more traditional mystical and magical materials rendered comic through the deflationary effects of his style and technique. For example, in Butler's eclectic vision, not only are the individual arts lumped together ("For mystick Learning, wondrous able / In Magick, *Talisman,* and *Cabal*"), but—owing to the nature of enthusiasm as a *"false conceit of inspiration"*—they are held to zealously and dogmatically by adherents such as Ralph: "Thus *Ralph* became infallible, / As three or four-legg'd Oracle, / The ancient Cup, or modern Chair; / Spoke truth pointblank, though unaware:" (1.1.519-22). It follows that Ralph should be well grounded in platonic cosmology and, like the "Hermetic Philosopher," he is "Deep-sighted in Intelligences" and the "intelligible" world, as opposed to the terrestrial one. The sources of his knowledge—Agrippa, *Anthroposophus* (i.e., Thomas Vaughan), Fludd, and Jacob Boehme—are, in Butler's deflationary couplet technique, "for profound / And solid Lying much renown'd" (1.1.533-36).

From the references to Vaughan and Fludd it is only a short step to the topic of Rosicrucianism, the real or imaginary brotherhood that Butler holds in special disrepute. Here, as in Samuel Parker's attack on the varying forms of Platonism, the Rosicrucians appear to function in Restoration England as a kind of objective correlative for the large and diverse occult milieu. Butler's identification of Ralph's knowledge with Rosicrucian lore is tantamount to designating it as absurd and useless; in his own note on "*Verè adeptus*" in the following quotation he states that the phrase means "one that has Commenc'd in their Fanatique extravagance."[54] Ralph is "In *Rosy-Crucian* Lore as learned, / As he that *Verè adeptus* earned. / He understood the speech of Birds / As well as they themselves do words:" (1.1.539-42), and his knowledge is often expressed in the form of fortune-telling and astrology, a motif that Butler will develop much further in the Sidrophel episode. In the present passage, Ralph's feigning of astrological skill based on the inner light merely serves the purpose of cheating others:

> He could foretell whats'ever was
> By consequence to come to pass.
> As Death of Great men, Alterations,
> Diseases, Battels, Inundations.
> All this without th'eclipse of Sun,
> Or dreadful Comet, he hath done,
> By inward light. [1.1.567-73]

With these powers he carries out his petty practice of astrology, physiognomy, and the casting of horoscopes: "Thus [with the New Light] was th'accomplish'd Squire endu'd / With Gifts and Knowledge, per'lous shrewd" (1.1.617-18).

But besides Hudibras and Ralph, Butler paints other characters and situations with enough of a varnish of occultism to render them ridiculous and enable them to serve in the debasement of knight and squire. Chief among these is the Rosicrucian Sidrophel, whose fortune-telling skills Hudibras seeks in order to discover his prospects for success in the wooing of the Widow. Nicolas H. Nelson has argued that this extended episode is Butler's response to the vigorous controversy over astrology and the many resulting publications both for and against it that appeared in England in the 1640s and 1650s; and, further, that astrology's most aggressive defenders were radical sectarians, who were rapidly emerging with the blessing and support of the Puritan regime.[55] While it is possible that Butler's Sidrophel may be drawn from hints in the life of William Lilly, the author of *England's propheticall Merline* (1644) and *Christian Astrology* (1647), who is referred to in the poem, John Wilders is correct in stating that the satire of astrology and experimental science is generalized and not limited to a particular individual.[56] Rather, Sidrophel, no less than the portrait of the Hermetic Philosopher, should be read in the context of the broader late seventeenth-century occult milieu that they, in part, embody.

Like Parker, whose *Free and Impartial Censure* followed the separately printed editions of parts 1 and 2 of *Hudibras* by only two or three years, Butler grounds his characters and action in the Sidrophel episode (part 2, canto 3) in the link between Rosicrucianism, astrology, and other occult arts, a connection that Butler announces in the canto's argument:

> *The* Knight *with various doubts possest*
> *To win the* Lady, *goes in Quest*
> *Of* Sidrophel *the* Rosy-crucian,
> *To know the Dest'nies resolution;*
> *With whom being met, they both chop* Logick,
> *About the Science* Astrologick. [p. 152]

Seeking information from Sidrophel concerning his possible success in wooing the widow, Hudibras, unlike the reader, is unaware of the trap that awaits him. Butler's imagery leading into this episode effectively suggests the myriad ways in which superstitiousness and chicanery can lead the ignorant to misadventure: there are images of birds being caught by strange noises, lights, and snares and of men being duped with promises of alchemical "*Med'cine,* and *Receit,*" or as the prey of crooked lawyers. Other men, like Hudibras, consult wizards "to foresee / What shall, and what shall never be" (2.3.25-26). Again, Butler's mock-heroic style effectively ridicules Hudibras by juxtaposing things great and small: "O that I could enucleate, / And solve the *Problems* of my *Fate;* / Or find by *Necromantick* art, / How farr the *Dest'nies* take my part" (2.3.93-96), a technique continued in the listing of the "deep importances" (ll. 105-24) that prompt people to seek out Sidrophel. He who "deals in *Destinies* dark *Counsels,*" we learn, is a cunning man and witch whose supernatural gifts enable the villagers to recover their lost silver or find cures for ailing livestock.

In contrast to these trivial exercises in the supernatural, Hudibras's quest is far more ambitious and daring, just as Butler's satire is morally more incisive. Hudibras seeks nothing less than advice from the devil, which, Ralph assures him, the Saints have every right to expect because there are many precedents for supernatural predictions and intervention on their behalf. In these passages, Ralph's argument is laced with personal names and places: Martin Luther, Matthew Hopkins, Edward Kelley, George Wither, Woodstock, and Sarum. References to political issues and military campaigns also heighten the overall satiric effect, deepening and rendering concretely (albeit humorously) the implications of witchcraft, astrology, magic, and devil worship as far as religious hypocrisy and social instability are concerned. For Hudibras, the decision to consult Sidrophel is obvious: "Quoth *Hudibras,* The case is cleer, / The *Saints* may 'mploy a *Conjurer;* / As thou hast prov'd it by their *practice*" (2.3.189-91). The thematic link with Jonson's avaricious Puritan brethren in *The Alchemist* is clear and direct: with the sanction of the inner light, human nature will go to any extreme to satisfy its desires.

To refer to Sidrophel merely as an astrologer or a magician is, however, to put the matter too simply and to distort the objective of Butler's satire. In addition to his occult interests, Sidrophel is a scientific projector, and Butler, as Swift was later to do, includes a full measure of satire on the experimental science of his day just as he attacked its occult interests. This extension of satire to "scientific" endeavors of the later seventeenth century marks a new and final direction in the tradition of alchemical satire that I have been tracing. What was Butler's position with respect to the emerging experimental science and the "institutionalization" of science as seen in the Royal Society? John Wilders has described it as follows:

> Holding as he did an essentially empirical view of knowledge, Butler might be expected to have sympathized with the growing interest in science and with the deliberations of the Royal Society. In fact, he had little or no respect for the scientists, exposing them to ridicule both in *Hudibras* and in his best minor poem, *The Elephant in the Moon*. It is true that he shared something of their practical, empirical attitude, but he could see little of value in their activities. They were, he believed, as prone to error and misapprehension as other men, and, in their over-exclusive concern for experiment and discovery, were apt to be absorbed by the trivial rather than the useful, or to seek for wonders at the expense of truth.[57]

To fit Sidrophel as the vehicle for this broader vein of satire, it was necessary that Butler provide him with a more comprehensive background than if he were a mere witch or quack astrologer. Although Butler ironically refers to him as a "Profound *Gymnosophist*" (2.3.196), the mystical and ascetic significations of this term are as inadequate as the word "*Conjurer*" (2.3.202) to describe the range of his interests and ambitions. Butler therefore endows him with qualifications that will position him within both the occult and scientific milieus, granting him expertise in mathematics, optics, philosophy, magic, horoscopy, and astrology. In addition he is an

>   old *Dog* at *Physiologie:*
> But, as a *Dog* that turns the spit,
> Bestirs himself, and plys his feet,
> To clime the *Wheel;* but all in vain,
> His own weight brings him down again:
>
> . . . .
>
> So in the *Circle* of the *Arts,*
> Did he advance his nat'rall Parts;
> Till falling back still, for retreat,
> He fell to *Juggle, Cant,* and *Cheat.* [2.3.208-12, 215-18]

For the success of Butler's satire on both the occult and scientific milieus, it is important that, along with Sidophel's breadth of background, a pervasive sense of futility attend his efforts. The images of a dog on a treadmill, trying to climb the wheel, like that of Sidrophel's attempted advancement in the "*Circle* of the *Arts*," are informed by the myth of Sisyphus and the idea of Fortune's wheel: "And still he's in the self same place, / Where at his setting out he was" (ll. 213-14). Futility and misspent effort are thus implicit in both types of endeavors.

Given Butler's skepticism about the utility of experimental science, it is essential that Sidrophel's endeavors be incontrovertibly impractical and useless in improving the human condition: this is the point Shadwell makes in *The Virtuoso*, as does Swift through the scientific projectors that Gulliver visits in the third voyage. For this reason, Butler presents in great detail the authors and works from which Sidrophel derives his knowledge, "authorities" that an elite audience might have regarded with derision. Roger Bacon and Robert Grosthead ("*Hodg Bacon*, and *Bob Grosted*") are included here (2.3.224), not for their philosophical and scientific achievements but for their reputations as learned magicians and conjurers. Although in the course of the seventeenth century, Bacon's reputation was steadily rehabilitated toward scientific respectability, nevertheless, in Butler's time, he would still have been best known as the magician-hero of Robert Greene's *Friar Bacon and Friar Bungay* and chapbook tradition.[58] Also among the important influences on Sidrophel are John Dee and Edward Kelley. Dee, however, is not cited for his extraordinary learning or skill in mathematics and medicine, but for the notoriety resulting from his dabblings in the spirit world in association with his "skryer" Kelley. An account of this unfortunate relationship had—to the destruction of Dee's reputation—been published by Meric Casaubon in 1659 while *Hudibras* was being written:[59] "H' [Sidrophel] had read *Dee's* Prefaces before / The *Dev'l*, and *Euclide* o're and o're. / And, all th'*Intregues*, 'twixt him and *Kelly*, / *Lescus* and th'*Emperor*, would tell yee" (2.3.235-38). As with his treatment of Roger Bacon, Butler's refashioning of Dee's reputation is achieved at the expense of Dee's scientifically valuable preface to the Billingsley translation of Euclid's *Elements* (1570), which Butler disparages through association with the petty intrigues with Kelley at the courts of the Polish prince Albert Laski and Emperor Rudolph II in Prague. And, continuing this pattern of diminution, commentary on Paracelsus is at this point limited to the prescription for making an artificial man (2.3.299-300).

Additional figures will be considered shortly; however, we may pause here to examine several tendencies in Butler's reductive approach to occult and scientific authorities and ideas. One obvious effect of the consistent debunking of such figures is to debase and trivialize the traditions and worldviews they represent. Butler is as skeptical of metaphysical abstruseness as he is of experimental science, and his principal objection to philosophical speculation is its remoteness from matters of genuine human concern and benefit. Early in the portrait of Sidrophel, for example, Butler calls attention to the astrologer's knowledge of the "*Intelligible world*," the abstract realm of ideas derived from platonic tradition, and then proceeds to describe sardonically the complex network of correspondences that obtain between macrocosm and microcosm:

> Th'*Intelligible world* he knew,
> And all, men dream on't, to be true:
> That in this *World,* there's not a *Wart,*
> That has not there [in the microcosm] a Counterpart;
> Nor can there on the *face* of Ground,
> An Individuall *Beard* be found,
> That has not, in that Forrain *Nation,*
> A fellow of the self-same fashion; [2.3.225-32]

Sharing Samuel Parker's distrust of platonically derived metaphysical speculation, Butler criticizes the substitution of the abstract "*Intelligible*" world for the
terrestrial one as the object of greatest human concern. This commonsense approach to human knowledge and need is revealed as well in Butler's enumeration of the absurd ways in which man attempts to utilize his knowledge.
Sidrophel, like Hudibras, would relish the use of "*Geometrick* scale" to calculate
the size of ale pots. We see his grotesque fascination with futile incongruities
throughout the portrait, but especially in his "practical" applications of astrology to daily life. For example, Sidrophel finds through astrology propitious times
for both planting and harvest, and, as village cunning man, he uses stellar influences to facilitate the art of healing: "When for anoynting *Scabs* or *Itches,* / Or
to the *Bum* applying *Leeches;*" (2.3.245-46).

Butler combines these satiric motifs most effectively in Sidrophel's fascination with the moon, with which he "was more familiar / Than e're was *Almanack-
well-willer*" (2.3.239-40). The moon is at once a symbol of Sidrophel's remoteness
from humanity, of the futility of abstract speculation and philosophizing, and,
most important, of madness itself. (Butler would not have been impressed with
Penseroso's nocturnal studies of the occult in the "high lonely Tow'r," and
Sidrophel is a kind of utterly debased, comic portrait of him.) Above all else,
Sidrophel is a lunatic. His removal from the terrestrial world to a realm of abstract speculation makes the moon a perfect habitation for him: in fact, the moon's
"Secrets [he] understood so clear, / That some believ'd he had been there"
(2.3.241-42), and, obsessed by the moon's visionary aspects, he proceeds to act
under her inspiration, becoming a kind of mad scientific projector, oblivious to
the impracticality and futility of his inventions and calculations:

> He made an *Instrument* to know
> If the *Moon* shine at full, or no,
> That would as soon as e're she shon, streit
> Whether 'twere Day or Night demonstrate;
> Tell what her *D'ameter* t'an inch is,
> And prove she is not made of *Green Cheese.* [2.3.261-66]

Although the "*Instrument*" Sidrophel has invented might tend to mark him as
an empiricist, it is without value because he fails to utilize it for human betterment; moreover, it cannot assist in the discovery of truth because he lacks the

ability to make accurate observations and to draw valid conclusions from them. Unable thus to discover truth through common sense and empirical investigation, Sidrophel's "knowledge" amounts to bizarre extrapolations from absurd, stubbornly held ideas. He is therefore a failure in his use of both induction and deduction; he is the chief victim of his own quackery.

While astrology underlies much of Sidrophel's absurdity, Butler is also at pains to present his follies as the confused efforts of an experimental scientist. To achieve this purpose, he will, at times, adopt the vocabulary of scientific reports: "demonstrat[ing]" (ll. 264, 267), "prov[ing]" (l. 266), "quot[ing]" and "detect[ing]" (ll. 283, 285), even "applying" "Med'cines, to th'*Imagination*" (ll. 287-88). Or, as Wilders notes, he will also satirize actual experiments by leading scientists of the time, as in the description of the use of the microscope to observe a flea's pulse, which is drawn from Robert Hooke's demonstrations before the Royal Society and was later published in his *Micrographia*:[60]

> Whether a *Pulse* beat in the black
> List, of a Dappled *Louse's* back:
> If *Systole* or *Diastole* move
> Quickest, when hee's in wrath, or love:
> . . . .
> Whether his *Snout* a perfect *Nose* is,
> And not an Elephants *Proboscis,* [2.3.305-8, 315-16]

Similarly, Butler's extensive appropriation of the vocabulary of the occult sciences, especially astrology, is most evident in the description of Whacham, Sidrophel's "Under-*Conjurer,* / Or Journey-man *Astrologer,*" who extracts information from clients, which they, in turn, will pay to receive from the conjurer (2.3.332-42). Whacham is also his master's poetaster, putting into "*Dogrel-Rimes* his *Spells,* / Which over ev'ry Month's blank-page / In th'*Almanack,* strange *Bilks* presage" (2.3.374-76). It is entirely possible that Butler's sardonic view of the poetaster's source of inspiration owes something to the link between enthusiasm and the poetic faculty that some of his scientific contemporaries were asserting.

Butler's satire encompasses a variety of other topics and authorities associated with the occult tradition. Along with Paracelsus and his *homunculus* referred to earlier, Butler also notes the possibility of "fir[ing] a Mine in *China,* here / With Sympathetick *Gunpowder*" (2.3.295-96), apparently a weapon akin in principle to Sir Kenelm Digby's "miraculous powder of Sympathy," believed to effect cures at great distances from the wound itself. The latter is, in fact, alluded to in part 3, canto 2, lines 1030-31. And near the dwelling of Sidrophel and Whacham there is an obelisk with an inscription, written "not in words, / But *Hieroglyphick* Mute of *Birds*" (2.3.405-6). More important, there is the notion, associated with the astrological omen of the fallen planet, that the end of the world was imminent. For Butler, the absurdity of this idea, here emphasized by the absurdity of its evidence, i.e., the image of a boy's kite as seen through the lens of Sidrophel's telescope, effectively combines religious millenarianism, science, and pseudoscience, reminding us of the historical connection between millenarianism and occultism in the minds of the radical sectarians. Scathing references also abound in the latter part of canto 3 to a range of occult and hermetic authorities who, as earlier noted, were subject to attack in the writings of proponents of the New Science and the Royal Society. Among these are "*Bumbastus*, [i.e., Paracelsus, who] kept a *Devil's Bird* / Shut in the Pummel of his Sword" (2.3.627-28), Edward Kelley who "did all his Feats upon / The Devil's *Looking-glass*, a *Stone*," Agrippa, and Boehme. This indictment extends to the earliest of the hermetic authorities and the *prisci theologi*, Hermes Trismegistus, Pythagoras, Zoroaster, and "*Appollonius* their Master" (2.3.656), as well as to such mid–seventeenth-century astrologers as John Booker, William Lilly, and Sarah Jimmers, identified as an author of astrological predictions and almanacs.[61] Later in the poem, there is incidental satire of Athanasius Kircher, the Jesuit authority on Egyptian hieroglyphics (3.2.1583-86), and hieroglyphics are themselves invoked to satirize the Rump parliament (3.2.1587-96). Clearly, the tendency to attack the varied forms of occultism collectively, which we have seen in the writings of Restoration intellectuals, is continued in *Hudibras*.

Butler's harshest satire is reserved for the Rosicrucians, who epitomize the most negative aspects of occultism. Hudibras, in conversation with Sidrophel concerning various means of conjuring the devil, begins this attack. He speaks of the superiority of the method used by the Rosicrucians, with its philosophical and cosmological ploys for capturing heavenly influences:

> The *Rosy-crucian* way's more sure,
> To bring the Devil to the Lure,
> Each of'em has a sev'ral Gin,
> To catch *Intelligences* in.
> Some by the *Nose* with fumes trapan 'em,
> . . . .
> Others with *Characters* and *Words*,
> Catch 'em as men in *Nets* do *Birds*.
> And some with *Symbols, Signs,* and *Tricks,*
> Engrav'd in *Planetary* nicks.
> With their own influences, will fetch 'em,
> Down from their Orbs, arrest and catch 'em. [2.3.613-17; 619-24]

In these lines Hudibras attributes to the Rosicrucians several means of calling down the spirit world, and immediately following he associates with the brotherhood a representative group of magicians who, by this time, had come to be identified with occultism in a general sense. These include Paracelsus, who was not a Rosicrucian,[62] Kelley, and Agrippa, each of whom, according to Hudibras, has his own means of demonic conjuration. Hudibras's inclusion of these three figures prompts an immediate response from Sidrophel, and thus begins their debate on the merits of astrology. Sidrophel at first defends Agrippa and Paracelsus against charges of demonic conjuration and proceeds to lighten Hudibras's charges against the Rosicrucians:

> To this, quoth *Sidrophello*, Sir,
> Agrippa was no *Conjurer,*
> Nor *Paracelsus*, no nor *Behman;*
> Nor was the Dog [of Agrippa] a *Cacodæmon,*
> But a true Dog, that would shew tricks,
> For th'*Emperor*, and leap o're sticks;
>
> . . . .
>
> As for the *Rosi-cross Philosophers,*
> Whom you will have to be but *Sorcerers;*
> What they pretend to, is no more,
> Then *Trismegistus* did before,
> *Pythagoras*, old *Zoroaster,*
> And *Appollonius* their Master; [2.3.641-46; 651-56]

Following this response to Hudibras, Sidrophel broadly defends the validity of astrology and omens of all sorts as means of predicting the future. Hudibras, who curiously appears to be Butler's spokesman, then counters with the argument that knowledge acquired through astrology or other forms of occultism is unlikely to contribute to the improvement of the human condition; or, to put the issue in the form of a question, can the follies imported to mankind from the moon exceed those that are already here in plentiful supply? His conclusion to this portion of the debate is thoroughly conventional:

> So when your Speculations tend
> Above their just and useful end,
> Although they promise strange and great
> *Discoveries* of things far fet,
> They are but idle *Dreams* and *Fancies*
> And savour strongly of the *Ganzas*. [2.3.777-82]

Butler would surely have agreed; he had no patience with dwellers in the "high lonely Tow'r."

Although the Sidrophel episode is Butler's most extended treatment of Rosicrucianism and hermeticism, he returns to these topics occasionally in later cantos. In the first canto of part 3 he refers to magical rites in which "Bewitch[ed] *Hermetique-men* . . . Run / Stark staring mad with *Manicon*," a kind of deadly nightshade. He then turns immediately to strange feats of the "*Mechanick Virtuosi* / [who] Can raise 'em *Mountains* in *Potosi*" (3.1.323-26). The presence of these two passages in a list of similar supernatural performances suggests again that Butler makes no important distinction between the virtuosi and ranker forms of occult charlatanism. Finally, in discussing the effects of irrational fears on the human mind, Butler draws together the idea of the diseased imagination and Rosicrucianism. Baseless fear, he states, has

> no possible Foundation,
> But merely in th'Imagination:
> And yet can do more Dreadful Feats,
> *Than Hags* with all their *Imps and Teats:*
> Make more bewitch and haunt themselves,
> Than all their *Nurseries of Elves.*
>
> . . . .
>
> Sets up communities of Senses,
> To chop and change Intelligences,
> As *Rosi-crusian Virtuoso's,*
> Can see with *Ears,* and hear with *Noses.*[63] [3.3.5-10, 13-16]

There is little doubt that the attacks on the varied forms of occultism and hermeticism present in "An Hermetic Philosopher" and *Hudibras* are accurate reflections of Butler's true views on these subjects. His range of reference—to ideas, authors, titles, quotations, topics, and relationships—is broad, surely indicating acquaintance with many of these materials and that his rejection of occultism was far more informed than that of a number of the earlier satirists I have considered. These assessments of Butler's views on the occult milieu are also corroborated by evidence from his *Prose Observations.* In one such reference Butler rejects the boasts of cabalists, especially Lull and Agrippa, of being able to impart vast quantities of knowledge to the ignorant quickly through the art of memory, so that "Illitterate and Decrepit old men, with Boys of Ten yeares of Age, have, in a short Space, been inabled, by this Sole Art to dispute with the wisest Doctors of his Times in all manner of Learning."[64] Similarly, he disparages those who claim to have derived occult learning by means of the art of memory, asserting that this is a state of profound delusion resulting from the operation of inspiration and imagination. Such are the fanciful stories of "Cardan, and Nicholas Flamell, who by buying two guilt Books of two Strangers whom they met by Accident, became immediatly learned; the first in the Latine Tongue, of which he was utterly Ignorant before; and the other, by the help of a Jew, and St James in the Philosophers Stone. . . . But these are but the Conceptions of wearyd Melancholy, like the Images which a Sick or Idle Fancy will observe in the fire, or such as Cardan saw upon a wall" (135).

Of Pythagoras and the tradition of the *prisci theologi* that he represents, Butler states that "No Sect of Philosophers ever lasted so long, or propagated so far as that of Pythagoras, although perhaps one of the most extravagant and Sensles of all others" (176). And, finally, the same scorn and skepticism, consistently present in Butler's statements on all forms of occult thought, appear again in both his short poem entitled "Chymistry," where the art becomes synonymous with deception and greed, and in his remark in the *Prose Observations* that "The Reasons and Arguments of Chymists are like their operations upon Mettles, They give a Tincture of Truth upon Error, and Falshood as they do, of Gold and Silver upon Copper, but it will not indure the Test."[65]

Thus Butler shares with many of his contemporaries in the universities and the Royal Society the idea that rampant zeal and enthusiasm were responsible for much of the political, religious, and social instability that had distressed England in the middle decades of the seventeenth century. They also agreed that the occult milieu—a notable manifestation of this enthusiasm—was broad and varied in extent and form and eminently in need of banishment if truth, reason, common sense, and stability were to be restored in society. However, at this point Butler and his scientific contemporaries part company. That he chose laughter and the sardonic wit of the mock-heroic and Hudibrastic style as his weapons in this attack marks one difference; no less important is the fact that he chose to direct these weapons against the absurdities of the New Science itself.

X

CAUDA PAVONIS

<hr>

The projector of this cell was the most ancient student of the Academy; his face and beard were of a pale yellow; his hands and clothes daubed over with filth. When I was presented to him, he gave me a close embrace (a compliment I could well have excused). His employment from his first coming into the Academy, was an operation to reduce human excrement to its original food, by separating the several parts, removing the tincture which it receives from the gall, making the odour exhale, and scumming off the saliva. He had a weekly allowance from the society, of a vessel filled with human ordure, about the bigness of a Bristol barrel.

—Jonathan Swift, *Gulliver's Travels,* part 3[1]

In 1667, the publication year of the first edition of *Paradise Lost* and some three hundred years after Chaucer began writing *The Canterbury Tales*, Thomas Sprat devoted a generous paragraph to the topic of "Chymists" (not "Alchemists") in his *History of the Royal Society.* The term itself had been introduced only in the latter part of the sixteenth century and steadily gained currency throughout the next. Sprat remarks on the numerousness of these "philosophers" and on their ability to achieve "great productions, and alterations" by means of fire; he then turns to ways of classifying and evaluating them:

> The next Philosophers, whom I shall touch upon, are the *Chymists*, who. . . . may be divided into three rancks: Such, as look after the knowledge of Nature in general: Such, as seek out, and prepare Medicines: and such, as search after riches, by Transmutations, and the great *Elixir.* The two first, have been very successful, in separating, compounding, and changing the parts of things: and in shewing the admirable powers of Nature, in the raising of new consistencies, figures, colors, and vertues of Bodies. And from their labors, the true *Philosophy* is like to receive the noblest Improvements. But the pretensions of the Third kind, are not onely to indow us, with all the benefits of this life, but with Immortality it self. And their success has been as small, as their design was extravagant. Their Writers involve them in such darkness; that I scarce know, which was the greatest task, to understand their meaning, or to effect it. And in the chase of the *Philosopher's Stone,* they are so earnest, that they are scarce capable

294

of any other thoughts. . . . This secret they prosecute so impetuously, that they believe they see some footsteps of it, in every line of *Moses, Solomon,* or *Virgil.* The truth is, they are downright *Enthusiasts* about it. And seeing we cast *Enthusiasm* out of Divinity it self, we shall hardly sure be perswaded, to admit it into Philosophy.[2]

Sprat's classification and assessment of chemists and chemistry serves not only to summarize many of the Restoration attitudes toward occult ideas discussed in chapter 9 but is also in a direct line of descent from what I have earlier called Francis Bacon's desire to purify or "de-alchemize" alchemy: his efforts to transmute it from an art to a science by purging it of the dross of "belief," "imagination," and corrupt methodology. In this respect, the remarks of the Royal Society's historian accurately reflect the direction in which chemical studies were moving in the seventeenth century and the attitudes toward alchemy that were coming to prevail. Alchemy and alchemists, no less than members of dissenting religious sects, were in need of purifying "distillation"; significant contributions to the "true *Philosophy*" could not result from experiments grounded in "*Enthusiasm*" or "the wild lightning of the others Brains," as Sprat later describes it.

But Sprat's reference to those "chymists" whose "success has been as small, as their design was extravagant" also provides a useful summation of the art and its practitioners as we have seen them mirrored in the literary art of the Middle Ages and early modern period. With few exceptions, until the time of Donne and Herbert, alchemists of literature are what he terms chemists of this "third kind," and it is the remarkable consistency with which English writers maintained this view that accounts for the tradition of alchemical satire. Throughout this period, as we have seen, alchemy's appearance in English literature is extremely common. It is used by major and minor writers alike, and the range of works in which it is found nearly coincides with the variety of literary genres that were cultivated at this time. Chaucer, far more than any of his contemporaries, is responsible for placing the subject matter of alchemy into the stream of popular literature. In the *Canon's Yeoman's Tale* he makes a distinction between two types of alchemy, the physical or exoteric and the spiritual or esoteric. It is his concentration on the former that lays the foundation for the satiric treatment of alchemy that dominates literature up to the earlier part of the seventeenth century. Chaucer's knowledge of the art—its claims, processes, materials, authorities, and characteristic idiom—*and* its adepts—their greed, charlatanism, poverty, and vulnerability to self-deception—are combined to produce a literary masterpiece that is humorous in effect and serious in intention. Thus, at the very beginning of the satirical tradition we have one of its finest examples.

Chaucer's contemporaries and fifteenth- and early sixteenth-century imitators are more narrowly concerned with the practical aspects of this art. In their works alchemy emerges, at best, as a futile pursuit of the philosopher's stone or the elixir, or more commonly as a means by which cheating knaves gull their victims, or as a symptom of the corruption present in the world at large. The popularity of works by Barclay, Douglas, Dunbar, and Skelton served effectively in transmitting the tradition of alchemical satire, but at the same time alchemy's literary potential was greatly diminished through the restriction of its meanings and associations.

This period of decline in the effective literary use of alchemy was short-lived. Beginning with the comic dialogues of Erasmus, the sixteenth century saw many original and richly variegated adaptations of the subject. That alchemy was taken seriously and was regarded as a social threat is evidenced by Scot's lengthy exposé in *The Discoverie of Witchcraft*, the effectiveness of which owes much to borrowings from Chaucer and Erasmus. But Elizabethan authors more often responded to it with laughter and irony rather than with ponderous and ill-humored diatribes. Although alchemical allusions continue to be overwhelmingly satirical, their contexts become increasingly and richly diverse: in the prose of Greene, Nashe, and Harvey alchemy is invoked to attack personal enemies, to render more vividly the operations of criminal elements in society, to epitomize folly, or to evoke bawdy humor. Although alchemy appears less frequently in Elizabethan drama and poetry than in prose, Lyly's *Gallathea,* passages in the plays of Marlowe, Greene, and Shakespeare, and in the poetry of Sidney, Shakespeare, Davies, and Hall serve to illustrate the persistence of alchemy's influence and the manifold ways in which it could be employed. In this latter group we also find foreshadowings of some of the new ways alchemy would be utilized in the next century.

The early years of the seventeenth century mark the culmination of the satirical tradition and the flourishing of other, totally different treatments and techniques. Taken together, Jonson's *Alchemist* and *Mercury Vindicated* are the longest, wittiest, and most devastating attacks on alchemy, alchemists, their victims, and the principle that art is superior to nature that can be found in English literature. However, as has been demonstrated in chapter 9, the tradition of alchemical satire does not end with Jonson; in the works of Samuel Butler, the meaning of occultism generally is narrowed through the reductive and simplifying means of farce and broad humor. However, even as literary alchemy was declining through Butler's caustic Hudibrastics and powerful forces within the Restoration intellectual milieu, the impulse behind this tradition was being transmuted and reshaped: through Butler's attacks on scientific projectors, Shadwell's on virtuosi like Sir Nicholas Gimcrack, and, most of all, in Swift's assault on the cult of scientific rationalism in Gulliver's third voyage. In each of these cases, satirical energy is often redirected from alchemy and occult interests to experimental science. Chaucer's Yeoman, Face, Subtle, Sidrophel, and all the rest live on as members of the Academy of Projectors in Lagado. The results of this transmogrification are predictably familiar: "The only inconvenience is, that none of these projects are yet brought to perfection, and in the mean time, the whole country lies miserably waste, the houses in ruins, and the people without food or clothes."[3]

Others who have not been transformed into grotesque caricatures of Royal Society members retain their own identities as alchemists, magicians, and adepts in *A Tale of A Tub* but are no less grotesque: there is the 984-year-old Artephius, whose experiments proceed "wholly by reincrudation," and he is followed by "Sendivogus, Behmen, or *Anthroposophia Theomagica*" (i.e., Thomas Vaughan), and "Bumbastus." And, in section 11, Jack insists on interpreting the plain meaning of his father's will, as if it were a "deeper and darker" cryptic code: "Gentlemen," said he, "I will prove this very skin of parchment to be meat, drink, and cloth, to be the philosopher's stone, and the universal medicine."[4]

Just as *The Canon's Yeoman's Tale* serves as the basis for the satirical tradition, it also provides an anticipatory glimpse of the philosophically and spiritually charged alchemical themes, images, and allusions that would begin to emerge more than two hundred years after its composition. The idea of alchemy as an art not only sanctioned by Plato but one that is "unto Crist . . . so lief and deere" foreshadows references in the poetry of Donne, Herbert, Milton, and Vaughan, which, although satirical at times, are for the most part purged of the unfavorable connotations and associations that had dominated English writers' handling of the subject throughout history. To the extent that in these poets it becomes a subtle and learned vehicle for expressing change, growth, regeneration, and salvation; that it figures forth important events in Christian history by means of alchemical allegory, and that it represents Christ as the philosopher's stone or "great elixir"—to this extent it might be said that "literary" alchemy had also become purified, but the perfection of the form in which it appears in mid-century was achieved only after processes occurring over nearly three centuries had been completed. In either case, whether it is used to promote humor and satire or as a richly suggestive basis for metaphor, alchemy's influence in English literature of the Middle Ages and sixteenth and seventeenth centuries was extensive and profound.

Notes

Introduction

1. In Ashmole's "Annotations and Discourses," in *Theatrum Chemicum Britannicum,* with a preface by C.H. Josten (London, 1652; reprint, Hildesheim: Georg Olms, 1968), 443. All references are to this edition.

2. Of published book-length studies of alchemy and English literature in the periods covered by this study, the most important is Lyndy Abraham, *Marvell and Alchemy* (Aldershot, England: Scolar, 1990). Charles Nicholl's *The Chemical Theatre* (London: Routledge & Kegan Paul, 1980) provides an alchemical interpretation of *King Lear*. Michael Srigley, *Images of Regeneration: A Study of Shakespeare's* The Tempest *and Its Cultural Background* (Uppsala: Almqvist & Wiksell, 1985), examines this play in light of alchemy, magic, and millenarianism in the era of Rudolph II. A very early study, Lothar Nowak's *Die Alchimie und die Alchimisten in der*

englischen Literatur, a dissertation written and published at Breslau in 1934, contains little analysis of the way alchemy functions in literary contexts, as evidenced by the fact that only about a page is given to analysis of alchemy in Donne's poetry. A series of articles by Edgar Hill Duncan growing out of an unpublished dissertation written at Vanderbilt University in 1940 contains often illuminating discussion of alchemy in the writings of Chaucer, Jonson, and Donne. Brief, often superficial, accounts of alchemy and selected literary authors and works are included in some of the background books by John Read included in note 3 of chapter 1. The number of relevant journal articles is, of course, substantially greater. Specific debts to these and other studies will be acknowledged as they occur.

Chapter 1. Backgrounds, Definitions, and Preliminaries

1. Chap. 1 of *The Mirror of Alchimy Composed by the Thrice-Famous and Learned Fryer, Roger Bachon,* ed. Stanton J. Linden, English Renaissance Hermeticism (New York and London: Garland Publishing, 1992), 3. All references to this treatise are taken from this edition, which is based on the text of the first English translation of the *Mirror,* published in London, 1597.

2. From Thomas Tymme's dedication to Sir Charles Blunt, Earle of Devonshire, Lord Montjoy, of Joseph Quersitanus, *The Practise of Chymicall, and Hermetical Physicke, for the preservation of health . . . . Translated into English by Thomas Timme, Minister* (London, 1605).

3. Useful accounts of the origins and early development of alchemy, emphasizing its cultural context, are included in John Read, *Prelude to Chemistry* (London: Bell, 1936), *The Alchemist in Life, Literature and Art* (London: Thomas Nelson, 1947), chap. 1, and *Through Alchemy to Chemistry* (New York: Harper and Row, 1963); E.J. Holmyard, *Alchemy* (Harmondsworth, Middlesex: Penguin, 1957); Wayne Shumaker, *The Occult Sciences in the Renaissance: A Study in Intellectual Patterns* (Berkeley: Univ. of California Press, 1972), esp. chap. 4; and, from the history of science perspective, in J.R. Partington, *A Short History of Chemistry,* 3d ed. (New York: Harper, 1960). A much fuller account is contained in Lynn Thorndike, *A History of Magic and Experimental Science,* 8 vols. (New York: Columbia Univ. Press, 1923-58). This chapter draws heavily upon these sources.

4. On the provenance, authorship, manuscripts, and early printed editions of the *Mirror of Alchimy,* see the introduction to my edition.

5. Quoted from Roger Bacon's *Opus Tertium,* in Holmyard, *Alchemy,* 120.

6. On Paracelsus's revolutionary influence in reorienting alchemy and placing chemistry in the service of medicine, see works by Read and Holmyard previously cited, and, especially, Allen G. Debus, *The English Paracelsians* (New York: Franklin Watts, Inc., 1966).

7. Quoted in Holmyard, *Alchemy,* 120.

8. Holmyard, *Alchemy,* 16.

9. A selection from this *Dialogue* is included in F. Sherwood Taylor, *The Alchemists: Founders of Modern Chemistry* (New York: Henry Schuman, 1949), 58-59.

10. Taylor, *The Alchemists,* 60-66.

11. "Some Spiritual Alchemies of Seventeenth-Century England," *JHI* 41 (April-June 1980): 293-318.

12. The nature and efficacy of "drinkable" gold, a popular Paracelsian medication, is clarified in the title of a work by Francis Anthonie: *The Apologie, or Defence of . . . Aurum Potabile, that is, the pure substance of Gold, prepared, and made Potable and Medicinable without corrosives, helpfully given for the health of Man in most Diseases, but especially available for the strengthening and comforting of the Heart and vitall Spirits the performers of health* (London, 1616).

Anthonie's oft-maligned practice was theoretically grounded in the idea that the equal and harmonious composition of gold makes it effective in treating diseases caused by *Intemperies* or distemperatures in the body.

13. "European Alchemy in the Context of a Universal Definition," in *Die Alchimie in der europäischen Kultur- und Wissenschaftsgeschichte,* ed. Christoph Meinel, Wolfenbütteler Forschungen, vol. 32 (Wiesbaden: Otto Harrassowitz, 1986), 16-17.

14. Read, *Through Alchemy to Chemistry,* 12.

15. Read, *Through Alchemy to Chemistry,* 7.

16. Read, *Through Alchemy to Chemistry,* 12.

17. Holmyard, *Alchemy,* 19.

18. Holmyard, *Alchemy,* 33.

19. Taylor, *The Alchemists,* 71. On the importance of potable gold and a "regenerative elixir" in Chinese alchemy, see the treatise by Ko Hung in Joseph Needham, "The Refiner's Fire; The Enigma of Alchemy in East and West," the second J.D. Bernal Lecture delivered at Birkbeck College, London, 4 Feb. 1971 (London: Birkbeck College, 1971), 23-24.

20. Holmyard, *Alchemy,* 38.

21. Holmyard, *Alchemy,* 40.

22. See the summaries of arguments for and against this view in Holmyard, *Alchemy,* 41-42, and Read, *Prelude to Alchemy,* 5-7. Joseph Needham, the leading authority on Chinese alchemy, states that "There can now be no doubt that the Arabic experimentalists and writers were deeply influenced by Chinese ideas and discoveries, perhaps indeed hardly less than by the Hellenistic aurifactive proto-chemistry which Byzantine culture had preserved" (*The Refiner's Fire,* 8).

23. Arthur John Hopkins, *Alchemy: Child of Greek Philosophy* (Morningside Heights, N.Y.: Columbia Univ. Press, 1934), 28.

24. Holmyard, *Alchemy,* 25; and Charles C. Gillispie, ed. *Dictionary of Scientific Biography* (New York: Charles Scribner's Sons, 1970), s.v. "Bolos of Mendes," by Jerry Stannard. Hereafter cited as *DSB.*

25. Holmyard, *Alchemy,* 25.

26. Holmyard, *Alchemy,* 26.

27. *DSB,* s.v. "Zosimos," by M. Plessner. For examples of the visions of Zosimos, see Taylor, *The Alchemists,* 60-66. For Taylor, they express "the wonderful analogies that the author sees between the great world with its seasons, and growth and death and regeneration, and the process of the alchemical work. It is, in fact, religious and technical, a sort of rejoicing in the wonderful phenomena of chemical change" (60). It is very unclear as to which surviving texts that pass under Zosimos's name are actually his.

28. See Read, *Prelude to Chemistry,* 40, where the Formula of the Crab is reproduced.

29. Holmyard, *Alchemy,* 27-28.

30. Holmyard, *Alchemy,* 63-66; see also Thorndike, *HMES,* 2:214.

31. Holmyard, *Alchemy,* 72.

32. For the controversy surrounding Jabir's identity and problems of attribution, see, especially, *DSB,* s.v. "Jabir ibn Hayyan," by M. Plessner. Brief discussion of these questions and of the "Brethren of Purity" is included in Taylor, *The Alchemists,* 78-85.

33. *DSB,* s.v. Plessner, "Jabir ibn Hayyan." Following the practice of Taylor and others, I am using the form "Jabir" to designate authorship of the earlier Arabian work, "Geber" to designate authorship of the later, Latin works. The similarity in the spelling and pronunciation of the two names is obviously another source of confusion.

34. Holmyard, *Alchemy,* 75.

35. Holmyard, *Alchemy,* 75; and Taylor, *The Alchemists,* 81.

36. Read, *Through Alchemy to Chemistry,* 18.

37. Read, *Through Alchemy to Chemistry,* 18.

38. See Holmyard, *Alchemy,* 86-92; and Taylor, *The Alchemists,* 86-87.

39. Holmyard, *Alchemy,* 95.

40. Taylor, *The Alchemists,* 91. Of the *Summa,* Taylor states that "we do not know whether it is a translation of an Arabic text or a summary of Arabic chemistry compiled in Latin by a Western writer" (91-92); he adds that its most important emphases are the sulphur-mercury theory, descriptions of chemical analysis, discussion and illustration of furnaces and other laboratory equipment, and the use of a miraculous transmuting agent, the philosopher's stone (91-93).

41. Still of value on these topics are such pioneering works as Basil Willey, *The Seventeenth Century Background* (London: Chatto and Windus, 1934); A.O. Lovejoy, *The Great Chain of Being* (Cambridge: Harvard Univ. Press, 1936); and E.M.W. Tillyard, *The Elizabethan World Picture* (London: Chatto and Windus, 1943).

42. From *The Sceptical Chymist by the Hon. Robert Boyle,* with an introduction by M.M. Pattison Muir (London: J.M. Dent, n.d.), 187.

43. *Timaeus,* in *The Dialogues of Plato,* trans. B. Jowett, 4th ed., 4 vols. (Oxford: Clarendon Press, 1953), 3:736.

44. Holmyard, *Alchemy,* 273.

45. On Boyle's alchemical interests and their links with magic and casuistry, see Michael Hunter, "Alchemy, Magic and Moralism in the Thought of Robert Boyle," *BJHS* 23 (1990): 387-410, esp. 404-5. On Newton's well-known alchemical interests, see Betty Jo Teeter Dobbs, *The Foundations of Newton's Alchemy or "The Hunting of the Greene Lyon"* (Cambridge: Cambridge Univ. Press, 1975).

46. In chap. 4 of *The Way to Bliss* (London, 1658), Elias Ashmole describes the subterranean, "sexual" production of metals as follows: "*Quick-silver* . . . if it meet with a fine *Brimstone,* to stay and fasten it, . . . proveth *Silver,* and then *Gold:* But if that curdling breath be foul and greasie, (as it is most commonly,) it turns *Quick-silver* into foul *Metals* first, and the work must tarry longer leisure to be made clean and perfect" (135).

47. *The Way to Bliss,* 134. Ashmole regards the "heat of heaven" and "the particular feed of the *Earth,*" apparently brimstone or sulphur (124, 128), as the "hot workmen"; "*Quick-silver* is the *Mother* of all the *Metalls*" (126).

48. Read, *Through Alchemy to Chemistry,* 22.

49. From *The Smaragdine Table of Hermes Trismegistus of Alchimy,* in *Mirror of Alchimy,* 16.

50. *Giordano Bruno and the Hermetic Tradition* (Chicago: Univ. of Chicago Press, 1964), 45.

51. Robert Fludd, *Utriusque cosmi maioris scilicet et minoris metaphysica, physica atque technica historia* (Oppenheim, 1617, 1619), 1:frontispiece. For additional commentary on this diagram, see Shumaker, *The Occult Sciences,* 122-23.

52. *A New Light of Alchymy: Taken out of the Fountain of Nature and Manual Experience. To which is added A Treatise of Sulphur. Written by Micheel Sandivogius* (London, 1674), 104-5.

53. Thomas Norton, *The Ordinall of Alchimy,* in Ashmole, *TCB,* 85-86.

54. Quoted in Yates, *Giordano Bruno,* 380. Animistic and anthropomorphic overtones are present in the fourth precept of the *Smaragdine Table,* where reference is to the philosopher's stone: "His father is the sun, his mother is the moone, the wind bore it in hir belly. The earth is his nurse" (*Mirror of Alchimy,* 16).

55. *A New Light of Alchymy,* 3.

56. According to Yates, "Mersenne is a modern; he has crossed the watershed and is on the same side of it as we are; belief in the power of magic images of the stars seems to him quite mad . . . . [He] completely discards astrology, . . . astral magic, the miraculous virtue of

plants, stones, images, and the whole apparatus upon which *magia naturalis* rested" (*Giordano Bruno*, 435).

57. *The Tillage of Light, or, A True Discoverie of the Philosophical Elixir, commonly called the Philosophers Stone* (London, 1623), 46.

58. From the *Fasciculus Chemicus: or Chymical Collections* (London, 1650), sig. aᵛ. Ashmole, under the pseudonym J. Hasolle, was the translator of this collection, which had originally been written in Latin.

59. Ashmole, prolegomena, *Fasciculus Chemicus*, sig. **4ᵛ.

60. Ashmole, prolegomena, *Fasciculus Chemicus*, sig. [A¹].

61. John French, dedication and preface to *The Art of Distillation* (London, 1651), sig. *2ᵛ ff.

62. *Basil Valentine His Triumphant Chariot of Antimony, with Annotations of Theodore Kirkringius (1678)*, ed. L.G. Kelly, English Renaissance Hermeticism (New York and London: Garland, 1990), 61. All references to Valentine are to this edition.

63. From Cooper's unpaginated dedication to his translation of Helvetius's *Golden Calfe*, in *The Philosophical Epitaph of W.C. Esquire, for a Memento Mori on his Tomb-stone* (London, 1673). Helvetius is Johann Friedrich Schweitzer (1625-1709), medical authority and physician to the Prince of Orange; his celebrated eyewitness account of transmutation (1666) is quoted in Holmyard, *Alchemy*, 259-67.

64. From the treatise *Hydropyrographum Hermeticum*, in John Frederick Houpreght, *Aurifontina Chymica: or, A Collection of Fourteen small Treatises concerning the First Matter of Philosophers* (London, 1680), 38-39. The volume is dedicated to Charles II, and a note on the title page of this first treatise identifies Houpreght as "a student of, and searcher into the wonderful Secrets of Hermes."

65. Cleidophorus Mystagogus, *Mercury's Caducean Rod; . . . or God's Vicegerent, Displayed*, 2d ed. (London, 1704), 16.

66. Paracelsus, *Nine Books of the Nature of Things*, in *A New Light of Alchymy* (London, 1674), 252.

67. William R. Newman's *Gehennical Fire: The Lives of George Starkey, an American Alchemist in the Scientific Revolution* (Cambridge: Harvard Univ. Press, 1994) was published too recently to be incorporated in this study. Newman's "Prophecy and Alchemy: The Origin of Eirenaeus Philalethes," *Ambix* 37:3 (Nov. 1990): 97-115, esp. 100-101, focuses on the identities of George Starkey and Eirenaeus Philalethes, their millenarian context, and the *Introitus apertus ad occlusum regis palatium*. A detailed earlier treatment of the Starkey/Philalethes relationship appears in a series of essays by Ronald S. Wilkinson, published in *Ambix* 1963-66 and 1972-73. On Eirenaeus Philalethes and William Cooper, see appendix 2 of my *William Cooper's A Catalogue of Chymicall Books, 1673-88: A Verified Edition* (New York and London: Garland Publishing, 1987).

68. The first of these characters is found in *Pyrotechny Asserted and Illustrated*, 57-62. See the *OED* for the meaning of "preposterous": i.e., "having or placing last that which should be first; inverted in position or order," therefore foolish, nonsensical, monstrous, etc.

69. Similarly, Basil Valentine enjoins the pious physician to address his invocation to God, "from the bottom of a pure and sincere Heart, and Conscience, free from all Ambition, Hypocrisie, and all other Vices, . . . as Arrogancy, Boldness, Pride, Luxury, Mundane Petulancy, Oppression of the Poor, and other dependent evils." Having done this, Valentine adds, man's body "may be transmuted into an Holy Temple of GOD, and be purged from every uncleanness" (*Basil Valentine His Triumphant Chariot of Antimony*, 4).

70. Scot, *Tillage of Light*, 2.

71. From the illustration facing p. 13 in Ashmole, *TCB.* I follow the translation supplied in Shumaker, *Occult Sciences in the Renaissance,* 172.

72. See "On the Function of Analogy in the Occult," in *Hermeticism and the Renaissance: Intellectual History and the Occult in Early Modern Europe,* ed. Ingrid Merkel and Allen G. Debus (Washington, D.C.: Folger Shakespeare Library, 1988), 265-92.

73. Ashmole, prolegomena, *Fasciculus Chemicus,* sigs. **ᵛ, **2.

74. On the links between occultism and seventeenth-century religious radicals, such as the Familists, Behmenists, Ranters, and Quakers, see a number of the works of Christopher Hill, e.g., *The Intellectual Origins of the English Revolution* (Oxford: Clarendon Press, 1965), *Milton and the English Revolution* (New York: Penguin, 1979), and *The World Turned Upside Down: Radical Ideas during the English Revolution* (London: Temple Smith, 1972). In the latter, Hill notes that during the period of the Civil War, "Chemistry became almost equated with radical theology. . . . astrology, alchemy and natural magic contributed, together with Biblical prophecy, to the radical outlook" (234). But see also J. Andrew Mendelsohn's important, revisionistic essay, "Alchemy and Politics in England 1649-1665," *Past and Present* 135 (May 1992): 30-78, which argues for the existence of strong Royalist sympathies and support for occult interests in the later seventeenth century.

75. *A Dialogue Philosophicall Wherein Natures Secret Closet is Opened* (London, 1612), 31.

76. From the title page of *A Dialogue Philosophicall* and 38.

77. See C.A. Patrides, "'Something like Prophetick strain': apocalyptic configurations in Milton," in *The Apocalypse in English Renaissance Thought and Literature,* ed. C.A. Patrides and Joseph Wittreich (Ithaca: Cornell Univ. Press, 1984), 207-37; and my "Alchemy and Eschatology in Seventeenth-Century Poetry," *Ambix* 31 (Nov. 1984): 102-24.

78. *A Dialogue Philosophicall,* 69. Tymme used a nearly identical version of this extended image in the epistle dedicatory to his previously cited translation of Quersitanus's *The Practise of Chymicall, and Hermetical Physicke,* which appeared seven years before *A Dialogue Philosophicall.*

79. On the general topic of millenarianism, see such standard works as Ernest Tuveson, *Millennium and Utopia* (Berkeley and Los Angeles: Univ. of California Press, 1949); and Norman Cohn, *The Pursuit of the Millennium,* rev. ed. (London: Temple Smith, 1970). Useful on the figure of Elias in millenarian thought is Herbert Breger, "Elias Artista—A Precursor of the Messiah in Natural Science," in *Nineteen Eighty-Four: Science between Utopia and Dystopia,* ed. Everett Mendelsohn and Helga Nowotny (Dordrecht, Holland: D. Reidel, 1984), 49-72.

80. From French's unpaginated preface "To the Reader," in *The Art of Distillation.* The Sendivogian passage to which French refers is included in the preface to *A Treatise of Sulphur,* as translated by French in *A New Light of Alchymy.* As part of the shifting view from God as Revelation to God as Manifestation, millenarian expectations were powerful in the last half of the century; here French's prophecy—like that of many others—is probably focused on 1657 as the anticipated beginning of the Last Days. On millenarianism at this time, see Paul J. Korshin, "Queuing and Waiting: the Apocalypse in England, 1660-1750," in *The Apocalypse in English Renaissance Thought and Literature,* esp. 240-45 ; also Korshin's *Typologies in England 1650-1820* (Princeton: Princeton Univ. Press, 1982), passim.

81. From the unpaginated "Epistle of W.C. to the Reader," which precedes Cooper's translation of Helvetius's *Golden Calfe* in *The Philosophical Epitaph.*

82. For example, chapter 4 of this dialogue includes the following statement by Elias: "I never shewed the Stone to any in the world, but to you, except one aged man, and henceforth shall not to any; but if any King, or other, (which I hope God will not permit) should Rack me to pieces, or burn me alive, I would not reveal it to them, neither directly nor indirectly, as

many circumferanious Physitians, Mountebanks, Vagabonds, and other pretend to do"
(Helvetius's *Golden Calfe* in *The Philosophical Epitaph,* 37).

83. Mystagogus, *Mercury's Caducean Rod,* 63.

84. Hill, *The World Turned Upside Down,* 235.

2. Chaucer and the Medieval Heritage of Alchemical Satire

1. Quoted in *The Riverside Chaucer,* ed. Larry D. Benson, 3d ed. (Oxford: Oxford Univ. Press, 1987), p. 275, ll. 915-17; p. 281, ll. 1464-69. All references to *The Canon's Yeoman's Tale* are to this edition. I have occasionally drawn upon notes included in *The General Prologue to The Canterbury Tales and The Canon's Yeoman's Prologue and Tale,* ed. A.V.C. Schmidt (New York: Holmes & Meier, 1976).

2. I am not suggesting that this worldview coincided precisely with the doctrines held by Renaissance Neoplatonists. Frances Yates notes, for example, that owing to the importance of the sun in his "astral magic," Ficino found its position according to the Egyptian ordering of planets more congenial than its more distant location in the Ptolemaic system. She adds, however, that there is no evidence that Ficino did in fact reject the Ptolemaic scheme. See *Giordano Bruno,* 152.

3. Dorothea Waley Singer, *Catalogue of Latin and Vernacular Alchemical Manuscripts in Great Britain and Ireland dating from before the XVI Century,* 3 vols. (Brussels: Union Académique Internationale, 1928-31).

4. Singer, *Catalogue,* 1:18-60. It is not surprising that many alchemical treatises should have been ascribed to Plato during the Middle Ages as the foundation of alchemy and other related occult arts rested largely on ideas that can be conveniently labeled under "Platonism." Thorndike, although noting that "the names of Plato and Aristotle had headed the lists of alchemists in Greek manuscripts" (*HMES,* 2:251), regards these attributions as spurious and places such writings in the post-Hellenic period. He states that "alchemy seems to have made its appearance in the ancient Greek-speaking and Latin world only at a late date. There seems to be no allusion to the subject in classical literature before the Christian era, the first mention being Pliny's statement that Caligula made gold from orpiment" (1:193).

5. Singer, *Catalogue,* 1:61-135. Thorndike cites Robert of Chester's latinization in 1144 of the eighth-century *Book of Morienus* as marking the beginning of the Arabian influence on Western alchemy (Thorndike, *HMES* 1:773).

6. Singer, *Catalogue,* 1:139-326.

7. "Some English Alchemical Books," *Journal of the Alchemical Society* 2 (Oct. 1913): 4.

8. Ferguson, "Some English Alchemical Books," 4. This listing of additional sixteenth-century alchemical authors is not intended as complete. See the following entries in the previously cited edition of *William Cooper's A Catalogue of Chymicall Books:* 72, 125, 127, 143, 161, 162, 163, 194, 221, 283, 284, 299, 309, 312, and 321. The sixteenth century saw publication of many books on medicine and distillation and collections of "secrets" that also contain alchemical material.

9. Thorndike, *HMES,* 5:532.

10. Read, *Through Alchemy to Chemistry,* 92.

11. Thorndike, *HMES,* 5:532-33.

12. Thorndike, *HMES,* 2:846.

13. Although beginning with the fourteenth century Lull is one of the most frequently cited alchemical authorities, Thorndike and others reject the authenticity of the alchemical treatises commonly ascribed to him. In fact, he cites works known to have been written by Lull in which statements opposing alchemy appear (*HMES,* 2:867). For a detailed examina-

tion of this question, see Michela Pereira, *The Alchemical Corpus Attributed to Raymond Lull,* Warburg Institute Surveys and Texts 18 (London: Warburg Institute, 1989).

14. Thorndike, *HMES,* 5:536.

15. Thorndike, *HMES,* 5:536.

16. Thorndike, *HMES,* 5:536-37.

17. Paracelsus was not the first to show interest in the use of minerals to cure diseases. A work printed in 1523 by a Neapolitan scholar, John Abiosus of Babnoli, discusses the medicinal properties of specially prepared gold and contains numerous references to classical, Arabian, and medieval Latin authorities, including Roger Bacon (Thorndike, *HMES,* 5:541).

18. Thorndike, *HMES,* 5:541.

19. The *Alchimia Volumen,* in fact, brought together the group of treatises that comprise the *Speculum Alchymie* or *Mirror of Alchimy* collection, which was translated into French in 1557 and English in 1597.

20. John Ferguson, *Bibliotheca Chemica* (1906; reprint, London: Derek Verschoyle, 1954), 1:19.

21. Ferguson, *Bibliotheca Chemica,* 1:341-42.

22. Ferguson, *Bibliotheca Chemica,* 1:52.

23. For a list of contents see Ferguson, *Bibliotheca Chemica,* 2:436-40.

24. Chaucer's eighteenth-century editor, Thomas Tyrwhitt, speculated "that some sudden resentment had determined Chaucer to interrupt the regular course of his work, in order to insert a Satire against the Alchemists," quoted in Charles Muscatine, *Chaucer and the French Tradition* (Berkeley and Los Angeles: Univ. of California Press, 1957), 214.

25. See, for example, Pauline Aiken, "Vincent of Beauvais and Chaucer's Knowledge of Alchemy," *SP* 41 (July 1944): 371-89; Edgar H. Duncan, "Chaucer and 'Arnold of the Newe Toun,'" *MLN* 57 (Jan. 1942): 31-33; "The Yeoman's Canon's 'Silver Citrinacioun,'" *MP* 37 (Feb. 1940): 241-62; and "The Literature of Alchemy and Chaucer's 'Canon's Yeoman's Tale': Framework, Theme, and Characters," *Speculum* 43 (1968): 633-56; J.L. Lowes, "The Dragon and His Brother," *MLN* 28 (Nov. 1913): 229; and Karl Young, "The 'secree of secrees' of Chaucer's Canon's Yeoman," *MLN* 58 (Feb. 1943): 98-105.

26. See, for example, Peter Brown, "Is the 'Canon's Yeoman's Tale' Apocryphal?" *English Studies* 64 (1983): 480-90; and Albert E. Hartung, "'Pars Secunda' and the Development of the *Canon's Yeoman's Tale,*" *ChauR* 12 (1977): 111-28. On possible relationships between the *CYT* and *The Second Nun's Tale,* see Robert M. Longsworth, "Privileged Knowledge: St. Cecilia and the Alchemist in the *Canterbury Tales,*" *ChauR* 27:1 (1992): 87-96, on the common theme of transformation; and James D. Pickering, "Chaucer's Alchemy: The Pilgrims Assayed," *Medieval Perspectives* 4-5 (1989-90): 140-49, on responses to test and trial in the two tales. For David Raybin, in "'And Pave it Al of Silver and of Gold': The Humane Artistry of the *Canon's Yeoman's Tale,*" in *Rebels and Rivals: The Contestive Spirit in The Canterbury Tales,* ed. Susanna Greer Fein et al. (Kalamazoo, Mich.: Medieval Institute Publications, 1991), 189-212, the *CYT* "offers an exaltation of artistic striving" (190); see also Eric Weil, "An Alchemical Freedom Flight: Linking the *Manciple's Tale* to the *Second Nun's* and *Canon's Yeoman's Tales,*" *Medieval Perspectives* 6 (1991): 162-70.

27. On these topics see, for example, Dorothee Finkelstein, "The Code of Chaucer's 'Secree of Secrees': Arabic Alchemical Terminology in *The Canon's Yeoman's Tale,*" *Archiv für das Studium der neueren Sprachen und Literaturen* 207 (1970-71): 260-76; Joseph E. Grennen, "The Canon's Yeoman and the Cosmic Furnace: Language and Meaning in the 'Canon's Yeoman's Tale,'" *Criticism: A Quarterly for Literature and the Arts* 4 (1962): 225-40; Jane Hilberry, "'And in Oure Madnesse Everemore We Rave': Technical Language in the *Canon's Yeoman's Tale,*" *ChauR* 21:4 (1987): 435-43.

28. Muscatine, *Chaucer and the French Tradition,* 216. Others who have developed this line of criticism in different ways include Bruce A. Rosenberg, "Swindling Alchemist, Antichrist," *Centennial Review* 6 (1962): 566-80, esp. 575-78; John Gardner, "*The Canon's Yeoman's Prologue and Tale:* An Interpretation," *PQ* 46 (Jan. 1967): 1-17, esp. 9-10; Lawrence V. Ryan, "The Canon's Yeoman's Desperate Confession," *ChauR* 8:4 (1974): 302ff.; and Duncan, "The Literature of Alchemy and Chaucer's 'Canon's Yeoman's Tale,'" 639.

29. See Muscatine, *Chaucer and the French Tradition,* 217; Gardner, "*The Canon's Yeoman's Prologue and Tale,*" 2; Robert Cook, "The Canon's Yeoman and His Tale," *ChauR* 22:1 (1987): 28-40; Donald Dickson, "The 'Slidynge' Yeoman: The Real Drama in the *Canon's Yeoman's Tale,*" *South Central Review* 2:2 (Summer 1985): 10-22; Ryan, "The Canon's Yeoman's Desperate Confession," 305; and Joseph E. Grennen, "Chaucer's Characterization of the Canon and His Yeoman," *JHI* 25 (April-June 1964): 279-84.

30. See Lee Patterson, "Perpetual Motion: Alchemy and the Technology of the Self," in *Studies in the Age of Chaucer,* ed. Lisa J. Kiser, vol. 15 (Columbus, Ohio: New Chaucer Society, 1993), 48.

31. S. Foster Damon is an early representative of this second point of view, stating that "Chaucer intended to attack false alchemists because he saw that they were becoming a public menace . . . but that under cover of this attack, he deliberately introduced material calculated to stimulate those rare experimenters who knew something of the real secret. And his scheme succeeded just as he wished. The public was warned off, while the adepts hailed him as a fellow initiate" ("Chaucer and Alchemy," *PMLA* 39 [Dec. 1924]: 782).

32. For an early account of this famous illustrated manuscript, see Edwin Ford Piper, "The Miniatures of the Ellesmere Chaucer," *PQ* 3 (Oct. 1924): 241-56.

33. That the Yeoman has undergone a kind of physical "transmutation" while in the Canon's service has been noted in Judith Herz's "*The Canon's Yeoman's Prologue and Tale,*" *MP* 58 (May 1961): 231-37, and by several other critics. On the contrasting transformations in the *CYT* and the *Second Nun's Tale,* see Longsworth, "Privileged Knowledge: St. Cecilia and the Alchemist in the *Canterbury Tales.*"

34. The Yeoman appears to recognize that the inevitable consequences of alchemy are poverty and madness, "empte his purs" and "his wittes thynne" (l. 741); nonetheless, he has learned that desperate poverty leads alchemists to infect others with "peyne and disese" in an attempt to relieve their own destitute condition and envy of others' well-being: "For unto shrewes joye it is and ese / To have hir felawes in peyne and disese" (ll. 746-47). For this reason, I am not convinced that the Yeoman is now morally reformed or, in fact, capable of attaining such a state, as is sometimes argued.

35. Most of these references have been noted in the previously cited essays by Gardner, Rosenberg, Ryan, and Herz.

36. This structural similarity has been noted by several critics, most recently by Cook, in "The Canon's Yeoman and His Tale," who observes that the tellers of each of these tales "begin by discussing topics that have loomed large in their personal lives (marriage, preaching, alchemy) and then provide illustrations from their past experience, before passing to tales which are meant to epitomize their 'doctrine'" (30).

37. A number of commentators believe that the pars secunda is flawed by an inconsistency in the point-of-view character. They believe that the Yeoman, who has been so vigorous in his denunciation of quack alchemists, could not plausibly admit to alchemy's existing in a purer form. Judith Herz, for instance, states that "the last lines are set in so radically different a key from all the preceding that one doubts if the same character is speaking them. The voice is serious and educated. The tone changes. No longer does it arise from a degraded world where all is trickery but which men endure on the slim chance that some good may yet come" (236).

38. I am in basic agreement with and indebted to the views of Ryan (302-3), Rosenberg (576-77), Dickson (17), Gardner (2, 8-9), and Muscatine (216), all of whom, although in varying degrees, call attention to Chaucer's association of the false Canon with the devil or, at least, with the demonic. I disagree with Gardner, however, that for the Yeoman alchemy is categorically a "false religioun." He is condemning its fraudulent practice only, and in the final fifty-six lines of the *Tale* he acknowledges the existence of a "true alchemy." Muscatine completely overlooks this final section in his discussion.

39. The Yeoman's use of the exotic rhetoric of alchemy is unquestionably important as "bait" in the confidence schemes he practices with the Canon, and such rhetoric becomes a constant motif in the tradition of alchemical satire. Nonetheless, I disagree with a recent critic who sees the Yeoman's fascination with alchemical language as the primary reason for his addiction to the art. See Hilberry, "'And in Oure Madnesse Everemore We Rave.'" As noted earlier, the "wan hope" of successful transmutation, at once dimmed by repeated failures and sharpened by desperate need, is at the heart of his addiction to the practice of alchemy. In this regard, my views are close to those of Dickson in "The 'Slidynge' Yeoman."

40. The book is identified as *Antichristus* (Hye hebt sich . . .) and has the British Library shelfmark IB 15343. It is thought to date from about 1480. For brief commentary on a similar illustration, see Will H.L. Ogrinc, "Western Society and Alchemy from 1200 to 1500," *Journal of Medieval History* 6 (1980): 117-18.

41. The correct attribution was made in J.L. Lowes, "The Dragon and His Brother," 229. See also Duncan, "The Literature of Alchemy and Chaucer's 'Canon's Yeoman's Tale,'" 652-56.

42. This is the thesis of Gardner's essay.

43. On the background of this treatise, see Duncan, "The Literature of Alchemy and Chaucer's 'Canon's Yeoman's Tale,'" 653-55.

44. This gloss is from Schmidt, *The General Prologue to The Canterbury Tales,* 122n.

45. These associations have been noted by Ryan in "The Canon's Yeoman's Desperate Confession," 302.

46. See especially Duncan, "The Yeoman's Canon's 'Silver Citrinacioun,'" 241-62.

47. All references are to the A-text printed in *The Vision of William concerning Piers Plowman,* ed. Walter W. Skeat, 2 vols. (London: N. Trübner & Co., 1867). Comparable material, but with a somewhat less detailed treatment of alchemy, is included in passus 10 of the B-text of Langland's poem; see *The Vision of Piers Plowman,* ed. A.V.C. Schmidt (London: J. M. Dent, 1978). I have cited major differences in the following notes.

48. The passage reads as follows in *Lydgate and Burgh's Secrees of Old Philisoffres,* ed. Robert Steele (London: K. Paul, Trench, Trübner & Co., 1894), 16: "With othir Crafftys / which that be secre, / Calculacioun / and Geomancye, / Difformacyouns / of Circes and meede, / lokyng of ffacys / and piromancye, / On lond and watir / Crafft of Geometrye, / Heyhte and depnesse / with al experience, / Therefore the kyng / desyryd his presence" (ll. 498-504). All references are to this edition.

49. H. Kurath and S.H. Kuhn, eds., *Middle English Dictionary* (Ann Arbor: Univ. of Michigan Press, 1952—).

50. Here, the Schmidt edition of the B-text reads, "fibicches in forceres of fele mennes makynge" (10:211), which is glossed as "tricks in boxes," *The Vision of Piers Plowman,* 107. See *Middle English Dictionary,* s.v. "febicchis." The B-text also contains no reference to Albertus Magnus's connection with alchemical experiments or to "Nigromancye," "perimancie," or the "pouke"; ll. 212-13 state simply: "Experiments of Alkenamye the peple to deceyve; / If thow thynke to dowel, deel therwith nevere!"

51. Ashmole, *TCB,* 467. It is not surprising that Ashmole and other Renaissance

hermeticists should have been keenly interested in the *Canon's Yeoman's Prologue* and *Tale* because, as I will show at the beginning of the next chapter, Chaucer's Renaissance image included authoritativeness in alchemy as one important component.

52. Ashmole, *TCB*, 469.

53. Ashmole, *TCB*, 470.

54. *The English Works of John Gower*, ed. G.C. Macaulay, 2 vols. (London: K. Paul, Trench, Trübner & Co., 1901), 1: bk. 4, ll. 2457-632. All references to Gower's works are to this edition.

55. Read, *Through Alchemy to Chemistry*, 17-18. We recall the *Mirror of Alchimy's* assertion that "the naturall principles in the mynes, are *Argent-vive* and *Sulphur*. All mettals and minerals, whereof there be sundrie and divers kinds, are begotten of these two" (4).

56. The agreement between Vincent of Beauvais and Chaucer (and Gower) strengthens Pauline Aiken's argument that much of Chaucer's knowledge of alchemy was derived from Vincent's *Speculum Naturale;* see "Vincent of Beauvais and Chaucer's Knowledge of Alchemy." Useful information on the "spirits" of alchemy is also contained in the article on "Alchemy" in the *Encyclopaedia Britannica*, 11th ed.

57. For example, the following passage from Arnald of Villanova's *Rosarium Philosophorum* is cited in Robert Steele's notes to the *Secrees of Old Philisoffres*: "*Tres sunt lapides, et tres sales sunt, ex quibus totum magisterium consistit: Scilicet mineralis, plantalis, & animalis. Et sunt tres aquae, scilicet Solaris, Lunaris, & Mercurialis. Mercurius est minera, Luna planta, quia recipit in se duos colores, albedinem et rubedinem. Et Sol est animalis, quia recepit tria, scilicet constrictionem, albedinem, & rubedinem, & vocatur animal magnum*" (93).

58. Ashmole, *TCB*, 484.

59. *Secrees of Old Philisoffres*, xv-xvi. For a more complete account of the history of this work, see vii-xxi.

60. Steele (*Secrees of Old Philisoffres*, xii-xiii) mentions a number of works that are either based on the *Secreta Secretorum* or patterned after it.

61. See Steele, *Secrees of Old Philisoffres*, xii-xiv.

62. See, for example, *Bazilica Chymica, & Praxis Chymiatricae or Royal and Practical Chymistry, . . . All faithfully Englished by a Lover of Chymistry* (London, 1670), 1.

Chapter 3. Sixteenth-Century Alchemical Satire

1. From Ashmole's "Annotations and Discourses" to the *TCB*, 483.

2. Ashmole, *TCB*, 470.

3. Gareth W. Dunleavy, "The Chaucer Ascription in Trinity College, Dublin MS. D.2.8," *Ambix* 13 (1965): 5. This view is strengthened by the likelihood that John Dee had owned the manuscript before its acquisition by the Trinity College Library.

4. "The Renaissance Chaucer as Alchemist," *Viator: Medieval and Renaissance Studies* 15 (1984): 305-33. I disagree with only one view expressed in Schuler's valuable study: he maintains that the problematical conclusion of the pars secunda is Chaucer's "joke" or satirization of the "habit of alchemical compilers to assemble passages on specific topics from different authorities, in order to clarify difficult or obscure terms and concepts" (309, also 311). As argued in chapter 2, I believe that the Yeoman, after rejecting the debased state of exoteric alchemy, is here seriously acknowledging the existence of a higher form that is dear to God. It is this sacred tradition that many of Schuler's sources, Ashmole foremost, point toward and would seek to place Chaucer within.

5. All references are to *William Dunbar, Poems*, ed. James Kinsley (Oxford: Clarendon

Press, 1958), 44-48; hereafter referred to as *Poems*. For additional information on Damien, see John Read, "Alchemy Under James IV of Scotland," *Ambix* 2 (Sept. 1938): 60-67.

6. *The Poetical Works of Gavin Douglas,* ed. John Small, 4 vols. (Edinburgh: William Paterson, 1874), 3:142-48.

7. *The Eclogues of Alexander Barclay,* ed. Beatrice White, Early English Text Society, vol. 93 (London: Oxford Univ. Press, 1928), xx. All references are to this edition.

8. *The Ship of Fools translated by Alexander Barclay,* ed. T.H. Jamieson, 2 vols. (Edinburgh: William Paterson, 1874), 2:219-23.

9. *Ane Satyre of the thrie Estaits, In Commendation of Vertew and Vituperation of Vyce,* ed. F. Hall, Early English Text Society, vol. 37 (London: N. Trübner and Co., 1869). All references are to this edition. For detailed discussion of the play's significance and the elaborateness of its first performance, see F.P. Wilson, *The English Drama, 1485-1585* (Oxford: Clarendon Press, l969), 15-21.

10. *John Skelton: The Complete English Poems,* ed. John Scattergood (New Haven: Yale Univ. Press, l983), 312-57.

11. Erasmus is quoted in the introduction to *The Praise of Folly By Desiderius Erasmus,* ed. and trans. Leonard F. Dean (New York: Hendricks House, 1969), 1.

12. Leonard F. Dean describes Brant's position in *The Ship of Fools* as being "essentially moralistic and conservative. It is a collection of pictorially illustrated aphorisms designed primarily to enforce conventional behavior. A fool is anyone who does not conform to the established order" (*Praise of Folly,* 16).

13. *The Praise of Folie* [translated] *By Sir Thomas Chaloner,* ed. Clarence H. Miller, Early English Text Society, vol. 257 (London: Oxford Univ. Press, 1965), 3. All references are to this edition.

14. See chap. 2 of Virgil Whitaker, *Shakespeare's Use of Learning* (San Marino: Huntington Library, 1953); and for a fuller account, T.W. Baldwin, *William Shakspere's Small Latine & Lesse Greeke,* 2 vols. (Urbana: Univ. of Illinois Press, 1944).

15. Baldwin, *William Shakspere's Small Latine,* 1:735. Craig R. Thompson lists Lyly, Webster, Nashe, Jonson, and probably Shakespeare among the Elizabethan writers whose works reveal familiarity with the *Colloquies.* See *The Colloquies of Erasmus,* ed. and trans. Craig R. Thompson (Chicago: Univ. of Chicago Press, 1965), xxxi. All references are to this edition.

16. In Frances Yates, *The Art of Memory* (Chicago: Univ. of Chicago Press, 1966), see plates 7a, 7b, 10, and 11 and figs. 4-7. It is clear from them that Erasmus's description, although greatly oversimplified for purposes of irony, is generally accurate.

17. The letter is quoted in Yates, *Art of Memory,* 130-31. For a detailed account of Camillo's mnemonic system and its philosophical context, see chap. 6 of this work and the diagram opposite p. 144.

18. Yates, *Art of Memory,* 151.

19. Quoted from the text included in Ashmole, *TCB,* 15.

20. William Salmon, trans. *Clavis Alchymiae: Or, Hermes Trismegistus, Kalid Arabs, and Geber Arabs,* in *Medicina Practica; or, practical physick* (London, 1692), 179.

21. From the text included in Salmon, *Medicina Practica,* 434.

22. Quoted in D. Geoghegan, "A Licence of Henry VI to Practice Alchemy," *Ambix* 6 (Aug. 1957): 10. For additional information on legal strictures and related matters, see Will H.L. Ogrinc, "Western Society and Alchemy from 1200 to 1500," esp. 114-23; and appendix 2, "Some references to alchemy and chemical craftsmanship in legal archives," in Singer's *Catalogue of Latin and Vernacular Alchemical Manuscripts,* 3:777-95. The manuscript documents

included in Singer have been translated by Robert Steele, in "Alchemy in England," *Antiquary* 24 (Sept. 1891): 99-105.

23. Thorndike, *HMES*, 4:349.

24. Steele, "Alchemy in England," 99.

25. These persecutions are reported in Holmyard, *Alchemy*, 223-38. John Lyly's *Pappe with an Hatchet* includes a humorous fiction about an alchemist in captivity, to be discussed later.

26. This treatise is one of twenty-two included in *The Hermetic Museum, Restored and Enlarged*, ed. Arthur Edward Waite, 2 vols. (London: James Elliot and Co., 1893), 1:167-68. Waite's version is an English translation based on earlier Latin editions that had appeared in 1625 and 1678.

27. *The Tract of Basilius Valentinus, the Benedictine, concerning the Great Stone of the Ancient Sages*, in Waite, *Hermetic Museum*, 1:315.

28. Waite, *Hermetic Museum*, 1:325.

29. *English Literature in the Sixteenth Century* (Oxford: Clarendon Press, 1954), 435.

30. Quoted in Hugh Ross Williamson's introduction to his facsimile edition of *The Discoverie of Witchcraft* (Carbondale, Ill.: Southern Illinois Univ. Press, 1964), 19. All references are to this edition.

31. In the following "quotation" from Chaucer (297), Scot draws on ll. 624-26, 672-73, 682-83, and 740-41 of *The Canon's Yeoman's Prologue* and *Tale*: "They take upon them to turne upside downe, / All the earth betwixt Southwarke & Canturburie towne, / And to pave it all of silver and gold, &c. / But ever they lacke of their conclusion, / And to much folke they doo illusion. / For their stuffe slides awaie so fast, / That it makes them beggers at the last, / And by this craft they doo never win, / But make their pursse emptie, and their wits thin."

32. The majority of Scot's terms are drawn directly from Chaucer, but are rearranged in different categories. The few differences appear to result from Scot's misspelling or misunderstanding of the items recorded in Chaucer: e.g., Chaucer's "grounden litarge," "citrinacioun," and "watres corosif, and of lymaille" become "groundlie large," "ritrination," and "waters corosive and lincall" in Scot.

33. In *Alchemy*, 95, Holmyard summarizes the skeptical view of Avicenna, who denied that transformation of one metal into another of a different nature was possible but agreed that alchemists were capable of producing excellent imitations of precious metals. My brief remarks on Avicenna in chapter 1 also indicate how well his position agreed with Scot's.

34. In a marginal note on 309, Scot identifies the source of the quotation as follows: "*Goschalcus Boll. ordinis S. August. in suo præceptorio*, fol. 244. col. b. c. d. & 1."

35. On 24 March 1593, *The English Phlebotomy* by Nicholas Gyer was so dedicated. See G.B. Harrison, ed., *The Elizabethan Journals*, 2 vols. (Garden City, N.Y.: Anchor Books, 1965), 1:177.

36. Lewis, *English Literature in the Sixteenth Century*, 670. Wing also lists editions of 1651 (S943/S943A) and 1654 (S944).

37. *The Life and Complete Works in Prose and Verse of Robert Greene, M. A.*, ed. Alexander B. Grosart, 12 vols. (London: Huth Library, 1881-83), 4:24. All references to Greene's writings are to this edition.

38. See Mordechai Feingold, "The occult tradition in the English universities of the Renaissance: a reassessment," in *Occult and scientific mentalities in the Renaissance*, ed. Brian Vickers (Cambridge: Cambridge Univ. Press, 1984), 81-82.

39. *The Works of Thomas Nashe*, ed. Ronald B. McKerrow, 5 vols. (Oxford: Basil Blackwell, 1958), 1:255. All references to Nashe's writings are to this edition.

40. "The Stone of the Philosophers: Embracing The First Matter and the Dual Process for the Vegetable and Metallic Tinctures," in *Collectanea Chemica: Being Certain Select Treatises on Alchemy and Hermetic Medicine* (London: James Elliott, 1893), 116. This anthology of alchemical tracts is a reprinting of some, but not all, of those included in a collection of the same name printed in 1684 by William Cooper.

41. *The Works of Gabriel Harvey, D.C.L.*, ed. Alexander B. Grosart, 3 vols. (London: Huth Library, 1884), 2:250-51. All references to Harvey's writings are to this edition, hereafter cited as *Works*.

42. Kelley's exploits are alluded to in Jonson's *Alchemist*, 4.1, and in canto 3 of *Hudibras*. Also in *Pierces Supererogation*, Harvey invokes Kelley for the purpose of ridiculing Nashe: "I wondred to heare, that Kelly had gotten the Golden Fliece [i.e., the philosopher's stone], and by vertue thereof was sodenly advaunced into so honorable reputation with the Emperours maiestye; but would have woondred more, to have seene a woorke of Supererogation from Nashe: whose witt must not enter the listes of comparison with Kelleyes Alchimy" (Harvey, *Works*, 2:68-69).

43. The details of Kelley's life are recounted in Holmyard, *Alchemy*, 204-9; see also the article in the *DNB*.

44. References to musical gold occur infrequently in literary treatments of alchemy. Nashe's mention of it in *Christ's Teares*, 2:185 (and numerous other obscure allusions to alchemy throughout his writings) suggest, I think, that he possessed a far more detailed knowledge than most of his contemporaries. According to Read, the connection between alchemy and music is derived from the Pythagorean idea of harmonious correspondences between the notes of the musical scale and the extension of this idea to the music of the spheres. Read also mentions musical compositions that accompanied early ceremonies and rituals in magic and necromancy; see *Through Alchemy to Chemistry*, 68-73. The primary example of the use of musical notation in an alchemical treatise/emblem book is the *Atalanta Fugiens* of Michael Maier, published in Oppenheim in 1617.

45. Nashe refers to the *Discoverie* in *Terrors of the Night*, (1:309, 351). For discussion of the influence of Erasmus, Scot, and other writers on Nashe, see McKerrow, "Nashe's Reading," (5:110-36).

46. I agree with McKerrow's general assessment that "Among modern authors the most surprising amount of borrowing is from *De Incertitudine et Vanitate Scientiarum* of Cornelius Agrippa, to which Nashe appears to be indebted more than seventy times—and some of the borrowings are passages of several lines in length, containing a number of distinct facts. It is hardly too much to say that the greater part of Nashe's apparent learning is transferred wholesale from Agrippa's work" (5:134-35).

47. *Henrie Cornelius Agrippa, of the Vanitie and uncertaintie of Artes and Sciences, Englished by Ja*[mes] *San*[dford] *Gent*. (London, 1569), 157.

48. *The Complete Works of John Lyly*, ed. R. Warwick Bond, 3 vols. (Oxford: Clarendon Press, 1902), 3:402.

49. *The Non-Dramatic Works of Thomas Dekker*, ed. Alexander B. Grosart, 5 vols. (London: Huth Library, 1884-86), 3:286-90. All references to Dekker's writings are to this edition.

50. Ashmole, *TCB*, 455.

51. References are to *The Poems of Sir Philip Sidney*, ed. William A. Ringler, Jr. (Oxford: Clarendon Press, 1962).

52. All references to Shakespeare's sonnets and plays are to *The Riverside Shakespeare*, ed. G. Blakemore Evans et al. (Boston: Houghton Mifflin, 1974).

53. *The Poetical Works of Edmund Spenser*, ed. J.C. Smith and E. de Selincourt (London: Oxford Univ. Press, 1950), 403.

54. In *The Poems of Sir John Davies,* ed. Robert Krueger (Oxford: Clarendon Press, 1975). All references are to this edition.

55. *The Collected Poems of Joseph Hall, Bishop of Exeter and Norwich,* ed. A. Davenport (Liverpool: Univ. Press, 1949), 27. All references are to this edition.

56. In *Prelude to Chemistry,* Read summarizes the innovations of Paracelsus: "Paracelsus (1493-1541), besides developing the theory of the *tria prima,* introduced a new era of iatrochemistry, or alchemy in the service of medicine . . . [He] expounded with great vigour seasoned with venom, the view that the chief object of the alchemist should be to aid the apothecary and the physician, rather than to make gold. His great achievement for alchemy lay not in the introduction of revolutionary theoretical ideas or practical advances, but in his determined attempt to liberate the incipient science from the narrow and sordid domination of the 'multipliers' and 'bellows-blowers'; he gave alchemy a new orientation and endowed it with a fresh stimulus" (29-30). An excellent account of the impact of Paracelsus on English medicine in the sixteenth and seventeenth centuries is Debus's *English Paracelsians.*

57. Debus, in *English Pracelsians,* observes that "Objecting to the belief that diseases could be identified by means of a simple inspection of the patient's urine, Paracelsus called instead for a 'chemical dissection' of the sample. Since urine is comprised of waste from the entire body the physician might expect a chemical dissection to give the same information obtained from a bodily dissection" (157).

58. Debus, *English Paracelsians,* 33-34.

59. Debus, *English Paracelsians,* 34.

60. Debus cites several vicious attacks by English authors against Paracelsus and his followers. One of the most vituperative was by William Foster, a clergyman, against Robert Fludd and his "weapon salve." Debus quotes a passage that concludes with these words against Fludd's Swiss master: "If this be not Witchcraft, I know not what is! Now then Paracelsus being a Witch, and this experiment being placed amongst his Diabolicall and magicall conclusions, it cannot choose but be Witchcraft, and come from the grand master of Witches, the Divell, if Paracelsus were (as most repute him) the Author and Founder of it" (122).

61. Debus notes that "Paracelsus stated that the basis of occult philosophy or magic should rest on the three pillars of prayer, faith, and imagination. Conjurations and ceremonies other than those used by the Church were to be rejected, but on the other hand the efficacy of black magic was never denied" (21). However, it would seem that Robert Fludd used conjuration or something closely resembling it.

62. Debus, *English Paracelsians,* 27.

63. Debus, *English Paracelsians,* 17.

64. Debus, *English Paracelsians,* 32.

65. In 2.3 of *All's Well that Ends Well,* Shakespeare enhances the miraculous nature of Helena's curing of the King by noting that France's recovery has been "relinquish'd" or abandoned by both Galenic and Paracelsian physicians, "all the learned and authentic fellows," to quote Lafew (l. 12). The contemporary medical implications of Helena's use of natural magic in this episode have been discussed in J. Scott Bentley, "Helena's Paracelsian Cure of the King: *Magia Naturalis* in *All's Well that Ends Well,*" *CaudaP* 5:1 (spring 1986): 1-4.

66. *The Works in Verse and Prose of Nicholas Breton,* ed. Alexander B. Grosart, 2 vols. ([Edinburgh]: Edinburgh Univ. Press, 1879), 1: sec. S.

67. *The Complete Works of Thomas Lodge,* ed. Sir Edmund Gosse, 3 vols. (Glasgow: Hunterian Club, 1883; reprint, New York: Johnson Reprint Corp., 1966), 3:66-70. All references to this poem are to this edition and volume.

68. Of this poem's indebtedness to Agrippa, Edgar H. Duncan has said it is "a versifying, with slight additions and some omission, of James Sandford's translation of Agrippa's chapter

on alchemy in the *Vanitate*" ("Alchemy in the Writings of Chaucer, Jonson and Donne," [Ph.D. diss., Vanderbilt University, 1940], 209). I have compared the two works closely and agree with Duncan's conclusion.

69. All references to Marlowe's plays are taken from *The Works of Christopher Marlowe,* ed. C.F. Tucker Brooke (Oxford: Clarendon Press, 1962).

70. Faustus is probably alluding slightly to alchemy at 1.1.140, when he states that the miracles of magic depend on the magician's being "grounded in Astrologie, / Inricht with tongues, [and] well seene [i.e., expert] in minerals." The works of Roger Bacon and "Abanus," i.e., Pietro Abano, a thirteenth-century alchemist, are referred to in l. 155.

71. Robert Greene, *Friar Bacon and Friar Bungay,* ed. Daniel Seltzer (London: Edward Arnold, 1963), 2.105-13.

72. For brief but suggestive comments on larger alchemical possibilities in this play, see T. McAlindon, *Shakespeare's Tragic Cosmos* (Cambridge: Cambridge Univ. Press, 1991), 238-39.

73. John Lyly, *Gallathea and Midas,* ed. Anne Begor Lancashire (Lincoln: Univ. of Nebraska Press, 1969). All references are to this edition.

74. These distortions are cited in the notes on 23-25 of this edition. It is also probable that Lyly drew on the Chaucerian materials included in the chapter on alchemy in Scot's *Discoverie of Witchcraft;* see R.W. Bond's introduction to *Gallathea* in *The Complete Works of John Lyly,* 2:423-24.

Chapter 4. Francis Bacon and Alchemy

1. *The Works of Francis Bacon, Baron of Verulam, Viscount St. Alban, and Lord High Chancellor of England,* ed. James Spedding, Robert L. Ellis, and Douglas D. Heath, 14 vols. (1872; reprint, New York: Garret Press, Inc., 1968), 3:496. All references to Bacon's writings are to this edition. An earlier version of this chapter appeared under this title in *JHI* 35 (1974): 547-60.

2. See Feingold, "The occult tradition," 73-94. On the degree of tolerance for such studies at this time, Feingold states: "University records suggest that the attitude of the universities to occult pursuits was similar to that of the state; private study was tolerated as long as it did not involve any unlawful casting of the nativities of monarchs or debasing of coins and did not result in any scandalous accusations of cheating or witchcraft" (77).

3. Although I have relied primarily on the text of Bacon's works in this chapter, the following, published after my original version, have been of special value in defining aspects of his intellectual milieu. Several works by Brian Vickers: a bibliographical essay, "Francis Bacon and the Progress of Knowledge," *JHI* 53 (July-Sept. 1992): 495-518; "Analogy versus Identity: the Rejection of Occult Symbolism, 1580-1680," in *Occult and scientific mentalities in the Renaissance,* 95-163 (a slightly different version appeared as "On the Function of Analogy in the Occult"); and "On the Goal of the Occult Sciences in the Renaissance," in *Die Renaissance im Blick der Nationen Europas,* ed. Georg Kauffmann, Wölfenbutteler Abhandlungen zur Renaissanceforschung, Band 9 (Wiesbaden: Harrassowitz, 1991), 51-93; Paolo Rossi, "Hermeticism, Rationality and the Scientific Revolution," in *Reason, Experiment, and Mysticism in the Scientific Revolution,* ed. M.L. Righini Bonelli and William R. Shea (London: Science History Publications, 1975), 247-73; Brian Copenhaver, "Astrology and Magic," in *The Cambridge History of Renaissance Philosophy,* ed. Charles B. Schmitt (Cambridge: Cambridge Univ. Press, 1988), 264-300; and John C. Briggs, *Francis Bacon and the Rhetoric of Nature* (Cambridge: Harvard Univ. Press, 1989).

See also several earlier studies of Bacon and alchemy: Joshua C. Gregory, "Chemistry and

Alchemy in the Natural Philosophy of Sir Francis Bacon, 1561-1626," *Ambix* 2 (1938): 93-111; Harold Fisch, "Bacon and Paracelsus," *Cambridge Journal* 5 (1952): 752-58; Paolo Rossi, *Francis Bacon: From Magic to Science,* trans. Sacha Rabinovitch (Chicago: Univ. of Chicago Press, 1968); Thorndike, *HMES,* 7:63-88, and "The Attitude of Francis Bacon and Descartes Towards Magic and Occult Science," in *Science, Medicine and History: Essays on the Evolution of Scientific Thought and Medical Practice written in honour of Charles Singer,* ed. E. Ashworth Underwood (Oxford: Oxford Univ. Press, 1953), 451-54; Muriel West, "Notes on the Importance of Alchemy to Modern Science in the Writings of Francis Bacon and Robert Boyle," *Ambix* 9 (1961): 102-14; and Graham Rees, "Francis Bacon's Semi-Paracelsian Cosmology," *Ambix* 22 (July 1975): 81-101.

4. Willey, *Seventeenth Century Background,* 34.

5. As quoted in Rossi, *Francis Bacon: From Magic to Science,* 16-17.

6. The nature of these forms is, to use Copenhaver's word, "obscure"; Bacon states that "In nature nothing really exists beyond individual bodies performing pure individual acts according to a fixed law. . . . And it is this law . . . that I mean when I speak of forms. . . . The form of a nature is such that given the form the nature infallibly follows" (quoted in Copenhaver, "Astrology and Magic," 298).

7. These three arts are commonly linked in Bacon and are said to possess the same weakness in foundation. For example, in book 1 of *The Advancement of Learning* he states: "The sciences themselves which have had better intelligence and confederacy with the imagination of man than with his reason, are three in number; Astrology, Natural Magic and Alchemy; of which sciences nevertheless the ends or pretences are noble" (3:289).

8. See Copenhaver, "Astrology and Magic," 297.

9. Bacon's attacks on authority and the schools are well known; particularly incisive are sections 90-96 of the *Novum Organum* (4:89-93) and the dedication to King James of book 2 of the *Advancement* (4:283-91).

10. *The Sceptical Chymist,* 113-14.

11. *The History of the Royal Society,* in *Critical Essays of the Seventeenth Century,* ed. J.E. Spingarn, 3 vols. (Oxford: Clarendon Press, 1907; reprint, Bloomington: Indiana Univ. Press, 1957), 2:118.

12. On these linguistic distinctions and other crucial oppositions between the occult and scientific outlooks, without special concentration on Bacon, see Vickers, "Analogy versus Identity" and "On the Goal of the Occult Sciences"; and Rossi's idea of the "refutation of [hermeticism's] priestly idea of knowledge" as a distinguishing mark of modern thought, in "Hermeticism, Rationality and the Scientific Revolution" (250).

13. In section 64 of the *Novum Organum,* Bacon again attacks the experimental methods of the alchemists. They are an example of "[T]he Empirical school of philosophy [which has given] birth to dogmas more deformed and monstrous than the Sophistical or Rational school. For it has its foundations not in the light of common notions, . . . but in the narrowness and darkness of a few experiments" (4:65).

14. This idea is often repeated in the *Sylva Sylvarum,* e.g., "All bodies have spirits and pneumatical parts within them" (2:528).

15. See Rees, "Francis Bacon's Semi-Paracelsian Cosmology," 85-6. In Bacon's cosmological system the four "pure" spirits are air, ether, and terrestrial and sidereal fire (86).

16. Rees, "Francis Bacon's Semi-Paracelsian Cosmology," 97.

17. Thorndike, "The Attitude of Francis Bacon and Descartes Towards Magic and Occult Science," 452.

18. This view is repeated in book 2 of the *Advancement:* "The ancient opinion that man

was Microcosmus, an abstract or model of the world, hath been fantastically strained by Paracelsus and the alchemists," (3:370).

19. Rees, "Francis Bacon's Semi-Paracelsian Cosmology," 88-91.

20. The passage from *De Sapientia* reads: "As for that golden branch, . . . they promise us by that same stone of theirs not only mountains of gold, but also the restitution of natural bodies as it were from the gates of the Infernals. Nevertheless for Alchemy and those that are never weary of their wooing of that stone, as I am sure they have no ground in theory, so I suspect that they have no very good pledge of success in practice" (6:760-61).

21. In *Francis Bacon and the Rhetoric of Nature*, John C. Briggs attributes Bacon's guarded optimism about alchemical success to reformations taking place *within* the alchemist's psyche more than in his practical methods as such (148-50); nonetheless, I agree with Briggs that for Bacon the "means" employed by the "old" alchemy were defective, not the goal it was attempting.

22. The passage from the *Historia Densi et Rari* reads: "The manufacture of gold, or the transmutation of metals into gold, is to be much doubted of. For of all bodies gold is the heaviest and densest, and therefore to turn anything else into gold there must needs be condensation." However, in two short passages that follow immediately, Bacon, characteristically, shifts to greater optimism about the "conversion" of quicksilver or lead into silver. Further, he adds that if baser metals could be transmuted into a superior metal that resembled gold in all respects except weight, "it would doubtless be both profitable and useful" (5:346-47).

23. This passage closely parallels several of Bacon's statements concerning the transmutation of metals, especially in its insistence on the practitioner's possession of knowledge: "So again the retarding of old age or the restoration of some degree of youth, are things hardly credible; yet it is far more probable that a man who knows well the nature of arefaction and the depredations of the spirits upon the solid parts of the body, and clearly understands the nature of assimilation and of alimentation, whether more or less perfect, and has likewise observed the nature of the spirits, and the flame as it were of the body, whose office is sometimes to consume and sometimes to restore, shall by diets, bathings, anointings, proper medicines, suitable exercises, and the like, prolong life, or in some degree renew the vigour of youth; than that it can be done by a few drops or scruples of a precious liquor or essence" (4:368).

24. West, "Notes on the Importance of Alchemy," 103.

Chapter 5. Ben Jonson and the Drama of Alchemy

1. In *Ben Jonson, Poems*, ed. Ian Donaldson (London: Oxford Univ. Press, 1975), 9. All references to Jonson's nondramatic poems are to this edition.

2. Sendivogius, *A New Light of Alchymy*, 32.

3. From the *Discoveries*, in *Ben Jonson*, ed. C.H. Herford and Percy and Evelyn Simpson, 11 vols. (Oxford: Clarendon Press, 1925-52), 8:567. Unless indicated, all references are to this edition. Jonson was not entirely consistent on the subject of nature's decline: in the section, *Sed seculi morbus* (8:572), he speaks of the prevalence of lying as "the disease of the Age" and continues, "and no wonder if the world, growing old, begin to be infirme: Old age it selfe is a disease. It is long since the sick world began to doate, and talke idly: Would she had but doated still; but her dotage is now broke forth into a madnesse, and become a meere phrency." Scholars have generally neglected the literature of alchemy in examining the Art-Nature debate; see, for example, Edward Tayler, *Nature and Art in Renaissance Literature* (New York: Columbia Univ. Press, 1964), where alchemy receives only a brief mention (76).

4. All quotations from and line references to this play are taken from the text included

in volume 5 of *Ben Jonson*. For notes on Jonson's alchemical sources and commentary, see volume 10 of this edition, 46-116.

5. I agree entirely with Edgar Hill Duncan's statement concerning "Jonson's remarkable knowledge of alchemy, a knowledge greater than that of any other major English literary figure, with the possible exceptions of Chaucer and Donne" ("Jonson's *Alchemist* and the Literature of Alchemy," *PMLA* 64 [Sept. 1946]: 699).

6. On the essentially new, "capitalistic" type of criminality represented in the play and, especially, its relationship to the contemporary London setting, see Jonathan Haynes, "Representing the Underworld: *The Alchemist*," *SP* 86 (winter 1989): 18-41. This study, and my own discussion, is indebted to the pioneering analysis of relationships among religion, sex, commerce, criminality, and alchemy reflected in the play's language and imagery in Edward B. Partridge, *The Broken Compass* (New York: Columbia Univ. Press, 1958), chap. 6.

7. Much has been written on the motivations of Jonson's gulls in the *Alchemist*. My method in discussing this play, although not my focus and objective, bears some resemblance to that used by Robert N. Watson in *Ben Jonson's Parodic Strategy: Literary Imperialism in the Comedies* (Cambridge: Harvard Univ. Press, 1987). Watson is concerned with showing how, for purposes ultimately of subversion, the dreams, aspirations, and actions of Jonson's foolish characters are shaped by the ambitions and visions of heroes of popular Elizabethan fiction and drama, such as those written by Dekker, Deloney, Heywood, Marlowe and Middleton. My concern is with showing how many aspects of the play creatively "recapitulate"—at times nearly parody—common themes and topics derived from alchemical writing and alchemical satire.

8. *Ben Jonson, Dramatist* (Cambridge: Cambridge Univ. Press, 1984), 137-38. However, I disagree with Barton's view of the role of the charlatans in the lives of their victims. She regards the gulls more sympathetically, as sufferers from limitations in their social and intellectual backgrounds (Face and Subtle may be able to "liberate and objectify their inchoate feelings of restriction and discontent," 138) rather than from powerful and diverse manifestations of greed, ignoble ambition, and sensualism, which the charlatans are concerned to exploit. Partridge, in *The Broken Compass*, also speaks of the absence of transforming features in the play's denouement: Face's last speech shows him to be unregenerate and there is a "sinister note" in his proffered exchange with the audience, which "may be there to judge his case, but . . . is also a nation to be exploited" (154-55).

9. See, for example, the summaries of problematic issues raised by Jonson's conclusion in Partridge, *The Broken Compass*, 152-56, and Donald Gertmenian, "Comic Experience In *Volpone* and *The Alchemist*," *SEL* 17 (1977): 247-58. Gertmenian's conclusion is that instead of offering moral affirmation, *The Alchemist* "invites us to take delight in Protean human energies that are quite amoral, so that . . . questions about affirmation of the ideal or of healthy stability in society are beside the point" (248). Somewhere between this view and the search for conventional morality in the play's ending is Watson's attractive interpretation, in *Ben Jonson's Parodic Strategy*, that Lovewit's triumph is that of energetic "innovative wit" over standardized moralizing (134).

10. Jonson's phrase, "Your crosse-lets, crucibles, and cucurbites?" (1.3.103), can be compared with Chaucer's "Violes, crosletz, and sublymatories, / Cucurbites and alambikes eek," *CYT*, pars prima, ll. 793-94. Adjacent references to beech coals in each passage may also be suggestive of borrowing on Jonson's part.

11. This is the so-called "philosopher's wheel," common in alchemical writing and deriving ultimately from Plato's *Timaeus*, 49 C.

12. *Discoveries*, 8:581. Of the many relevant passages in the *Discoveries*, see, for example, "Pure and neat Language I love, yet plaine and customary. A barbarous Phrase hath often

made mee out of love with a good sense" (8:620); "the chiefe vertue of a style is perspicuitie, and nothing [is] so vitious in it, as to need an Interpreter" (8:622).

13. *Discoveries,* 8:627; in this passage Jonson is consciously evoking book 1 of the *Advancement of Learning.* On Jonson's detestation of imposture, see also the section entitled *Impostorum fucus* (8:570).

14. See, for example, Subtle's specious fears that his efforts in behalf of Mammon will come to naught because of the knight's suspected immorality: his own thoughts, he tells Mammon, have "look'd no way, but unto publique good, / To pious uses, and deere charitie" (2.3.16-17). Watson, in *Ben Jonson's Parodic Strategy,* suggests reasonably that Mammon, on certain occasions as at 2.3.49-52, adopts the role of "public benefactor" in order to disguise his base motives from the supposedly pious Subtle (120-21).

15. On the question of the dates of the Hollands, see Herford and Simpson's note, *Ben Jonson,* 10:63.

16. The major recent study of Dee is Nicholas H. Clulee, *John Dee's Natural Philosophy* (London and New York: Routledge, 1988). See also Peter French, *John Dee: The World of an Elizabethan Magus* (London: Routledge & Kegan Paul, 1972). Despite Dee's appearance in Subtle's rebus, it is too much to claim, as several scholars have done, that Dee is the charlatan's original, a view that goes back as far as Margaret Cavendish, Duchess of Newcastle's *The Description of the World* (1668); for the relevant passage, see *Ben Jonson,* 10:47. For one example of the perpetuation of this tradition, see Frances A. Yates, *The Occult Philosophy in the Elizabethan Age* (London: Routledge & Kegan Paul, 1979), 161.

17. On Jonson's adaptation from his source, Chrysogonus Polydorus's preface to the collection *De Alchemia,* published at Nuremberg in 1541 and 1545, see Supriya Chaudhuri, "Jason's Fleece: The Source of Sir Epicure Mammon's Allegory," *RES,* n.s., 35 (1984): 71-73. See also the notes accompanying this passage in *Ben Jonson,* vol. 10, and Duncan, "Jonson's *Alchemist* and the Literature of Alchemy," 702-5.

18. The epigram reads in part, "It is a wonderful story . . . / They say that a gold rain descended from the clouds, / When Sol was united in love with the Cyprian goddess: / May then also, when Pallas breaks out of Jupiter's head, / The gold descend into the retort destined to it, like a rainshower," as translated in H.M.E. De Jong, *Michael Maier's Atalanta Fugiens: Sources of an Alchemical Book of Emblems* (Leiden: E.J. Brill, 1969), 181. Maier includes alchemical emblems of several other myths of the sort that Jonson mentions here, e.g., Ceres (411), Mercury and Venus (414), and Oedipus (415).

19. The existence of such linguistic modes has been noted by several critics, including Anne Barton, in *Ben Jonson, Dramatist,* 149, and, most recently, Cheryl Lynn Ross, "The Plague of *The Alchemist,*" *Renaissance Quarterly* 41:3 (autumn 1988): 454-57, who sees them as symptomatic of the play's tendencies toward colonization. On the "inflationary" and "awe-producing" qualities in the language of alchemy, see Wayne A. Rebhorn, "Jonson's 'Jovy Boy': Lovewit and the Dupes in *The Alchemist,*" *JEGP* 79 (1980): 361-64.

20. On Jonson's essentially conservative cast of mind, see Alvin B. Kernan, "Alchemy and Acting: The Major Plays of Ben Jonson," *Studies in the Literary Imagination* 6 (April 1973): 5-6. There is critical disagreement as to whether the explosion and the failed experiment that precipitates it are, in fact, "real" in the play. R.L. Smallwood sees Subtle's laboratory as existing only in the rhetoric of the charlatans and from thence in the imaginations of the dupes and audience; it is part of the play's pervasive *deceptio visus,* "created through pretence, through theatrical art, above all through the art of language" ("'Here, in the Friars': Immediacy and Theatricality in *The Alchemist,*" *RES,* n.s., 32 [1981]: 154). On the other hand, Anne Barton, on the basis of Lovewit's description of smoky walls, a furnace, and broken utensils (5.5.38-42), states that "it becomes plain that Mammon, Tribulation and the rest are not the only ones

who have been fooled by [the] art," (*Ben Jonson, Dramatist,* 152). The charlatans themselves have fallen victim to alchemy's promise of wealth.

21. See Christopher Hill, *Intellectual Origins of the English Revolution* and *The World Turned Upside Down;* Keith Thomas, *Religion and the Decline of Magic* (New York: Charles Scribner's Sons, 1971); Charles Webster, *The Great Instauration: Science, Medicine and Reform, 1626-1660* (New York: Holmes & Meier, 1976); and P.M. Rattansi, "Paracelsus and the Puritan Revolution," *Ambix* 11 (1963): 24-32.

22. On the appropriateness of Mammon's proposed activity and the prevailingly futuristic orientation of the play's action, see Gerard H. Cox, "Apocalyptic Projection and the Comic Plot of *The Alchemist,*" *ELR* 13:1 (winter 1983): 70-87, esp. 86. Otherwise useful, this essay fails to mention the popularity of eschatological and millenarian ideas and images in much alchemical writing of the sixteenth and seventeenth centuries, a link that helps account for the special trenchancy of Jonson's satire of the Puritans.

23. *Renaissance Magic and the Return of the Golden Age: The Occult Tradition and Marlowe, Jonson, and Shakespeare* (Lincoln and London: Univ. of Nebraska Press, 1989), 137; on Jonson's treatment of individual and religious radicalism in the *Alchemist,* see chap. 7.

24. In "An Execration upon Vulcan," which laments the loss of his library by fire in November, 1623, Jonson again associates alchemical experiments with madness: "Some alchemist . . . / May to thy name a *Vulcanale* say, / And for it lose his eyes with gunpowder, / As the other may his brains with quicksilver" (ll. 118, 120-22). Earlier in the same poem he speaks slightingly of alchemical, hermetic, and Rosicrucian works that deal "With the chimera of the Rosy Cross, / Their seals, their characters, hermetic rings, / Their gem of riches, and bright stone that brings / Invisibility, and strength, and tongues; / *The Art of Kindling the True Coal,* by Lungs," ll. 72-76, (Donaldson, *Ben Jonson, Poems,* [196]); such works, he states, would have better suited Vulcan's conflagration than his own books. Jonson was, nonetheless, to incorporate several of these magical and Rosicrucian themes in his masque, *The Fortunate Isles,* performed at court on 9 January 1624/25. The Rosicrucian manifestos had first been published in 1614-15.

25. Following several textual clues (e.g., 1.1.45, 64, 67-71, 78-79; 1.3.104; 2.3.96-98), a number of critics have observed that Jonson's characterization as well as other aspects of the play are likened to chemical properties and reactions occurring within an alchemist's alembic; perhaps the most thoroughgoing of such studies is Michael Flachmann, "Ben Jonson and the Alchemy of Satire," *SEL* 17 (1977): 259-80. See also Mebane, *Renaissance Magic,* 144, and Charles Nicholl, *The Chemical Theatre,* 111-12.

26. Typical is the expansion of Dapper's desire for a "rifling *flye*" into one for a charm that will attract "all the treasure of the realme" (1.2.80-103), a process that, he inadvertently confesses, will require him to "leave the law" (91).

27. This is not to say, however, that Surly escapes gulling. I am basically in agreement with David F. Finnigan, who finds that Surly "enters Lovewit's house as a rogue or rascal but is transformed into his final role as a gull" ("The Role of Surly in *The Alchemist,*" *PLL* 16 [1980]: 100).

28. The masque was performed on 1 and 6 January 1616; on the question of dating and first performance, see *Ben Jonson,* 10:545-47. All quotations are taken from the text in vol. 7 of this edition.

29. Thus he is termed by Herford and Simpson in *Ben Jonson,* 2:294.

30. See "The Alchemy in Jonson's *Mercury Vindicated,*" *SP* 39 (1942): 625-37, which is still useful for its tracing of sources and analogues.

31. These are John C. Meagher, *Method and Meaning in Jonson's Masques* (Notre Dame: Univ. of Notre Dame Press, 1966), 68, 88, 120; Stephen Orgel, *The Jonsonian Masque* (Cam-

bridge: Harvard Univ. Press, 1965), 99, and *The Illusion of Power: Political Theater in the English Renaissance* (Berkeley: Univ. of California Press, 1975), 53-54; Stephen Orgel and Roy Strong, *Inigo Jones: The Theatre of the Stuart Court,* 2 vols. (London and Berkeley: Sotheby Parke Bernet and Univ. of California, 1973), 1:23-4; and Douglas Brooks-Davies, *The Mercurian Monarch: Magical Politics from Spenser to Pope* (Manchester: Manchester Univ. Press, 1983), 90-91, which also discusses other masques and Renaissance literary works from a magical and hermetic perspective. See also Nicholl, *The Chemical Theatre,* 100-1. An earlier version of this section of the chapter appeared in my article, "Jonson and Sendivogius: Some New Light on *Mercury Vindicated from the Alchemists at Court,*" *Ambix* 24:1 (1977): 39-54.

    32. Orgel, *The Illusion of Power,* 43. For Orgel, this concept is centered in the idea of masques as celebrations of the ruler as an "exemplary figure," reflections of his life, "extension[s] of the royal mind," and "expressions of royal power" (42-45).

    33. Lists of "Books in Jonson's Library" are included in *Ben Jonson,* 1:250-71 and 11:593-603. See also David Mcpherson, "Ben Jonson's Library and Marginalia: An Annotated Catalogue," *SP* 71 (1974): 1-106.

    34. The following biographical sketch draws upon A.E. Waite, *Alchemists through the Ages* (London: Redway, 1888; reprint [of *Lives of Alchemystical Philosophers*], Blauvelt, N.Y.: Rudolf Steiner Publications, 1970), 171-81; John Read, *Humour and Humanism in Chemistry* (London: Bell, 1947), 50-65; and Holmyard, *Alchemy,* 223-38. Additional biographical and bibliographical information is included in Ferguson, *Bibliotheca Chemica,* 2:364-70; and Thorndike, *HMES,* 7:158-59 and passim.

    35. Read, *Humour and Humanism in Chemistry,* 53. For an excellent account of the occult milieu in Rudolf II's court, see R.J.W. Evans, *Rudolf II and His World: A Study in Intellectual History, 1576-1612* (Oxford: Clarendon Press, 1973), 196-242; for Sendivogius, 211-12.

    36. Holmyard, *Alchemy,* 236.

    37. Waite, *Alchemists through the Ages,* 180. Ferguson reports the death year as 1636 or 1646 (*Bibliotheca Chemica,* 2:369).

    38. "The Mystery of Alexander Seton, the Cosmopolite," in *Proceedings of the XIVth International Congress of the History of Science* (Tokyo-Kyoto: n.p., 1974), 2:397-400. On Scotto, see also the note in Herford and Simpson, *Ben Jonson,* 9:704.

    39. "The True Life of Michael Sendivogius," in *Actes du XI*ᵉ *Congrès international d'histoire des sciences, Varsovie-Cracovie, 24-31 August, 1965* (Warsaw: n.p., 1968), 4:31-35; and Hubicki's article in the *DSB* (1975), s.v. "Sendivogius," which states that the adventures of Seton and Sendivogius "seem to be a literary fiction, created years after his [Sendivogius's] death" (307).

    40. This statement is made in correspondence to the author.

    41. Hubicki, "The True life of Michael Sendivogius," 35.

    42. Hubicki, "The True Life of Michael Sendivogius," 32. Hubicki notes that according to one of Sendivogius's early biographers, Carolides a Carlsperga in *Praecepta Institutionis* (Prague, 1598), Sendivogius is supposed to have visited Cambridge University prior to 1598, while in the service of Rudolf II. Another link with England resulted from Sendivogius's purchase in 1597 of the Fumberg estate near Prague from the widow of the English alchemist Edward Kelley.

    43. As noted earlier in this chapter, the *Alchemist* reveals Jonson's acquaintance with both ancient authorities (2.1.80-104) and a number of recent or contemporary alchemists, e.g., the two fifteenth-century Dutch alchemists Isaac and John Isaac Hollandus (1.2.109), whose misfortunes at the court of Rudolf II are reminiscent of Seton's rumored experience with Christian II. In addition, Jonson's knowledge of contemporary Rosicrucian lore was wittily incorporated into *The Fortunate Isles,* designed for performance at court on Twelfth Night, 1625.

    44. Holmyard, *Alchemy,* 236.

45. Thorndike, *HMES*, 7:158. In footnote 25 on this page, Thorndike states that two other early editions of the *Novum Lumen*, printed in Frankfurt (1606) and Cologne (1610), are listed in Carl C. Schmieder, *Geschichte der Alchemie* (Halle, 1832).

46. Thorndike, *HMES*, 7:158-59.

47. Thorndike, *HMES*, 7:155.

48. Read, *Humour and Humanism in Chemistry,* 62.

49. Ferguson, *Bibliotheca Chemica,* 2:365.

50. Thorndike, *HMES*, 7:159 n. 29.

51. Ferguson, *Bibliotheca Chemica,* 2:369. Ferguson states that Sendivogius "is considered to have written: *Tractatus de Sulphure; Dialogus Mercurii, Alchymistæ et Naturæ; Aenigma philosophicum*. These, which appear sometimes separately, are usually all printed together."

52. *Theatrum Chemicum, Praecipuos Selectorum Auctorum Tractatus de Chemiae* (Strasburg, 1613), 4:509-17.

53. John W. Shirley, "The Scientific Experiments of Sir Walter Ralegh, the Wizard Earl, and the Three Magi in the Tower, 1603-17," *Ambix* 4 (Dec. 1949): 66.

54. See figura 27 in this edition.

55. *The Works of Sir Thomas Browne,* ed. Geoffrey Keynes, 4 vols. (Chicago: Univ. of Chicago Press, 1964), 2:106.

56. George Thor, *Cheiragogia Heliana. A Manuduction to the Philosopher's Magical Gold* (London, 1659), 29.

57. From the translation of Helvetius's *Golden Calf* included in William Cooper, *The Philosophical Epitaph of W.C. Esquire,* 37.

58. Houpreght, *Aurifontina Chymica,* sig. A3ᵛ.

59. Mystagogus, *Mercury's Caducean Rod,* 70.

60. See entry 338 in my *William Cooper's A Catalogue of Chymicall Books.*

61. Francis A. Yates, *The Rosicrucian Enlightenment* (London: Routledge & Kegan Paul, 1972), 31, 50, 84. Although rare, brief and humorously allegorical alchemical tracts of the *Dialogue* type appear occasionally from the Middle Ages through the seventeenth century. In addition to the few examples cited by Yates, see Jean de Meun's *A Demonstration of Nature, made to the Erring Alchemists* in Waite, *Hermetic Museum,* 1:121-41, which has important thematic and stylistic resemblances to both Sendivogius's *Dialogue* and *Mercury Vindicated*. See also Michael Maier's *A Subtle Allegory Concerning the Secrets of Alchemy* in the *Hermetic Museum,* 2:199-223; *[An Historical Account] of a Degradation of Gold Made by an Anti-Elixir* (London, 1678), by Robert Boyle; and Johann Joachim Becher's *Magnalia Naturae* (London, 1680).

62. All of the following quotations are taken from this edition.

63. See, for example, Thomas Tymme's *A Dialogue Philosophicall* (London, 1612) and Michael Maier's *Lusus Serius* (London, 1654). Thorndike cites other alchemical dialogues in *HMES,* 5:545; 7:166, 173, and the genre is discussed in Robert P. Multhauf, "Some Nonexistent Chemists of the Seventeenth Century: Remarks on the Use of the Dialogue in Scientific Writing," in *Alchemy and Chemistry in the Seventeenth Century: Papers Read by Allen G. Debus and Robert P. Multhauf at a Clark Library Seminar, March 12, 1966* (Los Angeles: William Andrews Clark Memorial Library, 1966), 31-50.

64. See the section "Of Sulphur" in the previously cited edition of 1650, pp. 126-42. This treatise is a close counterpart of the Mercury dialogue and takes the form of an exchange between a foolish alchemist, who is unable to reach a "conclusion," and a voice representing Saturn.

65. Duncan, "The Alchemy in Jonson's *Mercury Vindicated,*" 629-30.

66. This passage reveals Jonson's familiarity with the terminology and physical processes of the art as well as his skill in rendering its modes of thought and metaphorical idiom. "Crude" and "Sublimate," for example, refer to the common, material substance (quicksilver, in this case) and to the specially prepared "sophic" mercury, one of the proximate principles of the stone. The "male" and "female" and "hermaphroditic" qualities might refer either to the conjunction of opposites—king and queen, brother and sister, sol and luna, sulphur and mercury, etc.—that was a crucial stage in the alchemical process or to the bisexual principles inherent in mercury alone. The complexity of the alchemists' conception of mercury is summarized in Jung, *Psychology and Alchemy,* trans. R.F.C. Hull, 2d ed. (New York: Princeton Univ. Press, 1953), 292-93, 295.

67. Jung, *Psychology and Alchemy,* 65-6.

68. Orgel has stated that "Court masques were always topical; under Charles I they argued the royal case in current political and legal disputes with an energy and ingenuity that suggests that the king must have been actively involved in their composition" (*Illusion of Power,* 43). Further, in noting the commonness of magician-monarch figures in Jacobean masques, Brooks-Davies states that "clearly, James's hatred of witchcraft and the black arts was no hindrance to the resurgence of the cult of the monarch magus in his reign" (*Mercurian Monarch,* 87). The strength of James's feelings against witchcraft is reflected not only in its most famous expression, the *Demonology* of 1597, but also in the *Basilicon Doron,* where he states that "there [are] some horrible crimes that ye are bound in conscience never to forgive: suche as Witchcraft, wilfull murther, Incest (especiallie within the degrees of consanguinitie) Sodomy, Poysoning, and false coine" (*The Basilicon Doron of King James VI,* ed. James Craigie, 2 vols. [Edinburgh and London: William Blackwood, 1944, 1950], 1:65).

69. Cf. ll. 23, 37, 192, and especially 45-51: "Howsoever they may pretend under the specious names of *Geber, Arnold, Lully, Bombast of Hohenhein* [Paracelsus], to commit miracles in art, and treason again' nature. And, as if the title of *Philosopher,* that creature of glory, were to be fetch'd out of a furnace, abuse the curious and credulous *Nation* of metall-men through the world, and make *Mercury* their instrument."

70. Duncan, "The Alchemy in Jonson's *Mercury Vindicated,*" 637.

71. This reference to the number twelve marks a further similarity in the two works. In Sendivogius, Nature says that she has many sons, but of these, seven—those who correspond to the seven metals—are set apart, and of these Mercury is first (*Dialogue,* 73). There are also comparable references to Nature's daughters near the end of each work: Sendivogius's Nature notes that she has "many Sonnes, and many Daughters" (*Dialogue,* 73), while in Jonson, Prometheus's song following the first dance poses the question: "How many, 'mongst these Ladies here, / Wish now they such a mother were!"; Nature responds: "Not one, I feare, / And read it in their laughters. / There's more, I guesse, would wish to be my daughters" (ll. 226-30).

72. De Jong's translation, in *Michael Maier's Atalanta Fugiens,* of the motto reads: "May Nature, Reason, Exercise and Literature be the guide, staff, spectacles and lamp for him who participates in chemistry" (266).

73. Orgel has noted the antithetical spirit of the masque and satire: "The masque presents the triumph of an aristocratic community; at its center is a belief in the hierarchy and a faith in the power of idealization. . . . As a genre, it is the opposite of satire; it educates by praising, by creating heroic roles for the leaders of society to fill" (*The Illusion of Power,* 40).

Chapter 6. The Poetry of Donne and Herbert

1. *The Complete Poetry of John Donne,* ed. John T. Shawcross (Garden City, N.Y.: Anchor, 1967), 97.

2. William Cooper, *The Philosophical Epitaph,* 10.

3. See W.A. Murray, "Donne and Paracelsus: An Essay in Interpretation," *RES* 25 (1949): 115-23; Joseph Mazzeo, "Notes on John Donne's Alchemical Imagery," *Isis* 48 (1957): 103-23; Laurence Stapleton, "The Theme of Virtue in Donne's Verse Epistles," *SP* 55 (April 1958): 187-200, esp. 192-98; Edgar Hill Duncan, "Donne's Alchemical Figures," *ELH* 9 (1942): 257-85; and Eluned Crawshaw, "Hermetic Elements in Donne's Poetic Vision," in *John Donne: Essays in Celebration,* ed. A.J. Smith (London: Methuen, 1972), 324-48. Other more recent and specialized studies will be cited as applicable.

4. Charles Monroe Coffin, *John Donne and the New Philosophy* (1937; reprint, New York: Humanities Press, 1958), is still a valuable book on these topics.

5. My categories closely follow those used by Duncan in "Donne's Alchemical Figures." Though Duncan is largely concerned with the sources of Donne's alchemical ideas (his expressed aim is to "analyze the alchemical figures in Donne's poetry against a background of the theories and practices of alchemy as recorded in the compendious literature of the science current in the late sixteenth and early seventeenth centuries" [257]), I wish to acknowledge my indebtedness to this excellent essay. For the texts of the poems, I cite Shawcross, *Complete Poetry,* and have also drawn on the notes included in the following editions: *The Elegies and the Songs and Sonnets,* ed. Helen Gardner (Oxford: Clarendon Press, 1965); *The Poems of John Donne,* ed. Herbert J.C. Grierson, 2 vols. (1912; reprint, London: Oxford Univ. Press, 1963); *John Donne: The Complete English Poems,* ed. A.J. Smith (London: Penguin, 1971); *John Donne: The Anniversaries,* ed. Frank Manley (Baltimore: Johns Hopkins Univ. Press, 1963); and *John Donne: The Satires, Epigrams and Verse Letters,* ed. Wesley Milgate (Oxford: Clarendon Press, 1967).

6. Arthur F. Marotti, *John Donne, Coterie Poet* (Madison: Univ. of Wisconsin Press, 1986), 321 n. 89, places "Sunne Rising" in a group of poems associated with Ann More, but he also sees it as "more concerned with the judgment of peers than with the responses of a beloved" (139). John Cary, *John Donne: Life, Mind and Art,* new ed. (London: Faber and Faber, 1990), 95, also finds that the poem's "vaunting language" masks anxieties about Donne's unemployment arising from the marriage to Ann More.

7. Marotti, *John Donne,* 111. However, for Anthony Low, the poem reflects the age's increasing pragmatism and commercialism: "mining and alchemy illustrate a more cynical mood, as exploration, science, and the search for new wealth through technology prove to be failed enterprises that began in hope but end in disillusionment" ("Love and Science: Cultural Change in Donne's *Songs and Sonnets,*" *Studies in the Literary Imagination* 22:1 [spring 1989]: 9).

8. Shawcross, *Complete Poetry,* 126 n. 2.

9. Regarding this detail, Grierson quotes the following from one of Donne's letters to Sir Henry Goodyere: "My Lord Chancellor gave me so noble and so ready a dispatch, accompanied with so fatherly advice that I am now, like an alchemist, delighted with discoveries by the way, though I attain not mine end" (*Poems,* 2:36).

10. I agree with Gardner's gloss of the final couplet: "If you aren't willing to give it up I hope it poisons you" (*The Elegies and the Songs and Sonnets,* 119).

11. Grierson, *Poems,* 2:236. See also the background note in Smith, *The Complete English Poems,* 646.

12. Grierson traces the poem's background to a literary debate that was taking place, ca. 1597-98, within the Earl of Essex's circle concerning the superiority of life in the court, coun-

try, or city (*Poems,* 2:140-41). Marotti is certainly correct in calling attention to this poem's "strong strain of anticourtly and antiestablishment feeling" and Christian Stoicism (*John Donne,* 119).

13. See Grierson's note in *Poems,* 2:152.

14. Donne's poetry and the system of court patronage has, of course, been the subject of much recent critical interest. On this general topic and Donne's relationship with the Countess of Bedford, in particular, see Marotti, *John Donne,* esp. 202-32; Ted-Larry Pebworth, "John Donne, Coterie Poetry, and the Text of Performance," *SEL* 29 (1989): 61-75; Margaret Mauer, "The Real Presence of Lucy Russell, Countess of Bedford, and the Terms of John Donne's 'Honour is so Sublime Perfection,'" *ELH* 47 (summer 1980): 205-34, in which the Countess and her circle are presented in a sharply critical light; Patricia Thomson, "Donne and the Poetry of Patronage," in Smith, *John Donne: Essays in Celebration,* 308-23.

15. Marotti, *John Donne,* 208.

16. Stapleton, in "The Theme of Virtue in Donne's Verse Epistles," also identifies the Paracelsian images of a *balsamum* with platonic ideas of virtue in this and other verse letters (197). One of Donne's Whitsuntide sermons contains the following theological analogy: "Every thing hath in it, as Physitians use to call it, *Naturale Balsamum,* A naturall Balsamum, which, if any wound or hurt which that creature hath received, be kept clean from extrinsique putrefaction, will heale of it self. We are so far from that naturall Balsamum, as that we have a naturall poyson in us, Originall sin" (*The Sermons of John Donne,* ed. Evelyn M. Simpson and George R. Potter, 10 vols. [Berkeley and Los Angeles: Univ. of California Press, 1953], 6:116).

17. On the character and reputation of the Countess of Bedford and her circle in James's court, see Mauer, "The Real Presence of Lucy Russell."

18. Mauer, "The Real Presence of Lucy Russell," 225.

19. David Aers and Gunther Kress, "'Darke Texts Need Notes': Versions of Self in Donne's Verse Epistles," *Literature and History* 8 (autumn 1978): 139. My interpretation is indebted to this fine essay.

20. I summarize Aers and Kress, "'Darke Texts,'" 141-42. On the poem's dating, see Shawcross, *Complete Poetry,* 414.

21. See Shawcross, *Complete Poetry,* 414.

22. Cf. "Verse the fame enroules," the concluding phrase of *The First Anniversary,* l. 474. Pebworth notes, in "John Donne, Coterie Poetry, and the Text of Performance," that "[Donne] stands virtually alone among major English poets in apparently feeling little sense of poetic vocation and in almost never asserting the transcendent power of poetry" (64).

23. Milgate, *Satires, Epigrams,* 266. See also the entries for "Tinctura"/"Tincture" in Ruland's *A Lexicon of Alchemy,* trans. A.E. Waite (London: Westminster Press, 1893; reprint, London: John Watkins, 1964), 318, 429.

24. Milgate's gloss on this passage (*Satires, Epigrams,* 267) is similar to mine.

25. From the unpaginated, first printed edition of *The Compound of Alchymy. Or The ancient hidden Art of Archemie.* This quotation appears in the penultimate stanza of "Of Dissolution."

26. Marotti, *John Donne,* 226.

27. Grierson conjectures that Lady Bedford's deceased friend was either Lady Marckham or Mrs. Boulstred, both of whom died in 1609 (*Poems,* 2:133).

28. The identification of virtue with gold and the idea of becoming gold through the exercise of virtue is also present in "*A Letter to the Lady* Carey, *and Mrs.* Essex Riche, *From Amyens,*" dating from 1611: "to Gold we'are growne / When Vertue is our Soules complexion" (ll. 31-32).

29. See my "Alchemy and Eschatology in Seventeenth-Century Poetry."

30. See Milgate, *Satires, Epigrams,* 272.

31. Milgate, *Satires, Epigrams,* 273. On this theme, see Betty Jo Teeter Dobbs, *Alchemical Death & Resurrection: The Significance of Alchemy in the Age of Newton* (Washington, D.C.: Smithsonian Institution Libraries, 1990). Another brief example of the grave-alembic, death-resurrection motif is found in "Elegie: Death" ("Language thou art too narrow, and too weake," ll. 57-60), with its reference to a "*Lemnia,*" e.g., Lemnia Terra or earth of Lemnos, known in alchemical mythology as an antidote to poison or as a transmuting agent. On this topic, see Ruland, *Lexicon of Alchemy,* s.v. "Rubrica Sinopica"; also the notes in the editions of Grierson, *Poems,* 2:216, and Shawcross, *Complete Poetry,* 256.

32. The traditional identification of "E. of D." with Richard Sackville, third Earl of Dorset, has recently been challenged by Dennis Flynn in "'Awry and Squint': The Dating of Donne's Holy Sonnets," *John Donne Journal* 7 (1988): 35-46, who identifies "E. of D." as William Stanley, sixth Earl of Derby, or possibly Ferdinando Stanley, fifth Earl of Derby, both of whom had poetic as well as alchemical interests.

33. See Flynn, "'Awry and Squint,'" 41. Marotti, *John Donne,* 245, makes the suggestion that Donne's act of sending the six accompanying "Holy Sonnets" to "E. of D" was an appeal for patronage.

34. "Ode V, In commendation of the time we live under the Reigne of our gracious King Charles," *The Complete Works in Verse and Prose of Abraham Cowley,* ed. Alexander B. Grosart, 2 vols. (Edinburgh, 1881; reprint, New York: AMS Press, 1967), 1:31 ("Sylva" section). This poem was first printed in the second edition of Cowley's *Poetical Blossomes* (1636).

35. I am indebted to the commentary in Manley, *The Anniversaries,* and *John Donne: The Epithalamions, Anniversaries and Epicedes,* ed. W. Milgate (Oxford: Clarendon Press, 1978).

36. Manley is undoubtedly correct in seeing the presence of distillation or sublimation behind this image, *The Anniversaries,* 139. There may also be a connection between this image and the extraction of the "worlds soule" and driving it into the "glasses of your eyes" in ll. 40-41 of "The Canonization."

37. As quoted in Manley, *The Anniversaries,* 139.

38. Duncan cites a number of passages from medieval and Renaissance alchemical treatises that reveal the commonness of the identification of gold with perfection; see "Donne's Alchemical Figures," 264-66.

39. Quoted in Herford and Simpson, *Ben Jonson, Works,* 1:133.

40. *The Hermetic and Alchemical Writings of Aureolus Philippus Theophrastus Bombast, of Hohenhein, Called Paracelsus the Great,* ed. Arthur Edward Waite, 2 vols. (London: J. Elliott & Co., 1894; reprint, New Hyde Park, N.Y.: University Books, 1967), 1:114. Hereafter *Paracelsus.*

41. Waite, *Paracelsus,* 2:364.

42. From *The Poems and Letters of Andrew Marvell,* ed. H.M. Margoliouth, 3d ed., 2 vols. (Oxford: Clarendon Press, 1971), 1:16.

43. *John Milton: Complete Poems and Major Prose,* ed. Merritt Y. Hughes (Indianapolis: Odyssey, 1957), 273. All references to Milton's works are to this edition, hereafter cited as *Complete Poems.*

44. See, for example, Josef Lederer, "John Donne and the Emblematic Practice," *RES* 22 (July 1946): 194, who states that in this stanza it appears "as if Donne was running quickly through the pages of an emblem book," and Donald Guss, *John Donne, Petrarchist* (Detroit: Wayne State University Press, 1966), 157-61.

45. Guss, *John Donne, Petrarchist,* 159.

46. On the extraordinary range of meanings present in the fly, but excluding an alchemical one, see A.B. Chambers, "The Fly in Donne's 'Canonization,'" *JEGP* 65 (1966): 252-59.

47. Duncan cites Paracelsus: "in the space of forty days, you can . . . produce the Al-

chemical Phoenix. But it should be noted well that the Sulphur of Cinnabar becomes the Flying Eagle, whose wings fly away without wind, and carry the body of the Phoenix to the nest of the parent, where it is nourished by the element of fire, and the young ones dig out its eyes," ("Donne's Alchemical Figures," 270). For additional attempts to trace the provenance of Donne's birds in nonalchemical contexts, see John Louis Lepage, "Eagles and Doves in Donne and Du Bartas: 'The Canonization,'" *N&Q* 30 (Oct. 1983), 427-28; Brian Vickers, "Donne's Eagle and Dove," *N&Q* 32 (March 1985), 59-60; and John Manning, "The Eagle and the Dove: Chapman and Donne's 'The Canonization,'" *N&Q* 33 (Sept. 1986), 347-48.

48. The quoted phrase from Johannes Grasseus appears in Jung, *Psychology and Alchemy,* 340.

49. Jung, *Psychology and Alchemy,* 340, 342.

50. For example, see figures 134 and 178 in Jung, *Psychology and Alchemy,* and similar motifs within the roundels of the topmost design in several copies of the *Ripley Scrolls.*

51. Jung, *Psychology and Alchemy,* 436-37.

52. Jung, *Psychology and Alchemy,* 66.

53. Figures 20, 98, and 266 in Jung, *Psychology and Alchemy,* are examples of the "double" or hermaphroditic eagle.

54. "Donne and Propertius: Love and Death in London and Rome," in *The Eagle and the Dove: Reassessing John Donne,* ed. Claude J. Summers and Ted-Larry Pebworth (Columbia: Univ. of Missouri Press, 1986), 75.

55. On this image, see Lyndy Abraham, "'The Lovers and the Tomb': Alchemical Emblems in Shakespeare, Donne, and Marvell," *Emblematica* 5:2 (winter 1991): 301-20.

56. The illustration is reproduced in Jung, *Psychology and Alchemy,* 284, with commentary following on 285-87.

57. The verse beneath the *pictura* reads: "Let the Body be placed in horse-dung, or a warm bath, the Spirit having been extracted from it. The Body has become white by the process, the Spirit red by our Art. All that exists tends towards perfection, and thus is the Philosopher's Stone prepared," in Waite, *The Hermetic Museum, Restored and Enlarged,* 1:291.

58. *The Book of Lambspring,* in Waite, *The Hermetic Museum,* 1:290.

59. My alchemical reading is not intended to preclude other approaches to the poem. N.J.C. Andreasen in *John Donne: Conservative Revolutionary* (Princeton: Princeton Univ. Press, 1967), for example, sees it as exploring the Petrarchan theme of "the reaction of a lover who has loved a mortal woman inordinately, so inordinately that he is overwhelmed with grief and despair when her death reveals to him that she was only mortal" (152). I agree entirely with this view of the poem's intent, but I differ from Andreasen as to how it is achieved.

60. See Yates, *The Rosicrucian Enlightenment,* 31, 50, 84.

61. Boyle, *[An Historical Account],* 10.

62. Boyle, *[An Historical Account],* 14.

63. Also closer to Donne's time than Boyle's treatise is the caution contained in Ambrosius Siebmacher's *Hydrolithus Sophicus:* "If thou strivest unduly to shorten the time thou wilt produce an abortion. Many persons have, through their ignorance, or self-opinionated haste, obtained a Nihilixir instead of the hoped-for Elixir" (quoted in Nicholl, *The Chemical Theatre,* 134).

64. Duncan, "Donne's Alchemical Figures," 280. For Paracelsus in *The Fourth Book of the Archidoxies: Concerning the Quintessence,* quintessence "is a certain matter extracted from all things which Nature has produced, and from everything which has life corporeally in itself, . . . [T]he quintessence is, so to say, a nature, a force, a virtue, and a medicine. . . . The same is also the colour, the life, the properties of things" (quoted in Duncan, 281).

65. It is possible, as Peter D. Wiggins has recently argued, that the "nothingnesse" from

which the speaker has been "expressed" (pressed or squeezed) is "the erotic relationship that his beloved's death has since taught the speaker was not what he thought it was"; however, I think the poem is more an expression of the speaker's grief over the beloved's death than a remorseful self-condemnation for participating in an erotic relationship with her. See "Preparing Towards Lucy: 'A Nocturnall' as Palinode," *SP* 84 (1987): 489-90.

66. Duncan, "Donne's Alchemical Figures," 280.

67. Alchemical possibilities in "The Extasie" have been studied in two recent articles: Julia M. Walker, "John Donne's 'The Extasie' as an Alchemical Process," *English Language Notes* 20:1 (September 1982), 1-8; and Abraham, "'The Lovers and the Tomb,'" 311-18. See also Nicholl, *The Chemical Theatre*, 119-35, for brief discussion of "The Extasie" and a few other of the *Songs and Sonets*.

68. Ruland, *Lexicon of Alchemy*, 303. See also Shawcross, *Complete Poetry*, 117 n. 13.

69. Quoted by Grierson in *Poems*, 2:29. The following passage from George Ripley's *Marrow of Alchemy* illustrates what Donne has in mind in the lines from "*A Valediction of the booke*": "See what the Scripture saith, *He stroke the Stone, and water flowed out, and he brought forth oyl out of the Flinty rock.* We may note the whole composition of the Elixir in these four verses following. *He stretcheth forth the Heavens as a Curtain. The Water stood above the Mountains:* This is the Water which does cover Our Matter, and performs the dissolution thereof, causing a cloudy Ascension. *That does walk upon the Wings of the Wind.* This figures forth the sublimation of our Stone" (from the *Medulla Alchymiae, The Marrow of Alchemy, Written in Latin by George Ripley, Canon of Bridlington . . . Translated into English, . . . by William Salmon* (London, 1692), 664-65. Hereafter cited as *Ripley*).

70. Holmyard, *Alchemy*, 48.

71. Mazzeo, in "Donne's Alchemical Imagery," notes the popularity of alembic images in Donne's poetry; several of my examples receive some discussion in his essay and in Duncan, "Donne's Alchemical Figures."

72. Jung, *Psychology and Alchemy*, 236-38. See also H.J. Sheppard, "Egg Symbolism in Alchemy," *Ambix* 6 (August 1958): 140-48.

73. Jung, *Psychology and Alchemy*, 293.

74. Jung, *Psychology and Alchemy*, 293.

75. Translated in De Jong, *Michael Maier's Atalanta Fugiens*, 214.

76. These have been noted in De Jong, *Michael Maier's Atalanta Fugiens*, 217, 449.

77. Jung, *Psychology and Alchemy*, 276.

78. Ruland, *Lexicon of Alchemy*, 279.

79. For example, after recounting the casting of the three youths into the furnace, Jung states "King Nebuchadnezzar had a vision of a fourth, 'like the Son of God,' as we are told in Daniel 3:25. This vision is not without bearing on alchemy, since there are numerous passages in the literature stating that the stone is *trinus et unus*. It consists of the four elements, with fire representing the spirit concealed in matter. This is the fourth, absent and yet present, who always appears in the fiery agony of the furnace and symbolizes the divine presence—succour and the completion of the work" (*Psychology and Alchemy*, 346-47).

80. See Raymond-Jean Frontain, "Donne's Imperfect Resurrection," *PLL* 26:4 (fall 1990), 539-45.

81. All references to Herbert's poems are to *The Works of George Herbert*, ed. F.E. Hutchinson (Oxford: Clarendon Press, 1964).

82. See figures 98 and 178 in Jung, *Psychology and Alchemy*.

83. Ashmole, *TCB*, opposite 13; see also the illustration from Salomon Trismosin's *Splendour Solis*, reproduced in Jung as figure 166.

84. On the source and provenance of this image, see my "Herbert and the Unveiling of Diana: Stanza Three of 'Vanitie' (I)," *George Herbert Journal* 1:2 (1978): 30-37.

Chapter 7. Alchemy, Allegory, and Eschatology in the Seventeenth Century

1. *The Table Talk of Martin Luther,* trans. William Hazlitt (London: G. Bell, 1902), 326.

2. Quoted in William Haller, *The Rise of Puritanism* (New York: Columbia Univ. Press, 1938), 125.

3. This and the following companion poem are quoted from *The Poems English, Latin and Greek of Richard Crashaw,* ed. L.C. Martin, 2d ed. (Oxford: Clarendon Press, 1966), 345-46.

4. *Aureng-Zebe* in *John Dryden: Four Tragedies,* ed. L.A. Beaurline and Fredson Bowers (Chicago: Univ. of Chicago Press, 1967), 154.

5. My reading of these lines follows the text of the poem included in *Andrew Marvell: The Complete Poems,* ed. Elizabeth Story Donno (Harmondsworth, Middlesex: Penguin, 1978), 49, rather than that provided in Margoliouth, *The Poems and Letters of Andrew Marvell,* 1:5. Margoliouth places a semicolon after Mayern (l. 48), making him subject to Aesculapius's condemnation. However, Theodore de Mayerne properly belongs with the alchemical references of the next two lines. He was a physician to Charles I, Paracelsian and iatrochemical in orientation, and important in the founding and directing of the London Distillers' Company. Earlier, he had been instrumental in introducing the practice of chemical physic in Paris. See John Webster, *The Displaying of Supposed Witchcraft* (London, 1677), 5; and Walter Harris, *Pharmacologia Anti-Empirica* (London, 1683), 27-28; also Webster, *The Great Instauration,* 254, 273. On Marvell's extensive use of alchemy in "Upon Appleton House" and other poems, see the excellent study by Abraham, *Marvell and Alchemy.*

6. Ashmole, *TCB,* 95.

7. *The Poems of Henry King,* ed. Margaret Crum (Oxford: Clarendon Press, 1965), 184.

8. *The Poems of Thomas Carew with his Masque Coelum Britannicum,* ed. Rhodes Dunlap (Oxford: Clarendon Press, 1970), 51.

9. *The Dramatic Works of John Lacy, Comedian* (1874; reprint, New York: B. Blom, 1967). All references are to this edition.

10. In *Robert Burton, Philosophaster,* ed. and trans. Connie McQuillen (Binghamton, N.Y.: MRTS, 1993), see 47, 77, and 183 for mentions of Paracelsus; 107, 109, and 111 for the urinalysis motif; 85 for the squaring of the circle; and 131, 133, and 135 for Erasmus's deceptive methods of "longation" and "curtation." In this play, however, alchemy is only incidental to a great range of types of charlatanism.

11. Historians of Renaissance science and medicine agree that the training of physicians within the English universities lagged considerably behind education on the Continent. Thus it suffered from the same lack of emphasis that marked studies in mathematics and the experimental sciences at Oxford and Cambridge. As early as the first half of the sixteenth century, it was common for English medical students to visit Continental universities for specialized work in anatomy and dissection, clinical training, and exposure to "humanistic" medicine in general. See Webster, *The Great Instauration,* 120-23. Rattansi has noted that one consequence of inadequacies in English medical training was a severe shortage of licensed physicians, which led, in turn, to an increase in the amount of prescribing of medicines done by apothecaries. See "Paracelsus and the Puritan Revolution," 24-25. On the highly traditional nature of medical training in sixteenth-century England, see Debus, *The English Paracelsians,* 51-55.

12. The name is a probable pun on "authentic" as designating duly qualified members of the medical profession; cf. Lafew's mention of "all the learned and authentic fellows" (*All's Well that Ends Well,* 2.3.12).

13. According to Rattansi, despite the increasing need for physicians in London in the first forty years of the seventeenth century, the number actually licensed by the College of Physicians remained stable at about twenty-five per decade ("Paracelsus and the Puritan Revolution," 24-25). Webster notes that during this period, the number of graduates in medicine produced by Oxford and Cambridge was extremely small, averaging from 1 to 2.5 per year between 1620 and 1640 (*The Great Instauration,* 121).

14. Rattansi, "Paracelsus and the Puritan Revolution," 25.

15. Webster, *The Great Instauration,* 253.

16. Arthur Dee, "To the Students of Chemistry," *Fasciculus Chemicus,* sig. aᵛ. On Arthur Dee, see Lyndy Abraham, "Arthur Dee, 1579-1651: A Life," *CaudaP* 13:2 (fall 1994): 1-14, and the introduction to her edition of the *Fasciculus Chemicus,* forthcoming in the English Renaissance Hermeticism series.

17. From Ashmole's "Prolegomena" [to the *Fasciculus Chemicus*], sig. **4ᵛ.

18. French, *The Art of Distillation,* sig. *2.

19. French, "Dedication," *The Art of Distillation,* sig. A3.

20. From the "Dedication" to the *Art of Distillation,* sig. A3. While attacks upon the universities abound in the seventeenth century, the following charges by the chemical philosopher George Starkey are particularly powerful in support of the reformation in experimental method advocated by both Bacon and John French: "And this is the misery of our Schools and Academies, that the one teach barely words, the other bare notions, which indeed are nothing, and in application prove but empty shadowes; for he that seeks to apply them to practise, beyond vain disputations can proceed no farther" (*Natures Explication and Helmont's Vindication* [London, 1657], 114-15).

21. "Preface" to *The Art of Distillation,* sig. *2ᵛ.

22. J. F., "To the Reader," *The Divine Pymander of Hermes Mercurius Trismegistus, In XVII. Books. Translated . . . By that Learned Divine Doctor Everard* (London, 1650), sig. A2.

23. Ibid., sigs. A3, A4ᵛ.

24. Ibid., sig. A4.

25. Ferguson, "Some English Alchemical Books," 5.

26. On Cooper's career, see the Introduction to my *William Cooper's A Catalogue of Chymicall Books,* vii-xlvii. A brief account of Cooper's life is included in Henry R. Plomer, *A Dictionary of the Printers and Booksellers who were at work in England, Scotland and Ireland from 1668-1725* (1922; reprint, Oxford: Bibliographical Society, 1968), 80-81. The fullest account of Cooper's career as a book auctioneer is in chapter 2 of John Lawler, *Book Auctions in England in the Seventeenth Century (1676-1700)* (1898; reprint, Detroit: Gale Research, 1968).

27. From the "Epistle Dedicatory" to Thomas Tymme's translation of Joseph Duchesne [Quersetanus], *The Practise of Chymicall and Hermeticall Physicke* (London, 1605). Of the many works treating connections between religion, especially Christianity, and alchemy, see especially Jung, *Psychology and Alchemy,* 345-431, and Thomas S. Willard, "Alchemy and the Bible," in *Centre and Labyrinth: Essays in Honour of Northrop Frye,* ed. Eleanor Cook et al. (Toronto: Univ. of Toronto Press, 1983), 115-27.

28. From *A briefe Commentarie of Hortulanus the Philosopher, upon the Smaragdine Table,* in *The Mirror of Alchimy,* 25. On Hortulanus (and his identification or association with John of Garland and Martinus Ortholanus) and problems in determining the authorship of the

briefe Commentarie, see Ferguson, *Bibliotheca Chemica*, 1:419-22, and my introduction to *The Mirror of Alchimy*, especially xvi-xx.

29. The reasons for Tymme's attribution of the theory of the tria prima to Hermes Trismegistus rather than to Paracelsus may be similar to those which Robert Bostocke had in mind when he made Hermes a champion of chemically prepared medicines. Referring to Bostocke's *Difference betwene the Auncient Phisick . . . and the latter Phisicke* (1585), Debus states that the author "considered it his primary aim to point out that iatrochemistry was actually the ancient medicine which after the fall of man had steadily deteriorated until it had reached the depraved state in which Galen offered it. The original chemical physicians were to be sought in a line of sages that ran from Adam through the sons of Seth, Abraham, Moses, Hermes Trismegistus, Thales, Democritus, Pythagoras, and even Hippocrates" (see *The English Paracelsians*, 58, also 96). The fact that Paracelsus's character and reputation were at best dubious in many quarters in England would provide additional reason for Tymme's avoidance of mentioning him by name even while appropriating his theories.

30. Tymme was, for a time, rector of Hasketon, near Woodbridge, in Suffolk; for his writings, see the *DNB*.

31. A handwritten note opposite the title page of the Huntington Library copy (R230461) identifies the translator tentatively as Robert Napier Esquire (or of Edinburgh).

32. R.N.E.'s Epistle Dedicatory to John Baptista Lambye, *A Revelation of the Secret Spirit* (London, 1623), sig. A3ᵛ.

33. Ibid., 3-5.

34. Lambye treats these topics in chapters 1 and 2, respectively. Generalizing extravagantly, he also asserts that the universal medicine "appears in four forms, corresponding to the elements" (6-8).

35. *Pseuchographia Anthropomagica: or, A Magicall Description of the Soul* (London, 1652), 6-9.

36. Scot, *Tillage of Light*, 3

37. Cf. the previously noted alchemical salamander in l. 23 of Donne's "Satire III. Religion."

38. Thorndike reports that the original French version, *Le livre des figures hiéroglyfiques de Nicolas Flamel* (Paris, 1612), was "concocted" by Arnaud de la Chevalerie early in the century and fathered upon Flamel (*HMES*, 7:165-66).

39. Accounts of Flamel's extremely romantic life and career, most of which are based on materials from the *Exposition*, are included in Holmyard, *Alchemy*, 239-49; Read, *Through Alchemy to Chemistry*, 47-54; Waite, *Alchemists through the Ages*, 95-118, and, most recently, in the introduction to *Nicolas Flamel: His Exposition of the Hieroglyphicall Figures (1624)*, ed. Laurinda Dixon, English Renaissance Hermeticism (New York and London: Garland Publishing, 1994), which I have cited throughout. Dixon concludes that Flamel was a real person who may have practiced alchemy and probably died in 1417; however, "his reputation as an author and immortal adept must be accepted as an invention of the seventeenth century" (xvii). Flamel's tombstone is on display at the Musée de Cluny in Paris. One evidence of his reputation in England is that the 1624 translation of the *Exposition* is quoted extensively in Thomas Vaughan's *Magia Adamica*, published in 1650. See *The Works of Thomas Vaughan*, ed. Alan Rudrum (Oxford: Clarendon Press, 1984), 182-84.

40. Holmyard, *Alchemy*, 244.

41. Waite, *Alchemists through the Ages*, 108-09.

42. On Hester's role in popularizing Paracelsian medicine in the late sixteenth century, see Debus, *The English Paracelsians*, 65-69, passim.

43. *The Secrets of Physick and Philosophy, Divided into Two Bookes: . . . First Written in the German Tongue by the most learned Theophrastus Paracelsus, and now published in the English Tongue, by John Hester* (London, 1633), 107-8.

44. *Paracelsus his Dispensatory and Chirurgery . . . Faithfully Englished, by W. D.* (London, 1656), "To the Reader."

45. *Philosophy Reformed & Improved in Four Profound Tractates. . . . Both made English by H. Pinnell* (London, 1657), 84-85.

46. Many examples of this poetry, along with introductions and commentary, are included in Robert M. Schuler, ed., *Alchemical Poetry 1575-1700: From Previously Unpublished Manuscripts*, English Renaissance Hermeticism (New York and London: Garland Publishing, 1995).

47. From the poem "Crollius," inserted following the translator's apology, in *Philosophy Reformed & Improved.*

48. John Ferguson, *Bibliographia Paracelsica* (Glasgow: James Maclehose, 1890), 31-49.

49. On this author, see Ferguson, *Bibliotheca Chemica*, 2:383-85.

50. Johann Ambrosius Siebmacher, *The Water-Stone of the Wise Men*, in *Paracelsus his Aurora, & Treasure of the Philosophers . . . Faithfully Englished, and published by J. H. Oxon.* (London, 1659), 89, 92.

51. *The Complete Poetry of Robert Herrick*, ed. J. Max Patrick (New York: Norton, 1968), 512; see also the reference to "tincture" in l. 8 of "To God," 490.

52. French's respect for and indebtedness to this influential Polish alchemist is more apparent in his translated edition of Sendivogius, *A New Light of Alchymy.* In the "Epistle to the Reader" by J. F., French emphasizes the need for reason as a guide to truth in religion and philosophy, warning that "Men therefore that lay aside Reason in the reading of sacred Mysteries, do but un-man themselves, and become further involved in a Labyrinth of errours." The result, he continues, with a seeming thrust at the nonconforming sects, is that "Religion is degenerated into irrational Notions." The antidote is for men to study the "most profound Sandivogius": "*if any one should ask me, What one Book did most conduce to the knowledg of God and the Creature, and the Mysteries thereof, I should speak contrary to my Judgment, if I should not, next to the Sacred Writ, say Sandivogius.*" That French's charge that religion has degenerated into "irrational Notions" is an attack on the dissenting sects might be challenged by the fact that he practiced medicine for the Parliamentary army, eventually serving under General Fairfax. French took his B.A. and M.A. at Oxford (1637, 1640) and was the author of a variety of medical and hermetic treatises. On French, see the entry in the *DNB* and Webster, *The Great Instauration,* 128.

53. French, preface to *The Art of Distillation.*

54. The somewhat more detailed description in Sendivogius's original follows: "Now those times are coming, in which many Secrets of Nature will be revealed. Now that fourth Monarchy of the North is about to begin: Now the times are at hand; the Mother of Sciences will come: greater things shall be discovered than hath been done in these three last past Monarchies. . . . For we have in this Northern part a most wise Prince, and most warlike, whom none of the Monarchs doth go beyond in Victories, or excell in Humanity and Piety. In this Northern Monarchy God the maker of all things will, without doubt, bring to light greater Secrets in Nature than in those times, when Pagan and Tyrant Princes reigned. . . . In this Northern Monarchy, . . . Mercy and Truth are met together; Peace and Justice shall kiss each other: Truth shall rise out of the earth, and Justice shall look from Heaven. One Sheepfold and one Shepherd. Many Arts without Envy: All which I do earnestly expect" (80-81).

55. Eyraeneus Philaletha [Eirenaeus Philalethes], *Secrets Reveal'd: Or, An Open Entrance to the Shut Palace of the King* (London, 1669), 10. On this work and the identity of its author,

see Newman's "Prophecy and Alchemy" and *Gehennical Fire;* and R.A. Wilkinson, "The Problem of the Identity of Eirenaeus Philalethes," *Ambix* 12 (Feb. 1964): 24-43; on Philaletha's many writings and their popularity, see appendix 2, "William Cooper and the Works of Eirenaeus Philalethes," of my *William Cooper's A Catalogue of Chymicall Books,* 149-54.

56. Philaletha, *Secrets Reveal'd,* 7. This passage reads: "Our *Chalybs* . . . [is] the Miracle of the World, a Systeme of the superior virtues in the inferiors; and therefore the Omnipotent hath marked it with that notable Sign, whose Nativity is declared in the East. The Wisemen saw it in the East and were amazed, presently knew that a most Serene King was born into the World. Thou when thou beholdest his Star, follow him even to his Cradle, there shalt thou see a fair Infant by removing the defilements, honour the Kingly Child, open the Treasury, offer the gift of Gold, so at length (after death) he will give thee his Flesh and Blood, the highest Medicine in the three Monarchies of the Earth."

57. [W]illiam [C]ooper, *A Philosophicall Epitaph in Hierogliphicall Figures* (London, 1673), 10.

58. From Cooper's dedicatory remarks to his translation of Helvetius, i.e., "The Epistle of W.C. to the Reader"; this section of the *Philosophicall Epitaph* contains additional evidence of Cooper's keen interest in the Elias figure. He uses this sobriquet to identify the pseudonymous Eirenaeus Philalethes, "a most rare Anonymon (probably yet living) who like a miracle of nature, attained the *Elixir* at 23 years of Age, 1645. And as a true *Elias* (or fore-runner) hath taught the same, in his Book Entitled, *Secrets Revealed, or an open entrance to the shut Pallace of the King.*" The Helvetius section also includes a dialogue between "Elias the Artist, and the Physitian," in which the former is reputed to possess the power to reveal the secret of the stone to select individuals.

59. *The Works of the Highly Experienced and Famous Chymist, John Rudolph Glauber . . . Translated into English* (London, 1689), 51, 52. On the Jewish and Christian mystical tradition of the return of Elias as a foreshadowing of Christ's Second Coming, and its influence on Renaissance utopian, Rosicrucian, alchemical, and scientific thought, see Breger, "Elias Artista."

60. *Aurifontina Chymica,* sig. A3.

61. Mystagogus, *Mercury's Caducean Rod,* 24.

Chapter 8. Alchemy in the Works of Vaughan and Milton

1. *The Works of Sir Thomas Browne,* ed. Geoffrey Keynes, 4 vols. (Chicago: Univ. of Chicago Press, 1964), 1:50.

2. *Henry Vaughan and the Hermetic Philosophy* (Oxford: Basil Blackwell, 1932).

3. All subsequent references to Vaughan's poetry and prose are to L.C. Martin, ed., *The Works of Henry Vaughan,* 2d ed. (Oxford: Clarendon Press, 1963). Parallels between many of Vaughan's poetic ideas and images and passages from the *Hermetica* (Brian P. Copenhaver, ed. and trans., *Hermetica: The Greek "Corpus Hermeticum" and the Latin "Asclepius" in a new English translation* [Cambridge: Cambridge Univ. Press, 1992]) are also set forth in L.C. Martin's "Henry Vaughan and 'Hermes Trismegistus,'" *RES* 18 (1942): 301-7. Valuable later discussions that assume Vaughan's indebtedness to the *Hermetica* appear in M.M. Mahood, *Poetry and Humanism* (New York: Norton, 1970), 252-95, and Patrick Grant, *The Transformation of Sin* (Montreal and London: McGill-Queens Univ. Press, 1974), 134-69.

4. "Henry Vaughan and the Alchemists," *RES* 23 (1947): 107-22.

5. "The Influence of Alchemy in the Poems of Henry Vaughan," *PQ* 49 (1970): 469-80.

6. Rudrum, "The Influence of Alchemy," 479.

7. "The Private Imagery of Henry Vaughan," *RES,* n.s., 1 (1950): 214.

8. *Henry Vaughan: Experience and the Tradition* (Chicago: Univ. of Chicago Press, 1959), 62.

9. Garner states: "It seems clear, then, that 'Resurrection and Immortality' is not a Hermetic poem with a Christian twist but a Christian poem in which Christian dogma is experienced as an analogy to a natural process" (89).

10. Garner, *Experience and the Tradition*, 135.

11. R.A. Durr, *On the Mystical Poetry of Henry Vaughan* (Cambridge: Harvard Univ. Press, 1962), 24-25. It should be noted that in emphasizing mysticism—"the Christian life of prayer" (xi)—as the major informing context for Vaughan's poetry, Durr reduces the explicit influence of hermetic thought: Vaughan "was familiar with hermetical doctrine and symbol, to be sure, but most likely regarded them as only an eddy in the main stream of Christian mysticism" (15).

12. *Of Paradise and Light* (Cambridge: Cambridge Univ. Press, 1960), 72.

13. *Masques of God: Form and Theme in the Poetry of Henry Vaughan* (Pittsburgh: Univ. of Pittsburgh Press, 1972), 19. Similarly, in Jonathan F.S. Post's *Henry Vaughan: The Unfolding Vision* (Princeton: Princeton Univ. Press, 1982), the influence of hermeticism would appear to be denied altogether.

14. *Henry Vaughan: The Achievement of Silex Scintillans* (Newark, Del.: Univ. of Delaware Press, 1981), 109.

15. Calhoun, *The Achievement of Silex Scintillans*, 128.

16. Calhoun cites only the authors and sources referred to in Vaughan's translations of Henry Nollius, i.e., Paracelsus, Oswald Croll, and Quersetanus.

17. Unless otherwise noted, all quotations from the *Corpus Hermeticum* are taken from Copenhaver, *Hermetica*. The passage reads: "Since it is the visual ray itself, the sun shines all around the cosmos with the utmost brilliance, ... the sun enlivens and awakens, with becoming and change, the things that live in these regions of the cosmos. It brings transmutation and transformation among them, as in a spiral, when change turns one thing to another, from kind to kind, from form to form, ... For the permanence of every body is change:" *Corpus Hermeticum*, 16:[7]-[9], 59.

18. Robert Fludd, *Mosaicall Philosophy: Grounded upon the Essentiall Truth or Eternal Sapience* (London, 1659), from the address "To the Judicious and Discreet Reader."

19. See my article, "Herbert and the Unveiling of Diana."

20. See the compilation of these passages in the notes to the Martin (729-30) and Rudrum (534-36) editions. This stanza and, to a lesser degree, the one following, makes untenable Garner's statement that this "is not a Hermetic poem with a Christian twist but a Christian poem in which Christian dogma is experienced as an analogy to a natural process" (*Experience and the Tradition*, 89).

21. Martin, *Works*, 573.

22. Copenhaver, *Hermetica*, 25.

23. Copenhaver, *Hermetica*, Libellus 8.[1], 25.

24. The passage reads: "The recurrence of earthly bodies, by contrast, is {the dissolution} of their composition, and this dissolution causes them to recur as undissolved bodies—immortal, in other words. Thus arises a loss of awareness but not a destruction of bodies" (Copenhaver, *Hermetica*, Libellus 8.[4], 26.

25. "[W]e humans see the things that are in heaven as if through a mist, to the extent that we can, given the condition of human consciousness. When it comes to seeing great things, our concentration is quite confined, but once it has seen, the happiness of our awareness is vast" (Copenhaver, *Hermetica*, *Asclepius* [32], 87).

26. Cf. "Consider this for yourself: command your soul to travel to India, and it will be

there faster than your command. Command it to cross over to the ocean, and again it will quickly be there, not as having passed from place to place but simply as being there. Command it even to fly up to heaven, and it will not lack wings. . . . But if you wish to break through the universe itself and look upon the things outside . . . it is within your power" (Copenhaver, *Hermetica*, Libellus 11.[19], 41).

27. A valuable survey of this topos is included in Gordon W. O'Brien, "Milton, Hermes, and the Rhetoric of Mental Flight," *CaudaP* 7:1 (spring 1988): 1-8. Although Vaughan's poem is not discussed, I am indebted to this article for other examples.

28. Martin, *Works*, 195-96.

29. Copenhaver, *Hermetica*, Libellus 13.[3], [6], 49-50. Copenhaver uses { } to indicate "a word or words regarded as unintelligible or otherwise problematic."

30. See Martin, *Works*, 746n.

31. "Vaughan's 'Cock-crowing' and the Tradition," *ELH* 21 (1954): 94-106.

32. Allen, "Vaughan's 'Cock-crowing,'" 99.

33. See Durr, *On the Mystical Poetry of Henry Vaughan*, 32-33, and especially appendix A, "The Idea of the Divine Spark, or Seed," 125-30, where the Christian tradition of synteresis is traced.

34. See, for example, Plotinus's summary in *Ennead* 8, 6: "Thus, in sum, the soul, a divine being and a dweller in the loftier realms, has entered body; it is a god, a later phase of the divine," from *Plotinus, The Six Enneads,* trans. Stephen MacKenna and B.S. Page (Chicago: Encyclopaedia Britannica, 1952), 203. In the *Hermetica*, Hermes appeals to Tat to pray to God "to permit even one ray of his to illuminate your thinking" (Libellus 5.[2], 18); or "Few seeds come from god, but they are potent and beautiful and good—virtue, moderation and reverence" (Libellus 9.[4], 28).

35. On the role of images of sparks and seeds in Stoic thought, see Maryanne C. Horowitz, "The Stoic Synthesis of the Idea of Natural Law in Man: Four Themes," *JHI* 35 (Jan.-March 1974): 3-16, and especially 14-16. The influence of these images in French Renaissance thought is also discussed in Horowitz's "Natural Law as the Foundation for an Autonomous Ethic: Pierre Charron's *De la Sagesse,*" *Studies in the Renaissance* 21 (1974): 208-9.

36. Henry Vaughan's position on the concern that God exercises over the lower creatures is paralleled in the following passage from Thomas Vaughan's *Anima Magica Abscondita:* "For though his [God's] full-ey'd love shines on nothing but Man, yet everything in the world is in some measure directed for his preservation by a spice or touch of the first intellect" (*Henry Vaughan: The Complete Poems,* ed. Alan Rudrum [New Haven: Yale Univ. Press, 1976], 597n).

37. I agree with Rudrum's interpretation that the primary meaning of veil in this passage is "body"; see *Henry Vaughan: The Complete Poems,* 599n. Especially valuable is Mahood's discussion of this passage in *Poetry and Humanism,* 261-65; Mahood sees the veil as a symbol, not for the flesh alone, "but the whole fabric of the physical world [that] impedes the 'love-sick souls exalted flight'" (263).

38. Copenhaver, *Hermetica, Asclepius* 3.[32], 87.

39. From "To Amoret gone from him," ll. 19-20, in Martin, *Works,* 8.

40. From the untitled poem beginning "Sure, there's a tye of Bodyes!" in Martin, *Works,* 429.

41. For discussion of the role of "magnetism" in this poem and others, see Alan Rudrum, "An Aspect of Vaughan's Hermeticism: The Doctrine of Cosmic Sympathy," *SEL* 14 (winter 1974): 130-38, especially 135-36.

42. On the causes of the star's attraction to particular terrestrial objects, the following passage from Thomas Vaughan's *Magia Adamica* is illuminating: "Every thing therefore hath its Character pressed upon it by its Star for some peculiar effect, especially by that Star which

doth principally govern it: And these Characters contain, and retain in them the peculiar natures, vertues, and roots of their Stars, and produce the like operations upon other things, on which they are reflected" (Holmes, *Henry Vaughan and the Hermetic Philosophy,* 39).

43. On imagery of seeds and plants in Vaughan's poetry, see Durr, *On the Mystical Poetry of Henry Vaughan,* 29-53 especially, which presents an outline of major imagistic patterns in "Disorder *and* frailty" but little sustained analysis.

44. On Stobaeus's editing of these fragments, see the introduction to Walter Scott, ed. and trans., *Hermetica: The Ancient Greek and Latin Writings Which Contain Religious or Philosophic Teachings Ascribed to Hermes Trismegistus,* 4 vols. (Oxford: Clarendon Press, 1924-36; reprint, Boston: Shambhala, 1985), 1:82-86.

45. Scott, *Hermetica,* excerpt 6, sec. 15, 1:417.

46. From "The Smaragdine Table of Hermes Trismegistus of Alchimy," in Linden, *The Mirror of Alchimy,* 16.

47. Fludd, *Mosaicall Philosophy,* 7.

48. Copenhaver, *Hermetica,* Libellus 3.[1]-[2], 13. Copenhaver uses [ ] to indicate "removal of a word or words." Rudrum cites the following passage from Thomas Vaughan's *Magia Adamica* as apposite to the lines from "I walkt the other day": "*Hermes* affirmeth, that in the *Beginning* the Earth was a *Quakemire,* or quivering kind of *Jelly,* it being nothing els but *water congealed* by the *Incubation,* and heat of the *Divine spirit;* . . . When as yet the *Earth* was a *quivering, shaking substance,* the *Sun* afterwards *shining* upon it, did *compact* it, or make it *Solid*" (Rudrum, *Works of Thomas Vaughan,* 147).

49. Fludd, *Mosaicall Philosophy,* 58.

50. Fludd, *Mosaicall Philosophy,* 58.

51. Fairly representative of critical opinion on the shaping of "The Water-fall" is Simmonds' view that it is "an artificially constructed emblem representing temporal life, death, resurrection, and immortality" (*Masques of God,* 17-18).

52. Cf. the following passage from the *Magia Adamica:* "The *Holy Spirit* moving upon the *Chaos,* which *Action* some *Divines* compare to the *Incubation* of a *Hen* upon her *Eggs,* did together with his *Heat* communicat other *manifold Influences* to the *Matter;* For as wee know the *Sun* doth not onely dispense *heat,* but som other *secret Influx;* so did God also in the *Creation*" (Rudrum, *Works of Thomas Vaughan,* 148). Pettet, in *Of Paradise and Light,* 74, cites as an analogue to these lines Sir Thomas Browne's reference to "that gentle heat that brooded on the waters and in six days hatched the world" (*Religio Medici,* xxxii). On the complexities of meaning of the metaphor of the water-cycle in this poem and others, see Donald R. Dickson, *The Fountain of Living Waters: The Typology of the Waters of Life in Herbert, Vaughan, and Traherne* (Columbia: Univ. of Missouri Press, 1987), especially 160-65.

53. Mahood, *Poetry and Humanism,* 259.

54. The major exceptions are Rudrum and Calhoun, both of whom make distinctions between hermeticism and alchemy largely in accordance with a "practical"/"philosophical" opposition, or, in Calhoun's case, according to the theory and practice of Paracelsian medicine. See especially Calhoun, *The Achievement of Silex Scintillans,* 128-35, and Rudrum "The Influence of Alchemy," 469-71.

55. This resemblance is noted in Rudrum, *Henry Vaughan: The Complete Poems,* 536n.

56. Ruland, *Lexicon of Alchemy,* 137.

57. Ruland, *Lexicon of Alchemy,* 88.

58. See entries in Ruland, *Lexicon of Alchemy,* 69, 217.

59. On Nollius, see Ferguson, *Bibliotheca Chemica,* 2:140.

60. Martin, *Works,* 549-50.

61. Martin, *Works,* 551, 558, 562, 564, 580.

62. From Vaughan's translation of Henry Nollius's *Hermetical Physick*, in Martin, *Works*, 581; also quoted in Calhoun, *The Achievement of Silex Scintillans*, 128.

63. Calhoun, *The Achievement of Silex Scintillans*, 128.

64. Martin, *Works*, 592; this metaphor also appears again on 578 but is implicit throughout much of Nollius's work.

65. Martin, *Works*, 578.

66. While Vaughan's medical imagery is derived most often from the tradition of chemical cures, occasionally there are slight allusions to the medicinal properties of plants and flowers. For example, "Childe-hood" states "But flowers do both refresh and grace, / And sweetly living (*fie on men!*) / Are when dead, medicinal then" (ll. 14-16). Related images appear in the later version of "Death" (ll. 21-25), and "Misery" (ll. 49-51), in which God appears as a physician dispensing "healing sweets" into the sinner's wounds. It must be remembered, however, that the medicinal use of herbs and plants is not alone sufficient to make a physician a "Galenist" in the seventeenth century; Nollius, for example, observes that "the true Hermetical Physicians, do not at all times administer Minerals; but most commonly when they exhibite Minerals, they make use also of Medicines extracted out of Vegetables, or to quicken the operation of these latter, they give a competent and safe quantity of the former" (*Hermetical Physick*, in Martin, *Works*, 582).

67. On this topic, see my "Alchemy and Eschatology in Seventeenth-Century Poetry." For a more general discussion of Vaughan's eschatological poems, see John N. Wall, *Transformations of the Word: Spenser, Herbert, Vaughan* (Athens and London: Univ. of Georgia Press, 1988), 335-37; for "White Sunday," 351-53.

68. Pettet, *Of Paradise and Light*, 76-77.

69. Typical of this earlier approach, though still useful, are Kester Svendsen, *Milton and Science* (Cambridge: Harvard Univ. Press, 1956), 123-27, which treats *Paradise Lost*, 3:593-612, in metaphoric terms derived from references to alchemical processes and the "Arch-chemic Sun"; and Walter Clyde Curry, *Milton's Ontology, Cosmogony, and Physics* (Lexington: Univ. of Kentucky Press, 1966), which explicates the same passage in terms of traditional alchemical sources, 124-31, 137-43. For relevant scientific background to many of Milton's references to metals and minerals (including his use of alchemical lore), see Edgar Hill Duncan, "The Natural History of Metals and Minerals in the Universe of Milton's *Paradise Lost*," *Osiris*, 11 (1954): 386-421. Among more recent studies that depart from the history of science approach, Michael Lieb's valuable appendix, "Creation & Alchemy," to *The Dialectics of Creation: Patterns of Birth and Regeneration in "Paradise Lost"* (Amherst: Univ. of Massachusetts Press, 1970) "attempts to suggest the presence of alchemy in the universe of *Paradise Lost* and to show how alchemy is intimately related to the creational dimension of the poem" (229). The rather brief glances at alchemy and hermeticism in "Il Penseroso" and *Comus* have been interpreted politically, as Milton's views on monarchical government, in Douglas Brooks-Davies, *The Mercurian Monarch*, 124-49. Lee A. Jacobus gives slight attention to alchemy under the more general heading of thaumaturgy, "the science of wonder-working," concluding that Milton's thinking on this topic was usually more closely aligned to John Dee than to Francis Bacon; see *Sudden Apprehension: Aspects of Knowledge in "Paradise Lost"* (The Hague: Mouton, 1976), 70-78. Alchemy also receives brief mention in Stephen M. Fallon, *Milton among the Philosophers* (Ithaca and London: Cornell Univ. Press, 1991), 113-15, and in Harinder Singh Marjara, *Contemplation of Created Things: Science in Paradise Lost* (Toronto: Univ. of Toronto Press, 1992).

70. Fallon, *Milton among the Philosophers*, 115.

71. See Brooks-Davies, *The Mercurian Monarch*, 124, 138. While I agree that these companion poems should be read as a progression and that Milton privileges the "private contemplative idea" of "Il Penseroso" over the physical pleasures of "L'Allegro," it is nonetheless too

much to characterize "L'Allegro" as depicting a "corrupt court." Brooks-Davies sees alchemical possibilities in *Comus* primarily through the mysterious plant haemony that the Shepherd Lad receives from the Attendant Spirit (l. 618ff.)

72. In *Complete Prose Works of John Milton*, ed. Don M. Wolfe, 7 vols. (New Haven and London: Yale Univ. Press, 1953), 1:885. All references to Milton's prose are to this edition. For the poetry, I have used *John Milton: Complete Poems and Major Prose*.

73. Svendsen, *Milton and Science*, 124.

74. See *The Dialectics of Creation*, 230-44, esp. 230. In *Milton and Science*, Svendsen anticipated certain of the main lines of Lieb's argument: "The cosmological supremacy of the lordly sun, endlessly repeated in the poem, establishes it as a symbol of one kind of perfection in the world; . . . The failure of the philosophers to create the elixir is like Satan's failure" (126).

75. On the relevant scientific background for this passage and other mineralogical references, see Duncan's excellent article, "The Natural History of Metals and Minerals."

76. For Duncan's gloss on the following passage and his discussion of the sulphur-mercury theory in *Paradise Lost*, see especially 391-95, 400-401; Milton again draws upon theories of the origin of metals in *Paradise Lost* 6:477-81, 509-17.

77. Duncan, "The Natural History of Metals and Minerals," 403-4.

78. On the musical implications of alchemy, see Read, *Through Alchemy to Chemistry*, 68-73; and for connections among music, the divine, and alchemical ritual in myth and primitive society, see Mircea Eliade, *The Forge and the Crucible*, trans. Stephen Corrin (New York: Harper, 1962), 98-99.

79. *Of the Vanitie and uncertaintie of Artes and Sciences, Englished by Ja[mes] San[dford] Gent.* (London, 1569), 159.

80. For example, three versions of the *Cantilena Georgii Riplaei* are included in the Bodleian Library Ashmolean MS 1445: a Latin text with an English translation by Sir George Wharton (ff. 2b-12a) and an earlier translation, ff. 41-44. A printed version appeared in Ripley's *Opera omni chemica* (Cassellis, 1649), 421-26.

81. Quoted in Read, *Through Alchemy to Chemistry*, 71.

82. See also *Paradise Lost* 1:670-74, 5:300-302, and 6:472-83; and Duncan's commentary in "The Natural History of Metals and Minerals," 412-19, which suggests similarities to Robert Fludd's interpretation of the Creation.

83. D.P. Harding in *Milton and the Renaissance Ovid* identifies Milton's Carbuncle with Ovid's *pyropus* (90), as cited in *Complete Poems and Major Prose*, 273n. For discussion of other aspects of this passage, see Duncan, "The Natural History of Metals and Minerals," 413-15; Svendsen, *Milton and Science*, 123-27; and Lieb, *Dialectics of Creation*, 230-31.

84. Lieb, *Dialectics of Creation*, 230-31.

85. See Lev. 8:8; Num. 27:21; Deut. 33:8; 1 Sam. 28:6; Ezra 2:63; Neh. 7:65.

86. *The Interpreter's Bible*, 12 vols. (Nashville: Abingdon, 1980), 1:1042, which adds that it is "most probable that they were only names given to signify the clearness and certainty of the divine answers which were obtained by the high priest consulting God with his breastplate on, in contradistinction to the obscure, enigmatical, uncertain, and imperfect answers of the heathen oracles." On nonalchemical nuances in Milton's usage, see Linda Weinhouse, "The Urim and Thummim in *Paradise Lost*," *Milton Quarterly* 11:1 (March 1977): 9-12.

87. See Webster, *The Great Instauration*, 281, 304-5, for information on this collection.

88. However, in the notes to his edition of *Paradise Lost* (London and New York: Longman, 1971), Alastair Fowler states that the connection was made by "many" alchemical authors, among them Joachim Tancke (180n).

89. Milton retains the association with brilliant light in book 6 as Christ, mounted in the

"Chariot of Paternal Deity," prepares to do battle against the rebellious angels on the third day of the heavenly war: "Hee in Celestial Panoply all arm'd / Of radiant *Urim*, work divinely wrought" (ll. 760-61).

90. I disagree with Duncan, who regards Proteus as one of the "proximate material[s] of the philosopher's stone or transmuting elixir" (405). Curry, in *Milton's Ontology, Cosmology, and Physics,* also identifies Proteus with the "parent" sulphur (128-29). However, according to Francis Bacon in *The Wisdom of the Ancients,* 13 (6:725-26), and other works in the mythographic tradition, Proteus was associated with matter, the "one first matter" of the ontological passage in *Paradise Lost* 5:472. Noting the absence of references to Proteus in alchemical treatises, A.B. Chambers argues that Milton's identification of Proteus with prime matter is based on mythographic sources instead; see his "Milton's Proteus and Satan's Visit to the Sun," *JEGP* 62 (1963): 280-87. Although probably correct, Chambers's argument does not satisfactorily explain why Proteus has been used in this distinctly alchemical context. On Milton's Hermes and Proteus, see also Fowler, *Paradise Lost,* 181n.

91. Svendsen, *Milton and Science,* 127.

92. Parts of the discussion of this passage appeared in my article "'By gradual scale sublim'd': Jean d'Espagnet and the Ontological Tree in *Paradise Lost,* Book V," *JHI* 52:4 (Oct.-Dec. 1991): 603-15. Thorndike reports that Espagnet's *Enchyridion Physicae Restitutae* was first published in Paris in Latin in 1623; second and third editions appeared in 1638, and others followed in 1642, 1647, 1653, and 1702 (see *HMES,* 7:389).

93. In *Reason of Church Government,* Milton states that the angels, as described by the apostle John (Rev. 8-9), "are distinguisht and quaterniond into their celestiall Princedomes, and Satrapies, according as God himselfe hath writ his imperiall decrees through the great provinces of heav'n. The state also of the blessed in Paradise, though never so perfect, is not therefore left without discipline" (Wolfe, *Complete Prose,* 1:752).

94. The Renaissance view of a close and unbroken ordering of the scale of nature, which is, in part, the foundation for Milton's meliorism, is discussed at some length in C.A. Patrides, *Milton and the Christian Tradition* (Oxford: Clarendon Press, 1966), 60-68; however, Patrides notes only that Milton acknowledges the existence of "orders" and "degrees" in heaven (64). More to the point of my discussion, Lovejoy in *The Great Chain of Being* states that "the graded series of creatures down which the divine life in its overflow had descended might be conceived to constitute also the stages of man's ascent to the divine life in its self-contained completeness" (89).

95. On the relationship among motion, multiplicity, and the theme of praise in the morning hymn, see chapter 3 in Joseph H. Summers, *The Muse's Method* (Cambridge: Harvard Univ. Press, 1962). In his valuable discussion of Neoplatonic resonances in *Paradise Lost* 5:469-84, William G. Madsen (*From Shadowy Types to Truth* [New Haven and London: Yale Univ. Press, 1968]) notes that "Some words suggest that the scale of nature is dynamic . . . but at the same time it appears to be static" (120). Madsen does not suggest, however, what I think to be the case: that within the entire scale of creation, dynamism is largely confined to the terrestrial world and its interaction with the celestial; the positions of the celestial beings within their proper sphere is much more rigid.

96. Martin, *Works,* 582.

97. See Madsen, *From Shadowy Types to Truth,* 113-24.

98. Important discussions of possible sources of this image appear in Svendsen, *Milton and Science,* 114-15, where a similar tree image from Mercator's *Historia Mundi* is discussed; in Curry, *Milton's Ontology, Cosmology, and Physics,* chap. 7, especially 167-71, 223n, where a source in Duns Scotus is proposed; and William Brennan, "Robert Fludd as a Possible Source for *Paradise Lost,* V.469-470," *Milton Quarterly* 15 (1981): 95-97, where, expanding on ideas

proposed by Denis Saurat, a motto and engraving from Fludd's *Monochordum mundi* are suggested sources for the opening "Neoplatonic" movement of the Creator in Milton's passage. In "'By gradual scale sublim'd,'" I have traced the tree image to a similar one in Espagnet's *Enchyridion Physicae Restitutae*. Drawing on both biblical iconography and Neoplatonic thought, Jonathan Goldberg's "Virga Iesse: Analogy, Typology, and Anagogy in a Miltonic Simile," *Milton Studies* 5 (1973): 177-90, also contains valuable commentary.

99. Christopher Hill has termed Milton a "radical millenarian" and argues for the presence of other occult and hermetic connections in sketching the poet's background of political and religious radicalism; see *Milton and the English Revolution,* 106 and passim.

100. That Milton also sees the life of the individual Christian as subject to a process analogous to alchemical purification is shown in God the Father's disquisition to the Son at the time the expulsion is announced. Using images no doubt indebted to Malachi 3:2-3 as well as alchemical tradition, God speaks of man's attainment of eternal life following a mortal life "Tri'd in sharp tribulation, and refin'd / By Faith and faithful works" (11:63-64). Cf. Milton's use of medical imagery to suggest how books serve as "usefull drugs," "effective and strong med'cins," and "working mineralls," which are necessary correctives in the moral life of man in *Areopagitica* (Wolfe, *Complete Prose,* 2:521).

101. For a fuller explication of this engraving, see M.K. Corbett, "Ashmole and the Pursuit of Alchemy: The Illustrations to the *TCB,* 1652," *Antiquaries Journal* 63 (1983), 326-36. Corbett identifies the judge as Hermes Trismegistus on the basis of his Eastern-style cap and robe decorated with the pentagol, "seal of Solomon and symbol of wisdom"; the winged figures placed along the sides of the cresent are famous alchemists (333).

102. Yates, *Giordano Bruno and the Hermetic Tradition,* 398.

103. Brooks-Davies notes that "*Penseroso* here envisages himself enjoying demonic illumination under the power of a melancholic frenzy" (*Mercurian Monarch,* 130). Also relevant is the ancient topos of "mental flight" delineated by O'Brien in "Milton, Hermes, and the Rhetoric of Mental Flight" (6).

104. Brooks-Davies, *Mercurian Monarch,* 124.

Chapter 9. Alchemy, Poetry, and the Restoration Revolt against Enthusiasm

1. Joseph Glanvill, *Philosophia Pia; or A Discourse, of the Religious Temper, and Tendencies of the Experimental Philosophy* (London, 1671), 56-57. For Henry More, "*Enthusiasme* is nothing else but a misconceit of being *inspired.* Now to be *inspired* is, *to be moved in an extraordinary manner by the power or Spirit of God to act, speak, or think what is holy, just and true.* From hence it will be easily understood what *Enthusiasm* is, viz. *A full, but false, perswasion in a man that he is inspired*" (*Enthusiasmus Triumphatus,* in *A Collection of Several Philosophical Writings of Dr. Henry More,* 2d ed., vol. 1 (London, 1662; reprint, New York: Garland, 1978), 2. All references are to this edition.

2. More, *Collection,* 1:29.

3. Citing John Ferguson, "Some English Alchemical Books," Keith Thomas has stated that "more books on alchemy were published in England between 1650 and 1680 than before or afterwards" (*Religion and the Decline of Magic,* 227).

4. See Mendelsohn, "Alchemy and Politics in England 1649-1665."

5. From *The Anatomy of Melancholy,* ed. Thomas C. Faulkner, Nicolas K. Kiessling, Rhonda L. Blair, vol. 3 (Oxford: Clarendon Press, 1994), pt. 3., sec. 4, memb. 1, subsec. 1, pp. 330-31. All references are to this edition.

6. *Anatomy,* vol. 3, pt. 3, sec. 4, memb. 1, subsec. 1, p. 331.

7. The idea of enthusiasm as a kind of degenerate religious experience, common to all of these writers, is reflected in the title of Casaubon's work from which this definition is drawn: *A Treatise concerning Enthusiasme, As it is an Effect of Nature: but is mistaken by many for either Divine Inspiration, or Diabolical Possession* (London, 1654), 13.

8. On the importance of Latitudinarian thought in the quarrel between Henry More and Thomas Vaughan, see Frederic B. Burnham, "The More-Vaughan Controversy: The Revolt Against Philosophical Enthusiasm," *JHI* 35 (Jan.-March 1974): 33-49; see also Margaret Jacob, "Millenarianism and Science in the Late Seventeenth Century," *JHI* 37 (1976): 335-41.

9. More, *Collection*, 1:4. More emphasizes the involuntary nature of the imagination, which is often beyond the soul's power to control. For example, in a passage that serves as an excellent gloss on Adam's discussion of faculty psychology following Eve's troubling dream ("But know that in the Soul / Are many lesser Faculties" [*Paradise Lost,* 5:100-113]), he notes: "For what are *Dreams* but the Imaginations and Perceptions of one asleep? which notwithstanding steal upon the Soul, or rise out of her without any consent of hers; as is most manifest in such as torment us, and put us to extreme pain till we awake out of them" (1:3).

10. On the publication history of Paracelsus in England, especially the period 1650-74 which saw thirteen editions, see Ferguson, *Bibliographia Paracelsica,* part 3. Excellent evidence of the popularity of Paracelsus's writings in seventeenth-century England is present in *John Dee's Library Catalogue,* ed. Julian Roberts and Andrew G. Watson (London: Bibliographical Society, 1990), esp. appendix 5.

11. An indication of Boehme's popularity in England in the later seventeenth century is the occurrence of thirty-nine entries for his works in Wing's *Short-Title Catalogue, 1641-1700,* 2d ed. Casaubon's contemporary William Cooper includes four titles (entries 35-38), all dating from the 1650s, in his *Catalogue of Chymicall Books* and two additional titles in the supplementary lists that appeared in books he published.

12. From the preface to *Forty Questions of the Soul . . . Englished by John Sparrow* (London, 1665), sig. A3ᵛ.

13. Boehme, *Forty Questions,* sig. [A5].

14. Boehme, *Forty Questions,* sigs. [A8ᵛ-A9].

15. *Plus Ultra: Or, The Progress and Advancement of Knowledge Since the Days of Aristotle* (London, 1668), 11.

16. *Plus Ultra,* 10-12.

17. Thomas, *Religion and the Decline of Magic,* 227. However, for a challenge to this view, see Mendelsohn, "Alchemy and Politics in England 1649-1665," which demonstrates that some Royalist politicians were keenly interested in alchemy after the Restoration.

18. *A Free and Impartial Censure of the Platonick Philosophie, Being a Letter Written to his much Honoured Friend Mr. N. B.* (Oxford, 1666), 46-47. All references are to this edition. For an account of the author's life and works, see the *DNB*.

19. Ormsby-Lennon's valuable analysis of contrasting language and linguistic theories among midcentury scientists, Latitudinarians, Platonists, and hermeticists appears in "Rosicrucian Linguistics: Twilight of a Renaissance Tradition," in Merkel and Debus, *Hermeticism and the Renaissance,* 311-41.

20. From the *History of the Royal Society of London,* in *Critical Essays of the Seventeenth Century,* ed. J.E. Spingarn, 3 vols. (Oxford: Clarendon Press, 1907; reprint, Bloomington: Indiana Univ. Press, 1957), 2:118.

21. Or again, on the idea of forbidden knowledge and human arrogance, Parker states, "For Curiosity it self is a gallant and heroical Quality, and the natural Product of a Generous

Complexion, but when it aspires after the knowledge of things placed above its Reach, it degenerates into a vain and fruitless Ambition, or rather an unnatural lust of the mind after strange and extravagant Notions" (78).

22. In this section, Parker frequently devalues poetry because of its creation by a "bold and ungovern'd Imagination" (73), which seeks to cheat the rational faculty.

23. See Vickers, "On the Function of Analogy in the Occult."

24. Parker's attack on the seduction of the reason by a fancy stimulated by empty rhetoric, ironically metaphorical in its own right, is again reminiscent of Adam's summary of Renaissance faculty psychology as he explains the cause of Eve's dream in *Paradise Lost,* 5:100-113; Parker states: "Thus their wanton & luxuriant fancies climbing up into the Bed of Reason, do not only defile it by unchast and illegitimate Embraces, but instead of real conceptions and notices of Things, impregnate the mind with nothing but Ayerie and Subventaneous Phantasmes" (76).

25. Writing at about the same time, John Wilkins, in *An Essay towards a Real Character and a Philosophical Language* (London, 1668), is more charitable toward the purpose for which hieroglyphics were originally used: i.e., "to conceal from the vulgar the Mysteries of their Religion" (12). Kircher's *Oedipus Ægyptiacus. Hoc est Universalis Hieroglyphicæ Veterum* was published in Rome in four enormous folios in 1652-54. Its lavish illustrations, tables, emblems, cabalistic diagrams, maps, and passages in remote languages (e.g., Chinese, Arabic) would no doubt have fueled Parker's disdain for the arcane and exotic.

26. George Castle, *The Chymical Galenist: A Treatise Wherein The Practise of the Ancients is reconcil'd to the new Discoveries in the Theory of Physick* (London, 1667). From the Epistle Dedicatory to Dr. Thomas Millington, sig. [A6].

27. On Nedham's life, see Joseph Frank, *Cromwell's Press Agent: A Critical Biography of Marchamont Nedham* (Lanham, Md.: Univ. Press of America, 1980).

28. Walter Harris, *Pharmacologia Anti-Empirica: or a Rational Discourse of Remedies Both Chymical and Galenical* (London, 1683), sig. [A8]. Later, Harris announces one of his purposes as "to give a check to all malapert Pretenders, and to vindicate *Natural Remedies,* that are very good as Nature provides them, from being swallowed up, or over-powred with a *Scenical Parade,* as if nothing were good for any thing that had not undergone the *Test* of *Chymical Preparation*" (5).

29. See, for example, his use of extended military metaphor in chapter 1, entitled "*The Wars between* Chymists, *and* Galenists, *very fierce for some time; but end at last in a Peace*" (1).

30. Harris elaborates his criticism of "chymists'" style in chapter 5, noting that "It has been a general humour with *Chymists,* to affect hard and strained Words, to deliver themselves with a *Mysterious Obscurity,* to turn every thing almost into *Arcana,* and when they do bring them forth, after much Labour and Travel, the World is hardly big enough to contain them; . . . But this I have often observ'd, that the more Precious and Thundring a Name is bestowed on the *Preparation,* commonly the more *Dangerous* and Dreadful it is in reality" (38-39).

31. See the *OED* and, for Webster's chemical training and interests, chapter 12 of Webster's *Metallographia: or, An History of Metals* (London, 1671). Useful on the general subject of the Webster-Ward debate and its relation to educational reform in the seventeenth century is Allen G. Debus, *The Chemical Philosophy: Paracelsian Science and Medicine in the Sixteenth and Seventeenth Centuries,* vol. 2 (New York: Science History Publications, 1977), 393-410. It should be noted that Wing and the *British Library General Catalogue of Printed Books* identify the *Metallographia* and *Displaying of Supposed Witchcraft* as the work of a different John Webster ("metallist" / "Practitioner in Physick") from the one ("chaplain in the army") who authored the *Academiarum Examen.* On the other hand, the *DNB* considers all three works as being by the same author, as does Debus. I have adopted the *DNB*'s position in my discussion because I

find no inconsistencies on matters that concern me; on the other hand, I admit the distinct possibility of different authorship. This possibility is perhaps increased with the awareness that Webster refers to his "History of Metals" in the "Preface *or* Introduction," but there is no mention of the *Academiarum.*

32. In response to the question of whether the entire body of Aristotelian philosophy should be thrown away, Webster states: "No; for there are many things in his *History of Animals,* and some things in his *Politicks, Ethicks, Logick, Metaphysicks,* and *Rhetorick,* that are commodious and useful, yet do they all stand in need of reformation and amendment: But for his Natural *Philosophy,* and his *Astronomy* depending thereon, it admits of no reformation but eradication, that some better may be introduced in the place thereof. And for his Expositors, and Commentators, they instead of reforming what was amisse in his writings, carried with a blind zeal to make him the onely oracle of truth, have increased the corruption, and not supplyed the defects, nor removed the errours" (*Academiarum Examen, or the Examination of Academies* [London, 1654], 104).

33. Webster's defence of "that noble, and almost divine Science of natural Magick" (68) takes much the same form as his arguments in support of astrology and alchemy. He speaks, for example, of the present neglect of magic in the universities, of its honorable past when the term was "appropriated to those that the world accounted most wise and learned" (69), and of the benefits its study might confer, i.e., "that sublime knowledge whereby the wonderful works of the Creator are discovered, and innumerable benefits produced to the poor Creatures" (*Academiarum Examen,* 69-70).

34. Webster, *Academiarum Examen,* 51. The references here are to Elias Ashmole, compiler of the *TCB* and one of the best-known hermetic authorities of the period; William Lilly, astrologer, almanac maker, and supporter of the Parliamentary cause; John Booker, astrologer, almanac maker, and, during the period of Parliamentary control, official licenser of astrological works; Sanders is probably Richard Sanders ("Student in Physic," *British Library General Catalogue*), author of *Apollo Anglicanus* and other astrological works; Nicholas Culpepper was a prolific editor of medical works and an exponent of astrology.

35. Webster was not alone in his championing of academic reform and chemical studies. Noah Biggs's *Mataeotechnia Medicinae Praxeus. The Vanity of the Craft of Physick* (London, 1651), in fact, anticipates some of Webster's challenges by three years. Biggs's work is more narrowly focused on medical reforms, as its subtitle indicates: *A New Dispensatory. Wherein is dissected the Errors, Ignorance, Impostures and Supinities of the Schools, in their main Pillars of Purges, Blood-letting, Fontanels or Issues, and Diet, & c. and the particular Medicines of the Shops. With an humble Motion for the Reformation of the Universities, and the whole Landscap of Physick, And discovering the Terra incognita of Chymistrie.* Like Webster, Biggs's preface "To the Parliament of England" is Baconian in its demand for a reformation in learning and in chemical studies specifically; he asserts, using elaborate metaphor, that "Truth, and the once-lovely body of Learning, is become a deformed and ill-favoured Medusa, with her tresses full of Adders, and her limbs, like that of Osiris King of Argives mangled body, lies torn and scattered in as many pieces; and that they are as hard to finde and re-unite as his was" sig. [b^v].

36. Webster, from the preface to *Metallographia,* sig. [A4^v]. Later in the preface, Webster, no doubt reflecting greater caution as a result of the attacks upon him, worries that he "may have given too great Commendations to *Paracelsus, Helmont, Basilius,* and some other of the Adeptists" (B2^v).

37. Webster, *The Displaying of Supposed Witchcraft,* 5.

38. For Hall's life, see the *DNB.*

39. Thomas Hall, *Histrio-Mastix. A Whip for Webster (as 'tis conceived) the Quondom Player: Or, An examination of one John Websters delusive Examen of Academies* (London, 1654), 198. As

the title indicates, Hall confuses the author of the *Academiarum Examen* with John Webster, the "Author of Stage-plaies, but now the Tutor of Universities" (217).

40. On Ward's life, see the *DNB*.

41. [Seth Ward], *Vindiciae Academiarum: Containing Some briefe Animadversions upon Mr Websters Book, Stiled, The Examination of Academies* (Oxford, 1654), sig. A2.

42. The *Mensa Isiacae, Canopi, Obeliskes*, and *Thesaurus Hieroglyphicus* are major sections in the third tome of Athanasius Kircher's monumental *Oedipus Ægyptiacus*, published only two years before Ward's volume. Johann Baptist Grossschedel von Aicha's *Calendarium naturale magicum* appeared in Frankfurt in 1620.

43. Webster, *Academiarum Examen*, 105.

44. Philaletha, *Secrets Reveal'd*, 51-52.

45. John Wilkins, *Mathematicall Magick. Or, The wonders that may be performed by Mechanicall Geometry* (London, 1648), sigs. A4ᵛ-A5.

46. A brief background to the character genre is included in the introduction to *Samuel Butler 1612-1680, Characters*, ed. Charles W. Daves (Cleveland and London: Press of Case Western Reserve Univ., 1970). According to Daves, Butler's *Characters* were written "largely between 1667 and 1669," this dating having originally been proposed by Robert Thyer, Butler's eighteenth-century editor (4). All references are to this edition.

47. The connection with Thomas Vaughan has been recognized since Thyer's first publication of Butler's prose sketches; Daves includes the following note from Thyer's edition: "The Reader will from several Circumstances quickly perceive that the first Part of [the Character] is personal; and from the same one may with a good deal of Certainty pronounce, that it was intended for the Author of a Book entituled—MAGIA ADAMICA; or *the Antiquity of Magic, and its descent from* ADAM," i.e., Thomas Vaughan (139). There is, indeed, evidence for identifying the target of the attack as Vaughan because his works were all published, under the pseudonym Eugenius Philalethes, in the decade before Butler apparently wrote this character (1667-69): e.g., *Magia Adamica, Anima Magica Abscondita*, and *Anthroposophia Theomagica* (1650); *Lumen de Lumine* (1651); *The Fame and Confession of the Fraternity of R:C:* (1652); and *Euphrates, or the Waters of the East* (1655). Furthermore, Vaughan had gained considerable notoriety in the recent controversy with Henry More, who had written under the pseudonym Alazonomastix Philalethes.

48. Parker, *Free and Impartial Censure*, 72.

49. On this dispute, see Burnham, "The More-Vaughan Controversy."

50. For example, see the following in the *Fama Fraternitatis or a Discovery of the Fraternity of the Most Noble Order of the Rosy Cross*, in Yates, *The Rosicrucian Enlightenment*: "But now concerning (and chiefly in this our age) the ungodly and accursed gold-making, which hath gotten so much the upper hand, . . . Yea nowadays men of discretion do hold the transmutation of metals to be the highest point and *fastigium* in philosophy, this is all their intent and desire, and that God would be most esteemed by them, and honoured, which could make great store of gold, and in abundance, the which with unpremeditate prayers, they hope to attain of the all-knowing God, and searcher of all hearts. We therefore do by these presents publicly testify, that the true philosophers are far of another mind, esteeming little the making of gold, which is but a *parergon;* for besides that they have a thousand better things" (250).

51. *Samuel Butler, Hudibras*, ed. John Wilders (Oxford: Clarendon Press, 1967), xxxiii. For Wilders and most critics, the marks of Butler's style are obvious: "earthy, colloquial language, intentionally clumsy rhythms, and comic rhymes, which debase everything they describe" (xl). All references to the poem are to this edition.

52. This is not to say that he is modeled on or a comic version of any particular occult philosopher, as has sometimes been argued. On the question of possible originals for Ralph,

see the Wilders edition of *Hudibras,* 330, n. 451, and George R. Wasserman, *Samuel "Hudibras" Butler* (Boston: Twayne Publishers, 1976), 54, 57.

53. Parker, *Free and Impartial Censure,* 72-3.

54. Butler, *Hudibras,* 17n.

55. "Astrology, *Hudibras,* and the Puritans," *JHI* 37 (1976): 521-36.

56. Butler, *Hudibras,* 390n, 454.

57. Butler, *Hudibras,* xxv-xxvi. The earlier, octosyllabic version of "The Elephant in the Moon" is generally thought to have been written in 1675-76, the pentameter version slightly later; they were not published until Robert Thyer's edition of the *Genuine Remains* in 1759. For Butler's thoughts on science, especially as related to "The Elephant in the Moon," see also Wasserman, *Samuel "Hudibras" Butler,* 39-42.

58. On Roger Bacon's changing Renaissance reputation, see the introduction to my edition of *The Mirror of Alchimy,* xxxiii-xlvi.

59. See *A True and Faithful Relation of What passed for many Yeers Between Dr. John Dee . . . and Some Spirits* (London, 1659).

60. See Butler, *Hudibras,* 394n. and Wilders's other notes on this passage.

61. Butler, *Hudibras,* 403n. On these and other figures involved in the mid-seventeenth century debate on astrology, see Nelson, "Astrology, *Hudibras,* and the Puritans."

62. In the *Fama Fraternitatis,* the first of the Rosicrucian manifestos (printed in Cassel, 1614), Paracelsus is treated as one of congenial temperament, although he is not a member of the fraternity. See the English translation included in Yates, *Rosicrucian Enlightenment,* 241, 247.

63. The last two lines of this quotation recall a passage from the *Confessio Fraternitatis,* in which the author remarks on man's difficulty in reading the book of nature: "For as there is given to man two instruments to hear, likewise two to see, and two to smell, but only one to speak, and it were but vain to expect speech from the ears, or hearing from the eyes" (from the text included in Yates, *Rosicrucian Enlightenment,* 257).

64. *Samuel Butler: Prose Observations,* ed. Hugh De Quehen (Oxford: Clarendon Press, 1979), 135. All references are to this edition.

65. The text of "Chymistry" appears in *Samuel Butler: Satires and Miscellaneous Poetry and Prose,* ed. René Lamar (Cambridge: University Press, 1928), 198. See the related poems on "Magique" (199), "Geomancy" (201), and "Astrology" (202). The prose passage is from *Prose Observations,* 134.

Chapter 10. Cauda Pavonis

1. Jonathan Swift, *Gulliver's Travels, A Tale of a Tub, The Battle of the Books* (London: Oxford Univ. Press, 1956), 213; hereafter cited as *Works.*

2. Thomas Sprat, *History of the Royal Society by Thomas Sprat,* ed. Jackson I. Cope and Harold Whitmore Jones (St. Louis: Washington Univ. Press, 1958), 37-38.

3. From chap. 4 of "A Voyage to Laputa," in Swift, *Works,* 210.

4. Swift, *Works,* 418-19, 462, 510.

Bibliography

Works cited in the text or notes have been categorized in one of the following: I. Alchemical Bibliographies, Booklists, and Catalogs; II. Alchemical, Scientific, and Philosophical Treatises and Collections; III. Editions of Literary Works; IV. Secondary Sources. Abbreviations of journal titles are listed on page 298.

I. Alchemical Bibliographies, Booklists, and Catalogs

Duveen, Denis I., comp. *Bibliotheca Alchemica et Chemica: An Annotated Catalogue of Printed Books on Alchemy, Chemistry and Cognate Subjects in the Library of Denis I. Duveen.* London: E. Weil, 1949.

Ferguson, John, comp. *Bibliographia Paracelsica. Contributions Towards a Knowledge of Paracelsus and his Writings.* Part 3. Glasgow: Robert Maclehose, 1890.

Ferguson, John, comp. *Bibliotheca Chemica.* 2 vols. Glasgow: J. Maclehose and Sons, 1906. Reprint, London: Derek Verschoyle, 1954.

Linden, Stanton J., ed. *William Cooper's A Catalogue of Chymicall Books: A Verified Edition.* New York and London: Garland Publishing , 1987.

MacPhail, Ian. *Alchemy and the Occult; A Catalogue of Books and Manuscripts from the Collection of Paul and Mary Mellon given to Yale University Library.* 4 vols. New Haven: Yale Univ. Press, 1968-77.

Pereira, Michela. *The Alchemical Corpus Attributed to Raymond Lull.* Warburg Institute Surveys and Texts 18. London: Warburg Institute, 1989.

Roberts, Julian, and Andrew G. Watson, comp. *John Dee's Library Catalogue.* London: Bibliographical Society, 1990.

Singer, Dorothea Waley, comp. *Catalogue of Latin and Vernacular Alchemical Manuscripts in Great Britain and Ireland dating from before the XVI Century.* 3 vols. Brussels: Union Académique Internationale, 1928-31.

II. Alchemical, Scientific, and Philosophical Treatises and Collections

Agrippa, Henry Cornelius. *Henrie Cornelius Agrippa, of the Vanitie and uncertaintie of Artes and Sciences, Englished by Ja*[mes] *San*[dford] *Gent.* London, 1569.

Anthonie, Francis. *The Apologie, or Defence of . . . Aurum Potabile.* London, 1616.

Ashmole, Elias. *Theatrum Chemicum Britannicum.* London, 1652. Reprint, Hildesheim: Georg Olms, 1968.

Ashmole, Elias. *The Way to Bliss.* London, 1658.

Becher, Johann Joachim. *Magnalia Naturae: or, the Philosophers-stone lately expos'd to public sight and sale.* London, 1680.

Biggs, Noah. *Mataeotechnia Medicinae Praxeus. The Vanity of the Craft of Physick.* London, 1651.

Boehme, Jacob. *Forty Questions of the Soul . . . Englished by John Sparrow.* London, 1665.

Boehme, Jacob. *Signatura rerum.* Translated by John Ellistone. London, 1651.

Bonus, Petrus. *Pretiosa margarita novella.* Venice, 1546.

Bostocke, R. *The Difference betwene the Auncient Phisick . . . and the latter Phisicke.* London, 1585.

Boyle, Robert. *[An Historical Account] of a Degradation of Gold Made by an Anti-Elixir.* London, 1678.

Boyle, Robert. *The Sceptical Chymist by the Hon. Robert Boyle.* With an introduction by M.M. Pattison Muir. London: J.M. Dent, n.d.

Braunschweig, Hieronymus. *Liber de arte Distillandi de Compositis.* Strassburg, 1512.

Carpenter, Agricola. *Pseuchographia Anthropomagica: or, A Magicall Description of the Soul.* London, 1652.

Casaubon, Meric. *A Treatise concerning Enthusiasme, As it is an Effect of Nature: but is mistaken by many for either Divine Inspiration, or Diabolical Possession.* London, 1654.

Casaubon, Meric. A True and Faithful Relation of What passed for many Yeers Between Dr. John Dee . . . and Some Spirits. London, 1659.

Castle, George. *The Chymical Galenist: A Treatise Wherein The Practise of the Ancients is reconcil'd to the new Discoveries in the Theory of Physick.* London, 1667.

Charleton, Walter. *The Immortality of the Human Soul, Demonstrated by the Light of Nature.* London, 1657.

Cooper, William. *The Philosophical Epitaph of W.C. Esquire, for a Memento Mori on his Tomb-stone.* London, 1673.

Crollius, Oswald. *Philosophy Reformed & Improved in Four Profound Tractates . . . Both made English by H. Pinnell.* London, 1657.

Dee, Arthur. *Fasciculus Chemicus: or Chymical Collections.* London, 1650.

De Jong, H.M.E. *Michael Maier's Atalanta Fugiens: Sources of an Alchemical Book of Emblems.* Leiden: E.J. Brill, 1969.

Digby, Sir Kenelm. *A Late Discourse . . . Touching the Cure of Wounds by the Powder of Sympathy.* London, 1658.

Duchesne, Joseph. [Quersetanus]. *The Practise of Chymicall, and Hermetical Physicke, for the preservation of health. . . . Translated into English by Thomas Timme, Minister.* London, 1605.

Espagnet, Jean d'. *Enchyridion Physicae Restitutae, or Summary of Physicks' Recovery.* [Translated by Dr. Johann Everard]. London, 1651.

Flamel, Nicolas. *Le livre des figures hiéroglyfiques de Nicolas Flamel.* Paris, 1612.

Flamel, Nicolas. *Nicolas Flamel: His Exposition of the Hieroglyphicall Figures (1624).* Edited by Laurinda Dixon. English Renaissance Hermeticism. New York and London: Garland Publishing, 1994.

Fludd, Robert. *Mosaicall Philosophy: Grounded upon the Essentiall Truth or Eternal Sapience.* London, 1659.

Fludd, Robert. *Utriusque cosmi maioris scilicet et minoris metaphysica, physica atque technica historia.* 2 vols. Oppenheim, 1617, 1619.

French, John. *The Art of Distillation.* London, 1651.

Glanvill, Joseph. *Philosophia Pia; or A Discourse, of the Religious Temper, and Tendencies of the Experimental Philosophy.* London, 1671.

Glanvill, Joseph. *Plus Ultra: Or, The Progress and Advancement of Knowledge Since the Days of Aristotle.* London, 1668.

Glauber, John Rudolph. *The Works of the Highly Experienced and Famous Chymist, John Rudolph Glauber . . . Translated into English by Christopher Packe.* London, 1689.

Hall, Thomas. *Histrio-Mastix. A Whip for Webster (as 'tis conceived) the Quondom Player: Or, An examination of one John Websters delusive Examen of Academies.* London, 1654.

Hall, Thomas. *Vindiciae Literarum, The Schools Guarded.* London, 1654.

Harris, Walter. *Pharmacologia Anti-Empirica: or a Rational Discourse of Remedies Both Chymical and Galenical.* London, 1683.

Hartlib, Samuel. *Chymical, Medicinal and Chyrurgical Addresses, made to Samuel Hartlib, Esquire.* London, 1655.

Helvetius. *A Briefe of the Golden Calfe.* In William Cooper, *The Philosophical Epitaph of W.C. Esquire, for a Memento Mori on his Tomb-stone.* London, 1673.

Hermes Trismegistus. *The Divine Pymander of Hermes Mercurius Trismegistus, in XVII. Books. Translated . . . By that Learned Divine Doctor Everard.* London, 1650.

Hermes Trismegistus. *Hermetica: The Ancient Greek and Latin Writings Which Contain Religious or Philosophic Teachings Ascribed to Hermes Trismegistus.* Edited and translated by Walter Scott. 4 vols. Oxford: Clarendon Press, 1924-36. Reprint, Boston: Shambhala, 1985.

Hermes Trismegistus. *Hermetica: The Greek "Corpus Hermeticum" and the Latin "Asclepius" in a new English translation.* Edited and translated by Brian P. Copenhaver. Cambridge: Cambridge Univ. Press, 1992.

Hermes Trismegistus. *The Smaragdine Table of Hermes Trismegistus of Alchimy.* In *The Mirror of Alchimy.*

The Hermetic Museum, Restored and Enlarged. Edited by Arthur Edward Waite. 2 vols. London: James Elliot and Co., 1893.

Heydon, John. *The Wise-Mans Crown, or, the Glory of the Rosie Cross.* London, 1664.

Hortulanus. *A briefe Commentarie of Hortulanus the Philosopher upon the Smaragdine Table.* In *The Mirror of Alchimy Composed by the Thrice-Famous and Learned Fryer, Roger Bachon.* London, 1597.

Houpreght, John Frederick. *Aurifontina Chymica: or, A Collection of Fourteen small Treatises concerning the First Matter of Philosophers.* London, 1680.

Hydropyrographum Hermeticum. In Houpreght, *Aurifontina Chymica.*

Khunrath, Heinrich. *Amphitheatrum sapientiæ.* Hanover, 1609.

Kircher, Athanasius. *Oedipus Ægyptiacus: Hoc est Universalis Hieroglyphicæ Veterum.* 3 vols. Rome, 1652-54.

Lambye [Lambi], John Baptista. *A Revelation of the Secret Spirit.* London, 1623.

Libavius, Andreas. *Alchymia.* Frankfurt, 1606.

Maier, Michael. *Atalanta fugiens.* Oppenheim, 1617.

Maier, Michael. *Lusus Serius: or, serious passe-time.* London, 1654.

Maier, Michael. *A Subtle Allegory Concerning the Secrets of Alchemy.* In *The Hermetic Museum.* 2:199-223.

Maier, Michael. *Symbola aureæ Mensæ.* Frankfurt, 1617.

Maier, Michael. *Tripus aureus.* Frankfurt, 1618.

Meun, Jean de. *A Demonstration of Nature, made to the Erring Alchemists.* In *The Hermetic Museum.* 2:121-41.

The Mirror of Alchimy Composed by the Thrice-Famous and Learned Fryer, Roger Bachon. Edited by Stanton J. Linden. English Renaissance Hermeticism. New York and London: Garland Publishing, 1992.

More, Henry. *Enthusiasmus Triumphatus; or, A Brief Discourse of The Nature, Causes, Kinds, and Cure of Enthusiasm.* In *A Collection of Several Philosophical Writings of Dr. Henry More.* 2d ed. Vol. 1. London, 1662. Reprint, New York: Garland, 1978.

Mylius, Johann. *Philosophia reformata.* Frankfurt, 1622.

Mystagogus, Cleidophorus. *Mercury's Caducean Rod; . . . or God's Vicegerent, Displayed.* 2d ed. London, 1704.

Norton, Thomas. *The Ordinall of Alchimy.* In Ashmole, *Theatrum Chemicum Britannicum.* 1-106.

Paracelsus. *The Hermetic and Alchemical Writings of Aureolus Philippus Theophrastus Bombast, of Hohenhein, Called Paracelsus the Great.* Edited by Arthur Edward Waite. 2 vols. London: J. Elliott & Co., 1894. Reprint, New Hyde Park, N.Y.: University Books, 1967.

Paracelsus. *Nine Books of the Nature of Things.* In Michael Sendivogius, *A New Light of Alchymy.* London, 1674.

Paracelsus. *Paracelsus his Aurora, & Treasure of the Philosophers . . . Faithfully Englished. And published by J. H. Oxon.* London, 1659, 1674.

Paracelsus. *Paracelsus his Dispensatory and Chirurgery . . . Faithfully Englished, by W. D.* London, 1656.

Paracelsus. *The Secrets of Physick and Philosophy, Divided into Two Bookes: . . . First Written in the German Tongue by the most learned Theophrastus Paracelsus, and now published in the English Tongue, by John Hester.* London, 1633.

Parker, Samuel. *A Free and Impartial Censure of the Platonick Philosophie, Being a Letter Written to his much Honoured Friend Mr. N. B.* Oxford, 1666.

Philaletha, Eyraeneus. *Secrets Reveal'd: Or An Open Entrance to the Shut-Palace of the King.* London, 1669.

Philalethes, Eirenaeus Philoponos. *The Marrow of Alchemy . . . in Two Parts.* London, 1654-55.

Plato. *The Dialogues of Plato.* Translated by Benjamin Jowett. 4th ed. 4 vols. Oxford: Clarendon Press, 1953.

Plotinus. *Plotinus, The Six Enneads.* Translated by Stephen MacKenna and B.S. Page. Chicago: Encyclopaedia Britannica, 1952.

Ripley, George. *Cantilena Georgii Riplaei.* In Bodleian Library Ashmolean MS 1445.

Ripley, George. *The Compound of Alchymy. Or The ancient hidden Art of Archemie.* London, 1591.

Ripley, George. *Opera omni chemica.* Cassellis, 1649.

Rosarium Philosophorum. Frankfurt, 1550.

Ruland, Martin. *A Lexicon of Alchemy.* Translated by A.E. Waite. London: Westminster Press, 1893. Reprint, London: John Watkins, 1964.

Salmon, William. *Medicina Practica; or, practical physick.* London, 1692.

Scot, Patrick. *The Tillage of Light or, A True Discoverie of the Philosophicall Elixir.* London, 1623.

Scot, Reginald. *The Discoverie of Witchcraft.* Edited by Hugh Ross Williamson. Carbondale, Ill.: Southern Illinois Univ. Press, 1964.

Sendivogius, Michael. *A New Light of Alchymy: Taken out of the Fountain of Nature and Manual Experience. To which is added A Treatise of Sulphur . . . Translated out of the Latin by J[ohn] F[rench], M.D.* London, 1674.

Siebmacher, Johann Ambrosius. *The Water-Stone of the Wise Men.* In Paracelsus, *Paracelsus His Aurora.*

Sprat, Thomas. *History of the Royal Society by Thomas Sprat.* Edited by Jackson I. Cope and Harold Whitmore Jones. St. Louis: Washington Univ. Press, 1958.

Starkey, George. *Natures Explication and Helmont's Vindication.* London, 1657.

Starkey, George. *Pyrotechny Asserted and Illustrated, to be the surest and safest means for Arts Triumph over Natures Infirmities.* London, 1658.

"The Stone of the Philosophers: Embracing The First Matter and the Dual Process for the Vegetable and Metallic Tinctures." In *Collectanea Chemica: Being Certain Select Treatises on Alchemy and Hermetic Medicine.* London: James Elliott, 1893.

Theatrum Chemicum, Præcipuos Selectorum Auctorum Tractatus de Chemiæ. 4 vols. Strasburg, 1613.

Thor, George. *Cheiragogia Heliana. A Manuduction to the Philosopher's Magical Gold.* London, 1659.

Tymme, Thomas. *A Dialogue Philosophicall Wherein Natures Secret Closet is Opened.* London, 1612.

Valentine, Basil. *Basil Valentine His Triumphant Chariot of Antimony, with Annotations of Theodore Kirkringius (1678).* Edited by L.G. Kelly. English Renaissance Hermeticism. New York and London: Garland Publishing, 1990.

Vaughan, Thomas. *Anima Magica Abscondita or, A Discourse of the Universall Spirit of Nature . . . By Eugenius Philalethes.* London, 1650.

Vaughan, Thomas. *The Fame and Confession of the Fraternity of R:C: Commonly, of the Rosie Cross. With a Praeface annexed thereto . . . By Eugenius Philalethes* [Thomas Vaughan]. London, 1652.

Vaughan, Thomas. *Magia Adamica: or the Antiquity of Magic, and the Descent thereof from Adam downwards. . . . By Eugenius Philalethes* [Thomas Vaughan]. London, 1650.

Vaughan, Thomas. *The Works of Thomas Vaughan.* Edited by Alan Rudrum. Oxford: Clarendon Press, 1984.

Ward, Seth. *Vindiciae Academiarum: Containing Some briefe Animadversions upon Mr Websters Book, Stiled, The Examination of Academies.* Oxford, 1654.

Webster, John. *Academiarum Examen, or the Examination of Academies.* London, 1654.

Webster, John. *The Displaying of Supposed Witchcraft.* London, 1677.

Webster, John. *Metallographia: or, An History of Metals.* London, 1671.

Wilkins, John. *Mathematicall Magick. Or, The wonders that may be performed by Mechanicall Geometry.* London, 1648.

III. Editions of Literary Works

Alchemical Poetry 1575-1700: From Previously Unpublished Manuscripts. Edited by Robert M. Schuler. English Renaissance Hermeticism. New York and London: Garland Publishing, 1995.

Alciatus, Andreas. *Andreas Alciatus.* Index Emblematicus. Edited by Peter M. Daly. 2 vols. Toronto: Univ. of Toronto Press, 1985.

Alciatus, Andreas. *Les Emblemes de Maistre Andre Alciat.* Paris, 1540.

Bacon, Francis. *The Works of Francis Bacon, Baron of Verulam, Viscount St. Alban, and Lord High Chancellor of England*. Edited by James Spedding, Robert L. Ellis, and Douglas D. Heath. 14 vols. 1872. Reprint, New York: Garrett Press, Inc., 1968.

Barclay, Alexander. *The Eclogues of Alexander Barclay*. Edited by Beatrice White. Early English Text Society, vol. 93. London: Oxford Univ. Press, 1928.

Barclay, Alexander. *The Ship of Fools translated by Alexander Barclay*. Edited by T.H. Jamieson. 2 vols. Edinburgh: William Paterson, 1874.

Breton, Nicholas. *The Works in Verse and Prose of Nicholas Breton*. Edited by Alexander B. Grosart. 2 vols. [Edinburgh]: Edinburgh Univ. Press, 1879.

Browne, Sir Thomas. *The Works of Sir Thomas Browne*. Edited by Geoffrey Keynes. 4 vols. Chicago: Univ. of Chicago Press, 1964.

Burton, Robert. *The Anatomy of Melancholy*. Edited by Thomas C. Faulkner, Nicolas K. Kiessling, and Rhonda L. Blair. Vol. 3. Oxford: Clarendon Press, 1994.

Burton, Robert. *Philosophaster*. Edited and translated by Connie McQuillen. Binghamton, N.Y.: Medieval & Renaissance Texts & Studies, 1993.

Butler, Samuel. *Samuel Butler, Hudibras*. Edited by John Wilders. Oxford: Clarendon Press, 1967.

Butler, Samuel. *Samuel Butler, Prose Observations*. Ed. Hugh De Quehen. Oxford: Clarendon Press, 1979.

Butler, Samuel. *Samuel Butler: Satires and Miscellaneous Poetry and Prose*. Edited by René Lamar. Cambridge: University Press, 1928.

Butler, Samuel. *Samuel Butler 1612-1680, Characters*. Edited by Charles Daves. Cleveland and London: Press of Case Western Reserve Univ., 1970.

Carew, Thomas. *The Poems of Thomas Carew with his Masque Coelum Britannicum*. Edited by Rhodes Dunlap. Oxford: Clarendon Press, 1970.

Chaucer, Geoffrey. *The General Prologue to The Canterbury Tales and The Canon's Yeoman's Prologue and Tale*. Edited by A.V.C. Schmidt. New York: Holmes & Meier, 1976.

Chaucer, Geoffrey. *The Riverside Chaucer*. Edited by Larry D. Benson. 3d ed. Oxford: Oxford Univ. Press, 1987.

Cowley, Abraham. *The Complete Works in Verse and Prose of Abraham Cowley*. Edited by Alexander B. Grosart. 2 vols. Edinburgh, 1881. Reprint, New York: AMS Press, 1967.

Crashaw, Richard. *The Poems English, Latin and Greek of Richard Crashaw*. Edited by L.C. Martin. 2d ed. Oxford: Clarendon Press, 1966.

Davies, Sir John. *The Poems of Sir John Davies*. Edited by Robert Krueger. Oxford: Clarendon Press, 1975.

Dekker, Thomas. *The Non-Dramatic Works of Thomas Dekker*. Edited by Alexander B. Grosart. 5 vols. London: Huth Library, 1884-86.

Donne, John. *The Complete Poetry of John Donne*. Edited by John T. Shawcross. Garden City, N.Y.: Anchor, 1967.

Donne, John. *John Donne: The Anniversaries*. Edited by Frank Manley. Baltimore: Johns Hopkins Univ. Press, 1963.

Donne, John. *John Donne: The Complete English Poems*. Edited by A.J. Smith. London: Penguin, 1971.

Donne, John. *John Donne: The Elegies and the Songs and Sonnets*. Edited by Helen Gardner. Oxford: Clarendon Press, 1965.

Donne, John. *John Donne: The Epithalamions, Anniversaries and Epicedes*. Edited by W. Milgate. Oxford: Clarendon Press, 1978.

Donne, John. *John Donne: The Satires, Epigrams and Verse Letters.* Edited by Wesley Milgate. Oxford: Clarendon Press, 1967.

Donne, John. *The Poems of John Donne.* Edited by Herbert J.C. Grierson. 2 vols. 1912. Reprint, London: Oxford Univ. Press, 1963.

Donne, John. *The Sermons of John Donne.* Edited by Evelyn M. Simpson and George R. Potter. 10 vols. Berkeley and Los Angeles: Univ. of California Press, 1953.

Douglas, Gavin. *The Poetical Works of Gavin Douglas.* Edited by John Small. 4 vols. Edinburgh: William Paterson, 1874.

Dryden, John. *John Dryden: Four Tragedies.* Edited by L.A. Beaurline and Fredson Bowers. Chicago: Univ. of Chicago Press, 1967.

Dunbar, William. *William Dunbar, Poems.* Edited by James Kinsley. Oxford: Clarendon Press, 1958.

Erasmus, Desiderius. *The Colloquies of Erasmus.* Edited and translated by Craig R. Thompson. Chicago: Univ. of Chicago Press, 1965.

Erasmus, Desiderius. *The Praise of Folie* [translated] *By Sir Thomas Chaloner.* Edited by Clarence H. Miller. Early English Text Society, vol. 257. London: Oxford Univ. Press, 1965.

Erasmus, Desiderius. *The Praise of Folly By Desiderius Erasmus.* Edited and translated by Leonard F. Dean. New York: Hendricks House, 1969.

Gower, John. *The English Works of John Gower.* Edited by G.C. Macaulay. 2 vols. London: K. Paul, Trench, Trübner & Co., 1901.

Greene, Robert. *Friar Bacon and Friar Bungay.* Edited by Daniel Seltzer. London: Edward Arnold, 1963.

Greene, Robert. *The Life and Complete Works in Prose and Verse of Robert Greene, M.A.* Edited by Alexander B. Grosart. 12 vols. London: Huth Library, 1881-83.

Hall, Joseph. *The Collected Poems of Joseph Hall, Bishop of Exeter and Norwich.* Edited by A. Davenport. Liverpool: Univ. Press, 1949.

Harvey, Gabriel. *The Works of Gabriel Harvey, D.C.L.* Edited by Alexander B. Grosart. 3 vols. London: Huth Library, 1884.

Herbert, George. *The Works of George Herbert.* Edited by F.E. Hutchinson. Oxford: Clarendon Press, 1964.

Herrick, Robert. *The Complete Poetry of Robert Herrick.* Edited by J. Max Patrick. New York: Norton, 1968.

James I. *The Basilicon Doron of King James VI.* Edited by James Craigie. 2 vols. Edinburgh and London: William Blackwood, 1944, 1950.

Jonson, Ben. *Ben Jonson.* Edited by C.H. Herford and Percy and Evelyn Simpson. 11 vols. Oxford: Clarendon Press, 1925-52.

Jonson, Ben. *Ben Jonson, Poems.* Edited by Ian Donaldson. London: Oxford Univ. Press, 1975.

King, Henry. *The Poems of Henry King.* Edited by Margaret Crum. Oxford: Clarendon Press, 1965.

Lacy, John. *The Dramatic Works of John Lacy, Comedian.* 1874. Reprint, New York: B. Blom, 1967.

Langland, William. *The Vision of Piers Plowman.* Edited by A.V.C. Schmidt. London: J.M. Dent, 1987.

Langland, William. *The Vision of William concerning Piers Plowman.* Edited by Walter W. Skeat. 2 vols. London: N. Trübner & Co., 1867.

Lindsay, David. *An Satyre of the thrie Estaits, In Commendation of Vertew and Vituperation of Vyce.* Edited by F. Hall. Early English Text Society, Vol. 37. London: N. Trübner and Co., 1869.

Lodge, Thomas. *The Complete Works of Thomas Lodge.* Edited by Sir Edmund Gosse. 3 vols. Glasgow: Hunterian Club, 1883. Reprint, New York: Johnson Reprint Corp., 1966.

Luther, Martin. *The Table Talk of Martin Luther.* Translated by William Hazlitt. London: G. Bell, 1902.

Lydgate, John. *Lydgate and Burgh's Secrees of Old Philisoffres.* Edited by Robert Steele. London: K. Paul, Trench, Trübner & Co., 1894.

Lyly, John. *The Complete Works of John Lyly.* Edited by R. Warwick Bond. 3 vols. Oxford: Clarendon Press, 1902.

Lyly, John. *Gallathea and Midas.* Edited by Anne Begor Lancashire. Lincoln: Univ. of Nebraska Press, 1969.

Marlowe, Christopher. *The Works of Christopher Marlowe.* Edited by C.F. Tucker Brooke. Oxford: Clarendon Press, 1962.

Marvell, Andrew. *Andrew Marvell: The Complete Poems.* Edited by Elizabeth Story Donno. Harmondsworth, Middlesex: Penguin, 1978.

Marvell, Andrew. *The Poems and Letters of Andrew Marvell.* Edited by H.M. Margoliouth. 3d ed. 2 vols. Oxford: Clarendon Press, 1971.

Milton, John. *Complete Prose Works of John Milton.* Edited by Don M. Wolfe. 7 vols. New Haven and London: Yale Univ. Press, 1953.

Milton, John. *John Milton: Complete Poems and Major Prose.* Edited by Merritt Y. Hughes. Indianapolis: Odyssey, 1957.

Milton, John. *Paradise Lost.* Edited by Alastair Fowler. London and New York: Longman, 1971.

Nashe, Thomas. *The Works of Thomas Nashe.* Edited by Ronald B. McKerrow. 5 vols. Oxford: Basil Blackwell, 1958.

Shakespeare, William. *The Riverside Shakespeare.* Edited by G. Blakemore Evans et al. Boston: Houghton Mifflin, 1974.

Sidney, Sir Philip. *The Poems of Sir Philip Sidney.* Edited by William A. Ringler Jr. Oxford: Clarendon Press, 1962.

Skelton, John. *John Skelton: The Complete English Poems.* Edited by John Scattergood. New Haven: Yale Univ. Press, 1983.

Spenser, Edmund. *The Poetical Works of Edmund Spenser.* Edited by J.C. Smith and E. de Selincourt. London: Oxford Univ. Press, 1950.

Spingarn, J.E., ed. *Critical Essays of the Seventeenth Century.* 3 vols. Oxford: Clarendon Press, 1907. Reprint, Bloomington: Indiana Univ. Press, 1957.

Swift, Jonathan. *Gulliver's Travels, A Tale of A Tub, The Battle of the Books.* London: Oxford Univ. Press, 1956.

Vaughan, Henry. *Henry Vaughan: The Complete Poems.* Edited by Alan Rudrum. New Haven: Yale Univ. Press, 1976.

Vaughan, Henry. *The Works of Henry Vaughan.* Edited by L.C. Martin. 2d ed. Oxford: Clarendon Press, 1963.

IV. Secondary Sources

Abraham, Lyndy. "Arthur Dee, 1579-1651: A Life." *Cauda Pavonis: Studies in Hermeticism* 13:2 (fall 1994): 1-14.

Abraham, Lyndy. "'The Lovers and the Tomb': Alchemical Emblems in Shakespeare, Donne, and Marvell." *Emblematica* 5 (winter 1991): 301-20.

Abraham, Lyndy. *Marvell and Alchemy.* Aldershot, Hants.: Scolar Press, 1990.

Aers, David, and Gunther Kress. "'Darke Texts Need Notes': Versions of Self in Donne's Verse Epistles." *Literature and History* 8 (autumn 1978): 138-58.

Aiken, Pauline. "Vincent of Beauvais and Chaucer's Knowledge of Alchemy." *Studies in Philology* 41 (July 1944): 371-89.

Allen, Don Cameron. "Vaughan's 'Cock-crowing' and the Tradition." *ELH* 21 (1954): 94-106.

Andreasen, N.J.C. *John Donne: Conservative Revolutionary.* Princeton: Princeton Univ. Press, 1967.

Baldwin, T.W. *William Shakspere's Small Latine & Lesse Greeke.* 2 vols. Urbana: Univ. of Illinois Press, 1944.

Barton, Anne. *Ben Jonson, Dramatist.* Cambridge: Cambridge Univ. Press, 1984.

Bentley, J. Scott. "Helena's Paracelsian Cure of the King: *Magia Naturalis* in *All's Well that Ends Well.*" *Cauda Pavonis: Studies in Hermeticism* 5:1 (spring 1986): 1-4.

Breger, Herbert. "Elias Artista—A Precursor of the Messiah in Natural Science." In *Nineteen Eighty-Four: Science between Utopia and Dystopia,* edited by Everett Mendelsohn and Helga Nowotny, 49-72. Dordrecht, Holland: D. Reidel, 1984.

Brennan, William. "Robert Fludd as a Possible Source for *Paradise Lost,* V.469-470." *Milton Quarterly* 15 (1981): 95-97.

Briggs, John C. *Francis Bacon and the Rhetoric of Nature.* Cambridge: Harvard Univ. Press, 1989.

Brooks-Davies, Douglas. *The Mercurian Monarch: Magical Politics from Spenser to Pope.* Manchester: Manchester Univ. Press, 1983.

Brown, Peter. "Is the 'Canon's Yeoman's Tale' Apocryphal?" *English Studies* 64 (1983): 480-90.

Burnham, Frederic B. "The More-Vaughan Controversy: The Revolt Against Philosophical Enthusiasm." *Journal of the History of Ideas* 35 (Jan.-Mar. 1974): 33-49.

Calhoun, Thomas O. *Henry Vaughan: The Achievement of Silex Scintillans.* Newark: Univ. of Delaware Press, 1981.

Cary, John. *John Donne: Life, Mind and Art.* New ed. London: Faber and Faber, 1990.

Chambers, A.B. "The Fly in Donne's 'Canonization.'" *JEGP* 65 (1966): 252-59.

Chambers, A.B. "Milton's Proteus and Satan's Visit to the Sun." *JEGP* 62 (1963): 280-87.

Chaudhuri, Supriya. "Jason's Fleece: The Source of Sir Epicure Mammon's Allegory." *RES,* n.s., 35 (1984): 71-73.

Clulee, Nicholas H. *John Dee's Natural Philosophy.* London and New York: Routledge, 1988.

Coffin, Charles Monroe. *John Donne and the New Philosophy.* 1937. Reprint, New York: Humanities Press, 1958.

Cohn, Norman. *The Pursuit of the Millennium.* Rev. ed. London: Temple Smith, 1970.

Cook, Robert. "The Canon's Yeoman and His Tale." *Chaucer Review* 22 (1987): 28-40.

Copenhaver, Brian. "Astrology and Magic." In *The Cambridge History of Renaissance Phi-*

losophy, edited by Charles B. Schmitt, 264-300. Cambridge: Cambridge Univ. Press, 1988.

Corbett, M.K. "Ashmole and the Pursuit of Alchemy: The Illustrations to the *Theatrum Chemicum Britannicum, 1652." Antiquaries Journal* 63 (1983): 326-36.

Cox, Gerard H. "Apocalyptic Projection and the Comic Plot of *The Alchemist." ELR* 13:1 (winter 1983): 70-87.

Crawshaw, Eluned. "Hermetic Elements in Donne's Poetic Vision." In *John Donne: Essays in Celebration,* edited by A.J. Smith, 324-48. London: Methuen, 1972.

Cunnar, Eugene R. "Donne's 'Valediction: Forbidding Mourning' and the Golden Compasses of Alchemical Creation." In *Literature and the Occult: Essays in Comparative Literature,* edited by Luanne Frank, 72-110. University of Texas at Arlington Publications in Literature. Arlington: Univ. of Texas Arlington Press, 1977.

Curry, Walter Clyde. *Milton's Ontology, Cosmogony, and Physics.* Lexington: Univ. of Kentucky Press, 1966.

Damon, S. Foster. "Chaucer and Alchemy." *PMLA* 39 (December 1924): 782-88.

Debus, Allen G. *The Chemical Philosophy: Paracelsian Science and Medicine in the Sixteenth and Seventeenth Centuries.* 2 vols. New York: Science History Publications, 1977.

Debus, Allen G. *The English Paracelsians.* New York: Franklin Watts, Inc., 1966.

Dickson, Donald. "The 'Slidynge' Yeoman: The Real Drama in the *Canon's Yeoman's Tale." South Central Review* 2 (summer 1985): 10-22.

Dickson, Donald R. *The Fountain of Living Waters: The Typology of the Waters of Life in Herbert, Vaughan, and Traherne.* Columbia: Univ. of Missouri Press, 1987.

Dobbs, Betty Jo Teeter. *Alchemical Death & Resurrection: The Significance of Alchemy in the Age of Newton.* Washington, D.C.: Smithsonian Institution Libraries, 1990.

Dobbs, Betty Jo Teeter. *The Foundations of Newton's Alchemy or "The Hunting of the Greene Lyon."* Cambridge: Cambridge Univ. Press, 1975.

Duncan, Edgar H. "The Alchemy in Jonson's *Mercury Vindicated." Studies in Philology* 39 (1942): 625-37.

Duncan, Edgar H. "Alchemy in the Writings of Chaucer, Jonson and Donne." Ph.D. diss., Vanderbilt University, 1940.

Duncan, Edgar H. "Chaucer and 'Arnold of the Newe Toun.'" *MLN* 57 (Jan. 1942): 31-33.

Duncan, Edgar Hill. "Donne's Alchemical Figures." *ELH* 9 (1942): 257-85.

Duncan, Edgar Hill. "Jonson's *Alchemist* and the Literature of Alchemy." *PMLA* 64 (Sept. 1946): 699-710.

Duncan, Edgar H. "The Literature of Alchemy and Chaucer's 'Canon's Yeoman's Tale': Framework, Theme, and Characters." *Speculum* 43 (1968): 633-56.

Duncan, Edgar Hill. "The Natural History of Metals and Minerals in the Universe of Milton's *Paradise Lost." Osiris* 11 (1954): 386-421.

Duncan, Edgar H. "The Yeoman's Canon's 'Silver Citrinacioun.'" *MP* 37 (Feb. 1940): 241-62.

Dunleavy, Gareth W. "The Chaucer Ascription in Trinity College, Dublin MS. D.2.8." *Ambix* 13 (1965): 2-21.

Durr, R.A. *On the Mystical Poetry of Henry Vaughan.* Cambridge: Harvard Univ. Press, 1962.

Eliade, Mircea. *The Forge and the Crucible.* Translated by Stephen Corrin. New York: Harper, 1962.

Evans, R.J.W. *Rudolf II and His World: A Study in Intellectual History, 1576-1612.* Oxford: Clarendon Press, 1973.

Fallon, Stephen M. *Milton among the Philosophers.* Ithaca and London: Cornell Univ. Press, 1991.

Feingold, Mordechai. "The occult tradition in the English universities of the Renaissance: a reassessment." In *Occult and Scientific Mentalities in the Renaissance,* edited by Brian Vickers, 73-94. Cambridge: Cambridge Univ. Press, 1984.

Ferguson, John. "Some English Alchemical Books." *Journal of the Alchemical Society* 2 (1913): 2-16.

Finkelstein, Dorothee. "The Code of Chaucer's 'Secree of Secrees': Arabic Alchemical Terminology in *The Canon's Yeoman's Tale.*" *Archiv für das Studium der neueren Sprachen und Literaturen* 207 (1970-71): 260-76.

Finnigan, David F. "The Role of Surly in *The Alchemist.*" *Papers on Language and Literature* 16 (1980): 100-104.

Fisch, Harold. "Bacon and Paracelsus." *Cambridge Journal* 5 (1952): 752-58.

Flachmann, Michael. "Ben Jonson and the Alchemy of Satire." *SEL* 17 (1977): 259-80.

Flynn, Dennis. "'Awry and Squint': The Dating of Donne's Holy Sonnets." *John Donne Journal* 7 (1988): 35-46.

Frank, Joseph. *Cromwell's Press Agent: A Critical Biography of Marchamont Nedham.* Lanham, Md.: Univ. Press of America, 1980.

Frontain, Raymond-Jean. "Donne's Imperfect Resurrection." *Papers on Language and Literature* 26 (fall 1990): 539-45.

Gardner, John. "*The Canon's Yeoman's Prologue and Tale*: An Interpretation." *Philological Quarterly* 46 (Jan. 1967): 1-17.

Garner, Ross. *Henry Vaughan: Experience and the Tradition.* Chicago: Univ. of Chicago Press, 1959.

Geoghegan, D. "A Licence of Henry VI to Practice Alchemy." *Ambix* 6 (Aug. 1957): 10-17.

Gertmenian, Donald. "Comic Experience In *Volpone* and *The Alchemist.*" *SEL* 17 (1977): 247-58.

Gillispie, Charles C., ed. *Dictionary of Scientific Biography.* New York: Charles Scribner's Sons, 1970. S.v. "Bolos of Mendes," by Jerry Stannard; "Jabir ibn Hayyan," by M. Plessner; "Sendivogius," by Włodzimierz Hubicki."

Goldberg, Jonathan. "Virga Iesse: Analogy, Typology, and Anagogy in a Miltonic Simile." *Milton Studies* 5 (1973): 177-90.

Grant, Patrick. *The Transformation of Sin.* Montreal and London: McGill-Queens Univ. Press, 1974.

Gregory, Joshua C. "Chemistry and Alchemy in the Natural Philosophy of Sir Francis Bacon, 1561-1626." *Ambix* 2 (1938): 93-111.

Grennen, Joseph E. "The Canon's Yeoman and the Cosmic Furnace: Language and Meaning in the 'Canon's Yeoman's Tale.'" *Criticism: A Quarterly for Literature and the Arts* 4 (1962): 225-40.

Grennen, Joseph E. "Chaucer's Characterization of the Canon and His Yeoman." *Journal of the History of Ideas* 25 (April-June 1964): 279-84.

Guss, Donald. *John Donne, Petrarchist.* Detroit: Wayne State Univ. Press, 1966.

Haller, William. *The Rise of Puritanism.* New York: Columbia Univ. Press, 1938.

Harrison, G.B., ed. *The Elizabethan Journals.* Garden City, N. Y.: Anchor Books, 1965.

Hartung, Albert E. "'Pars Secunda' and the Development of the *Canon's Yeoman's Tale.*" *Chaucer Review* 12 (1977): 111-28.

Haynes, Jonathan. "Representing the Underworld: *The Alchemist.*" *Studies in Philology* 86 (winter 1989): 18-41.

Herz, Judith. "*The Canon's Yeoman's Prologue and Tale.*" *MP* 58 (May 1961): 231-37.

Hilberry, Jane. "'And in Oure Madnesse Everemore We Rave': Technical Language in the *Canon's Yeoman's Tale.*" *Chaucer Review* 21 (1987): 435-43.

Hill, Christopher. *The Intellectual Origins of the English Revolution.* Oxford: Clarendon Press, 1965.

Hill, Christopher. *Milton and the English Revolution.* New York: Penguin, 1979.

Hill, Christopher. *The World Turned Upside Down: Radical Ideas during the English Revolution.* London: Temple Smith, 1972.

Holmes, Elizabeth. *Henry Vaughan and the Hermetic Philosophy.* Oxford: Basil Blackwell, 1932.

Holmyard, E.J. *Alchemy.* Harmondsworth, Middlesex: Penguin, 1957.

Hopkins, Arthur John. *Alchemy: Child of Greek Philosophy.* Morningside Heights, N.Y.: Columbia Univ. Press, 1934.

Horowitz, Maryanne C. "Natural Law as the Foundation for an Autonomous Ethic: Pierre Charron's *De la Sagesse.*" *Studies in the Renaissance* 21 (1974): 204-27.

Horowitz, Maryanne C. "The Stoic Synthesis of the Idea of Natural Law in Man: Four Themes." *Journal of the History of Ideas* 35 (Jan.-March 1974): 3-16.

Hubicki, Włodzimierz. "The Mystery of Alexander Seton, the Cosmopolite." In *Proceedings of the XIVth International Congress of the History of Science.* Tokyo-Kyoto: n.p., 1974.

Hubicki, Włodzimierz. "The True Life of Michael Sendivogius." In *Actes du XIe Congrès international d'histoire des sciences, Varsovie-Cracovie, 24-31 August, 1965,* 257-85. Warsaw: n.p., 1968.

Hunter, Michael. "Alchemy, Magic and Moralism in the Thought of Robert Boyle." *British Journal for the History of Science* 23 (1990): 387-410.

The Interpreter's Bible. Edited by George Arthur Buttrick. 12 vols. Nashville, Tenn.: Abingdon, 1980.

Jacob, Margaret. "Millenarianism and Science in the Late Seventeenth Century." *Journal of the History of Ideas* 37 (1976): 335-41.

Jacobus, Lee A. *Sudden Apprehension: Aspects of Knowledge in "Paradise Lost."* The Hague: Mouton, 1976.

Jung, C.G. *Psychology and Alchemy.* Translated by R.F.C. Hull. 2d ed. New York: Princeton Univ. Press, 1953.

Kermode, Frank. "The Private Imagery of Henry Vaughan." *RES,* n.s., 1 (1950): 214.

Kernan, Alvin B. "Alchemy and Acting: The Major Plays of Ben Jonson." *Studies in the Literary Imagination* 6 (April 1973): 5-6.

Kurath, H. and S.H. Kuhn, eds., *Middle English Dictionary.* Ann Arbor: Univ. of Michigan Press, 1952- .

Lederer, Josef. "John Donne and the Emblematic Practice." *RES* 22 (July 1946): 194.

Lepage, John Louis. "Eagles and Doves in Donne and Du Bartas: 'The Canonization.'" *Notes and Queries* 30 (Oct. 1983): 427-28.

Lewis, C. S. *English Literature in the Sixteenth Century.* Oxford: Clarendon Press, 1954.

Lieb, Michael. *The Dialectics of Creation: Patterns of Birth and Regeneration in "Paradise Lost."* Amherst: Univ. of Massachusetts Press, 1970.

Linden, Stanton J. "Alchemy and Eschatology in Seventeenth-Century Poetry." *Ambix* 31 (Nov. 1984): 102-24.

Linden, Stanton J. "'By gradual scale sublim'd': Jean d'Espagnet and the Ontological Tree in *Paradise Lost,* Book V." *Journal of the History of Ideas* 52 (Oct.-Dec. 1991): 603-15.

Linden, Stanton J. "Francis Bacon and Alchemy: The Reformation of Vulcan." *Journal of the History of Ideas* 35 (Oct.-Dec. 1974): 547-60.

Linden, Stanton J. "Herbert and the Unveiling of Diana: Stanza Three of 'Vanitie' (I)." *George Herbert Journal* 1 (1978): 30-37.

Linden, Stanton J. "Jonson and Sendivogius: Some New Light on *Mercury Vindicated from the Alchemists at Court.*" *Ambix* 24 (1977): 39-54.

Longsworth, Robert M. "Privileged Knowledge: St. Cecilia and the Alchemist in the *Canterbury Tales.*" *Chaucer Review* 27 (1992): 87-96.

Lovejoy, A.O. *The Great Chain of Being.* 1936. Reprint, New York: Harper, 1960.

Low, Anthony. "Love and Science: Cultural Change in Donne's *Songs and Sonnets.*" *Studies in the Literary Imagination* 22 (spring 1989): 5-16.

Lowes, J.L. "The Dragon and His Brother." *MLN* 28 (Nov. 1913): 229.

Madsen, William G. *From Shadowy Types to Truth.* New Haven and London: Yale Univ. Press, 1968.

Mahood, M.M. *Poetry and Humanism.* New York: Norton, 1970.

Manning, John. "The Eagle and the Dove: Chapman and Donne's 'The Canonization.'" *Notes and Queries* 33 (Sept. 1986): 347-48.

Marjara, Harinder Singh. *Contemplation of Created Things: Science in Paradise Lost.* Toronto: Univ. of Toronto Press, 1992.

Marotti, Arthur F. *John Donne, Coterie Poet.* Madison: Univ. of Wisconsin Press, 1986.

Martin, L.C. "Henry Vaughan and 'Hermes Trismegistus.'" *RES* 18 (1942): 301-7.

Mauer, Margaret. "The Real Presence of Lucy Russell, Countess of Bedford, and the Terms of John Donne's 'Honour is so Sublime Perfection.'" *ELH* 47 (summer 1980): 205-34.

Mazzeo, Joseph. "Notes on John Donne's Alchemical Imagery." *Isis* 48 (1957): 103-23.

McAlindon, T. *Shakespeare's Tragic Cosmos.* Cambridge: Cambridge Univ. Press, 1991.

McPherson, David. "Ben Jonson's Library and Marginalia: An Annotated Catalogue." *Studies in Philology* 71 (1974): 1-106.

Meagher, John C. *Method and Meaning in Jonson's Masques.* Notre Dame: Univ. of Notre Dame Press, 1966.

Mebane, John S. *Renaissance Magic and the Return of the Golden Age: The Occult Tradition and Marlowe, Jonson, and Shakespeare.* Lincoln and London: Univ. of Nebraska Press, 1989.

Mendelsohn, J. Andrew. "Alchemy and Politics in England, 1649-1665." *Past and Present* 135 (May 1992): 30-78.

Multhauf, Robert P. "Some Non-existent Chemists of the Seventeenth Century: Remarks on the Use of the Dialogue in Scientific Writing." In *Alchemy and Chemistry in the Seventeenth Century: Papers Read by Allen G. Debus and Robert P. Multhauf at a Clark Library Seminar, March 12, 1966.* 31-50. Los Angeles: William Andrews Clark Memorial Library, 1966.

Murray, W.A. "Donne and Paracelsus: An Essay in Interpretation." *RES* 25 (1949): 115-23.

Muscatine, Charles. *Chaucer and the French Tradition.* Berkeley and Los Angeles: Univ. of California Press, 1957.

Needham, Joseph. *The Refiner's Fire; The Enigma of Alchemy in East and West.* In *The Second J.D. Bernal Lecture Delivered at Birkbeck College, London, 4 Feb. 1971.* London: Birkbeck College, 1971.

Nelson, Nicolas H. "Astrology, *Hudibras,* and the Puritans." *Journal of the History of Ideas* 37 (1976): 521-36.

Newman, William R. *Gehennical Fire: The Lives of George Starkey, an American Alchemist in the Scientific Revolution.* Cambridge: Harvard Univ. Press, 1994.

Newman, William R. "Prophecy and Alchemy: The Origin of Eirenaeus Philalethes." *Ambix* 37 (Nov. 1990): 97-115.

Nicholl, Charles. *The Chemical Theatre.* London: Routledge & Kegan Paul, 1980.

O'Brien, Gordon W. "Milton, Hermes, and the Rhetoric of Mental Flight." *Cauda Pavonis: Studies in Hermeticism* 7 (spring 1988): 1-8.

Ogrinc, Will H.L. "Western Society and Alchemy from 1200 to 1500." *Journal of Medieval History* 6 (1980): 103-32.

Orgel, Stephen. *The Illusion of Power: Political Theater in the English Renaissance.* Berkeley: Univ. of California Press, 1975.

Orgel, Stephen. *The Jonsonian Masque.* Cambridge: Harvard Univ. Press, 1965.

Orgel, Stephen, and Roy Strong. *Inigo Jones: The Theatre of the Stuart Court.* 2 vols. London and Berkeley: Sotheby Parke Bernet and Univ. of California, 1973.

Ormsby-Lennon, Hugh. "Rosicrucian Linguistics: Twilight of a Renaissance Tradition." In *Hermeticism and the Renaissance: Intellectual History and the Occult in Early Modern Europe,* edited by Ingrid Merkel and Allen G. Debus, 311-341. Washington, D.C.: Folger Shakespeare Library, 1988.

Partington, J.R. *A Short History of Chemistry.* 3d ed. New York: Harper, 1960.

Partridge, Edward B. *The Broken Compass.* New York: Columbia Univ. Press, 1958.

Patrides, C.A. *Milton and the Christian Tradition.* Oxford: Clarendon Press, 1966.

Patrides, C. A. "'Something like Prophetick strain': apocalyptic configurations in Milton." In *The Apocalypse in English Renaissance Thought and Literature,* edited by C.A. Patrides and Joseph Wittreich, 207-37. Ithaca: Cornell Univ. Press, 1984.

Patterson, Lee. "Perpetual Motion: Alchemy and the Technology of the Self." In *Studies in the Age of Chaucer,* edited by Lisa J. Kiser, 25-57. Vol. 15. Columbus, Ohio: New Chaucer Society, 1993.

Pettet, E.C. *Of Paradise and Light.* Cambridge: Cambridge Univ. Press, 1960.

Pickering, James D. "Chaucer's Alchemy: The Pilgrims Assayed." *Medieval Perspectives* 4-5 (1989-90): 140-49.

Piper, Edwin Ford. "The Miniatures of the Ellesmere Chaucer." *Philological Quarterly* 3 (Oct. 1924): 241-56.

Plomer, Henry R. *A Dictionary of the Printers and Booksellers who were at work in England, Scotland and Ireland from 1668-1725.* 1922. Reprint, Oxford: Bibliographical Society, 1968.

Post, Jonathan F.S. *Henry Vaughan: The Unfolding Vision.* Princeton: Princeton Univ. Press, 1982.

Rattansi, P.M. "Paracelsus and the Puritan Revolution." *Ambix* 11 (1963): 24-32.

Raybin, David. "'And Pave it Al of Silver and of Gold': The Humane Artistry of the *Canon's Yeoman's Tale.*" In *Rebels and Rivals: The Contestive Spirit in The Canterbury Tales*, edited by Susanna Greer Fein et al., 189-212. Kalamazoo, Mich.: Medieval Institute Publications, 1991.

Read, John. *The Alchemist in Life, Literature and Art.* London: Thomas Nelson, 1947.

Read, John. "Alchemy Under James IV of Scotland." *Ambix* 2 (Sept. 1938): 60-67.

Read, John. *Humour and Humanism in Chemistry.* London: Bell, 1947.

Read, John. *Prelude to Chemistry.* London: Bell, 1936.

Read, John. *Through Alchemy to Chemistry.* New York: Harper and Row, 1963.

Rebhorn, Wayne A. "Jonson's 'Jovy Boy': Lovewit and the Dupes in *The Alchemist.*" *JEGP* 79 (1980): 361-64.

Rees, Graham. "Francis Bacon's Semi-Paracelsian Cosmology." *Ambix* 22 (July 1975): 81-101.

Revard, Stella P. "Donne and Propertius: Love and Death in London and Rome." In *The Eagle and the Dove: Reassessing John Donne*, edited by Claude J. Summers and Ted-Larry Pebworth, 69-79. Columbia: Univ. of Missouri Press, 1986.

Roberts, Gareth. *The Mirror of Alchemy: Alchemical Ideas and Images in Manuscripts and Books from Antiquity to the Seventeenth Century.* Toronto: Univ. of Toronto Press, 1994.

Rosenberg, Bruce A. "Swindling Alchemist, Antichrist." *Centennial Review* 6 (1962): 566-80.

Ross, Cheryl Lynn. "The Plague of *The Alchemist.*" *Renaissance Quarterly* 41 (autumn 1988): 454-57.

Rossi, Paolo. *Francis Bacon: From Magic to Science.* Translated by Sacha Rabinovitch. Chicago: Univ. of Chicago Press, 1968.

Rossi, Paolo. "Hermeticism, Rationality and the Scientific Revolution." In *Reason, Experiment, and Mysticism in the Scientific Revolution*, edited by M.L. Righini Bonelli and William R. Shea, 247-73. London: Science History Publications, 1975.

Rudrum, Alan. "An Aspect of Vaughan's Hermeticism: The Doctrine of Cosmic Sympathy." *SEL* 14 (winter 1974): 130-38.

Rudrum, Alan. "The Influence of Alchemy in the Poems of Henry Vaughan." *Philological Quarterly* 49 (1970): 469-80.

Ryan, Lawrence V. "The Canon's Yeoman's Desperate Confession." *Chaucer Review* 8:4 (1974): 297-310.

Schuler, Robert M. "The Renaissance Chaucer as Alchemist." *Viator: Medieval and Renaissance Studies* 15 (1984): 305-33.

Schuler, Robert M. "Some Spiritual Alchemies of Seventeenth-Century England." *Journal of the History of Ideas* 41 (April-June 1980): 293-318.

Schultz, Howard. *Milton and Forbidden Knowledge.* New York: Modern Language Association, 1955.

Sheppard, H.J. "Egg Symbolism in Alchemy." *Ambix* 6 (August 1958): 140-48.

Sheppard, H.J. "European Alchemy in the Context of a Universal Definition." In *Die Alchimie in der europäischen Kultur- und Wissenschaftsgeschichte*, edited by Christoph Meinel, 13-17. Wolfenbütteler Forschungen, vol. 32. Wiesbaden: Otto Harrassowitz, 1986.

Shirley, John W. "The Scientific Experiments of Sir Walter Ralegh, the Wizard Earl, and the Three Magi in the Tower, 1603-17." *Ambix* 4 (Dec. 1949): 52-66.

Shumaker, Wayne. *The Occult Sciences in the Renaissance: A Study in Intellectual Patterns.* Berkeley: Univ. of California Press, 1972.

Simmonds, James D. *Masques of God: Form and Theme in the Poetry of Henry Vaughan.* Pittsburgh: Univ. of Pittsburgh Press, 1972.

Smallwood, R.L. "'Here, in the Friars': Immediacy and Theatricality in The Alchemist." *RES,* n.s., 32 (1981): 142-60.

Srigley, Michael. *Images of Regeneration: A Study of Shakespeare's* The Tempest *and Its Cultural Background.* Acta Universitatis Upsaliensis 58. Uppsala: Almqvist & Wiksell, 1985.

Stapleton, Laurence. "The Theme of Virtue in Donne's Verse Epistles." *Studies in Philology* 55 (April 1958): 187-200.

Steele, Robert. "Alchemy in England." *Antiquary* 24 (Sept. 1891): 99-105.

Summers, Joseph H. *The Muse's Method.* Cambridge: Harvard Univ. Press, 1962.

Svendsen, Kester. *Milton and Science.* Cambridge: Harvard Univ. Press, 1956.

Tayler, Edward. *Nature and Art in Renaissance Literature.* New York: Columbia Univ. Press, 1964.

Taylor, F. Sherwood. *The Alchemists: Founders of Modern Chemistry.* New York: Henry Schuman, 1949.

Thomas, Keith. *Religion and the Decline of Magic.* New York: Charles Scribner's Sons, 1971.

Thomson, Patricia. "Donne and the Poetry of Patronage." In *John Donne: Essays in Celebration,* edited by A.J. Smith, 308-23. London: Methuen, 1972.

Thorndike, Lynn. "The Attitude of Francis Bacon and Descartes Towards Magic and Occult Science." In *Science, Medicine and History: Essays on the Evolution of Scientific Thought and Medical Practice written in honour of Charles Singer,* edited by E. Ashworth Underwood, 451-54. Oxford: Oxford Univ. Press, 1953.

Thorndike, Lynn. *A History of Magic and Experimental Science.* 8 vols. New York: Columbia Univ. Press, 1923-58.

Tillyard, E.M.W. *The Elizabethan World Picture.* London: Chatto and Windus, 1943.

Tuveson, Ernest. *Millennium and Utopia.* Berkeley and Los Angeles: Univ. of California Press, 1949.

Vickers, Brian. "Analogy versus Identity: the Rejection of Occult Symbolism, 1580-1680." In *Occult and scientific mentalities in the Renaissance,* edited by Brian Vickers, 95-163. Cambridge: Cambridge Univ. Press, 1984.

Vickers, Brian. "Donne's Eagle and Dove." *Notes and Queries* 32 (March 1985): 59-60.

Vickers, Brian. "Francis Bacon and the Progress of Knowledge." *Journal of the History of Ideas* 53 (July-Sept. 1992): 495-518.

Vickers, Brian. "On the Function of Analogy in the Occult." In *Hermeticism and the Renaissance: Intellectual History and the Occult in Early Modern Europe,* edited by Ingrid Merkel and Allen G. Debus, 265-92. Washington, D.C.: Folger Shakespeare Library, 1988.

Vickers, Brian. "On the Goal of the Occult Sciences in the Renaissance." In *Die Renaissance im Blick der Nationen Europas,* edited by Georg Kauffmann, 51-93. Wölfenbutteler Abhandlungen zur Renaissanceforschung, vol. 9. Wiesbaden: Harrassowitz, 1991.

Waite, A.E. *Lives of Alchemystical Philosophers.* London: Redway, 1888. Reprint, *Alchemists through the Ages.* Blauvelt, N.Y.: Rudolf Steiner Publications, 1970.

Walker, Julia M. "John Donne's 'The Extasie' as an Alchemical Process." *English Language Notes* 20 (Sept. 1982): 1-8.

Wall, John N. *Transformations of the Word: Spenser, Herbert, Vaughan*. Athens and London: Univ. of Georgia Press, 1988.

Walters, Richard H. "Henry Vaughan and the Alchemists." *RES* 23 (1947): 107-22.

Wasserman, George R. *Samuel "Hudibras" Butler*. Boston: Twayne Publishers, 1976.

Watson, Robert N. *Ben Jonson's Parodic Strategy: Literary Imperialism in the Comedies*. Cambridge: Harvard Univ. Press, 1987.

Webster, Charles. *The Great Instauration: Science, Medicine and Reform, 1626-1660*. New York: Holmes & Meier, 1976.

Weil, Eric. "An Alchemical Freedom Flight: Linking the *Manciple's Tale* to the *Second Nun's* and *Canon's Yeoman's Tales*." *Medieval Perspectives* 6 (1991): 162-70.

Weinhouse, Linda. "The Urim and Thummim in *Paradise Lost*." *Milton Quarterly* 11 (March 1977): 9-12.

West, Muriel. "Notes on the Importance of Alchemy to Modern Science in the Writings of Francis Bacon and Robert Boyle." *Ambix* 9 (1961): 102-14.

Westman, Robert S., and J.E. McGuire. *Hermeticism and the Scientific Revolution*. Papers read at a Clark Library Seminar, March 9, 1974. Los Angeles: William Andrews Clark Memorial Library, 1977.

Whitaker, Virgil. *Shakespeare's Use of Learning*. San Marino: Huntington Library, 1953.

Wiggins, Peter D. "Preparing Towards Lucy: 'A Nocturnall' as Palinode." *Studies in Philology* 84 (1987): 483-93.

Wilkinson, R.A. "The Problem of the Identity of Eirenaeus Philalethes." *Ambix* 12 (Feb. 1964): 24-43.

Willard, Thomas S. "Alchemy and the Bible." In *Centre and Labyrinth: Essays in Honour of Northrop Frye,* ed. Eleanor Cook et al., 115-27. Toronto: Univ. of Toronto Press, 1983.

Willey, Basil. *The Seventeenth Century Background*. London: Chatto and Windus, 1934.

Wilson, F.P. *The English Drama, 1485-1585*. Oxford: Clarendon Press, 1969.

Yates, Frances. *The Art of Memory*. Chicago: Univ. of Chicago Press, 1966.

Yates, Frances. *Giordano Bruno and the Hermetic Tradition*. Chicago: Univ. of Chicago Press, 1964.

Yates, Frances A. *The Occult Philosophy in the Elizabethan Age*. London: Routledge & Kegan Paul, 1979.

Yates, Frances A. *The Rosicrucian Enlightenment*. London and Boston: Routledge & Kegan Paul, 1972.

Young, Karl. "The 'secree of secrees' of Chaucer's Canon's Yeoman." *MLN* 58 (Feb. 1943): 98-105.

Index

Aaron, 250-51, 252
Abraham, 20, 329 n 29
Abraham, Lyndy, 4
Academiarum Examen (Webster), 81, 271-72, 274, 275
Adam, 126, 253
Advancement of Learning (Bacon), 107, 266, 314-15 n 18; alchemy in, 109, 115, 117, 314 n 7. *See also Augmentis Scientiarum*
Aeneid, 66-67
Aers, David, 164
"Affliction" (H. Vaughan), 245
"Agreement" (H. Vaughan), 245
Agrippa, Cornelius, 106, 213, 279, 283; and alchemy, 89, 248-49; attacks on, 290, 291, 292; influence of, 89, 91-92, 93, 97, 98, 224, 311 n 46, 312-13 n 68
Albertus Magnus, 38, 40, 41, 55, 84
Alchemia Volumen (Petreium), 41-42
alchemical literature, 1, 2, 4, 5, 296; alchemy linked with the demonic in, 50, 53; creation accounts in, 201-2; and human representation, 24, 26-27; and metaphysical poetry, 155-56; motifs of, 6-7, 14, 53. *See also* alchemical satire
alchemical satire, 36, 190, 193; alchemy and alchemists portrayed in, 14, 141, 144-45, 155, 193, 282, 295; charlatanism in, 52, 64, 155, 198, 211; in Elizabethan drama, 2, 98-103; in Elizabethan poetry, 2, 92-98; in fifteenth century, 38, 295; in fourteenth century, 42; origins of, 38, 44, 295; and Paracelsian ideas, 195-98; during Renaissance, 62, 63; and rhetoric of obscurity, 33-34, 307 n 39; scientific endeavors included in, 282-83, 286; in seventeenth century, 104-5, 167, 193, 194-95, 211; in sixteenth century, 63, 84, 92-103, 104-5. *See also* alchemical literature
alchemical treatises, 42; literary influences in, 29-31; revelation and concealment in, 31-33, 261; in seventeenth century, 193-94, 200, 204
Alchemist (Jonson), 99, 142, 146, 150, 276; alchemical idiom in, 121-22, 124-25, 126-27; alchemical knowledge in, 119, 120-21, 122-23, 125, 126, 127, 153; and alchemical satire, 118, 119, 296, 316 n 7; alchemy portrayed in, 130-31, 144-45, 318 n 25; and *Canon's Yeoman's Tale*, 53, 121, 316 n 10; charlatanism in, 79, 118, 125, 128, 130, 131, 316 n 8; and controversy concerning Art and Nature, 121, 122, 123, 132, 296; explosion in, 53, 128, 130, 317-18 n 20; human nature portrayed in, 119-20, 125, 126, 131, 285, 316 n 98, 318 n 26; millenarianism in, 128, 130; the obscure explained by the more obscure in, 122, 124-25, 127-28; occult linked with radical protestantism in, 128, 130; philosopher's stone in, 123, 124, 128, 130; transformation in, 120, 128, 316 n 8
"Alchemist" (Matham), 126
alchemy: as art, 4, 29, 36, 54, 181, 297; changing colors in, 14, 86-87; definition of, 6, 7-11; demise of, 18-19, 34; esoteric, 7-8, 9-10, 26, 36, 80, 194, 213, 251, 263, 295; etymology of, 12; exoteric, 7-8, 10, 26, 36, 44, 80, 105, 116, 295; four elements theory of, 13, 17, 21, 24, 34, 37; goals of, 6, 11; hostility and skepticism toward, 26-28, 270; in literature *(see* alchemical literature); and microcosm-macrocosm correspondence, 13, 17, 19-22, 24, 37, 60, 80, 111-12, 114, 169; and nature, 19, 21, 111-12, 181; origin and development of, 6, 11-16, 304 n 4; and prima materia, 17, 19-20, 24, 169, 257; punishment of adepts of, 79, 310 n 25; and purity in life of the adept, 79-80; rhetoric of, 33-34, 272, 276; as sacred, 62, 200-201, 215; as science, 29, 36; and souls of metals, 158; spiritual and philosophical aspects of, 211, 214, 224, 251; and spiritual growth, purification, and regeneration, 3, 26; sulphur-mercury theory of, 15-16, 17, 19, 23-24, 37, 57, 142, 176; symbolism of, 175-76, 178, 179, 186-87; and transmutation, 212, 213, 224, 241; and university, 313 n 2; writings on *(see* alchemical treatises)